THE JEWISH YEAR BOOK
2014

Jewish Year Book Editors

1896–1899	Joseph Jacobs
1900–1924	Isidore Harris
1925–1934	Rev. Solomon Levy
1935–1938	Rev. Solomon Levy & Cecil Roth
1939	Cecil Roth
1940–1952	Albert Hyamson
1953–1968	Hugh Harris
1969–1983	Michael Wallach
1984–1989	Roger Japhet
1990–2009	Stephen Massil
2010–	Elkan Levy & Derek Taylor

We are very grateful to the Dorset Foundation for their support for the 2014 Jewish Year Book.

The Jewish Year Book

Founded 1896

2014

5774–5775

Edited by
Elkan D. Levy & Derek Taylor

VALLENTINE MITCHELL
LONDON • PORTLAND, OR

Published in 2014 by Vallentine Mitchell

Middlesex House	920 NE 58th Avenue, Suite 300
29/45 High Street	Portland, Oregon,
Edgware, Middlesex HA8 7UU	97213-3786
UK	USA

www.vmbooks.com
info@vmbooks.com

Copyright © 2014 Vallentine Mitchell

British Library Cataloguing in Publication Data
An entry can be found on request

ISBN 978 0 85303 987 7 (cloth)
ISBN 978 0 85303 898 6 (Ebook)
ISSN 0075-3769

Printed by CPI Group (UK) Ltd, Croydon, CR0 4YY

CONTENTS

A YEAR TO REMEMBER

It is a very special year when Prince Charles is the guest of honour at the retirement dinner for one Chief Rabbi and then attends the installation of the next incumbent. Resplendent in his Prince of Wales *kippah*, with his crest of three white feathers emblazoned on the front, it was a proud moment for the community when he graced the induction of Chief Rabbi Ephraim Mirvis, a worthy successor to Lord Sacks in September. Chief Rabbi Mirvis is the 11th British Chief Rabbi since Aaron Hart first started advising provincial communities after 1705.

The installation was, however, only the culmination of a very pleasing year for British Jews. There were new Jewish peers, worthy members received awards in the Honours Lists, and the latest census shows that our numbers have stabilised at around a quarter of a million. That satisfactory result owes a great deal to the growing Charedi community. The new Manchester *eruv* is the largest in the country. By contrast, in America, a recent study has suggested that 70 per cent of non-Orthodox weddings involving Jews are out of the faith.

Our numbers were also increased by the considerable number of French Jews who have emigrated to Britain. Anti-Semitic incidents increased by 58 per cent in France in 2012 and 26 per cent of French Jews were reported to be considering leaving the country. There are now regular French *minyanim* at St Johns Wood Synagogue in London.

During the year a provincial German judge held that circumcision should be illegal as it caused babies grievous bodily harm. The German parliament were appalled and moved swiftly to approve circumcision by 434 to 100 votes. There may be a case for French Jews to think of moving to the benevolent protection of the Bundestag.

Making up just 0.4 per cent of the UK population, the A-level performance of Jewish school pupils in the non-selective comprehensive category was a cause for heartiest congratulations. Of the top 12 places in the country, Jewish schools won four; JFS was 4th, Yavneh 5th, Hasmonean 9th and King David High School 12th. According to the census nearly 20 per cent of the working Jewish community are in executive jobs. This is about three times the norm for the best of the other ethnic communities. For those less fortunate Jews, Norwood found the funds to resurrect Drugsline, which had done such sterling work in helping those struggling with addiction.

There were, of course, a number of negative incidents. One of the most serious was the advice given to a child abuse victim by a senior Charedi rabbi. He counselled the boy not to go to the police. An article by Rabbi Harvey Belovski in this volume states the *din* on the subject, which is not in accordance with the advice given. Hopefully, a clearer understanding of the *din* may prevent members of the Charedi community discriminating against the victims, if they do tell the authorities. The Union of Orthodox Hebrew Congregations (UOHC) should protect the victims and roundly condemn those who would defend the criminals.

A further cause célèbre has been the charging of a senior Charedi rabbi after complaints by women. An independent Beth Din has yet to give a ruling after many months of deliberation. The North Hendon Adath Synagogue has withdrawn from the UOHC as a result. Just as it was decided to ban television from Charedi homes 50 years ago, there is now concern that the Internet is offering the same world-view, both potentially enlightening and corrupting.

Other sections of the community have had their problems as well. Discussions are ongoing between the Board of Deputies and the Jewish Leadership Council (JLC) to see whether there could be benefits from closer cooperation. The Board of Deputies has represented the views of the community to the government since 1760, covers a wide section of the community, and the Deputies are democratically elected. The most important aspect of dealing with government is to be united in the messages sent out. The alternative is to confuse the politicians and enable them to reject requests simply because there are alternative views provided. It is to be hoped that the discussions will come to some useful conclusions.

In particular, the Board of Deputies is now paying even more attention to the needs of small communities and the JLC has been very helpful in covering half the costs of the Community Partnership Project to support them. Rabbi Major Reuben Livingstone is now both the Minister for Small Communities and the Senior Jewish Chaplain to the Forces.

The United Synagogue elections in the spring saw nine women become Chair of their synagogues. There are, however, 49 synagogues in all in the organization, so parity has yet to be achieved.

Overall, the community has been highly gratified by the unstinting praise lavished on Chief Rabbi Lord Sacks on his retirement. The press and TV coverage was vast for the leader of such a small section of the population, which says a great deal for the esteem in which Lord Sacks is held throughout the country. He left his post with the key question he both asked and answered: 'who is going to lead the community forward? The Jews who abandon Judaism, or the Jews who abandon the world? Neither.' In the twentieth century British Jews remained Orthodox largely because the United Synagogue was middle-of-the-road. It still is, but its support has dwindled from its peak.

Lord Sack's popularity has not, however, prevented continuing attacks by sections of the Church on the alleged mistreatment of Palestinians in Israel. This at a time when most Arab countries are suffering from civil war or near-civil war, and Christian communities – notably Copts – are being attacked and massacred in many parts of the Middle East. The basic Church and Israel problem is, of course, insoluble; the holiest sites in Christendom are now part of a Jewish State. This was not the objective of the Crusades and it is offensive to many devout members of the church around the world.

It is deeply ironic, therefore, that the only part of the Middle East where Christians live in peace, fully protected by the State and, as a result, increasing in numbers, is Israel. The State receives little credit for this and the Church of Scotland is only the latest to issue a highly critical report. The Jewish organizations in Scotland have broken off relations with them as a result. A joint Board of Deputies/Oxfam project on relieving hunger is also in danger from the charity not abiding by prior agreements.

The community always has difficulty in keeping such problems in perspective. For instance, a minor Liberal Democrat MP with a tiny majority has a major Moslem section of his electorate. His attack early in the year on alleged atrocities against Palestinian people by the Israelies might have garnered some votes in the future, but hardly deserved the attention it received. However, of more importance was the appointment of Grant Shapps as Chair of the Conservative Party, which was largely overlooked by the *Jewish Chronicle*.

Well over a million viewers enjoyed Simon Schama's television series *The History of the Jews*, which became required viewing on Sunday evenings in September, thankfully after the *Antiques Roadshow*. A conflict of interests was thus narrowly avoided.

Although minor efforts continue to be made to boycott Israeli products, imports from Israel to the UK rose by over 50 per cent, year-on-year. Trade relations are excellent. In Saudi Arabia favourable comments on Israel are showing a new sense of realism. One professor at King Saud University said that, since 1967, Israel has managed to build eight public universities and 200 museums that receive nearly four million tourists a year. It has also become a rival to the United States in the programming and software industries. Praise like that in Saudi Arabia only comes with government approval. A Moslem peer, however, said in Pakistan that Jews controlled the press in Britain. He was thrown out of the Labour party.

Another satisfactory principle was reiterated in July. An Orthodox Jew had been denied unemployment benefit because he refused to take a job which involved working on Shabbat. His claim was upheld and he was awarded £1,500 damages against the Department of Work & Pensions.

Kosher meat sales have been said to be buoyant since horsemeat was discovered in the general public's food chain. DEFRA, the government body who decides on animal slaughter, has said that there will be no change to the government's acceptance of the continuation of Shechita in this country. The Dutch have drawn back from banning it after discussions with their Jewish community leaders, as have the New Zealand government. It should be emphasized that there remains no definitive scientific evidence that Shechita has been improved on over the centuries as the most humane way of killing animals.

After the assassination of a British soldier in London by Moslem terrorists, there were 150 anti-Moslem incidents across the country in 48 hours. Totally disgraceful attacks on 15 Mosques had to be dealt with by the police. By contrast, in all of 2012 the Community Security Trust reported that there had been only two acts of extreme violence against Jews in this country and no destruction of buildings. The number of anti-Semitic incidents also dropped in the first half of 2013. There was no violence at all over the *yomim tovim*.

Very properly, the community extended its sympathy to its Moslem counterparts and, appropriately at Yom Kippur, World Jewish Relief joined with Save the Children to provide medical supplies, housing and food for about 70,000 Syrian refugee children in Jordan. *Tzedokah* remains at the heart of Judaism. Two adolescent Moslem boys were segregated at school for growing beards. What would the headmaster and governors say about *payas*? The boys should be allowed to grow beards if that is required in their religion.

On campus, there are still anti-Semitic incidents, but universities are rightly intent on maintaining the importance of free speech while ensuring that behavioural issues are kept under control. A hotel in St Andrews which cancelled a Jewish Society dinner booking after a threat to demonstrate by Palestinian supporters was roundly condemned.

The differences between the Orthodox and Progressive movements continue to grow. The Progressives have approved gay marriages and mixed faith burials. The Board of Deputies naturally rejected a request to ask parliament to ban same-sex marriages – it's a free country. Chief Rabbi Mirvis has assured Jewish gays and lesbians that they will always be welcome in his synagogues, but the Orthodox will go no further. It's a free country. The Chief Rabbi will also be setting a precedent by attending Limmud.

Mixed faith burial is, in fact, not a new problem but it can work both ways. Lord Rosebery, the Victorian Prime Minister, was most upset when his wife, Hannah de Rothschild, gave instructions she was to be buried in Willesden rather than with her husband.

In Israel the general election saw the Right and Left blocks with an identical number of seats. A coalition government, with 68 seats out of 120, was formed in which, for the first time in many years, the Ultra-Religious parties were not members. It consists of Likud, the ultra-nationalist Yisrael Beitenu, HaBayit HaYehudi, Yesh Atid and Tzipi Livni's new Hatnua party. Renewed peace talks with the Palestinians were begun under American auspices.

The successful candidates in the election included 12 Arabs. There have always been Arab MPs in the Knesset since the birth of the State. The present group are members of different parties, but include Druze, Bedouin, Christian and Sunni Moslem representatives. A move to rehouse 40,000 Bedouins from their ancestral homes in the Negev has aroused great opposition in many parts of the world. It's somewhat like asking gypsies to settle down permanently in Milton Keynes. The Bedouins would have a higher standard of living but they want to live their lives in their own way.

Israel remains under great pressure but there are positives. The 90 per cent success rate of their Iron Dome antimissile defence system shows just how advanced is their own technology. In addition, Egypt has destroyed much of the tunnel infrastructure by which Hamas brought in military supplies to Gaza. The civil wars in the region are forcing Arab armies to concentrate on sustaining their governments rather than attacking Israel.

Iran has a new Prime Minister who might exchange nuclear enrichment for the removal of sanctions from his country. If the Americans needed any persuading, the events in the Middle East show just how sensible it is for them to maintain Israel as a close friend in the region.

The best news from Israel, however, was the size of the offshore gas fields which have been located in their territorial waters, 60 miles west of Haifa. These are estimated to contain enough gas to produce 2 billion cubic metres for the next 30 years, but these figures will, no doubt, be adjusted in the future. Whatever the final total, the help to the Israeli economy is bound to be substantial.

The new Jewish community centre in Finchley Road, London opened at the end of September to much acclaim, thanks to the munificence and hard work of Lady Duffield and many generous supporters.

In September there was a public discussion on whether the word Yid should be used by supporters at Tottenham Hotspur FC. It was pointed out by the Prime Minister that to do so in public, if it was a hate word, was a criminal offence. This ruling presumably also covers Shikser, Goy, Yok and Schwartzer.

A major row erupted in October when the *Daily Mail* accused Ed Miliband's late father of hating Britain. This was obviously untrue and clumsy anti-Labour rhetoric. It did have the heart-warming result of every political leader publicly supporting Mr Miliband's defence of his father.

In October eight Nobel Prizes were awarded for Science. Six went to Jews. James E. Rothman and Randy W. Schekman won the prize for Physiology or Medicine; François Englert was awarded the Physics prize; and Martin Karplus, Michael Levitt and Arieh Warshel shared the Nobel Prize for Chemistry.

Many famous names in the community have died this year. Among them, Irving Patnick, the MP, Michael Sherrard, the lawyer, Eric Hobsbawm, the historian and, from the world of entertainment, David

Jacobs, Michael Winner and Mike Winters. We have also lost five centenarians in Sidney Jacque, Gertrude Landy, Rita Levi-Montalcini, Stella Mann and Maksymilian Treister. Please G-d by us.

This year marks the 50th anniversary of John Fischer's production of the Calendar section of the Year Book. We would like to offer him our congratulations on reaching this milestone and our sincere thanks for the impeccable correctness of each year's contribution.

Elkan Levy
Derek Taylor
Editors
November 2013

ABBREVIATIONS

Ad. – Address
Admin. – Administrative; administration; administrator
Adv. – Advisory; adviser
Asst. – Assistant

B. – Born
Bd. – Board
BoD – Board of Deputies
Br. – Branch

C. – Council
Ch. – Chairman, chairmen, chair
Cllr. – Councillor
Coll. – College
Com. - Communal; community; commission(er)
Comp. – Company
Cttee. – Committee

Dep. – Deputy
Dept. – Department(s)
Dev. – Development
Dir. – Director
Distr. – District

Eccl. – Ecclesiastical
Ed. – Editor
Educ. – Education; educationist; educational
Emer. – Emeritus
Exec. – Executive

Fdr. – Founder
Fed. – Federation; federal
Fel. – Fellow; fellowship
Fin. – Finance; financial
Form. – Former; formerly

Gen. – General
Gov. – Governor; governing
Govt. – Government

H. – Honorary
Hist. – History; historical; historian
Hd. – Head, Headmaster, Head Teacher
Hon. T. – Honorary Treasurer
Hon. S. – Honorary Secretary

Imm. - Immediate
Instit. – Institute; institution(al)
Intl. – International

Jt - Joint

Lab. – Labour; laboratory
Lect. – Lecturer; lecture(ship)
Libr. – Librarian
Lit. – Literature
LJ – Liberal Judaism

M. – Minister
Man. – Manager; management; managing
Med. – Medical; medicine
Mem. - Member/membership
Min. – Ministry; ministerial
MEP – Member of European Parliament
MP – Member of Parliament

Nat. – National; nationalist; nation(s)
NGO - Non Government organisation

Off. – Officer; office
Org. – Organiser

Parl. – Parliament; parliamentary
Pol. – Political
Pres. – President(s)
PM – Prime Minister
Princ. – Principal
Prof. – Professor
Publ. – Publication; publicity; publishing

Reg. – Registrar; register(ed); region(al)
Res. – Research; residence; resource
RM – Reform Movement

SAE - Stamped Addressed Envelope
Sch. – School(s)
Sec. – Secretary
Soc. – Society; social; sociology
Snr. – Senior
Supt. – Superintendent

T. – Treasurer
Tech. – Technical; technology, -ical
Tru. – Trustee(s); trust

UK – United Kingdom
US – United Synagogue

V. – Vice
Vis. – Visitation; visitor; visiting
Vol. – Voluntary; volunteer; volume

GLOSSARY

AJA – Anglo-Jewish Association
AJEX – Association of Jewish Ex-Servicemen and Women

BMA – British Medical Association

CBF-WJR – Central British Fund for World Jewish Relief
CCJ – Council of Christians and Jews
C of E – Council of Europe

IJPR – Institute for Jewish Policy Research

JBS – Jewish Blind Society

JEDT – Jewish Educational Development Trust
JMC – Jewish Memorial Council
JNF – Jewish National Fund
JWB – Jewish Welfare Board

TAC – Trades Advisory Council

ORT – Organisation for Resources and Technical Training

WIZO – Women's International Organisation
WJC – World Jewish Congress
WZO – World Zionist Organisation

The Installation Address of
Chief Rabbi Ephraim Mirvis

COME WITH ME

'Ze hayom asa Hashem nagila venismecha vo' – 'This is the day
that the Lord has made, let us be glad and rejoice thereon'.

Prayers

On this auspicious and historic occasion, when I humbly take on the
mantle of the 11th Chief Rabbi since 1704, I offer two prayers. First,
a prayer of thanksgiving. I express my gratitude to the Holy One,
Blessed Be He, who has guarded and protected me from the time of
my birth and upbringing in South Africa, through to the years of my
studies in Israel, on to the time when I had the privilege to lead great
communities in Ireland and the UK, through to this special day, filled
with joy and charged with opportunity – *Baruch Atah shehecheyanu
vekiyemanu vehigiyanu lazeman hazeh*.

And I also offer a prayer of supplication. May Almighty God bless
me and those who will work with me so that we shall succeed in our

quest. *Lehagdil Torah uleha'adira* – to magnify Torah and bring glory to its name, *lekadesh Shem Shamayim* – to sanctify the Name of God in heaven, may we have the privilege to enhance lives, to transform communities and to make a contribution of value to our society. *Vihi noam Hashem Elokenu alenu uma'aseh yadenu konena aleinu uma'aseh yadenu konenehu* – May the pleasantness of the Lord our God be upon us and the work of our hands, for good, for life and for peace, Amen.

Distinguished Guests

Looking around the Synagogue right now, I'm so touched to see so many of you who have made great efforts to come and celebrate with us today from many countries right around the world. But first and foremost, Your Royal Highness. Your presence here today is a great honour, not just an honour for me personally, but a great honour for our entire community. It is a reflection of the passion you have to work with the faith communities in this country; it is an expression of your desire to bring unity and to promote all the good things that we stand for. Your input and your inspiration go a long way. May I avail of this opportunity on behalf of all present and indeed on behalf of our entire Jewish community, to warmly congratulate you on the recent birth of your first grandchild, HRH Prince George Alexander Louis of Cambridge. Mazeltov!

We are honoured here today to welcome the Leader of Her Majesty's Opposition, Ed Miliband, together with representatives of the Prime Minister and the Deputy Prime Minister and I note that you're all sitting on the same front bench in our Synagogue, and that is together with notable members of the Commons and of the Lords. I think that we shouldn't read too deeply into this, but rather it is a reflection of the fact that in this house we are all on the same side. Thank you so much for gracing this event with your presence here today.

A warm welcome to distinguished national leaders and communal leaders, revered and esteemed faith leaders, the President and Trustees of the United Synagogue and our good friends from other synagogal bodies.

Beruchim habaim, to close to 200 Dayanim, Chief Rabbis and Rabbis, from Britain and many countries around the world. And in particular it is my great pleasure today to celebrate this moment in the presence of my esteemed colleagues, the Dayanim of the London Beth Din, the Court of the Chief Rabbi. Our community is blessed to have Dayanim, who are Torah scholars of the highest calibre, who are totally committed to the future success of our community and it will now be my pleasure and privilege to work with them.

A special warm welcome to His Excellency, the Ambassador of the State of Israel. As a passionate supporter of Israel and as the first Chief Rabbi to be a product of Israeli Yeshiva academies, and the first to have been ordained in Israel, I am delighted that in our country, as is the case in our community, we have strong, close and warm ties with the State of Israel.

My three immediate predecessors were all installed into office at momentous times in the history of the State. Chief Rabbi Sir Israel Brodie gave his inaugural address in the New Synagogue, Egerton Road in 1948, in the midst of the War of Independence, just six weeks after the creation of the State. Chief Rabbi Lord Jakobovits gave his inaugural address from this pulpit in 1967, just weeks before the outbreak of the Six Day War. And Chief Rabbi Lord Sacks spoke from this pulpit 22 years ago to the day, and he delivered his inaugural address just after the conclusion of the Gulf War.

As I stand before you today, hostility is rife in Syria and we are witnessing some terrible atrocities. And also at this time, Israel and the Palestinians are set on holding negotiations with an eye towards establishing a true and lasting peace. In the years to come, I would love people to look back on this day and associate it with the time when finally we were on the path to beating swords into ploughshares, in Israel and throughout the Middle East. May Almighty God bless our leaders with the wisdom, to make wise and responsible decisions through these days, weeks and months of challenge. *Oseh shalom bimromav hu ya' aseh shalom aleynu*. May he who makes peace in high places, bring peace for us all, Amen.

Emeritus Chief Rabbi Lord Sacks. Thank you so much for your prayers, for your warm wishes, for your kind sentiments. Thank you for your friendship and for your encouragement. You have presided over a remarkable era of Jewish growth and renewal. You have become a leading spokesman for Judaism in our generation. Through the sheer brilliance of your writings and your speeches, you have touched the hearts and moulded the minds of thousands upon thousands of people, in this country and indeed throughout the world. And we in your community have basked in the radiance of your success, as our ambassador par excellence.

Your legacy will be with us for generations to come. This is the second time that I am succeeding you and the first was when you became Chief Rabbi and I then became Rabbi of Western Marble Arch and now, as was the case then, I'm in the privileged position to build on your successes.

On behalf of us all, I extend to you warm and fond wishes, may you and Lady Sacks benefit from the showering of blessings from the Almighty, for *beracha vehatzlacha* – blessing and success in all your future endeavours on behalf of the Jewish people, Amen.

Family

Valerie and I are delighted to celebrate this day with our dear family. Our sons, Hillel, Danny, Noam and Eitan, our daughters-in-law, Melanie and Althea, together with Jonny and Batya.

We are blessed with wonderful, darling grandchildren: Kinneret and Elitzur; Naama and Tamara; Raphael and Liora.

We thank the Almighty that our respective fathers are here to witness this day. My father, *Avi Mori* Rabbi Dr Lionel Mirvis with Raisel. It is from my father that I received my passion for communal leadership and my yearning for the Rabbinate. And my father-in-law, Dr Stanley Kaplan with Pia. They have all given us much support and encouragement.

There are two remarkable women of blessed memory, about

whom I think many times, each and every day. My mother, Freida Mirvis *z'l*, taken from us at all-too-young an age. In her pious and selfless ways, she taught us the lesson, that when all is said and done, what matters most in life, is not what titles you have had, but rather what kind of a *mensch* you have been. And our daughter Liora *z'l*. Her deep-rooted faith, her remarkable courage, her joy of life and the light that she brought into the lives of many, provide us with ongoing inspiration. She taught us the lesson, that in a short amount of time you can do some incredible things.

A Time for Change

At this moment, I am thinking of the High Priest, who entered into the Holy of Holies on the Holy day of Yom Kippur, to stand before the Almighty and pray for his people, the people he loved. And so too at this moment, I enter into this sacred office and I stand before the Almighty on behalf of my community, the community I love, and our community will always be our top priority.

We are standing on the threshold of a new Jewish year. The Hebrew for year is *shana*, meaning 'repetition', as we have in the *Shema*, where the term *veshinantam*, means to educate by rote through repetition. *Shana* therefore represents everything that comes time and again in a predictable way, year in and year out. The same months, the same seasons, the same festivals. And within a *shana* we have *chodashim*, months, coming from the root *chadash* which means 'new'. And this is because, with the advent of every new month, the moon appears afresh and anew.

We therefore have two interlinked concepts; *shana* and *chodesh*. The constant and the new – fused together to provide us with our unique recipe for fulfilling religious experience. We are blessed to have a framework of immutable and timeless truths which transcend the fads and fashions of the era, which anchor us in the dawn of time, which link us up with successive generations that take us back to the origins of our faith. Built into that framework we have a mechanism for rebirth and renewal.

Every generation faces its own challenges and every generation must provide its response to the challenges it faces. With our minds turned to the past, and our eyes fixed firmly on the future, rooted in our traditions and in touch with the world around us, governed by *halacha*, Jewish law, we must find the necessary tools to transform our challenges into opportunities, as we hold on ever so tightly to our spiritual legacy, which passes through our hands en-route to the generations to come.

Times do change. Twenty-two years ago, when my illustrious predecessor stood on this pulpit, that was a very different world from the one we have today. The Iron Curtain then, was still falling, the Internet was not an integral part of our lives and Arsenal were still winning trophies.

Yes, times do change.

The beauty of our tradition, the majesty of our heritage, the thrill of a Jewish way of life, accompanied by joy and fulfilment, all of these need to be transmitted, conveyed and articulated in a way that suits our times. I am so excited to be the first Chief Rabbi to be inducted into office in the digital age, providing us with breathtaking opportunities to reach homes and hopefully to reach the hearts of people within those homes, right around the world.

My Vision

So, what are the challenges that we are facing in this second decade of the twenty-first century? There is so much that we can be proud of, and at the same time there is lots of room for concern.

We can be proud of the fact that there is today a renaissance of Jewish life, added commitment to Jewish learning and practice, and so we have seen increased levels of attendance in many of our synagogues. This, however, is accompanied by the fact that in the last national census 26 per cent of those who proudly responded that they are Jewish are not members of any synagogue whatsoever. Such a high level of disengagement must be a cause for concern.

We are encouraged by the increase of Jewish children attending Jewish schools. The number has close to trebled within one single generation, what a stunning statistic. But that is coupled by record levels of assimilation.

Within our society, we benefit from the comforts of modern living, and from the breathtaking advances in science, medicine and technology, but how can we ever rest when we know there are so many that have been impoverished, who need assistance, who are weak and who are vulnerable.

And within our community, we have succeeded in some spectacular ways together, however we have suffered damage from totally unnecessary communal infighting and ill-will.

So, what can be done?

When the cantor takes the Torah scroll out of the Ark, he declares *Gadlu laShem iti uneromema Shemo yachdav*. Come with me to do great things for the Lord and let us exalt His name together.

Today I issue an invitation to you all: *Gadlu laShem iti* – Come with me to do great things for the Lord. Come with me as I embark on my Chief Rabbinate. Come with me on an exciting and fulfilling journey.

And as we embark on this journey we will be confronted by many challenges and numerous hurdles that we will need to negotiate. We will take on many of them, but in particular, I would like us to focus on three priorities.

In the Ethics of the Fathers we are taught: The world stands upon three things: *Torah* –Jewish education, *Avodah* – service of God through community, *Gemilut Chasadim* – acts of love and kindness. These will be the three major pillars of my Chief Rabbinate:

First of all, *Torah* – Enhancing and deepening Jewish education for one and all.

Secondly, *Avodah* – Building and developing great Jewish communities in the UK and throughout the Commonwealth.

And thirdly, *Gemilut Chasadim* – Enabling us to achieve our potential for personal and communal social responsibility.

So come with me as we embark on this journey, prioritising these three areas.

Education

Gadlu laShem iti. Come with me, as we deepen and enhance Jewish education for one and all.

The term Rabbi means teacher. As Chief Rabbi, I will be the senior teacher of the community and I see in our Rabbis, my partners. We have a dual responsibility, to be there for those who are already committed and also to reach out to those who do not yet fully appreciate the beauty of their heritage. We will be there for one and all, we will stand there with open arms and a smile on our faces, letting everyone know that in Synagogue you have a home away from home.

During the past six months, I have had the great pleasure of visiting the majority of United Synagogue Rabbis and Rebbetzens in their homes, and I am looking forward to the pleasure of meeting all of our Rabbinic couples throughout the country as soon as I can. I have been deeply impressed to witness the high calibre of Rabbinic leadership that is being provided to our communities. I would like to empower our Rabbis further to provide Rabbinic excellence and I would like us to have world-class spiritual leadership, in all of our communities.

I would like ours to be a learning community. That is why I have chosen for the motto of my Chief Rabbinate the verse '*Etz chayim hi lamachazikim ba*' – 'It is a tree of life for those who grasp hold of it'.

We shall not seek to impose our traditions on anyone, nor to push our religion down people's throats. The Torah is there as a tree of life for those who grasp it. We will provide you with great opportunities and invite you to avail of them and to grasp hold of these opportunities to enhance your personal lives, and through your lives to strengthen communities, and through great communities to contribute to our wonderful society.

And therefore, my call to you is: come learn with me. Come and learn with your Rabbi. Come and learn with your friends and soon enough you will realize the truth of what is taught in the ethics of the fathers. '*Hafoch ba vehafoch ba dekula ba*'. Take the Torah, turn it this way and that and you will discover that it provides you with the potential to achieve your greatest dreams.

Community Development

Gadlu laShem iti. Come with me, as we highlight the importance of building and strengthening and developing our communities.

There are many terms in Hebrew which are used for the gathering of people. In the Torah there are primarily two; they are *edah* and *kehilla*. What's the difference between them? An *edah* is a group of people who have come together at one time, in one place, for one specific purpose. They might never have met one another before, nor are they interested in meeting one another again but right now they have a common goal. A fine example of an *edah* setting is an audience at the theatre. When you enter into the theatre to take your seat, is it expected of you to say 'good evening' to the person sitting next to you? It is not really expected but if you do so you will probably receive a polite good evening in return. Is it expected of you in addition to then say 'How are you? Family alright? Everything OK?'. No, it is not. That could be quite unsettling for the person next to you. And if in addition you say 'After the show, would you like to come to our home for coffee?' that would be highly suspicious.

A *kehilla*, however, is something very different. A kehilla is a group of like-minded individuals who share a set of values and a vision for their future. They have met one another on many occasions in the past and will be thrilled to be in the presence of one another on many occasions in the future. And through participation within the *kehilla* dynamic, each individual is empowered to do far more than he or she could ever have done alone. When you enter into the *kehilla* context and you take your seat, is it expected of you to turn to your neighbour and say 'Shabbat Shalom'? Most definitely. And you will receive a hearty 'Shabbat Shalom' in return. And if you add to that: 'How are you, is everything alright?' then your neighbour would engage you in a long conversation, regardless of where we are at in the service. And if, in addition, you say 'After the service, would you like to come to our home for Kiddush?' that would be just wonderful because that is what the *kehilla* is all about.

In the Book of Exodus we are taught *'Vayakhel Moshe et kol adat Bnei Yisrael.'* 'Moses congregated the assembly of the children of Israel.' Moses transformed an *edah* into a *kehilla*. When we were in Egypt, we were a loosely bonded collection of souls who were descended from the same ancestors. When we arrived at Mount Sinai, we were transformed into a kingdom of priests and a holy nation and, through the Torah, we were given a common mandate for life. We arrived at Sinai as an *edah* and we emerged from there as a *kehilla*.

So let us take a leaf out of the book of Moses, who transformed our people, into a viable and vital community. Traditionally, many of our synagogues have been just houses of prayer. I would like to transform our synagogues into powerhouses of Jewish religious, educational and cultural experience which will enhance the lives of one and all. And the key to our success will be our Rabbis. Great Rabbis will make great communities.

Social Responsibility

Gadlu laShem iti. Come with me as we take seriously our social responsibility, caring for the weak, the needy and the vulnerable.

The Torah introduces us to the concept of *machatzit hashekel*, the half shekel piece, the one coin per person that the nation was invited to contribute to the Sanctuary – that public space belonging to the entire people. The coins were then counted and as a result a census figure was known. Consequently, you were only counted, if you gave. Descartes said 'I think, therefore I am'. Jewish tradition teaches 'I give, therefore I am.'

And it is in this context that we discover the hallmark of British Jewry. Today I am privileged to become the spiritual head of a most wonderful and remarkable community which fully appreciates the value of giving. A community which is there not only for members of our own community who are needy, but which is there for those who require assistance throughout the country. And so we need to be committed to one and all. We have a great concept in our tradition, called *tikun olam*, healing the world; making it into a better world. *Tikun olam* is based on the premise that we appreciate and recognize that every human soul is sacred.

The Jerusalem Talmud asks the question: 'What is the most important verse of the entire Torah?' Ben Azzai gives the answer: 'Genesis chapter 5 verse 1, which reads: "This is the book of the generations of man on the day that God created man, in the image of God he formed him."' Ben Azzai wants us to know that the greatest pillar of our faith is recognition of the fact that every human being is created in the image of God.

We must be there for one and all with compassion, giving to our society, engaging in social action of the highest calibre.

If you would ask me, amongst all the great Rabbis of the last few centuries, do I have a role model, somebody, who I try to emulate in my life, my answer readily would be to tell you about a great man who lived from 1810 to 1883. He was given the name at birth, Yisrael Lipkin. And because he was raised in the town of Salant, he became popularly known as Reb Yisrael Salanter. He founded the Mussar Movement and he advocated a life of ethical values.

Let me share with you one anecdote, which encapsulates his mindset and his world view. In the 1840s Reb Yisrael Salanter was a Rabbi in Vilna in Lithuania. A matzah manufacturer desperately wanted his *hechsher*, his Rabbinic seal of approval, for his matzah products in anticipation of the festival of Passover. So the Rabbi was invited to inspect the plant. He came to the matzah factory, he was shown around and it was explained to him how the minutiae of Jewish law were being applied. At the end of his tour he was brought into the office of the owner, who turned to him with great expectation and said 'Well Rabbi, can I expect your seal of approval?' The Rabbi said 'No'. The owner said, 'What do you mean "no"? Haven't you noticed, we apply every single stringency in the book, in this plant.' The Rabbi replied, 'I'm sorry, you won't have my seal of approval.' The owner asked why and the Rabbi explained: 'While I was engaged in my tour of the plant I spoke to some of your workers. They told me about the conditions in which they work and the shabby treatment they are given. I will not allow my name to be associated with your products.'

Kosher is not only a concept which relates to what we eat and drink. Kosher is a way of life. Let us adopt a kosher way of life with compassion, with understanding, with tolerance, with warmth, with love to one and all, through social responsibility of the highest order. The Talmud teaches that if there is a person who believes in God but does not act in ways of loving kindness, it is as if that person has no God.

So these then, are the three great pillars of my Chief Rabbinate. *Torah*, high quality Jewish education for one and all. *Avodah*, the building and strengthening of great Jewish communities. *Gemilut chasadim*, acts of loving kindness.

Friends, I cannot do it by myself. I need your help.

When the High Priest stood in the Holy of Holies, while he was praying to the Almighty on behalf of the people, the people gathered in the courtyard outside to will him on with prayer. They worked together, in order to get results. And so too, please, will you work together with me. Let us not allow *sinat chinam*, the type of causeless hatred which brought about the destruction of our Temple and the exile in its wake, to stand in our way. Instead, let us follow the advice of the first Chief Rabbi of the Holy Land, Rabbi Kook who taught that with *ahavat chinam*, unconditional love, we will ultimately achieve our goal of reaching redemption.

This is the second time as well that I am succeeding Lord Jakobovits. He preceded me as well as Chief Rabbi of Ireland. I grew to love and revere Lord Jakobovits. And I recall him once commenting on the *Sim Shalom* prayer, which we say three times a day. Within this prayer when we ask God for peace between ourselves and our enemies. we say: *'Barechenu Avinu kulanu ke'echad'*. 'Bless us, our Father, all of us, as one.' Lord Jakobovits asked, why, while we pray for peace between ourselves and our enemies without, do we speak about peace between ourselves within. And he answered, we can only seek peace with those who seek to harm us from without, if, in the first instance, we work together as a united people within.

Sadly, in our post-Holocaust era, there are still those who seek our harm from without. I am proud of the many communal organizations who are seeking to combat the spread of anti-Semitism but most of all, I'm proud of the fact that in our country, the fight against anti-Semitism is being led by successive governments and parliament. That is because it is correctly recognized that a threat against the Jews is a threat against our society.

The values of working together, unity and togetherness also underpin the relationship that we should have with other faiths. And I'm so delighted that already there are warm and cordial ties between our community and other faith groups in this country and I will passionately be involved in strengthening those bonds further. At times we become confused between uniformity and unity. We presume that in order to have peace, everybody should say the same and think the same. That is uniformity. It was Chief Rabbi Kook who spoke about real unity, through the imagery of a symphony orchestra. In an orchestra, you have different instruments, each providing their own unique sound. Under the baton of the conductor, they blend together to produce a beautiful harmony. And so too within a society, when we respect differences and when we work together under the baton of cooperation, we can produce a beautiful and marvellous harmony for our entire society.

That is my vision for a bright and great future for us all. Come with me to focus on the three great pillars of my Chief Rabbinate.

Conclusion

Torah – Jewish education of the highest caliber. *Avodah* – strengthening our community, creating great communities. *Gemilut chasadim* – social responsibility.

Etz chayim hi lamachazikim ba. The Torah is a tree of life for all those who grasp it. Today I issue this call to you: Come and grasp hold of the opportunities you will have from this day forward and work together with me, to ensure that we will have a thrilling and wonderful future.

Gadlu laShem iti uneromema Shemo yachdav. Come with me to do great things for the Lord and let us exalt His name together.

Come with me, *lehagdil Torah uleha'adira*, to magnify Torah and bring glory to its name.

Come with me *lekadesh Shem Shamayim*, to sanctify the name of God in Heaven.

Come with me to build and develop great Jewish communities.

Come with me to engage with love and understanding, compassion and tolerance towards all others.

Come with me to celebrate the achievements of the State of Israel and to work towards a lasting peace in the entire Middle East.

Come with me to engage in *tikun olam*, as we will make this into a better world.

May we do all this and much more in good health and in happiness.

Venimtza chen vesechel tov be'einei Elokim veadam, and may we find grace and favour in the eyes of God and of man.

Vechen yehi ratzon, and so may it be His will, and let us say, Amen.

Rabbi Harvey Belovski

JEWISH LAW ON CHILD ABUSE

Introduction

There have recently been a number of deeply uncomfortable commentaries surrounding attitudes to reporting sexual abuse within the Jewish community in the UK and overseas. These have appeared in both Jewish and mainstream media. They have called attention to the reality that, for some British Jews, admitting that domestic and child abuse occur within our community, albeit at no greater frequency than in any other sector of society, remains unthinkable. It is understandably difficult to accept that members of one's own tribe could be involved in such abhorrent activities. It can be devastating when faced with incontrovertible evidence or even persistent rumours of sexual abuse by a family member or religious leader.

These exposés, as well as a number of unsavoury high-profile allegations, have focused on the conduct of certain members and leaders of the strictly Orthodox (Haredi) community. They have consciously highlighted their attitude to reporting sexual and domestic abuse to the police and social services. The issue is not unique –

whistle-blowers have often been treated with contempt in, for example, the military, universities and businesses. A further complication, however, is that Orthodox informers must also contend with accusations of *mesirah* – informing on a fellow Jew – and their ramifications.

In this essay, I will explore the thorny issue of *mesirah* and ascertain how it applies to allegations of domestic or sexual abuse. I will determine appropriate Jewish juridical guidelines for reporting, that are responsive to the demands of Jewish law, contemporary sensitivities and mandatory requirements.

Background

Even a cursory examination of early Jewish sources produces an overwhelmingly negative picture of reporting a fellow Jew to non-Jewish authorities, whatever the alleged offence. The Talmud lists the *moser* (informer) among the worst sinners – apostates and those who incite others to sin – and declares that they descend to *Gehinnom* (Hell) and are judged there for many generations.[1] Rashi, the foremost talmudic commentator, narrowly defines informers as those who hand Jewish money to idolators.[2] The informer was understood to be someone who reported any actual (or fabricated/exaggerated) wrongdoing of his or her co-religionists to non-Jewish authorities. The Talmud itself explains that non-Jewish authorities were ruthless when dealing with Jews who were handed to them for even minor infraction. It actually sanctions eliminating informers, in extremis, where they pose a direct danger to the Jewish community.[3] Maimonides (d.1204, Spain and Egypt) codifies a broad understanding of the term: there are two types of *mosrim* – (a) one who hands a fellow Jew to gentiles who will kill or beat him; and (b) one who hands the property of a fellow Jew to gentiles; neither has a portion in the World to Come.[4] This antagonistic attitude to reporting reflects the political and social realities of Jewish life under the Roman Empire and during the Middle Ages.

However serious the allegation against a Jew, the consequences of reporting him or her to unprincipled, exploitative and often Jew-hating authorities were worse. Jews were commonly singled out for inequitable treatment and handed sentences incommensurate with the offence committed. Worse, handing Jews, their property or even information about the workings of Jewish communities to the non-Jewish authorities could compromise Jewish self-determination. It could imperil the Jews precarious economic and social position.

In many cases, Jewish communities had no option but to handle offenders internally. Jewish authorities resorted to trials, sentencing and severe sanctions, however unsatisfactory the outcome. Understandably, the *moser* was the most despised member of early Jewish societies – reviled, excluded and, in some cases, eliminated. The fear that the *moser* engendered is illustrated by a responsum of Rabbenu Asher (d.1329, Germany and Spain), which describes how the community is extremely frightened of an individual who frequently handed exaggerated reports about Jewish criminality to the ruling Moslem authorities.[5] Rabbenu Asher permitted the Jews to take whatever steps necessary to rid themselves of the *moser*, as the entire Jewish community was imperilled by his actions.

This is coded by the authoritative *Shulhan Arukh* (Rabbi Yosef Karo, d.1575, Spain and Israel), where it states that: it is forbidden to hand a Jew into the hands of an idolater, whether for his person or his property, even if he is a wicked and sinful person and even if he is causing others distress and upset. Anyone who does this has no portion in the World to Come. It is permitted to kill an informer anywhere, even today, and it is permitted to kill him before he informs.[6]

Continuation of Traditional Approach

This draconian approach has been bolstered by harsh experience over the centuries since the publication of the *Shulhan Arukh*. Jewish communities have frequently endured persecution, discrimination and unjust treatment at the hands of anti-Semitic authorities. Examples of these inequities are too numerous to list. Even within the last 200 years, however, infamous cases include the kidnapping of Edgardo Mortara, a Jewish boy removed from his family by the Papal authorities to be raised as a Catholic; the Cantonists, Jewish boys forcibly conscripted into the Russian army, a practice that continued well into the nineteenth century; the Dreyfus Affair, in which a Jewish army officer was wrongly convicted of treason by the French military; and the Beilis Trial, in which a Ukrainian Jew was accused of ritual murder. Jews from Arab lands frequently fared little better.[7] Haunted by these communal experiences, it is hardly surprising that Jews whose ancestors hailed from European and North African countries and fled persecution there, should retain a visceral negativity towards those who might report their co-religionists to the authorities; irrespective of the nature of the allegation.

And, of course, the more recent horrors of the Holocaust, during which reporting the slightest movements of fellow Jews could lead to their torture and execution, remains deeply embedded in people's collective memory.

Understanding Contemporary Haredi Attitudes

The combination of extreme hostility to reporting found in classic sources and the ghastly legacy of anti-Semitic persecution has informed the contemporary attitude to reporting, found in some segments of the Orthodox community.

As such, there are members of traditional communities who are convinced that *mesirah* is a heinous crime, an offence that will certainly consign both the reporter and the Jewish community at large to a dreadful fate. And in parochial village communities, non-conformity, especially in an area such as reporting, may be treated very harshly. Informers can be ostracized from their community, risking their professional, personal and social lives. It is not unknown for potential informers to fear that their children's schooling and marriage options will be severely compromised, should they go to the authorities rather than allowing the matter to be dealt with internally. Sadly, even intimidation is not unknown.

Some rabbis insist that sexual abuse allegations be handled internally. Indeed, in most situations, it is actually forbidden to turn to secular authorities when a viable Jewish alternative is available. Yet Jewish courts today are not equipped (or, most jurisdictions, empowered) to deal with accusations of abuse. Even those communities whose leaders vehemently disapprove of reporting have failed to create any type of credible court or system to handle them.

Yet since for the members of insular communities, identification with the group is the central and defining feature of their lives, the threat of exclusion can be utterly devastating. So much so that even those contemplating reporting horrible abuse may be willing to reconsider. This, despite the obvious reality, that in a world where Jewish authorities have no real powers, failure to report allegations of sexual abuse focuses blame on victims, protects perpetrators and encourages reoffending.

Mesirah in Sexual Abuse Cases

Our study thus far may help to understand the resistance in some quarters to the reporting of even the most serious allegations. Yet notwithstanding the overwhelming negativity we have encountered, further enquiry reveals that the true picture with regard to allegations involving vulnerable people is more nuanced, and in tune with modern sensitivities. Indeed, I will show that reporting in most sexual abuse cases is actually mandated by Jewish law.

To investigate this further, I will consider the following points in turn: (a) whether the concept of *mesirah* applies in non-discriminatory jurisdictions; (b) whether classic sources forbidding *mesirah* were ever, in fact, germane to allegations of sexual abuse; (c) whether statutory reporting obligations impact on Jewish legal considerations.

(A) Does Mesirah Apply in Non-Discriminatory Jurisdictions?

I have already considered the impact of the hostile non-Jewish environments in which Jews commonly lived on the issue of *mesirah* – reporting co-religionists to the authorities. While some contemporary sources interpret the laws of reporting virtually unchanged from their antecedent texts,[8] others take a different approach. Among them is the great Lithuanian scholar Rabbi Yehiel Mikhel ha-Levi Epstein (d.1908, Belarus), who writes that:

It is widely known to historians that in times of old in far-away places, no-one had any assurance in the safety of his life or property because of pirates and bandits, even if they took upon themselves the appearance of government. It is known that this is true even today in some places in Africa where the government itself is grounded in theft and robbery. Yet we can mention favourably the sovereigns of Europe, especially our great ruler, the Tsar of Russia and his predecessors, and the Kings of Great Britain, who have spread their influence over many distant lands, so that everyone will have confidence in the security of his life and property. The wealthy do not need to hide themselves so that others will not loot or kill them. On this rests all the laws of the reporter and informer that appear in the Talmud and codes.[9]

It is left to later scholars to debate whether R. Epstein wrote his curious praise of the Tsar merely to bypass the Russian censor.[10] His formulation, however, is of great importance, as it indicates that the classic laws of *mesirah* may not apply where Jews live under non-discriminatory regimes, such as the British Empire, where people feel secure in person and property. This approach is accepted in principle by Rabbi Eliezer Waldenberg (d.2006, Israel), a leading judge in the Supreme Rabbinical Court of Jerusalem.[11]

(B) Are Classic Sources About Mesirah *Germane to Sexual Abuse Allegations?*

A careful examination of classic texts reveals that the extreme animus directed towards the *moser* may never have applied to situations in which the alleged offender poses a risk to individuals or to society.

Numerous classic sources, from the Talmud onwards, identify someone who threatens the physical welfare of members of the community as a *rodef* (a pursuer). This individual must be eliminated by whatever means necessary, and certainly, when it will be effective, by handing him or her over to the civil authorities.[12] This applies even when there is a doubt as to whether the allegation is true, and, therefore, whether the person concerned is, in fact a *rodef*. This implements the biblical requirement not to stand idly by one's brother's blood.[13] According to Maimonides,[14] even someone who harasses the community may be handed to the authorities; it is obvious that sexual abuse is far worse than mere harassment.

In his gloss to the *Shulhan Arukh*, Rabbi Moshe Isserles (d.1572, Poland) records a view, based on mediaeval sources, that someone who has been attacked by a fellow Jew may report him to non-Jewish authorities; even if this causes the attacker great loss.[15] R. Isserles also writes that when someone is occupied with deceit and the like, and there is a concern that he will harm the public, it is permitted to report him.[16] This is certainly true where reporting him will prevent him from attacking his victim again.[17] In a responsum dealing with reporting child abuse, R. Waldenberg points out that when the *Shulhan Arukh* forbids informing on an alleged offender, even if he is a wicked and sinful person, this does not apply to situations where the offender poses a threat, such as in sexual abuse allegations. R. Waldenberg explains that in such cases, the purpose of reporting is: 'to rescue [the victim or potential victim] so that [the perpetrator] cannot actualise his evil intention; hence it is permitted to report him; cases such as those before us [child abuse] are much worse than physical violence'.[18] R. Waldenberg concludes his paragraph with the poignant phrase: 'the court is the parent of minors' – the legal system exists to protect children and other vulnerable members of society from predators.

This view, which is rooted firmly in early sources, applies irrespective of the considerations raised in section (A) above. As such, even in circumstances where the authorities treat offenders unjustly, as was certainly the case in R. Isserles time, concern for the welfare of the alleged perpetrator is supplanted by the need to protect society from evil individuals who ruin the lives of others.

(C) Does Statutory Reporting Impact on Jewish Legal Considerations?

In most countries today, statutory reporting obligations pertain in a range of circumstances. A UK example is the provision under Section Seven of the Proceeds of Crime Act 2002, requiring those working in certain regulated professions to report suspicions of money laundering to the authorities. Another common example is the requirement for medics to report cases of suspected domestic or sexual abuse. A number of rabbinic authorities discuss whether such mandatory reporting requirements create a Jewish legal imperative, irrespective of the laws of *mesirah*.[19] These include Rabbis Shemuel Wosner (b.1913, Israel),[20] and Moishe Sternbuch (b.1926, South Africa and Israel),[21] both world-renowned experts in Jewish law, who state that statutory obligations are to be taken very seriously and include them in their evaluation of due process.

I have demonstrated that it is doubtful that the laws of *mesirah* were ever intended to be applied in jurisdictions governed by demo-cratic, equitable laws. Nor is it likely that they were ever germane in cases where the offender poses a threat to individuals or society. I have also noted that according to major contemporary authorities, statutory reporting requirements are vital in determining how to proceed in the event of an allegation. As such, notwithstanding the vigorous opposition to *mesirah* found in classic sources, it seems that in principle, Jewish law requires its adherents to report allegations of sexual abuse to the authorities.

In the final section of this study, I will examine the approach in practice of modern Jewish authorities to reporting abuse and demon-strate that the normative Jewish legal position is, in fact, that reporting is mandatory.

The Views of Contemporary Experts

I now turn to contemporary approaches to reporting abuse. I will examine the view of a number of contemporary Haredi experts and then look at the policy statements of two major rabbinical organizations.

The Position of Rabbi Moishe Sternbuch and other Leading Haredi Authorities

Rabbi Sternbuch, the vice-president of the rabbinical court of the Edah Haredit (strictly Orthodox separatist authority in Jerusalem), is well known for his outspoken views on reporting allegations of abuse. While far from being a lone voice in the Haredi world, he has written and pronounced widely on the topic, making his view especially instructive.

In this matter, R. Sternbuch is aided by Rabbi Dr Daniel Eidensohn, a psychologist and author of three published volumes on the issues of child and domestic abuse in the Jewish community. These incorporate and promote R. Sternbuch's opinions.[22] The following summary of R. Sternbuch's opinions is drawn from his written responsa and also from R. Eidensohn's understanding of R. Sternbuch's position as presented in his works on child abuse.

By way of introduction, R. Sternbuch acknowledges that there have been serious errors in dealing with abuse allegations within the observant community. Some people were concerned that publicizing such incidents would harm the reputation of the community and its institutions. Others mistakenly believed that those who had been molested would get over the abuse in time; that the damage to the reputation of others was more harmful and embarrassing than the hurt and shame experienced by victims.[23]

Add to this the fear of the crime of *mesirah*, and it was not unusual for community leaders to force an abuser to move districts, or a teacher under suspicion to switch schools They even directed the victim and his or her family not to reveal the reason for the change, especially to the secular authorities. It was not unheard of for the family of a victim who had chosen to report a molester, to be ostracized and driven from the community for supposedly disregarding its welfare.

Rejecting this approach as horribly mistaken, R. Sternbuch offers well-defined, unequivocal guidelines. He makes it clear that (a) the majority of Jewish authorities permit going to the police when there is a clear threat of physical or sexual abuse; (b) this is the only appropriate course of action in sexual abuse cases, and the community should not attempt to handle such allegations internally; (c) historic abuse cases must also be reported, as the vast majority of abusers have a strong propensity to reoffend; (d) where, as is the case in most countries today, the law requires suspected abusers to be reported, at least by doctors, teachers and psychologists, it follows that complying with the law is a Torah obligation; and (e) where there is clear evidence of abuse and a rabbi advises not to go to the police, he should be ignored – indeed, any rabbi who suggests sacrificing innocent people to avoid negative consequences to others is not acting as a rabbi at all.

Furthermore, in a responsum, R. Sternbuch clarifies the obligation of a school principal to protect his or her students even if this means listening to rumours and gossip about alleged abusers (something ordinarily forbidden), since these allegations might be true. R. Sternbuch emphasizes that there is no prohibition of listening to rumours when there is a possibility of danger to others.[24]

Yet it is clearly extremely important to exercise caution. R. Sternbuch reminds his readers that malicious accusations certainly occur. As such, it is correct for the sake of objectivity that a competent rabbi – one fully appraised of the gravity of sexual abuse and its ramifications for its victims – be consulted before informing the authorities. Of course, this is only possible when there is no imminent threat, and the short delay caused by consulting with a rabbinical expert will make no difference. R. Sternbuch makes it clear that when there is pressing danger to a child or other potential victim, the requirement to discuss the matter with a rabbi is waived and the matter should be reported directly and immediately to the police.

Other major contemporary authorities from the Haredi sector who mandate reporting abuse to the police include Rabbis Yehudah Silman (Israel),[25] and Hayyim Yisrael Belsky (USA),[26] as well as the greatest expert of his time, Rabbi Shalom Yosef Eliashiv (d.2012, Israel).[27] Rabbi Eliashiv is cited as having said that abuse destroys a child s soul.

The Rabbinical Council of America (RCA) and the Court of the Chief Rabbi

In 2010, the leading rabbinical organization in the USA, the RCA, issued a strongly-worded statement about reporting abuse allegations:

The lives and futures of many of these victims and their families are harmed in significant ways: suicide, post traumatic stress syndrome, inability to form healthy relationships, inability to develop healthy intimate relationships, etc. Many victims of abuse in our community still remain silent and do not come forward to accuse perpetrators or seek help for fear of stigma, personal and familial consequences, or perceived *halakhic* concerns. The Rabbinical Council of America has resolved through past resolutions its condemnation of abuse and its censure of abusers, and has affirmed, under the guidance and direction of its *poskim* (rabbinic decisors), that the prohibitions of *mesirah* (reporting crimes to the civil authorities) and *arka ot* (adjudication in civil courts) do not apply in cases of abuse and in fact, it is *halakhically* obligatory to make such reports.[28]

In 2013, the RCA published the following clarification:

For many years the RCA has condemned the efforts of many parts of the Jewish community to cover up or ignore allegations of abuse, viewing these efforts as against Jewish law, illegal and irresponsible to the welfare of the victims and the greater community. The RCA strongly advocates, as a matter of Jewish law, the reporting of reasonable suspicions of all forms of child abuse to the authorities and full cooperation with the criminal justice system. The RCA decries any invocation of Jewish law or communal interests as tools in silencing victims or witnesses from reporting abuse, or from receiving therapeutic and communal support.[29]

In early 2013, the Court of the Chief Rabbi (London Beth Din) issued a comparable statement:

We have an obligation to safeguard the children of our community and we have to accept that, even within our own communities, there are those who steal the innocence of our children through criminal activity. We are acutely aware that sexual abuse can (apart from being inherently abhorrent) destroy lives and cause a break-down in relationships. It is therefore essential that when abuse has occurred, the police must be informed without delay. Local communities should not attempt to deal with the situation internally. Delays in reporting abuse can cause vital evidence to be lost, allowing the abusers to continue violating our children: the children of our communities will be protected by reporting abuse to the authorities whenever it take place.

It is clear that the guidelines published by the major American and British Jewish religious authorities broadly concur with R. Sternbuchs treatment of reporting as mandatory. It is hard to escape the conclusion that those rabbis who advise otherwise are not following normative Jewish law, but do so because of ignorance of the devastating impact of abuse or for social/political reasons.

Conclusion

In this brief study I have attempted to explain the deeply hostile attitude prevalent in some traditional circles to those who repor fellow Jews to the authorities, even for the most serious crimes. I have demonstrated that this attitude exists at the complex interface between genuine religious imperative rooted in classic sources, communal politics and the realities of historic persecution.

Yet I have clarified that the law of the informer may not be relevant to those who live within equitable, just democracies, especially those that have statutory reporting obligations and certainly does not apply to people whose behaviour renders them a threat to others. Based on these principles, I have shown that major contemporary Jewish legal experts, as well as leading rabbinical authorities in the USA and the UK are clearly of the view that reporting sexual and domestic abuse to the police without delay is a religious duty.

Rabbi Dr Harvey Belovski has been rabbi of Golders Green Synagogue since 2003. He received *semicha* from Gateshead Yeshiva and gained a PhD in hermeneutics from the University of London. In addition to his rabbinical duties, he is principal of Rimon Jewish Primary school, the rabbinic mentor for University Jewish Chaplaincy, a teaching and research fellow at the London School of Jewish Studies, Rosh of the Midrasha for Women, the rabbi of Kisharon and Pal and a lecturer at the JLE. He is a relationship counsellor and rabbinic

advisor. Rabbi Belovski is also a mediator and organizational consultant and the author of three books. He is married and has seven
children.

Notes

1. Talmud Bavli, Rosh HaShanah 17a.
2. Rashi in ibid.
3. Talmud Bavli, Bava Kamma 177a.
4. Mishneh Torah (Maimonides), Laws of Repentance 3:12.
5. Responsa ha-Rosh 17:1.
6. *Shulhan Arukh*, Hoshen Mishpat 388:9–10.
7. See Martin Gilbert, *In Ishmael s House: A History of Jews in Muslim Lands* (New Haven, CT and London: Yale University Press, 2010).
8. See, for example *Pithey Hoshen* (Blau) vol.5 4:2, which asserts that the full force of the law of the *moser* applies even today. See also *Diney Mamonot* (Batzri) 4:93, which claims that even in a jurisdiction in which they bring all matters to the court, through interrogations and police, people can be destroyed. Despite the rather reactionary tone of these 20th/21st century sources, it would be naive to assume that even in the great democracies, all people are treated fairly by the police, courts and prison systems.
9. *Arukh ha-Shulhan* (Epstein) Hoshen Mishpat 388:7.
10. R. Epstein published the Hoshen Mishpat section of his work in the 1880s, during the reign of the autocratic, reactionary Alexander III.
11. Responsa Tzitz Eliezer (Waldenberg) 19:52. Even though R. Waldenberg accepts that R. Epstein wrote his statement for the government, he accepts R. Epstein s central principle.
12. See Talmud Bavli, Bava Kama 117a; Talmud Bavli, Berakhot 58a; Responsa ha-Rashba 1:181, Responsa ha-Rosh 17:1.
13. VaYikra 19:16.
14. Mishneh Torah, Laws of Injurer and Damager 8:11.
15. Gloss to *Shulhan Arukh*, Hoshen Mishpat 388:7.
16. Ibid., 12.
17. Shakh gloss to Isserles (Kohen) in ibid., 45.
18. Waldenberg, ibid.
19. Jewish law includes the principle '*dina de-malkhuta dina*' – the law of the land is the law (Tal-mud Bavli, Nedarim 28a et al.). Scholars have debated for centuries whether this principle applies to all areas of law, only just laws or merely to financial law, as well as what to do when the law of the land explicitly contradicts Jewish law.
20. Responsa Shevet haLevi (Wosner) 2:58.
21. Rabbi Sternbuch's approach to reporting allegations of abuse will be discussed in detail in the next section.
22. Daniel Eidensohn, *Child and Domestic Abuse*, 3 vols (CreateSpace Independent Publishing Platform: vols I & II – 2010, vol. III – 2011). Rabbi Dr Eidensohn has been most helpful in revising and improving this essay, something I gratefully acknowledge.
23. While to those familiar with contemporary thinking about the devastating long-term consequences to the victim of sexual abuse, this attitude seems absurd, it was common throughout society (not just within religious communities) until relatively recently. It is also important to note that contrary to popular belief, most abuse is perpetrated by someone known to and trusted by the victim.
    As such, the victim often believes that no-one will believe the accusations. This is

compounded by the fact that rabbis often dismiss charges against pillar of the community types, such as rabbinical colleagues, doctors and teachers, because they know them and cannot believe that they are capable of such heinous acts.

24. Responsa Teshuvot ve-Hanhagot (Sternbuch) 5:398.
25. Yeschurun, vol. 15.
26. Although there is controversy surrounding Rabbi Belsky's position, it is clear that he advocates reporting to the authorities; see http://www.rabbis. org/news/article.cfm?id =105755.
27. See http://daattorah.blogspot.co.uk/2008/09/child?abuse?calling?police?rav?eliashiv.html.
28. http://www.rabbis.org/news/article.cfm?id=105544.
29. http://www.rabbis.org/news/article.cfm?id=105757.

Maureen Kendler

WOMEN IN THE COMMUNITY

If this was an audio recording, it would begin with the opening bars of Stravinsky's *The Rite of Spring*. This year, two Jewish organizations, setting the scene for new women's initiatives, used the exciting, unexpected sounds of the music for the *The Rite of Spring* ballet and other orchestral works by the Russian composer as their opening gambit. One occasion was the launch of the UK branch of the American organization, the Jewish Orthodox Feminist Alliance (JOFA), and the other was the ordination in America of three women as 'Maharat'. Maharat is a Hebrew acronym for Manhiga Hilkhatit Rukhanit Toranit – a female teacher, legal scholar and spiritual leader.

I will return to JOFA and Maharat: but first, why *The Rite of Spring*? The ballet, *The Rite of Spring*, was first performed a hundred years ago. Written for the 1913 Paris season of Sergei Diaghilev's Ballets Russes company, it was choreographed by Vaslav Nijinsky and designed by Nicholas Roerich. When first performed, at the Théâtre des Champs-Élysées, the avant-garde nature of the music, sets and choreography caused a sensation and a near-riot in the audience. The shock of the new seemed insupportable, outrageous and utterly confusing to the audience. The work – despite its roots in folk tradition – was greeted with disbelief, the derision and the catcalls accompanying the first performance drowned out the orchestra, who gamely continued playing.

The Rite of Spring was a revolutionary work for a revolutionary time. Now the piece is recognized as a masterwork, and part of the international orchestral repertoire. Its place in the cultural canon is secure and its influence celebrated and appreciated. Since 1913 generation after generation of composers have felt impelled to face the challenges it set. The two Jewish events that used this music as their statement fanfare were making a clear comparison about Jewish women's involvement and role in the community. Sometimes it takes revolutionary rather than evolutionary moves to change things. Although so many establishment groups are naturally conservative and resist change; eventually change happens, is accepted as inevitable, necessary and even welcomed, integrated into the mainstream and – with hindsight – seen as beneficial.

It seems that Jewish women in the UK may be on the cusp of change that might be less dramatic than being booed off the communal arena with accompanying violence, but a change that may be equally decisive in terms of long-term influence. Are attitudes to Jewish women reflecting the re-evaluation of women's roles in the wider community, and are they taking hold of their own destiny in a new way?

The year 2013 has seen women in the media spotlight. The centenary of suffragette struggles, the Church's turmoil over appointing women bishops, and disturbing statistics about the reality of glass ceilings in the workplace have dominated the headlines. The lack of visibility of women in public life, discrimination of older women in the media, and power sharing in the boardroom have caused hard, searching questions to be asked. Inevitably, this debate has reached the Jewish community. Male and female members have had to think about how this affects them and their institutions. What sort of changes in our community do we want? What is concomitant with halacha and tradition? There are challenges being made with possible inroads upon centuries of practise in areas of governance and religious practices. Religious authority itself is being brought into question over women's issues.

Inevitably, one response is that we don't want any changes at all. In the more traditional synagogue organizations, such as the Union of Orthodox Hebrew Congregations of England (founded in 1926 with the stated mission 'to protect traditional Judaism'), they see their role as resisters of all such changes. Women are not able to be members of their synagogues, so therefore have no voting rights or representation on synagogue boards. Their one-vote-per-family policy does not extend to families where women head the household. They have no plans to change their policy and see their role as to uphold the Haredi way of life, with its very distinct gender roles. Women have a much more minor role in synagogue life than men: women can exercise relative autonomy in their traditionally designated areas of education and communal welfare, and the very last thing the Union would do is change their rules in response to secular pressures.

The Federation of Synagogues now allows women to vote, apparently as a response to requests from single women – especially widows – who wish to have their voices heard. While Rabbinic sources are not monolithic on this topic, certain sources permit full membership rights of religious organizations: indeed such sources have been relied upon to enable women's voting in Israeli elections.

The United Synagogue has taken a step further and changed their constitution to allow women to be Chairs. Women have risen to this challenge with enthusiasm: at the time of writing there are nine women Chairs and 15 women serving as Vice-chairs. Three are female Chair and Vice-chair teams.

The next stage is allowing them to be trustees of the United Synagogue, which is currently under discussion. There are two issues here: one halachic and one that might be described as meta-halachic. The halachic issue is oddly enough the more straight-forward. Back in the 1930s, Rabbi Yehiel Ya'akov Weinberg, one of the great rabbinic authorities of the twentieth century, conceded that there was no halachic bar to women being elected as heads of communities, but since there was a consensus that it was not generally welcomed, or appropriate, he felt that there should be no change in public policy. In the 1960s, Rabbi Moshe Feinstein gave permission for women to serve in leadership roles. Yet synagogues did not instantly change their policies because it felt wrong, too new, it was not done. What is uncomfortable, unfamiliar and potentially dangerous is resisted for complex, deep reasons that may be far more powerful than a positive halachic ruling. In whose interests is it to change the seat of power?

The gap between women's achievements in their secular education, work and economic independence and their roles in communal life are becoming, for many, a chasm that must be bridged. For many there is a desire to make the most of the possibilities.

There are many examples of women being denied or not being given opportunities to take part in Orthodox ritual which fall into this 'not done' category. But recently women have been taking the initiative themselves to become more informed and empowered to make changes. This has often been done in the face of Rabbinic hostility at worst, and indifference at best. Rabbinic encouragement for these endeavours in mainstream Orthodox synagogues is very rare.

For many years there have been individual women and small groups exploring areas of potential change. But now there has been much more public discussion, arenas for education where women can learn about these matters, and an understanding that change may be best made by those that want it, rather than waiting for permission from authority.

One example is the proliferation of women-only Megillat Esther readings for the festival of Purim. This year there were eight women-only Megilla readings in United synagogues, and several more were held in private homes. Often these were held on private premises because the local Rabbi had not permitted them to be held on synagogue premises. Maybe ten years ago the women would have abandoned the idea: now they went ahead anyway without Rabbinic approval. Mostly the women had made independent arrangements outside their community to learn to read the Megilla and to study the laws of how such a reading should be conducted. Such educational initiatives have raised awareness, boosted confidence, and given spiritual satisfaction and a new sense of community involvement.

A more contentious phenomenon has been the Partnership *minyanim*. Partnership *minyan* is a term describing a prayer group conforming to the strictures of Orthodox halacha while still allowing for parts of the services to be led by both men and women. A new and relatively small initiative within Modern Orthodox Judaism, there are currently about 30 in the Jewish world, the most established situated in Jerusalem and New York. Recently there have been a few Partnership *minyanim* held in the UK, run in a private capacity.

There has been considerable opposition to these, amongst the Rabbinate. Rabbi Schochet of Mill Hill United Synagogue wrote a stern warning against them in the 16 June 2013 edition of the *Jewish Chronicle* under the headline: 'Orthodox Feminism must Know its Limits': Partnership *minyanim* – where women can read from the *Sefer Torah* – are a step too far. He states that those who push the boundaries and look for some rabbi somewhere that would give them the nod to perhaps even step over the boundaries, are, without doubt, coming with an ulterior motive. The feminist movement is blamed for encouraging such ideas and he also claims that legitimate Rabbinic support anywhere in the world would be difficult to find.

One such Orthodox defendant of Partnership *minyanim* is Rabbi Marc Shapiro who holds the Weinberg Chair in Judaic Studies at the University of Scranton, Pennsylvania. He argues that although opponents of such *minyanim* will use halachic arguments to argue they should not happen, this is not a clear matter of permission or prohibition. In other words although halachic permission for a Partnership *minyan* may fall into a minority category, the truth is that many of the most important things traditional Jews do and don't do have nothing to do with halacha; communities should focus on what direction is best for Judaism.

There are other synagogue-based issues which might best be described as purely sociological: two examples are women giving sermons and the wearing of a *tallit*. Lindsey Taylor-Guthartz, currently completing a PhD on the spiritual expression of Orthodox women, commented to me: 'you would be hard-pressed to find an orthodox rabbi in this country who could find any clear halachic grounds for the prohibition of women wearing a *tallit* and you would be equally hard pressed to find a rabbi who would permit it in his congregation'.

Historically, within Orthodox synagogues there has been an absence of women's voices, so there is a residual resistance in some communities to hearing women teaching or speaking to a congregation: so although it may *feel* wrong to hear a woman delivering a sermon to substitute for the rabbi, this is not a halachic-based argument.

However, progress has been made in response to requests from women in other areas of ritual. There has definitely been a shift in mourning customs to include women. Funeral and *shiva* custom can carry emotional power, particularly when their origins come from a benign impulse to protect women. Although some Orthodox organizations still do not permit women to attend even family funerals or stand by the graveside, most have relaxed rules on this. Women mourners will often say *Kaddish* and will shovel earth on to the grave. There does not seem to be a landmark ruling on this matter, it has just slowly evolved.

The non-Orthodox community have recently brought several women into senior roles, including Rabbi Laura Janner-Klausner who became the Reform Judaism Movement's first Rabbi in January 2012. She felt that the Reform Movement's aim was to achieve a gender balance in leadership, rather than having either men or women's voices dominating the agenda. She is convinced that the input of women at senior level has been transformative for the movement in a positive way.

The Commission on Women in Jewish Leadership – an initiative of the Jewish Leadership Council – was set up this year to strengthen the community by addressing this gender imbalance in Jewish communal leadership. A 2011 survey showed that women comprise only a fifth of all trustees, a quarter of chief executives and a quarter of members of the elected Body, the Board of Deputies. They believe that by taking a strategic and coordinated approach, that change can and should take place by actively bringing more women into roles of lay and professional leadership into the community. One Commission project is the imminent launch of the organizational Award for Change which will attempt to redress the issue of all-male representation in the public arena for Jewish organizations.

In America, the pace of change is moving faster, more decisively and with more impact. This summer, in a New York ceremony, the Orthodox community ordained three Maharat graduates. One of them, a 32-year-old Chicago woman, was the first ordained woman to be hired at an Orthodox synagogue. All the graduates have been offered employment in the community. These women are qualified and equipped as a new kind of leader in the Orthodox community and beyond – not exactly a rabbi, but close enough. Yeshivat Maharat has 14 students enrolled in their current training programme, and although they are few in number, these women loom large in their influence – and legacy. JOFA, the Jewish Orthodox Feminist Alliance which has done pioneering work for Orthodox women in the USA, opened a UK branch this year and held a well-attended inaugural conference where the issues of women's education, leadership and participation were discussed with passion and intensity.

The Jewish community's struggles about women do not exist in a vacuum in this country. It is instructive to read Robert McCrum's recent comments in the *Observer* about the how the traditionalists in the Church of England were jubilant when the vote allowing women to be bishops collapsed – because the House of Laity, opposing the ordained clergy, staged a revolt. Its 64 per cent vote for women bishops fell just six votes short of the required majority. McCrum recalls: among the bishops and clergy there was shock, disbelief, anger and despair at a historic wrong turn. One journalist wrote in the 23 July 2013 edition of the *Observer Magazine*: 'I have just watched the Church of England commit suicide.' Religious organizations do not like change, particularly in the area of women's roles, and that resistance can come from the grassroots as well the leadership. Somehow the issue of women's roles and leadership form a very sensitive barometer for the spiritual temperature of a community.

And in Israel, controversies abound over Women At the Wall, the group of women who gather as a prayer group on *Rosh Chodesh* at the Kotel. Although this is a specifically Jerusalem-based conflict, with much of its conflict revolving around civil/religious law, communities here have reflected on what have been bitter and violent scenes at the holy site. The sight of women in *tallit* and tefillin, their voices raised in song, may seem on the one hand an unnecessary provocation to the Haredi worshippers at the Wall; others have been shocked by the rough treatment of women, with the threat of prison sentences for what they see as simply women exercising their religious rights. Equally, the sight of members of the Haredi community hurling abuse – and stones – at the women has for others served as a shocking wake-up call for the level of intolerance on this matter.

In many ways, Orthodoxy feels itself buffeted on all sides by the demands of modernity and often threatened by it. This has necessitated tough decisions about how to maintain a dearly cherished tradition together with allowing and even encouraging its members to feel part of the modern world. The groundswell of women's voices have recently become a potentially unignorable sound. Women make up 52 per cent of the community, but as long as this is seen as a women's issue nothing will change. A more equal sharing of power, decision-making, inclusivity and participation would have to be seen as beneficial to everyone.

So many men are unaware of the problems faced by Jewish women, and thus women are either bypassed or not considered; not necessarily by intention but because thinking equally about women at leadership level is not instinctive in our community. (This is particularly true with regard to appointing women to leadership roles or engaging them as spokespeople.)

But also – as we saw from the reception to *The Rite of Spring* – people fear change. People fear the unknown. The Orthodox community especially fears losing its traditions and fading into secular society. But to hold on tightly with a closed fist without listening to the women, or engaging properly in the debate, separating halacha from custom and accepting that a higher level of education for women will indeed bring consequences of more involvement, then British Jewry may well be trying to hold on to a handful of sand, and the tighter they hold on to it, the more it will fall away. The answer without explanation of *es passt nicht* – the Yiddish expression best translated as 'it is unseemly' – to a question put by a woman about her future in the Jewish community will no longer be acceptable as an end to the conversation. Our religious leaders may have to take their hands from their ears: *The Rite of Spring* is playing on.

Maureen Kendler is Head of Education at the London School of Jewish Studies.

David J. Graham

THE 2011 CENSUS: A REMARKABLE RESOURCE REVEALING A DECADE OF JEWISH POPULATION CHANGE

Introduction

The census is a remarkable, if underappreciated, gift to Britain's Jewish community. Its vast archives offer insights into multiple aspects of Jewish life in Britain in unprecedented detail. Here we explore some of the findings from the 2011 Census with a particular focus on how the community changed over the decade.

With the introduction of a religion question in Britain's 2001 Census, the 2011 Census provided not only a second deluge of data on Jews but, for the first time, an opportunity to precisely track a decade of communal change. And much did change between April 2001 and March 2011.

This decade witnessed the 9/11 terror attacks in the US (2001), the 7/7 terror attacks in London (2005), the end of Tony Blair s premiership (2007), the global financial crisis (2008), the election of Barack Obama (2009), and the election of a Conservative/Liberal Democrat coalition government (2010).

The religion question's introduction formed part of a broader effort by the nation's statistical agencies to better understand the complexities of identity in contemporary British society. This commenced with the introduction of a question on ethnic group in the 1991 Census, supplemented in 2001 with a question on religion. For 2011, further questions were added including one on national identity.

As in 2001, the census asked a voluntary question: 'What is your religion?'; the only example of an exemption in an otherwise compulsory questionnaire. Although the precise number of Jewish people choosing not to respond is unknown, we do know that on average about 7 per cent of people chose not to respond. In addition, communal surveys and other datasets provide confidence that the enumerated count is not too wide of the mark and claims that the census is missing hundreds of thousands of self-defined Jews are without empirical grounds.

Yet Britain's census currently hangs in the balance, and at the time of writing, the Office for National Statistics (ONS) was in the midst of a consultation period exploring cheaper and more frequent alternatives to the decennial census. Nevertheless, the current decennial format has yet to be definitely ruled out and indeed remains one of two favoured options.

Britain s Jewish Population in Context

The 2011 Census enumerated 269,568 people who gave their religion as Jewish in the United Kingdom. By contrast, there were over 37 million Christians and almost 2.8 million Muslims (see Table 1). Jews make up less than 0.5 per cent of the national population, or 1 in 230 people.

TABLE 1.
RELIGIOUS GROUPS BY COUNT AND PERCENTAGE CHANGE, 2001 TO 2011.

Group	2011 count	Percent of total population in 2001	Percent of total population in 2011	Percent change in group size 2001-2011
Christian	37,583,962	71.60%	59.50%	-10.70%
Muslim	2,786,635	2.70%	4.40%	75.10%
Hindu	835,394	1.00%	1.30%	49.50%
Sikh	432,429	0.60%	0.70%	28.60%
Jewish	269,568	0.50%	0.40%	1.10%
Buddhist	261,584	0.30%	0.40%	72.30%
Other religion	262,774	0.30%	0.40%	46.90%
No religion*	16,221,509	15.90%	25.70%	73.70%
Religion not stated	4,528,323	7.30%	7.20%	5.60%
Total	63,182,178	100.00%	100.00%	7.50%

* This category was labelled 'None' in 2001.

Source: 2001 ONS Table KS07; 2011 ONS Table KS209EW, GROS Table KS209SC, NISRA Table QS218NI.

Between 2001 and 2011 the Jewish UK count increased slightly by 2,828 people, a statistically small (or even insignificant) 1.1 per cent, but crucially, this was not a decline and the importance of that finding matters since the Jewish community had been steadily contracting throughout the second half of the twentieth century.

These figures also tell us something interesting about the way British society has changed over the decade. Although the Christian count remains by far the largest – 60 per cent of the population ticked Christian in 2011 – it has experienced a considerable 11 per cent decline since 2001 (Table 1). By contrast, one in four people in the UK ticked 'No Religion' in 2011, an increase of 74 per cent since 2001 reflecting a general move away from organized religion in Britain.

But the census offers us so much more than a simple totting up of the population. Indeed, when we focus less on the totals and more on the details within the vast data archives that comprise a census, our knowledge grows exponentially.

Geography

For example, the fact that 1 in 230 people in the UK is Jewish may be surprising, especially for those who live in Jewish areas. But this is simply due to the fact that most Jews choose to live or congregate near each other, resulting in an illusion of high numbers. For example, over half (55 per cent) of Jews live in London (GLA boundaries) compared with just 13 per cent of the general population. And almost 70 per cent of Jews live in London and the contiguous districts of Hertfordshire and Surrey. But even this fails to paint the full picture of Jewish residential congregation. As Map 1 shows, Jews are highly concentrated within the capital region forming a fan of congregation spreading out from central London into southern Hertfordshire. By contrast, the rest of London has a rather sparsely distributed Jewish population.

MAP 1.
THE JEWISH POPULATION DISTRIBUTION IN LONDON AND CONTIGUOUS REGIONS.

Source: ONS Table KS209EW; Map Copyright Jewish Policy Research.

In terms of change, of the 31 areas listed in Table 2, nine experienced a Jewish population increase but 22 experienced a decrease over the decade. Thus, even as the total size of the Jewish population grew (albeit slightly) at the national level between 2001 and 2011, Jews became more spatially concentrated.

The largest proportionate gains were in Gateshead (92 per cent), Hackney (44 per cent) and Haringey (34 per cent). And it is no coincidence that Jews in these three areas are largely Haredi, as this community has maintained very high birth rates for over 20 years. Nevertheless, it should also be noted that Hertsmere, adjacent to the London Boroughs of Barnet and Harrow, also experienced strong growth (33 per cent) in the period, as did Barnet itself (16 per cent), but this growth is likely to be a result of migration rather than very high birth rates.

Jewish population decline, on the other hand, was more spatially widespread. The London Boroughs of Brent and Redbridge experienced the greatest contractions: 33 per cent and 31 per cent respectively. And Redbridge experienced the largest absolute decline of almost 4,600 between 2001 and 2011. Regional communities also experiencing significant decline were as spatially dispersed as Merseyside and Brighton, both contracting by 21 per cent.

Jewish Families and Households

Switching the focus to the Jewish family, the 2011 census tells us there are 110,726 Jewish households in England and Wales with an average size of 2.4 persons, the same as in the general population. The most common Jewish household type is married couples which are more prevalent among Jews than the population at large (38 per cent versus 33 per cent respectively) (see Table 3). In addition, one in three Jewish households consists of a lone person and Jews are half as likely to live in cohabiting couple households as the general population (5 per cent versus 10 per cent respectively) and almost half as likely to live in lone parent households (6 per cent versus 11 per cent respectively). All of this is testament to the continuing relative strength of the nuclear family among Jews.

TABLE 2.

JEWISH POPULATION DISTRIBUTION AND CHANGE BY AREA, 2001 TO 2011.*

	2011 count	Percent of 2011 total	Change from 2001 to 2011	Percentage change 2001 to 2011
Barnet	54,084	20.10%	7,398	15.80%
Hackney	15,477	5.70%	4,745	44.20%
Harrow	10,538	3.90%	-2,574	-19.60%
Redbridge	10,213	3.80%	-4,583	-31.00%
Camden	9,823	3.60%	-1,330	-11.90%
Haringey	7,643	2.80%	1,919	33.50%
Westminster	7,237	2.70%	-495	-6.40%
Enfield	4,412	1.60%	-924	-17.30%
Brent	4,357	1.60%	-2,107	-32.60%
Kensington and Chelsea	3,320	1.20%	-230	-6.50%
Rest of London	21,498	8.00%	-3,006	-12.30%
Hertsmere	14,293	5.30%	3,581	33.40%
Epping Forest	3,972	1.50%	257	6.90%
Rest of East of England	16,565	6.10%	625	3.90%
Greater Manchester	25,013	9.30%	3,280	15.10%
Merseyside	3,014	1.10%	-789	-20.70%
Rest of North West	2,390	0.90%	-48	-2.00%
Surrey	3,055	1.10%	-174	-5.40%
Brighton and Hove	2,670	1.00%	-688	-20.50%
Rest of South East	12,036	4.50%	-414	-3.30%
Leeds	6,847	2.50%	-1,420	-17.20%
Rest of Yorkshire and the Humber	3,082	1.10%	-205	-6.20%
Gateshead	3,004	1.10%	1,440	92.10%
Rest of North East	1,499	0.60%	-88	-5.50%
Birmingham	2,205	0.80%	-138	-5.90%
Rest of West Midlands	2,416	0.90%	-218	-8.30%
South West	6,365	2.40%	-382	-5.70%
East Midlands	4,254	1.60%	179	4.40%
Wales	2,064	0.80%	-192	-8.50%
Scotland	5,887	2.20%	-561	-8.70%
Northern Ireland	335	0.10%	-30	-8.20%
UK total	**269,568**	**100%**	**2,828**	**1.10%**

* For communities greater than 2,000 Jewish people (3,000 in London) in 2011.

Source: 2001 ONS Table KS07 (2001); 2011 ONS Table KS209EW (2011), GROS Table KS209SC, NISRA Table QS218NI.

Overall, the number of Jewish households declined by 5 per cent, despite the Jewish population increasing, thus the average Jewish household size also increased (from 2.2 persons in 2001 to 2.4 in 2011). Looking more closely at the data we see that the number of Jews living alone fell by 13 per cent whilst the number of couple households increased (by 3 per cent for both married and cohabiting couples) (Table 3). In other words, the proportion of Jews living in family households increased (from 57 per cent to 60 per cent).

TABLE 3.
HOUSEHOLD COMPOSITION JEWISH AND GENERAL POPULATION BY HRP*, 2001–2011.

		2011 Jewish count	Change 2001 to 2011	Percentage change 2001 to 2011	Percent of all Jewish households 2011	Percent of all general households 2011
Lone person household		36,537	-5,509	-13.10%	33.00%	30.20%
	All aged 65 and over	11,873	-1,613	-12.00%	10.70%	8.20%
Family	Married couple‡	42,223	1,344	3.30%	38.10%	33.20%
household	Cohabiting couple	5,558	155	2.90%	5.00%	9.80%
	Lone parent	6,205	-244	-3.80%	5.60%	10.60%
Other households		8,330	263	3.30%	7.50%	7.90%
Total		110,726	-5,604	-4.80%	100.00%	100.00%

* HRP: Household Reference Person.

‡ Includes couples in same-sex civil partnerships

Source: ONS Table DC1202 (2011) and S151 (2001).

As in 2001, Jews in 2011 were more likely to own their home than the general population (73 per cent v 64 per cent respectively) and they were far less likely to live in socially rented property (8 per cent v 18 per cent respectively) (see Table 4). However, as was also seen in 2001, many Jews live in privately rented homes; indeed a slightly higher proportion of Jews do so than in the general population (19 per cent v 18 per cent respectively).

But the data on changes in Jewish house tenure are especially interesting. The proportion of Jewish householders who own their own home decreased by 9 per cent in the period, and the proportion living in social rental housing was down by 20 per cent (Table 4). However, even that shift is modest compared with the change in size of the Jewish private rental sector which experienced a substantial increase of 27 per cent: there were almost 4,600 more privately rented Jewish households in 2011 than in 2001. This may be a reflection of the average level of wealth among Jews declining over the decade.

TABLE 4.
CHANGE IN JEWISH TENURE BY HOUSEHOLD*, 2001 TO 2011.

Tenure type	Jewish Tenure type 2011	Jewish Tenure type percent 2011	General Tenure type percent 2011	Change in Jewish tenure 2001 to 2011	Percentage change in Jewish tenure 2001 to 2011
Owned	81,162	73.30%	64.30%	-8,078	-9.10%
Social rented	8,384	7.60%	17.60%	-2,087	-19.90%
Private rented	21,180	19.10%	18.00%	4,561	27.40%
Total	110,726	100.00%	100.00%	-5,604	-4.80%

* Jewish household is based on the Household Reference Person.

Source: ONS Table DC4204 (2011) and S156 (2001).

This is not the place to enter into a detailed examination about why this has might have occurred other than to speculate that it is likely to be the outcome of a number of factors. Many Haredim privately rent their homes and any increase in the size of this community could lead to an increase in the Jewish private rental sector; older people are more likely to own their homes than younger people so any contraction in the size of this group (as is suggested by the decline in lone pensioner households) would reduce the size of the home-owned sector; and any squeeze on the availability of housing finance caused by the financial crisis of 2008 may have restricted younger Jewish people's ability to get onto the housing ladder.

Identity

Finally, we take a look at what the 2011 census tells us about Jews and identity. Although we must still rely on communal surveys to investigate Jewish religious identity, the census data nevertheless warrant our attention. In Britain, ethnicity has tended to be defined in terms of the multicultural politics it informs. Therefore, the census defines ethnic group or background along the lines of skin colour and nationality. For Jews, this definition is problematic since the vast

majority (92 per cent) are White (or a variation thereof) and English
or British (see below). But communal surveys tell us that most Jews
feel culturally, if not ethnically, distinct from the general White (i.e.
Anglo Saxon) population. Nevertheless, census data on ethnic group
do reveal some interesting findings. While over three-quarters (78 per
cent) of Jews defined their ethnic group/background as White in the
census, this represents a decrease of 7 per cent since 2001 (see Table 5).
On the other hand, the number of non-White Jews increased by almost
half (47 per cent) and the number of Jews reporting 'Other' ethnic
group virtually quadrupled between 2001 and 2011. These changes
suggest an increase in the racial and ethnic diversity of Britain's Jewish
population.

TABLE 5.
ETHNIC GROUP – JEWS – ENGLAND AND WALES 2001–2011.

Source: ONS Table DC2201 (2011) and S104 (2001).

	2011 count	Change from 2001 to 2011	Percent Change 2001 to 2011	2011
White	203,981	-15,490	-7.10%	77.50%
Other White	39,319	7,155	22.20%	14.90%
Mixed/Black/Asian	8,628	2,738	46.50%	3.30%
Other	11,418	9,016	375.40%	4.30%
Total	263,346	3,419	1.30%	100.00%

Part of this increased diversity may be a result of a large increase
in the size of the non-UK born Jewish population (increasing by 6,135
or 12.3 per cent) and a slight decrease in the size of the UK-born
Jewish population between 2001 and 2011 (declining by 2,717 or 1.3
per cent). The greatest non-UK born increase (33 per cent) was Jews
born in the Middle East, of which the majority were presumably born
in Israel (see Figure 1). Thus, the Jewish population of England and
Wales appears to have become not only more ethnically diverse but
also more internationally diverse over the decade. Nevertheless,
although there are other ways of defining Israeli in the British context
(such as holding an Israeli passport) these Middle East figures tell

us that claims of there being 50,000 or even more Israelis in Britain cannot be substantiated, at least by country of birth data.

FIGURE 1.
PLACE OF BIRTH (NON-UK BORN), 2001 AND 2011, SIZE OF JEWISH POPULATION IN ENGLAND AND WALES.
Source: ONS Table DC2207 (2011) and S150 (2001).

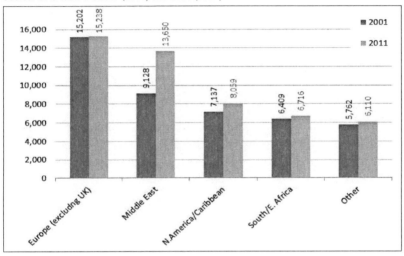

The census's broadening of its identity questions in 2011 provides some brand new data that was unavailable in 2001. For example, a question on national identity was included for the first time and this found that Jews are more likely to consider themselves British than the general population (25 per cent versus 19 per cent respectively) but less likely to consider themselves English (53 per cent versus 58 per cent respectively) despite the proportion of Jews born in England being almost the same as in the general population. This poses more questions than it answers but it may reflect, for some Jews, a feeling that the term 'British' is more inclusive than the narrower term 'English' which, like 'White', is perhaps more readily associated with an Anglo-Saxon heritage not shared by Britain's Jews.

TABLE 6.
SELF-DEFINED NATIONAL IDENTITY, JEWS AND THE GENERAL POPULATION, 2011.

National Identity	General population N=56,075,912	Jewish population N=263,346
British only	19.10%	24.60%
English only	57.70%	53.40%
English and British only	8.70%	9.70%
Other British identity	5.70%	1.30%
Other national identity	8.80%	11.00%
Total	100.00%	100.00%

Source: ONS Table DC2204.

Concluding Comments

It is still early days in analysis of the 2011 census but we have already learnt more about the Jewish population than we could have achieved with conventional surveys. And the unique aspect of the 2011 Census is that for first time we have been able to compare two consecutive censuses and therefore measure change. The community is extremely fortunate to be able to access this kind of data which addresses the national, regional and local picture and that includes data for every synagogue, Jewish school and care facility in the country.

The figures from the 2011 Census firmly establish that the British Jewish community is no longer contracting; that the Jewish nuclear family goes from strength to strength; and that a shift away from home ownership (the dominant group) towards private renting has occurred, possibly suggesting a decrease in average communal wealth. We have also discovered the Jewish population has become more ethnically and internationally diverse and that it is more British than the British but less English than the English.

In the coming months and years, more and more census data will be analysed including information on Jewish health, economic well-being, intermarriage, education, languages spoken, Israelis, schools, Jewish ethnicity, and migration. Jewish Policy Research (JPR) is spearheading this effort and is committed to continue exploring the census data on behalf of the community, its constituent bodies and interested parties.

It regularly produces summary reports on new census data releases which are freely available from its website jpr.org.uk.

Dr David J. Graham is a Research Fellow at the Institute for Jewish Policy Research, admin@jpr.org.uk.

Elkan D. Levy

BRITISH JEWRY IN THE GREAT WAR

The Board of Deputies came together for its regular meeting on 19 July 1914 and passed a resolution 'to send an address of sympathy to the Emperor or of Austria on the assassination of the Archduke Franz Ferdinand'. Few people at that meeting thought that the Sarajevo killing would be any different from the various political assassinations that had occurred in Europe. Within three weeks war had broken out.

The Jewish population of Great Britain at this time was about 350,000, of whom about three-fifths lived in London. Provincial Jewry was divided into a mass of small communities with the great industrial towns – Manchester, Leeds, Birmingham, Glasgow – as the main centres. There were also small communities in the mining areas of South Wales and the mining and shipbuilding towns of the North East.

The community was still ruled by a number of related families, known to historians as the Cousinhood. The first Lord Rothschild still presided over New Court with his brothers and ruled the community as a benevolent, though much feared, despot. Representatives of this group were making their way in English life; Herbert Samuel was in the Liberal cabinet formed by Asquith at the beginning of the war and his cousin Edwin Montagu joined him there soon after. The Lord Chief Justice of England, Rufus Isaacs, was the first Jew to hold the position.

Below them was the mass of middle-class Jews, mostly professional and mercantile, who formed a large part of the organized community although not yet of its leadership. First or second generation English born, and increasingly anglicized, they formed the backbone of the United Synagogue and the franchise of the Board of Deputies.

Finally there were the Jews of London's East End and the other ghettos of Britain. The immigrants formed an almost self-contained artisan community of their own. Religiously they were more positively orthodox than the United Synagogue but maintained a grudging admiration and respect for the institutions of Anglo-Jewry. The more assimilated Jews in return had made the cause of the immigrants their own and devoted their talents and energies towards the anglicization of the East End and the amelioration of the conditions of the ghetto.

Major institutions including the Chief Rabbinate, the United Synagogue, the Board of Deputies and the Board of Guardians all tended to keep the community together despite the latent fissiparous tendencies of Jewish organizational life. A most powerful common denominator was the *Jewish Chronicle*, by then a very Zionist paper. Widely read in upper-class Jewish homes, it also engendered queues of readers in the Whitechapel Public Library. So highly was it regarded that when a ghetto teacher, attempting to instil the glorious moments of English naval history into his small pupils, asked how Nelson gave his famous message at Trafalgar, back came the answer, 'Please Sir, he put it in the *Jewish Chronicle*'!

Sentiment in the community was firmly against Britain's entry into the war, and especially against Britain's alliance with Russia, the arch persecutor of the Jews at that time. The *Jewish Chronicle*'s first editorial after the outbreak of war hurriedly reversed its policy and spoke of 'the futility of those who cry peace, peace, when there is no peace'.

One of the immediate problems which faced the community was the nationality of the large number of immigrants. Passports were rarely carried or held and often the immigrant Jew had no evidence of citizenship. Britain was embarking on her first continental war in a century and foreigners were immediately suspected of being the enemy. German and Austrian citizens were interned, mainly on the Isle of Man, as were Turkish nationals. There was at one time a separate Jewish internment camp, and two of those who died there still repose in a Manx churchyard.

The Board of Deputies declined to get involved in exempting Jewish enemy aliens from internment or repatriation because it regarded the whole question as not being specifically Jewish, and attempted to pass its responsibilities onto one of the friendly societies. The *Jewish Chronicle*, and its correspondence columns, attacked this attitude with great vigour, describing the board's attitudes as 'ridiculously Gilbertian' and the provincial councils stepped in vigorously where the Board had failed to act.

By the beginning of 1915 anti-foreign attitudes had considerably diminished only to be revived after the torpedoing of the Lusitania on 7th May.

The outbreak of war was seen by the *Jewish Chronicle*, undoubtedly reflecting the predominant sentiment of the community, as a chance for Anglo-Jewry to repay England for her kindness and hospitality. 'England has been all she could be to Jews, Jews will be all they can to England' was the slogan in their opening wartime editorial. This slogan was painted on a large sign board outside the *JC* offices in Finsbury Square and remained there throughout the war. At Whitechapel recruiting station on Wednesday 5th August the great crowd included over 500 young Jews and the community encouraged enlistment. Chief Rabbi Hertz issued a recruiting message: 'Israel expects every son of Israel to do his duty', and synagogues throughout the land held recruiting meetings.

There was a popular belief that Jews did not make good soldiers, which in due course led Chief Rabbi Hertz to pay an official visit to the Western Front. Sir John French, the commander-in-chief, in a despatch gratifyingly mentioned 'the large Jewish community now serving with the Army in the field'. At this stage about 40 per cent of Jewish recruits were rejected on health grounds, although towards the end of the war standards were lowered.

The war produced an unusually virulent strain of anti-foreign feeling. Throughout the war *The Times* maintained a policy of using the terms 'German' and 'Jew' synonymously. Many leading figures in English life came under suspicion. Sir Alfred Mond received an official call at his London home asking why he kept *carrier* pigeons in his garden. They were Hyde Park pigeons which gathered there because they were fed.

The Sephardi community, in an excess of patriotic Englishness, developed a dislike of Ashkenazi Jews because they were German, and even considered withholding funds from the Judith Montefiore College at Ramsgate in case any of those studying there were enemy aliens. The United Synagogue, containing many Ashkenazim of fairly recent immigration, avoided anti-German hysteria, although one of its ministers questioned the fact that it maintained the 'German-Polish ritual'.

Many of those with German names considered a change: for example, the Minister of the Liverpool Old Hebrew Congregation in Princes Road abandoned his surname of Friedberg in favour of Frampton, a Dorset village.

Economically the beginning of the war brought hardship among immigrant workers. Food prices rose rapidly, and the *JC* complained that while the price of the bagel remained stationary 'its circumference has become suspiciously less'. However the expansion of the Armed Forces meant huge clothing contracts of which the East End and other immigrant areas received a fair share. One little pageboy at a ghetto wedding arrived in an officer's uniform, complete to the smallest detail, which his father had no doubt fashioned from khaki clippings! Manchester Jewry supplied most of the army's ground sheets and the khaki boom generally brought prosperity to the tailoring and dressmaking trades.

The Board of Guardians found its support much in demand, but generally helped to alleviate the most severe poverty without receiving support either from government or national funds. Most charities however found their income falling, the demand for their assistance rising, and the position made worse by a shortage of voluntary workers. Some 3,500 Belgian Jewish refugees came to Britain at the beginning of the war, many of whom had been very prosperous but now needed assistance.

Most synagogue bodies waived contributions from men on active service, while the Federation of Synagogues relieved all those on active service of their subscriptions to the Burial Society while still receiving the benefits!

The senior Jewish chaplain, the Revd Michael Adler, was in civilian life the Minister of the Central Synagogue in Great Portland Street. In January 1915 he went to France and a number of Anglo-Jewish ministers served as chaplains in the field. In 1916 Rabbi A.I. Kook, formerly Chief Rabbi of Jaffa, who had been stranded in Switzerland by the outbreak of war, became the Rav of the Machzike Hadass Synagogue in Brick Lane.

By the summer of 1916 the nation, conscious of its huge losses in the incredible slaughter of the Western Front and the general failure of such slaughter to produce any positive reactions, looked for fresh sources of manpower. Almost the only unwounded young men in London by then were the young Jews of Whitechapel who were not liable for English conscription and, as Herbert Samuel told the House of Commons, there was a distinct feeling that allied subjects of military age 'ought either to serve in the army of the country of their birth or in the army of the country of their adoption'.

The feeling was so strong that anti-Jewish riots broke out in the summer of 1917. These lasted three days in Leeds in June, and there were a further two days in Bethnal Green in September. Senior figures within Anglo-Jewry hoped that if the law was changed to allow friendly aliens to volunteer for the British forces the ghetto would volunteer before it was conscripted. A small number of Jews returned to Russia to fight with Kerensky's government, but the majority refused, no doubt influenced by the heavy casualty figures whose existence could no longer be denied. Fearful of further anti-Jewish riots, Samuel persuaded the government to bring in compulsory conscription for non-British nationals in the summer of 1917.

Before the outbreak of the war the immigrant populations, which vastly outnumbered the indigenous and acculturated Jews, had relied upon them to represent their views and their requirements to wider society whose language they did not speak and whose attitudes they did not comprehend. By the summer of 1916 all had changed.

Before the war most of the acculturated members of the community had sent their sons to public school. With the rapid expansion of the army at the outbreak of war and the need for junior officers, public schoolboys received an automatic commission and subsequently the junior officers bore the brunt of the casualties. By the summer of 1916 many of the younger members of the community who had devoted time and efforts to the immigrants were dead.

At the same time the increase in wartime regulations, and the close relationship between the immigrants and the government on matters such as clothing contracts, gave the ghetto increasing confidence in its dealings with the outside non-Jewish world. Suddenly they realized that they could survive without the Jews of the West End.

In many ways the year of 1917 was viewed by the community as an *annus mirabilis*. Since the early days of the war it had been clear to the British government that an attack on the Ottoman Empire would both take pressure off the Western Front and bring many other benefits to the war effort. Two attempts to defeat the Turkish armies at the first and second battles of Gaza in April 1917 had failed miserably, and Prime Minister Lloyd George felt that a much-needed military success would come in the Middle East far sooner than in France. One of his most successful generals was Allenby and in June 1917 he was sent to the Middle East.

Allenby neither underestimated the Turks nor dismissed the problems of the theatre of war. Having made careful preparations, and having received an instruction from the Prime Minister to 'give Jerusalem to the British people as a Christmas present', Allenby attacked at the end of October and on 9 December Jerusalem surrendered. This was the first major success of British arms in the whole war.

Relations between the Jewish community and the government particularly in respect of Jewry in foreign countries had been handled since 1878 by the Conjoint Foreign Committee, a joint organization of the Board of Deputies and the Anglo Jewish Association. The presidents of the two bodies, D. L. Alexander KC and Claude G. Montefiore, were assisted by Lucien Wolf, secretary of the committee, considered by the Foreign Office as spokesman of the Jews. All three shared an inability to understand or appreciate the immigrant or Jewish nationalist viewpoint.

By the early summer of 1917 the government was considering a declaration in support of Zionist aims. On this the community was split between the immigrants and their few Zionist supporters within upper-class Jewry on the one hand, and the acculturated Jewish community which feared that Zionism would destroy its hard-won standing and privileges in English society on the other. Matters came to a head in May 1917 when the president of the Board of Deputies and the president of the Anglo Jewish Association wrote a letter to *The Times* in an attempt to strangle the declaration before its birth. With great courage Chief Rabbi Hertz wrote a letter in strong refutation and the president of the Board of Deputies was forced to resign. On 2 November 1917 the Balfour Declaration was duly issued to wild rejoicing among the pro-Zionist sections of the community.

At the same time the community was grappling with the question of a specifically Jewish military unit. Attempts to form such a unit had been resisted both by the War Office and by the community itself, but the formation of the Zion Mule Corps and its record at Gallipoli had somewhat weakened the opposition. There was real concern in the community at how such a unit might behave under fire; there had after all been no Jewish military units since the Maccabees. It was therefore agreed that they would become the 38th Royal Fusiliers, despite which the unit was always known as 'the Judeans'. Subsequently the 39th was raised in Palestine and the 40th in New York. All three battalions fought creditably and are commemorated on the Royal Fusiliers Memorial in Holborn, the only war memorial in the UK which contains the word 'Jewish'.

The war dragged on to its miserable end in November 1918. The vast social changes which it had brought within British society were reflected in the Jewish community. Old certainties had gone, the old leaders were weary, many of the younger men who would be expected to take their place were dead, the East End was no longer subservient to the West End and British Jewry along with its non-Jewish counterparts faced with uncertainty the problems of the interwar years.

Derek Taylor

COMETH THE HOUR, COMETH THE MAN. CHIEF RABBIS FACE DIFFERENT PROBLEMS

What should be the objectives of a British Chief Rabbi? The answer has always been to solve the problems facing the community at the time of their installation. These problems have changed radically over the years. There are common threads, however, and the same challenges emerge more than once in our 350-year history.

The first Chief Rabbi was Jacob Sasportas (1664–65) who was the Sephardi Haham. His challenge was to create a congregation out of a group of Jews who had been forbidden to practice their religion in the Spanish and Portuguese empires more than 150 years before. By the time of Charles II they had forgotten a great deal of the religious laws. Sasportas even had to explain, for example, that he couldn't allow them to be part of the congregation if they hadn't been circumcised. He had to look at the education of the children as well and he started the Gates of Hope School. He also recognized the importance of charity and formed the Hebra de Bikur Holim e Gemilut Hasadim, to take care of the sick and bury the impoverished dead.

The spiritual seniority of Sasportas was established, but there were rows between Hahamim and the Mahamad for the next 300 years.

Sasportas left London when the plague struck and it wasn't until 1670, when the pestilence was but a bad memory, that he was replaced by a friend from Amsterdam, Joshua da Silva (1670–79). Da Silva was a safe pair of hands at a time when the community was settling down. The lay leaders of the Sephardim wanted to keep their heads well below the parapet and, in particular, they didn't want to get into any arguments with the Church of England. The enmity of the church had created nothing but trouble in the Middle Ages. Over a million Jews had died just as a result of the first Crusade.

A church that looked kindly upon the Jews was another matter. Clerics in the Church of England wanted to prove the Catholics wrong and that involved intense bible study. Their problem was that much of it was originally written in Aramaic and even those who knew Hebrew didn't know Aramaic. Many called on da Silva for advice. Relations improved still further.

When da Silva died in 1679 he was replaced by Jacob Abendana (1681–85). Like so many rabbis at the time, Abendana coupled his spiritual responsibilities with a commercial occupation; he was a book seller, in partnership with his brother, Isaac. They were also notable scholars. The Church of England still needed help to understand important parts of Judaism and the brothers translated the Mishnah into Spanish and Latin. Isaac went to Cambridge and was paid by the university. His Latin translation is still in the University library.

Abendana died in 1685 and wasn't replaced for four years. Then along came a glib, charming rabbi called Solomon Ayllon (1689–1700). He was seen as the ideal man to raise the profile of the community, but they found out too late that he also had leanings towards the prime Jewish heresy of the day, Sabbateianism. Sabbatei Zevi was a rabbi who started by teaching his followers to make a few small changes in the religion. By the time he died, a convert to Islam, he had given instructions that Tisha b'Av was to be a joyous festival because he was born on that day! The Sephardi community back in London was not to be moved from its traditional beliefs and by 1700 Ayllon was back in Amsterdam.

The Sephardim didn't want to make another mistake. They realized the need now was for a traditional Orthodox Jewish scholar to ensure the community kept to the halachah. The Mahamad, the lay leaders, found him in David Nietto (1700–28). He was probably the most learned Haham the Sephardim ever had and he was responsible for cementing the community's position as loyal citizens of the country.

When Queen Anne died in 1715 and the Old Pretender, the son of James II, was set on invading Britain and regaining the throne, the country was split. Many wanted him, as he had both the best claim and the support of the powerful French. The British Government wanted the King of Hanover, who was 45th in line of succession, but the first Protestant.

Who the Jews backed was going to define their allegiance. If they chose wrongly, they could be expelled again. Nietto was consulted. He pointed out a third century din: *dina de malchuta dina* - that the community should support whichever government was in power in the country in which they lived. The Mahamad voted to support George of Hanover by 18–2. When he won, the loyalty of the Jewish community had been proved up to the hilt.

By this time the Ashkenazim had also come to Britain, primarily from Europe after the disastrous 30 Years War (1618–48). In that chaos two thirds of the total German population perished from slaughter in battle and from disease. It took 200 years for Germany to recover. Jewish Refugees arrived in Britain and the main Ashkenazi synagogue, the Great Synagogue, was built. Their rabbi, Aaron Hart, had little problem with the lay leader, Moses Hart, because they were brothers. For Aaron Hart (1705–56) the task was to enable the Ashkenazim to settle down like the Sephardim.

It was in his time that new communities started to be formed in many other parts of the country. Congregations, like Portsmouth, couldn't afford their own rabbi and they began to look to Aaron Hart to give them spiritual guidance and rulings. This made Hart the first Chief Rabbi, if the term is defined as the religious leader whose word is accepted in more than one community. When the Penzance community prayed for past Chief Rabbis, Hart was the first on their list. At the installation of the current Chief Rabbi, Ephraim Mirvis, he referred to himself, correctly, as the 11th Chief Rabbi in the country.

Under Hart the Ashkenazim grew in number and stayed faithful to their continental *minhagim*. His successor, Hart Lyon (1756–63), wanted to tackle the need for a greater degree of learning in the community but he received little support in his endeavours. After only seven years he resigned to go to Halberstadt in Germany, taking a 40 per cent cut in salary, but gaining a guarantee of 12 students to help him form a Yeshiva.

After David Nietto died, his son Isaac held the fort until 1751. The problem with the Sephardim was the desire of the Mahamad to make all the major decisions for the community and this time it was Isaac Nietto who resigned when he refused to tolerate it any longer. When Moses Gomez de Mesquita became Haham, Isaac Nietto condemned his appointment as he felt it disregarded what he considered de Mesquita's want of merit or qualifications for the post. He was a good family rabbi, though, and gave the Mahamad little competition in the leadership of the community. It would be ten years before a successor was appointed to replace de Mesquita. The Sephardi community in New York now looked to the London

Haham for religious rulings and continued to do so after the American War of Independence

There have often been arguments about the depth of Talmudic expertise of our spiritual leaders; Hermann Adler and Israel Brodie are two modern examples. The same applied to the next Haham, Moses Cohen Dazavedo (1761–84) but it depends on what is considered the norm. In Dazavedo's time Bishop Kennett was trying to make sense of the different translations of the Bible that existed. One of his advisers who he found most helpful, as he gratefully acknowledged, was Dazevedo. He may not have been Maimonides, Caro or Nietto, but he could hold his own with less expert theologians.

When Hart Lyon left, there were two London rabbis who competed for Ashkenazi leadership. It was David Tevele Schiff (1765–91) who came out on top and, under his leadership, the reputation of British Jewry on the international stage improved markedly. Schiff was an excellent scholar and his opinion was sought, as head of the London Beth Din, by Jews all over the world. He was a good diplomat and he brought the separate Jewish communities in Britain closer together. As it said on his tombstone:

> He planned the future to lead the ignorant in the ways of uprightness and rebuked them with bruises of love. For those near and far he was an adviser ... true Torah was in his mouth with a sweet golden tongue ... they testified about him as to his pleasant deeds.

Solomon Hirschell (1802–42) applied to succeed Schiff with the unusual qualification of actually being British by birth. To this day only three Chief Rabbis and Hahamim have been born in Britain. Hirschell was the son of Hart Lyon and had been educated by his learned father. The Ashkenazim waited to appoint him until the Peace of Amiens had brought a temporary halt to the Napoleonic Wars and the cost of a Chief Rabbi was more sustainable.

During his long tenure, Hirschell was well known for creating a major traffic jam in the City of London every Rosh Hashanah. At that time he would lead large numbers of the community to the Thames to perform *tashlich*. He also worked well for many years with one of his congregants, Nathan Mayer Rothschild, and he died the richest of the Chief Rabbis.

Hirschell was 80 when he passed away in 1842 and his last years were clouded by the intention of some senior members of the community to set up a synagogue in the West End of London. No new synagogue was permitted by the rules of the Sephardim at the time and this was the beginning of the movement which would develop into Reform Judaism over the next 100 years. After endless fruitless discussions, the new congregation was formed and, as a result, its members were excluded from the community by Hirschell and his Sephardi counterpart, David Meldola. Meldola's father, Raphael Meldola had been the Haham from 1805–28 but his incumbency had been marred by severe arguments with the Mahamad.

When Hirschell died, the overwhelming need was for a new Chief Rabbi to bind up the wounds, and to lay down the law for the majority of the community who were doubtful about the legitimacy of the new breakaway community. The favourite candidate at the outset was Samson Raphael Hersch. The 'what if' school of history would have a field day discussing the possibilities, if he had been the choice. The successful candidate, however, was Nathan Marcus Adler, then the Chief Rabbi of Hanover. The King of Hanover had also been King of England since George I, and the royal Duke of Sussex, the current king's close relation, had been taught Hebrew by Solomon Hirschell. Nathan Marcus Adler also had a close friend at the university – Prince Albert of Saxe Coburg Gotha – and when Albert was organizing the 1851 Great Exhibition, he asked Adler to serve on the committee.

Adler's lay leader was Sir Moses Montefiore, a Sephardi, and they worked together to ensure that there would only be one spiritual authority in British Jewry, and that would be the Chief Rabbi. The Board of Deputies, which had been founded in 1760, had this in its founding document. When the United Synagogue was formed in 1870, the same rule was agreed. In spiritual matters, the Chief Rabbi's decision was, and remains, law.

Benjamin Artom (1866–79) took over as Haham from Meldola after a lapse of nearly 40 years. Unhappily he died young and was succeeded by Moses Gaster (1887–1917), a brilliant scholar and the only Ashkenazi to be appointed Haham. It was Gaster who supported Theodor Herzl and the Zionists when nobody else of importance would believe in the impossible dream of a National Home in Israel. To Gaster belongs a lot of the credit for the Balfour Declaration.

Adler was succeeded by his son, Hermann, who was impeccably British and much favoured by King Edward VII, though he never lost a strong guttural accent. Hermann Adler's main task was to try to avoid the passing of an Aliens Act which would stop Jewish refugees entering the country. The numbers of Jews grew from about 35,000 in 1880 to about 350,000 in 1914. The problem for Hermann Adler was that he had no real contact with the refugees, and his successor would need to try to integrate them within the United Synagogue. For this task Lord Rothschild, President of the United Synagogue, insisted that Joseph Herman Hertz (1913–46) be chosen. It was the American Hertz who could communicate with the East Europeans as he had done in South Africa, from where, after a short stint in New York, he was recruited.

Hertz's main problem was that the future head of the United Synagogue, Sir Robert Waley Cohen, wanted to repair the rift with the Reform movement. After 80 years, there was still very little difference between Orthodox and Reform theology. This would change radically in the 1930s, but the possibility of coming together existed when Hertz was appointed. Hertz fought Waley Cohen to a standstill over more than 30 years. By the end, the two men could only communicate through intermediaries, but the bulk of the community remained in the Orthodox camp.

When Hertz died, Waley Cohen's objective was to have a more

malleable successor appointed. Also one whose British credentials were totally credible while hostilities raged in Palestine. Israel Brodie (1948–65) was born in Newcastle, went to Balliol College, Oxford, and was a Chaplain to the Forces in both World Wars. He was a fine speaker and turned out to be equally determined to protect the authority of his office after Waley Cohen died.

Solomon Gaon served as Haham from 1949–77 but, again, the Sephardim had difficulty in marrying the authorities of the Haham and the Mahamad. No Haham has been appointed since Gaon retired.

Lord Jacobovits was the only Chief Rabbi who didn't want the job. He took it because he felt it was his duty to do so, and he gave the community an image in the country it had never before enjoyed. He became a good friend of Prime Minister Margaret Thatcher because he shared some of her views, and he was sent to the House of Lords as a result. It was Jacobovits' leadership which led to the growth of Jewish schools in this country, something he would undoubtedly have considered his greatest achievement. He followed in the footsteps of Rabbi Dr Solomon Schonfeld who had led the way.

Jonathan Sacks (1991–2013) was the best communicator ever to lead British Jewry. Where the community had kept its head down for hundreds of years, Chief Rabbi Sacks, who was also made a peer, became one of the most important moral voices of the nation.

Over the years, Jewry in Britain has become fully acculturated and integrated but not assimilated. The numbers have stabilized at about 250,000, with a substantial contribution through the growth of Charedi families. While it is impossible to foretell the future, Chief Rabbi Mirvis begins his term of office with the community in pretty good shape.

Kenneth Collins

THE GLASGOW JEWISH
REPRESENTATIVE COUNCIL

The Glasgow Jewish Representative Council will be celebrating its centenary in 2014.

During the nineteenth century, communication between the Glasgow Jewish community and the wider society was handled by the Glasgow (later Garnethill) Hebrew Congregation. As long as there was only one Jewish community in Glasgow this arrangement was satisfactory. However, with the growth of the Jewish population around the turn of the century, new structures were necessary.

Of course, the Garnethill leadership, which had long experience of dealings with the civic and religious bodies of Victorian Glasgow, continued to take a prominent position in its relations with the outside world.

Garnethill Synagogue led the United Synagogue of Glasgow, which operated between 1898 and 1906, and brought together the various synagogues, based in the immigrant areas of the Gorbals. When the United Synagogue was dissolved an attempt was made to set up a new community body, the Glasgow Jewish Communal Council.

This was representative only of the Gorbals community, though with tacit support from Garnethill. This Council succeeded in the appointment of Rabbi Samuel Hillman as Communal Rabbi in 1908 but was less successful in solving other problems, such as paying for pauper burials and the supervising of kosher meat.

The communal leadership vacuum continued to be filled by Garnethill Synagogue and it became clear that there was a need for a new community organization. This would bring together the religious, educational, cultural and welfare bodies in a single structure, which could speak authoritatively for all the Jews of Glasgow.

In 1913 the catalyst for such a body was the widespread concern in both the Jewish and wider community over the Mendel Beilis blood libel case in Kiev. Revd Phillips, the minister at Garnethill, and Michael Simons, a former Glasgow Bailie (Senior City Councillor) and the most prominent member of the Jewish community, led the Jewish efforts on behalf of Beilis during the early protests. However, further action, and a mass rally led by the Lord Provost and the Roman Catholic Archbishop, saw input from a new generation of Gorbals leadership.

Following Beilis' acquittal it was agreed that a Glasgow Jewish Representative Council should be formed. The Representative Council came into being in January 1914 with Joseph Hallside as its first President. Though the new body aimed for a careful balance of members from Gorbals and Garnethill, the exclusion of Michael Simons led to the initial absence of Garnethill Synagogue and some of its associated bodies from the Representative Council. However, in major issues, Michael Simons was often called on to lead the community and the Representative Council often formed a joint delegation with Garnethill. The synagogue continued to describe itself as the leading and most representative synagogue in Scotland.

From the beginning the Representative Council took an activist role. It advocated the establishment of a Jewish day school through negotiations with the Glasgow Corporation's Education Department. Despite discussions, which went on for over a decade, it was not until 1962 that a Jewish Day School, Calderwood Lodge Jewish Primary School, was opened in Glasgow.

The Council provided almost 2,000 affidavits for alien Jews to prevent their internment during the First World War. It helped sponsor a service at the synagogue in South Portland Street in 1916 to emphasize the Jewish patriotic contribution to the British war effort. It also raised funds to support the dependants of Jews who had decided to enlist in the Russian army after the introduction of conscription in 1917.

During 1917 the Representative Council joined with local Zionist bodies in protesting the action of the soon to be discredited Conjoint Committee of the Board of Deputies. This had publicly repudiated Zionism on the eve of the Balfour Declaration. The Declaration was greeted with great enthusiasm in Glasgow, and the Representative Council mobilized the community in support of the Zionist movement. It also attracted wider support from the Moderator and General Assembly of the Church of Scotland and the *Glasgow Herald*.

The Council's main focus during its first years was dealing with outbreaks of anti-Semitism and it monitored threats from extreme religious and political groups. In the 1930s, although the British Union of Fascists only had a small foothold in Scotland, their posters and street presence scared the community. The Council's response to threats, formulated by Bailie Michael Simons, was to use 'a maximum of reasonable persistency and a minimum of fuss'. Thus Representative Council responses were always quiet and measured, and usually conducted out of public sight.

The Representative Council was also involved during the inter-war years with helping community members with naturalization papers where immigrant parents had not obtained British nationality.

By the 1930s the Representative Council was established as the

official body of the community and virtually all communal organizations were affiliated. During these years, the largest group of affiliates
were the synagogues and the Jewish friendly societies, which
provided social and welfare facilities for their members.

The Representative Council promoted a public boycott of Nazi
German goods. This was despite fears that such a boycott, along with
the presence of increasing numbers of Jewish refugees in Glasgow,
might increase anti-Jewish feeling. A Glasgow Jewish Refugee
Children's Aid Society was established. Discreet moves continued to
provide support and employment for refugees, and to support a
hostel in Glasgow for Kindertransport refugee children.

During the war years the Representative Council sponsored the
establishment of a Committee for Christian-Jewish Understanding
which brought the Church of Scotland into its first dialogue with the
Jewish community. A branch of the Council of Christians and Jews, with
all the Christian denominations, had to await improvements in relations
between the Church of Scotland and the Catholic Church in the 1980s.

The post-war years saw the beginning of major changes in the shape
of the community, as numbers reached a peak of around 14,000 in the
early 1950s. The Gorbals community was now in decline and the
establishment of synagogues at Giffnock, Clarkston and Newton
Mearns indicated that the core of the community was moving
southwards.

The Representative Council celebrated its Golden Jubilee in 1964
with a major event in the City Chambers. It could reflect that it was
now well established as the representative body and not just for the
Jews of Glasgow. It was widely consulted on matters of Scottish
interest by the Scottish civil service in Edinburgh.

The Presidency of Dr Jack E. Miller in the 1960s was associated
with a major improvement in the Representative Council's ability to
respond to the challenge of leading and representing the community.
The Council now employed a part-time office secretary and set up
an office in the Jewish Welfare Board building. This had meeting

rooms, a kosher restaurant for small Council events, and a hall for larger meetings. It also served as the base for the Jewish dramatic society, the Avrom Greenbaum Players.

The establishment of the Glasgow Jewish Community Trust in the 1960s began an era of more targeted help for community organizations. It had a body of trustees, which always included at least one, and usually more, former presidents of the Representative Council. Thus, the Council had a key role in encouraging funding for key institutions and informing the other trustees about community priorities.

The 1967 Six-Day War saw a wave of emotional and financial support for Israel from the Jews of Glasgow. Many volunteers from the city went to work in Israel's farms and industries, to take over the duties of reserve soldiers. At the same time the plight of Soviet Jewry became an important part of Representative Council activity. This increased over the final two decades of Communist rule with regular 'write-in' events and international phone calls, trying to maintain contact with refuseniks.

In the 1970s the Representative Council became seriously involved in interfaith and multicultural activities. The new communities, especially from the Indian subcontinent, were continuing to expand. The network of new inclusive voluntary bodies gave the Representative Council an opportunity to provide leadership and expertise. Led by Harry Crivan and Judith Tankel, the Representative Council was active in the Glasgow Sharing of Faiths programmes, as well as in various ethnic minority organizations. The Council's involvement in interfaith activities increased with the establishment of a dialogue group with the Church of Scotland. This followed an invitation from the Church to Chief Rabbi Jakobovits. The group discussed Jewish and Christian theology in a spirit of respect and understanding. This led to a former Council President, Henry Tankel, addressing the General Assembly of the Church of Scotland in Edinburgh in 1984.

The role of the Glasgow Jewish Representative Council in fostering new organizations was exemplified in 1987 with the establishment of the Scottish Jewish Archives Centre at Garnethill Synagogue. The

Representative Council provided the initial funding for the organization until it was able to function independently. The Council acted as publishers for *Aspects of Scottish Jewry*, edited by Dr Kenneth Collins, the first book on Scottish Jewry to appear in 40 years.

In 1988 the Glasgow Garden Festival had an Israel Week, with Israel-themed events and an Israel Garden, with Representative Council input into the programme. This was repeated in 1990 when Glasgow was European City of Culture. The newly formed Glasgow Jewish Arts ran an ambitious cultural programme covering almost every area of Jewish art and culture. This was complemented by an exhibition of Treasures of the Holy Land, staged by Glasgow Museums. The exhibition was the brainchild of Henry Diamond, head of public relations for the Glasgow City Council, and an adviser on public relations to the Representative Council.

In 1992 the new Chief Rabbi Dr Jonathan Sacks paid his first pastoral visit to Glasgow and issued a challenge for community involvement. This challenge was realized, under the direction of the Representative Council, as Glasgow Jewish Community Week. The programme of the week enabled many organizations to showcase their activities. Some groups combined to produce events and the level of involvement ensured a great community 'buzz'.

Also in 1992 the community was faced with the loss of the *Jewish Echo*, the community newspaper which had been printed every Friday since 1929. The Representative Council explored different options for keeping a local community paper. The *Jewish Chronicle* offered to print a Scottish section and the Council tried to keep an informative newsletter going. It was, however, the Manchester-based *Jewish Telegraph* which moved into the city, found its own premises in Giffnock, and published a dedicated Scottish edition every week.

The opening of the Scottish Parliament in 1999 marked a major shift in the organization of Jewish representation in Scotland. The informal Scottish Jewish Standing Committee, under whose banner the Glasgow and Edinburgh communities had met, was transferred into the Scottish Council of Jewish Communities (SCoJeC). This led to the Representative Council playing a leading role within SCoJeC while reducing its own focus to Glasgow, East Renfrewshire and the West of Scotland generally. The concentration of the community within the local authority boundary of East Renfrewshire, which partners Jewish Care Scotland and runs Calderwood Lodge Jewish Primary School, fostered ever closer ties between local authority and Jewish community.

The changing demographic structure of the community, graphically illustrated by the reduction in numbers revealed in the 2001 Census, prompted a number of synagogue closures and some communal reorganization. The Representative Council has taken the lead over the past 20 years in focussing communal attention on changing require-ments and the need to meet the needs of the next generations.

As the Representative Council approaches its centenary it is one of the oldest organizations in the Glasgow Jewish community. Like many other established bodies, it faces the common problem in recruiting young leadership. The Representative Council has continued to sponsor further Jewish Community Weeks under the banner of JFest, and its public meetings include an annual event for Yom Hashoah. It also holds regular Delegate Meetings which provide an opportunity for communal debate and discussion.

The Representative Council has taken the lead in planning for the future, to balance the smaller size of the community with the facilities required in future years. It takes pride in its achievements and those of the community it represents. The oldest Jewish Representative body in Britain outside London, it remains at the forefront of community life.

Dr Kenneth Collins is a former President of the Glasgow Jewish Representative Council and has been Chair of the Scottish Jewish Archives Centre since it opened in 1987. He has written a number of books on Jewish and medical history in Scotland. A former GP in Glasgow he is currently Visiting Professor in the History of Medicine at the Hebrew University of Jerusalem.

ANGLO-JEWISH INSTITUTIONS

BOARD OF DEPUTIES OF BRITISH JEWS
6 Bloomsbury Square, London WC1A 2LP
Tel 020 7543 5400 *Fax* 020 7543 0010
Email info@bod.org.uk *Website* www.bod.org.uk
BoD Charitable Foundation (Reg. Charity No. 1058107).
Founded in 1760 as a joint committee of the Sephardi and Ashkenazi communities in London, the BoD of British Jews has flourished in its role as the elected representative body of the British Jewish community. It has been involved in all issues affecting the political and civil rights of British Jewry and, in many cases, in times of crisis, in affairs overseas. It conveys the views of the community to Government and other public bodies on political and legislative matters which affect British Jewry, and provides information about the Jewish community and Israel to the non-Jewish world. The Board examines legislative proposals in Britain and the European Union which may affect Jews, and ensures the political defence of the community. It collects statistical and demographic information and undertakes research on and for the community. It maintains contact with, and provides support for, Jewish communities around the world and promotes solidarity with Israel. It counters bias in the media and ensures that Jews enjoy the full rights of all British citizens.

The Board plays a co-ordinating role in key issues affecting the Jewish community, and promotes co-operation among different groups within the community The basis of the Board's representation is primarily synagogal, although the body itself has no religious affiliations. All properly constituted synagogues in Great Britain are entitled to representation, as are other significant communal organisations, such as the Regional Representative Councils, youth organisations and other communal bodies, including major charities. The Charedi community have their own representative body that works closely with the Board of Deputies. The Board meets most months in London, but holds one meeting a year in a regional community. *Pres.* Vivian Wineman; *Snr. V. Pres.* Laura Marks; *V. Pres.* Alex Brummer, Jonathan Arkush; *T.* Laurence Brass; *Chief Exec.* Jon Benjamin

The work of the Board is channelled through four Divisional boards, each chaired by an Honorary Officer and supported by a professional Director.

International Division *Ch.* Paul Edlin; *Dir.* Elizabeth Harris-Sawczenko
Community Issues *Dir.* Colin Spanjar
Finance and Organisation *Dir.* Adam Joelson
Defence Policy and Group Relations Division *Ch.* Jonathan Arkush; *Dir.* Mike Whine
Regional Assembly *Ch.* Ephraim Borowski
Public Affairs *Dir.* Elizabeth Harris-Sawczenko
Community Policy Research Unit (Est. 1965). Carries out demographic and other research on various aspects of the community *Email* research@bod.org.uk
Trades Advisory Council Affiliated to the BoD, the Council seeks to combat causes of friction in industry, trade and commerce, and discrimination in the workplace, where these threaten good relations where Jews are concerned. The TAC offers arbitration and conciliation facilities in business disputes and advice to employees who consider that they have suffered discrimination. *Dir.* Martin Frey
Jewish Community Information Provides information to the Jewish and non-Jewish public on all aspects of the Jewish Community in the UK.
Tel 020 7543 5421 *Email* jci@bod.org.uk
Communal Diary Designed to minimise clashes between events organised by different communal organisations. *Email* diary@bod.org.uk
Jewish Community Services - Ombudsman c/o The Board of Deputies of British Jews, *Tel* 020 7543 0105 (answerphone). (Reg. Charity No: 269525). The Ombudsman is available to deal with disputes or complaints concerning Jewish community services, i.e. any institutions in the Jewish community. It is an independent service, for which no fee is charged.
Ombudsman, Paul Shaerf *Email* ombudsman@bod.org.uk

JEWISH REPRESENTATIVE COUNCILS

BERKSHIRE JEWISH REPRESENTATIVE COUNCIL

(Est. 1995). Representing Maidenhead Synagogue, Reading Hebrew Congregation and Reading Liberal Jewish Community. *Contact* Myer Daniels *Email* mdaniels@globalnet.co.uk

REPRESENTATIVE COUNCIL OF BIRMINGHAM & WEST MIDLANDS JEWRY

Email jewishbirmingham@talktalk.net *Website* www.jewishbirmingham.org
(Est. 1937). *Pres.* Sir B. Zissman; *Ch.* R. Jacobs; *Hon. S.* Leonard Jacobs *Tel* 0121 236 1801; *Admin.* c/o BHC, Singers Hill, Ellis Street, Birmingham, B1 1HL *Tel* 07768 761 930

BOURNEMOUTH JEWISH REPRESENTATIVE COUNCIL (incorporating Southampton)

Email info@bournemouthjewishcommunity.co.uk
Website www.bournemouthjewishcommunity.co.uk
Ch. Jonathan Kay *Tel* 01202 557 748

GLASGOW JEWISH REPRESENTATIVE COUNCIL

Jewish Community Centre, 222 Fenwick Road, Giffnock, Glasgow G46 6UE
Tel 0141 577 8200 *Fax* 0141 577 8202
Email office@glasgowjewishrepcouncil.org *Website* www.glasgowjewishrepcouncil.org
Pres. Paul H. Morron; *Admin.* Julia Tatarenko; *Hon. S.* Fiona L. Brodie

HULL JEWISH REPRESENTATIVE COUNCIL

Pres. J. Rose *Tel* 01482 655367; *Hon. S.* Prof. J. Friend, 9 Allanhall Way, Kirk Ella, HU10 7QU
Tel 01482 658930 *Email* j.friend@cj2f.karoo.co.uk

THE INTERFAITH COUNCIL FOR WALES

c/o Cytun, 58 Richmond Road, Cardiff CF24 3UR
Email info@interfaithwales.org *Website* www.interfaithwales.org
Sec. Rev Aled Edwards OBE *Tel* 02920 464 204

LEEDS JEWISH REPRESENTATIVE COUNCIL

Marjorie & Arnold Ziff Community Centre, 311 Stonegate Road, Leeds LS17 6AZ
Tel 0113 269 7520
Website www.leedsjewishcommunity.com
Pres. Simon Jackson; *V. Pres.* Alan Dunwell, Abigail Levin; *Hon. T.* Keith Ackerman; *Hon. S.* (*acting*) Jonathan Rose

JEWISH REPRESENTATIVE COUNCIL OF GREATER MANCHESTER & REGION

Jewish Community Centre, Bury Old Road, M7 4QY
Tel 0161 720 8721
Email office@jewishmanchester.org *Website* www.jewishmanchester.org
Pres. Frank Baigel BA B Dent Sc; *V. Pres.* Sharon A. Bannister, Jacky Buchsbaum BSc ACA CTA; *Hon. T.* Philip A. Langer; *Hon. S.* Filis Rosenberg, Ray Cook BA(Hons); Ex-officio, Lucille M. Cohen MA; *H. Media Analyst*, Frank R. Baigel. *Publ.* Year Book, Newsletter *RepPresents*

MERSEYSIDE JEWISH REPRESENTATIVE COUNCIL

433 Smithdown Road, L15 3JL
Tel 0151 733 2292 *Fax* 0151 734 0212
Email repcouncil@mjccshifrin.co.uk *Website* www.liverpooljewish.com
(Reg. Charity No. 1140569). *Pres.* Prof. Julian Verbov, JP; *Ch. of the Council* Ian S. Cohen; *Hon. S.* S. Sprince *Publ.* Year Book

REPRESENTATIVE COUNCIL OF NORTH EAST JEWRY

Email repcouncilpresident@northeastjewish.co.uk *Website* www.northeastjewish.org.uk
(Reg. Charity No. 1071515). *Co-Pres.* B. Mark *Tel* 0191 284 2808, E. Joseph *Tel* 0191 285 7654; *Hon. S.* B. Joseph 21 Church Avenue, Newcastle upon Tyne NE3 1AN *Tel* 0191 285 7654; *Hon. T.* W. Knoblauch *Email* walter@total-accounting.com; *Pres.* and *PR*, c/o E. Joseph *Tel* 0191 285 7654

SOUTH WALES JEWISH REPRESENTATIVE COUNCIL
9 Holmwood Close, Cyncoed, Cardiff CF23 6BT
Tel 029 2048 8198
Email swjewishrepcouncil@gmail.com
Ch. Stanley Soffa; *Hon. S.* Ruth Levene *Tel* 07920 585 848

SOUTHPORT JEWISH REPRESENTATIVE COUNCIL
Pres. Sonia Abrahamson 65 Beach Priory Gardens, PR8 2SA *Tel* 01704 540 704; *Hon. S. R.* Jackson 33 The Chesters, 17-19 Argyle Road PR9 9LG *Tel* 01704 532 696

SUSSEX JEWISH REPRESENTATIVE COUNCIL
Tel 07789 491 279
Email info@sussexjewishrepresentativecouncil.org
Website www.sussexjewishrepresentativecouncil.org
Nearly every synagogue, charitable organisation, social and cultural institution, as well as the communities in Eastbourne, Hastings, Bexhill and Worthing, are affiliated to this Council, and meetings are held quarterly. *Pres.* Beryl Sharpe; *Sec.* Jessica Rosenthal *Corr.* P.O. Box 2178, Hove, BN3 3SZ

COMMUNAL ORGANISATIONS

ANGLO-JEWISH ASSOCIATION
JHUB, 152 West End Lane, London NW6 1SD
Tel 020 7449 0909
Email info@anglojewish.org.uk *Website* www.anglojewish.org.uk
(Est. 1871. Reg. Charity No. 256946). Membership of the Association is open to all British Jews who accept as their guiding principle loyalty to their faith and their country. Its aim is to promote the education of Jews in the UK and elsewhere. It offers scholarships to Jewish UK university students who can demonstrate academic excellence and financial need. *Pres.* Jonathan Walker; *Ch. Ed. Comm.* Julia Samuel

ASSOCIATION OF JEWISH WOMEN'S ORGANISATIONS IN THE UNITED KINGDOM
6 Bloomsbury Square, London WC1A 2LP
Tel 020 7242 8300 *Fax* 020 7242 8313
Email contact@ajwo.org *Website* www.ajwo.org
(Est. 1965). To further communal understanding. To promote the achievement of unity among Jewish women of differing shades of opinion, belonging to autonomous organisations with different aims. *Affiliate orgs:* Agunot Campaign; US Women; B'nai B'rith Women; British Emunah; Friends of Hebrew University of Jerusalem Women's Group; Friends of Ort Women's Division; Jewish Women's Aid; Jewish Women's Network; League of Jewish Women; Liberal Judaism; Masorti Judaism; Paperweight; Reform Judaism; Sephardi Women (Lauderdale Road Synagogue Association); WIZO.uk; *Ch.* Penelope Conway; *V. Ch.* Anne Lyons; *Hon. S.* Marilyn Lehmann; *Hon. T.* Helen Reisman

BICOM: BRITISH ISRAEL COMMUNICATIONS AND RESEARCH CENTRE
Tel 020 7636 5500 *Fax* 020 7636 5600
Email info@bicom.org.uk *Website* www.bicom.org.uk
(Est. 2001). To provide a better understanding of Israel in the UK; to create a more positive environment for Israel in the UK. *Chief Exec.* Dermot Kehoe *Email* francescai@bicom.org.uk *Twitter* @BritainIsrael; *Donor Relations & Events Man.* Ruth Fisher *Email* ruthf@bicom.org.uk; *Press Off.* JJ Hodari *Email* jonathanh@bicom.org.uk *Twitter* @JJ_Hodari; *Dir. Israel Off.* Richard Pater *Email* richardp@bicom.org.uk *Twitter* @Richard_Pater

COMMUNITY SECURITY TRUST (CST)
Head Office, London and Southern Region P.O. Box 35501, London NW4 2FZ
Tel 020 8457 9999
Manchester and Northern Region P.O. Box 245, Manchester M7 2WY
Tel 0161 792 6666
Email Enquiries@thecst.org.uk *Website* www.thecst.org.uk
(Reg. Charity No. 1042391). CST believes that the fight against antisemitism and terrorism is vital to help ensure a vibrant Jewish community. CST provides physical security, training and advice for the protection of British Jews. CST also assists victims of antisemitism and monitors antisemitic activities and incidents. CST represents British Jewry to Police, Government and media on the subjects of antisemitism, terrorism and security.

JEWISH LEADERSHIP COUNCIL (formerly Jewish Community Leadership Council)
6 Bloomsbury Square, London WC1A 2LP
Tel 020 7242 9734
Email email@thejlc.org *Website* www.thejlc.org
Northwest London Office, Shield House, Harmony Way, NW4 2BZ
(Est. 2006. Reg. Charity No. 1115343). As a 'coalition of organisations', the Jewish Leadership Council helps its member organisations. It does this by organising projects that all its member organisations can benefit from and by supporting member organisations in their own strategic goals. JLC works to ensure the health of the Jewish voluntary sector,

both through internal strategic planning for the future and, where necessary, through external campaigning and lobbying. The JLC plans for the future of the UK Jewish community. It does this through commissioning research, holding seminars and supporting leadership development. The Council also works to ensure that there is a positive public policy environment for the British Jewish community. It coordinates internally so that the Jewish community has a connected and forward-looking approach to policy.

In addition to its central operations the JLC incorporates two subsidiary Divisions. Partnerships for Jewish Schools (PaJeS) and LEAD (Jewish Leadership Excellence and Development). PaJeS Division: *Ch.* Jonathan Goldstein; *Exec. Dir.* Alastair Falk; LEAD Division: *Ch.* Nigel Layton; Exec. Dir. Nicky Goldman

The JLC comprises the heads of the major institutions in each sector of British Jewish life, together with significant individual leaders of British Jewry. *Publ.* The Future of Jewish schools (2008); The Big Society and the UK Jewish Community (2010); The Future of Jewish Schools: Three Years On (2011); Inspiring Women Leaders: Advancing Gender Equality in Jewish Communal Life (2012). *Ch. of Council of Membership,* Vivian Wineman (BoD.); *Ch. of Bd. of Tru.* Mick Davis, Poju Zabludowicz; *V. Pres.* Sir Victor Blank, Sir Trevor Chinn CVO, Michele Vogel, Gilllian Merron, Lord Stanley Fink, Henry Grunwald OBE QC, Lord Greville Janner, Howard Leigh, Leo Noé, Lord Harry Woolf; *Council of Members,* Frank Baigel (Representative Council of Greater Manchester and Region), Bill Benjamin (UJIA), Adrian Cohen (London Jewish Forum), David Dangoor, Spanish & Portuguese Jews Congregation; Rhea Wolfson, Harry Jardine (ZYC); Jonathan Goldstein (PaJeS), Joe Tarsh (UJS), Lucian J. Hudson (Liberal Judaism), Brian Kerner (Cross Communal Group), Debbie Klein (JCC), Nigel Layton (LEAD), Steven Lewis (New Leadership Network/Jewish Care), James Libson (New Leadership Network/World Jewish Relief), Simon Jackson (Leeds Jewish Representative Council), Bernie Myers (Norwood), Stephen Pack (United Synagogue), Robert Weiner (Movement for Reform Judaism), Gerald M. Ronson CBE (CST), Harvey Rosenblatt (Nightingale Hammerson), Jill Shaw (WIZO), Lord David Young (Ch. Jewish Museum), Edward Mizrahi (BICOM), Michael Ziff (Maccabi GB)

LEAGUE OF JEWISH WOMEN
6 Bloomsbury Square, London WC1A 2LP
Tel 020 7242 8300 *Fax* 020 7242 8313
Email office@theljw.org *Website* www.theljw.org
(Est. 1943. Reg. Charity No. 1104023). Voluntary service organisation to unite Jewish women of every shade of opinion who live in the UK; to intensify in each Jewish woman her Jewish consciousness and her sense of responsibility to the Jewish community and the community generally; to stimulate her personal sense of civic duty and to encourage her to express it by increased service to the country. *Pres.* Yvonne Brent; *Hon. S.* Marilyn Herman
    Groups operate in the following centres:

Greater London
Barnet; Bushey Heath; Central; Chigwell & Hainault; Coombe & District; Harrow & Kenton; JMUMS; London North West; Newbury Park & District; North & East London; Northwood; Oakwood & Winchmore Hill; Pinner; Radlett; Southgate; Stanmore & Edgware; Surrey; Prime Time (single women).

Outside London
Bournemouth; Cardiff; Glasgow; Leicester.

North West Region (centred at Manchester)
Bowdon & Hale; Brantwood; Bury & Whitefield; Cheadle & Gatley; Fylde; Kingsway; Park & Windsor; Prestwich; Sale & Altrincham.

In addition to groups of women throughout the UK, there are focussed groups for young mums, JMums, and women on their own, Prime Time. Men can join as associate members, League Associate Division (LADS). LJW is the UK Affiliate of the International Council of Jewish Women.

ORT HOUSE CONFERENCE CENTRE
126 Albert Street, London NW1 7NE
Tel 020 7485 5847 *Fax* 020 7446 8651
Email ort@pavpub.com *Website* www.orthouse.co.uk
(Est. 1996). A Jewish conference centre and IT Suite. Capacity 120. Suitable for business, community or social events. *Org.* Natalie Campbell

WORKING PARTY ON JEWISH MONUMENTS IN THE UK & IRELAND
c/o Board of Deputies, 6 Bloomsbury Square, London WC1A 2LP
Email heritage_wp@bod.org.uk
(Est. 1991). To act as a forum, bringing together people with a wide interest, expertise, and involvement in maintaining and supporting Jewish Heritage Institutions in the UK. *Ch.* David Jacobs

INTERFAITH REPRESENTATIVE BODIES
COUNCIL OF CHRISTIANS AND JEWS
21 Godliman Street, London EC4V 5BD
Tel 020 7015 5160
Email cjrelations@ccj.org.uk *Website* www.ccj.org.uk
(Est. 1942. Reg. Charity No. 238005). Patron: Her Majesty the Queen. The Council brings together the Christian and Jewish Communities in a common effort to fight the evils of prejudice and intolerance, especially antisemitism. It is neither a missionary nor a political organisation. It runs projects nationally and through its 35 regional branches. *Pres.* The Archbishop of Canterbury; The Chief Rabbi; The Archbishop of Westminster; The Greek Orthodox Archbishop of Thyateira and Great Britain; The Moderator of the Church of Scotland; The Free Churches' Moderator; The Head of the Movement for Reform Judaism, The Chief Executive of LJ, the Senior Rabbi, Assembly of Masorti Synagogues, and The Spiritual Head of the Spanish and Portuguese Jews' Congregation. *Ch.* The Lord Bishop of Manchester; Rt. Rev. Nigel McCulloch. *C.E.O.* David Gifford, *Publ.* Common Ground.

3FF (formerly **The Three Faiths Forum**)
Star House, 104-108 Grafton Road, London NW5 4BA
Tel 020 7482 9549
Email info@3ff.org.uk *Website* www.3ff.org.uk
(Est. 1997. Reg. Charity No. 1092465). 3FF, the Three Faiths Forum builds understanding and lasting relationships between people of all faiths and beliefs; It runs education, engagement and action programmes that bring diverse communities together. Its main focus is in the UK, but it also works internationally to create new models for intercultural cooperation, particularly in the EU, USA and Middle East. Its work involves teachers, students and young professionals, faith organisations, artists and galleries, political leaders in Parliament and upcoming leaders still at university. *Trustees: Co. Fdr.* Sir Sigmund Sternberg KC*SG; *Co. Fdr.* Revd. Dr. Marcus Braybrooke MA MPhil, *Ch.* Michael Sternberg QC FRSA KFO, Solicitor of the Senior Courts of England and Wales, Farmida Bi MA (Cantab), Barbara Mills LLB, Dilwar Hussain

JOSEPH INTERFAITH FOUNDATION
75 North End Road, London NW11 7RL
Tel 020 8458 9081 *Mobile* 07816 814 691
Email info@josephinterfaithfoundation.org *Website* www.josephinterfaithfoundation.org
(Est. 2006. Reg. Charity 1119284). An officially registered joint Muslim-Jewish interfaith organisation. It is committed to fostering constructive and sustained interaction through academic and educational programmes and a deeper understanding of both faiths in Britain. *Tr.* Sir David Michels, Lord Sheikh; *Exec. Dir.* Mehri Niknam, MBE

JEWISH PRESS, RADIO AND INFORMATION SERVICES

The following is a selection of the major national publications. Many synagogues and communal organisations publish newsletters and magazines.

JEWISH PRESS

AJR JOURNAL (Monthly)
Jubilee House, Merrion Avenue, Stanmore, Middlesex HA7 4RL
Tel 020 8385 3070 *Fax* 020 8385 3080
Email enquiries@ajr.org.uk *Website* www.ajr.org.uk

BELFAST JEWISH RECORD (Quarterly)
42 Glandore Avenue, Belfast BT15 3FD
Tel 028 9077 9491
(Est. 1953). *Ed. Bd. Hon. S. N.* Simon

BIMAH (Three issues annually)
18 St Edeyrns Road, Cyncoed, Cardiff CF23 6TB
Tel 0292 076 2689
(Est. 1994). The Platform of Welsh Jewry. *Ed.* Barbara Michaels
Email barbara.michaels@btopenworld.com

BIRMINGHAM JEWISH RECORDER (Monthly)
P.O. Box 13512, Birmingham B32 9BX
Tel 0121 428 3347
Email admin@recorder.org.uk
(Est. 1935).

EDINBURGH STAR (Two issues a year)
31/3 Rattray Grove, Edinburgh EH10 5TL
Email michelinebrannan@msn.com
(Est. 1989). Community journal. *Ed.* M. Brannan

ESSEX JEWISH NEWS (Three issues a year)
Barbara Newman *Tel* 07866 607 437 *Email* essexjewishnews@gmail.com
Accounts *Email* office.ejn@gmail.com

EUROPEAN JUDAISM (Two issues a year)
Leo Baeck College, 80 East End Road, London N3 2SY
Tel 020 8349 5600 *Fax* 020 8349 5619
Email editorial@journals.berghahnbooks.com *Website* www.journals.berghahnbooks.com/ej/
(Est. 1966). *Ed.* Rabbi Prof. J. Magonet

JEWISH CHRONICLE (Weekly)
28 St Albans Lane, London NW11 7QE
Website www.thejc.com
(Est. 1841). *Ed.* Stephen Pollard

JEWISH NEWS (Weekly)
Unit 611, Highgate Studios, 53-79 Highgate Road, London NW5 1TL
Tel 020 7692 6929
Website www.totallyjewish.com

JEWISH QUARTERLY (incorporating Jewish Book News and Reviews) (Quarterly)
ORT House, 126 Albert Street, London NW1 7NE
Email info@jewishquarterly.org *Website* www.jewishquarterly.org
Twitter @JewishQuarterly
(Reg. Charity No. 268589). The Jewish Quarterly is a London-based literary journal of ideas and culture boasting among its contributors the greatest writers and minds of the Jewish and non-Jewish world. Founded in 1953, it is loved for its fine writing and editorial integrity. *Ed.* Rachel Lasserson

JEWISH RENAISSANCE: MAGAZINE OF JEWISH CULTURE (Four issues a year)
P.O. Box 28849, London SW13 0WA
Tel 020 8876 1891
Email editor@jewishrenaissance.org.uk *Website* www.jewishrenaissance.org.uk
(Est. 2001). *Ed* Janet Levin; *Ch.* Lionel Gordon

JEWISH SOCIALIST (Quarterly)
JS Publications, BM3725, London WC1N 3XX
Website www.jewishsocialist.org.uk
(Est. 1985). Magazine of the Jewish Socialists' Group

JEWISH TELEGRAPH (Published weekly)
Telegraph House, 11 Park Hill, Bury Old Road, Prestwich, Manchester M25 OHH
Tel 0161 741 2631 (Newsdesk) *Tel* 0161 740 9321 (Switchboard) *Fax* 0161 740 9325
Email manchester@jewishtelegraph.com *Website* www.jewishtelegraph.com
(Est 1950). In Glasgow: glasgow@jewishtelegraph.com Leeds: leeds@jewishtelegraph.com
and Liverpool: liverpool@jewishtelegraph.com *Ed.* P. Harris

JEWISH TRIBUNE (Weekly)
97 Stamford Hill, London N16 5DN
Tel 020 8800 6688 *Fax* 020 8800 5000
Email editor@j-tribune.co.uk
(Est. 1962). English and Yiddish. *Ed.* Dan Levy (Agudas Yisroel of Great Britain)

LEO BAECK COLLEGE YEAR BOOK (Annually)
2nd Floor, Arts Two Building, Queen Mary, University of London, Mile End Road,
London E1 4NS
Email info@leobaeck.co.uk
(Est. 1956). *Ed.* Professor R. Gross, Dr. Cathy Gelbin

MENORAH
A magazine for Jewish members of H.M. Forces and Friends of Jewish Servicemen and
Women. *Ed.* Col. M. Newman DL
Tel 0161 766 6479 *Email* martin.newman@armymail.mod.uk

THE SCRIBE: JOURNAL OF BABYLONIAN JEWRY (Annually)
4 Carlos Place, London W1K 3AW
Tel 020 7399 0850
Email scribe@dangoor.com *Website* www.thescribe.info
(Est. 1971). *Ed.* Dr. N.E. Dangoor, CBE

SUSSEX JEWISH NEWS (Monthly)
P.O. Box 2178, Hove BN3 3SZ,
Tel 07906 955 404
Email editor@sussexjewishnews.com info@sussexjewishrepresentativecouncil.org
Admin. Bernard Swithern subscription £20 p.a. /£15 online

WESSEX JEWISH NEWS (Six issues a year)
3 De Lisle Road, Bournemouth, BH3 7NF
Email edwjn@onetel.com

JEWISH RADIO PROGRAMMES

JEWISH HOUR

Radio weekly show for and about the Jewish Community in Manchester. Every Monday evening from 7-8pm online, and on 94.4 FM. Listen again at www.jewishhour.co.uk *Editor* and *Producer* Basil Herwald *Email* Herwald_law@hotmail.com

TIKKUN SPECTRUM JEWISH RADIO

4 Ingate Place, Battersea, London SW8 3NS
Tel 020 7627 4433 Phone-In: 020 7627 8383 *Fax* 020 7627 3409
Email tikkunspectrum@spectrumradio.net *Website* www.spectrumradio.net
Facebook spectrum radio *Twitter* @spectrumradio
Producer and Presenter Michael Milston. Other Presenters Jon Kaye, Laurence Kilshaw, Ervin Landau and Joanne Simmons. One weekly hour programmes of news, views and discussion. Programme accessible for one week on the internet, Smart Phone and Tablet. See Website for programme details weekly.

INFORMATION SERVICES

BRIJNET

Website www.brijnet.org

Provider of UK Jewish communal internet services. Creates awareness of the use and benefits of the Internet in the community through training and assistance with all Internet tools. Creates and maintains a useful, quality, communal, electronic information database. Published electronic listings including: brij-announce, daf-hashavua.

JEWISH COMMUNITY INFORMATION

6 Bloomsbury Square, London WC1A 2LP
Tel 020 7543 5421 *Fax* 020 7543 0010
Email jci@bod.org.uk

A service of the Board of Deputies, providing information to the Jewish and non-Jewish public on all aspects of the Jewish community in the UK.

RELIGIOUS ORGANISATIONS

THE CHIEF RABBINATE

The Chief Rabbinate of Britain has evolved from the authority of the Rabbi of the Great Synagogue in London. From the early years of the 18th century he was acknowledged as the spiritual leader of the majority of the London community, a recognition also accorded by the provinces and overseas. Jonathan Sacks was inducted into office in 1991. Previous holders of the office were: Aaron Hart (1709–1756); Hart Lyon (1756–1764); David Tevele Schiff (1765–1791); Solomon Herschell (1802–1842); Nathan Marcus Adler (1845–1890); Hermann Adler (1891–1911); Joseph Herman Hertz (1913–1946); Israel Brodie (1948–1965); Immanuel Jakobovits (1967–1991); Jonathan Sacks (1991-2013). The formal designation (1845–1953) of the office was 'Chief Rabbi of the United Hebrew Congregations of the British Commonwealth of Nations' and subsequently 'Chief Rabbi of the United Hebrew Congregations of the Commonwealth'.

Chief Rabbi Ephraim Mirvis
Office of the Chief Rabbi: 305 Ballards Lane, London N12 8GB
Tel 020 8343 6301 *Fax* 020 8343 6310
Email info@chiefrabbi.org *Website* www.chiefrabbi.org
Exec. Dir. Ari Jesner

Marriage Authorisation Office of the Chief Rabbi, 305 Ballards Lane, London N12 8GB
Tel 020 8343 6313 *Fax* 020 8343 6310 *Dir.* Rabbi Dr J. Shindler

UNITED SYNAGOGUE

305 Ballards Lane, London N12 8GB
Tel 020 8343 8989 *Fax* 020 8343 6262
Website www.theus.org.uk
Pres. Stephen Pack; *V. Pres.* Stephen Fenton, Russell Kett, Jonathan Miller; *T.* Stephen Lubinsky, Brian Markeson R. Tenzer; *Chief Exec.* Jeremy Jacobs
(Reg. Charity No. 242552). For accurate contact information for all our synagogues and for further information about the US, please visit the website.

While the Act of Parliament under which it was created bears the date July 14, 1870, the US had its origin much earlier in the history of London Jewry. Of the five Constituent Synagogues which joined to form the US, the oldest – the Great Synagogue – was early 18th Century; the Hambro dated from 1707, while the New Synagogue was founded in 1761. The Member Synagogues now number 45, there is also one associate and a small number of affiliate communities within the London area, providing religious facilities for over 100,000 Jews in the greater London area. For Member and Affiliated Synagogues, *See* London and the Home Counties.

The US is the main contributor towards the maintenance of the Chief Rabbinate.

The **Community Services Division** *Tel* 020 8343 5680. This department is the interface between the US Centre and the local synagogue communities. The department provides a range of activities including US Cares, Project Chesed and Tribe – Young US.

Tribe *Tel* 020 8343 5656 provides a range of activities for its members, including After School activities at Tribe Clubs across London. There are Residential Summer camps and Summer Day schemes, as well as comprehensive training and support for member synagogues, with their youth provision and employees. **Project Chesed** carries out a wide range of activities, including its annual Pesach food parcel delivery to members. *Dir.* David Collins

The **Kashrut Division** *Tel* 020 8343 6255 *Fax* 020 8343 6254
Website www.kosher.org.uk *Dir.* Rabbi J. Conway, BA; *Kashrut Admin.* N. Lauer
Publ.: The Really Jewish Food Guide, Kosher Nosh Guide, Passover Supplement.

The **Visitation Committee** provides a caring service for all Jews who unfortunately find themselves in hospital, in prison or who are bereaved (*See* p. 156). The Jewish Bereavement Counselling Service has a team of trained bereavement counsellors available to meet the needs of all members of the Jewish community. *Tel* 020 8457 9710

The **External Services Division** The Division includes the US Legal department as well

as Burial, Hospital and Prison visitation. *Tel* 020 8343 8989 *Dir.* David Frei
Burial Society *Tel* 020 8950 7767
(All Cemeteries) *Dir.* Melvyn Hartog; *Man.* Bushey Office Marcia Wohlman

CEMETERIES
Willesden, Beaconsfield Road, NW10 2JE *Tel* 020 8459 0394 *Fax* 020 8830 4582 (Opened 1873); East Ham, Marlow Road, High Street South, E6 3QG *Tel* 020 8472 0554 *Fax* 020 8471 2822 (Opened 1919);
Bushey, Little Bushey Lane, Herts, WD2 3TP *Tel* 020 8950 7767 *Fax* 020 8420 4973 (Opened 1967);
Waltham Abbey, Upshire Hall, Honey Lane, Essex, EN9 3QT *Tel* 01992 714 492 *Fax* 01992 650 735 (Opened 1960);
Plashet, High Street North, E12 6PQ (Opened 1896);
West Ham, Buckingham Road, Forest Lane, E15 1SP *Tel* 020 8472 0554 (Opened 1857);
Alderney Road, E1 (Opened for Great Synagogue in 1696. Disused);
Brady Street, E1 (Opened for the New Synagogue, in 1761; subsequently used also by Great Synagogue. Disused);
Hackney, Lauriston Road, E9 (Opened for Hambro' Synagogue in 1788. Disused).

BETH DIN (COURT OF THE CHIEF RABBI)
305 Ballards Lane, London N12 8GB
Tel 020 8343 6270 *Fax* 020 8343 6257
Email info@bethdin.org.uk
Dayanim Rabbis Menachem Gelley, Ivan Binstock, BSc., Yonason Abraham, Shmuel Simons, *Registrar* D. Frei, LLB
The Beth Din fulfils the following functions: (i) dispute arbitration and mediation; (ii) supervision of Jewish religious divorces, adoptions and conversions; (iii) certification of religious status; (iv) supervision of shechita and kashrut.
General enquiries may be made from 9am-5pm (Monday to Thursday). You need an appointment to attend the Beth Din. Messages left on the answerphone will be dealt with as soon as possible.
The London Beth Din (Court of the Chief Rabbi) is an integral part of the US.

INITIATION SOCIETY
Website www.initiationsociety.org.uk
(Est. 1745. Reg. Charity No. 207404). To train Mohalim and to supply Mohalim in cases where they are needed. For a list of Mohalim practising in the British Isles and registered with the Society, you should contact the Secretary.
Med. Off. Dr. J. Spitzer *Tel* 020 8802 2002 *Email* j.spitzer@doctors.org.uk *Sec.* M. Levenson 22 Wentworth Road, London NW11 0RP *Tel* 020 8455 5059
Email mlev@parl.org.uk

JEWISH COMMITTEE FOR H.M. FORCES
12 Conisborough Place, Manchester M45 6EJ
Tel 0161 766 6479
Email afjc@armymail.mod.uk
The Committee is officially recognised by the Minister of Defence for appointing Jewish chaplains and to provide for the religious needs of Jewish members of H.M. Forces.
Pres. Lt. Cdr. Alan Tyler RN; *V. Pres.* Brig. Simon Bell TD, Rear Admiral Lord Sterling, Capt. Solomon Levy MBE ED; *Ch.* Col. Martin Newman DL FCIPR; *V. Ch.* Judge Stuart Taylor; *Hon. T.* Major Rob Pollock; *Jewish Chaplain to H.M. Forces* Rabbi Reuben Livingstone CF(V); *Hon. S.* Brian Bloom; *Faith Adv.* Rabbi Dr. Abraham Levy OBE *Publ.* Menorah.

JEWISH MEMORIAL COUNCIL
Begbies Chettle Agar, Epworth House, 25 City Road, London, EC1Y 1AR
Tel 020 7628 5801 *Fax* 020 7628 0390
Email admin@begbiesaccountants.co.uk *Website* www.begbieschettleagar.co.uk

(Est. 1919). To commemorate the services rendered by Jews in the UK and British Empire in the war of 1914-18 by establishing an organisation which will carry on Jewish tradition as a permanent ennobling force in the lives of Jews in this country. *Ch.* E. Astaire; *Tru.* J. Guttentag, S. Bentley, S. Cohen

JMC PENSIONS FUND
Admin 25 Enford Street, London W1H 1DW
Tel 020 7724 7778
Email jmcpf@btinternet.com
JMC Pension Fund is separate from the Jewish Memorial Council and now is a closed scheme for Jewish Communities. *Tru. Ch.* T. Simon

NATIONAL COUNCIL OF SHECHITA BOARDS
Elscot House, Arcadia Avenue, London N3 2JU
Tel 0800 035 0466 *Fax* 0800 035 0467
Email ncsb@shechita.co.uk *Website* www.shechitauk.org
Shechita UK PR Office: *Tel* 020 7284 6969 *Email* shechita@theproffice.com
Provides information on all matters relating to the performance and administration of Shechita. It also acts as liaison between all Shechita Boards and the Government and agencies affecting shechita and the kosher meat and poultry industry, throughout the UK and abroad. The National Council registered a trade mark in 1955, and re-registered in 1995 a warranty of Kashrus. This testifies that the holder of this trade mark is a purveyor of kosher meat and/or poultry and is licensed by a recognised Shechita Board affiliated to the Council and under the supervision of a Rabbinical Authority. Shechita UK is its information arm. *Pres.* Henry Grunwald QC; *Jt. V. Pres.* J. Lobenstein, I. R. Singer; *Jt. T.* B. Sandler, R. Stern; *Exec. Dir.* D. J. Rose

RABBINICAL COMMISSION FOR THE LICENSING OF SHOCHETIM
Established in respect of Welfare of Animals Regulations (1995). This provides for the shechita of animals and poultry by a shochet, duly licensed for the purpose by the Rabbinical commission. Membership of the Rabbinical Commission is as follows: The Chief Rabbi, who is the permanent Chair; one member appointed by the Spanish and Portuguese Synagogue (London), who is a Vice Chair; three members appointed by the Beth Din (London); two members appointed by the Federation of Synagogues (London); one member appointed by the Union of Orthodox Hebrew Congregations (London); two members appointed by the Pres. of the BoD to represent regional congregations. *Ch.* The Chief Rabbi; *Hon. S.* Stuart Taylor 305 Ballards Lane, London N12 8GB *Tel* 020 8343 6301 *Email* info@chiefrabbi.org

SHATNEZ CENTRE TRUST
22 Bell Lane, Hendon, London NW4 2AD
Tel 020 8202 4005
(Est. 1990. Reg. Charity No. 1013840). To provide Shatnez checking at the Shatnez Centre and promote Shatnez observance in the community. *T.* A. E. Bude, David Rabson

SMALL JEWISH COMMUNITIES COUNCIL
c/o Board of Deputies, 6 Bloomsbury Square, London WC1A 2LP
Tel 020 8459 4372
To provide appropiate help to small communities that do not have a Minister. *M.* The Rev Malcolm Weisman OBE, MA

SPANISH AND PORTUGUESE JEWS' CONGREGATION
Website www.sandp.org
The community of Spanish and Portuguese Jews in London was founded by Marranos in the middle of the seventeenth century. The congregation 'Sahar Asamaim', worshipped in Creechurch Lane (where a tablet records the site) from 1657 to 1701, when the Bevis Marks

Synagogue was built. It is the oldest extant synagogue building in Britain except for the medieval synagogue of Lincoln. The first branch synagogue of the congregation in the West End was established in Wigmore Street in 1853, and in 1861 removed to Bryanston Street; in 1896 the existing building in Lauderdale Road, Maida Vale was opened. In 1977 another branch of the Spanish & Portuguese Jews' Congregation was opened in Wembley. The congregation is run by a board of Elders as well as a Mahamad (six members) who act as an Executive. An assessment (Finta) is levied on the Yehidim, and congregational affairs are regulated by laws, termed Ascamot, the first code of which was drawn up in 1663.

The congregation maintains the Medrash of Heshaim (founded in 1664). Hebrew religious instruction is given at the Communal Centre, Ashworth Road, W9

A brotherhood Mikveh Israel (Lavadores), established 1678, and a Burial Society, Hebrat Guemilut Hassadim (1665), attend to the last rites to the dead. A number of charitable and educational trusts exist for the benefit of Sephardim. Previous holders of the office of Haham were: Jacob Sasportas (1664-5); Joshua da Silva (1690-9); Jacob Abendana (1681-5); Solomon Ayllon (1689-1700), David Nietto (1702-28), Isaac Nietto (1733-41), Moses Gomez de Mesquita (1744-51); Moses Cohen Dazevedo (1761-84); Raphael Meldola (1805-28); Benjamin Artom (1866-79); Moses Gaster (1887-1917); Solomon Gaon (1947-77).

Pres. of Elders, D. Dangoor; *V. Pres. of Elders*, R. Leon; *Chief Exec.* Howard Miller *London Sephardi Trust*. Office, 2 Ashworth Road, Maida Vale, W9 1JY
Tel 020 7289 2573 *Fax* 020 7289 2709 *Admin.* H. Miller *Email* howardmiller@spsyn.org.uk
Rosh Beth Din Dayan S. Amor.
(Reg. Charity No. 212517). Synagogues and organisations are listed in the London and the Home Counties section.

Burial Society
2 Ashworth Road, W9 1JY
Tel 020 7289 2573

CEMETERIES
253 Mile End Road, E1 4BJ. (Opened in 1657. Disused), The oldest Jewish burial ground in the United Kingdom
329 Mile End Road, E1 4NT (Opened 1725. Disused)
Hoop Lane, Golders Green, NW11 7EU *Tel* 020 8455 2569 *Email* director@ejbb-jbc.org.uk
Edgwarebury Lane, Edgware HA8 8QP *Tel* 020 8958 0090 *Email* director@ejbb-jbc.org.uk
Dytchleys, Coxtie Green, Brentwood. (Disused)

FEDERATION OF SYNAGOGUES
65 Watford Way, NW4 3AQ
Tel 020 8202 2263 *Fax* 020 8203 0610
Email info@federationofsynagogues.com *Website* www.federationofsynagogues.com
The Federation of Synagogues, then embodying 16 small Synagogues in the East End of London, was established in 1887. It now comprises 14 Constituent Synagogues and 10 Affiliated congregations situated in most parts of Greater London and Manchester. The objects of the Federation include: To provide the services of Orthodox rabbis, ministers and Dayanim; the provision of a Burial Society; to assist synagogues in the erection, reconstruction or redecoration of their Houses of Worship, to assist in the maintenance of Orthodox religious instruction in Talmud Torahs and Yeshivot; to obtain and maintain Kashrut; to support charitable and philanthropic works; to further the progress of Eretz Yisrael. *Pres.* A. Finlay; *V. Pres.* H. Dony, B. Mire; *T. L.* Newmark, M. Greenbaum; *Chief Exec.* Dr. Eli Kienwald
Constituent and affiliated synagogues are listed in the London and the Home Counties and Manchester sections.
Associated Bodies
Beth Din of the Federation of Synagogues
Dayan Yisroel Yaakov Lichtenstein, Rosh Beth Din, Dayan M.D. Elzas; *Reg.* Rabbi S. Z. Unsdorfer

Kashrus Board
Kashrus Dir. Dayan M. D. Elzas; *Pres.* A. Finlay
Federation Burial Society
Tel 020 8202 3903 *Fax* 020 8203 0610
Office: 65 Watford Way, Hendon NW4 3AQ *Tel* 020 8202 3903 *Fax* 020 8203 0610
Admin. T. Zelmanovits; *Sexton* N. Kahler; *T.* Rabbi J. Cohen, M. Ezra
Hamaor Magazine (Two issues a year)
Federation of Synagogues, 65 Watford Way, London NW4 3AQ
(Est. 1962). *Ed.* E. Chapper

CEMETERIES
Montagu Road, Edmonton, N18 2NF *Tel* 020 8807 2268
Foreman Paul Beasley *Tel* 020 8807 2268
416 Upminster Road North, Rainham, Essex RM13 9SB *Supt.* Rev. M. Brown *Tel* 01708 552
825; *Foreman* Mark Stonely *Tel* 01708 552 825, Mobile 07960 349 382

UNION OF ORTHODOX HEBREW CONGREGATIONS
140 Stamford Hill, N16 6QT
Tel 020 8802 6226 *Fax* 020 8809 6590
(Est. 1926. Reg. Charity No. 249892). The Union of Orthodox Hebrew Congregations was
founded by the late Rabbi Dr. Victor Schonfeld to protect traditional Judaism. It comprises
synagogues and institutions, which retain their independence but accept the authority of
the rabbinate of the union. Synagogues are entitled to representation on the Council of the
Union, through their delegates who elect the executive committee.
   Rabbinate Rabbi Ephraim Padwa (Principal Rabbinate Authority), Dayan A. D. Dunner,
Rabbi Z. Feldman, Dayan S. Friedman, Dayan D. Grynhaus, Rabbi Ch. Halpern, Rabbi E.
Halpern, Rabbi P. Roberts, Dayan J. Padwa; *Court Registrar* J. R. Conrad, *Pres.* Rabbi D.
Frand, *Exec. Co-ord.* Chanoch Kesselman, *Gen. Sec.* C. Z. Schneck
Constituent and affiliated synagogues are listed in the London and the Home Counties
section.
Details of the Eruv in Edgware are given on p.172

Associated Bodies
Kashrus Committee-Kedassia
140 Stamford Hill, N16 6QT *Tel* 020 8800 6833 *Fax* 020 8809 7092
Ch. Sinitsky; *Admin.* Y. Feldman, Y. Y. Frankel
Central Mikvaot Board
140 Stamford Hill, N16 6QT
Tel 020 8802 6226
Adath Yisroel Burial Society
40 Queen Elizabeth's Walk, N16 0HH *Tel* 020 8802 6262/3 *Fax* 020 8800 8764
Sec. D. Lobenstein

CEMETERIES
Carterhatch Lane, Enfield *Tel* 020 8363 3384; Silver Street, Cheshunt, Herts *Tel* 01707 874 220

MASORTI

MASORTI JUDAISM
Alexander House, 3 Shakespeare Road, Finchley, London N3 1XE
Tel 020 8349 6650
Email enquiries@masorti.org.uk *Website* www.masorti.org.uk
Masorti means Traditional Judaism for Modern Jews. Masorti Judaism is the umbrella body
that serves all Masorti communities in Britain. It acts as a central co-ordinating body with
responsibility for developing Masorti communities, providing social, cultural and
educational opportunities for youth, students and young adults, and for promoting
Masorti values. Masorti Judaism provides a network of welcoming, inclusive Jewish

Communities, Noam - Masorti Youth, Marom - Masorti Young Adults, the European Masorti Bet Din, a range of leadership training programmes, adult education courses, and resources for educators. *Jt. Ch.* Clive Sheldon QC, Nick Gendler; *Ch. Exec.* Matt Plen. Constituent synagogues are listed in the London and the Home Counties section. *See also* Bournemouth, Leeds and Oxford.

European Masorti Beth Din (form. **Bet Din of the Assembly of Masorti Synagogues**) Alexander House, 3 Shakespeare Road, Finchely, London N3 1XE
Tel 020 8349 6650
Email office@europeanmasortibetdin.org *Website* www.europeanmasortibetdin.org
(Est. 2005). Provides Bet Din services (conversion, Divorce, Kashrut Supervision) in Masorti communities in the UK and across Europe. *Av Bet Din and Dir.* Rabbi Chaim Weiner *Email* director@europeanmasortibetdin.org

REFORM

THE MOVEMENT FOR REFORM JUDAISM
The Sternberg Centre for Judaism, 80 East End Road, London N3 2SY
Tel 020 8349 5640 *Fax* 020 8349 5699
Email admin@reformjudaism.org.uk *Website* www.reformjudaism.org.uk
The Movement for Reform Judaism was formed in 2005 as successor to the Reform Synagogues of Great Britain, founded in 1942 with just 6 synagogues. The Movement for Reform Judaism in Britain now consists of 42 synagogues with more than 35,000 members (approximately 20 per cent of UK synagogue affiliations). The Movement is a major supporter of the Leo Baeck College where its rabbis and educators are trained. Akiva Primary School is under the auspices of the Reform and Liberal Movements and Clore Tikva and Clore Shalom Primary School are under Reform, Liberal and Masorti auspices. The Movement sponsors the RSY-Netzer Youth Movement and supports the Jewish Cross Communal Secondary School. The Movement for Reform Judaism seeks to reach out to and engage with Jews 'where they are', understand their Jewish needs and facilitate a wide range of continuing Jewish journeys. It offers pluralist Judaism, rooted in tradition yet in dialogue with modernity.
Life Pres. Sir Sigmund Sternberg; *Pres.* Rabbi Dr. Tony Bayfield; *Movement Rabbi*, Laura Janner-Klausner
Constituent Synagogues are listed in the London and home counties section. *See also* Blackpool; Bournemouth; Bradford; Brighton & Hove; Cambridge; Cardiff; Cheshire; Glasgow; Hull; Liverpool; Maidenhead; Manchester; Milton Keynes; Newcastle; Leeds; N. Manchester; Sheffield & District; Southend & District; South Hampshire; Southport; Thanet & District; Coventry; Darlington; Swindon; Totnes; Cornwall.

Assembly of Rabbis *Ch.* Rabbi Sybil Sheridan
Rabbinical Court (Beit Din) *Tel* 020 8349 5657 *Convenor*, Rabbi Jaqueline Tabick
Associated Schools Akiva Finchley, Clore Shalom Shenley, Clore Tikva Redbridge
RSY-Netzer (The Movement for Reform Judaism's Youth Movement)
See under Organisations Concerned with Jewish Youth

Jewish Joint Burial Society (serving Reform & Masorti communities)
1 Victory Road, Wanstead E11 1UL
Tel 020 8989 5252 *Fax* 020 8989 6075
Email admin@jewishfunerals.org.uk
(Est. 1968; Reg. Charity No. 257345). *Sexton* C.R. Joseph, *Asst. Sexton* M. Kalinsky

THE STERNBERG CENTRE FOR JUDAISM
80 East End Road, N3 2SY
Tel 020 8349 5640 *Fax* 020 8349 5699
Email admin@manorhousetrust.org.uk
(Manor House Trust, Est. 1982. Reg. Charity No. 283083). A European centre for the

promotion of Jewish religious, educational, intellectual and cultural matters. The Centre includes a Holocaust Memorial Garden and a mikveh; it houses the Akiva School; Assembly of Reform Rabbis UK; Leo Baeck College; Manor House Books; Manor House Centre for Psychotherapy & Counselling; Pro-Zion; Reform and Liberal Association of Mohalim; The Movement for Reform Judaism; the Masorti New North London Synagogue. *Ch. of Trs.* Sir Sigmund Sternberg, KCSG, JP; *T. G.* Rothman; *Movement Ch.* Robert Weiner; *V. Ch.* Gary Copitch

LIBERAL JUDAISM (formerly ULPS)
The Montagu Centre, 21 Maple Street, London W1T 4BE
Tel 020 7580 1663 *Fax* 020 7631 9838
Email montagu@liberaljudaism.org *Website* www.liberaljudaism.org
(Reg. Charity No. 236590). Est. 1902 for the advancement of Liberal Judaism and to establish and organise Congregations, Groups and Religion Schools on Liberal Jewish principles. *Ch.* Lucien J. Hudson; *Chief Exec.* Rabbi Danny Rich *Tel* 020 7631 9830 *Email* d.rich@liberaljudaism.org; PA to Chief Exec. Alex Wakely *Tel* 020 7631 9830 *Email* awakely@liberaljudaism.org
Constituent Synagogues are listed in the London and the Home Counties section. *See also* Bedfordshire; Birmingham; Brighton & Hove; Bristol & West; Crawley; Dublin; East Anglia; Eastbourne; Edinburgh; Gloucestershire; Herefordshire; Kent; Leicester; Lincolnshire; Manchester; Nottingham; Peterborough; Suffolk; Reading; Amersham (South Bucks).

LJY Netzer
Liberal Judaism's Youth Department LJY-Netzer
Tel 020 7631 0584 *Email* ljynetzer@liberaljudaism.org *Admin* Selina O'Dwyer

Rabbinic Conference
The Montagu Centre, 21 Maple Street, London W1T 4BE
Tel 020 7580 1663
Email montagu@liberaljudaism.org
Ch. Rabbis Aaron Goldstein and Shulamit Ambalu

Associate Communities
Oxford, Beit Ha'Chiddush (Amsterdam) and Wessex Liberal Jewish Group (Bournemouth)
For further information look at the respective headings.

CEMETERIES
Funeral-Dir. Martin Broad and Son. *Tel* 020 8445 2797 *Fax* 020 8343 9463
Edgwarebury Lane, Edgware, Middlesex HA8 8QP *Cemetery Dir.* Paul van der Hulks *Tel* 020 8958 0090/07967 656 733 *Email* director@ejbb-jbc.org.uk
Liberal Jewish Cemetery, Pound Lane, Willesden, NW10 *Supt.* A. O'Brian *Tel* 020 8459 1635
Western Cemetery, Bulls Cross Ride, Cheshunt, Herts EN7 5HT *Supt.* A. Harris *Tel* 01992 717 820

ASSOCIATION OF REFORM AND LIBERAL MOHALIM
The Sternberg Centre for Judaism, 80 East End Road, London N3 2SY
Tel 020 8349 5645 *Fax* 020 8349 5699
(Est. 1988). You can get a full list of Mohalim from constituent synagogues, from Reform Judaism (020 8349 5657), LJ (020 7580 1663) or by writing to the Association at the Sternberg Centre.

WELFARE ORGANISATIONS

BRITISH TAY-SACHS FOUNDATION
Now under the administration of Jewish Care (*See* p. 91, 185). *Tel* 020 8922 2000

CHAI CANCER CARE
142-146 Great North Way, London NW4 1EH
Tel Office 020 8202 2211 *Helpline Freephone* 0808 808 4567 *Fax* 020 8202 2111
Email info@chaicancercare.org *Website* www.chaicancercare.org
(Reg. Charity No. 1978956). Chai Cancer Care is the community's cancer support organisation, providing a range of services including: counselling for families, individuals and couples; complementary therapies; children, teenage and family services; Medical Outpatient Rehabilitation and Palliative Care Service; home support services; group activites and support groups. Services are available to patients in the flagship North West London centre, South London, Essex, South Manchester, North Manchester, Liverpool, Leeds and Glasgow. *Pres.* Lord Young; *Ch.* L. Hager; *Chief Exec.* Lisa Steele

CHILDREN'S AID COMMITTEE CHARITABLE FUND
P.O. Box 68019, Hendon, NW4 9HN
Email info@thecac.org.uk *Website* www.thecac.org.uk
(Est. 1955. Reg. Charity No. 302933). *Ch.* M. Herman; *Sec.* A. Littman; *Admin* Michele Stern

EZER LEYOLDOS LTD
Unit 2, 2a Northfield Road, London N16 5RN
Tel 020 8880 2488 *Fax* 020 3137 5708
Email mail@ezerleyoldos.co.uk *Website* www.ezerleyoldos.co.uk
(Est. 1986. Reg. Charity No. 1132971). Based in the Hackney and Haringey area, Ezer Leyoldos's aim is to provide support to families with short term difficulties; enable families with ongoing difficulties to function; educate and empower parents by teaching parenting skills; provide support to dysfunctional families. *Dir.* Malke Sterlicht 136 Stamford Hill London N16 6QT; *Ch.* Aron Emanuel Bude 10 Parkway London NW11 0EX; *V. Ch.* Rabbi Abraham Pinter 6 Northdene Gardens London N15 6LX; *Sec.* Michael Posen 46 Riverside Road London N15 6DA

FINNART HOUSE SCHOOL TRUST
Radius Works, Back Lane, London NW3 1HL
Tel 07804 854 905
Email info@finnart.org *Website* www.finnart.org
(Est. 1901. Reg. Charity No. 220917). A charitable trust that provides scholarships and bursaries to Jewish young people. *Ch. of Tru.* Dame Hilary Blume

JAT (Jewish Action and Training for Sexual Health)
c/o 2a Dunstan Road, London NW11 8AA
Tel 07546 429 885
Website www.jat-uk.org
(Reg. Charity No. 327936). JAT is the only charity in the UK providing support for Jewish people from across the whole Jewish community and their families/carers who are living with HIV and AIDS. *Patrons* Prof. Michael Adler, CBE, Clive Lawton, Lady Morris of Kenwood, Lord Sacks of Aldgate; *Client Support*, Janine Clements; *Ch.* Ruth Hilton

JEWISH ASSOCIATION FOR MENTAL ILLNESS – JAMI
Olympia House, Armitage Road, London NW11 8RQ
Tel 020 8458 2223 *Fax* 020 8731 7395
Email info@jamiuk.org *Website* www.jamiuk.org
(Est. 1980. Reg. Charity No. 1003345). JAMI provides mental health services to the Jewish community. These range from day services for those with severe and enduring ill-health,

to education for our children, to ensure they seek help quickly and effectively and so help to prevent just such problems. Other services include befriending; cultural and religious activities; advice and information; social events; outreach and hospital visiting. One in four people will experience mental health difficulties at some time. JAMI helps people to recognise the symptoms and know where and how to seek help. JAMI runs a range of activities to help regain confidence and vital skills, and offers what is for many the only hot, nutritious daily meal that they will eat. JAMI provides a lifeline by enabling people to come to a place which is free of judgement, prejudice and stigma.

JEWISH CARE

Amélie House, Maurice and Vivienne Wohl Campus, 221 Golders Green Road, London NW11 9DQ
Tel 020 8922 2000 Jewish Care Direct (Helpline) 020 8922 2222 *Fax* 020 8201 3897
Email jcdirect@jcare.org *Website* www.jewishcare.org
(Est. 1990. Reg. Charity No. 802559). Jewish Care is the largest social care and health charity for the Jewish community in London and the South-east. Staff and volunteers help and support over 7,000 people every week through a range of 70 services. Jewish Care wants to make a positive impact on the lives of Jewish people by creating and providing excellent social care that enhances wellbeing and inspires them to stay connected to their community. Its ambition is to work collaboratively, initiate debate, be a catalyst for change, a channel for advancement and a voice across the sector. Jewish Care – promoting meaningful lives for our community.
Jewish Care was formed on 1 January 1990 by the merger of the Jewish Blind Society and the Jewish Welfare Board. Jewish Care has since merged its activities with a number of other Jewish organisations. These include: the Jewish Home and Hospital at Tottenham, Food for the Jewish Poor, British Tay Sachs Foundation, Waverley Manor (Friends of the London Jewish Hospital), Brighton & Hove Jewish Home, Stepney Jewish (B'nai Brith) Clubs and Settlements, and the Redbridge Jewish Youth and Community Centre (Sinclair House), and most recently a collaboration with JAMI. *Pres.* Lord Levy; *Ch.* Steven Lewis; *Chief Exec.* Simon Morris

JEWISH CHILD'S DAY (JCD)

707 High Road, London N12 0BT
Tel 020 8446 8804 *Fax* 020 8446 7370
Email info@jcd.uk.com *Website* www.jcd.uk.com
(Est. 1947. Reg. Charity No. 209266). Raises funds to distribute to agencies providing services to Jewish children in need of special care throughout the world. Provides equipment of all kinds and supports specific projects for children who are blind, deaf, mentally or physically disabled, orphaned, neglected, deprived, abused, refugee or in need of medical care. *Life Pres.* J. Jacobs; *Ch.* J. Moss MBE; *T. S.* Moss, CBE; *Exec. Dir.* Melanie Klass

JEWISH GENETIC DISORDERS UK (JGD UK)

P.O. Box 65520, London, N3 9BU
Tel 020 8123 5022
Email info@jgduk.org *Website* www.jewishgeneticdisordersuk.org
(Est. 2010. Reg. Charity No.1134935). JGD UK is dedicated to making a real difference to the prevention, diagnosis and management of Jewish genetic disorders in the UK. It focuses on genetic conditions that are more common among people of Jewish ancestry relative to the general population - including disorders that are fatal in childhood and others associated with chronic disability.
JGD UK aims to raise awareness of Jewish genetic disorders across the Jewish and healthcare professional communities; and to help those affected and at risk, to access the best available information, services and support.
Its core activities include: awareness raising, information provision and referral, and facilitating access to responsible genetic testing services. *Exec. Dir.* Katrina Sarig; *Ch. of Tru. Bd.* Peter Jacobs

JEWISH HELPLINE LTD

(*Admin. Office*) Cardinal Point, Park Road, Rickmansworth, Herts WD3 1RE
Tel 0800 652 9249
Email jewishhl@live.co.uk
Serving MIYAD (first est. 1988), JLINE (opened in 2004) (Reg. Charity No. 1101612). Telephone crisis lines for Jewish children and adults, manned by professionally trained volunteers. *Tru.* R. Rosenberg, M. Stalbow, P. Caplan

JEWISH MARRIAGE COUNCIL

23 Ravenshurst Avenue, NW4 4EE
Tel 020 8203 6311
Email info@jmc-uk.org *Website* www. jmc-uk.org
(Est. 1946). The Council provides the following services: a counselling service for couples, individuals and families - nobody is turned away through lack of funds. Divorce Mediation. (*Tel* 020 8203 6311); support group for divorced/divorcing women *Tel* 020 8203 5207

JEWISH WOMEN'S AID (JWA)

JWA, P.O. Box 2670, London N12 9ZE
Tel Office, 020 8445 8060 *Fax* 020 8445 0305
Confidential Helpline Freephone 0808 801 0500 Monday-Thursday 9.30am-9.30pm
Email info@jwa.org.uk For *Email* advice advice@jwa.org *Website* www.jwa.org.uk
(Est. 1992. Reg. Charity No. 1047045). Jewish Women's Aid (JWA) is a charity for Jewish Women, and their children, who are affected by domestic violence. JWA has two core aims; First, to provide confidential, accessible, empowering and culturally sensitive advocacy and support for Jewish women and children who are affected by domestic violence. Second, through education, training and awareness raising, to ensure that all sectors of the Jewish community recognise and speak out against domestic violence.
JWA has a team of dedicated professional staff and volunteers who run the organisation's core services; a national freephone helpline; a refuge for Jewish women and their children; a community support and children's service, free counselling services, and education and awareness raising programmes.
Hon. Pres. Judith Usiskin; *Ch.* Francis Turner; *Exec. Dir.* Emma Bell

JSENSE

21 Marchbank Drive, Gatley, Cheadle, Cheshire SK8 1QY
Email services@jsense.org.uk *Website* www.jsense.org.uk
(Reg. Charity No. 1151197). Support for education of Jewish Children with special educational needs. *Ch.* Malcolm Joels

LANGDON

PO Box 640, Edgware, Middlesex HA8 4GL
Tel 0845 600 6562 (ext. 4, admissions), (ext. 5, fundraising/events)
Email info@langdonuk.org *Website* www.langdon.info
(Est. 1992. Reg. Charity No. 1142742). Langdon provides education, employment and supported living for Jewish young and adults in both Manchester and London.
CEO, Alison Rosen; *Ch.* Barry Welck; *T.* Laurence Tish; *Patrons Ch.*, Jonathan Joseph.
London Centre: Maccabi House, Gideon Close, Manor Park Crescent, Edgware, Middlesex HA8 7FR *Dir.* Robert Mutch
Manchester Office: 44 Rectory Lane, Prestwich, Manchester, M25 1BL *Dir.* Robert Mutch
Langdon College: 9 Leicester Avenue, Salford, Manchester, M7 4HA *Princ.* Christopher Mayho

THE MANOR HOUSE CENTRE FOR PSYCHOTHERAPY AND COUNSELLING (MHCPC)

The Sternberg Centre, 80 East End Road, N3 2SY
Tel 020 8371 0180
Email admin@manorhousecentre.org.uk *Website* www.manorhousecentre.org.uk

(Reg. Charity No. 1131804). The Centre provides counselling training for people working or planning to work, in both paid and voluntary positions in the community. A counselling service is also provided for those seeking help for emotional distress.

RESOURCE (formerly **Employment Resource Centre**)
8 Dancastle Court, 14 Arcadia Avenue, London N3 2JU
Tel 020 8346 4000 *Fax* 020 8346 4433
Email office@resource-centre.org *Website* www.resource-centre.org
(Est. 1992. Reg. Charity No. 1106331). A service for the Jewish community offering opportunities for the unemployed to gain skills and training for the job market.
Ch. Exec. Cttee. Emma May; *Centre Dir.* Alan Shapiro

TAY-SACHS SCREENING CENTRE
Genetics 7th Floor, Borough Wing, Guy's Hospital, Great Maze Pond, London SE1 9RT
Tel 020 7188 1364 *Fax* 020 7188 1369
Website www.guysandstthomas.nhs.uk
Provides information, carrier testing and genetic counselling for Tay-Sachs disease, and a walk-in clinic on Monday morning. Additional private test now offered for 8 other genetic conditions that are common in the Ashkenazi Jewish population. *Sec.* Debbie Wyndham; *Genetic Counsellor* Sara Levene

REFUGEE ORGANISATIONS

45 AID SOCIETY
10 York House, Royal Connaught Drive, Bushey, Herts WD23 2RF
Tel 07786 240 309
Email max.kim@hotmail.co.uk
(Est. 1963). The Society consists mainly of Holocaust survivors who came to England in 1945/6 and others who have immigrated subsequently. It maintains close links with members who have emigrated to Israel, USA, Canada and other countries. The Society is active in the community, helps members as well as others in need. It furthers Holocaust education and other charitable causes. *Pres.* Sir Martin Gilbert; *Ch.* Ben Helfgott MBE D.Univ; *V. Ch.* Angela Cohen; *T.* Alan Greenberg; *Sec.* Kim Stern

ACJR (Association of Children of Jewish Refugees)
Tel 020 8201 7986
Email info@acjr.org.uk *Website* www.acjr.org.uk
A cultural and social group for those whose parents were victims of, or who fled from, Nazi persecution in the 1930s and 1940s. *Publ.* Monthly newsletter. *Ch.* Anthony Abbey

AJR CHARITABLE TRUST (Association of Jewish Refugees in Great Britain)
(Head Office) Jubilee House, Merrion Avenue, Stanmore, Middlesex HA7 4RL
Tel 020 8385 3070 *Fax* 020 8385 3080
(AJR Centre) Belsize Square Synagogue, 51 Belsize Square, London NW3 4HX
Tel 020 7794 3949
Email enquiries@ajr.org.uk *Website* www.ajr.org.uk
(Reg. Charity No. 211239). The AJR provides social and welfare services to Holocaust survivors and refugees and their families. Alongside its team of dedicated social care workers, the AJR operates a nationwide network of regional groups for members to enjoy entertainment. The AJR Volunteers department looks after the interests of many AJR members who still live in their own homes, including arranging for regular visits from a befriender and helping out at regional groups and Head Office. The AJR offers advice and assistance with claims for Holocaust-era compensation and the restitution of appropriated assets. The Paul Balint AJR Centre now meets on Tuesdays and Thursdays at the Belsize Square Synagogue (51 Belsize Square, London NW3 4HX). As well as serving freshly prepared meals, the centre offers a wide range of activities and entertainment for its members. The AJR arranges frozen kosher meals to be delivered once a week to members in the North West London area. The Kindertransport and the Child Survivors Association (CSA) are Special Interest Groups of the AJR. All members receive the monthly *AJR Journal*, which combines topical news analysis with feature articles as well as book, theatre and film reviews.
Chief Exec. Michael Newman; *Dir.* Carol Rossen, David Kaye. *Publ.*: *AJR Journal* (monthly), *Kindertransport Newsletter* (quarterly), *Child Survivors Association* (bi-monthly).

HOLOCAUST SURVIVORS' CENTRE (HSC)
(Jewish Care with the support of World Jewish Relief)
Corner of Parson Street/Church Road, London NW4 1QA
Tel 020 8202 9844 *Fax* 020 8202 2404
Email hsc@jcare.org
A Jewish social centre for survivors who were in Europe during the Second World War, or came to the UK as refugees after November 1938 and on the Kindertransport.
It offers a friendly, safe place where elderly survivors can meet and socialise, and where they can benefit from a full therapeutic programme. The centre offers a wide range of social activities for members, six days a week, Sunday-Friday. Testimonies are also recorded and survivors visit schools, colleges and universities to talk about their experiences. It is the only centre designed specifically for Holocaust survivors in the UK.
Dir. Aviva Trup; *Co-ord.* Rachelle Lazarus, Melanie Gotlieb

SHALVATA

Parson Street/Corner of Church Road, London NW4 1QA
Tel 020 8203 9033 *Fax* 020 8201 5534
Email shalvata@jcare.org

Associated with the Holocaust Survivors' Centre. Testimonies are recorded. Shalvata is a counselling and social work service. It is also known as a training and consultation service for professionals working with war trauma. In conjunction with World Jewish Relief, Shalvata is currently working with a group of Bosnian refugees.

ORGANISATIONS CONCERNED WITH THE JEWS OF EASTERN EUROPE

COMMUNITY CONNECTIONS (Formerly **Exodus 2000**)
European Union for Progressive Judaism, Sternberg Centre, 80 East End Road, London N3 2SY
Tel 020 8349 5651
Email exodus2000@eupj.org   *Website* www.eupj.org/exodus-2000
Community Connections' aims to support Progressive Judaism in Eastern Europe. It works under the aegis of the European Union for Progressive Judaism (part of the WUPJ). Community Connections has a national executive and groups in many Reform and Liberal synagogues. Its major areas of work are: (i) supporting the growth of Progressive Judaism in the former Soviet Union; (ii) establishing and facilitating twinnings between UK Progressive Communities and those in Russia, Ukraine and Belarus; (iii) sending Rabbis and lay educators to teach. Community Connections works closely with the World Union of Progressive Judaism in Israel and America.

ZIONIST ORGANISATIONS

ISRAEL EMBASSY
2 Palace Green, Kensington, W8 4QB
Tel 020 7957 9500 (Consulate telephone hours: Monday-Thursday 2-5pm)
Email info@london.mfa.gov.il *Website* www.embassyofisrael.co.uk
Consulate opening hours Monday-Thursday 10am-1.15pm, Friday 10am-12pm (See website for full details). *Ambassador to the Court of St James's, HE* Daniel Taub; *Min. Plenipotentiary* Alon Roth-Snir

JEWISH AGENCY FOR ISRAEL
7th Floor, Central House, 1 Ballards Lane, London N3 1LQ
Aliyah: *Tel* 020 8371 5250 *Fax* 020 8371 5251
Education: *Tel* 020 8371 5270 *Fax* 020 8371 5271
Treasury & Administration: *Tel* 020 8371 5300 *Fax* 020 8371 5301
Email londonoffice@jafi.org *Website* www.jewishagency.org
The Jewish Agency for Israel in Great Britain is one of eight delegations worldwide. In partnership with the Zionist Youth Movements and Jewish Communities around the world, the Jewish Agency's main activities are focused on encouraging and nurturing Aliyah to Israel. It also works to reinforce Jewish Zionist education and strengthen the connection between the Diaspora and the State of Israel. *Ch. of the Exec.* Natan Sharansky; *Ch. of the Bd of Gov.* Richard L. Pearlstone; *Dir. Gen.* Alan Hoffman

JEWISH LABOUR MOVEMENT (incorporating Poale Zion)
P.O. Box 695, Harrow, HA3 0HF
Tel/Fax 020 8621 4574
Email info@jlm.org.uk *Website* www.jlm.org.uk
The Jewish Labour Movement, launched officially in July 2004, is the successor to Poale Zion. As such it retains its Labour Zionist ideals and affiliation to the Labour Party, where it acts as a link between Labour and the Jewish community. It also works within communal organisations, such as the Board of Deputies. Its main campaigning activities focus on the peaceful conclusion of the Israel-Palestine conflict, on the basis of a two-state solution, and combating racism and antisemitism. *Ch.* Louise Ellman MP; *V. Ch.* Neil Nerva, Jerry Lewis; *Hon. S.* Dr Judith Bara; *Hon. T.* Edwin Strauss

JNF CHARITABLE TRUST
Head Office, JNF House, Spring Villa Park, Spring Villa Road, Edgware, Middlesex HA8 7ED
Tel 020 8732 6100 *Fax* 020 8732 6111
Website www.jnf.co.uk
CEO David Goodman; *Ch.* Samuel Hayek; *V. Ch.* Dr. Michael Sinclair

KKL Charity Accounts
Head Office, JNF House, Spring Villa Park, Spring Villa Road, Edgware, Middlesex HA8 7ED
Tel 020 8732 6134/3 *Fax* 020 8732 6111
Email giving@kkl.org.uk
Administration of charity accounts and payroll giving.

KKL Executor & Trustee Co. Ltd
JNF House, Spring Villa Park, Spring Villa Road, Edgware, Middlesex HA8 7ED
Tel 020 8732 6121 *Fax* 020 8732 6111
Email wills@kkl.org.uk
Will writing, Estate planning and Executorship services.

LIKUD-HERUT MOVEMENT OF THE UNITED KINGDOM
Email mail@Likud-Herut.org.uk *Website* www.likud-Herut.org.uk
(Est. 1970). To promote the Zionist ideology as conceived by Ze'ev Jabotinsky. Member of World Likud. *Life Pres.* Eric Graus; *Ch.* Zalmi Unsdorfer

Affiliated Organisations: Young Likud-Herut; (Brit Nashim Herut Women's League); Betar-Tagar, Brit Hashmonayim.

MERETZ UK For equality, human rights and peace (part of World Union of Meretz)
Hashomer House, 37A Broadhurst Gardens, London NW6 3BN
Tel 020 7328 5451/020 3286 1616
Email info@meretz.org.uk *Website* www.meretz.org.uk
Social, cultural, educational and political programme, stressing humanistic values of Judaism and progressive Zionist elements.

NEFESH B'NEFESH
65 Watford Way, Hendon, London NW4 3AQ
Tel 0800 075 7200
Website www.nbn.org.il
Established in 2002 with the aim of revitalising western Aliyah (immigration to Israel) from USA and Canada. In May 2006, in response to numerous requests from British Jewry, Nefesh B'Nefesh expanded its services to the UK. Working together with the Jewish Agency and the Government of Israel, Nefesh B'Nefesh assists Olim (immigrants to Israel) throughout the entire Aliyah process, from the planning stage to well beyond arrival in Israel. By removing or minimising the financial, professional, logistical and social obstacles that potential Olim face, Nefesh B'Nefesh helps ensure their successful absorption in Israel. To date, the organisation has brought over 30,000 Olim (new immigrants) from North America and the UK.
Dir. of UK Aliyah Dov Newmark *Email* dov@nbn.org.il

PRO-ZION: PROGRESSIVE RELIGIOUS ZIONISTS
The Sternberg Centre for Judaism, 80 East End Road, N3 2SY
Tel 020 8349 5640
Email info@prozion.org.uk *Website* www.prozion.org.uk
(Est. 1978). To work for full legal and religious rights for Progressive Judaism in Israel, to affirm the centrality in Jewish life of the State of Israel. Affiliated to the Zionist Federation, LJ and the Movement for Reform Judaism. Associated with the Israel Movement for Progressive Judaism. A constituent of Arzenu. *Co-Ch.* D. Needlestone, C. Gluckman; *Hon. S.* M. Silverman; *Hon. T.* S. Michaels; *Admin.* P. Lewis *Publ.* Shema, Progressive Jewish News

UJIA (United Jewish Israel Appeal)
37 Kentish Town Road, London NW1 8NX
Tel 020 7424 6400 *Fax* 020 7424 6401
Email central@ujia.org *Website* www.ujia.org
(Reg. Charity No. 1060078. Reg. Company No. 3295115). UJIA's strategy is designed to help guarantee a sustainable and positive future for the people of the Galil and the Jewish community of the UK. Our programme is built around young people and education, which we see as the key to securing our future. We believe that the future of Israel and the Jewish Diaspora are dependent on each other. UJIA creates the 'Living Bridge' between the communities. *Hon. Pres.* Lord Sacks, Lord Levy, Lord Woolf; *Hon. V. Pres.* Lord Janner QC, Gerald M. Ronson; *Pres.* Sir Trevor Chinn, CVO, David M. Cohen, Brian Kerner; *V. Pres.* Michael Bradfield, Stanley Cohen, OBE, Alan Fox, Dov Hamburger, Ronald Preston, Stephen Rubin, OBE, Sir Harry Solomon, Anthony Spitz, Michael Ziff; *Ch.* Mick Davis; *Chief Exec.* Douglas Krikler; *Company Sec.* Maurice Stone FCA; *Fin. Dir.* Eyal Samuel

WIZOUK
Charles House, 108-110 Finchley Road, London NW3 5JJ
Tel 020 7319 9169 *Fax* 020 7486 7521
Email central@wizouk.org *Website* www.wizouk.org

(Est. 1918. Reg. Charity No. 1125012. Reg. Company No. 6634748). The largest women's society in the UK and Ireland. WIZOᴜᴋ is the UK Branch of World WIZO, the leading provider of social welfare and educational services for disadvantaged families and children in Israel. It has over 90 affiliated women's groups with over 9,000 members. Its mission is to help support and strengthen Israeli citizens through fundraising. *Pres.* Loraine Warren; *Ch.* Jill Shaw; *Hon. S.* M. Pollock; *T.* Helen Reisman, Hanni Seifert; *Exec. Dir.* Linda Boxer *Publ.* WIZOᴜᴋ newsletter (Two issues a year).

WORLD ZIONIST ORGANISATION
BM Box 1948, London WC1N 3XX
Tel 020 8202 0202 *Fax* 020 8202 0233
Email zion-fed@dircon.co.uk Website www.zionist.org.uk
The WZO was established by the first Zionist Congress, which met in Basle on August 29, 1897. The aim of the Organisation, as defined in the programme adopted by the Basle Congress, was to secure for the Jewish people a home in Palestine guaranteed by public law. At the Congress, a constitution providing for a self-governing World Organisation, with the Zionist Congress as the supreme body, was adopted.
The aims of Zionism, as enunciated in the 'New Jerusalem Programme' adopted by the 27th World Zionist Congress in June, 1968, are:
The unity of the Jewish People and the centrality of Israel in Jewish Life;
The ingathering of the Jewish people in its historic homeland, Eretz Israel, through Aliya from all countries;
The strengthening of the State of Israel which is based on the prophetic vision of justice and peace;
The preservation of the identity of the Jewish people through the fostering of Jewish and Hebrew education and of Jewish spiritual and cultural values. *UK contact,* Alan Aziz

ZIONIST FEDERATION OF GREAT BRITAIN AND IRELAND
Box 1948, 116 Ballards Lane, London N3 2DN
Tel 020 8202 0202
Email office@zfuk.org *Website* www.zionist.org.uk
(Est. 1899). The Zionist Federation was founded in 1899 and helped create support for the establishment of the State of Israel. Today we are Britain's largest grass-roots Israel movement. We are supported by over seventy affiliated organisations, representing a wide range of political and religious views and ages. The ZF aims to educate and entertain the British public, by presenting events about Israeli history, politics, film, music, science, tourism etc.
Executive *Ch.* Harvey Rose; *V. Ch.* Jonathan Hoffman, Paul Charney; *Hon. T.* Harvey Rose; *Pres.* Prof. Eric Moonman OBE, Joy Wolfe MBE; *Dir.* Alan Aziz; *Asst. Dir./ Dir. Israel Connect* Gary Sakol; *Fin.* Rowena Rosenberg; *Admin* Melissa Harris
Committee Chairmen *Constitution,* Jonathan Kramer; *Fin.* John Barnett; Yom Ha'atzmaut, Estelle Gilston; Israel Connect, David Cohen

OTHER ORGANISATIONS CONCERNED WITH ISRAEL AND ISRAELI ORGANISATIONS

ACADEMIC STUDY GROUP ON ISRAEL AND THE MIDDLE EAST

PO Box 42763, London NW2 0YJ
Tel 020 8444 0777 *Fax* 020 8444 0681
Email info@foi-asg.org
(Reg. Charity No. 801772). An academic organisation which aims at forging and expanding research contacts between academics in this country and their colleagues in Israel. Organises Anglo-Israel Research Workshops in Israel and the UK. *Pres.* Sir Walter Bodmer, Oxford University; *T.* Aviva Petrie, Eastman Dental Instit.; *Dir.* J. D. A. Levy

AKIM

(Est. 1964. Reg. Charity No. 241458). To assist with the rehabilitation of mentally handicapped children in Israel. *Pres.* Sir Sidney Samuelson CBE. *V. Pres.* Judge B. Lightman; *Ch.* A. Broza; *V. Ch.* J. Samad; *Hon. T.* V. Cohen. *Corr.* 22 Golf Close, Stanmore, Middlesex HA7 2PP *Tel* 020 8954 2772 *Email* info@akim.org.uk *Hon. S.* B. Kober

ALL-PARTY-BRITISH ISRAEL PARLIAMENTARY GROUP

c/o Lord Janner of Braunstone, QC, House of Lords, London, SW1A 0PW
Tel 020 7219 8988
Email lordj@grevillejanner.org.uk *Ch.* Lord Janner of Braunstone, QC; *V. Ch.* Louise Ellman; *T.* Mike Freer; *Sec.* Matthew Offord

ANGLO-ISRAEL ARCHAEOLOGICAL SOCIETY

2nd Floor, Supreme House, 300 Regents Park Road, London N3 2JX
Tel 020 8349 5754
Email sheilarford1@sky.com *Website* www.aias.org.uk
(Reg. Charity No. 220367). Lectures on recent archaeological discoveries in Israel, publishes an annual research bulletin entitled Strata and awards travel grants to students to participate in excavations in Israel. *Ch.* Prof. Martin Goodman, Oriental Institute, Pusey Lane, Oxford OX1 2LE; *Admin.* Sheila Ford

ANGLO-ISRAEL ASSOCIATION

P.O. Box 47819, London NW11 7WD
Tel 020 8458 1284 *Fax* 020 8458 3484
Email info@angloisraelassocation.com *Website* www.angloisraelassocation.com
(Est. 1949. Reg. Charity No. 313523). The purpose of the Association is to promote a wider and more positive understanding of Israel in the UK; to encourage exchanges in both directions; and generally to support activities which foster goodwill between the two countries. The AIA administers two educational Trust Funds. The Wyndham Deedes Memorial Travel Scholarship provides British Students with the opportunity to study in Israel. The Kenneth Lindsay Scholarship Trust provides scholarships for Israeli students to study in the UK. *Fdr.* The late Brigadier-General Sir Wyndham Deedes, CMG, DSO; *Hon. Pres.* The Israeli Ambassador; *Ch. of C.* Lady Sainsbury; *Ch. Exec. Cttee.* Lord Bew; *Hon. T.* A. Epton; *Exec. Dir.* R. Saunders

THE BALFOUR DIAMOND JUBILEE TRUST

67 Addison Road, London W14 8JL
Tel 020 7603 5847
Email strage@compuserve.com
(Est. 1977. Reg. Charity No. 276353). To consolidate and strengthen cultural relations between the UK and Israel. Provides the community with a diverse programme of topical activities throughout the year in literature and the arts. Makes financial support available to individuals and small organisations – both in the UK and Israel – whose work will make an enduring cultural contribution.

BANK LEUMI (UK) plc
London Office, 20 Stratford Place, London W1C 1BG
Tel 020 7907 8000
Email info@bankleumi.co.uk *Website* www.bankleumi.co.uk
Bank Leumi (UK) is a subsidiary of Bank Leumi Le-Israel B.M., which was established in London in 1902 as the financial instrument of the Zionist Movement (under the name of Jewish Colonial Trust). Today the bank specialises in providing corporate and private banking services via its offices in London (Head Office) and Leeds. The bank has two subsidiaries in Jersey, C.I., Bank Leumi (Jersey,) Ltd. and Leumi Overseas Trust Corp. Ltd. and an asset based lending subsidiary in Brighton, Leumi ABL Ltd. *Ch.* Y. Mintz; *CEO* L. Weiss

BEN-GURION UNIVERSITY FOUNDATION
Ort House, 126 Albert Street, London NW1 7NE
Tel 020 7446 8558
Email bengurion.foundation@bguf.org.uk *Website* www.bguf.org.uk
(Est. 1974. Reg. Charity No. 276203). To promote and raise awareness of Ben-Gurion University of the Negev, Israel's youngest University founded in 1969 with a special mandate to develop the Negev. BGU is a University with a conscience, where high standards of research are integrated with community involvement. The University has five Faculties: Health Sciences, Humanities and Social Sciences, Natural Sciences, Engineering Sciences and the Guilford Glazer Faculty of Business and Management. There is also the Kreitman School of Advanced Graduate Studies. Ben-Gurion University is privileged to have the only National Jean Monnet Centre of Excellence in European Studies in Israel. *V. Pres.* Lord George Weidenfeld, Suzanne Zlotowski; *Ch.* Harold Paisner; *Admin. Dir.* Hannah Allen; *Tr.* Eric Charles

BRITISH & EUROPEAN MACHAL ASSOCIATION
3 Moorcroft Court, Bibsworth Road, London N3 3RE
Tel/Fax 020 8343 3508
Email stanleymedicks@email.uk.com *Website* www.machal.org.il
To inform and publicise the inaugeration of a Machal Exhibition at Beit Hatfusot (Museum of Diaspora) on the Campus of Tel Aviv University. The exhibition depicts the heroic endeavour and sacrifice of Machal (Volunteers from the Diaspora) in the 1948 Israel War of Independence. *Co-ordinator* Stanley Medicks

BRITISH FRIENDS OF THE ART MUSEUMS OF ISRAEL
Euston Tower, Floor 33, 286 Euston Road, London NW1 3DP
Tel 020 3463 8715
Email info@bfami.org *Website* www.bfami.org
(Est. 1948. Reg. Charity No. 313008). BFAMI raises funds to help support art museums in Israel. The main focus is on educational activities and the projects sponsored enrich the lives of children from Israel's multi-cultural backgrounds. The versatility of these projects engages individuals as well as communities and offers activities which are open to everyone especially the disadvantaged. BFAMI also acquires works of art and antiques for the museum as well as sponsoring exhibitions. *Patrons* H.E. The Ambassador of Israel, Sir Anthony Caro OM CBE, Dame Vivien Duffield DBE, Sir Anish Kapoor, Sir Timothy Sainsbury PC; *Ch.* Wendy Fisher; *Exec. Dir.* Michelle Hyman

BRITISH FRIENDS OF BAR ILAN UNIVERSITY
109 Baker Street, London W1U 6RP
Tel 020 7486 7394 *Fax* 020 7935 1192
Email info@bfbiu.org *Website* www.bfbiu.org
(Est. 1957. Reg. Charity No. 314139). (*See* p. 248). (BFBIU) promotes Israel's fastest-growing university through a variety of activities designed to advance its academic programmes, research, and continued growth. The Bar-Ilan family numbers 33,000

students pursuing their BA, MA and PhD degrees on the University's award-winning campus just outside Tel Aviv and its four regional colleges throughout the country. Recently Bar-Ilan opened a new Medical School in Sfat, This is a National Israeli project. Combining academic excellence with a commitment to Jewish enrichment and values, Bar-Ilan has achieved an international reputation in the sciences and humanities. *Ch.* Romie Tager QC; *Exec. Dir.* Shlomo Rechtschaffen; *Asst. Dir.* Nadia Nathan; *Chancellor* Rabbi Prof. Emanuel Rackman; *Pres.* Prof. Moshe Kaveh; *Rector* Prof. Teitelbaum

BRITISH FRIENDS OF BOYS TOWN JERUSALEM

6 Bloomsbury Square, London WC1A 2LP
Tel 020 7404 1437
Email office@boystownjerusalem.co.uk
(Est. 1963. Reg. Charity No. 1100332). To help and enrich the lives of over 900 disadvantaged Jewish students who study and live at Boys Town Jerusalem (Kiryat Noar, Bayit Vegan). *Ch.* L. Reuben; *Dev. Dir.* L. Stein

BRITISH FRIENDS OF HAIFA UNIVERSITY

c/o Jewish memorial Council, 26 Enford Street, London W1H 1DW
Tel 020 7724 3777
Email friends@haifa-univ.org.uk *Website* www.haifa-univ.org.uk
(Reg. Charity No. 270733). To further the interests and development of Haifa University (*See* p.276) by donations, books, equipment and subscriptions. The British Founders are represented on the board of Governors of Haifa University *Co.-Ch.* Peter Kadas, Jonathan Lux; *Exec Dir.* Tali Sayar

BRITISH FRIENDS OF THE HEBREW UNIVERSITY OF JERUSALEM

Supreme House, 300 Regents Park Road, London N3 2JX
Tel 020 8349 5757 *Fax* 020 8349 5750
Website www. bfhu.org.uk
(Est. 1926. Reg. Charity No. 209691. Reg. Company No. 6350828). To promote and fundraise on behalf of the Hebrew University of Jerusalem, Israel's leading academic and research centre. The Hebrew University works for the benefit of all Israel's citizens while benefiting nations across the globe and enhancing Israel's reputation. The University boasts an impressive 8 Nobel Prize Laureates, over 258 Israel Prize winners, 12 Wolff Prizes and is the only Israeli university ranked in the Top 100 of world universities (Shanghai Jiao Tong Rankings). *Pres.* John Sacher CBE; *Chief Exec.* Nigel Salomon. The British and Irish Friends are represented on the Hebrew University Board of Governors. **Groups** Legacies; Students/Alumni; Women's Group; Legal; Young Legal and various Regional Groups including Glasgow friends.

BRITISH FRIENDS OF THE ISRAEL FREE LOAN ASSOCIATION

c/o K.C. Keller FCA, 25 Lodge Avenue, Elstree, Herts WD6 3NA
Tel 020 8207 2627
Email ifla@freeloan.org.il *Website* www.freeloan.org.il
(Reg. Charity No. 1009568). Provides interest-free loans to Russian and Ethiopian immigrants in Israel and other needy Israelis, including small business loans, emergency housing, medical loans, and loans to families with handicapped children. Established in Jerusalem in 1990, and in 1992 in London. *Ch.* Kenneth Keller *Email* kennethk53@gmail.com; *Hon. T.* A. Druce; *Patrons*, Lord Sacks.

BRITISH FRIENDS OF THE ISRAEL GUIDE DOG CENTRE FOR THE BLIND

P.O. Box 756, Borehamwood, Herts WD6 9JE
Tel 07702 316 423
Website www.israelguidedog.org
(Reg. Charity No. 1027996). Office hours Monday-Thursday 9.30am-3.30pm *Projects Co-Ord.* Jess Green *Email* bfigdcb-jessgreen@sky.com

BRITISH FRIENDS OF ISRAEL WAR DISABLED
45 Ealing Road, Wembley, Middlesex HA0 4BA
Tel 020 8903 8746 *Fax* 020 8795 2240
(Est. 1974. Reg. Charity No. 269269). A non-political organisation dedicated to helping disabled soldiers rebuild their lives. Aid is given in purchasing rehabilitation equipment at Beit Halochem. Working with the ZAHAL Disabled Veterans' Organisation, we bring groups of injured soldiers to the UK to stay with caring families. *Ch.* F. M. Weinberg; *H. Solicitor* L. Curry; *Hon. T.* C. Niren

BRITISH FRIENDS OF PEACE NOW
P.O. Box 35583, London NW4 4QY
Tel 020 8621 7172
Website www.peacenowuk.org
(Est. 1982. Reg. Charity No. 297295). Peace Now is a grass roots Israeli movement dedicated to Israeli–Palestinian and Israeli–Arab peace. Peace Now organises pro-peace activities and monitors Israel's settlement policy on the West Bank and Gaza Strip. The first and primary goal of Peace Now is to press the Israeli government to seek peace – through negotiations and mutual compromise – with Israel's Arab neighbours and the Palestinian people. British Friends of Peace Now mobilises support for the Israeli peace movement and the peace process among British Jews and the wider community. It is a membership organisation. Membership expresses support for the many Israelis actively working for peace, security, justice and reconciliation in the Middle East.

BRITISH FRIENDS OF RAMBAM MEDICAL CENTRE
1 Opal Court, 120 Regents Park Road, London, N3 3HY
Tel 020 8371 1500
Email anita@rambamuk.co.uk *Website* www.rambamuk.co.uk
(Reg. Charity No. 028061). Raising funds for the purchase of medical equipment for all hospital departments and in particular for Paediatric Nephrology, Oncology and Incubators for at risk babies in the Neo Natal Department. Also funding scholarships for research. *Patron* Chief Rabbi Lord Sacks; *Dir.* Anita Alexander-Passe

BRITISH FRIENDS OF REUTH
PO Box 57702, London NW7 0GL
Tel 07983 543 494
Email info@reuth.org.uk *Website* www.reuth.org.uk
(Reg. Charity No. 1126124). Reuth: providing cutting edge rehabilitation and long-term care for all in Israel since 1937 (the Reuth Medical Center, community housing, senior residences and day centers, Reuth Information Center). British Friends of Reuth are supporting the Reuth Medical Center, which provides world class rehabilitation for long term and chronic care patients, and is the only hospital of its kind in Tel Aviv. *Patrons* Chief Rabbi Lord Sacks, Lord Pannick QC, Peter Sheldon OBE; *Ch.* N. Ferber; *Projects Co-ord.* J. Dayan

BRITISH FRIENDS OF SARAH HERZOG MEMORIAL HOSPITAL (EZRATH NASHIM), JERUSALEM
37 The Avenue, Radlett, WD7 7DQ
Tel 01923 850 100
(Reg. Charity No. 1024814). Israel's foremost centre for geriatric and mental health care, Sarah Herzog Hospital offers exceptional medical care and has outstanding research achievements. The Hospital, with over 100 years experience, treats the effects of advancing age and mental instability with the best medical technologies. With 350 beds, the Hospital is the third largest in Jerusalem. Its Israel Centre for the Treatment of Psychotrauma and Community Mental Health Centre have leading roles in helping individuals affected by terrorist attacks. *Ch.* D. Halpern, QC

BRITISH FRIENDS OF SHUVU
Investing in Jewish Children in Israel
17 Golders Court, Woodstock Road, London NW11 8QG
Tel 020 8209 3010 *Fax* 0870 460 4997
Email shuvuuk@aol.com *Website* www.shuvu.org
(Est. 2003. Reg. Charity No. 1100984). Shuvu is an educational and welfare network. It provides disadvantaged immigrant and native Israeli children with excellence in secular and Jewish Studies within a supportive, warm and nurturing environment. Shuvu's network spans 68 schools and kindergartens, educating some 15,000 children and assisting families through counselling, financial, and medical assistance. *Ch.* David Blachman

BRITISH FRIENDS OF UNITED HATZALAH OF ISRAEL (formerly Hatzolah Jerusalem)
c/o Joseph Kahan Associates, 923 Finchley Road, London, NW11 7PE
Tel 020 8209 0159
(Reg. Charity No. 1101329)

BRITISH FRIENDS OF ZAKA
223a Golders Green Road, London NW11 9ES
Tel 020 8458 5391 *Fax* 020 8458 5398
Email info@zaka.org.uk *Website* www.zaka.org.uk
(Est. 2003. Reg. Charity No. 1099639). Provides support for the Israel Emergency Service, Zaka, ('Chessed shel Emet') whose purpose is the succour and relief of the victims of natural and unnatural disasters. *Patrons* Rabbi Lord Sacks, C. Morris, Lord David Alliance, Sir Victor Blank, David Brecher, Sir Trevor Chinn, Lord Stanley Fink, Lord Michael Levy, Gerald Ronson; *Tru.* Joshua Wahnon, Flora Frank, Herbert N. Frank; *Exec. Dir.* David Rose

CONSERVATIVE FRIENDS OF ISRAEL
45b Westbourne Terrace, W2 3UR
Tel 020 7262 2493 *Fax* 020 7224 8941
CFI works to promote its twin aims of supporting Israel and promoting Conservatism. It organises numerous events in and around Westminster, takes Conservative parliaments and candidates on delegations to Israel, campaigns hard for Tory candidates in target seats, and works to ensure that Israel's case is fairly represented in Parliament. *Exec. Ch.* Andrew Heller; *Exec. Dir.* Stuart Polak

FEDERATION OF JEWISH RELIEF ORGANISATIONS
HRS, Danescroft Avenue, Hendon, London NW4 2NA
Tel 020 8457 9169
Email fjro@btinternet.com
(Reg. Charity No. 250006). *Tr.* Alfred Garfield FCA, A. Lando; *Gen. Sec.* B. Shepherd

FRIENDS OF ALYN
88 Ossulton Way, London N2 0LB
Tel 020 8883 4716
Email alynuk@ip3.co.uk *Website* www.alyn.org
(Est. 1962. Reg. Charity No. 232689). To financially assist in the work of the Alyn Pediatric and Adolescent Rehabilitation Centre in Jerusalem, *Hon. S.* Maureen Lowry

FRIENDS OF THE BIKUR CHOLIM HOSPITAL, JERUSALEM & BRITISH AID COMMITTEE
c/o G. Rose, 34 Cleveland Square, London W2 6DD
Tel 020 7706 2666
Bikur Cholim, Jerusalem's oldest hospital, is now the largest medical centre in the heart of the city. *Ch.* G. Rose

FRIENDS OF THE ISRAEL CANCER ASSOCIATION

c/o Berwin Leighton Paisner LLP, Adelaide House, London Bridge, EC4R 9HA
Tel 020 3400 2361 *Fax* 020 3400 1111
Email jonathan.morris@blplaw.com
(Est. 1955. Reg. Charity No. 260710). Raises funds for the Israel Cancer Association (ICA).
ICA plays a prominent role in the fields of detection, research, treatment and education. It
supports oncological institutes, nationwide screening, patient care and information
services. *Pres.* Vered Aaron; *V. Pres.* Dame Vivien Duffield, CBE, Lady Alliance; *Hon. T.*
Jonathan Morris

FRIENDS OF ISRAEL EDUCATIONAL FOUNDATION

PO Box 42763, London N2 0YJ
Tel 020 8444 0777 *Fax* 020 8444 0681
Email info@foi-asg.org
(Reg. Charity No. 1095303). To promote and advance the education of the public in the
knowledge of the country of Israel and its citizens. F.O.I.E.F. undertakes an extensive UK
education programme and sponsors a variety of young adult and professional scholarships
in Israel. *Bd.* Jeremy Manuel, Hon. Gerard Noel, Peter Oppenheimer, David Kaye, Larry
Levine, Marcus Rebuck; *Dir.* John D. A. Levy

FRIENDS OF ISRAEL SPORT CENTRE FOR THE DISABLED

1 Marylebone High Street, London W1U 4LZ
Tel 020 7935 5541 *Fax* 020 7935 6638
Email fiscd@btinternet.com
(Est. 2001. Reg. Charity No. 1086205). Building hope and renewal through sporting
achievement. Formed in 1961, the Israel Sports Centre for the disabled in Ramat Gan is a
world-leading facility for rehabilitation. Spread over four acres, the facilities offer
everything from swimming pools and gymnasiums to cultural activities. The centre is
currently rehabilitating over 2,500 people per week from all denominations, most of them
children, including many victims of terrorists attacks. It is the Centre's goal to help
everyone into full integration and involvement in Israeli society. The Centre's funding
comes almost entirely from kind and generous donations. *Ch.* Brian Harris; *V. Ch.* Irwyn
Yentis; *T.* Jeremy Harris; *Sec.* Jane C. Jukes

FRIENDS OF JERUSALEM BOTANICAL GARDENS

Upper Unit, 100 Green Lane, Edgware, Middlesex HA8 8EJ
Tel 020 8238 2779
Email friendsjbg@gmail.com *Website* www.friendsjbg.org.uk
(Reg. Charity No. 1151347). To provide annual scholarships for horticultural graduates
from around the world to work and study at the Jerusalem Botanical Gardens; organising
working holidays there, supporting educational programmes and special projects.

FRIENDS OF YESHIVAT DVAR YERUSHALAYIM (Jat: The Jerusalem Academy Trust)

Office, 1007 Finchley Road, London NW11 7HB
Tel/Fax 020 8458 8563
(Reg. Charity No. 262716). London Cttee: *Jt. Ch.* A. Maslo, BCom; FCA, and M.A. Sprei,
MA (Cantab), MSc; *Patrons* Lord Sacks; *Princ.* Rabbi B. Horovitz, MA

FUNDING FOR PROGRESSIVE JUDAISM (FPJ)

PO Box 3998, Gerrards Cross, Bucks, SL9 1AS
Tel 01753 886220
Email admin@fpjie.org.uk
(Reg. Charity No. 241337). Friends of Progressive Judaism in Israel and Europe.
Admin. Neil Drapkin

HADASSAH
26 Enford Street, London W1H 1DW
Tel 020 7723 1144 *Fax* 020 7723 1222
Email uk.office@hadassah.org *Website* www.hadassahuk.org
(Reg. Charity No. 1040848). Hadassah UK is a registered charity, dedicated to supporting the Hadassah Medical Organisation in Jerusalem and promoting its medical and scientific excellence. *H. Pres.* Lady Wolfson; *Ch.* Carolyn Simons; *Dir.* Mark Addleman

HOLYLAND PHILATELIC SOCIETY (formerly British Association of Palestine Israel Philatelists)
Email holylandphilatelicsociety@yahoo.com
(Est. 1952). For the study and encouragement of all branches of the philately of Palestine and the State of Israel, and of other countries connected with the postal history of the region. *H. Mem. Sec.* A. Tunkel 3 Stone Buildings, Lincoln's Inn, London WC2A 3XL *Tel* 020 7242 4937 *Fax* 020 7405 3896 *Email* atunkel@3sb.law.co.uk

ISRAEL DISCOUNT BANK, London Branch
65 Curzon Street, London W1J 8PE
Tel 020 7499 1444 *Fax* 020 7499 1414
Website www.israeldiscountbank.co.uk
The London branch is part of the Israeli Discount group, a major financial group in Israel, with subsidiaries in Switzerland, the US and South America. The branch first opened as a representative office in 1982 and achieved full branch status in 1999. It offers various services such as: property lending, corporate and trade finance as well as treasury services. It also operates an Israeli desk for Hebrew-speaking clients based in Israel and the UK. Authorised and regulated by the Bank of Israel and the Prudential Regulation Authority. Subject to regulation by the Financial Conduct Authority and limited regulation by the Prudential Authority. Details about the extent of their regulation by the Prudential Regulation Authority are available on request.

ISRAEL GOVERNMENT TOURIST OFFICE
UK House, 180 Oxford Street, London W1D 1NN
Tel 020 7299 1100 *Fax* 020 7580 7325
Email info@igto.co.uk *Website* www.thinkisrael.com
(Est. 1954). *Dir.* N. Oryan-Kaplan. The office provides information about Israel as a tourist destination, and assistance to the British and Irish travel trade wishing to promote Israel as a holiday destination.

ISRAEL PHILATELIC AGENCY IN GREAT BRITAIN
P.O. Box 5, Poole, Dorset BH12 9GF
Tel 01202 711 371 *Fax* 01202 711 372
Email enquiries@harryallen.com
Official Agents of the Philatelic Service, Israel Postal Authority, Tel Aviv-Yafo, Israel, for the distribution and promotion of postage stamps and related products of Israel (in the UK). *New Issues Man.* Aileen Walshe, on behalf of Harry Allen (Intl. Philatelic Agencies).

THE JERUSALEM FOUNDATION
Administered by Prism the Gift Fund, 20 Gloucester Place, London W1U 8HA
Tel 020 009 9649 *Fax* 020 7224 2744
(Reg. Charity No. 258306). The Jerusalem Foundation works toward creating an open, equitable and modern society by responding to the needs of residents and improving their quality of life through a comprehensive approach centred on community vitality, cultural life and coexistence for all Jerusalem's residents. *Ch.* Peter Halban; *Admin, Prism The Gift Fund,* Anna Josse; *Dir., UK Desk* Neil Greenbaum

JEWISH BLIND IN ISRAEL ASSOCIATION

c/o K. C. Keller F.C.A., 25 Lodge Avenue, Elstree, Herts WD6 3NA
Tel 020 8207 2627
Email kennethk53@gmail.com
(Reg. Charity No. 1006756). Provides financial support and equipment to the Jewish registered blind in Israel. Adv: Prof. Lutza Yanko & Prof. Eliezer D. Jaffe, Dr. Ben-Zion Silverstone (Jerusalem), Joseph S. Conway, F.R.C.S. (London). Ch. K.C. Keller

JEWISH INSTITUTE FOR THE BLIND (British Aid Committee)

71 Eyre Court, Finchley Road, London NW8 9TX
Tel 0207 722 0887
Email info@jewishblind.org Website www.jewishblind.org
(Est 1964. Reg. Charity No. 222849). The British Aid Committee for the Jewish Institute for the Blind, Jerusalem (Est. 1902) has provided aid to the Institute since 1964 and undertakes work and support through legacies and donations.

LABOUR FRIENDS OF ISRAEL

BM LFI, London, WC1N 3XX
Tel 020 7222 4323
Email mail@lfi.org.uk Website www.lfi.org.uk

LANIADO HOSPITAL UK

2nd Floor, Shield House, Harmony Way, London NW4 2BZ
Tel 020 8201 6111 Fax 020 8201 6222
Email admin@laniado.co.uk Website www.laniado.co.uk
(Reg. Charity No. 1126356). Raising vital funds for Laniado Hospital in Netanya, Israel. Ch. Jerry Kohn; Chief Exec. Simon Silver; Manchester Ch. Dov Hamburger; Leeds Ch. Carl Evans

LIBERAL DEMOCRAT FRIENDS OF ISRAEL

LDFI, PO Box 57769, London NW11 1GF
Corres: 1 View Point, 1475 High Road, London NZ0 9PL
Tel 020 8455 5140 Email admin@ldfi.org.uk
Open to all supporters of the Liberal Democrats in the UK who recognise the right of Israel to a free, independent, permanent and prosperous existence as a member state of the United Nations. The Association exists to foster good relations and understanding between Britain and the State of Israel. Pres. Rt. Hon. Sir Alan Beith, MP; V. Pres. Lord Monroe Palmer OBE, Sarah Ludford MEP; Ch. G. Stollar; V. Ch. J. Davies

LIFELINE FOR THE OLD

(Reg. Charity No. 232084). To assist the work of Lifeline for the Old in Jerusalem, which aims to help the aged in Israel by providing training in occupational skills. Also to improve the welfare and quality of life of Jerusalem's elderly and disabled. Leeds Branch: Jt. Ch. Dr. Marjorie E. Ziff, 626 Harrogate Road, Leeds LS17 8EW, London Branch Denise Cohen, 3 Bryanston Court, George Street, London W1H 7HA

MAGEN DAVID ADOM UK

Shield House, Harmony Way, off Victoria Road, London NW4 2BZ
Tel 020 8201 5900 Fax 020 8201 5901
Email info@mdauk.org Website www.mdauk.org
(Reg. Charity No. 1113409). Magen David Adom is Israel's only National ambulance and medical emergency service. For over 60 years Magen David Adom UK has raised funds for medical equipment, ambulances, bloodmobiles and stations to benefit all the citizens of Israel - Arabs, Christians, Druze and Jews. The organisation also collects and supplies

300,000 units of blood each year and is responsible for all Israel's first aid and pre-hospital medical emergency training. As a member of the International Federation of Red Cross and Red Crescent Societies, Magen David Adom works internationally to give its support and share its expertise with those in need around the world. Magen David Adom is a non-Governmental, not-for-profit organisation that depends on the generosity of its supporters to save more lives. Magen David Adom UK also provides first aid training and equipment to schools, youth and community groups throughout the UK. *Ch.* R. Ellison; *Jt. Hon. T. J.* Ward, FCA, T. Shasha; *Chief Exec.* Daniel Burger. Groups in many districts of London and the Regions.

MEDICAL AID COMMITTEE FOR ISRAEL (MAC-I)
Email lbl@120harley.co.uk
(Est. 1969. Reg. Charity No. 258697). To provide medical and laboratory equipment and offer technical and professional advice. To assist and promote health and welfare projects in Israel. Applications from the Director of International Relations, Israel Min. of Health, 2 Ben Tabai Street, Jerusalem 93591. *Chief Exec.* Dr. Lionel P. Balfour-Lynn, MA, MD (Cambs), FRCPCH, DCH c/o 69 Hampstead Way, London NW11 7LG

MIZRAHI TEFAHOT BANK LTD
30 Old Broad Street, London EC2N 1HQ
Tel 020 7448 0600 *Fax* 020 7448 0610
Email umb.main@umtb.co.uk *Website* www.umtb.co.uk
Branch of Mizrahi Tefahot Bank in Israel. *Branch Man.* Itzik Coriat

NEW ISRAEL FUND
25-26 Enford Street, London W1H 1DW
Tel 020 7724 2266 *Fax* 020 7724 2299
Email info@uknif.org
(Est. 1992. Reg. Charity No. 1060081). The New Israel Fund (NIF) supports Israelis who work to realise Israel's founding vision of a free and democratic society by protecting civil and human rights, fostering religious tolerance, tackling poverty and disadvantage, promoting Jewish-Arab coexistence and preserving the environment. NIF provides hundreds of Israeli non-profit organisations with financial support and professional training each year, thus assisting them in building a brighter future within the framework of the best Jewish and democratic values. *Ch.* Nicholas Saphir; *CEO* Adam Ognall

ONE TO ONE PROJECT (formerly Jewish AID Committee)
Carradine House, 237 Regents Park Road, London N3 3LF
Tel 020 8343 4156 *Fax* 020 8343 2119
Email admin@one-to-one.org *Website* www.one-to-one.org
(Reg. Charity No. 801096). The JAC (formerly the 35's) formed the One to One project in 1991. It was responding to the mass immigration of Soviet Jews to Israel and to the economic situation of some of Israel's poorest families (Druse, Bedouin, Muslim, Christian and Jewish). Funds are raised through sponsored treks, the Annual Backgammon/Poker Event in May, individual donations and grant making trust/foundations. *Co-Ch.* Rita Eker MBE, Margaret Rigal

OPERATION WHEELCHAIRS COMMITTEE
1 Opal Court, 120 Regents Park Road, London, N3 3HY
Tel 020 8371 1500
Email alexanderpasse@tiscali.co.uk
(Est. 1970. Reg. Charity No. 263089). Voluntary organisation providing rehabilitation and general medical equipment to hospitals in Israel. *Ch.* Anita Alexander-Passe

POALE AGUDAT ISRAEL
Unites Orthodox religious workers to build up Eretz Yisrael in the spirit of the Torah. **World**

Central Office: 64 Frishman Street, Tel Aviv *Pres.* Rabbi A. Werdiger. **European Office and Great Britain**: P.A.I., 2A Alba Gardens, NW11 9NR *Tel/Fax* 020 8458 5372 *Corr.* D. Winter

SHAARE ZEDEK UK
766 Finchley Road, London NW11 7TH and P.O. Box 202, Salford, M7 4WS
Tel 020 8201 8933 *Fax* 020 8201 8935
Email office@shaarezedek.org.uk *Website* www.shaarezedekuk.com
(Hospital est. Jerusalem 1902. Reg. Charity No. 1143272). Shaare Zedek UK's sole purpose is to raise much needed funds for The Shaare Zedek Medical Centre in Jerusalem. This is Jerusalem's busiest hospital and it is imbued throughout with the warmth of traditional Jewish values. The hospital cares equally for anyone and everyone regardless of race, religion or financial circumstances - treating all with the same unparalleled degree of care, compassion and medical excellence. Shaare Zedek does not receive any government funding for the equipment and development which is vital to enabling the world class medical staff to save lives on a daily basis and so it is only with the support of the hospital's friends from around the world that these essential elements can be provided. *Ch.* M. Sorkin; *Hon. T.* A. Stechler, ACA

STAND WITH US UNITED KINGDOM
Email uk@standwithus.com
Websites www.standwithus.com www.standwithus.co.uk www.standwithus.co.il
(Reg. Charity No. 1115343). StandWithUs is an international organisation based in Los Angeles with 17 regional offices around the world of which the UK is one. Its mission is to counter misconceptions and prejudices about Israel and the Arab-Israel conflict through education about Israel. Using print materials, speakers, programmes, conferences, missions to Israel, campaigns, social media and internet resources, StandWithUs brings Israel's story of achievements and its on-going challenges to campuses, communities, the media, churches and schools around the world.

StandWithUs UK office is in London, but serves the whole of the UK. It has three main strands of activity, work with students, work in the community (Jewish and non Jewish) and pro Israel campaigning. The StandWithUs team is available to create Israel education and advocacy events with students and communities. *Ch.* Joy Wolfe MBE; *Leadership Team: Community Dir.* Irene Naftalin; *Campus Dir.* Shlomie Liberow

STATE OF ISRAEL BONDS
Development Company for Israel (UK) Ltd
ORT House, 126 Albert Street, London NW1 7NE
Tel 020 7446 8670 *Fax* 020 7446 8675
Email info@israelukbonds.com *Website* www.israelukbonds.com
(Est. 1981). Promotes and sells State of Israel Bonds (Israel's gilt-edged securities). *Man. Dir.* Moti Besser

TECHNION UK
62 Grosvenor Street, London W1K 3JF
Tel 020 7495 6824 *Fax* 020 7355 1525
Email info@technionuk.org *Website* www.technionuk.org
also on FaceBook and Twitter
(Est. 1951. Reg. Charity No. 1092207). Technion UK supports the Technion, Israel Institute of Technology in Haifa, one of the world's leading technology universities. The society brings Technion expertise to the UK through a series of events, seminars and networking sessions with Israel's foremost scientific, education and business leaders. Our funds have provided research centres and equipment, as well as student facilities and scholarships. *H. Patron* The Ambassador of Israel; *V. Pres.* L. Peltz, Sir Michael Heller, *Exec. Dir.* A. Bernstein; *Ch.* D. Peltz; *Sec.* S. Posner

TEL AVIV UNIVERSITY TRUST
ORT House, 126 Albert Street, London NW1 7NE
Tel 020 7446 8790 *Fax* 020 7446 8795
Email info@tau-trust.co.uk
(Reg. Charity No. 314179). The principal aim of the Trust is to raise funds to promote the work of Tel Aviv University and to encourage support for academic projects, scholarships and campus development. The Trust also advises those who may wish to study at the University. *H. Pres.* Dame Shirley Porter; *Ch. D.* Levin; *Exec. Dir.* Cara Case

TRADE UNION FRIENDS OF ISRAEL (TUFI)
BCM TUFI, London, WC1N 3XX
Tel 020 7222 4323 *Fax* 020 7222 4324
Website www.tufi.org.uk
Established to strengthen the links between the Histadrut (the Israeli TUC), the Palestinian General Federation of Trade Unions (PGFTU) and the British Trade Union Movement. It aims to build support for the Middle East peace process in the UK Labour movement, promote efforts towards finding a just and lasting peace settlement for both Israelis and Palestinians, initiate dialogue by taking British delegations to meet with both Israeli and Palestinian trade unionists, build support for the Peace Process in the UK by providing meetings and briefings for British Trade Unionists, engage trade unionists on a variety of issues beyond the Israeli-Palestinian conflict and aims to provide practical assistance that helps Israeli and Palestinian workers. *Pres.* Lord Clarke of Hampstead, CBE, KSG; *Ch.* Roger Lyons

UK FRIENDS OF THE ASSOCIATION FOR THE WELLBEING OF ISRAEL'S SOLDIERS
Tel 020 3210 3060 *Fax* 020 3210 3075
Email ukawis@ukawis.net *Website* www.ukawis.co.uk
(Est. 2001. Reg. Charity No. 1084272). To support the work of the Association in Israel, by raising funds for the wellbeing, education and culture of Israel's soldiers. *Tr.* Peter Sussmann, Julian Kemble, Zeev Remez, David Tucker; *Exec. Dir.* E. Hellerstein

UK ISRAEL BUSINESS
Tel 020 3510 0002
Email info@ukisraelbusiness.co.uk
UK Israel Business is a member-led organisation promoting bilateral business, trade, industry and investment between the UK and Israel. It works closely with the UK Embassy in Tel Aviv and the Israeli Embassy in London. Its network includes more than 2,000 companies and an extensive database of over 10,000 entrepreneurs, investors, senior executives, professional advisers and financiers. It organises and provides a host of activities and services in the UK and Israel, aimed at creating new business opportunities for members. *Hon. Pres.* Sir Victor Blank, Sir Trevor Chinn CVO. *Bd. Members,* Marc Worth (*Ch.*), Hugo Bieber (*CEO*) Yitz Applbaum, Nicola Cobbold, Stuart Lewis, Jonathan Morris, Neil Stone, Larry Weiss, Paul Winter

UK SOCIETY FOR THE PROTECTION OF NATURE IN ISRAEL
P.O. Box 67678, London NW11 1LD
Tel 020 7048 6057
Email ukspni@spni.org.il
(Est. 1986. Reg. Charity No. 327268). To generate interest in the beauty of Israel's natural landscapes and to muster support for the conservation lobby in Israel. *Trs.* Michael Green, John D. A. Levy

WEIZMANN UK
9 Hampstead Gate, 1a Frognal, London NW3 6AL
Tel 020 7424 6860 *Fax* 020 7431 2165

Email post@weizmann.org.uk *Website* www.weizmann.org.uk
(Est. 1956. Reg. Charity No. 232666). To stimulate financial, scientific and cultural support in the UK for the Weizmann Institute of Science in Rehovot. *Ch. of Exec. Cttee.* Martin Paisner CBE; *V. Ch.* Dame Vivien Duffield, DBE; *Hon. S.* J. Kropman; *Hon. T.* Howard Stanton; *Dir.* S. Gould

YAD VASHEM - UK FOUNDATION
Contact, Stirling House, Breasy Place, 9 Burroughs Gardens, London NW4 4AU
Tel 020 8359 1146
Email office@yadvashem.org.uk *Website* www.yadvashem.org.uk
(Est 1978. Reg. Charity No. 1099659). Incorporated in 2003, to represent Yad Vashem, Jerusalem (*See* p. 281). *Life Pres.* Ben Helfgott MBE; *Ch.* Simon Bentley; *Operational Man.* Evelynne Garbacz

YOUTH ALIYAH-CHILD RESCUE
Trojan House, 34 Arcadia Avenue, Finchley, London N3 2JU
Tel 020 8371 1580
Email info@youthaliyah.org.uk *Website* www.youthaliyah.org.uk
(Est. 1933. Reg. Charity No. 1077913). Object: to offer a secure home for under-privileged and deprived refugee, immigrant and native Israeli children. Five Youth Villages offer residential community care. *Jt. Ch.* Stephen Barry, Melvin Robinson; *Admin. Exec. Dir.* Nelly Ebert *Email* nelly@youthaliyah.org.uk; *Project Associate* Eva Burker *Email* eva@youthaliyah.org.uk; *Dir. of Develpopment* Martin Mason *Email* martin@youthaliyah.org.uk

EDUCATIONAL AND CULTURAL ORGANISATIONS

Hebrew and Religion Classes are attached to most of the synagogues listed.
For University Centres and Institutions *See* pp. 119-122.

ANNE FRANK TRUST UK

Star House, 104-108 Grafton Road, London NW5 4BA
Tel 020 7284 5858 *Fax* 020 7428 2601
Email info@annefrank.org.uk *Website* www.annefrank.org.uk
(Est. 1990, Reg. Charity No. 1003279). The Anne Frank Trust draws on the power of Anne
Frank's life and diary to challenge anti-semitism, racism and all forms of prejudice and
discrimination. Working in some of the UK's most difficult areas, the Trust does this by
taking exhibitions and educational programmes into schools, prisons and community
venues. The exhibitions are enhanced by educational activities such as workshops and
peer educator training for teenagers. The Trust's Anne Frank Ambassador Scheme, with
over 200 participants a year, increases knowledge and confidence in young people.

BRITISH ORT

126 Albert Street, London NW1 7NE
Tel 020 7446 8520 *Fax* 020 7446 8654
Email info@britishort.org *Website* www.britishort.org
Facebook British ORT
(Est. 1921. Reg. Charity No. 1105254). British ORT is the UK arm of World ORT, the
world's largest Jewish education and training charity. Currently operating in 56 countries,
ORT helps vulnerable communities to become self-sufficient by educating and training
their members in skills they need for life. *Pres.* Sir David Sieff; *Ch.* Simon Alberga; *Exec. Dir.*
Dan Green

CHAZAK

379 Hendon Way, London NW4 3LP
Tel 020 8457 4444
Email info@chazak.org.uk
There exists a proud established network of Sephardic communities spanning the UK who
have successfully guarded and transmitted the grand traditions of Spain, Portugal, India,
Aden, Syria, Egypt, Iraq, Persia, Tunisia and Morocco. Chazak's goal is to work alongside
and in conjunction with all existing communities and organisations in order to further
inspire young British Jews of Sephardic descent with a pride and commitment to their
culture, heritage and continuity. *Dir.* Rabbi S. Farhi; *Man.* Rabbi M. Levy

DAVAR, The Jewish Institute in Bristol and the South West

Suite 431, 179 Whiteladies Road, Clifton, Bristol, BS8 2AG
Tel/Fax 0117 970 6594
Email davarbristol@yahoo.co.uk *Website* www.davarbristol.com
DAVAR provides a wide programme of cultural, educational and social activities. A regular
newsletter is available, and Jewish groups in the area advertise their own events via the
mailing list. *Ch.* Martin Weitz

THE HOLOCAUST CENTRE

Laxton, Newark, Notts NG22 0PA
Tel 01623 836 627 *Fax* 01623 836 647
Email office@holocaustcentre.net *Website* www.holocaustcentre.net
(Est. 1978, as Beth Shalom Limited. Reg. Charity No. 509022). Holocaust education and
commemoration. *Off.* Dr. James M. Smith, Helen Whitney

HOLOCAUST EDUCATIONAL TRUST

BCM Box 7892, London WC1N 3XX
Tel 020 7222 6822 Fax 020 7233 0161
Email info@het.org.uk Website www.het.org.uk

(Est. 1988. Reg. Charity No. 1092892 England and Wales, SC042996 Scotland). The Holocaust Educational Trust works with schools, colleges and communities across the UK to educate about the Holocaust and its contemporary relevance. Work includes the Lessons from Auschwitz project for post-16 students, which includes a one-day visit to Auschwitz-Birkenau. The Trust arranges for Holocaust survivors to speak in schools, delivers innovative educational and teacher training programmes and produces groundbreaking resources. Patrons Most Rev. and Rt. Hon. Lord Carey of Clifton, Lord Dholakia OBE, Rt. Hon. Lord Mackay of Clashfern, Lady Merlyn-Rees JP, Prof. Elie Wiesel KBE; Bd. of Tru. Founding Patron. Lord Janner of Braunstone QC; Pres. R. Stephen Rubin OBE; H. V. Pres. Rt. Hon Lord Hunt of Wirral MBE; T. Paul Berlyn; Ch. Paul Phillips, Oliver Blechner, David Gryn, Richard Harrington MP, Kitty Hart-Moxon, OBE, Ben Helfgott MBE, Helen Hyde, Michael Karp, Sir Ivan Lawrence QC, Nigel Layton, Edward Lewin, Kirsty McNeill, Lord Jon Mendelsohn, Martin Paisner CBE, Alberta Strage; C. James Clappison MP, Louise Ellman MP, Rt. Hon Andrew Lansley CBE, MP, Sir Antony Sher KBE, Stephen Twigg MP; Chief Exec. Karen Pollock MBE

INCLUSIVE JEWISH SCHOOLS PARTNERSHIP (IJSP)

c/o, Akiva School, The Sternberg Centre For Judaism, 80 East End Road, N3 2SY
Tel 020 8349 4980 Fax 020 8349 4959
Email ijsp@akivaschool.org

(Est. 2012). A network of schools that teach the full range of Jewish values, beliefs and practises with equivalence and include all memebrs of hte Jewish community. Schools included in the partnership: JCoSS, Akiva, Clore Shalom, Clore Tikva, Eden Primary, South London Jewish Primary School, Finchley Jewish Primary School. Co-ord. Susy Stone MA

ISRAEL ZANGWILL MEMORIAL FUND

c/o, The Sternberg Centre For Judaism, 80 East End Road, N3 2SY
Tel 020 8349 5640
Email admin@reformjudaism.org.uk

(Est. 1929). To assist poor Jews engaged in research into special areas of Jewish music or art.

ISRAELI DANCE INSTITUTE

Suite 8, Time House, 56b Crewys Road, NW2 2AD
Tel 020 8209 3155
Email info@idi.org.uk Website www.idi.org.uk

The Israeli Dance Institute uses dance as a tool to promote Jewish and Israeli culture. It does this through an annual training seminar, Machol Europa, and training and support programmes that include an annual dance festival for schools across the country. The Institute's performance troupes represent the community in interfaith and multi-cultural events. Ch. M. Stone

JEWISH BOOK COUNCIL

ORT House, 126 Albert Street NW1 7NE
Tel 020 7446 8771
Email Info@jewishbookweek.com Website www.jewishbookweek.com
Admin. Pam Lewis Tel 020 7446 8771

(Est. 1947. Reg. Charity No. 293800). To stimulate and encourage the reading of books on Judaism and on every aspect of Jewish thought, life, history and literature; organises an annual Jewish Book Week, now Europe's largest Jewish literary festival, and associated events. Administers a triennial prize for Hebrew translation and an annual children's poetry prize. Pres. Anne Webber; Co-Ch. Gail Sandler, Lucy Silver

JEWISH COMMUNITY DAY SCHOOL ADVISORY BOARD
c/o Leo Baeck College, Sternberg Centre, 80 East End Road, London N3 2SY
Tel 020 8349 5620 *Fax* 020 8349 5639
Email sharon@silver-myer.com
(Est. 1998). Promotion and development of Jewish cross-community day schools through-
out the UK. *Ch.* Jon Epstein; *Admin.* S. Silver-Myer

JEWISH GENEALOGICAL SOCIETY OF GREAT BRITAIN
33 Seymour Place, London W1H 5AU
Membership: *Email* membership@jgsgb.org.uk *Website* www.jgsgb.org.uk
(Est. 1992. Reg. Charity No. 1022738). To promote and encourage the study of Jewish
genealogy. The Society organises lectures, seminars and family history workshops; it
publishes *Shemot*, and guides to the study of Jewish genealogy; it promotes research; and
operates a library. *Pres.* Dr Saul Issroff; *Pres. Emer.* Dr Anthony Joseph; *Ch.* Doreen Berger;
T. P. Roth; *Sec.* R. Moulding; *Membership Sec.* Hazel Atlass. *Regional Groups:* Leeds (Ann
Lightman, J. Williams), Manchester (Lorna Kay), South West London (Ena Black), East of
London (Raymond Montanjees), Chilterns and the Home Counties (S. Rose), Midlands
(David Harrison), South East Essex (Anne Marcus)

JEWISH HERALDIC FOUNDATION
73 Newberries Avenue, Radlett WD7 7EL
Tel 0845 519 3451 *Fax* 0845 519 3452
Email info@jewishheraldicfoundation.com *Website* www.ourjewishidentity.com
The Jewish Heraldic Foundation runs Jewish Identity Projects, benefiting young people
with interactive sessions of educational value aimed at strengthening Jewish identity. *Dir.*
Rabbi Ariel Abel, MSc, MCMI

JEWISH HERITAGE UK
Room 204, Ducie House, 37 Ducie Street, Manchester, M1 2JW
Tel 0161 238 8621
Email director@jewish-heritage-uk.org *Website* www.jewish-heritage-uk.org
(Est. 2004. Reg. Charity No. 1118174). To care for the historic buildings and sites of
Britain's Jewish community and to promote the Jewish-built heritage through education and
public access. *See* pp. 325-328. *Dir.* Dr. Sharman Kadish; *Consult. Architects*, Viorica Feler-
Morgan, Hedy Parry-Davies

JEWISH HISTORICAL SOCIETY OF ENGLAND
33 Seymour Place, W1H 5AP
Tel 020 7723 5852
Email info@jhse.org *Website* www.jhse.org
(Est. 1893. Reg. Charity No. 217331). *Pres.* Dr. Piet van Boxel; *Exec. Ch.* David Jacobs; *Hon
T.* Dr. Alan Swarc
Branches: Birmingham Dr.Anthony Joseph *Email* birmingham@jhse.org; **Essex** Sheila
Lassman *Email* lassmans@aol.com; **Herts and Middlesex** Norman Gerald *Email*
geraldn@btinternet.com; **Israel** Dr.Kenneth Collins *Email* drkcollins@gmail.com; **Leeds**
Murray Winer *Email* murraywiner@ntlworld.com; **Liverpool** Arnold S. Lewis. *Email*
arnoldslewis@gmail.com; **Sussex** Godfrey Gould *Email* g.gould915@btinternet.com

JEWISH LITERARY TRUST
ORT House, 126 Albert Street, London NW1 7NE
Tel 020 7267 9442
Website www.jewishquarterly.org
(Est. 1984. Reg. Charity No. 268589). Established on the death of Jacob Sonntag,
(founding Ed.), to ensure the continuity of the Jewish Quarterly. *Patrons* David and
Marion Cohen, The John S. Cohen Foundation, Elizabeth and Stanley Corob, Sir Trevor

Chinn, Daniel and Elizabeth Peltz, Robin and Inge Hyman, The Dorset Foundation, The Humanitarian Trust, Lord Kalms, Simon Ryde, Roger Wingate; *Co-Ch.* Mark Goldberg, Lance Blackstone; *Hon. T.* Stanley Salter; *Exec. Cttee.* James Freedman, Michael Green, Andrew Renton, Jodie Myers; *Ed.* Rachel Lasserson; *Man. Ed.* Susannah Okret. *Publ.* Jewish Quarterly (*See* Jewish Press).

JEWISH MUSIC INSTITUTE

SOAS University of London, Thornhaugh Street, Russell Square, London WC1H 0XG
Tel 020 7898 4308
Email jewishmusic@jmi.org.uk *Website* www.jmi.org.uk
(Reg. Charity No. 328228). Based at the University of London, the Jewish Music Institute (JMI) is a European Centre for the study, practical training and performance of Jewish music at all levels from schools to postgraduate level. Activities include:
Support of the Joe Loss Lectureship in Jewish Music at SOAS University of London: Some scholarships are available for postgraduate study in Jewish Music at SOAS.
Practical training: JMI runs Summer schools, evening classes and workshops at London University and outreach programmes across the country in Yiddish song, klezmer, Sephardi and cantorial music.
Consultation: JMI is available for consultation and advice to the media and scholars and the general public.
Music Suppressed by the Nazis: JMI researches, performs and records music by composers banned, exiled or murdered by the Third Reich.
Jewish Music Institute Library at SOAS: Providing resources in the form of books, manuscripts, scores and recordings for scholars, musicians and the general public.
Artistc Dir. Sophie Solomon; *Ch.* Jennifer Jankel; *Admin.* Louise Shiels *Email* louise.shiels@jmi.org.uk

THE JEWISH TEACHERS' ASSOCIATION (JTA)

C/o Board of Deputies of British Jews, 6 Bloomsbury Square, London WC1A 2LP
Tel 020 7543 5400 *Fax* 020 7543 0010
Email info@jewishteachers.org.uk *Website* www.jewishteachers.org.uk
Twitter @jewishteacher *Facebook* UK Jewish Teachers
(Est. 2007). The Jewish Teachers' Association (JTA) is a membership organisation for Jewish teachers, trainee teachers, teaching assistants and educational psychologists as well as those working in informal education, such as youth workers and tutors. The JTA exists to protect the rights of Jewish teachers; provide continual professional development through training and resources; offer support on issues of discrimination in the work place and encourage balanced teaching about Judaism and the state of Israel. *Ch.* FRH. Richards

KESHER – THE LEARNING CONNECTION

933 Finchley Road, London NW11 7PE
Tel 020 8458 5836 *Fax* 020 8201 9537
Email connect@kesher.org.uk *Website* www.kesher.org.uk
(Est. 1997. Reg Charity No. 1061689). Social, educational, communal and outreach programming for Jews of all backgrounds. *Dir.* Rabbi Rashi Simon, MA. International, Shabbat and Festival Services. (Orthodox)

LEO BAECK COLLEGE

The Sternberg Centre for Judaism, 80 East End Road, London N3 2SY
Tel 020 8349 5600
Email info@lbc.ac.uk *Website* www.lbc.ac.uk
(Est. 1956. Reg. Charity No. 209777). Established for the study of Judaism and the training of rabbis and teachers, under the joint auspices of the Movement for Reform Judaism and Liberal Judaism *Princ.* Rabbi Dr Deborah Kahn-Harris; *Ch., Bd. of Govs.* Alasdair Nisbet; *Exec. Dir.* Stephen Ross; *Dir. Jewish Studies,* Rabbi Dr Charles Middleburgh; *Dir. Jewish*

Education, Jo-Ann Myers; *Hd of Academic Services* G. Ruppin; *Hd. of HR and Support Services* Rhona Lesner; *Hd. Student Services*, Irit Burkeman

The Department of Rabbinic and Higher Jewish Studies
Tel 020 8349 5600 *Email* info@lbc.ac.uk

Offers a five-year programme leading to Rabbinic Ordination, full-time and part-time degrees. It also caters for those wishing to further their Jewish knowledge, and it supports Progressive communities in developing their own programmes.

The Department of Jewish Education
Tel 020 8349 5620 *Fax* 020 8349 5639
Email admin@lbc.ac.uk

This department of Leo Baeck College serves the Progressive movements, providing services to part-time religion schools and primary schools. It offers teacher training, community/family education, Hebrew programming, outreach projects, a purchasing service for text books for schools, and a Resource Centre. Starting 2013-14, this department will also offer an MA degree course in Jewish Education and BA (Hons) in Jewish Education. Consultants are available to visit communities and offer programmes around the country.

LIMMUD
1A Hall Street, North Finchley, London N12 8DB
Tel 020 3115 1620
Email office@limmud.org *Website* www.limmud.org

(Reg. Charity No. 1083414). Limmud is a volunteer-led cross-communal, multi-dimensional education organisation. Its flagship event is the week long winter residential Limmud Conference. It also organises Limmud Fest in the summer; Regional Day Limmuds in 14 communities across the UK; the Limmud on One Leg weekly cross-communal parasha commentary; and the annual Chavruta project. Through its Limmud International team, Limmud supports the development of over 65 Limmud communities in 28 countries outside of the UK. *Ch.* Kevin Sefton; *Exec. Dir.* Shelley Marsh; *Admin.* Cathryn Sweid

LONDON ACADEMY OF JEWISH STUDIES
2-4 Highfield Avenue, NW11 9ET
Tel 020 8455 5938/020 8458 1264

(Est. in 1975). To assist post-Yeshiva students to further their Jewish education and engage in advanced Talmudic research. Graduates are expected to take up rabbinical and teaching posts in the community. The Kolel also serves as a Torah-study centre for laymen. Its specialised library is open to the general public throughout the year including Shabbat and Yom Tov. *H. Princ.* Rabbi G. Hager

LONDON JEWISH CULTURAL CENTRE
Ivy House, 94-96 North End Road, London, NW11 7SX
Tel 020 8457 5000 *Fax* 020 8457 5024
Email admin@ljcc.org.uk *Website* www.ljcc.org.uk

(Est 2000. Reg. Charity No. 1081014). The London Jewish Cultural Centre is a vibrant centre of education, the Arts and cultural activity throughout the year. Inclusive and independent, the centre welcomes c2,000 people of all ages each week to engage with Jewish life, language, identity and heritage through the broadest range of courses, events and activities, including tours to places of Jewish interest. The Holocaust Education department works to challenge prejudice wherever it is found; represents the UK on the Task Force for International Cooperation on Holocaust Education, educates teachers around the world in how to teach the Holocaust and provides survivor enrichment programmes. The LJCC has also developed a unique Holocaust education website for secondary school children www.theholocaustexplained.org. FUSION, the Centre's innovative youth programme, offers creative, interactive schemes and activities both during term and during school holidays. In the new on-site building, the Catherine Lewis Centre, the programme is expanding to include activities for FUSION Parents. *Publ.* Prospectus and FUSION and Ivy House. *Chief Exec.* Louise Jacobs

LONDON SCHOOL OF JEWISH STUDIES (formerly **Jews' College**)
Schaller House, Wohl Campus for Jewish Education, 44A Albert Road, London NW4 2SJ
Tel 020 8203 6427 *Fax* 020 8203 6420
Email info@lsjs.ac.uk *Website* www.lsjs.ac.uk
London School of Jewish Studies is a world-class Centre of Jewish Scholarship and teaching that inspires our community with lifelong love of Jewish learning and practices. *Pres.* Chief Rabbi Lord Sacks; *Dep. Pres.* Rabbi Dr. Abraham Levy, OBE; *Ch. of the C.* Prof. Anthony Warrens; *Dean* Rabbi Dr. Raphael Zarum; *CEO* Jason Marantz

MAROM (MASORTI YOUNG ADULTS)
Alexander House, 3 Shakespeare Road London N3 1XE
Tel 020 8349 6650
Email students@masorti.org.uk
Twitter @MaromUK
Facebook Marom Coordinator (*Young Adults*)   Marom Fieldworker (*students*)
Marom builds grassroots communities, whilst developing young adults and engaging them with positive Masorti experiences. Marom is composed of two parts: Marom on Campus and Marom Young Adults. It supports many social events, initiatives, such as communal Shabbat dinners, Masorti programming on UK campuses, and learning experiences in Israel and Europe. Marom is part of an international movement of young Masorti Jews, empowering young emerging leaders within the Masorti movement.

POLACK'S HOUSE EDUCATIONAL TRUST CLIFTON COLLEGE
32 College Road, Bristol BS8 3JH
Tel 0117 315 7000
Email jgreenbury@clifton-college.avon.sch.uk
Website www.cliftoncollegeuk.com/upper/pupilcare www.polackshousetrust.org
(Reg. Charity No. 1040218). The Trust supports the education of Jewish pupils at Clifton College, and in so doing continues a tradition going back to 1878. Jewish Studies, Jewish Worship and kosher food for boys and girls aged 3-18. Scholarships and bursaries available. *Hd. Jewish Studies* Jonathan Greenbury (Hd. Sixth form)

SCOPUS JEWISH EDUCATIONAL TRUST (formerly **ZFET**)
54 Welbeck Street, London W1G 9XS
Tel 020 7935 0100 *Fax* 020 7935 7787
(Est. 1953. Reg. Charity No. 313154). To raise funds by way of endowment, legacy, bequest, gift or donation in order to provide a first-class education in Jewish Studies and Hebrew throughout its national network of day schools; all of which have a Zionist ethos and emphasise the centrality of Israel in Jewish life. *H. Pres.* Stanley S. Cohen, OBE; *Ch.* Peter Ohrenstein; *Hon. T.* Jonathan M. Kramer; *Hon. S.* Brenda Hyman. School: **London** Harry & Abe Sherman Rosh Pinah School, Mathilda Marks-Kennedy School, Ella & Ernst Frankel Kindergarten, Simon Marks School, Simon Marks Sherman Nursery; **Leeds** Brodetsky Primary and Nursery School; Deborah Taylor Playgroup; **Manchester** North Cheshire Primary School.

Seed UK
Mowbray House, 58-70 Edgware Way, Edgware, Middlesex, HA8 8DJ
Tel 020 8958 0820 *Fax* 020 8958 0821
Email info@seed.uk.net *Website* www.seed.uk.net
(Est. 1980. Reg. Charity No. 281307 Project SEED). To provide Jewish adult education through courses, weekend residential seminars and one-to-one study throughout the year. Working also with school and parents - specialising in the interests of parents and young

children. *Dir.* Rabbi J. Grunfeld; *London contact* for One to One Rabbi A. Lazarus; *Manchester* contact Rabbi A. Hassan: *Educ. London Programmes* contact Rabbi M. Herman, Manchester A. Bar Ilan *Tel* 0161 792 4457

THE SEPHARDI CENTRE

2 Ashworth Road, Maida Vale, London W9 1JY
Tel 020 7266 3682 *Fax* 020 7289 5957
Email scadmin@spsyn.org.uk
(Est. 1994. Reg. Charity No. 1039937). The Centre's aim is to promote Sephardi culture. Courses, open to all, focus on Religion, History, Music, Art and Cuisine. A library and reading room, specialising in Sephardi literature, is open to the public (*See* p. 135). *Admin.* Joanne Reich

SOCIETY FOR JEWISH STUDY

1A Church Mount, London N2 0RW
Website www.sjslondon.org.uk
(Est. 1946. Reg. Charity No. 283732). The Society presents academic research in Jewish religion, literature, history and the arts. *Sec.* Rosemary Goldstein

THE SPIRO ARK

788-790 Finchley Road, London NW11 7TJ
Tel 020 7289 6321 *Fax* 020 7289 6825
Email education@spiroark.org *Website* www.spiroark.org
(Est. 1998 Reg. Charity No.1070926). The Spiro Ark was established to continue the educational and cultural work of Nitza and Robin Spiro at the Spiro Institute (now known as the London Jewish Cultural Centre). It uses innovative teaching methods in order to encourage a learning community mainly based on Jewish History and Culture. Hebrew and Yiddish are taught at all levels. The Spiro Ark also specialises in providing extremely enjoyable Hebrew learning programmes to children of all ages. In addition there are regular outstanding cultural events, plus tours of Jewish interest. *Fdrs and developers, The Spiro Institute and Spiro Ark,* Nitza and Robin Spiro; *Admin.* Rozy Fis

SPRINGBOARD EDUCATION TRUST

32 Foscote Road, London NW4 3SD
Tel 020 8202 7147 *Fax* 020 8203 8293
Email aumie@hotmail.co.uk
(Est. 1979. Reg. Charity No. 277946). Specialising in reminiscence and stimulation programmes for senior citizens, Springboard has extended its range of audio-visual and film productions to cover Jewish and Zionist history, synagogue and home traditions and interfaith projects.

Springboard also produces low-cost DVD/film programmes for other organisations and provides seminars for teachers and welfare workers in the use of its programmes, with substantial back-up materials. *Dirs.* Aumie and Michael Shapiro

UK JEWISH FILM

5.09 Clerkenwell Workshops, 27-31 Clerkenwell Close, London EC1R 0AT
Tel 020 3176 0048
Email info@ukjewishfilm.org *Website* www.ukjewishfilm.org
(Est. 1997. Reg. Charity No. 1072914). The UK Jewish Film is the major exhibitor of films with Jewish themes in the UK and Europe. UK Jewish Film aims to entertain, educate and enlighten diverse audiences in London and in towns and cities across the UK, with both Israeli and worldwide films on Jewish culture, history and identity. The annual UK Jewish Film Festival is held in early November in cinemas across London and cities around the UK. The organisation also screens Films at the annual Limmud conference, runs the Pears Short Film Fund at UK Jewish Film Award, its series of 'all year round' screenings, Interfaith and Holocaust Education events. *Fdr. and Exec. Dir.* Judy Ironside; *Man. Dir.* Michael Etherton; *Ch.* Stephen Margolis

UNIVERSITY CENTRES AND ORGANISATIONS
(*See also* Organisations concerned with Jewish students and Libraries).

BRITISH ASSOCIATION FOR JEWISH STUDIES
Email LF309@cam.ac.uk *Website* britishjewishstudies.org
(Est. 1975). Membership is open to scholars concerned with the academic pursuit of Jewish studies in the British Isles. The Association promotes and defends the scholarly study of Jewish culture in all its aspects and organizes an annual conference. *Pres.* (2012) Prof. Sacha Stern, UCL Hebrew and Jewish Studies, Gower Street, London WC1E 6BT *Sec.* Dr. Lars Fischer, CJCR Wesley House, Jesus Lane, Cambridge, CB5 8BJ; *T.* Dr. Maria Diemling, Theology and Religious Studies, Canterbury Christ Church University, North Holmes Road, Canterbury CT1 1QU

CENTRE FOR GERMAN-JEWISH STUDIES
University of Sussex, Falmer, Brighton, East Sussex BN1 9QN
Website www.sussex.ac.uk/cgjs
Dir. Dr. Gideon Reuveni *Tel* 01273 877 344 *Email* g.reuveni@sussex.ac.uk; *Centre Man.* Diana Franklin *Tel* 01273 678 771 *Email* d.franklin@sussex.ac.uk; London Office *Tel/Fax* 020 8455 4785

CENTRE FOR JEWISH STUDIES (University of Leeds)
Leeds LS2 9JT
Tel 0113 343 5197 *Fax* 0113 245 1977
Email e.frojmovic@leeds.ac.uk *Website* www.cjs.leeds.ac.uk
(Est. 1995). Teaching Jewish Studies at undergraduate and postgraduate level and supervising research degrees. *Dir.* Dr Eva Frojmovic

CENTRE FOR JEWISH STUDIES (University of London)
School of Oriental and African Studies, Thornhaugh Street, Russell Square, London WC1H 0XG
Tel 020 7898 4358
Email cs52@soas.ac.uk *Website* www.soas.ac.uk/centres/jewish
The Centre seeks to promote modern Jewish and Israeli studies. It seeks to foster research seminars and to collaborate with other institutions of higher education. Through public lectures and conferences, the Centre endeavours to bring areas of academic interest to the wider community. In the multi-cultural atmosphere that is unique to the SOAS, it provides a forum for discussion and dialogue. In 2008 it staged an International Conference 'Israel and the Great Powers 1948–2008'. In 2009, the centre staged a weekly series of lectures to commemorate the founding of Tel Aviv in 1909, in conjunction with Tel Aviv University. In 2010, its speakers have included Anthony Julius, Mohammed Dara Washe, Ed Husain, Sami Zubeida, Robert Fine; *Ch.* Dr. Y. Wallach

CENTRE FOR JEWISH STUDIES (University of Manchester)
University of Manchester, Oxford Road, Manchester M13 9PL
Tel 0161 275 3614
Email cjs@manchester.ac.uk *Website* www.manchesterjewishstudies.org
(Est. 1997). The Centre seeks to maximise the teaching - undergraduate and postgraduate - of Jewish Studies in the University of Manchester, to foster collaborative research between staff of the University of Manchester and others in the region, through research seminars and research projects, to bring the results of academic work in Jewish Studies to the wider community through public lectures (including the Sherman Lectures) and conferences; and to disseminate the results of these activities on the internet, and through its on-line journal: Melilah. *Co-Dirs* Prof. Daniel Langton, Prof. Alexander Samely

CENTRE FOR MODERN HEBREW STUDIES

Faculty of Asian and Middle Eastern Studies, Sidgwick Avenue, Cambridge CB3 9DA
Tel 01223 335 117 *Fax* 01223 335 110
The Centre functions within the Faculty of Asian and Middle Eastern Studies where degree courses include options in classical, medieval and modern Hebrew studies. The Centre's principal activities include the provision of open language classes in Modern Hebrew, seminars on Israeli literature and culture, and weekly screenings of Israeli films; also, an annual ten-day summer Ulpan. *Contact* R. Williams, Dr. M. Marzanska-Mishani

INSTITUTE OF JEWISH STUDIES

University College London, Gower Street, WC1E 6BT
Tel 020 7679 3520 *Fax* 020 7679 2766
Email ijs@ucl.ac.uk *Website* www.ucl.ac.uk/ijs
(Est. 1953. Reg. Charity No. 213114). Founded by the late Prof. Alexander Altmann, IJS is now located within the Department of Hebrew and Jewish Studies at University College, London, while retaining its autonomous status. It is funded by the private sector. The programme of activities is dedicated to the academic study of all branches of Jewish history and civilisation, including public lectures, seminars, symposia, major international conferences, and publications, especially of its conference proceedings. It brings together scholars, students, and academic institutions from all sections, inside and outside the University of London and the scholarly scene in the UK and worldwide. All activities are free and open to the public. The conference topic for 2012 is Time, Astrology, and Calendars in Jewish Tradition. A publications and events programme is available by email or on the website. *Patrons* Lord Moser, Lord Woolf; *Board of Govs:* Ch. Philip L. Morgenstern MA; *Hon. Tru.* Daniel Peltz MA, David J. Lewis BSc, FRICS, Edward M. Lee BSc (Econ), Stuart Roden, J. Caplan FCA (also *Hon. S.*); *Dir.* Prof. Mark J. Geller. The Tr. of the Institute of Jewish Studies, a non-profit making company limited by guarantee, registered in England No. 2598783.

LEO BAECK INSTITUTE

Second Floor, Arts Two Building, Queen Mary, University of London, Mile End Road, London E1 4NS
Tel 020 7882 5690 *Fax* 020 7882 6901
Email info@leobaeck.co.uk *Website* www.leobaeck.co.uk
(Est. 1955. Reg. Charity No. 235163). Research and publications on history of Central European German-speaking Jewry. *Ch.* Prof. Peter Pulzer; *Dir.* Prof. R. Gross; *Hon. T. D.* Goldsmith; *Dep. Dir.* Dr. D. Wildmann. *Publ.:* Year Book (*Ed.* Prof. R. Gross, Dr. Cathy Gelbin), symposia, lectures, etc.

OXFORD CENTRE FOR HEBREW AND JEWISH STUDIES

Yarnton Manor, Yarnton, Oxford, OX5 1PY
Tel 01865 377946 *Fax* 01865 375079
Email enquiries@ochjs.ac.uk *Website* www.ochjs.ac.uk/home

Hebrew and Jewish Studies Unit

Oriental Institute, University of Oxford, OX1 2LE
01865 288216 *Fax* 01865 278190
Website www.orinst.ox.ac.uk/nme/hjs/index.shtml
The Centre, together with the Unit which it funds, is one of Europe's leading teaching and research institutions in the area of Jewish studies. Its work includes Jewish history and literature, ancient, medieval and modern; Jewish/Christian relationships in all periods; Hebrew and Yiddish language and literature; and Jewish theology. It provides instruction in Jewish studies towards the Oxford University BA, M.St., M. Phil, M.Litt and D. Phil degrees. The Centre initiated and runs the one-year Masters of Studies (M.St.) in Jewish Studies at Oxford.

Publ.: Journal of Jewish Studies (half-yearly); and numerous books and articles by Fellows past and present. The termly listing of lectures, seminars and classes, Newsletter and the Annual Report of the Centre are available on request. *Pres.* David Ariel; *Co-Ch. Bd. Gov.* Stanley Fink. G. Pinto (The Centre also houses the Leopold Muller Memorial Library, *See* p. 133).

PARKES INSTITUTE FOR THE STUDY OF JEWISH/NON-JEWISH RELATIONS
History, School of Humanities, Avenue Campus, University of Southampton, SO17 1BJ
Tel 02380 592 261 *Fax* 02380 593 131
Website www.parkes.soton.ac.uk

The Parkes Institute is an inter-disciplinary community of scholars, librarians, students and curators, whose work is based around the resources of the Parkes Library and archive. This is dedicated to the study of Jewish/non-Jewish relations throughout the ages and to the development of Jewish Studies with the School of Humanities at the University of Southampton. Through our research, publications, conferences, teaching and outreach work, we seek to bring the vision of James Parkes, pioneering campaigner against antisemitism and historian of Jewish/non-Jewish relations, to new generations; to provide a world-class centre for the study of Jewish culture and history; to study the experience of minorities, refugees and outsiders; and to examine the power of prejudice from antiquity to the contemporary world. A new area of research, in accordance with the School of Humanities, is dedicated to Jewish Maritime Studies. Members teach courses in Jewish history, literature, religion and cultural practice at undergraduate level. We offer an innovative MA programme in Jewish History and Culture in Southampton and London. PhD studies in the broad field of Jewish/non-Jewish relations from antiquity to the present. Publications linked to the Institute include three journals (*Patterns of Prejudice, Jewish Culture and History,* and *Holocaust Studies*). *Hd. of Instit.* Prof. Tony Kushner

SCHOOL OF ORIENTAL AND AFRICAN STUDIES (SOAS)
Department of the Languages and Cultures of the Near and Middle East, Thornhaugh Street, Russell Square, London WC1H OXG
Tel 020 7898 4320 *Fax* 020 7898 4359
Website www.soas.ac.uk/nme

SOAS has one of the world's greatest concentrations of expertise on Africa and Asia. The Near & Middle East Department offers a B.A. in Hebrew & Israeli Studies and degrees combining Hebrew with Law, Economics, Management, Arabic and with many other subjects – all affording a year's study at the Hebrew University of Jerusalem. The one-year MA in Israeli Studies caters for postgraduates from around the world seeking an entrée into the field. Doctorates in Israeli and Modern Jewish Studies can be researched. These programmes have the benefit of one of the largest open-stack Jewish Studies libraries in Europe. Also based at SOAS is the Centre for Jewish Studies, which hosts lecture series and symposia on a wide range of issues (*See* p. 199). In 2011, the European Association of Israeli Studies was established and is currently based at SOAS. *Contact* Professor Colin Shindler *Tel* 020 7898 4358 *Email* cs52@soas.ac.uk

STANLEY BURTON CENTRE FOR HOLOCAUST STUDIES
School of History, University of Leicester, Leicester LE1 7RH
Tel 0116 2522800 *Fax* 0116 2523986
Website www.le.ac.uk/hi/centres/burton

To promote the study of, and research, into the Holocaust. *Acting Dir.* Dr A. Korb; *Dep. Dir.* Dr. O. Jensen

UNIVERSITY COLLEGE LONDON
Department of Hebrew and Jewish Studies
Gower Street, WC1E 6BT
Tel 020 7679 7171 *Fax* 020 7679 2766
Email jewish.studies@ucl.ac.uk *Website* www.ucl.ac.uk/hebrew-jewish/home/index.php

The largest University department in the UK and Europe for obtaining honours degrees in Hebrew and Jewish Studies. There are single subject BA degrees in Hebrew and Jewish Studies; Jewish Studies or Jewish History; combined degrees in History (Central and East European) and Jewish Studies, Modern Languages, Modern Languages Plus and Language and Culture; MA in Hebrew and Jewish Studies, Holocaust Studies; Israeli Studies or Jewish History; MPhil or PhD. Fields of teaching and research include: the Ancient Near East; Biblical Languages and Literature; Rabbinic Literature; Ancient, Medieval and Modern Jewish History and Culture; Jews in Central and Eastern Europe; Comparative European Jewish History; Modern Hebrew Judeo-Spanish (Ladino) and Yiddish Language and Literature; Modern Israeli Politics; Jewish Mysticism and Spirituality, especially Hasidism, Women in the Jewish Tradition; the Holocaust in Historical Perspective. Undergraduate students spend a year of the course at the Hebrew University of Jerusalem. All degrees are available as full- or part-time programmes. The department often hosts visiting staff from abroad on an annual basis. It comprises nine full-time and seven part-time members of staff and hosts the Institute of Jewish Studies (*See* p. 120) *Hd.* Prof. Sacha Stern

WOOLF INSTITUTE
Wesley House, Jesus Lane, Cambridge CB5 8BJ
Tel 01223 741 048
Email enquiries@woolf.cam.ac.uk *Website* wwwwoolf.cam.ac.uk
(Reg. Charity No. 1069589). The Woolf Institute is a global leader in addressing one of the most pressing and rewarding challenges of our time: the current historical relationships that exist between the faith-traditions of Judaism, Islam and Christianity, with special reference to Europe and the Middle East. Established in Cambridge (UK) in 1998, with close links to the city's famous University, the institute comprises the Centres for the study of Jewish-Christian Relations and Public Education. Its work highlights the importance of shared values whilst acknowledging difference in order to further understanding between the communities and enhance the wider public good. *Exec. Dir.* Dr E. Kessler MBE; *Dep. Dir.* Dr Shana Cohen

ORGANISATIONS CONCERNED WITH JEWISH YOUTH

BBYO
Shield House, Harmony Way, London NW4 2BZ
Tel 020 8202 6698
Email bbyo@bbyo.org.uk *Website* www.bbyo.org.uk
BBYO is a unique, peer-led Zionist youth organisation. It promotes Zionism, Judaism, leadership, welfare and social awareness in a pluralist, open and totally youth-led environment. There are weekly meetings in 10 chapters, national events, an Israel summer tour, The 'Atid' Leadership tour, a one-year and 6 month programme in Israel. *Admin.* Tanya Seshold

FJL (Forum for Jewish Leadership)
379 Hendon Way, London NW4 3LP
Tel 020 8457 2115
Email info@jewish-leadership.com
(Reg. Charity No. 1139858). FJL offers outstanding educational opportunities to intelligent and ambitious future leaders of the Jewish community. Its range of courses and programmes provide an in-depth understanding of the theory and practice of Jewish leadership, as well as Jewish perspectives on a host of legal, political and social issues associated with the modern world. *Dir.* Rabbi A. Savage

FRIENDS OF JEWISH YOUTH (formerly Old Boys' Association)
Martin Shaw, c/o A.J.Y., 128 East Lane, Wembley, Middlesex
Tel 020 8908 4747 *Fax* 020 8904 4323

GIFT
379 Hendon Way, London NW4 3LP
Tel 020 8457 4429
Email shimon@jgift.org *Website* www.jgift.org
(Est. 2003, Reg. Charity No. 1107334). GIFT (Give It Forward Today) inspires and educates young people in the value of 'Giving' and 'volunteering'. GIFT finds tailor-made opportunities for young people in the community including rescuing and redistributing food to over 1,700 people every week, helping children from disadvantaged families with homework etc and arranging group visits to old age homes to provide entertainment. *Dir.* Michelle Barnett; *Man.* Shimon Gillis

J-ROOTS
379 Hendon Way, London NW4 3LP
Tel 020 8457 2121
Email info@jroots.org.uk
(Est. 2006, Reg. Charity No. 1136532). J-Roots was established to empower today's generation of Jews, to meaningfully connect with its past in order to shoulder responsibility for its future. J-Roots offers an all-inclusive journey through our heritage, looking at the past, the present and future. J-Roots combines the collective expertise and experience drawn from the most prolific educational tour operators and providers of informal education in the Jewish world. The J-Roots executive team is comprised of individuals responsible for facilitating over 200 Jewish journeys to destinations such as Poland, Belarus, Lithuania, Morroco, Prague, Israel and Ukraine, involving thousands of Jewish students and members of the community. *Dir.* Tzvi Sperber, Rabbi N. Schiff

JENERATION (Students and Young Adults)
The Sternberg Centre, 80 East End Road, N3 2SY
Tel 020 8349 5666
Email aly@jeneration.org *Website* www.jeneration.org

JEWISH GUIDE ADVISORY COUNCIL (JGAC)
JGAC furthers Girl Guiding within the Jewish community.
National Ch. Lucinda Glasser 21 West Avenue, London NW4 2LL *Tel* 07967 110 028
Email lucindaglasser@yahoo.co.uk

JEWISH LADS' AND GIRLS' BRIGADE (JLGB)
HQ: Camperdown, 3 Beechcroft Road, South Woodford, E18 1LA
Tel 020 8989 8990 *Fax* 020 8530 3327
Email getinvolved@jlgb.org *Website* www.jlgb.org
(Est. 1895. Reg. Charity No. 286950). JLGB has trained and developed tens of thousands of young people to reach their potential through active citizenship, within both the Jewish and wider community, empowering them to become future leaders. Through local weekly groups across the UK, the JLGB encourages friendship through achievement, recognition and personal development programmes. The JLGB helps to prepare and enable young Jewish people to develop the essential life skills needed to help their transition from young person to adult life.
It is the only Jewish Operating Authority for the Duke of Edinburgh's Award and works with almost every Jewish school in the UK promoting the Award scheme. *Pres.* Lord Levy; *Colonel Commandant* B/Col Jill Attfield; *Ch.* Norman Terrett, JP; *Chaplain* Rabbi A. Plancey; *Chief Exec.* N.S. Martin, BSc (Hons), MA

JEWISH SCOUT ADVISORY COUNCIL
Mrs Ellis *Tel* 01923 855 514
Furthers Scouting in the Jewish community.

JEWISH YOUTH FUND
C/o 3rd Floor, Chiswell Street, London, EC1Y 4YX
Tel 020 7449 0909
Email info@jyf.org.uk *Website* www.jyf.org.uk
(Est. 1937. Reg. Charity No. 251902). Provides funds to promote the social education of Jewish young people through the provision of leisure time facilities to clubs, movements and other Jewish youth organisations in the UK. *Co-Ch.* Stephen Spitz, Philippa Strauss; *Dir.* Julia Samuel

LJY–NETZER (Liberal Jewish Youth, Progressive Zionist Youth)
The Montagu Centre, 21 Maple Street, W1T 4BE
Tel 020 7631 0584
Email ljynetzer@liberaljudaism.org *Website* www.ljy-netzer.org
The Liberal Jewish youth movement, offering events and leadership training for young people aged eight to 23, all within a Progressive Zionist framework.
Movement Workers Graham Carpenter *Email* g.carpenter@liberaljudaism.org; Tom Francies *Email* t.francies@liberaljudaism.org; Bethany Stone *Email* b.stone@liberaljudaism.org; *Admin.* S. O'Dwyer *Email* selina@liberaljudaism.org

MACCABI GB
Shield House, Harmony Way, Hendon, London NW4 2BZ
Tel 020 8457 2333 *Fax* 020 8203 3237
Email enquiries@maccabigb.org *Website* www.maccabigb.org
To support the long-term future of British Jewry by engaging and developing the entire community, and especially young people, in a broad range of Jewish sporting, educational and social activities, whilst actively promoting the centrality of Israel.
Ch. M. Ziff; *CEO* M. Berliner

NOAM (NOAR MASORTI)
Alexander House, 3 Shakespeare Road, London N3 1XE

Tel 020 8349 6650
Email noam@masorti.org.uk *Website* www.noam.org.uk
(Est. 1985. Reg. Charity No. 801846). NOAM is the Zionist youth movement of Masorti Judaism. It runs a wide variety of fun educational and social activities for 4-18 year olds. These range from summer camps, both residential and Kaytana day camp, Shabbat services for kids, weekend outings, clubs, Israel tour, and more. NOAM also runs the MERKAZ NOAM Teenage Centre for years 9-13, which develops and trains young Jewish leadership. Over the summers, participants become *madrichim* (leaders) on Noam camps, go on Israel Tour, or run the Kaytana day camp. Each year Noam undertakes a charity fundraiser project for the Ruth Schneider Memorial Trust and another charity chosen by the movement. In July 2012, Noam leaders cycled to Brighton and in May 2013, each member of the NOAM office ran 10km. Mazkir 2012-2013: Sam Schryer.

OXFORD & ST. GEORGE'S
120 Oakleigh Road North, N20 9EZ
Tel 020 8446 3101
(Est. in 1914. Reg. Charity No. 207191). Oxford & St George's Jewish Youth Trust, formerly known as Oxford & St George's Jewish Youth & Community Centre, was established with the sole aim of running a Jewish youth and community centre. Over the years, because of a decline in membership, these activities have ceased and it is now a grant making organisation. The closure of the vast majority of Jewish youth clubs in the UK has restricted the grant making potential of the charity. The few Jewish youth clubs that still exist are aware of the facilities available and many have successfully applied for grants.

RSY-NETZER (Movement for Reform Judaism Youth Movement)
The Sternberg Centre, 80 East End Road, N3 2SY
Alyson Joseph *Tel* 020 8349 5666
Email admin@rsy-netzer.org.uk *Website* www.rsy-netzer.org.uk
RSY-Netzer is the Youth Movement of The Movement for Reform Judaism. Every year, it runs events and activities for over 800 10-18 year olds, offering fun and social experiences in a safe and supportive environment. RSY-Netzer is proud of its reputation for high quality fun events, Shemesh summer and Sheleg winter camps, leadership course, Israel tour and Shnat gap year and activities in local Reform Synagogues.

TRIBE (Young United Synagogue)
305 Ballards Lane N12 8GB
Tel 020 8343 5656
Email info@tribeuk.com *Website* www.tribeuk.com
Exec. Dir. David Collins

UJIA Informal Education Department
37 Kentish Town Road, London NW1 8NX
Tel 020 7424 6472
The UJIA Informal Education houses world-class educators who assist volunteers and professionals in the fields of Jewish Education and youth work in partnership with the Jewish Agency for Israel. It is the community's main centre for youth leadership training, offering seminars, conferences, mentoring and training and support for Israel engagement programmes and strategies. the Department also supports Jewish activities in mainstream schools and runs the University campus preparation programme in partnership with the Union of Jewish Students. *Dir.* A. Ashworth-Steen S. Marsh

YOUNG JEWISH CARE (YJC)
Tel 020 8922 2822
Email jwilson@jcare.org *Website* www.jewishcare.org
Young Jewish Care is a dynamic and interactive part of Jewish Care, playing a key role

in the fundraising successes of the charity through a mixture of initiatives and events. YJC supports and encourages young people to develop committees and fulfill their leadership potential through organising events that cover a wide range of interests.

The following groups are associated with the Zionist Movement.

BNEI AKIVA
2 Hallswelle Road, London NW11 0DJ
Tel 020 8209 1319 *Fax* 020 8209 0107
Email mazkir@bauk.org *Website* www.bauk.org
(Est. 1939). Bnei Akiva inspires and empowers young Jews with a sense of commitment to the Jewish people, the Land of Israel and the Torah. As the largest Jewish youth movement in the UK, Bnei Akiva runs weekly activities, summer and winter camps, tours and gap years to Israel and so much more. It is an inclusive youth movement, so whilst it has high religious standards, everyone is welcome. Bnei Akiva has branches in 37 countries all over the world. *Mazkir* Ben Dov Salasnik; *Rabbi* Rav Ari Faust; *Admin.* Sharon Kenley

  Regional centres: 72 Singleton Road, Salford M7 4LU *Tel* 0161 740 1621 *Fax* 0161 740 8018 *Email* north@bauk.org Shlichim Mickey & Ortal Flaumenhaft

EZRA YOUTH MOVEMENT
British and European Office: 2a Alba Gardens, London, NW11 9NR
Tel/Fax 020 8458 5372
Associated with Poale Agudat Israel. An Orthodox Jewish movement based in London, with a branch in Manchester and in Israel and other parts of the world.

FEDERATION OF ZIONIST YOUTH (FZY)
25 The Burroughs, Hendon, London NW4 4AR (Head Office)
Tel 020 8201 6661 (Head Office) *Tel* 0161 721 4782 (Northern Office)
Email office@fzy.org.uk *Website* www.fzy.org.uk
FZY is a Zionist youth movement for those aged 14 and above. It operates within a pluralist framework and educates its members around Jewish and Zionist themes, with the intention of fulfilling the four aims of FZY: Aliyah Nimshechet, Magen (defence of Jewish rights), Tzedakah and Tarbut (Jewish culture). FZY trains its members in leadership skills and encourages them to involve themselves as leaders in the wider Jewish community. The movement is part of the Atid partnership which also incorporates Young Judaea in USA and the Israeli Scouts. *Pres.* Paul Lenga; *Mazkir* Darren Wogman; *Dir. of Summer Programmes,* Nikki Horesh; *Dir. of 12-16 Programming,* Katie Frankel; *Shaliach,* Matan Hemo; *Northern Shaliach* Or Katzman; *Office Man.* Louise Jacobs; *Year Course Co-ord.* Vivienne Stone; *Tour Admin.* Fiona Prince. *Publ.* The Young Zionist.

FRIENDS OF BNEI AKIVA (BACHAD) (formerly **Bachad Fellowship**)
2 Hallswelle Road, London NW11 0DJ
020 8458 9370 *Fax* 020 8209 0107
(Est. 1942 Reg. Charity No. 1109706). To promote and organise Jewish religious educational activities in the UK and Israel, with a view to preparing the youth of Bnei Akiva for a life in Israel. To provide scholarships for students wishing to attend Bnei Akiva's gap year programme in Israel, and grants for children wishing to go to Bnei Akiva's activities. Maintains Youth Centres in London and Manchester. *Hon Pres.* Chief Rabbi Lord Sacks, Arieh L. Handler z''l; *Ch.* D. Kestenbaum; *V. Ch.* Lawrence Susser; *T. S.* Renshaw

HABONIM–DROR
Platinum House, Gabriel Mews, Crewys Road, London NW2 2GD
Tel 020 8209 2111 *Fax* 020 8209 2110
Website www.habodror.org.uk

(Est. 1929). Habonim was founded in the East End of London, and became the leading international socialist Zionist Jewish youth movement, merging with Dror in 1979. Habonim-Dror's ideology is centred around meaningful, cultural Judaism, socialism and Zionism. It educates members, aged 9–23, towards strong Jewish identities, striving for a more equal and compassionate Israeli society. Weekly activities around the UK focus on informal education. Habonim Dror's Shnat Hachshara involves living together as a community in Israel and engaging in social activism projects, intensive educational and leadership-training seminars, and tours of Israel. *Pres.* Ruth Lady Morris of Kenwood; *Admin.* Rosey Daniels; *Nat. Sec.* Lucy Travis. *Publ.* Koleinu.

Offices

London Platinum House, Gabriel Mews, Crewys Road, London NW2 2GD
Email lucy@habodror.org.uk
Manchester 28 Wilton Road, Crumpsall, Manchester M8 4WQ
Email jonny@habodror.org.uk
Birmingham c/o Central Office; **Glasgow** c/o Central Northern Office **Leeds** c/o Central Northern Office; **Oxford** c/o Central Office

HANOAR HATZIONI

Central House, 7th Floor, 1 Ballards Lane, London N3 1LQ
Tel 0208 371 5288
Email email@hanoar.co.uk *Website* www.hanoar.co.uk
Hanoar Hatzioni is a non-political Zionist Youth Movement catering for people between the ages of 7 and 23. Groups are run all over the country. Annual events include Summer and Winter Camps, Israel Tours for 16 year olds, outings, educational and social programmes. Hanoar Hatzioni also run the Shnat Sherut Year Scheme in Israel.
Admin. Hannah Kleinfeld; *Racaz Tnuati*, Jack Mayorcas

JNF FUTURE

JNF House, Spring Villa Park, Spring Villa Road, Edgware, Middlesex HA8 7ED
Tel 020 8732 6146 *Fax* 020 8732 6148
Email melanie@jnf.co.uk
(Est. 1998). To support the work of the JNF in Israel in afforestation, land reclamation, environmental and ecological issues, by fund-raising events organised for and by young people (21–35) nationwide. *Co-ord.* M. Lax

KIBBUTZ REPRESENTATIVES

16 Accommodation Road, London NW11 8ED
Tel 020 8458 9235 *Fax* 020 8455 7930
Website www.kibby.org.uk
(Reg. Charity No. 294563). Representing all the Kibbutz movements in Israel. The organisation arranges Working Visits on Kibbutz for those aged 18–40; Enquirers are requested to send SAE for information packs.

ORGANISATIONS CONCERNED WITH JEWISH STUDENTS

UJS - UNION OF JEWISH STUDENTS (UK and Ireland)
Office 1, 353-359 Finchley Road, London NW3 6ET
Tel 020 7424 3288
Email office@ujs.org.uk *Website* www.ujs.org.uk
(Est. 1919. Reg. Charity No. 313503). *Ch.* Sir Victor Blank; *Hon. T. P.* Keane; *Exec. Dir.* David Brown; *Dir. of Finance and Operations*, Lindsay Davidson; *Pres.* Joe Tarsh
   Residential and social facilities are available at **Hillel Houses** in the following locations:
   Birmingham: Bella Lupasco *Tel* 0121 777 3505; **Cardiff**: Lisa Gerson *Tel* 029 2075 9982; **Liverpool** Gareth Jones *Tel* 0151 280 0551; **London**: *Golders Green* Debbie Jackson *Tel* 020 8731 0914; **Manchester**: Sydney Baigel *Tel* 0161 740 2521; **Sheffield**: Jeffrey Shaw *Tel* 0114 266 9936

UNIVERSITY JEWISH CHAPLAINCY
305 Ballards Lane, London N12 8GB
Tel 020 8343 5678
Email office@mychaplaincy.co.uk *Website* www.mychaplaincy.co.uk
(Reg. Charity No. 1126031). Our chaplains are there for all Jewish students at universities across the UK. Chaplains live in the heart of the campus and provide emotional and welfare support, practical help and spiritual and educational guidance. *H. Pres.* Rabbi Lord Sacks; *Ch.* Uri Goldberg; *Dir. of Operations*, Suzy Richman *Email* suzy@mychaplaincy.co.uk *Chaplains* Birmingham & West Midlands, Rabbi Fishel Cohen *Tel* 07771 653 717 *Email* fishel@mychaplaincy.co.uk; Brighton and South Coast, *Associate Chaplain*, Rabbi Joe Kaye *Tel* 07929 953 511 *Email* joe@mychaplaincy.co.uk; Bristol & Western, *Associate Chaplain* Rabbi Jonathan Hughes, *Tel* 07969 318 699 *Email* rabbijonny@mychaplaincy.co.uk; Cambridge & East Anglia; Rabbi Yisrael & Elisheva Malkiel *Tel* 07916 139 974 *Email* yisrael@mychaplaincy.co.uk; Leeds & Yorkshire, Rabbi Yonasan & Braha Bender *Tel* 07815 108 260 *Email* yonasan@mychaplaincy.co.uk; London, Rabbi Gavin Broder *Tel* 07811 286 664 *Email* rabbibroder@mychaplaincy.co.uk; Manchester, Liverpool and Norht West, Rabbi Mati & Vanessa Kos *Tel* 07819 250 557 *Email* mati@mychaplaincy.co.uk; Newcastle, Rabbi Aaron Lipsey *Tel* 07793 746 454 *Email* aaron@mychaplaincy.co.uk; Nottingham & East Midlands, Rabbi Zvi and Esther Bloom *Tel* 07980 955 026 *Email* zvi@mychaplaincy.co.uk; Oxford, Rabbi Michael & Tracey Rosenfeld-Schueker *Tel* 07717 742 835 *Email* michael@mychaplaincy.co.uk; Scotland, Rabbi Yossi and Sarah Bodenheim *Tel* 07791 292 790 *Email* yossi@mychaplaincy.co.uk

WINGATE YOUTH TRUST
(Est. 1975. Reg. Charity No. 269678). To provide facilities for youth, for recreation and leisure. *Ch.* Martin Stone; 135-137 The Broadway, Mill Hill, London NW7 4TD *Sec.* Peter Rebak

LIBRARIES, MUSEUMS AND EXHIBITIONS

ANGLO-JEWISH ARCHIVES

A registered charity under the auspices of the Jewish Historical Society of England. The genealogical collections have been deposited at the Society of Genealogists and the main archive collection has been deposited with the Hartley Library, University of Southampton (*See* p.131). *Hon. S.* (JHSE), 33 Seymour Place, London W1H 5AP *Tel/Fax* 020 7723 5852 *Email* info@jhse.org

BEN URI ART, IDENTITY AND MIGRATION

The London Jewish Museum of Art, 108a Boundary Road, off Abbey Road, London NW8 0RH
Tel 020 7604 3991 *Fax* 020 7604 3992
Email reply@benuri.org.uk *Website* www.benuri.org.uk (for opening times and programmes)
(Est. 1915. Reg. Charity No. 280389. Reg. Museum No. 973). Founded by Lazar Berson as an Art society in Whitechapel in London's East End to collect works by Jewish artists and provide support to Jewish (often émigré) artists who were outside the British mainstream. Today a proud representative of the Jewish Community in Britain's cultural mainstrean, the objectives of the museum are to promote learning of the Jewish experience through art, enjoyment and outreach between communities. This is achieved through exhibitions that tour internationally; publications that are distibuted internationally; learning modules for schools and special needs, accessible to 25,000 Schools nationwide through the National education Network; social health 'art' for the elderly and those with Dementia; an extensive artist development programme and wide use of the internet and Social Media. Ben Uri explores and tells the stories of the life and work of artists of European Jewish descent, alongside their artist peers, within both the artistic and social history contexts. *Ch.* David Glasser (Executive); *Deputy Ch.* Mike Posen; *Fin. Dir. Co. Sec.* Keith Graham, Simon Bentley; *Advisor,* David Franks; *Ch. of Exhibitions Cttee.* Rachel Dickson; *Ch. of Collection Cttee.* Sarah MacDougall; *Education Man.* Alix Smith; *Development Management,* Kate Ferrie, Stephen Goldman; *Business Man.* Tania Talaga

BIESENTHAL COLLECTION

Special Collections Centre, Univeristy Library, Bedford Road, Aberdeen, AB24 3AA
Tel 01224 272 598
Email speclib@abdn.ac.uk
Consists of some 2,000 volumes. It has one of Britain's finest Rabbinical collections acquired in 1872. The Special Libraries and Archives also feature the collections and papers of Malcolm Hay of Seaton, which include material on Zionism and correspondence in Hebrew.

BODLEIAN LIBRARY

Broad Street, Oxford OX1 3BG
Tel 01865 277000
Email cesar.merchan-hamann@bodleian.ox.ac.uk
The Hebrew and Yiddish collections has 3,000 manuscript volumes and 60,000 printed books, including many incunabula, fragments from the Cairo Genizah and the Oppenheimer Library, the finest collection of Hebrew books and manuscripts ever assembled. Intending readers should always contact the Admissions Office in advance. Open to holders of a reader's ticket Monday to Friday 9am–7pm, Saturday 10am–4pm *Hebrew Specialist Libr.* Dr. Cesar Merchan-Hamann

THE BRITISH LIBRARY

African and Asian Studies, 96 Euston Road, London NW1 2DB
Tel 020 7412/7646 *Fax* 020 7412 7641
Email opac-enquiries@bl.uk *Website* http://www.bl.uk/reshelp/findhelplang/hebrewcoll/index.html
The Hebrew collection has over 3,000 manuscript volumes and 10,000 fragments (incl.

Moses Gaster's collection and many fragments from the Cairo Genizah). Its Hebrew printed books, amount to about 73,000 titles, incl. some 100 incunabula, rabbinic and modern Hebrew literature; Yiddish, Ladino, Judeo-Arabic and Judeo-Persian books; some 1,000 Hebrew and Yiddish periodicals and newspapers. The Asian and Africa Studies Reading Room is open to holders of readers' passes. (Opening hours may be revised at any time. Normal opening: Monday 10am–5pm; Tuesday-Saturday 9.30am–5pm). Some Hebrew manuscripts are on permanent display in the British Library Exhibition Galleries, open (free of charge): Monday, Wednesday to Friday 9.30am–6pm, Tuesday 9.30am–8pm, Saturday 9.30am–5pm, Sunday and English public Holidays 11am–5pm. The Golden Haggadah and Lisbon Bible are included in the electronic 'Turning the Pages' programme on www.bl.uk *Hebrew Specialist* Ilana Tahan, M.Phil. OBE *Email* ilana.tahan@bl.uk

BROTHERTON LIBRARY
University of Leeds, Leeds LS2 9JT
Tel 0113 3435518 *Fax* 0113 3435561
Email special-collections@library.leeds.ac.uk *Website* www.leeds.ac.uk/library
Holdings include substantial materials for Hebrew and Jewish studies and the Travers Herford Collection on Judaism and Talmudic studies. The primary Judaica collection is the Roth Collection which has the manuscripts and printed books from the Library of Cecil Roth, including 350 manuscripts, 900 printed books (pre-1850) 6,000 modern books and other archival material. Available to bona fide scholars, who should write to the library in the first instance, enclosing an appropriate recommendation. *Libr.* Margaret Coutts; *Asst. Libr. Publ.* Selig Brodetsky lecture series.

CAMBRIDGE UNIVERSITY LIBRARY
West Road, Cambridge CB3 9DR
Tel 01223 333 000 *Fax* 01223 333 160
Email library@lib.cam.ac.uk *Website* www.lib.cam.ac.uk
Dir. A. Jarvis. The Hebraica and Judaica collections have c. 190,000 Cairo Genizah fragments; 1,000 complete Hebrew codices (*See* S. C. Reif, Hebrew Manuscripts at Cambridge University Library, CUP, 1997); approximately 40,000 printed books. Available to members of the University and bona fide scholars by application. Reading rooms open Monday-Friday 9am–7pm, Saturday 9am-4.45pm; Admissions Office Monday-Thursday 9am–12.45pm, 2–5pm, Friday 9am–12.45pm, 2–4.45pm, Saturday 9am–1pm, 2–4pm. For more information see www.lib.cam.ac.uk/admissions *Hd. Genizah Res. Unit.* Dr B. M. Outhwaite; *Hebraica Librarian* Ms Y. Faghihi

CZECH MEMORIAL SCROLLS CENTRE (Memorial Scrolls Trust)
Kent House, Rutland Gardens, London SW7 1BX
Tel 020 7584 3741 *Fax* 020 7581 8012
Email czech.scrolls@virgin.net *Website* www.czechmemorialscrollstrust.org
(Reg. Charity No. 278900). This permanent exhibition tells the unique story of the rescue from Prague, in 1964, of 1,564 Torah Scrolls and of their restoration and distribution on permanent loan to communities throughout the world. The exhibits include some of the scrolls, a display of Torah binders, some dating from the 18th century, and other reminders of the vanished communities of Bohemia and Moravia. The centre is open on Tuesdays and Thursdays from 10am-4pm. Other times and Sundays are by arrangement. *Admin.* Rabbi Ariel J. Friedlander

DAUBE COLLECTION
Special Collections Centre, Univeristy Library, Bedford Road, Aberdeen, AB24 3AA
Tel 01224 272 598
Email speclib@abdn.ac.uk
Consists of some 30,000 printed volumes dating from 16th to 20th centuries on ancient law (especially Roman and Jewish), rabbinical subjects and history. Personal working

library of David Daube, (1909-1999), jurist and scholar. Daube, who spent much of his career as a law professor at University of California Berkeley, served as professor or Jurisprudence at Aberdeen from 1951-1955. The printed collection was donated by Daube's family with a substantial body of archival material in 2004, and is currently being catalogued.

THE HARTLEY LIBRARY
University of Southampton, Highfield, Southampton SO17 1BJ
Contact Tel 023 8059 3335 (Parkes), 023 8059 2721 (Archives) Fax 023 8059 3007
Email libenqs@soton.ac.uk (Parkes); archives@soton.ac.uk (Archives)
Website www.southampton.ac.uk/archives
Holdings of the Special Collections Division include (i) the **Parkes Library,** founded by the late Revd. Dr. James Parkes in 1935 to promote the study of relations between the Jewish and the non-Jewish worlds. It now contains 27,000 books and periodicals; (ii) more than 950 collections of manuscripts, of around 3.5 million items, relating to Anglo-Jewry (incorporating the collections of the **Anglo-Jewish Archives**). These manuscript collections encompass the papers of the Anglo-Jewish Association; records of the London Board of Shechita; archives of the Jewish Board of Guardians and the Jewish Association for the Protection of Girls, Women and Children; papers of the International Military Tribunal and the Nuremberg Military Tribunals; Zangwill and Henriques family papers,; papers of Sir Robert Waley Cohen, Lady Swaythling and Rabbi Solomon Schonfeld; the archives of Leo Baeck College, the Reform Synagogues of Great Britain and the West London Synagogue; the archives of the British Section of the World Jewish Congress and of the Institute of Jewish Affairs (now the Institute for Jewish Policy Research). The holdings of the Parkes Library are listed in the library WebCat http://www-lib.soton.ac.uk/ A guide to the archive collections is available at www.southampton.ac.uk/archives Visits to the Archives and Manuscripts reading room need to be arranged in advance. Snr. Archivist, K. Robson

HEBRAICA LIBRARIES GROUP
Website http://www.lib.cam.ac.uk/hebraica/hebraicam2.htm
(Est. 1976). The Group brings together representatives of all the major Judaica and Hebraica collections in Great Britain and Ireland, together with other academic libraries with an interest in the field. Membership is open to specialist librarians in academic libraries, specialists in public or private institutions, as well as scholars and researchers with an interest in the Hebrew book. It holds an annual meeting as well as visits to libraries and collections in the area of Hebraica and Jewish studies, and is affiliated to the National Committee for Information Resources on Asia (NACIRA). It offers expertise in all aspects of Hebraica collections, their preservation, security, conservation, cataloguing, computer systems and collection development. Convenor Vanessa Freedman, Hebrew and Jewish Studies Librarian, UCL Tel 020 7679 2598 Email v.freedman@ucl.ac.uk

THE HIDDEN LEGACY FOUNDATION
Kent House, Rutland Gardens, London SW7 1BX
Tel 020 7584 2754 Fax 020 7584 6896
(Est. 1988. Reg. Charity No. 326032). Devoted to promoting the awareness of provincial (English) and rural (German) Jewish history, as seen through buildings and artefacts. It has become particularly identified with German Genizot. It organises exhibitions: Genizah (1992), Mappot (1997), The Jews of Devon and Cornwall (2000). Having been active in Germany, it is now working in England, cataloguing Judaica. Library, slide and photo archives on rural German Jewry. Exec. Dir. Evelyn Friedlander

IMPERIAL WAR MUSEUM HOLOCAUST EXHIBITION
Lambeth Road, London SE1 6HZ
Dept. of Research Tel 020 7416 5286
Website www.iwm.org.uk
Holocaust Exhibition Hd. of Research, Suzanne Bardgett; Curator, Emily Fuggle; Founding

Patrons Lord Bramall, Sir Martin Gilbert, Ben Helfgott, Lord Moser, Lord Rothschild, Lord Weidenfeld, Lord Wolfson of Marylebone, Stephen Rubin; *Advisory Gp.* Prof. D. Cesarani, Sir Martin Gilbert, Ben Helfgott, Antony Lerman, Martin Smith. This major national exhibition was opened by H.M. the Queen in 2000. To discuss any exhibition-related enquiries please contact *Curator*, Emily Fuggle *Tel* 020 7416 5286

JEWISH MILITARY MUSEUM
Shield House, Harmony Way, Hendon, London NW4 2BZ
Tel 020 8201 5656 *Fax* 020 8202 9900
Email visit@thejmm.org.uk *Website* www.thejmm.org.uk
Curator, Roz Currie; *Museum Ch.* Ron Shelley MBE; *Fdr. Pres.* H. Morris; *Archivist* M. Sugarman. A History of the Jewish contribution to the Armed Forces of the Crown over three centuries. Displays of unique medals, photos, badges, letters, documents, uniforms and much other persona memoribilia of all kinds and a large archive available to reseachers by appointment. Please ring if you would like to visit.

JEWISH MUSEUM - LONDON
Raymond Burton House, 129-131 Albert Street, Camden Town, London NW1 7NB
Switchboard Tel 020 7284 7384
Email admin@jewishmuseum.org.uk *Website* www.jewishmuseum.org.uk

(Est. 1932. Reg. Charity No. 1009819). The Jewish Museum opened in 2010 following a £10 million investment. Here you can explore Jewish culture, heritage and identity. The Jewish story is placed in the wider context of British history. There are exhibitions, education programmes and activities available. The additional objectives are to build interfaith understanding, inspire people to take a stand against racism and to look at the world from a different point of view.
Open: daily, 10am–5pm, except Friday 10am-2pm. *Chief Exec.* Abigail Morris; *Ch.* Lord Young of Graffham; *T.* Mike Frankl

JEWS' COLLEGE LIBRARY
London School of Jewish Studies, Schaller House, 44A Albert Road, London NW4 2SJ
Tel 020 8203 6427 *Fax* 020 8203 6420
Email info@lsjs.ac.uk

150th anniversary in 2010. This is one of the most extensive Judaica and Hebraica libraries in Europe. With about 70,000 volumes and manuscripts. Open, free of charge: Monday 9am-4pm, Tuesday to Thursday, 9am-1pm. *Consultant Libr.* Erla Zimmels

JOHN RYLANDS LIBRARY
150 Deansgate, Manchester M3 3EH
Tel 0161 306 0555
Email jrul.special-collections@manchester.ac.uk
Website www.manchester.ac.uk/library/deansgate
Admission is free to all visitors and readers. Visitor opening hours are Sunday and Monday 12-5pm, Tuesday-Saturday 10am-5pm. Those wishing to consult rare books, manuscripts or archives should provide a suitable letter of introduction as well as proof of their address; advance notice of any visit is advisable. The Hebraica and Judaica has over 10,500 fragments from the Cairo Genizah; manuscripts and codices from the Crawford and Gaster collections; Samaritan manuscripts from the Gaster collection; 6,600 items of printed Hebraica and talmudic literature in the Marmorstein collection; 1,000 volumes of the Haskalah collection; the Moses Gaster collection; and some 5,000 volumes in the Near Eastern collection in the Main University Library dealing with Hebrew language and literature. *Hd. of Special Collection and Research Service Man.* (archives and manuscripts) John Hodgson

KEREN HATORAH BOOK LIBRARY AND TAPE LIBRARY
97 Stamford Hill, London N16 5DN
Tel 020 8800 6688
A comprehensive collection of Torah literature for the whole family, and over ten thousand cassette recordings including the complete Talmud in English and Yiddish and a range of other Torah and Jewish topics. Operates as a lending library.
Book Library open Sunday, Tuesday, Thursday, 10am-12.30pm, Monday 3.30-5.30pm
Tape Library for opening hours please phone.

LEO BAECK COLLEGE LIBRARY
80 East End Road, N3 2SY
Tel 020 8349 5610/1 *Fax* 020 8349 5619
Email Library@lbc.ac.uk
Est. 1956 to provide a library for Jewish Studies and research. Holdings: 60,000 vols; 40 current periodicals; 10,000 pamphlets; 180 rabbinic and MA theses; 500 rare books; Hyams collection of Jewish Children's literature. Range: Bible, rabbinic literature, codes, liturgy, education, literature, history, Holocaust and post-Holocaust studies, Israel and Zionism, Interfaith, historic children's books. Open to members and occasional readers from Monday–Thursday 10am–5pm, Friday 10am–1pm. Closed on Jewish Festivals, bank holidays and during the last week of December. During July and August, visits can be made only by appointment with the library For regular access to the library a yearly contribution of £40 is charged. *Hd. Libr.* Annette M. Boeckler, PhD; *Asst. Libr.* P. Claiden and volunteers

LEOPOLD MULLER MEMORIAL LIBRARY
Oxford Centre for Hebrew & Jewish Studies, Yarnton Manor, Yarnton, Oxford OX5 1PY
Tel 01865 377 946 (library office ext. 117; library ext. 120) *Fax* 01865 375 079
Email muller.library@ochjs.ac.uk *Website* www.ochjs.ac.uk
(Reg. Charity No. 309720). The Leopold Muller Memorial Library is an open access lending library of about 90,000 volumes and 80 current periodicals, covering the full range of Hebrew and Jewish studies, with special focus on Hebrew literature of the 19th and 20th centuries, Haskalah, modern Jewish history, Zionism, Israeli and Hebrew bibliography. Special collections: the Foyle-Montefiore Library, including the library of Leopold Zunz; the Louis Jacobs collection; the Copenhagen Collection (on Dutch Jewry and the Holocaust); the largest collection of *Yizkor* books in Europe; the Arthur Sebag-Montefiore Archive and the Shandel-Lipson Archive, containing materials on Sir Moses Montefiore; the Western Hebrew Library; the Hugo Gryn collection; an extensive microfiche collection containing the Montefiore collection of Manuscripts, the manuscripts and rare books collections of the Jewish Theological Seminary of America and the Harvard College Library, the *Dokumentation zur jüdischen Kultur in Deutschland 1840–1940: Die Zeitungsausschnittsammlung Steiniger* and the *Jüdisches Biographisches Archiv*; an archive of 40,000 newspaper cuttings on 12,000 Jewish personalities and on the early Yishuv in Palestine, as well as representative samples of the Hebrew and Yiddish press. For opening times, access and borrowing rights, see website. *Dir.* Dr César Merchán-Hamann; *Dep. Dir.* Milena Zeidler; *Assist. Libr.* Jane Barlow, Dr Zsófia Buda

LONDON METROPOLITAN ARCHIVES
40 Northampton Road, London EC1R 0HB
Tel 020 7332 3820 *Fax* 020 7833 9136
Email ask.lma@cityoflondon.gov.uk *Website* www.cityoflondon.gov.uk/lma
LMA is the regional archive for Greater London. The collections within it of Jewish interest include: BoD of British Jews, Office of the Chief Rabbi, US, London Beth Din, Jews Free School, Jews Temporary Shelter, London School of Jewish Studies, World Jewish Relief and the Spanish & Portuguese Jews' Congregation. Many collections are available to researchers only with the prior permission of the depositor, so please contact LMA in advance for the relevant addresses. Opening Hours: Monday 9.30am-4.45pm; Tuesday, Wednesday, Thursday

9.30am-7.30pm; closed Friday, selected Saturdays 9.30am-4.45pm (Please call for open dates or see website).

LUBAVITCH LENDING LIBRARY
1Northfield Road, London N16 5RL
Tel 020 8800 5823
Email library@lubavitch.co.uk
Established in 1972 to help the Jewish public study traditional Jewish culture and aid scholarship. The library contains 18,000 volumes in Hebrew, English and Yiddish. Services include a reference library, a children's library and postal lending. Lectures and displays organised anywhere. New expanded Library opened in Summer 2010. Loans free. Normal opening times Sunday 11am-8pm; Monday-Thursday 10.30am-5.45pm, 7.15pm-8.30pm; Friday 8.30am-1pm (Winter), 9.30am-4.30pm (Summer). *Librarian* Z. Rabin, MBE

NATIONAL LIFE STORIES at The British Library
96 Euston Road, London, NW1 2DB
Tel 020 7412 7404 *Fax* 020 7412 7441
Email oralhistory@bl.uk *Website* www.bl.uk/nls
(Est. 1987. Reg. Charity No. 327571). To 'record first-hand experiences of as wide a cross-section of present-day society as possible'. As an independent charitable trust within the Oral History Section of the British Library, NLS's key focus and expertise has been oral history fieldwork. *Lead Curator, Oral History Director of National Life Stories*, Rob Perks *Tel* 020 7412 7405; *Oral History Curator, Deputy Director of National Life Stories*, Mary Stewart *Tel* 020 7412 7406; *Oral History Archive Asst*, Elspeth Millar *Tel* 020 7412 7404

LIVING MEMORY OF THE JEWISH COMMUNITY (C410) is a major collection with a primary focus on pre-Second World War Jewish refugees to Britain, those fleeing from Nazi persecution during the Second World War and Holocaust survivors. The collection has recently expanded to include interviews with children of survivors. The collection complements other sound archive material on Jewish life, notably the Holocaust Survivors' Centre interviews (C830), Central British Fund Kindertransport interviews (C526), Testimony: Video Interviews with British Holocaust Survivors (C533) and London Museum of Jewish Life oral history interviews (C525).

PORTON COLLECTION OF JUDAICA
Business and Research Department, Central Library, Calverley Street, Leeds LS1 3AB
Tel 0113 2478282 *Fax* 0113 395 1833
Email businessandresearch@leedslearning.net *Website* www.leeds.gov.uk/libraries
The Porton Collection of Judaica has its roots in volumes originally housed in Rabbi Moses Abrahams Memorial Library in Leeds. The collection was enlarged over the years and presented to Leeds City Council in 1965 by Mr Porton's son Leslie, along with Mr Joseph Porton's Judaica collection. The collection covers all aspects of the religion and culture of the Jewish people and includes works in English, Hebrew and Yiddish, in all some 3,500 items. The collection is strong in theological works and religious texts, Jewish and Anglo-Jewish History and biography and also contains archives of the Jewish Year Book, Jewish Chronicle and Jewish Gazette. Rare books and pamphlets, largely in Hebrew and Yiddish, and published in the nineteenth century, are a feature of the collection. Some items are available for loan.

SCHOOL OF ORIENTAL AND AFRICAN STUDIES (University of London)
Thornhaugh Street, Russell Square, London WC1H 0XG
Tel 020 7898 4154 *Fax* 020 7898 4159
Website www.soas.ac.uk/library
The Ancient Near East, Semitics and Judaica Section of the SOAS Library. The Semitics and Judaica collections comprise about 15,000 Hebrew items, covering the fields of

modern Hebrew language and literature (one of the finest collections in Europe), biblical and intertestamental studies, Judaism, the Jewish people, and the land of Israel. There are also a considerable number of books in Western languages covering these fields. In addition, largely owing to the acquisition of the Stencl and Leftwich collections in 1983 and some books from the Whitechapel collection in 1984, there are about 3,000 books on Yiddish language and literature. Periodicals, of which the library holds about 200 Hebrew titles, are shelved separately. The transfer of the Joe Loss Lectureship in Jewish Music from the City University to SOAS has also brought the Harry Rosencweig Collection of Jewish Music to the library. For details of services, please refer to the Library's web pages.

SPANISH & PORTUGUESE JEWS' CONGREGATION ARCHIVES
2 Ashworth Road, W9 1JY
Tel 020 7289 2573 *Fax* 020 7289 2709

Archives The archives of the Spanish & Portuguese Jews' Congregation, London, and its institutions, which date from the mid-17th century, include Minute and Account Books, Registers of Births, Circumcisions, Marriages and Burials. Most of the Registers have now been published and copies may be purchased from the Congregation's office. The archives are not open to the public. Most of the Congregation's archive material is now located at London Metropolitan Archives. Queries and requests for access to the material at LMA from bona fide researchers should be submitted in writing to the Hon. Archivist. Advice and help will be given to general enquirers wherever possible. A search fee may be charged. *Hon. Archivist* Miriam Rodrigues-Pereira. **Shasha Library** (Est 1936) Designed to contain books on Jewish history, religion, literature and kindred interest from the Sephardi standpoint. It contains over 1,200 books. These collections are available at the Sephardi Centre by appointment only. (*See* p. 118).

UNIVERSITY COLLEGE LONDON LIBRARY (UCL)
University College London, Wilkins Building, Gower Street, WC1E 6BT
Tel 020 7679 2598 *Fax* 020 7679 7373
Email library@ucl.ac.uk *Website* www.ucl.ac.uk/library
The Hebrew and Jewish Studies collection comprises around 25,000 volumes in the fields of Jewish history, Israel and Zionism, Hebrew and Semitic languages, Bible, Rabbinic literature, mysticism, Jewish philosophy, Hebrew literature and Yiddish language and literature. In addition there are over 185,000 items of rare and archival material. The collection incorporates the Mocatta Library, Altmann Library and the William Margulies Yiddish Library. See website for opening times and access arrangements. *Hebrew and Jewish Studies Libr.* Vanessa Freedman

THE WIENER LIBRARY FOR THE STUDY OF HOLOCAUST AND GENOCIDE
29 Russell Square, London WC1B 5DP
Tel 020 7636 7247 *Fax* 020 7436 6428
Email info@wienerlibrary.co.uk *Website* www.wienerlibrary.co.uk
(Reg. Charity No. 313015). Founded by Dr. A. Wiener in Amsterdam, 1933, and since 1939 in London. Research library and Institute on contemporary European and Jewish history, especially the rise and fall of the Third Reich; survival and revival of Nazi and fascist movements; antisemitism; racism; the Middle East; post-war Germany. Holds Britain's largest collection of documents, testimonies, and books on the Holocaust. Active educational programme of lectures, seminars and conferences. *Ch. of Bd.* A. Spiro; *Dir.* B. Barkow

PROFESSIONAL ORGANISATIONS

ASSOCIATION OF MINISTERS (CHAZANIM) OF GREAT BRITAIN

Ch. Rev. S. I. Brickman 3 Chatsworth Close, Borehamwood, Herts WD6 1UE *Tel* 020 8387 9962; *Sec.* Rabbi D. A. Katanka; *T.* Rev. M. Haschel

ASSOCIATION OF ORTHODOX JEWISH PROFESSIONALS OF GREAT BRITAIN

53 Wentworth Road, London NW11 0RT

(Est. 1962). To promote research in matters of common interest, and the general acceptance of Torah and Halacha as relevant and decisive in all aspects of modern life and thought. *Ch.* H. J. Adler

JEWISH NURSES & MIDWIVES ASSOCIATION

32 Wykeham Road, London NW4 2SU

Tel 020 8203 2241 *Mobile* 07932 730 944

Email sara@smbarnett.com

(Est. 1993). A social, educational and support group for all Jewish nurses, midwives and members of allied professions. *Ch.* Sara Barnett

RABBINICAL COUNCIL OF NORTH-EAST LONDON

Co-ord. Rev G. Newman *Tel* 07932 166 733 *Email* reverendnewman613@hotmail.co.uk

RABBINICAL COUNCIL OF THE PROVINCES

Pres. Rabbi Lord Sacks; *Ch.* Rabbi Shlomo Odze; *Hon. T.* Rabbi Yoinosson Golomb; *M.* Rev. N. Fagelman 1 Sale Synagogue, 12a Hesketh Road, Sale, Cheshire M33 5AA *Tel* 0161 222 4478

RABBINICAL COUNCIL OF THE UNITED SYNAGOGUE

305 Ballards Lane, London N12 8GB

Tel 020 8343 6313 *Fax* 020 8343 6310

Email rabbi.shindler@chiefrabbi.org

Ch. Rabbi B. Davis; *V. Ch.* Rabbi N. Wilson, Rabbi D. Lister; *Exec. Dir.* Rabbi Dr J. Shindler, MSc; *Hon. T.* Rabbi D. Mason; *Hon. S.* Rabbi P. Hackenbroch

UNITED SYNAGOGUE ADMINISTRATORS' ASSOCIATION

305 Ballards Lane, London N12 8GB

Tel 020 8343 8989 *Fax* 020 8343 6236

Ch. Charles Loeb

VAAD HARABBONIM

Organisation of all the rabbis of the synagogues under the auspices of the Union of Orthodox Hebrew Congregations. *Hon. S.* Rabbi D. Halpern 3 The Approach, London NW4 2HU

MISCELLANEOUS ORGANISATIONS

ALAN SENITT MEMORIAL TRUST
13 Chestnut Avenue, Edgware, Middlesex HA8 8AB
Tel 07714 960 212
Email admin@alansenitt.org *Website* www.alansenitt.org
Facebook Alan Senitt Memorial Trust *Twitter* @senitttrust
(Est. 2006. Reg Charity No. 1117111). A Trust established to be a testimony to and the perpetuation of the life, work and aspirations of Alan Charles Senitt (1978-2006) for the benefit of future generations. The Trust runs a Community Leadership Programme for Year 10 pupils, of all faiths, running in 8 High Schools, provides funding for innovative educational programmes in Youth work, Community Leadership, Interfaith and Israel Programmes. It also partners UJS-Hillel in many activities, including the Alan Senitt Student Hardship Fund and the UJS Student Award for Outstanding Achievement. *Ch.* Emma Senitt; *V. Ch.* Jamie Senitt; *Hon. T. R.* Chaplin; *Hon. S.* Karen Senitt

ASSOCIATION OF JEWISH EX-SERVICEMEN AND WOMEN (AJEX)
Shield House, Harmony Way, Hendon, London NW4 2BZ
Tel 020 8202 2323 *Fax* 020 8202 9900
Email headoffice@ajex.org.uk *Website* www.ajex.org.uk
(Est. 1923). *Nat. Ch.* J. Fox; *Exec. Dir.* J. Weisser; *H. Chaplain* Rabbi Reuben Livingstone CF (U). A list of London and Regional Branches can be obtained from the Office. For the Jewish Military Museum contact the Curator, Roz Currie; *Museum Ch.* Ron Shelley MBE; *Fdr. and Pres.* Henry Morris; *Archivist,* Martin Sugarman (*See* p. 132).

ASSOCIATION OF JEWISH GOLF CLUBS & SOCIETIES
Pres. Clive Leveson, 4 College House, South Downs Road, Bowden, Cheshire WA14 3DZ
Email clive@thelevesons.co.uk; *Sec./T.* Alan Simons 12 Purcells Avenue, Edgware HA8 8DT
Email alsimcon@gmail.com; *Tournament Sec.* David Futerman 24 The Ridgeway, Finchley, London N3 2PH *Email* david.futerman@virgin.net

THE BIG GREEN JEWISH WEBSITE
25-26 Endford Street, London W1H 1DW
Tel 020 3603 8120
Email info@biggreenjewish.org *Website* www.biggreenjewish.org
The Big Green Jewish Website is a resource for Jewish People. It is the on-line meeting point between Jewish and environmental ethics. It seeks to educate about climate change and aims to inspire you to make a difference to the planet. *Staff* Oliver Marcus, David Brown

THE BURNING BUSH
19 Patshull Road, London NW5 2JX
Tel 020 7485 3957
Email lucieskeaping@hotmail.com *Website* www.theburningbush.co.uk
(Est. 1990). 3–6 musicians, traditional Klezmer, Yiddish, Sephardi, Israeli music and song. Weddings, Barmitzvahs, private parties and concerts. *Dir.* Lucie Skeaping

CAMPAIGN FOR THE PROTECTION OF SHECHITA
Elscot House, Arcadia Avenue, London NW3 2JU
Tel 0800 035 0466
Email david@shechita.co.uk
(Est. 1985). To protect the freedom of Jews to perform Shechita; to make representations to Government on proposed legislation or other measures which may affect the proper performance of Shechita. *Nat. Co-ord. and Hon. Solicitors* Neville Kesselman; *Reg. Coord.* Chanoch Kesselman, London; *Rabbinical Adv.* Rabbi Benjamin Vorst and Rabbi Dr David Miller, MA, MSc, DPhil (Oxon)

CELEBRITIES GUILD OF GREAT BRITAIN

The Studio, 16 Covert Way, EN4 0LT
Tel 020 8449 1234 weekdays 10am–4pm *Fax* 020 8441 8430
Email info@celebritiesguild.org.uk *Website* www.celebritiesguild.org.uk
(Est. 1977. Reg. Charity No. 282298). A social and fund-raising Guild of prominent people in British Jewry who organise events to raise funds to provide equipment for disabled and handicapped people. *H. Exec. Dir:* Ella Glazer, MBE; *Hon. T. Pres.* David Jacobs, CBE, DL; *Master Guilder* Mike Sarne

EDGWAREBURY JOINT BURIAL BOARD (EJBB)

Edgwarebury Cemetery, Edgwarebury Lane, Edgware, HA8 8QP
Edgwarebury Cemetery comprises 23 acres and was opened in 1973, it is owned by the Spanish & Portuguese Jews' Congregation, West London Synagogue, Liberal Judaism and Belsize Square Synagogue. *Tel* 020 8958 0090

FRIENDS OF JEWISH SERVICEMEN AND WOMEN

Freepost RSHG-JLJH-XZYY, JCHMF, 12 Conisborough Place, Manchester M45 6EJ
Email afjc@armymail.mod.uk
(Est. 1956. Reg. Charity No. 267647). Supports the Jewish Committee for H.M. Forces (*See* p. 84) in funding and ministering to the religious needs of serving Jewish personnel. *Ch.* Dr P. Wagerman; *Pres.* Lt Col. Mordaunt Cohen TD DL; *Hon. T.* Major Rob Pollock; *Hon. S.* Brian Bloom; *Tru.* Col. M Newman DL, Lt. Cdr. A. Tyler RN; *Tru.* Dr P. Wagerman

INDEPENDENT JEWISH VOICES (IJV)

Tel 020 8883 7063
Email info@ijv.org.uk *Website* www.ijv.org.uk
(Est. 2007). To promote expression of alternative Jewish voices, particularly with respect to Israel, based on commitment to universal human rights and social justice. *Sec.* Ann Jungman

JEWISH ASSOCIATION FOR BUSINESS ETHICS

2nd Floor, Mowbray House, 58-70 Edgware Middlesex HA8 8DJ
Tel 020 8905 4048 *Fax* 020 8905 4658
Email info@jabe.org *Website* www.jabe.org
(Reg. Charity No. 1038453). JABE aims to encourage honesty, integrity and social responsibility in business and the professions, operating within the corporate world and the education system to achieve this. JABE regularly delivers high-profile seminars, educational events and thought provoking publications, in addition to its highly successful 'Money and Morals' School Programme. *Ch.* Alan Tapnack; *Exec. Dir.* Lorraine Spector

JEWISH ASSOCIATION OF SPIRITUAL HEALERS

Email jashhealing@hotmail.com *Website* www.jashhealing.com
(Est. 1966. Reg. Charity No. 275081). Aims: (1) To attempt to relieve sickness and suffering; (2) To demonstrate that Spiritual Healing is in keeping with the teachings of Judaism. *Ch.* Stephen Sharpe *Tel* 020 8866 9332; *Sec.* Francine Benjamin *Tel* 07956 261 738; *News Ed.* Yetta and Maurice Powell *Tel* 020 8954 0787

THE JEWISH COUNCIL FOR RACIAL EQUALITY

P.O. Box 47864, London NW11 1AB
Tel 020 8455 0896
Email admin@jcore.org.uk *Website* www.jcore.org.uk
(Est. 1976. Reg. Charity No. 1132666). JCORE provides a Jewish voice on race and asylum issues in the UK and works with both the Jewish and wider community to promote a positive, multi-ethnic UK, free from all forms of racism. JCORE delivers race-equality education and publications for all ages; campaigns for the right of asylum seekers

and refugees; and provides practical support for destitute asylum seekers, unaccompanied child refugees and refugee doctors. JCORE works closely with other ethnic minority, refuge, anti-racism and interfaith organisations, bringing together people from Black, Jewish and Asian communities for dialogue, joint projects and campaigning. *Exec. Dir.* Dr Edie Friedman

JEWISH FRIENDLY SOCIETIES
Grand Order of Israel and Shield of David
11 The Lindens, Prospect Hill, Waltham Forest, London E17 3EJ
Tel 020 8520 3531
Email info@goisd.org.uk *Website* www.goisd.org.uk
(Est. 1896). The membership is contained in three Lodges in the Metropolitan area and one in Birmingham.

JEWISH GAY AND LESBIAN GROUP
BM-JGLG, London WC1N 3XX
Tel 07504 924 742
Email info@jglg.org.uk *Website* www.jglg.org.uk
(Est. 1972). Social group for Jewish gay men, lesbians and bisexuals of all ages. *Pres.* Sonia Lawrence

JEWISH SOCIALISTS' GROUP
BM 3725, London WC1N 3XX
Email jsg@jewishsocialist.org.uk *Website* www.jewishsocialist.org.uk
(Est. 1974). Political, cultural and campaigning organisation committed to socialism, diasporism and secularism, aiming to unite the Jewish community with other oppressed/persecuted minorities. Active on local, national and international issues. National Committee (collective leadership).

JEWISH VOLUNTEERING NETWORK (JVN)
The Wohl Campus for Jewish Education, 44a Albert Road, London NW4 2SJ
Tel 020 8203 6427
Email info@jvn.org.uk *Website* www.jvn.org.uk
Facebook JewishVolunteeringNetwork *Blog* www.jvnblog.com
(Est. 2007). JVN helps to match Jewish volunteers with volunteering opportunities in charities and organisations across England; provides training and support to Volunteer Co-ordinators and Trustees in the community and raises the profile of volunteers and volunteering across the UK Jewish community generally. *Pres.* Rosalind Preston OBE; *Dir.* Leonie Lewis; *Ch.* David Lazarus; *Fdr.* Judy Citron z'l

JEWS FOR JUSTICE FOR PALESTINIANS
P.O. Box 46081, London W9 2ZF
Email jfjusticefp@yahoo.co.uk *Website* www.jfjfp.com
(Est. 2002). JFJFP is a network of Jews who are British or live in Britain, practising and secular, Zionist and not. JFJFP opposes Israeli policies that undermine the livelihoods, and human, civil and political rights of the Palestinian people, while supporting the right of Israelis to live in freedom and security within Israel's 1967 borders. JFJFP is the largest group of British Jews openly critical of Israeli alleged human-rights abuses and transgressions of international law. JFJFP draw on Jewish values of justice, tolerance and mutal respect, and is motivated by concerns to combat antisemitism and to protect the long-term future of both peoples. JFJFP rejects any routine labeling of Israel's critics as antisemitic and promotes factually-based, open discourse on the conflict within British society, cooperating with other organisations on specific issues, without necessarily endorsing everything they do. JFJFP is a founding member of *European Jews for a Just Peace* and is a member of the Jewish Human Rights Network. *Contact* Deborah Maccoby

JOINT BURIAL COMMITTEE (JBC)
Hoop Lane Cemetery, London NW11 7EU
Hoop Lane cemetery is owned by the Spanish & Portuguese Jews' Congregation and West London Synagogue, The cemetery opened in 1897 and is one of the oldest operational Jewish cemeteries in London.
There are many notable interments within the grounds. *Tel* 020 8455 2569

LONDON CANTORIAL SINGERS
c/o 166 Regal Way, Harrow, Middx HA3 0SQ
Tel/Fax 020 8907 0616
Email info@tlcs.org.uk *Website* www.tlcs.org.uk
(Est.1995). Choir performing Synagogue, Israeli and Yiddish music. *Musical Dir.* David Druce; *Chazanim*, David Shine; *Rev Cantor*, David Rome; *Patron*, Rev Reuben Turner

NE'IMAH SINGERS
c/o St. John's Wood United Synagogue, 37-41 Grove End Road, London NW8
Tel 020 7286 3838
Email info@neimah.com *Website* www.neimah.com
(Est. 1993). Choir performing Synagogue music. *Fdr. and Conductor* Marc Temerlies; *Co-Fdr.* and *Co-Conductor* Jonathan Weissbart *Tel* 07973 424 306; *Asst. Chazan* Moshe Haschel

OPERATION JUDAISM
95 Willows Road, Birmingham B12 9QF
Tel 0121 440 6673 (24 hour ansaphone) *Fax* 0121 446 4199
Email operationjudaism@lubavitchuk.com
(Est. 1986). The community's defence against missionary attack. It operates nationally an information and counselling service. Information and support for those involved with cults. Management committee consists of representatives from: Office of the Chief Rabbi, BoD and Lubavitch Foundation.

PARENTS OF JEWISH GAYS AND LESBIANS
Tel 07806 636089
Email parentsjgl@gmail.com *Website* www.parentsofjewishgaysandlesbians.co.uk
(Reg Charity No. 1079918). Affiliated to FFLAG (Families & Friends of Lesbians & Gays) A support Group to help the parents of Jewish Gays and Lesbians.

PAVEL HAAS FOUNDATION UK
7 Roma Read Close, London SW15 4AZ
Tel 020 8785 4772
(Est. 2002). To promote the performance of the works of Pavel Haas (1899-1944) and Holocaust education. *Exec. Dir.* Jacqueline Bowen Cole

START YOUR DAY THE TORAH WAY
c/o Kehillas Ohel Moshe, 102 Leeside Crescent, London NW11 0LA
Email info@torahway.org.uk *Website* www.torahway.co.uk
(Est. 2005). Morning courses for men. Sunday and Bank Holiday 9.20-9.50am, Monday to Friday 8.30-9am. *Dir.* M. D. Salczman

SUPPORT GROUP FOR PARENTS OF JEWISH GAYS AND LESBIANS
59 Mowbray Road, Edgware, Middlesex HA8 8JL
Tel 020 8958 4827
Email kenmowbray@aol.com
(Est. 1996). To give support and help to parents of Jewish gays and lesbians. *Hon. S.* Kenneth Morris

SZYMON LAKS FOUNDATION UK
7 Roma Road Close, London SW15 4AZ
Tel 020 8785 4772
Email szymonlaks@viktorullmann.freeserve.co.uk *Website* www.musiciansgallery.com
(Est. 2005). To honour and celebrate the life and work of composer Szymon Laks (1901-1983). *Fdr. and Artistic Dir.* Jacqueline Bowen Cole *Tel* 07508 876 194; *Hon Patron* Dr. Y. Bauer. *Hon. Adr. Exec. Cttee.* Dr. G. Fackler, F.H. Wuthenow, Prof. Andre Laks

TJSPN
P.O. Box 33317, London NW11 9FR
Tel 020 8632 0216 *Fax* 020 8458 3261
Email jr6287@yahoo.co.uk
The Jewish Single Parent Network aims to assist single parents with a range of services focusing on the practical difficulties of single parenting. enquiries to R. Zrihen

TZEDEK (Jewish Action for a Just World)
25-26 Enford Street, London W1H 1DW
Tel 020 3603 8120
Email info@tzedek.org.uk *Website* www.tzedek.org.uk
(Est. 1990. Reg. Charity No. 1016767). Tzedek is an overseas development and educational charity working in some of the poorest countries in Africa and Asia. It aims to provide direct support to small-scale, self-help, sustainable development projects, regardless of race or religion, whilst educating the UK Jewish community about the causes and effects of poverty and the Jewish obligation to respond. *Chief Exec.* Jude Williams; *Ch.* Jonny Persey

UNITED KINGDOM ASSOCIATION OF JEWISH LAWYERS & JURISTS
P.O. Box 568 Edgware, Middlesex HA8 4BY
Tel 020 8958 6110 *Fax* 020 8905 4406
Website www.jewishlawyers.co.uk
(Est. 1990). The objectives of the Association are: to contribute towards the establishment of an international legal order, based on the Rule of Law, in relations between all nations and states; to promote human rights and the principles of equality of all and the right of all states and peoples to live in peace; to act against racism and anti-semitism, where necessary, by legal proceedings; to promote the study of legal problems affecting the world's Jewish communities; to promote, in consultation with the legal profession within Israel, the study of legal problems of particular concern; to promote the study of Jewish law in comparison with other laws, and facilitate the exchange of any information resulting from research among member groups; to collect and disseminate information concerning the *de facto* and *de jure* status of the Jewish communities and other minority ethnic and religious groups throughout the world, to give help and support pursuant to human rights treaties; to promote and support co-operation and communication between the Association's member groups; to concern itself with any other matter of legal interest considered of relevance by any of the member groups.
Pres. Lord Woolf; *V. Pres.* Lord Neuberger, Lord Justice Rix; *Ch.* HH D. Levy, QC; *Admin.* Liza Tilley

VIKTOR ULLMANN FOUNDATION UK
7 Roma Read Close, London SW15 4AZ
Tel 07936 268 804
Website www.viktorullmannfoundation.org.uk
(Est. 2002). To remember and celebrate the genius of Viktor Ullmann, (1898–1944), and to promote his music in association with the Terezin Music Memorial Foundation, the Jewish Music Institute, the International Forum for Suppressed Music and other bodies. *Exec. Cttee.* Anita Lask Wallfisch, Father Yves Dubois, Alexander Knapp, Gloria Tessler; *Artistic Dir.* Jacqueline Cole

INTERNATIONAL ORGANISATIONS

JEWISH ORGANISATIONS HAVING CONSULTATIVE STATUS WITH THE ECONOMIC AND SOCIAL COUNCIL OF THE UNITED NATIONS

Agudas Israel World Organisation; Coordinating Board of Jewish Organisations (comprising the British BoD, the South African BoD, and the B'nai B'rith); Consultative Council of Jewish Organisations (comprising the Anglo-Jewish Association, the Alliance Israélite Universelle, and the Canadian Friends of the Alliance); W.J.C. International Council on Jewish Social and Welfare Services (comprising American Joint Distribution Committee, World Jewish Relief, Jewish Colonization Association, European Council of Jewish Community Services, United Hias Service, World ORT Union); International Council of Jewish Women.

AGUDAS ISRAEL WORLD ORGANISATIONS

The organisation was founded in Kattowitz in 1912. Its programme was defined as being 'the solution – in the spirit of the Torah – of problems which periodically confront the Jewish people in Eretz Yisroel and the Diaspora'. This object was to be fulfilled 'by coordination of Orthodox Jewish effort throughout the world ... by the representation and protection of the interests of Torah-true Jewish communities'. The programme was formulated by our ancestors for the unconditional acceptance by all Jewish generations of the Biblical injunction 'And ye shall be unto Me a kingdom of priests and a holy nation'. The organisation seeks to implement this injunction by its endeavours. It opposes assimilation and different interpretations of Jewish nationhood. Consultative status with United Nations, New York and Geneva, and Unesco in Paris.

Main contact 42 Broadway, 14th Floor, New York NY 10004
Tel +1 (212) 797 9000 *Fax* +1 (646) 254 1640
Email sbloom@agudathisrael.org

Agudas Israel of Great Britain
97 Stamford Hill, N16 5DN
Tel 020 8800 6688 *Fax* 020 8800 5000
Presidium, Rabbi Y. M. Rosenbaum *Publ.* Jewish Tribune (weekly).

Zeire Agudas Israel
95 Stamford Hill, N16 5DN; 35a Northumberland Street, Salford 7
Ch. J. Schleider

Agudas Israel Community Services
97 Stamford Hill, N16 5DN
Tel 020 8800 6688 *Fax* 020 3240 0110
Email mposen@agudas.org.uk
(Est. 1980. Reg. Charity No. 287367), To help find suitable employment for observant Jews, including immigrants and Yiddish speakers. Also an advice centre dealing with welfare benefits and immigration advice, plus other social services. *Dirs.* Y. Silkin, M. M. Posen

Jewish Rescue and Relief Committee
215 Golders Green Road, NW11 9BY
Tel 020 8458 1710
(Reg. Charity No. 1120311). *Ch.* A. Strom

Society of Friends of the Torah Ltd
97 Stamford Hill, London N16 5DN
Tel 020 3240 0106 *Fax* 020 8800 5000
215 Golders Green Road, London NW11 9BY
Tel 020 8458 9988 *Fax* 020 8458 8425
Email accounts@softorah.com
(Reg. Charity No. 1140838). *Ass. Dir.* S. Bowden

ALLIANCE ISRAELITE UNIVERSELLE
45 rue La Bruyère, Paris 75009
Tel +33 (01) 53 32 88 55 *Fax* +33 (01) 48 74 51 33
Email info@aiu.org *Website* www.aiu.org *Library Website* www.aiu.org/bibli
(Est. 1860). This educative and cultural-oriented organisation essentially works through its network of schools in France, but also in Belgium, Canada, Israel, Morocco, Spain and North America. Active in the field of European Jewish Education, with the Alliance Europe Project, as well as with the European Emmanuel Levinas Institute. It has defended human rights before governmental and international institutions all over the world. Its library with more than 150,000 books in the field of Hebraica-Judaica, and its College des Etudes Juives, make it one of the most important Jewish centres in Europe. *Pres.* Marc Eisenberg; *Dir.* J. Tolédano.

AUSTRALIA/ISRAEL AND JEWISH AFFAIRS COUNCIL (AIJAC)
Level 1, 22 Albert Road, South Melbourne, Victoria 3205
Tel +61 (3) 9681 6660 *Fax* +61 (3) 9681 6650
Email aijac@aijac.org.au
The AIJAC is the premier public affairs organization for the Australian Jewish Community Through research, commentary, analysis and representation, AIJAC promotes the interests of the Australian Jewish Community to Government and other community groups and organizations. It has professionals dedicated to analysis and monitoring development in the Middle East, Asia and Australia. AIJAC is associated with the American Jewish Committee. in a global partnership designed to bring about a greater understanding of the issues and challenges lying ahead for Jewry. The former Australian Institute of Jewish Affairs, now operating as a division of AIJAC, maintains its programme of social and cultural activities, and holds important public functions and briefings throughout Australia. It also retains a role in South East Asia. *Publ.* Australia/Israel Review (monthly); *Exec. Dir.* Dr. Colin Rubenstein, AM; *Contact* L .Kahn

B'NAI B'RITH INTERNATIONAL
(Est. 1843). The world's largest Jewish human rights, philanthropic and community action group, bringing Jews to work in harmony for the common good, to help the poor and oppressed, and to become active in cultural and humanitarian projects. It is active in 58 countries around the world, with its head office in Washington DC. It has NGO status at the United Nations in New York, an office at the European Union in Brussels, and a World Centre in Jerusalem.

B'nai B'rith UK
A division of B'nai B'rith Europe, with headquarters in Brussels and comes under the overall umbrella of B'nai B'rith International in Washington.
The Core Objectives of B'nai B'rith in the United Kingdom are:
• to foster friendship through social, cultural and recreational programmes;
• to support the State of Israel and World Jewry;
• to work for charitable endeavours;
• to initiate and develop community projects;
• to strengthen B'nai B'rith links across Europe.
  B'nai B'rith UK's London Bureau of International Affairs visits Embassies and the Foreign Office on a regular basis to advance the cause of Jews and Israel. It works with corresponding B'nai B'rith groups in Brussels, Paris and Washington.
  B'nai B'rith UK's annual European Days of Jewish Culture and Heritage arranges for synagogues and places of Jewish interest to be open to the public. The rich Jewish history is showcased by cultural events, guided walks and heritage trails. B'nai B'rith works with other Jewish organisations across Europe.
  B'nai B'rith UK is actively involved in a number of projects to help disadvantaged Jews and Righteous Gentiles in other countries. It raises funds and takes a keen interest in making sure that those funds are put to the best possible use. Each fund has a project leader and there are regular visits for members to see how the funds benefitting recipients.

B'nai B'rith UK has three lodges in the North of England and 12 in London. The lodges and the new BB2545 group offer social events to enable Jews across the whole spectrum of observance to meet and enjoy a wide range of activities.

B'nai B'rith International HQ 2020 K Street, NW, 7th Floor, Washington, DC 20006, USA
Tel + 1 (202) 857 6600
Website www.bnaibrith.org

B'nai B'rith Europe Rue Dautzenberg 36, B-1050 Brussels, Belgium
Tel +32 (2) 646 9298
Email secretariat@bnaibritheurope.org *Website* www.bnaibritheurope.org
Pres. Ralph Hofmann

B'nai B'rith UK ORT House, 126 Albert Street, London NW1 7NE
Tel 020 7446 8660
Email office@bnaibrithuk.org *Website* www.bbuk.org
(Reg Charity No. 1061661). *Nat. Pres.* Eve Swabe

> **London Bureau of International Affairs** ORT House, 126 Albert Street, London NW1 7NE
> *Ch.* Richard Sotnick; *Dir.* Helene Briskman *Email* lbia2000@hotmail.co.uk

CCJO. René Cassin
The JHub, 152 West End Lane, London NW6 1SD
Tel 020 7443 5130
Email info@renecassin.org *Website* www.renecassin.org
(Est. 2000. Reg. Charity No. 1117472). René Cassin is a human rights non-governmental organisation that works to promote and protect universal human rights drawing on Jewish experience and values. It does this this by campaigning for change in defined human rights areas through a combination of advocacy, policy analysis, public campaigning and education; and building the capacity of activists and lawyers to promote and protect human rights. *Dir.* Shauna Leven; *Ch.* Maya Jaffe

CENTRAL REGISTRY OF INFORMATION ON LOOTED CULTURAL PROPERTY 1933–1945
76 Gloucester Place, London W1U 6HJ
Tel 020 7487 3401 *Fax* 020 7487 4211
Email info@lootedart.com *Website* www.lootedart.com
(Est. 2001. Reg. Charity No. 309720. IRS No. 13-2943469). Provides a centre of research, expertise and information on cultural objects looted between 1933 and 1945 - paintings, drawings, books, manuscripts, Judaica, silver, porcelain, etc. *Dir.* Anne Webber

COMMISSION FOR LOOTED ART IN EUROPE
76 Gloucester Place, London W1U 6HJ
Tel 020 7487 3401 *Fax* 020 7487 4211
Email info@lootedartcommission.com *Website* www.lootedartcommission.com
(Est. 1999). Non-profit, expert representative body which negotiates restitution policies and procedures, and assists families, communities and institutions internationally to locate and recover Nazi-looted cultural property. Represents the European Council of Jewish Communities and the Conference of European Rabbis. *Co-Ch.* David Lewis, Anne Webber

COMMITTEE FOR THE PRESERVATION OF JEWISH CEMETERIES IN EUROPE
34a Fairholt Road, London N16 5HW
Tel 020 8802 6853 *Fax* 020 8802 3756
Email cpjce@btconnect.com
(Est 1991. Reg. Charity No. 1073225). Preservation of Jewish burial sites in Europe to ensure that they are maintained according to Jewish law and tradition. *Pres.* Rabbi E. Schlesinger; *Hon. S.* Y. Marmorstein; *Hon. T.* A. Goldman. *Exec. Dir.* A. Ginsberg

COMMONWEALTH JEWISH COUNCIL AND TRUST
BCM Box 6871, London WC1N 3XX
Tel 020 7222 2120
Email info@cjc.org.uk *Website* www.cjc.org.uk
(Est. 1982, Reg. Charity No. 287564). To provide links between Commonwealth Jewish communities; to provide a central representative voice for Commonwealth Jewish communities and to help preserve their religious and cultural heritage; to seek ways to strengthen Commonwealth Jewish communities in accordance with their individual needs and wishes and to provide mutual help and cooperation. The Council undertakes charitable projects in Jewish communities throughout the Commonwealth, with special emphasis on the smaller communities. *Fdr. and Pres.* Lord Janner of Braunstone, QC; *Pres.* Michael Ellis MP; *V. Pres.* Paul Secher, Rev. Malcolm Weisman, OBE; *Tru.* Marlene Bethlehem (South Africa), Mitchell Coen, Jason Holt, Samuel Marshall (India), Dorothy Reitman (Canada), Gideon Wittenberg; *Dir.* Maureen Gold; *Co-ord.* Alanna Cawston
There are 38 members, including those in Antigua, Australia, Bahamas, Barbados, Belize, Bermuda, Botswana, Canada, Cayman Islands, Cyprus, Gibraltar, Guernsey, India, Isle of Man, Jamaica, Jersey, Kenya, Mauritius, Namibia, New Zealand, Seychelles, Singapore, Sri Lanka, Trinidad & Tobago, Turks & Caicos Islands, United Kingdom, Zambia. Obeservers: Hong Kong and Zimbabwe.

CONFERENCE OF EUROPEAN RABBIS
Website www.confeurorabbis.org
Exec. Dir. Rabbi Elimelech van Zetter; *Pres.* Rabbi Pinchas Goldschmidt; *Ch. Presidium,* Rabbi Joseph Sitruck; *Ch. European Rabbinical Court,* Dayan Chanoch Ehrentreu; *Assoc. Pres.* Chief Rabbi Lord Sacks; *V. Pres.* Rabbi Gilles Bernheim, Rabbi Menachem Gelley Senior Judge, Rabbi Yaakov Dov Bleich, Rabbi Riccardo DiSegni, Rabbi Rene Sirath
(Est. 1957). To provide a medium for co-operation on matters of common concern to rabbis of European communities.

CONFERENCE ON JEWISH MATERIAL CLAIMS AGAINST GERMANY, Inc
1359 Broadway, Room 2000, New York, NY 10018
Tel +1 (646) 536 9100 *Fax* +1 (212) 679 2126
Email info@claimscon.org *Website* www.claimscon.org
(Est. 1951). Represents world Jewry in negotiating for compensation and restitution for victims of Nazi persecution and their heirs. More than 500,000 Holocaust survivors in 67 countries have received payments from Germany and Austria due to the work of the Claims Conference. Administers compensation funds, recovers unclaimed Jewish property and allocates funds to institutions that provide social welfare services to Holocaust survivors, and preserves the memory and lessons of the Shoah. *Ch.* Julius Berman; *Exec. V. Pres.* Greg Schneider

EAST EUROPEAN JEWISH HERITAGE PROJECT
25 Plantation Park, Keele, Staffs ST5 5NA
Email eejhp@voluntas.org *Website* www.eejhp.netfirms.com
(Reg. Charity No. 10616229). The East European Jewish Heritage project is active in Belarus, Lithuania and Ukraine. In addition to its humanitarian assistance programmes, it encourages Jewish leadership in civil society through participation in projects which benefit the broader community. The EEJHP provides travel programmes for those interested in their ancestral past as well as genealogy services. Over the past ten years the EEJHP has engaged with many western organisations and universities in the restoration of derelict Jewish cemeteries. *Exec. Dir.* F. J. Swartz; *Dirs.* D. Solomon, K. G. Cushing

EMUNAH (Child Resettlement Fund)
Shield House, Harmony Way, off Victoria Road, London NW4 2BZ
Tel 020 8203 6066 *Fax* 020 8203 6668
Email info@emunah.org.uk *Website* www.emunah.org.uk
(Est. 1933. Reg. Charity No. 215398). Emunah cares for those children in Israel whose

lives are at risk, and whom no one else wants. Through its network of residential children's homes, therapy centres, day care and community centres, Emunah is recognised as one of Israel's leading provider of family welfare services. Emunah's members in the UK work tirelessly in a voluntary capacity to raise funds to support the vital projects in Israel. British Emunah currently helps to support 36 projects in Israel. *H. Pres.* Lady Sacks; *Found. Pres.* Gertrude Landy; *Exec. Pres.* Guggy Grahame, Daphne Kaufman; *Exec. V. Pres.* Vera Garbacz, Gertrude Compton, Rochelle Selby; *Ch.* Camille Compton; *Israel Projects Ch.* Lilian Brodie; *Admin. Ch.* Rosalyn Liss; *Hon. S.* Estelle Berest; *Hon. T.* Rachelle Greenwood; *Publ.* Helen Kon; *Dir.* Deborah Nathan

EUROPEAN ASSOCIATION FOR JEWISH CULTURE
Paris office: 19 Rue de la Tour d'Auvergne, 75009 Paris Tel +33 (0)1 4878 5892
London office: 7/8 Market Place, London W1W 8AG
Email eajc@jewishcultureineurope.org *Website* www.jewishcultureineurope.org
(Est. 2001). An independent grant-making body, which fosters and supports artistic creativity and promotes digital access to Jewish culture in Europe. *Pres.* Peter L. Levy OBE; *Sec.* Jean-Jacques Wahl; *Dir.* Lena Stanley-Clamp

EUROPEAN ASSOCIATION FOR JEWISH STUDIES
Oxford Centre for Hebrew and Jewish Studies, Yarnton Manor, Yarnton, Oxon OX5 1PY
Tel 01865 377946 (x111) *Fax* 01865 375079
Email admin@eurojewishstudies.org *Website* www.eurojewishstudies.org
Admin. Dr. G. Gilmour; *Pres.* Prof. Judith Olszowy-Schlanger; *Sec.* Prof. Daniel Langton; *T.* Prof. Gad Freudenthal *Publ.* European Journal of Jewish Studies.

EUROPEAN COUNCIL OF JEWISH COMMUNITIES (ECJC)
Oscar Joseph House, 54 Crewys Road, London, NW2 2AD
Tel 020 8455 8392 *Fax* 0 208 209 0583
Email info@ecjc.org *Website* www.ecjc.org www.presidents-meeting.ecjc.org
www.arachim.ecjc.org, www.jewisheritage.org www.european-encounters.ecjc.org
ECJC is a non-government organisation (NGO) established as a non-profit association in accordance with the laws of Belgium as a "Vereniging Zonder Winstoogmerk". It has its registered office at Centraal Beheer van Joods Weldadigheid, Antwerp. The first statutes were adopted in 1968 in London. ECJC represents Jewish national communal organisations from over 40 countries in Europe. The ECJC enjoys participative NGO status with the Council of Europe and has consultative NGO status recognition with the European Union. *Pres.* Jonathan Joseph; *Chief Exec.* Neville Kluk. *Contact.* Michelle Kathan *Email* michelle@ecjc.org Full list of board members on websites.

EUROPEAN JEWISH CONGRESS (previously **The European Branch of the World Jewish Congress**)
78 Avenue des Champs-Elysées, 75008 Paris
Tel +33 (01) 43 59 94 63 *Fax* +33 (01) 42 25 45 28
Website www.eurojewcong.org
(Est. 1986). Federates and co-ordinates the initiatives of 38 communities in Europe and acts as their spokesman. Has consultative status with the Council of Europe, European Commission and Parliament. Current concerns are the democratic development of Eastern Europe and the problems of racism and antisemitism throughout Europe. *Pres.* Moshe Kantor; *Sec. Gen.* Serge Cwajgenbaum

EUROPEAN UNION OF JEWISH STUDENTS
3 ave Antoine Depage, B-1000, Brussels, Belgium
Tel 010 32 2 647 72 79 *Fax* 010 32 2 648 24 31
Email info@eujs.org *Website* www.eujs.org
(Est. 1978). For co-ordination purposes between nat. unions in the 36 countries of Europe (and Turkey). It represents more than 180,000 European Jewish students in international

Jewish and non-Jewish forums, dealing with cultural and political matters, and opposes all forms of racism and fascism. The EUJS is also a 'service organisation' for students. It helps with courses abroad, supplies material on different subjects for university students and organises visits and seminars. *H. Pres.* Simone Veil, Maram Stern; *H. Mems.* Lord Janner, David Susskind (Belgium), Suzy Jurysta (B.), Laslov Kadelburg (Yu.); *Pres.* Benjamin Zagzag; *Exec. Dir.* Deborah Abisror; *Programme Dir.* Adam Mouchtar

HIAS
333 7th Avenue, 16th Floor, New York, NY 10001, USA
Tel +1 (212) 967 4100
Website www.hias.org
(Est. 1954, through the merger of the Hebrew Sheltering and Immigrant Aid Society (HIAS), United Service for New Americans (USNA) and the migration service of the American Joint Distribution Committee. (AJDC).)
Est. 1881, HIAS, the Hebrew Immigrant Aid Society, is America's oldest international migration and refugee resettlement agency. HIAS assists Jewish and other migrants and refugees to countries of freedom and security, helps newcomers to integrate into their new communities, and reunites family members. It advocates for, and works with government and other agencies to promote fair migration policies and increased opportunities. HIAS' activities have always mirrored world events. In the past decade alone, the organisation has worked to help refugees and immigrants from Afghanistan, Bosnia, Bulgaria, Czech Republic, Democratic Republic of the Congo, Ethiopia, Haiti, Hungary, Iran, Morocco, Nigeria, Poland, Romania, Sudan, Tunisia, Vietnam, successor states to the former Soviet Union, and other countries where persecution and absence of liberty have forced people to seek new lives in America and other welcoming nations. *Pres.* Gideon Aronoff; *Ch.* Marc Silberberg

INSTITUTE FOR JEWISH POLICY RESEARCH (JPR)
7-8 Market Place, London W1W 8AG
Tel 020 7436 1553 *Fax* 020 7436 7262
Email jpr@jpr.org.uk *Website* www.jpr.org.uk
JPR is an independent think-tank which informs and influences policy, opinion and decision-making on issues affecting Jewish life worldwide. This is done by conducting and commissioning research, developing and disseminating policy proposals and promoting public debate. JPR's public activities include lectures, policy seminars and conferences. *Hon. Pres.* Lord Rothschild, OM; *Pres.* Lord Haskel; *Ch.* Harold Paisner; *T.* Brian Smouha; *Exec. Dir.* Jonathan Boyd; *Development Dir.* Judith Russell. *Publ.* JPR Reports and Policy Debate papers

INTERNATIONAL COUNCIL OF CHRISTIANS AND JEWS
Martin Buber Haus, Werlestrasse 2, Postfach 1129, D-64646, Heppenheim, Germany
Tel +49 6252 689 6810 *Fax* +49 6252 68331
Email info@iccj.org *Website* www.iccj.org
Established 1947 to strengthen Jewish–Christian understanding on an international basis and to co-ordinate and initiate programmes and activities for this purpose. Now increasingly engaged in trilateral dialogue of Jews, Christians and Muslims. *Pres.* Dr. Deborah Weissman; *Patron* Sir Sigmund Sternberg

INTERNATIONAL COUNCIL OF JEWISH WOMEN
5655 Silver Creek Valley Road #480, San Jose, CA 95138, USA
Tel +1 408 274 8020 *Fax* +1 408 274 0807
Website www.icjw.org
ICJW is made up of 43 Jewish women's organisations in 40 countries, covering between them almost the whole spectrum of the Jewish world. The core purpose of ICJW is to bring together Jewish women from all walks of life in order to create a driving force for social justice for all races and creeds. ICJW has consultative status with ECOSOC at the United Nations and is represented on many international organisations. *Pres.* Sharon Gustafson

INTERNATIONAL COUNCIL ON JEWISH SOCIAL AND WELFARE SERVICES
The Forum, 74-80 Camden Street, London NW1 0EG
Tel 020 7691 1771 *Fax* 020 7691 1780
Email info@wjr.org.uk
(Est. 1961). Member Organisations: American Joint Distribution Committee; WJR; European Council of Jewish Community Services; HIAS; World ORT Union. *Chief Exec.* P. Anticoni

INTERNATIONAL JEWISH GENEALOGICAL RESOURCES (IJGR(UK))
Judith Joseph 344 Quinton Road, Birmingham B17 0RE *Email* josephj-2007@hotmail.co.uk
Dr. A.P. Joseph 3 Edgbaston Road, Smethwick, West Midlands, B66 4LA
(Est. 1988). Provides guidance on Jewish genealogy; has a library including material on Anglo-Jewry/Anglo-Australasian Jewry; microfilm of Jewish Chronicle, etc. Research undertaken.

INTERNATIONAL JEWISH VEGETARIAN SOCIETY
Bet Teva, 853/855 Finchley Road, NW11 8LX
Tel 020 8455 0692
Email info@jvs.org.uk *Website* www.jvs.org.uk
Facebook The Jewish Vegetarian Society *Twitter* jewishvegsociety
(Est. 1965. Reg. Charity No. 258581). Affiliated to the international Vegetarian Union. Branches: North and South America, South Africa, Israel, Australia. *Dir.* Suzanne Barnard; *Sec.* Shirley Labelda; *Hon. T.* Michael Freedman FCA; *Tru.* Adam Jackson, Rabbi David Rosen, Stanley Rubens

IRANIAN JEWISH CENTRE
1 Dukes Mews, London W1U 3ET
Tel 020 7414 0069 *Fax* 020 7491 4804
Email ijc@ijc.org.uk *Website* www.ijc.org.uk
(Est. 1981. Reg. Charity No. 287256). Fundraising to support Iranian Jewish communities in Britain, Iran and the USA. Promotion of Iranian/Jewish heritage and culture. *Ch.* Hamid Sabi

JCA CHARITABLE FOUNDATION
c/o Victoria Palace Theatre, Victoria Street, SW1E 5EA
Tel 020 7828 0600 *Fax* 020 7828 6882
Email thejcafoundation@aol.com *Website* www.ica-is.org.il
(Reg. Charity No. 207031). Charitable company established in 1891 by Baron Maurice de Hirsch to assist poor and needy Jews. The JCA was instrumental in promoting the emigration from Russia of thousands of Jews who were settled in farm 'colonies' in North and South America, Palestine/Israel and elsewhere. Today JCA's main efforts are in Israel in rural areas where it supports schools, institutes of higher learning, agricultural research and helps to promote the subsistence of needy Jews. *Pres.* Sir Stephen Waley-Cohen, Bt; *Man.* Y. Lothan

JEWISH AFFILIATES OF THE UNITED NATIONS ASSOCIATION AND PRO-ACTIVE GROUP
Email davidmjacobs@waitrose.com
(Est. 1971). A co-ordinating group of Jewish organisations and individuals affiliated to the United Nations Association. Members of the group represent their organizations at the UNA where they have two functions. First, to promote the interests of Israel and the Jewish People, and second, to present the Jewish view on general international and humanitarian issues. In addition the group acts as an umbrella organization for opposing Anti-Israel activity. *Ch.* David M. Jacobs; *Hon. S.* Prof Gerald Adler

JEWISH RECONSTRUCTIONIST FEDERATION (JRF, formerly FRCH)
Beit Devora, 101 Greenwood Ave, Suite 430, Jenkintown, PA 19046, USA
Tel +1 (215) 885 5601 *Fax* +1 (215) 885 5603

Email info@jrf.org *Website* wwwjrf.org
(Est. 1955). JRF is the congregational arm of the Reconstructionist movement, representing 103 affiliates in North America and internationally. Dedicated to the concept of Judaism as an evolving religious civilization, JRF provides outreach, consulting, programmatic and educational support to its congregations and havurot. JRF is the publisher of a new Haggadah and a variety of books, magazines and the *Kol Haneshamah* prayer book series.

MACCABI WORLD UNION
Kfar Maccabiah, Ramat Gan 52105, Israel
(Est. 1921). The union is a co-ordinating body for the promotion and advancement of sports, educational and cultural activities among Jewish communities worldwide. *Pres.* R. Bakalarz; *Pres.* Jeanne Futeran (South Africa); *Ch.* Oudi Recanati; *Ch. European Maccabi Confederation* Leo Dan-Bensky; *Ch.* Igal Carmi (Israel); *Exec. Dir.* E. Tiberger; *V. Ch. Hd. of European Confederation*, Stuart Lustigman. Maccabi Associations, *See* p. 124.

MEMORIAL FOUNDATION FOR JEWISH CULTURE
50 Broadway, 34th Floor, New York, NY 10004
Tel +1 (212) 425 6606 *Fax* +1(212) 425 6602
Email office@mfjc.org *Website* www.mfjc.org
(Est. 1965). Supports Jewish cultural and educational programmes all over the world in co-operation with educational research and scholarly organisations, and provides scholarship and fellowship grants in Jewish fields. Sponsors the International Nahum Goldmann Fellowship. *Pres.* Prof. I. Schorsch; *Exec. V. Pres.* Dr. J. Hochbaum

SIMON WIESENTHAL CENTRE
European office: 66 rue Laugier, 75017 Paris, France
Tel +33 (1) 4723 7637 *Fax* +33 (1) 4720 8401
London office: Simon Wiesenthal Centre UK, 27 Old Gloucester Street, WC1N 3XX
Tel 020 7419 5014 *Fax* 020 7831 9489
Email csweurope@gmail.com *Website* www.wiesenthal-europe.com
(Est. Los Angeles, 1979. Reg. Charity No. 1030966). To study the contemporary Jewish and general social condition in Europe by drawing lessons from the Holocaust experience. To monitor, combat and educate against anti-semitism, racism and prejudice. *Ch.* Graham Morris *Int. Dir.* Rabbi Marvin Hier; *Ch. Board of Tru.* Larry Maizel; *Dir. for Int. Relations* Dr. Shimon Samuels. 400,000 members. Headquarters: Los Angeles. Offices in: New York, Washington DC, Toronto, Jerusalem, Paris and Buenos Aires

WORLD COUNCIL OF CONSERVATIVE/MASORTI SYNAGOGUES
Israel: 32 Pierre Koenig Street, Jerusalem, Israel 93469
Tel +972 (02) 624 7106 *Fax* +972 (02) 624 7677
Email mail@masortiolami.org
USA: 3080 Broadway, New York, NY 10027
Tel +01 (212) 280 6039 *Fax* +1 (212) 678 5321
Email worldcouncil@masortiworld.org
(Est. 1957). To build, renew and strengthen Jewish life throughout the world, focusing on Europe, Latin America, the FSU, Africa, Asia and Australia. It works with all arms of the Conservative/Masorti movement. Emphasizing the study of Torah in its fullest sense, and its transmission from generation to generation. It is also concerned with the centrality of the synagogue, Israel and the Hebrew language and centrist, dynamic Jewish practice, based on *halacha* and *mitzvot*. It encourages the values of egalitarianism, pluralism and tolerence within this framework

WORLD JEWISH CONGRESS
Email info@worldjewishcongress.org *Website* wwwworldjewishcongress.org
(a) To co-ordinate the efforts of its affiliated organisations, in respect of the political, economic, social, religious and cultural problems of the Jewish people; (b) to secure the

rights, status and interests of Jews and Jewish communities and to defend them wherever they are denied, violated or imperilled; (c) to encourage and assist the creative development of Jewish social, religious and cultural life throughout the world; (d) to represent and act on behalf of its affiliated organisations before governmental, intergovernmental and other international authorities in respect of matters which concern the Jewish people as a whole. *Fdr Pres.* Late Dr N. Goldmann; *Pres.* Ronald S. Lauder; *Ch. Gov. Bd.* Eduardo Elsztain; *Sec. Gen.* Daniel Diker; *Ch. of Regional affiliates:* **North America** Evelyn Sommer, **Latin America** Jack Terpins, **Europe** Moshe Kantor; **Israel** Shai Hermesh, MK; **Euro-Asia** Vadim Shulman.

Principal Offices New York, 501 Madison Avenue, New York, NY 10022 *Tel* +1 (212) 755 5770; Brussels, 84 rue de Stassart, 1050 Brussels *Tel* +32 (02) 552 09 00 *Fax* +32 (02) 552 09 11 *Email* protocol@wjc.eu; Jerusalem, P.O.B. 4293, Jerusalem 91042. *Tel* +972 (02) 633 3000 *Email* wjc@wjc.co.il. *Publ.* Dateline World Jewry (monthly), WJC Email Newsletter (daily).

WORLD JEWISH RELIEF
Oscar Joseph House, 54 Crewys Road, London NW2 2AD
Tel 020 8736 1250 *Fax* 020 8736 1259
Email info@wjr.org.uk *Website* www.wjr.org.uk
(Est. 1933. Reg. Charity No. 290767 Member: Fundraising Standards Board). World Jewish Relief (WJR) is the leading UK Jewish international agency, responding to the needs of primarily, but not exclusively Jewish communities at risk or in crisis, outside the UK and Israel. At times of major international disaster, it leads the UK Jewish community's emergency response to others in need. *Ch.* James Libson; *Chief Exec.* Paul Anticoni; *Pres.* Henry Grunwald OBE, QC

WORLD ORT
1 Rue de Varembé, 1211 Geneva 20, Switzerland
Tel +41 (22) 919 4234 *Fax* +41 (22) 919 4232
(Est. 1880, Reg. Charity No. 1042541). Over three and a half million students have been trained since 1880, and currently some 300,000 students are being trained in more than 60 countries in different parts of the world.
Operational Headquarters in UK World ORT Trust, 126 Albert Street, London NW1 7NE
Tel 020 7446 8500
Email wo@ort.org *Website* www.ort.org

WORLD UNION FOR PROGRESSIVE JUDAISM
13 King David Street, 94101 Jerusalem
Tel +972 (02) 6203 447 *Fax* +972 (02) 6203 467
Website www.eupj.org
(Est. 1926). To foster the international growth and practice of Progressive Judaism, and to co-ordinate the activities of its autonomous constituent organisations. *Ch.* S. Bauman. European Union for Progressive Judaism: The Sternberg Centre, 80 East End Road, London N3 2SY *Tel* 020 8349 5651 *Fax* 020 8349 5699 *Email* kathrynmichael@eupj.org *Ch.* Rabbi Dr. Andrew Goldstein; *Sec.* Kathryn Michaels

ZIONIST COUNCIL OF EUROPE
Box 1948, 116 Ballards Lane, Finchley, London N3 2DN
Tel 020 8202 0202 *Fax* 020 8202 0233
Email zion-fed@dircon.co.uk
(Est. 1980). An umbrella organisation, consisting of the Zionist Federations from around Europe, with the aim of co-ordinating Zionist activities and developing young leadership on the continent. *Ch.* Harvey Rose; *Dir.* Alan Aziz

LONDON AND THE HOME COUNTIES

SYNAGOGUES

United Synagogue

For contact details: *See under* Religious Organisations.
Constituent and Affiliated Synagogues of the United Synagogue.

MEMBER SYNAGOGUES
Alei Tzion
LSJS, 44a Albert Road, London NW4 2SJ
Email info@aleitzion.co.uk aleitzion@theus.org.uk *Website* www.aleitzion.co.uk
M. Rabbi D. Roselaar; *Admin.* J. Cowan
Barnet Synagogue
Eversleigh Road, New Barnet, Herts EN5 1ND
Tel 020 8449 0145
Email administrator@barnetsynagogue.org.uk *Website* www.barnetsynagogue.org.uk
Office hours: Sunday-Thursday 9.30am-12.30pm *M.* Rabbi Barry Lerer; *Admin.* Susie Shaw
Belmont Synagogue
101 Vernon Drive, Stanmore, Middlesex HA7 2BW
Tel 020 8426 0104
Email office@belmontsynagogue.org.uk *Website* www.belmont.theus.org.uk
M. Rabbi Elchonon Feldman; *Admin.* C. Fletcher
Borehamwood & Elstree Synagogue
P.O. Box 47, Croxdale Road, Borehamwood, Herts WD6 4QF
Tel 020 8386 5227 *Fax* 020 8386 3303
Email info@borehamwoodshul.org *Website* www.borehamwoodshul.org
(Est. 1955). Mikveh on the premises. *Emer. M.* Rabbi A. Plancy; *Snr. Interim M. Rabbi* S.D.
Silkin; *Associate M. Rabbi* B. Boudilovsky; *Fin. Mem.* N. Arnold; *Snr. Admin.* H. Phillips;
Comm. Care Co-ord. R. Brummer; *Youth Dirs.* Josh and Katie Schwartz
Brondesbury Park Synagogue
143 Brondesbury Park, NW2 5JL
Tel 020 8459 1083 *Fax* 020 8459 5927
(Est. 1934). *R.* Rabbi B. Levin; *Admin.* S. Littner
Bushey & District Synagogue
177/189 Sparrows Herne, Bushey, Herts WD23 1AJ
Tel 020 8950 7340
Email adminstrator@busheyus.org
Daily Services held. *M.* Rabbi Z. M. Salasnik, BA, FJC, *Email* zm@salasnik.net; *Snr. Admin.*
M. Chambers; *Associate Rabbi.* Rabbi Y. Richards *Email* rabbi.richards@busheyus.org
Central Synagogue
(Great Portland Street), 36-40 Hallam Street, W1W 6NW
Tel 020 7580 1355 *Fax* 020 7636 3831
Email administrator@centralsynagogue.org.uk *Website* www.centralsynagogue.org.uk
(Consecrated 1870, destroyed by enemy action May 1941, rebuilt 1958). *Admin. Office* 36
Hallam Street, W1W 6NW; *M.* Rabbi B. Marcus; *R.* S. Leas; *Admin.* C. Levison
Chigwell and Hainault Synagogue
Limes Avenue, Chigwell, Essex IG7 5NT
Tel 020 8500 2451 *Fax* 020 8500 4345
Email chshul@btinternet.com *Website* www.chigshul.net
Regular Services held. *M.* Rabbi B. Davis; *Admin.* W. Land
Clayhall Synagogue
Sinclair House, Woodford Bridge Road, Ilford, Essex IG4 5LN
Tel 020 8551 6533 *Fax* 020 8551 9803
Email clayhallsynagogue@hotmail.com *Website* www.clayhallsynagogue.org.uk
M. Rabbi N. Wilson; *Admin.* A. Petar

Cockfosters & North Southgate Synagogue
Old Farm Avenue, Southgate, N14 5QR
Tel 020 8886 8225
Email office@ourshul.co.uk *Website* www.cnss.co.uk www.ourshul.co.uk
(Est. 1948. Consecrated Dec. 1954). *M.* Rabbi Y. Fine, BA

Dollis Hill Synagogue
No longer functioning (Sept 2011). All enquiries to United Synagogue, 305 Ballards Lane, London N12 8GB

Ealing Synagogue
15 Grange Road, Ealing, W5 5QN
Tel 020 8579 4894 *Fax* 020 8567 2348
Email office@ealingsynagogue.org.uk *Website* www.ealingsynagogue.com
M. Rabbi H. Vogel, MA; *Admin.* J. M. Gilford

Edgware Synagogue
Parnell Close, Edgware, Middlesex HA8 8YE
Tel 020 8958 7508 *Fax* 020 8905 4449
Email office@edgwareu.com *Website* www.edgwaresynagogue.org www.edgwareu.com
M. Rabbi D. Lister; *Asst. Rabbi*, Rabbi A. Zeidman; *Admin.* L. J. Ford, T. Harman

Enfield & Winchmore Hill Synagogue
53 Wellington Road, Bush Hill Park, Middlesex EN1 2PG
Tel 020 8363 2697
(Est. 1950). *Ch. Bd.* Tony Flacks *Email* tflacks@hotmail.com; *M.* Rabbi I.H. Sufrin
Email yitzips@gmail.com

Finchley Synagogue
Kinloss Gardens, N3 3DU
Tel 020 8346 8551 *Fax* 020 8349 1579
Email office@kinloss.org.uk *Website* www.kinloss.org.uk
(Consecrated 1935). *M.* Rabbi E. Mirvis

Finsbury Park Synagogue
220 Green Lanes, N4 2JG
Tel 020 8802 7004
Email fpsynagogue@yahoo.co.uk *Website* www.wix.com/i34725/finsburyparksynagogue
M. Rabbi A. Cohn; *R.* Rev. E. Krausher; *Admin.* H. Mather

Golders Green Synagogue
41 Dunstan Road, NW11 8AE
Tel 020 8455 2460 *Fax* 020 8731 9296
Email office@ggshul.org.uk
(Consecrated 1922). *M.* Rabbi H. Belovski *Tel* 020 8458 8824; *Admin.* N. Hill; *Jt. Youth Dirs.* Sammy Epstein and Jenny Mays

Hadley Wood Synagogue
Tel 020 8886 8285
Email office@hwjc.org.uk
M. Rabbi Yoni Birnbaum; *Admin.* F. Cohen *Tel* 07850 638 326

Hackney & East London Synagogue
2a Triangle Road, E8 3RP
Tel 020 7254 0183 *Fax* 020 7249 8210
Email office@hackneysynagogue.org.uk
M. Rev. N. Tiefenbrun; *Admin.* M. Fraser

Hampstead Garden Suburb Synagogue
Norrice Lea, N2 0RE
Tel 020 8455 8126 *Fax* 020 8201 9247
Email office@hgss.org.uk *Website* www.hgss.org.uk
(Consecrated 1934). *M. Rabbi* D. Kaplan; *Associate M. Rabbi* A. Knopf; *Youth and Community Dir.* Rabbi M. Levene, R. Chazan, A. Freilich; *Office Man.* S. Drucker

Hampstead Synagogue
Dennington Park Road, West Hampstead, NW6 1AX
Tel 020 7435 1518 *Fax* 020 7431 8369
Email admin@hampsteadshul.org.uk www.hampsteadshul.org
(Consecrated 1892). *M.* Rabbi Dr M. J. Harris; *R.* Rev. S. R. Gerzi; *Admin.* I. Nadel
Highams Park and Chingford Synagogue
81a Marlborough Road, London E4 9AJ
Tel 020 020 8368 1109
M. Rabbi A. Kahan; *Sec.* S. Smokler
Hendon Synagogue
18 Raleigh Close, NW4 2TA
Tel 020 8202 6924 *Fax* 020 8202 1720
Email admin@hendonus.org.uk
(Consecrated 1935). *M.* Rabbi M.S. Ginsbury; *Exec. Sec.* L. Cohen.
Highgate Synagogue
57 North Road, Highgate, N6 4BJ
Tel/Fax 020 8340 7655
Email highgateshul@ic24.net
(Est. 1929). *M.* Rabbi N. Liss *Tel* 020 8341 1714; *Admin.* Rachel Cohen
Ilford Synagogue
22 Beehive Lane, Ilford, Essex IG1 3RT
Tel 020 8554 5969 *Fax* 020 8554 4543
Email office@ilfordsynagogue.co.uk *Website* www.ilfordsynagogue.co.uk
(Est. 1936). *M.* Rabbi G. Hyman; *Admin.* A. Lever
Kenton Synagogue
Shaftesbury Avenue, Kenton, Middlesex HA3 0RD
Tel 020 8907 5959 *Fax* 020 8909 2677
Email admin@kentonsynagogue.org.uk *Website* www.kentonsynagogue.org
M. Rabbi Y. Black; *Admin.* I. Gold
Kingsbury Synagogue
Hool Close, Kingsbury Green, NW9 8XR
Tel 020 8204 8089
Email kinsyn@btinternet.com *Website* www.brijnet.org/kingsyn
M. Rabbi Z. Cohen; *Admin.* Ivan Gold
Mill Hill Synagogue
Brockenhurst Gardens, NW7 2JY
Tel 020 8959 1137 *Fax* 020 8959 6484
Email office@millhillsynagogue.co.uk *Website* www.shul.co.uk
M. Rabbi Y. Y. Schochet; *Admin.* Charles Loeb and Karyn Orchant, Alyson Sharron
Muswell Hill Synagogue
31 Tetherdown, N10 1ND
Tel 020 8883 5925
Email office@muswellhillsynagogue.org.uk *Website* www.muswellhillsynagogue.org.uk
(Est. 1911). *M.* Rabbi D. Mason; *Admin.* Joanna Cowen
New Synagogue
Victoria Community Centre, Egerton Road, Stamford Hill, N16 6UB
Office: 2a Triangle Road, London E8 3RP *Tel* 020 7254 0183 *Fax* 020 7249 8210
(Est. Leadenhall Street, 1761). Morning services held, throughout Shabbat and Yom Tov as
well as every weekday morning. *Admin.* Michelle Fraser; *Fin. Representative,* J. Yeshooa
Tel 07812 394 267
New West End Synagogue
St Petersburgh Place, Bayswater, W2 4JT
Tel 020 7229 2631 *Fax* 020 7229 2355
Email nwes@newwestend.org.uk *Website* www.newwestend.org.uk
(Consec. 1879). Services held weekdays 7am, Sunday and Bank Holidays 8.30am, Shabbat
9.15am. *M.* Rabbi G. Shisler; *Beadle* Eli Ballon; *Admin.* Mesod Wahnon

Newbury Park Synagogue
23 Wessex Close, off Suffolk Road, Newbury Park, Ilford, Essex IG3 8JU
Tel 020 8597 0958 *Fax* 020 8590 2919
M. Rev. G. Newman; *Admin.* K. Levy *Email* newburypk@spitfireuk.net

Northwood Synagogue
21-23 Murray Road, Middlesex HA6 2YP
Tel 01923 820 004 *Fax* 01923 820 020
Email admin@northwoodus.org
M. Rabbi Dr Moshe Freedman; *Admin.* E. Granger

Palmers Green and Southgate Synagogue
Brownlow Road, N11 2BN
Tel 020 8881 0037
Email palmgrnsyn@yahoo.co.uk
M. Rabbi E. Levy, BA(Hons); *Admin.* F. Cohen

Pinner Synagogue
1 Cecil Park, Pinner, Middlesex HA5 5HJ
Tel 020 8868 7204
Website http://pinnershul.org
Regular daily services held. Rabbi D. Bergson; *Community Admin.* Carolyn Abrahams
Email admin@pinnershul.org

Potters Bar Synagogue
78 Sunnybank Road, Potters Bar, Herts EN6 2NF
Tel/Fax 01707 656 202
Email office@pottersbarshul.org.uk *Website* www.pottersbarshul.org.uk
M. Rabbi A. S. Hill

Radlett
22 Watling Street, P.O. Box 28, Herts. WD7 7PN
Tel 01923 856 878 *Fax* 01923 856 698
Email office@radlettus.org *Website* www.radlettus.org
M. Rabbi L. Dee; *Admin.* A. Primhak, R. Hart

Richmond Synagogue
Lichfield Gardens, Richmond-on-Thames, Surrey TW9 1AP
Tel 020 8940 3526 *Fax* 020 8945 6586
(Est. 1916). *M.* Rabbi Hughes; *Admin.* The Hon. Mrs J.M. Fellows JP

St Albans United Synagogue
Oswald Road, Herts AL1 3AQ
Tel 01727 854 872
Email info@stalbanssynagogue.org.uk *Website* www.stalbanssynagogue.org.uk

St John's Wood Synagogue
37/41 Grove End Road, St John's Wood, NW8 9NG
Tel 020 7286 3838
Email office@shulinthewood.com *Website* www.shulinthewood.com
(Est. in Abbey Road 1882; present building consecrated 1964). *M.* Dayan I. Binstock,
BSc; *R. Rev.* M. Haschel; *Associate Rabbi*, Rabbi Ari Shainfield; *Admin.* Jennifer Weider

Shenley Synagogue
c/o 305 Ballards Lane, London N12 8GB
Tel 020 8343 5671
Email shenley@theus.org.uk *Website* www.shenleyunited.org
Shabbat and Yom Tov services only

South Hampstead Synagogue
21-22 Eton Villas, Eton Road, NW3 4SG
Tel 020 7722 1807 *Fax* 020 7586 3459
Email rachel@southhampstead.org *Website* www.southhampstead.org
M. Rabbi S. Levin, Rabbi E. Levin; Rabbi S. Odze; *Admin.* R. Perez-Arwas

South London Synagogue
45 Leigham Court Road, SW16 2NF
Tel 020 8677 0234
Email admin@sls1.org.uk *Website* www.slsl.org.uk
M. Rabbi Y. Grunewald, M.A.; *Admin.* T. Goldman

South Tottenham Synagogue
111-113 Crowland Road, N15 6UR
Tel 020 8809 2555
Email admin@stsynagogue.org.uk
(Est. 1938). *M.* Rabbi C. M. Biberfeld; *Snr. Warden.* M. Milner

Stanmore and Canons Park Synagogue
London Road, Stanmore Middlesex HA7 4NS
Tel 020 8954 2210
Email mail@stanmoresynagogue.org
M. Rabbi M. Lew; *R.* J. Turgel; *Community Dev. Rabbi* Rabbi A. Shaw; *Asst. Community Rabbi*
Rabbi B. Landau; *Admin.* B. S. Dresner

Sutton & District Synagogue
14 Cedar Road, Sutton Surrey SM2 5DA
Tel 020 8642 5419
Email sutton@theus.org.uk *Website* www.suttonsynagogue.org.uk
M. Rabbi M. Lev; *Admin.* W. Land *Tel* 020 8343 5684

Wanstead and Woodford Synagogue
20 Churchfields, London, E18 2QZ
Tel 020 8504 1990
Email ww@shul-ww.org
M. Rabbi B. Fleischer; *Admin.* L. Appleby

Watford Synagogue
16 Nascot Road, Watford, Herts WD17 4YE
Tel 01923 222 755
Email secretary@watfordsynagogue.org.uk
(Est. 1946). *M.* Rabbi E. Levine; *Admin.* C. Silverman

Wembley Synagogue
Forty Avenue, Wembley, Middlesex HA9 8JW
Tel 020 8904 6565 *Fax* 020 8908 2740
Email office@wembleysynagogue.org.uk *Website* www.wembleysynagogue.org.uk
M. Rabbi S.Y. Harris, BA Hons, Mst. (Oxon); *Admin.* E. Weiner

Woodside Park Synagogue
Woodside Park Road, N12 8RZ
Tel 020 8445 4236 *Fax* 020 8446 5515
Email admin@woodsidepark.org.uk *Website* www.woodsideparksynagogue.org.uk
Regular daily services held. *M.* Rabbi P. Hackenbroch; *Asst. M.* Rabbi G. Wayland; *Ch.* D.
Conway; *Admin.* D. Bruce

AFFILIATE SYNAGOGUE
Western Marble Arch Synagogue
32 Great Cumberland Place, W1H 7TN
Tel 020 7723 9333 *Fax* 020 7224 8065
Email office@marblearch.org.uk *Website* www.marblearch.org.uk
Successor to the Western Synagogue (Est. 1761) and the Marble Arch Synagogue. *M.*
Rabbi L. Rosenfeld; *Pres.* Stanley Simmonds; *Admin.* Gina Drew-Davis. Affiliated for burial
rights with United Synagogue and Western Charitable Foundation.
Affiliated Organisations: Western Charitable Foundation. *Ch.* H. Pasha; *T.* A.H. Yadgaroff

AFFILIATED SYNAGOGUES
These are synagogues. belonging to US by means of a scheme for small and newly established congregations.

Barking and Becontree (Affiliated) Synagogue
200 Becontree Avenue, Dagenham, Essex RM8 2TR
Tel 020 8590 2737
R. Ch. B. J. Lazarus; *Hon. S.* B. Berman

Catford & Bromley Affiliated Synagogue
6 Crantock Road, SE6 2QS
Enq. P.O. Box 4724, London SE6 2YA
Tel 020 8698 9496
(Est. 1937). *M.* Rev. D. G. Rome *Email* minister@catfordsynagogue.org.uk *Admin.* P. Tomlinson
Tel 020 8658 0090 *Email* administrator@catfordsynagogue.org.uk

Chelsea Affiliated Synagogue
Smith Terrace, Smith Street, Chelsea, SW3 4DL
Tel 020 7351 6292
Email office@chelseasynagogue.co.uk
(Reg. Charity No. 1101862). *M.* Rabbi Y. Efune *Tel* 07972 261 229; *Admin.* G. Gean *Tel* 020 7351 6292/ 07980 965 171

Harold Hill and District Affliliated Synagogue
Trowbridge Road, Harold Hill, Essex RM3 8YW
(Est. 1953). *T.* D. Jacobs *Tel* 020 8924 8668; *Hon. S.* Miss D. Meid, 4 Portmadoc House, Brosely Road, Harold Hill, Essex RM3 9BT *Tel* 01708 348 904

Kingston, Surbiton and District Affiliated Synagogue
33-35 Uxbridge Road, Kingston on Thames, Surrey KT1 2LL
Tel 020 8339 2689
(Est. 1947). *M.* Rabbi Samuel Landau; *H. Admin.* C. Abrahams 15 Albany Reach, Queens Road, Thames Ditton, KT7 0QH
Tel 020 8224 2073 *Email* carol.abrahams@btinternet.com

Peterborough Affiliated Synagogue
Tel 01733 264 151 *Admin.* C. Salamon

Romford and District Affiliated Synagogue
25 Eastern Road, Romford, Essex RM1 3NH
Tel 01708 741 690
(Est. 1929). *M.* J.R. Rose, *M.* Rev. L. Sunderland

Ruislip and District Affiliated Synagogue
9 Shenley Avenue, Ruislip Manor, Middlesex HA4 6BP
Tel 01895 622 059 *Fax* 01895 622 059
Email secretary@ruislipsynagogue.org.uk *Website* www.ruislipsynagogue.org.uk
(Est. 1946). *M.* Rabbi S. Coten

Staines Synagogue
Westbrook Road, South Street, Middlesex TW18 4PR
Tel 020 8890 0016
Email staines.synagogue@btinternet.com *Website* www.staines-synagogue.org.uk
Officiant David Kale; *Admin.* Eric Fenton

Federation of Synagogues

For contact details: *See under* Religious Organisations.
Constituent and Affiliated Synagogues of the Federation of Synagogues

CONSTITUENT SYNAGOGUES
Beis Hamedrash Nishmas Yisroel
62 Brent Street, Hendon, London NW4 2ES
Tel 07931 575 292

Website www.bhny.co.uk
Daily services held. *M.* Rabbi D. Tugendhaft; *Sec.* A. Krausz; *Ch.* S. Unsdorfer

Clapton Federation Synagogue (Sha'are Shomayim). (Incorporating Yavneh Synagogue) (in association with Springfield Synagogue). Services held at Springfield Synagogue 202 Upper Clapton Road, E5 9DH *Sec.* R. Jacobs *Tel* 020 8530 5816

Croydon & District Synagogue
The Almonds, 5 Shirley Oaks Road CRO 8YX
Website www.croydonsynagogue.org.uk
(Est. 1908; present synagogue consecrated 1995). Services held Friday night and Shabbat morning at 10am *M.* Rabbi Natan Asmoucha; *Hon. S.* Beila Harris *Tel* 020 8726 0179

East London Central Synagogue
30/40 Nelson Street, E1 2DE
Tel 020 7790 9809
Regular Shabbat Services at 10am *M.* Rabbi Y. Austin *Sec.* J. Beninson *Tel* 07983 931 178; *Pres.* L. Silver

Finchley Central Synagogue
Redbourne Avenue, N3 2BS
Tel 020 8346 1892
Website www.finchleyfed.org.uk
Regular weekday services: Shacharit Sunday 8am, Monday and Thursday 7.05am, Tuesday, Wednesday, Friday 7.15am; Mincha/Maariv 7.30pm; Shabbat services at Pardes House School, Hendon Lane, N3; Friday night 7.15pm or start of Shabbat if earlier; Shabbat morning 9.15am. *Rav.* Rabbi Y. Hamer; *Sec.* P. Wittner

Hendon Beis Hamedrash
65 Watford Way NW4 3AQ
Mincha and Ma'ariv services Monday - Friday at 1.40pm and Shabbat *M.* Dayan Y.Y. Lichtenstein; *Contact* P. Burns *Tel* 020 8203 7757

Ilford Federation Synagogue
The Dennis Centre, 84 Beehive Lane, Ilford, Essex IG1 3RS
Tel 020 8554 5289 *Fax* 020 8554 7003
Email ilfordfedsynagogue@btconnect.com *Website* www.ilfordfeds.org
(Est. 1927). Daily services held. *M.* Rabbi A. Chapper; *Sec.* L. Klein

Machzike Hadath Synagogue
1-4 Highfield Road, NW11 9LU
Tel 020 8455 9816
Services held daily morning and evening. *M.* Rabbi C. Z. Pearlman; *Sec.* R. Shaw *Tel* 020 8958 0499

Netzach Israel Community Centre
281 Golders Green Road, NW11 9JJ
Daily services held. *M.* Rabbi D. Ahiel *Admin.* Rabbi Adam Mather *Tel* 020 8455 7725

Ohr Yisrael Synagogue
31-33 Theobald Street, Borehamwood, Herts WD6 4RN
Website www.ohr-yisrael.org.uk
Daily services held. *M.* Rabbi R. Garson *Tel* 020 8953 8385 *Sec.* Jo Kay *Tel* 020 8207 4702

Shomrei Hadath Synagogue
64 Burrard Road, NW6 1DD
Tel 020 7435 3765
Website http://shomrei-hadath.com
Services held Shabbat, Yom Tov, Sunday, Monday, Thursday, Rosh Chodesh, Taanis. *Sec.* P. Schotten *Tel* 020 7435 6906

Sinai Synagogue
54 Woodstock Avenue, NW11 9RJ
Tel 020 8455 6876
(Est. 1935). Daily services held. *Rab.* Rabbi B. Knopfler; *Sec.* E. Cohen *Tel* 020 8458 8201

Yeshurun Synagogue
corner of Fernhurst Gardens and Stonegrove, Edgware, Middlesex HA8 7PH
Tel 020 8952 5167 *Fax* 020 8905 7439
Email admin@yeshurun.org *Website* www.yeshurun.org
(Est. 1946). Daily services held. *Emer. Rab.* Dayan G. Lopian; *Rab.* Rabbi A. Lewis; *Sec.* Lisa Denby

AFFILIATED SYNAGOGUES
Aish Community Synagogue
379 Hendon Way, NW4 3LP
M. Rabbi J. Roodyn *Tel* 020 8457 4444

Congregation of Jacob
351/353 Commercial Road, E1 2PS
Tel 020 7790 2874
Email info@congregationofjacob.org *Website* www.congregationofjacob.org
(Est. 1903). Regular Shabbat and Yom Tov services held. Contact D. Brandes and D. Behr

Fieldgate Street Great Synagogue
41 Fieldgate Street, E1 1JU
Tel 020 7247 2644
Secs. F. Treep, L. Michaels; *Pres.* H. Michaels

Finchley Road Synagogue (Sassover)
1a Helenslea Avenue, NW11 8NE
(Est. 1941). *Rab.* Rabbi S. Freshwater *Tel* 020 8455 2588
Contact S. Halpern *Tel* 020 8455 1814

Leytonstone & Wanstead Synagogue
2 Fillebrook Road, E11 4AT
Sec. Cllr. L. Braham *Tel* 020 8989 0978

Loughton Synagogue
Borders Lane, Loughton, Essex IG10 1TE
Email admin@loughtonsynagogue.com *Website* http://loughtonsynagogue.com
Regular Shabbat services are held Friday evening at 7pm and Shabbat morning at 9am *Ch.* B. Cohen; *Rav* Rabbi Zvi Portnoy; *Admin.* M. Lewis *Tel* 020 8508 0303

Springfield Synagogue
202 Upper Clapton Road, E5 9DH
Tel 020 8806 3167 (office)
(Est. 1929). Regular daily services held. *Rab.* Dayan I. Gukovitski

Stamford Hill Beis Hamedrash
50 Clapton Common, London E5 9AL
M. Dayan D. Grynhaus; *Ch.* M. Chontow *Tel* 020 8800 7369

Waltham Forest Hebrew Congregation
140 Boundary Road, E17 8LA
Tel 020 8509 0775 *Fax* 020 8518 8200
Email secretary@wfhc.co.uk
(Est. 1902) *M.* Rev. S. Myers; *Ch.* Mark Phillips; *Admin.* B. Rose

West End Great Synagogue
32 Great Cumberland Place, W1H 7TN
Tel 020 7724 8121 *Fax* 020 7723 4413
Email wegs@clara.co.uk
Regular Shabbat morning services are held in the Mintz Beth Hamidrash on the first floor at 9.45am. *M.* Rev. Ari Cohen; *Admin. N. Singer*

East End synagogues are served by Rev. Gingold *Tel* 020 7790 5287

Union of Orthodox Hebrew Congregations

For contact details: *See under* Religious Organisations.
Synagogues Associated with the Union of Orthodox Hebrew Congregations or the Burial Society.

Adath Yisroel Synagogue
40 Queen Elizabeth's Walk, N16 0HH
Tel 020 8802 6262/3 *Fax* 020 8800 8764
Rabbi Dovid Lewis; *Delegates*, M. T. Bibelman, M. Lobenstein

Adath Yisroel Tottenham Beth Hamedrash
55/57 Ravensdale Road, N16 6TJ
Tel 020 8800 3978
Dayan A. D. Dunner; *Delegate*, Dr S. Springer

Ahavat Israel Chasidey Wiznitz Synagogue
Wiznitz House, 89 Stamford Hill, N16 5TP
Tel 020 8800 9359
Rabbi A. Weiss; *Delegates*, R. Bergman JP LLB, Y. Feldman, Y. Zieg

Beis Gavriel Lubavitch
54 Parsons Street, NW4 1TP
Rabbi M. M. Junik; *Delegate*, M. Freundlich

Beis Hamedrash Avreichim Golders Green
211 Golders Green Road, NW11 9BY
Rabbi Y. Y. Lev

Beis Hamedrash Biala (Birkas Zvi)
45-47 Moundfield Road, N16 6DT
Rabbi B. L. Rabinowitz; *Delegate*, A. Schechter

Beis Hamedrash Maharim Dushinsky
1b Braydon Road, N16 6QL
Delegate, S. Z. Reizner

Beis Hamedrash Noam Hatorah
38a Braydon Road, N16 6QB
Delegate, Y. N. Schimanowitz

Beis Hamedrash 'Oraysoh'
102 Darenth Road, N16 6ED
Tel 020 8802 0103
Rabbi M. D. Weiss; *Delegate*, Y. Reichman

Beis Hamedrash Sharei Shulem Tchabe
23 Portland Avenue, N16 6HD
Rabbi A. E. Schwartz; *Delegate*, Y. Moster

Beis Kossov
96 Lewis Gardens, N16 5PJ
Tel 020 8809 6534
Rabbi M. Monderer; *Delegate*, B. Z. Goldstein

Beis Sholem D'Shotz
42 St. Kilda's Road, N16 5BZ
Rabbi S. Deutsch; *Delegates*, F. Gluck, Z. Singer

Beis Yitzchak Dovid, Avreichei Gur
26 Amhurst Parade, Amhurst Park, N16 5AA
Tel 020 8800 6615
Delegates, D. Piller, A. M. Royde

Beth Abraham (Goschalks) Synagogue
46 The Ridgeway, NW11 8QS
Tel 020 8455 2848
Rabbi C. Schmahl; *Delegate*, S. Chonton

Beth Chodosh Synagogue
51 Queen Elizabeth's Walk, N16 5UG
Tel 020 8809 4820
Rabbi H. Frankel; *Delegate*, Rabbi H. Frankel

Beth Hamedrash Cheishev Hoeifod
Brenner Centre, 91-93 Stamford Hill, N16 5TP
Rabbi Y. Padwa; *Delegate*, Y. M. Mann

Beth Hamedrash D'Chasidei Wiznitz
126 Stamford Hill, N16 6QT
Rabbi G. Spitzer; *Delegate*, E. Bretler

Beth Joseph Zvi
Schonfeld Square, Lordship Road, N16 0QQ
Tel 020 8802 7477
Delegate, Ch Konig

Beth Shmuel Synagogue
171 Golders Green Road, NW11 9BY
Tel 020 8458 7511
Rabbi E. Halpern; *Delegates*, S. Feiner, L. Frankel, I. Gabay, A. Heilpern

Beth Talmud Centre
78 Cazenove Road, N16 6AA
Tel 020 8806 8103
Delegate, N. Freedman

Beth Yisochor Dov Beth Hamedrash
4 Highfield Avenue, NW11 9ET
Tel 020 8458 1264
Rabbi G. Hager; *Delegates*, W. Grant, W. Held, Dr P. Mett

Biala Chelkas Yehoshua Beth Hamedrash
110 Castlewood Road, N15 6BE
M. Glausiusz

Bridge Lane Beth Hamedrash
44 Bridge Lane, NW11 0EG
Tel 020 8458 8364
Rabbi S. Winegarten *Burial Society Affiliate*

Chasidey Alexander Me'oron Shel Yisroel Beth Hamedrash
99 Clapton Common, E5 9AB
Delegate, S. Leichtag

Chasidey Belz Beth Hamedrash
99 Bethune Road, N16 5ED
Tel 020 8802 2151
Rabbi E. D. Friedman; *Delegates*, B. Bard, Rabbi D. Frand, Y. Gluck
117 Clapton Common, N16 6AB
Delegate, L. Weiser

Chasidey Belz Beth Hamedrash
96 Clapton Common, E5 9AL
Tel 020 8802 8233
Rabbi J. D. Babad; *Delegates*, M. Grosskopf, N. Merlin, B. Roth
49 St. Kilda's Road, N16 5BS
Tel 020 8211 0213
Rabbi N. B. Eckstein; *Delegates*, D. Y. Gluck, Y. S. Grosz
26 Lampard Grove, N16 6XZ
Rabbi M. Galitsky; *Delegate*, G. Schwartz

Chasidey Bobov Beth Hamedrash
73 Clapton Common, E5 9AA
Delegates, A. M. Lensky, C. Rudzinski

Chasidey Bobov D'Ohel Naphtoli and **Yeshiva Bnei Zion Beth Hamedrash**
87 Eagerton Road, N16 6UE
Tel 020 8809 0476
Rabbi B. Z. Blum; *Delegates*, Y. C. Blau, M. Just, M. Rothfeld

Chasidey Ryzhin Beth Hamedrash
33 Paget Road, N16 5ND
Tel 020 8800 7979
Delegate, M. Erlich

Chasidey Ryzhin-Sadigur Or Yisroel Beth Hamedrash
269 Golders Green Road, NW11 9JJ
Rabbi Y. M. Friedman; *Delegates*, N. Bude, P. Smus

Chasidey Sanz-Klausenburg Beth Hamedrash
124 Stamford Hill, N16 6QT
Tel 020 8802 1149
Delegate, Y. M. Klein

Chasidey Skver Beth Hamedrash
47 East Bank, N16 5PZ
Tel 020 8800 8448
Rabbi Y. Friesel; *Delegate*, M. Ciment

Chasidey Wizintz-Monsey Imrei Chaim Beth Hamedrash
121 Clapton Common, E5 9AB
Tel 020 8800 3741
Rabbi D. Hager; *Delegates*, Y. M. Cohen, Rabbi Zishe Fuchs

Cheishev Sofer D'Pressburg Beth Hamedrash
103 Clapton Common, E5 9AB
Tel 020 8809 1700
Rabbi S. Ludmir; *Delegate*, U. Low

Chevras Shass Zichron Shlomo Beth Hamedrash
11 Elm Park Avenue, N15 6UE
Tel 020 8809 7850
Rabbi S. Meisels; *Delegate*, Y. Y. Meisels

Congregation Chovevei Torah
76 Princes Park Avenue, NW11 0JX
Tel 020 8381 4227
Rabbi Y. Levenberg

Divrei Chaim Beth Hamedrash
71 Bridge Lane, NW11 0EE
Tel 020 8458 1161
Rabbi Chaim A. Z. Halpern; *Delegates*, M. Aisenthal, P. M. Grossnass

Etz Chaim Yeshiva
83-85 Bridge Lane, NW11 0EE
Rabbi Z. Rabi; *Delegate*, B. Manson

Golders Green Beth Hamedrash Congregation
The Riding, NW11 8HL
Tel 020 8455 2974
Rabbi Y. M. Greenberg *Burial Society Affiliate*

Gur Beiss Hachasidim
98 Bridge Lane, NW11 0ER
Tel 020 8458 6243
Delegate, A. Weingarten

Gur Beiss Hachasidim
2 Lampard Grove, N16 6UZ
Tel 020 8806 4333
Delegates, Y. M. Cymerman, Y. S. Goldman, Y. Traube

Heichal Hatorah
27 St. Kilda's Road, N16 5BS
Tel 020 8809 4331
Rabbi L. Rakow; *Delegate*, A. M. Schwartz

Heichal Leah
62 Brent Street, NW4 2ES
Tel 020 8203 6210
Rabbi M. Nissim; *Delegates*, C. Kohali, Rabbi M. Nissim

Heichal Menachem
209 Golders Green Road, NW11 9BY
Rabbi Y. M. Hertz; *Delegate*, Rabbi N. Cohen

Hendon Adath Yisroel Congregation
11 Brent Street, NW4 2EU
Sec. M. Moller *Tel* 020 8202 9183; *Rabbi* Rabbi P. Roberts

Hendon Beth Hamedrash
3 The Approach, London NW4 2HU
Tel 020 8202 5499
Rabbi D. Halpern; *Delegate*, J. Gertner

Kehal Chareidim Beth Hamedrash
99 Clapton Common, E5 9AB
Rabbi A. Y. Rubinfeld; *Delegates*, S. B. Gluck, D. Margulies

Kehal Chasidim D'Munkatch
85 Cazenove Road, N16 6BB
Delegate, C. L. Lipschitz

Kehal Chassidim Beth Hamedrash
213 Golders Green Road, NW11 9BY
Tel 020 8731 9583
Rabbi Y. E. Brief; *Delegate*, D. Ost

Kehillas Ohel Moshe
102 Leeside Crescent, NW11 0JN
Tel 020 8800 3868
Rabbi Dovid Stern; *Delegate*, M. Berger

Kingsley Way Beth Hamedrash
3-5 Kingsley Way, N2 0EH
Tel 020 8458 2312
Rabbi Y. M. Hertz; *Delegate*, F. Hager

Knesset Yehezkel Beth Hamedrash
187 Golders Green Road, NW11 9BY
Tel 020 8455 4722/3591
Rabbi A. Bassous *Burial Society Affiliate*

Knightland Road Synagogue
50 Knightland Road, E5 9HS
Tel 020 8802 7684 (Office)
Rabbi M. Halpern; *Delegate*, Y. Taub

Kol Ya'akov Beth Hamedrash
47 Mowbray Road, Edgware, Middlesex HA8 8JL
Tel 020 8905 3853
Rabbi S. Joseph

Lieger Beth Hamedrash Torath Chaim
37 Craven Walk, N16 6BS
Tel 020 8800 3868
Rabbi J. Meisels; *Delegate*, A. Reifer

Lieger Beth Hamedrash Torath Chaim
145 Upper Clapton Road, E5 9DB

Tel 020 8806 8405
Rabbi M. Meisels
Lubavitch Synagogue
107-115 Stamford Hill, N16 5RP
Tel 020 8800 0022
Rabbi N. Sudak, Dayan L. Y. Raskin; *Delegates*, B. Hackner, S. Herzog
Lubavitch Synagogue of Edgware
230 Hale Lane, Edgware, Middlesex HA8 9PZ
Tel 020 8905 4141
Rabbi L. Y. Sudak; *Delegate*, T. Brooks
Machzikei Hadass Edgware Beth Hamedrash
296 Hale Lane, Edgware, Middlesex HA8 8NP
Tel 020 8958 1030
Rabbi E. Schneelbalg; *Delegates*, B. Gordon, H. L. Sacks
Mesifta Synagogue
82-84 Cazenove Road, N16 6AB
Tel 020 8806 1775
Delegate, P. Ostreicher
Nachlei Emunah Chasidey Kretchnif
122 Cazenove Road, N16 6AH (Rav Tov)
Rabbi L. Kahane; *Delegate*, M. B. Kraus
Nadvorna Beth Hamedrash
45 Darenth Road, N16 6ES
Tel 020 8806 3903 *Fax* 020 8806 9590
Rabbi M. Leifer; *Delegate*, M. Z. Landau
North Hendon Adath Yisroel Synagogue
Holders Hill Road, NW4 1NA
Tel 020 8203 2390
Rabbi D. Cohn; *Delegate*, A. H. Ehreich
Ohel Israel (Skolyer) Beth Haedrash
11 Brent Street, NW4 2EU
Rabbi Y. Royde; *Delegate*, K. Kessleman, M. Meyer
Ohel Yaakov Beiss Hamedrash (Pshevorsk)
26 Lampard Grove, N16 6XB
Rabbi N. E. Leiser; *Delegate*, S. Z. Berger
Sasover Finchley Road Synagogue
1 Helenslea Avenue, NW11 8ND
Tel 020 8455 4305
Rabbi S. Y. Freshwater; *Delegates*, B. Freshwater, N. Rokach
SATMAR - KEHAL YETEV LEV
Rabbi M. Pollack, Rabbi E. M. Stolzberg, Rabbi H. Schneck
Beth Hamedrash Kehal Yetev Lev
86 Cazenove Road, N16 6AB
Tel 020 8806 2633
Delegates, B. Berger, Y. Z. Gross, S. Laufer, Sh. Seidenfeld
Beis Hamedrash Kehal Yetev Lev
42 Craven Walk, N16 6BU
Tel 020 8806 2932
Delegates, C. Y. Gluck, B. Kisch
Beis Hamedrash D'Chasidei Satmar
57 Bethune Road, N16 5EE
Delegates, A. Grunhut, S. Matyas
Beis Hamedrash Tehillois Yoel
148 Upper Clapton Road, E5 9JZ
Delegate, Y. Reiner

SATMAR - KEHAL YETEV LEV
Beth Hamedrash Kehal Yetev Lev
26 Clapton Common, E5 9BA
Tel 020 8880 8930
Dayan S. Low, Dayan Ch. Inzlicht
Beis Hamedrash V'Yoel Moshe
(67 Heathland Road) 91 Amhurst Park, N16 5DL
Tel 020 8809 0446
Harav S. B. Krausz; Dayan M. Markovits
Sdei Chemed D'Nitra Beth Hamedrash
113 Clapton Common, E5
Tel 020 8806 4828
Rabbi L. Braun; *Delegate*, L. Weiss
Spinke Beth Hamedrash
36 Bergholt Crescent, N16 6JE
Tel 020 8809 6903
Rabbi M. M. Kahana; *Delegate*, Y. Tunk
Stamford Hill Beth Hamedrash
50 Clapham Common, E5 9AL
Tel 020 806 8070
Dayan D. Grynhaus; *Delegate*, M. Chontow
Stanislowa Beth Hamedrash
93 Lordship Park, N16 5UP
Tel 020 8800 2040
Rabbi E. Aschkenazi; *Delegate*, M. Spiegel
Stolin Karlin
4 Castlewood Road, N16 6DW
Tel 020 8809 7454
Delegate, Y. Dreyfus
Tiferes Amrom Beth Hamedrash
3 Northdene Gardens, N15 6LX
Rabbi A. Jungreis; *Delegate*, B. Stroh
Torah Etz Chayim Beth Hamedrash
69 Lordship Road, N16 0QX
Tel 020 8800 7726
Rabbi Z. Feldman; *Delegates*, I. Hoffman, R. Spitzer
Yeshivas Ahavas Torah
10-18 Craven Park Road, N15 6AB
Tel 020 8809 5884
Rabbi B. Weisz; *Delegate*, M. Block
Yeshivas Horomoh Beth Hamedrash
100 Fairholt Road, N16 5HN
Tel 020 8800 6778
Rabbi E. Schlesinger; *Delegate*, S. Singer
Yeshivas Ohr Torah
Wellbury House, Great Offley, near Hitchin, Herts
Tel 01462 768 698 & 768 925
Rabbi Y. M. Stern; *Delegate*, B. Z. Weissman
Yeshivas Toras Chesed
118 Cazenove Road, London N16
Tel 020 8880 8026
Rabbi C. Y. Babad; *Delegate*, Y. Kornbluh
Yeshuath Chaim Synagogue
45 Heathland Road, N16 5PQ
Tel 020 8800 2332
Rabbi C. Pinter; *Delegates*, Rabbi A. Pinter, A. Rand

Yesodey Hatorah Beth Hamedrash
2-4 Amhurst Park, N16 5AE
Delegate, J. Teller
Zeire Agudath Yisroel Beth Hamedrash
69 Lordship Road, N16 0QX
Delegate, Ch. Kesselman
Zeire Agudath Yisroel Beth Hamedrash
95 Stamford Hill, N16 5DN
Rabbi M. J. Kamionka; *Delegates*, S. C. Grussgott, S. Just
ADATH YISROEL CHEVRA KADISHA
Adath Yisroel Synagogue, 40 Queen Elizabeth's Walk, London N16 0HH
Tel 020 8802 6262; Mobile 07973 622 350 *Fax* 020 8800 8764
Gabbai. K. Berkovits; *V. Gabbai* M. M. Brief; *Ch.* E. M. Hochhauser, *T.* S.B. Stern; L Wosner,
Hon. S. D. Lobenstein; *Cttee.* N. Berkovitz, A. Gluck, S. Grosz, C. L. Lieber, S. Sinitsky
GOLDERS GREEN BETH HAMEDRASH CHEVRA KADISHA
Tel 020 8455 5918

Masorti Judaism

For contact details: *See under* Religious Organisations.

Buckhurst Hill Masorti Synagogue
The Woollard Centre, Loughton Way, Buckhurst Hill, Essex IG9 4AB
Tel 07922 090 180
Email office@bhmasorti.org.uk *Website* www.bhmasorti.org.uk
Edgware Masorti Synagogue
Synagogue Office/Post/Weekly entrance: Pearl Community Centre, Stream Lane, Edgware
HA8 7YA
Shabbat entrance: Bakery Path (off Station Road), Edgware HA8 7YE
Tel 020 8905 4096
Email admin@masorti.org.uk
(Reg. Charity No. 1117623). *M.* Rabbi Dr Jeremy Collick; *Co-Ch.* J. Mitchell, M. Schraer;
T. S. Maisel; *Admin.* L. Lassman
Elstree & Borehamwood Masorti Community
Borehamwood & Elstree Childrens Centre (BECC), Shakespeare Drive, Borehamwood,
Herts WD6 2FD
Tel 07843 792 133
Email info@ebmc.org.uk *Website* www.ebmc.org.uk
Hatch End Masorti Synagogue
PO Box 326, Pinner, HA5 5UX
Tel 020 8866 0320
Email office@hems.org.uk *Website* www.hems.org.uk
Co-Ch. A. Goldner, P. Austin; *Admin.* K. Grout
Kol Nefesh Masorti Synagogue
Jewish Care, Rectory Lane, Edgware, Middlesex HA8 7LF
Enq. *Tel* 07768 117 145
Email convenor@kolnefesh.org.uk *Website* www.kolnefeshmasorti.org.uk
(Reg. Charity No. 1081444). *Co-ord.* James Burns; *M.* Rabbi Joel Levy
New London Synagogue
33 Abbey Road, NW8 0AT
Tel 020 7328 1026 *Fax* 020 7372 3142
Email office@newlondon.org.uk *Website* www.newlondon.org.uk
New North London Synagogue
80 East End Road, N3 2SY
Tel 020 8346 8560
Email office@nnls-masorti.org.uk *Website* www.nnls-masorti.org.uk

(Est. 1974). *M.* Rabbi J. Wittenberg; *Co-Ch.* D. Raff, T. Isaacs; *T.* S. Adler; *Off.* C. Mandel; *Com. Co-ord.* R. Gottlieb

New Stoke Newington Shul
Website www.newstokenewingtonshul.org
New Stoke Newington Shul (NSNS) is a growing Masorti community serving Stoke Newington and the wider Hackney area as well as Highbury, Islington, Shoreditch, Hoxton, Tower Hamlets, Haringey and beyond. We welcome newcomers of all generations, afflictions or levels of knowledge. *Contact* Paul Craven *Email* pcraven@pcraven.net

St Albans Masorti Synagogue
Unit 9, The Dencora Centre, Campfield Road, St Albans, Herts AL1 5HN
Email info@e-sams.org *Website* www.e-sams.org
Tel 01727 860 642

Sephardi

For contact details: *See under* Religious Organisations

SYNAGOGUES
Bevis Marks
EC3A 5DQ
Tel 020 7626 1274
Website www.bevismarks.org.uk
(Est. 1701).

Lauderdale Road Synagogue
Maida Vale, W9 1JY
Tel 020 7289 2573 *Fax* 020 7289 2709
Website www.lauderdaleroadsynagogue.org
(Est.1896). Daily services held. *Rabbi* Rabbi I. Elia

Wembley Spanish and Portuguese Synagogue
46 Forty Avenue, Wembley, Middlesex HA9 8LQ
Tel 020 7289 2573
Email secretary@wsps.org.uk *Website* www.wsps.org.uk
M. Rev. J. Houri

OTHER INSTITUTIONS
Welfare Board
2 Ashworth Road, W9 1JY
Tel 020 7432 1305
(Est. 1837)

Sephardi Kashrut Authority
2 Ashworth Road, W9 1JY
Tel 020 7432 1321
Ch. E. Cohen; *Dir.* D. Steinhof

Communal Centre
Montefiore Hall, 2 Ashworth Road, W9 1JY
Tel 020 7289 2573

Beth Hamedrash Heshaim
2 Ashworth Road, W9 1JY
Tel 020 7289 2573
(Instituted 1664). *T.* Dr. J. Schonfield

Montefiore Endowment (incorporating the **Judith Lady Montefiore College Trust**)
2 Ashworth Road, W9 1JY
Tel 020 7289 2573
Established by Sir Moses Montefiore in 1866. The purpose of the Endowment (reviewed by the Charity Commission in 1989) 'is the maintenance of the Synagogue, the Mausoleum and the Jewish Cemetery in Ramsgate'. Also 'the promotion of the advanced study of the Holy Law as revealed on Sinai and expounded by the revered sages of the Mishna and

Talmud' through its own Semicha programme and by making grants to charitable institutions and Rabbis and by awarding scholarships to trainees.

The Mausoleum, with the remains of Sir Moses and Lady Montefiore is situated next to the Synagogue in Ramsgate (*See* Regions). Sir Moses's seats in Bevis Marks and Ramsgate Synagogues are still preserved.

Edinburgh House (Beth Holim)
36/44 Forty Avenue, Wembley
Tel 020 8908 4151
Email enquiries@edinburghhouse.org.uk
(Est. 1747). Home for the Aged. *Hd. of Home* Paula Peake

Independent Sephardi Synagogues

Aden Jews' Congregation
117 Clapton Common, E5
Hon. S. B. Jacobs *Tel* 020 8806 1320

David Ishag Synagogue
Neveh Shalom Community, 352-4 Preston Road, Harrow, Middlesex HA3 0QJ
Hon. S. E. Myers *Tel* 020 8346 8744, M. Rose *Tel* 020 8907 0572

Heichal Leah
62 Brent Street, NW4 2ES
Tel 07966 258 160 (Gabbai-Haim Kohali)
Rabbi, Rabbi Assaf Portal

Jacob Benjamin Elias Synagogue
140 Stamford Hill, N16 6QT
(Reg. Charity No. 291531). *M.* Rabbi C. Tangy; *Hon. S.* E. Solomon

Levy Kelaty Synagogue OD Yosef Hai
50 Finchley Lane, NW4 1DJ
Dayan A. David *Tel* 020 8202 8374/020 8203 5701
Nancy Reuben Banqueting Suite Moshe King *Tel* 07969 959 933

Ohel David Eastern Synagogue
4-14 Broadwalk Lane, Golders Green Road, NW11 8HD
Tel 020 8455 3491, 07989 387 881
Email info@oheldavid.org *Website* www.oheldavid.org
(Reg. Charity No. 243901). Services held Monday and Thursday 6.30am, 6.45am; during week, Mincha and Arbit 7.30pm. *M.* Rabbi Asher Seebag

Persian Hebrew Congregation
5a East Bank, Stoke Newington, N16 5RX
Tel 020 8802 7339

Spanish & Portuguese Synagogue, Holland Park
8 St James's Gardens, W11 4RB
Tel 020 7603 7961/3232 *Fax* 020 7603 9471
Email admin@hollandparksynagogue.com *Website* www.hollandparksynagogue.com
(Est. 1928 under Deed of Association with Spanish and Portuguese Jews' Congregation. Reg. Charity No. 248945). Services are held Shabbat and Yamim Tovim. *M. Rabbi* Avraham Lavi

Reform

(Constituents of the Movement for Reform Judaism)
For contact details: *See under* Religious Organisations

West London Synagogue of British Jews
34 Upper Berkeley Street, W1; Office: 33 Seymour Place, W1H 5AU
Tel 020 7723 4404 *Fax* 020 7224 8258
Email admin@wls.org.uk

(Reg. Charity No. 212143). The congregation was organised April 15, 1840, to establish a synagogue 'where a revised service may be performed at hours more suited to our habits and in a manner more calculated to inspire feelings of devotion, where religious instruction may be afforded by competent persons, and where, to effect these purposes, Jews generally may form a united congregation under the denomination of British Jews.'

Snr. Rabbi Rabbi Julia Neuberger; *Principal Rabbi* Rabbi Helen Freeman; *Rabbis*, Rabbi David Mitchell and Rabbi Benjamin Stanley; *Ch.* Mark Fox, Alexander Landau; *Exec. Dir.* Simon Myers

Funerals: Tel 020 7723 4404 *Fax* 020 7224 8258

Cemeteries:

Golders Green, Hoop Lane, NW11 7EU *Tel* 020 8455 2569 *Email* linda@ejbb-jbc.org.uk

Edgwarebury, Edgwarebury Lane, Edgware, Middlesex HA8 8QP *Tel* 020 8958 0090 *Email* irene@ejbb-jbc.org.uk

Bromley Reform Synagogue
28 Highland Road, Bromley, Kent BR1 4AD

Tel 020 8460 5460

M. Rabbi Jason Holtz; *Admin.* J. Burlem *Email* janet@bromleyshul.org.uk

Edgware and District Reform Synagogue
118 Stonegrove, Edgware, HA8 8AB

Tel 020 8238 1000

Email admin@edrs.org.uk *Website* www.edrs.org.uk

(Est. 1934. Reg. Charity No. 1038116). Shabbat services Friday 6.30pm and Sundays 10.30am. Regular Children's/Youth Services, Nagila Nursery School, regular Youth Clubs and holiday play schemes, children's and adult education. Halls available for hire. *M.* Rabbi A.D. Smith, MA; *Assoc. M.* Rabbi N. S. Kraft, MA; *Exec. Dir.* J.A. Clements; *Admin.* K. B. Senitt

Finchley Reform Synagogue
101 Fallow Court Avenue, North Finchley, N12 0BE

Tel 020 8446 3244 *Fax* 020 8446 5980

Email frs@frsonline.org

Princ. Rabbi Miriam Berger; *Cantor* Zöe Jacobs; *Rabbi* Howard Cooper; *Emer. Rabbi* Jeffrey Newman; *Office.* Annie Simmons

Harlow Jewish Community
Harberts Road, Hare Street, Harlow, Essex CM19 4DT

Tel 01279 432503; 01279 792926

Email admin@harlowjewishcommunity.org.uk *Website* www.harlowjewishcommunity.org.uk

M. Rabbi Irit Shillor; *Sec.* Scott Pollack

Hendon Reform Synagogue
Danescroft Avenue, NW4 2NA

Tel 020 8203 4168 *Fax* 020 8203 9385

Email office@hendonreform.org.uk *Website* www.hendonreform.org.uk

(Est. 1949). *Snr. M.* Rabbi Steven Katz; *Admin.* R. Bloom

Cemeteries: Edgwarebury Lane, New Southgate Cemetery, Brunswick Park Road, N11 *Tel* 020 8203 4168

Kol Chai-Hatch End Jewish Community
434 Uxbridge Road, Hatch End, Middlesex HA5 4RG

Tel 020 8421 5482

Email admin@kolchai.org *Website* www.kolchai.org

(Reg. Charity No. 299063). Services held weekly Friday night 7pm, Shabbat morning 10.30am. *M.* Rabbi Dr. M. Hilton; *Admin.* D. Levy

Middlesex New Synagogue
39 Bessborough Road, Harrow, HA1 3BS

Tel 020 8864 0133

Email admin@mns.org.uk

(Est. 1959). *M.* Rabbi K. de Magtige-Middleton; *Sec.* A. Simon

North West Surrey Synagogue
Horvath Close, Rosslyn Park, Oatlands Drive, Weybridge, Surrey KT13 9QZ
Tel/Fax 01932 855400
Email admin@nwss.org.uk *Website* www.nwss.org.uk
(Est. 1956. Reg Charity No. 256232). *M.* Rabbi Jacqueline Tabick; *Hon. S. S.* Barnett; *Admin. L.* Bateman

North Western Reform Synagogue
Alyth Gardens, Finchley Road, NW11 7EN
Tel 020 8455 6763 *Fax* 020 8731 8175
Email mail@alyth.org.uk *Website* www.alyth.org.uk
(Est. 1933; Reg. Charity No. 247081). Regular services held Friday 6.30pm, Saturday 10.30am and daily. *M.* Rabbi M. Goldsmith, Rabbi J. Levy

Radlett & Bushey Reform Synagogue
118 Watling Street, Herts. WD7 7AA
Tel 01923 856 110
Email office@rbrs.org.uk *Website* www.rbrs.org.uk
Rabbis, Rabbi Paul Freedman, Rabbi Celia Surget; *Synagogue Man.* Madeleine Turner

Sha'arei Tsedek: North London Reform Synagogue
120 Oakleigh Road North, Whetstone N20 9EZ
Tel 020 8445 3400
Email info@shaarei-tsedek.org.uk *Website* www.shaarei-tsedek.org.uk
(Reg. Charity No. 1076670). *Snr. Min.* C. Eimer; *Synagogue Man.* Perry Newton; *Rabbis*, James Baaden, Judith Levitt; *Admin.* Antonia Reed.
    Alonim Kindergarten *Tel* 020 3115 1610 *Email* info@alonim.co.uk

Shir Hayim (Hampstead Reform Jewish Community)
37a, Broadhurst Gardens, NW6 3QT
Email mail@shirhayim.org.uk
M. Rabbi L. Tabick; *Contact* M. Teper *Tel* 020 7794 8488

South West Essex and Settlement Reform Synagogue
Oaks Lane, Newbury Park, Essex IG2 7PL
Tel 020 8599 0936
Email admin@swesrs.org.uk *Website* www.swers.org.uk
(Est. 1956. Reg. Charity No. 236663). *Emer.* Rabbi H. Goldstein; M.A. Michaels, *M.* Rabbi Nancy Morris; *Off.* Cheryll Gardiner

Sukkat Shalom Reform Synagogue
1 Victory Road, Hermon Hill, Wanstead, E11 1UL
Tel 020 8530 3345
Email admin@sukkatshalom.me.uk *Website* www.sukkatshalom.org.uk
(Reg. Charity No. 283615). *Rabbi*, Rabbi Larry Becker; *Admin.* Fiona Godson

Wimbledon and District Synagogue
1 Queensmere Road, Wimbledon Parkside, SW19 5QD
Tel 020 8946 4836 *Fax* 020 8944 7790
Email office@wimshul.org *Website* www.wimshul.org
(Est. 1949. Reg. Charity No. 1150678). *M.* Rabbi Sylvia Rothschild, Rabbi Sybil Sheridan; *Admin.* Ms J. Penn

Liberal Judaism

For contact details: *See under* Religious Organisations

Beit Klal Yisrael
c/o The Montagu Centre, 21 Maple Street, London W1T 4BE
Tel 07505 477459
Website www.bky.org.uk
Rabbi, Rabbi Judith Rosen-Berry; *Email* bkymail@gmail.com

Bet Tikvah Synagogue (Barkingside)
129 Perrymans Farm Road, Ilford, Essex IG2 7LX
Tel 020 8554 9682 office hours Tuesday and Wednesday 10am-4pm, Thursday 10am-3pm, Sunday 10am-12pm
Email bettikvah@talktalkbusiness.net *Blog* http://bettikvah.blogspot.com
(Reg. Charity No. 283547). Services held every Friday night and Shabbat morning and on the evening and first morning of every festival. Phone Shul office for times. Bet Tikvah welcome non-members to all High Holy Day Services. Please contact the synagogue office. *M.* Rabbi D. Hulbert; *Admin.* Anne Fishman

Ealing Liberal Synagogue
Lynton Avenue, Drayton Green, Ealing, W13 0EB
Tel 020 8997 0528
Email office@ealingliberalsynagogue.org.uk *Website* www.ealingliberalsynagogue.org.uk
(Est. 1943. Reg. Charity No. 1037099). *M.* Rabbi J. Burden; *Admin.* D. Martin

Finchley Progressive Synagogue
54 Hutton Grove, N12 8DR
Tel 020 8446 4063
Email administrator@fps.org *Website* www.finchleyprogressivesynagogue.org
(Est. 1953. Reg. Charity No. 1071040). *M.* Rabbi R. Qassim Birk

Harrow & Wembley Progressive Synagogue
39 Bessborough Road, Harrow, HA1 3BS
Tel 020 8864 5323
Email info@hwps.org *Website* www.hwps.org
(Est. 1947. Reg. Charity No. 251172). *M.* Rabbi Frank Dabba Smith; *Admin.* A. Simon

Kehillah North London (formerly **North London Progressive Jewish Community**)
Postal Add. Office 8, 10 Buckhurst Road, Bexhill on Sea TN40 1QF
Tel 020 7403 3779
Email nlpjc@liberaljudaism.org *Website* www.nlpjc.org.uk
(Est. 2002). Services held first and third Saturday of each month and fourth Friday evening. *M.* Rabbi Shulamit Ambalu *Admin.* Melanie Young

Kingston Liberal Synagogue
Rushett Road, Long Ditton, Surrey, KT7 0UX
Tel 020 8398 7400
Email office@klsonline.org *Website* www.klsonline.org
(Reg. Charity No. 270792). *M.* Rabbi C. Baginsky; *Ch.* Mr. Barnato; *Admin.* M. McHale

The Liberal Jewish Synagogue
28 St. John's Wood Road, London, NW8 7HA
Tel 020 7286 5181 *Fax* 020 7266 3591
Email ljs@ljs.org *Website* www.ljs.org
(Reg. Charity No. 235668). Established 1910 by the Jewish Religious Union, the LJS, as it is known, was the first Liberal synagogue in the UK. Synagogue rebuilt 1991. *Ch.* M. Hart; *Rabbi Emer.* Rabbi D.J. Goldberg OBE; *Snr. Rabbi* Rabbi A. Wright; *M.* Rabbi N. Janes; *Dir.* C. A. Bach

The Liberal Synagogue Elstree (formerly **Hertsmere Progressive**)
Elstree High Street, Elstree, Herts WD6 3EY
Tel 020 8953 8889
Email office@tlse.org.uk *Website* www.tlse.org.uk
M. Rabbi P. Tobias; *Hon. S.* R. Elman; *Man.* R. Davey

Northwood and Pinner Liberal Synagogue
Oaklands Gate, Green Lane, Northwood, Middlesex HA6 3AA
Tel 01923 822 592
Email admin@npls.org.uk *Website* www.npls.org.uk
(Est. 1964. Reg. Charity No. 243618). Services held Erev Shabbat, Shabbat and Yom Tovim. *M. Emer.* Rabbi Dr. A. Goldstein; *Snr. Rabbi* A. Goldstein; *Rabbi,* Rabbi L. Mühlstein; *Hon. S.* S. Frais

South London Liberal Synagogue
P.O. Box 14475, 1 Prentis Road, Streatham, SW16 1ZW
Tel 020 8769 4787 (admin. office: Tuesday and Friday 11am-4.30pm) *Fax* 020 8664 6439
Email office@southlondon.org *Website* www.southlondon.org
(Est. 1929. Reg. Charity No. 2367711). Services: Friday evening Kabbalat Shabbat 7.30pm
(6.30pm on the first Friday of the month); first and third Fridays are bring and share
Chavurah suppers; Shabbat morning service 11am; Religion school is on Shabbat morn-
ing at 9.45am, toddlers group to Kabbalat Torah class. *Rabbi* Janet Darley

Southgate Progressive Synagogue
75 Chase Road, N14 4QY
Tel 020 8886 0977
Email sps@liberaljudaism.org *Website* www.sps.uk.com
(Est. 1943. Reg. Charity No. 239096). *Sec.* B. Martin

West Central Liberal Synagogue
The Montagu Centre, 21 Maple Street, W1T 4BE
Tel 020 7636 7627 *Fax* 020 7631 9838
Email wcls@liberaljudaism.org *Website* www.wcls.org.uk
(Congregation Est. 1928; present synagogue opened 1954). Services held every Saturday
3pm, programmes for families at intervals throughout the year, Kabbalat Shabbat on some
Friday nights. Please check website for details. *M.* Rabbi Janet Burden; *Cantor* Rev. A.
Harman ALCM; *Ch.* Dr Julia Wendon; *Hon. S.* Dr. Peter Philips

Woodford Liberal Synagogue
Marlborough Road, South Woodford, E18 1AR
Tel 020 8989 7619
Email info@woodfordliberal.org.uk *Website* www.woodfordliberal.org.uk
(Est. 1960. Reg. Charity No. 232980). Weekly Shabbat and Erev services held. *M.* Rabbi
R. Jacobi; *Ch.* B. Kamall; *Hon. S.* S. Muscovitch; *Hon. T.* M. Millenbach, J. Rabin

Independent Congregations

Belsize Square Synagogue
51 Belsize Square, London NW3 4HX
Tel 020 7794 3949 *Fax* 020 7431 4559
Email office@synagogue.org.uk *Website* www.synagogue.org.uk
(Est. 1939. Reg. Charity No. 1144866). An Independent Synagogue combining traditional
forms of worship with progressive ideals. *M.* Rabbi Dr. Stuart Altshuler; *Admin.* Lee Taylor;
Co-Ch. Suzanne Goldstein, John Abramson; *Hon. S.* V. Pollins; *T.* Steve Abbott

Edgware Adath Yisroel Congregation
265 Hale Lane, Edgware, Middlesex HA8 8NW
Tel 020 8238 2491
Email admin@eayc.org *Website* www.eayc.org
Rabbi Z. H. Lieberman *Burial Society Affiliate*

Ner Yisrael
The Crest (off Brent Street), Hendon, NW4 2HY
Tel 020 8202 6687 *Fax* 020 8203 5158
Email louise@neryisrael.co.uk *Website* www.neryisrael.co.uk
Services held three times a day. *M.* Rabbi A.A. Kimche. *Tel* 020 8202 6687; *Admin.* L. Brayam

Porat Yosef Synagogue and Community Centre
3 Bell Lane, London, NW4 2BP
Tel 020 8202 6058
Email info@poratyosef.com *Website* www.poratyosef.com
(Est. 1988). Moroccan Hebrew Congregation. *Pres.* Jacques Onona; *Sec.* B. Benarroch

Saatchi Synagogue
37-41 Grove End Road, NW8 9NG
Tel 020 7289 2367
Email hayley@saatchishul.org *Website* www.saatchishul.org
(Est. 1998. Reg. Charity No. 289066). Rabbi Mendel Cohen; *Admin.* H. Bartman

Sandys Row Synagogue, Spitalfields
4a Sandy's Row, E1 7HW
Tel 0207 377 6196
Email info@sandysrow.org.uk *Website* www.sandysrow.org.uk
(Est. 1854). Services: Mincha Monday-Thursday 1.30pm; Shabbat every two weeks. See website for details. *Pres.* H. Rifkind; *T.* H. Freedman FCA; *Admin* E. Granger; *Warden* H. Gilbert

Sarah Klausner Synagogue
10A Canfield Gardens NW6
Tel 020 7722 6146

Synagogue Française de Londres (La)
101 Dunsmure Road, N16 5HT; Le Grand Rabbin Henri Brand, 54 Bethune Road, N16 5BD
Tel 020 8800 8612
Hon. T. Rabbi C. Pinter; *Hon. S.* I. Kraus

Walford Road Synagogue
99 Walford Road, Stoke Newington, N16 8EF
Tel 020 7249 1599
(Reg. Charity No. 1101200). Rabbi Avraham Citron; *Sec.* S. Raymond

Waltham Forest Hebrew Congregation
140 Boundary Road, E17 8LA
Tel Office 020 8509 0775 *Fax* 020 8518 8200
Email secretary@wfhc.co.uk
(Est. 1902). *M.* Revd. S. Myers; *Pres.* Mark Phillips; *Admin.* B. Rose

West End Great Synagogue (formerly in Dean Street, now in Great Cumberland Place)
32 Great Cumberland Place, W1H 7TN
Tel 020 7724 8121 *Fax* 020 7723 4413
Email wegs@clara.co.uk
(Est. 1880). *M.* Ari Cohen; *Admin.* N. Singer

Westminster Synagogue
Rutland Gardens, Knightsbridge, SW7 1BX
Tel 020 7584 3953 *Fax* 020 7581 8012
Email secretary@westminstersynagogue.org *Website* wwwwestminstersynagogue.org
(Est. 1957). *M.* Rabbi T. Salamon; *Hd. Education*, N. Young; *Pres.* H.D. Leigh; *Ch.* L. Derriey

Religious Organisations

The London Eruvim

The North West London Eruv Committee was inaugurated in February 2003. The area covered by the eruv includes virtually all of NW4 and NW11, most of N2 and N3; and small parts of NW2, NW3 and NW7. This Eruv is under the supervision of the Dayanim of the London Beth Din. *Contact*: North West London Eruv Committee, 84 Edgeworth Close, NW4 4HN
Tel 020 8202 ERUV/020 8202 3788 (recorded message with Eruv status)
Email info@nwlondoneruv.org *Website* www.nwlondoneruv.org *Twitter* @nwlondoneruv
The **Edgware Eruv** was inaugurated in 2006. The area covered by the eruv includes parts of HA8 and NW7. This eruv is under the supervision of Rabbi Zvi Lieberman of the Edgware Adath Yisroel Congregation and has the support and approval of the London Beth Din.
Contact: Edgware Eruv Committee, P.O. Box 594, Edgware, Middlesex HA8 4EE
Website www.edgwareeruv.org
(Reg. Charity No. 1111850). Both websites offer detailed maps of their jurisidictions. The Eruvim are inspected every week to check they are intact. This can be ascertained by visiting the respective websites after 12 noon on Friday. Observers of the Eruvim are invited to subscribe to the respective services maintained.

London Board for Shechita

Elscot House, Arcadia Ave, London N3 2JU
Tel 020 8349 9160 *Fax* 020 8346 2209
Email info@shechita.co.uk *Website* www.shechita.org
(Est. 1804. Reg. Charity No. 233467). Administer the affairs of Shechita in London,

having an elected membership from the United Synagogue, the Federation of Synagogues and the Spanish and Portuguese Jews' Congregation. *Rabbinical Authority*, Dayan Y.Y. Lichtenstein, Dayan M. Gelley, Dayan S. Amor; *Tru.*, *Pres.* Elliot Renton, *V. Pres.* Isaac S. Levy, Benjamin Mire, *Hon. T.* Leo Winter FCA; *Exec. Dir.* David J. Rose

Sabbath Observance Employment Bureau
Unit 2, 107 Gloucester Place, London W1U 6BY
Tel 020 7224 3433
(Est. 1909. Reg. Charity No. 209451). To obtain employment for those who want to observe the Sabbath and Holy-days. *Tr* I. M. Katz, S.D. Winegarten; *Man.* E. Statham; *Ch.* D. Winter, FCA

United Synagogue Women
c/o United Synagogue, 305 Ballards Lane, London N12 8GB
Tel 020 8343 8989 *Fax* 020 8343 6236
Email uswomen@theus.org.uk *Website* www.youandus.theus.org.uk
(Est. 1968). US Women is the representative organisation for women members of the United Synagogue. It liaises directly with the United Synagogue Trustees in all matters relating to women in the United Synagogue. It promotes, facilitates and communicates the interests and full involvement of women as an integral part of the United Synagogue, and at local United Synagogue/community level. It has representation on other Jewish organisational bodies. *Pres.* Lady Elaine Sacks; *Co-Ch.* Dalia Cramer, Leonie Lewis

Ritual Baths (Mikvaot)

Central Mikvaot Board
See under Religious Organisations

Borehamwood & Elstree Mikveh
Croxdale Road, Borehamwood, WD6 4QF
Tel 07504 927 066; 020 8387 1945
Email mikveh@borehamwoodshul.org *Website* www.borehamwoodshul.org

Edgware & District Communal Mikveh
Edgware United Synagogue, Edgware Way, Edgware, Middlesex
Tel 020 8958 3233 *Fax* 020 8958 4004
Email mikveh@estrin.co.uk
(Reg. Charity No. 281586). Enquiries: Mandy Estrin *Tel* 020 8958 4488, 0780 133 2508

Ilford Mikveh
463 Cranbrook Road, Ilford, IG2 6EW
Appointments and correspondence 367 Cranbrook Road, Ilford, IG1 4UQ *Tel* 020 8554 8532

Kingsbury Mikveh *See* United Synagogue Mikveh

Friends of the Kingsbury Mikveh – Educational and Support Group
Kingsbury United Synagogue, Hool Close, NW9 8UG
Tel 020 8204 6390 *Enquiries* 07890 932 340 (daytime only)
(Reg. Charity No. 1041629). *Hon. T.* Helene Leigh, 474 Kenton Road, Kenton, Middlesex HA3 9DN *Tel* 020 8206 1512

Mikveh of the Movement for Reform Judaism
Sternberg Centre, 80 East End Road, N3 2SY
Appointments essential. *Tel* 020 8349 5645

New Central London Mikveh
21 Andover Place, NW6 5ED
Appointments *Tel* 07870 696 570, 07989 858 615

North London Mikveh
adjoining 40 Queen Elizabeth's Walk, N16 (entrance Grazebrook Road)
Tel 020 8802 2554 *Fax* 020 8800 8764
Hon. S. M. Mannes

North West London Communal Mikvah
40 Golders Green Crescent, NW11 8LD

Tel 020 8457 5900, 020 8731 9494
10a Shirehall Lane, Hendon, NW4
Tel 020 8202 1427 (only open Friday nights and Yom Tov, by appointment)
Satmar Mikveh
62 Filey Avenue, N16
Tel 020 8806 3961
South London Mikveh
42 St. George's Road, Wimbledon SW19 4ED
Tel 07985 757 517
Email s@dubov.org
(Reg. Charity No. 1009208). By appointment only. *Hon. S. L. Cohen. Contact:* S. Dubov
Stamford Hill Mikveh
26 Lampard Grove, N16 (entrance in Margaret Road)
Tel 020 8806 3880
United Synagogue Mikveh
Kingsbury United Synagogue, Hool Close, NW9 8UG
Tel 020 8204 6390
Ch. F. Frank; *General Enq. Tel* 07890 932 340 (*See also* Friends Group, p.155)

Cemeteries

US = United Synagogue. F = Federation of Synagogues. UO = Union of Orthodox Hebrew Congregations. SP = Spanish and Portuguese Synagogue. W = Western Marble Arch Synagogue. WG = West End Great Synagogue. R = Reform. L = Liberal.

Alderney Road Cemetery (historic). Alderney Road, E1
Tel 020 8790 1445 Opened 1696–1853. Opening hours by appointment only (US)
Brady Street Cemetery (historic). Brady Street, E1
Opened 1761–1858. Opening hours by appointment only. (US)
Bullscross Ride Cemetery (current). Bulls Cross Ride, Cheshunt, Herts
Tel 01992 717820 Opened 1968. Opening hours 8am–4pm (W, L and WG)
Bushey Cemetery (current). Little Bushey Lane, Bushey, Herts
Tel 020 8950 6299. Opened 1947. Opening hours 8am–5pm (US)
East Ham Cemetery (reserves only). Marlow Road, E6 3QG
Tel 020 8471 2822 Opened 1919. Opening hours 9am–4.30pm (US)
Edgwarebury Lane Cemetery (current). Edgwarebury Lane, Edgware, HA8 8QP
Opened 1973. *Cemetery Dir.* Paul Van der Hulks 020 8958 0090/07967 656 733 *Email* director@ejbb-jbc.org.uk(SP, R, L, Independent (Belsize Square))
Edmonton Cemetery (current) Montagu Road, Edmonton, N18 2NF
Tel 020 8807 2268. Opened 1889. Opening hours 9am–3.30pm (F)
Enfield Cemetery (current), Carterhatch Lane, Enfield, Midlesex
Tel 020 8363 3384. Opened 1920s. Opening hours 8am–6pm (UO)
Hackney Cemetery (historic). Lauriston Road, E9
Tel 020 8985 1527. Opened 1788–1886 (US)
Hoop Lane Cemetery (current) Hoop Lane, NW11 7EU
Tel 020 8455 2569. Opened 1897. *Cemetery Dir.* Paul Van der Hulks *Tel* 020 8455 2569/07967 656 733 *Email* director@ejbb-jbc.org.uk Opening hours 8.30am–5pm. (SP and R)
Kingsbury Road Cemetery Kingsbury Road (off Balls Pond Road), N1
Opened 1840–1951 (R)
Liberal Jewish Cemetery (current) The Lodge, Pound Lane, NW10 2HG
Opened 1914. Opening hours 8am–5pm (L)
Mile End Road (Velho) (historic) behind 253 Mile End Road, E1
Tel 020 8958 3388 Opened 1657–1735. Opening hours by appointment. Key available from Superintendent (SP)
Mile End Road (Novo Beth Chaim) (historic) 329 Mile End Road, E1
Tel 020 8958 3388 Opened 1733–1918. Opening hours by appointment. Key available from Superintendent (SP)

Plashet Cemetery (reserves only) 361 High Street North E12 6PQ
Tel 020 8472 055 Opened 1896. Opening hours 9am–3pm. Nobody available on site.
Call East Ham to confirm open (US)
Queen's Elm Parade Cemetery (historic) Queen's Elm Parade, Chelsea SW3
Opened 1815–1884. Opening hours by appointment. Key available from Head Office *Tel* 020
7724 7702 (W)
Rainham Cemetery (current) Upminster Road North, Rainham, Essex
Tel 01708 552 825 Opened 1936. Opening hours 9am–3.30pm (F)
Rowan Road Cemetery (current) 3 Rowan Road, SW16 5JF
Opened 1915. Opening hours 8am–4pm. Head Office *Tel* 020 7724 7702 (WG)
Silver Street Cemetery (current) Silver Street, Goffs Oak, Cheshunt, Herts
Tel 020 8802 6262, 01707 874 220. Opened 1963. Opening hours 8am–6pm (UO).
Waltham Abbey Cemetery (current) Skillet Hill (Honey Lane), Waltham Abbey, Essex,
EN9 3QS
Tel 01992 714492 *Fax* 01992 650735 Opened 1857. Opening hours 9am–2.30pm. There
is nobody available on site. Call East Ham to confirm open (US).
West Ham Cemetery (reserves only) Buckingham Road, Forest Gate, E15
Tel 020 8472 0554 (US).
Western Synagogue Cemetery (current) Montagu Road, Edmonton N18 2NF
Opened 1890s. Opening hours 8am–4pm. Next to Federation cemetery. Head Office
Tel 020 7724 7702 (W).
Willesden Cemetery (reserves only) Glebe Road, NW10 2JE
Tel 020 8459 0394. Opened 1873. Opening hours 9am–5pm (US).

Memorials

AJEX memorial and **Special Forces plot** with a huge Magen David shaped table in memory
of Vera Atkins aka Rosenberg and all the Jewish SOE and SAS/Special Forces men and
women served in British Forces in WW2, Arboretum at Alrewas
Blue Plaque Memorial to Muriel Byck Bayfort Mansions, Warren Road Torquay.
Boer War Memorial Union Jack Club, Waterloo Road
Firemans' Memorial Peters Hill, Embankment, South Side
Holocaust Memorial and Garden Hyde Park, near Hyde Park Corner
Opened in July 1983, on a site given to the BoD by the British Government
Holocaust Memorial Waltham Abbey Cemetery, Upshire Hall, Honey Lane, Essex, EN9 3QS
Consecrated 1985 under US auspices.
Holocaust Memorial Rainham Cemetery, Upminster Road North, Rainham, Essex
Holocaust Memorial Sternberg Centre, 80 East End Road, Finchley N3
Kindertransport Statue Liverpool Street Station
Kindertransport Plaque House of Commons.
Memorial to the 5000 German and Austrian Jewish refugee soldiers, who fled the Nazis,
who trained at Richborough Camp, nearby, in 1939-41 Barbican arch in Sandwich, Kent
Memorial with Magen David and description of his act of bravery, to Major Simmon
Latutin, GC holder, Royal Academy of Music foyer, Marylebone Rd
Memorials in the Park Square by local art students to the hundreds of Jewish refugee
artists and musicians who were interned in the camp 1940-42, Hutchinson Square,
Douglas, Isle of Man
Memorial in Willesden Jewish Cemetery Beaconsfield Road, NW10
To Jewish Servicemen and Women in the British Armed Forces who died in the two World
Wars and have no known graves. Annual service organised by Ajex.
Memorial Plaque Arthaus Hackney.
In memory of the Israeli athletes murdered at the 1972 Olympics.
National Jewish Memorial (AJEX) Alrewas, Litchfield, Staffs
Prisoners' Memorial Gladstone Park, Dollis Hill Lane, NW2
To those who died in prisoner-of-war camps and concentration camps during WW II.
Annual service jointly organised by Ajex and the Royal British Legion.

RAF Church crypt of St Clements Danes, Strand
Memorial plaque with 12 tribes emblems to British and Israeli RAF personnel in the Second World War.

Raoul Wallenberg Statue Great Cumberland Place

Royal Fusiliers City of London Regiment Memorial High Holborn, by City boundary
The names of the 38th, 39th and 40th Battalions are inscribed on the monument, together with all other battalions who served in the First World War. Ajex is represented at the annual service.

Educational Organisations

Withdrawal on Friday Afternoons
When the Sabbath begins at 5pm or earlier, parents of Jewish children attending either State or State-aided schools can request that their children be withdrawn at such time as to reach their homes before the commencement of the Sabbath. Such requests should be submitted to the Head in writing.

GENERAL

Ackerman Resource Centre
Redbridge JCC, Woodford Bridge Road, Ilford, Essex, IG5 4LN
Tel 020 8551 0017 *Fax* 020 8551 9027
The Resource Centre was created for informal Jewish and Israel education. The Centre has operated in the community for 20 years as a resource for educators who need support and advice in this field. The Resource Centre is a focus for leadership training in the community. *Com. Res. Worker,* Mia Davis

Aish UK
379 Hendon Way, NW4 3LP
Tel 020 8457 4444 *Fax* 020 8457 4445
Email info@aish.org.uk *Website* www.aish.org.uk
(Est 1992; Reg. Charity No. 1069048). Nationwide innovative and dynamic social, educational and leadership opportunities for otherwise unaffiliated young Jews aged 17-35. Including Jewish identity travel to Israel and other destinations for hundreds of participants annually. Independently authenticated by MORI as effectively combating intermarriage and assimilation in the UK. Igniting Jewish commitment and the shouldering of responsibility in the community amongst its graduate student body. Hundreds of alumni subsequently involved in Jewish leadership/pursuing careers in community. Full time branches in Birmingham, City of London, Essex, Edgware, Manchester and Hendon. *Dir.* Rabbi N. Schiff; *Ch.* J. Faith

Binoh (part of **Norwood's Education Service**)
Tel 020 8809 8809 *Fax* 020 8203 8233
Email binoh@norwood.org.uk *Website* www.norwood.org.uk
(Registered as Hope Charity. Reg. Charity No. 1056674). Binoh is a specialist education and therapy service, run by Norwood, which provides specialist multi-professional support to children with additional and/or special education needs. Binoh works with children within their own school environment or through services provided from Norwood's Children & Family Centres in Hendon and Hackney. Binoh also provides early years services for the under-fives and a transition programme for students aged 16-19. Binoh offers art therapy, educational psychology, occupational therapy, teaching services (including religious studies) and speech and language therapy. In addition to directly supporting children, Binoh also supports schools, professionals and families. Services include consultations, INSET (in-service training) and mentoring.

The Hope Centre
228 Walm Lane, London NW2 3BS
Tel 020 8809 8809
Email hope@norwood.org.uk *Website* www.hope-centre.org.uk

(Reg. Charity No. 1056674). The Hope Centre is run by Norwood and provides services for children and young people, aged 3-19, with a wide range of learning disabilities and educational needs. Hope's multi-professional staff specialise in developing children's thinking skills and give students the tools to become confident and independent learners. Hope offers a wide range of services, including dynamic assessment, speech and language therapy and occupational therapy. Tuition is provided either on a one-to-one basis or in small groups. Training packages are also available for professionals and parents. *Hd. of Service* Luci Austin

Interlink Foundation
Fourth Floor Offices, 97 Stamford Hill, N16 5DN
Tel 020 8802 2469 *Fax* 020 8800 5153
Email admin@interlink-foundation.org.uk *Website* www.interlink-foundation.org.uk
(Reg. Charity No. 1079311, Company Limited by guarantee Reg. No. 3852756). The Interlink Foundation is an umbrella development agency for the Orthodox Jewish voluntary sector. Services include: capacity-building (including training) with groups, an information/monthly newsletter, policy and regeneration work. *Chief Exec.* Chaya Spitz

J-Link
c/o Aish, 379 Hendon Way, Hendon, London NW4 3LP
Tel 020 8457 2117 *Fax* 020 8457 4445
Email info@jlink.org.uk
(Est. 1993; Reg. Charity No. 1062551). Schools' J–Link aims to raise the sense of identity and commitment of Jewish pupils in non-Jewish secondary schools. It runs school assemblies and classes, less formal Jewish society meetings and lunch-and-learn sessions, and totally informal parties at Succot, Purim and other occasions. It offers a broad Jewish input by co-opting rabbis, youth workers, representatives of Jewish organisations and visiting speakers from abroad. It also runs training programmes for non-Jewish teachers who are teaching Judaism. Schools' J-Link operates in 60 schools in the London area and several provincial towns, and communicates with upwards of 6,000 Jewish youngsters each year. *Dir.* Rabbi B. Landau

Jewish Community Centre for London
6 Park End, NW3 2SE
Tel 020 7431 9866 *Fax* 020 7431 6483
Email info@jcclondon.org.uk *Website* www.jcclondon.org.uk
(Reg. Charity No. 1105622). *Ch.* Debbie Klein; *Chief Exec.* Nick Viner

Jewish Learning Exchange (JLE)
152-154 Golders Green Road, NW11 8HE
Tel 020 8458 4588 *Fax* 020 8458 4587
Email jle@jle.org.uk *Website* www.jle.org.uk
(Est. 1988. Reg. Charity No. 292886). The JLE is an educational and social centre for Jews of all backgrounds between the ages of 18-35. Through its wide variety of classes, events and trips, it allows its students to connect to their traditional roots and to meet like-minded people in a warm and welcoming environment. *Dir.* Rabbi Danny Kirsch; *Dir. Education,* Rabbi Reuven Stepsky; *Dir. Campus,* Rabbi Avi Hill; *Dir. Young Professionals,* Rabbi Benjy Morgan

Jewish Resource Centre (JRC)
University of Roehampton, The Froebel College, School of Education, Roehampton Lane, SW15 5PJ
www.roehampton.ac.uk/jrc
Contact Judy Weleminsky *Email* judyweleminsky@roehampton.ac.uk
(Est. 1996). Serves as a resource for all sections of the Jewish community in South London, as well as for the non-Jewish teaching community. The JRC has one of the University's Special Collections which can be accessed online or for research, study and personal interest if you make an appointment. The JRC hosts educational and cultural events. Staff are available to visit synagogues, religion schools/hederim and schools in the area to run events.

SCHOOLS

Akiva School
The Sternberg Centre, 80 East End Road, N3 2SY
Tel 020 8349 4980 *Fax* 020 8349 4959
Email admin@akivaschool.org *Website* www.akivaschool.org
(Est. 1981). Voluntary aided State Primary with a progressive Jewish Ethos. Education for pupils, aged 4-11 years. *Hd.* Susy Stone MA

Avigdor Hirsch Torah Temimah Primary School
Parkside, Dollis Hill, London NW2 6RJ
Tel 020 8450 4377 *Fax* 020 8208 7998
Email admin@torahtemimah.brent.sch.uk
(Est. 1989. Reg. Charity No. 100146). Voluntary-aided (London Borough of Brent) Orthodox Jewish Primary School and Nursery for boys aged 3-11. *Menahel* Rabbi E. Klyne MA(Ed); *Hd.* Rabbi Y. Freeman B.Sc; *Ch. of Govs.* U. Kaplan

Beth Jacob Seminary of London
196–198 Lordship Road, N16 5ES
Tel 020 8800 4719 *Fax* 020 8800 6067
(Reg. Charity No. 312913). Teacher Training College and finishing school for Hebrew Studies and vocational qualifications. *Princ.* Rabbi B. Dunner

Bushey Ganim
177–189 Sparrows Herne, Bushey, Herts, WD23 1AJ
Tel 020 8386 1515 *Mobile* 07733 068 358
Email head@busheyganim.org
Website www.busheyganim.org.uk
(ages 2-rising 5). *Hd.* Ms D. Boder-Cohn Cert. Ed.

Clore Shalom School
Hugo Gryn Way, Shenley, Herts WD7 9BL
Tel 01923 855 631 *Fax* 01923 853 722
Email admin@cloreshalom.herts.sch.uk
(Est. 1999). Voluntary-aided primary school (3-11). Pluralist Jewish day school. *Hd.* Sheree Oxenham

Clore Tikva School Redbridge
115 Fullwell Avenue, Ilford, Essex IG6 2JN
Tel 020 8551 1097 *Fax* 020 8551 2070
(Est. 1999). Community, state-aided primary school (4-11), under Reform, Masorti and Liberal auspices. *Hd.* L. Rosenberg; *Admin.* Valerie Garnelas

Hasmonean High School:
  Boys' Campus, 11/18 Holders Hill Road, NW4 1NA *Tel* 020 8203 1411 *Fax* 020 8202 4526
  Girls' Campus, 2/4 Page Street, NW7 2EU *Tel* 020 8203 4294 *Fax* 020 8202 4527
Website www.hasmonean.co.uk
Voluntary Aided, London Borough of Barnet. *Exec. Hd.* Rabbi D. Meyer, BA, MBA, NPQH

Hasmonean Pre-Nursery
8-10 Shirehall Lane, NW4 2PD
Tel 020 8201 6252 *Fax* 020 8202 1605
(children ages 2-3). *Man.* J. Truman

Hasmonean Primary School
8-10 Shirehall Lane, NW4 2PD
Tel 020 8202 7704 *Fax* 020 8202 1605
Email admin@hasmonean-pri.barnet.sch.uk
(Boys and Girls ages 3-11) *Princ.* Rabbi M. Ginsbury; *Hd.* A. Shaw, BA (Hons.), MA Cert Ed.

Hertsmere Jewish Primary School
Watling Street, Radlett, Herts WD7 7LQ
Tel 01923 855857 *Fax* 01923 853399

Email admin@hjps.herts.sch.uk
Hd. Steven Isaacs; *Admin.* K. Thomas. Voluntary-aided primary school for ages 3-11.

Ilford Jewish Primary School
Forest Road, Ilford, Essex IG6 3HB
Tel 020 8498 1350/1351
Email admin@ijpsonline.co.uk *Website* www.ijpsonline.co.uk
Hd. R. Levin

Immanuel College (The Charles Kalms, Henry Ronson Immanuel College)
Elstree Road, Bushey, Herts WD23 4EB
Tel 020 8950 0604 *Fax* 020 8950 8687
Email enquiries@immanuel.herts.sch.uk *Website* www.immanuelcollege.co.uk
(Reg Charity No. 803179). Founded by Chief Rabbi Jakobovits, Orthodox. Immanuel College opened in 1990 with a pupil roll of 38. There are now 470 pupils in the senior school, of whom 125 are in the Sixth Form. The Immanuel College Preparatory School opened in September 2011. The college is characterised by academic excellence, expert pastoral care and inspiring Jewish education. *Hd.* Charles Dormer MA (Cantab); *Dep. Hd. Academic* Martin Blain MA (Cantab); *Dep. Hd. Pastoral* Beth Kerr (BSc); *Dep. Hd. Jewish Life and Learning*, Rabbi David Riffkin BA, MA

Independent Jewish Day School
46 Green Lane, NW4 2AH
Tel 020 8203 2299
Email office@ijds.co.uk
(Est. 1979). Orthodox Primary School & Kindergarten. *Ch.* A. Levey; *Princ.* A. A. Kimche, BA; *Hd.* Miss A. Lando

JCOSS (Jewish Community Secondary School)
Castlewood Road, New Barnet, Herts EN5 9GE
Tel 020 8344 2220
Email admin@jcoss.barnet.sch.uk *Website* www.jcoss.org
(Reg. Charity No. 1107705). Secondary School for 11-19 year olds.

Jewish Secondary Schools Movement
11/18 Holders Hill Road, NW4 1NA
Tel 020 8203 1411 *Fax* 020 8202 4526
(Est. 1929).

J.F.S. School
The Mall, Kenton HA3 9TE
Tel 020 8206 3100
Email admin@jfs.brent.sch.uk
(Est. 1732). *Hd.* J. Miller, BSc (Hons), MA, NPQH; *Clerk to Govs.* Dr. A. Fox

Kerem School (including **Kerem Early Years Unit**)
Norrice Lea, N2 0RE
Tel 020 8455 0909
Email admin@kerem.org.uk
(Boys and Girls rising 4-11) *Hd.* A. Burns

King Solomon High School
Forest Road, Barkingside, Ilford, Essex IG6 3HB
Tel 020 8498-1300 *Fax* 020 8498 1333
Email info@kshsonline.com
Hd. S. Lewis; *Ch. of Govs.* S. Sollosi; *Denominational Body:* United Synagogue; *Authority* London Borough of Redbridge

Kisharon Organisation
Head Office, 54 Parson Street, NW4 1TP
Tel 020 8203 2233 *Fax* 020 8731 7005
Email info@Kisharon.org.uk *Website* www.kisharon.org.uk
(Reg. Charity No. 271519). *Chief Exec.* Dr Beverley Jacobson; *Ch. of Govs.* Phillip Goldberg

Kisharon Day School
1011 Finchley Road, Golders Green, NW11 7HB
Tel 020 8455 7483
Sora Kopfstein *Email* kisharondayschool@kisharon.org.uk
Tuffkid Nursery
3 Western Avenue, London NW11 9HG
Tel 020 8201 8488
Janice Marriott *Email* tuffkid@kisharon.org.uk
Law of Truth Talmudical College
50 Knightland Road, E5 9HS *Corr.* 31 Leadale Road, London N16 6BZ
Tel 020 8802 7684 *Fax* 020 8806 9318. Students: 020 8806 6642
Email schneidersyeshivah@gmail.com
(Est. by Rabbi M. Szneider in Memel, 1911, Frankfurt 1918, London 1938. Reg. Charity
No. 312845). *Princ.* Rabbi M. Halpern
Lubavitch Children's Centre
1 Northfield Road, N16 5RL
Tel 020 8809 9050
Website www.lubavitchchildrenscentre.com
Admin. D.L. Sudak
Lubavitch Foundation
107-115 Stamford Hill, N16 5RP
Tel 020 8800 0022 *Fax* 020 8809 7324
Email mail@chabad.org.uk *Website* www.chabad.org.uk
(Est. 1959). To further Jewish religious education, identity and commitment. Separate
departments for adult education, summer and day camps, youth clubs and training, univer-
sity counsellors, publications, welfare, and organisations concerned with Israel. *Princ.* Rabbi
N. Sudak, OBE; *Admin.* Rabbi I. H. Sufrin. Lubavitch House School *Tel* 020 8809 7476; Girls'
Senior, 107/109 Stamford Hill, N16 *Tel* 020 8800 0022; *Hd.* Rabbi S. Lew. Boys', 133/135
Clapton Common E5 *Tel* 020 8800 1044; Girls' Primary, 111-115 Stamford Hill, N16 5RP
Tel 020 8800 0022 *Fax* 020 8809 7324; *Hd.* F. Sudak. Kindergarten, 107 Stamford Hill, N16
5RP *Tel* 020 8800 0022; *Admin.* B. Raskin; *Libr.* Zvi Rabin, ALA *Tel* 020 8800 5823; Vista
Vocational Training, 1 Northfield Road, N16 5RL *Tel* 020 8802 8772; *Man.* H. Lew.
Women's Centre, 19 Northfield Road, N16 5RL *Tel* 020 8809 6508; *Admin.* R. Bernstein
Menorah Foundation School
Abbots Road, Burnt Oak, Edgware HA8 0QS
Tel 020 8906 9992 *Fax* 020 8906 9993
Orthodox. *Hd.* C. Neuberger, BSc, PGCE, NPQH; *Princ.* Rabbi D. Roberts; *Ch.* Joe Holder
Menorah Primary School (and Menorah Nursery)
The Wohl Campus, 1-3 The Drive, NW11 9SP
Tel 020 8458 1276
(Est. 1944). Voluntary Aided (London Borough of Barnet) for Boys & Girls ages 3-11. *Princ.*
Rabbi Y. M. Greenberg; *Hd.* J. Menczer
Michael Sobell Sinai School
Shakespeare Drive, Kenton, Harrow, Middlesex HA3 9UD
Tel 020 8204 1550
Email admin@sinai.brent.sch.uk
(Est. 1981). Orthodox. Voluntary aided primary school for boys & girls, aged 3-11. *Ch. Govs.*
L. Glassar; *Hd.* R. Leach *Denominational body* Board of Religious Education; *Authority* London
Borough of Brent. *School Rabbi* Rabbi David Lister.
MST College
240-242 Hendon Way, NW4 3NL
Tel/Fax 020 8202 2212
Orthodox teacher training college offering a range of accredited Degree courses leading to
Qualified Teacher Status. *Princ.* Michael Cohen BA, M.Phil, PGCE; *Reg.* Dr. Abbott Katz
MA Ph.D; *College Man.* Bernice Black

Naima Jewish Preparatory School (Independent)
21 Andover Place, NW6 5ED
Tel 020 7328 2802 *Fax* 020 7624 0161
Website www.naimajps.co.uk
(Reg. Charity No. 289066). For children aged 2-11 years offering a broad secular curriculum together with rich programme of Orthodox Jewish studies. Catering for children of all abilities through flexible learning programme. *Hd. Princ.* Rabbi Dr A. Levy; *Hd.* B. Pratt

Nancy Reuben Primary School
48 Finchley Lane, Hendon NW4 1DJ
Tel 020 8202 5646
Email office@nrps.co.uk
Princ. A. Haye

North West London Jewish Day School
180 Willesden Lane, NW6 7PP
Tel 020 8459 3378 *Fax* 020 8451 7298
Email admin@nwljds.org.uk *Website* www.nwljds.org.uk
(Est. 1945). Voluntary Aided. Modern Orthodox Primary school and nursery for boys and girls, 3-11 *Princ.* Dayan I. Binstock; *Ch. of Govs.* P. Gottlieb; *Hd.* Rabbi D.S. Kerbel, MA, NPQH

Pardes House Grammar School
Hendon Lane, N3 1SA
Tel 020 8349 4222
Email admin@phgrammar.co.uk
Hd. Princ. Rabbi E. Halpern; *Hd. M.* Rabbi D. Dunner

Pardes House Kindergarten
Hendon Lane, N3 1SA
Tel 020 8371 8292
Hd. Y. Wajnstock

Pardes House Primary School
Hendon Lane, N3 1SA
Tel 020 8343 3568
Email office@pardeshouse.com
H. Princ. Rabbi E. Halpern; *Hd.* J. Sager; *Menahel* Rabbi G. Abeless

Rosh Pinah Primary School
(Est. 1956). Glengall Road, Edgware, Middlesex HA8 8TE
Tel 020 8958 8599 *Fax* 020 8905 4853
Email admin@rpps.org.uk *Website* www.rpps.org.uk
H. Princ. Rabbi Y.Y. Schochet; *Hd.* A. Wolfson, B.Ed(Hons), MA, M.Ed, NPQH; *Admin.* S. Stern. Voluntary aided Orthodox Jewish Primary School in the London Borough of Barnet for boys and girls aged 3-11.

Sharon Kindergarten
Finchley Synagogue, Kinloss Gardens, N3 3DU
Tel 020 8346 2039
Email info@sharonkindergarten.org
(For children ages 2½-5) *Man.* T. E. Elek

Side by Side Kids Ltd
9 Big Hill, E5 9HH
Tel 020 8880 8300 *Fax* 020 8880 8341
Email school@sidebysidekids.org.uk
Side by Side is an integrated nursery and special needs school providing therapy and education for children and a support network for their families. *Hd.* Gerald Lebrett

Torah Centre Trust
84 Leadale Road, N15 6BH
Tel 020 8802 3586
(Est. 1975). To provide full or part-time facilities for children, in particular those from uncommitted' families, to enable them to further their secular and Hebrew education
Educ. Dir. Rabbi M. Bernstein, B.Ed

Wolfson Hillel Primary School
154 Chase Road, Southgate, N14 4LG
Tel 020 8882 6487 *Fax* 020 8882 7965
Email schooloffice@wolfsonhillel.enfield.sch.uk *Website* wwwwolfsonhillel.enfield.sch.uk
(Est. 1992). Voluntary aided primary school for boys & girls aged 3-11. *Ch. Govs.* H. Cohen;
Hd. K. Jowett (*Authority* London Borough of Enfield)

Yeshiva Gedola Lubavitch
3/5 Kingsley Way, N2 0EH
Tel 020 8458 3212
Rosh Yeshiva Rabbi I. M. Hertz

Yeshivah Ohel Moshe Etz Chaim
85 Bridge Lane, NW11
Tel 020 8458 5149
(Reg. Charity No. 312232). *Princ.* Rabbi Z. Rabi

Yesodey Hatorah Schools
2 and 4 Amhurst Park, N16 5AE
Tel 020 8800 8612
(Est. 1943). Chassidish. *Princ.* Rabbi A. Pinter; *V. Pres.* Rabbi C. Pinter
Nursery, 2 Amhurst Park, N16 SAE *Tel* 020 8800 9221 *Hd.* Shine
Kindergarten, 2 Amhurst Park, N16 5AE *Tel* 020 8800 8612 *Matron* Mrs Shine.
Primary School (Boys), 2 Amhurst Park, N16 5AE *Tel* 020 8800 8612 *Princ.* Rabbi A.
Pinter; *Menahel* Rabbi P. Rosenberg
Senior School (Boys), 4 Amhurst Park, N16 5AE *Tel* 020 8800 8612 *Princ.* Rabbi A. Pinter;
Menahel Rabbi D. Weiler
Primary School (Girls), 153 Stamford Hill, N16 5LG *Tel* 020 8800 8612 *Princ.* Rabbi A.
Pinter; *Hd.* D. Luria
Senior School (Girls), Egerton Road, N16 6UB *Tel* 020 8826 5500 *Princ.* Rabbi A. Pinter;
Hd. R. Pinter

Welfare Organisations

Abbeyfield Camden (Jewish) Society
59 Belmont Road, Bushey, Herts WD23 2JR *Tel* 01923 213 964
House Man. Margaret Kazanecka *Email* belmontlodge@virginmedia.com *Admin.* G. Benson
Tel 020 8423 1351
Website www.jewishabbeyfield.org.uk
The Society runs one small supported sheltered home for elderly residents.
House: Belmont Lodge, 59 Belmont Road, Bushey, Herts WD23 2JR

Agudas Israel Housing Association Ltd
206 Lordship Road, N16 5ES
Tel 020 8802 3819 *Fax* 020 8809 6206
Email info@aihaltd.co.uk
(Reg. Charity No. 23535). *Chief Exec.* Ita Symons, MBE

Schonfeld Square Foundation
1 Schonfeld Square, Lordship Road, N16 0QQ
Tel 020 8802 3819 *Fax* 020 8809 6206
Email info@aihaltd.co.uk
(Reg. Charity No. 1049179). *Co-ord.* Ita Symons, MBE
Includes ownership of: **Beenstock Home** (Home for the Frail and Elderly)
19–21 Northumberland Street, Salford, M7 4RP *Tel* 0161 792 1515 *Fax* 0161 792 1616
Care Man. C. Laurence

Beis Brucha (Mother and Baby Home)
208 Lordship Road, N16 5ES
Tel 020 8211 8081
Man. M. Hirschler *Email* management@beisbrucha.co.uk

Beis Pinchos (Residential and Nursing Home for the Frail and Elderly), and

Fradel Lodge (Sheltered Accommodation for the Frail and Elderly)
Schonfeld Square, Lordship Road, N16 0QQ
Tel 020 8802 7477 *Fax* 020 8809 7000
Email schonfeld@aihaltd.co.uk
Care Man. Barbara Carzolio; *Social Man.* H. Pesach

Beis Rochel (Supported Housing for Vulnerable Women)
52 Lordship Park, N16 5UD
Tel 020 8802 2160 (Office), 020 8802 2909 (Residents)
Email lordship52@btinternet.com

30 Dunsmure Road
N16 5PW (Supported Housing for Vulnerable Men)
Tel (Office) 020 8800 2860, (Residents) 020 8802 0073
Email info@aihaltd.co.uk

Ahada Bereavement Counselling
370 Cranbrook Road, Gants Hill, Ilford, Essex IG2 6HY
Tel 07758 727 328
Email admin@empathy.uk.net *Website* www.empathy.uk.net
(Est. 1986. Incorporated into Empathy Counselling Services, 2012. Reg. Charity No. 1118894). Offers free confidential counselling and support for members of the Jewish community who are experiencing difficulties as a result of bereavement. Provides trained voluntary counsellors who are professionally supervised. Covers Redbridge, neighbouring Boroughs and other areas of Essex. *Tru.* Dr. David Hamilton, Robert Jackson, Rabbi Maurice Michaels, Marc Preston

Arbib Lucas Charity
(Reg. Charity No. 208666). Arbib Lucas responds to requests for small grants to help needy women in the community with specific practical items to benefit their day-to-day living in the long term. *Hon. S.* Marianne Temple, 17 Heronsforde, W13 8JE

Brenner Jewish Community Centre
Raine House, 91-93, Stamford Hill, N16 5TP
Tel 020 8442 7750
Email brenner@jcare.org *Website* www.jewishcare.org
(Reg. Charity No. 802559). Administered by Jewish Care. Community Centre for the local Jewish community *Centre Man.* L. M. Harris

Camp Simcha
The House, 12 Queens Road, NW4 2TH
Tel 020 8202 9297 *Fax* 020 8202 6670
Email office@campsimcha.org.uk www.campsimcha.org.uk
(Charity No. 1044685). A charity aiming to enhance the quality of life for Jewish children in the UK with cancer and other life threatening conditions. *Chief Exec.* N. Goldschneider

Chevrat Bikkur Cholimx (Chevrat Bikkur Cholim)
463a Finchley Road, NW3 6HN
Tel 020 7435 0836
Email info@ukfos.org *Website* www.ukfos.org
(Est. 1947. Reg. Charity No. 91468A). Provides home helps/carers to the sick, needy and elderly. *Pres.* S. Sackman; *Hd.* M. Wechsler; *Gen. Sec.* N. Brotzen

Empathy Counselling Services
370 Cranbrook Road, Gants Hill, Ilford, Esses IG2 6HY
Tel 07758 727 328
Email admin@empathy.uk.net *Website* www.empathy.uk.net
(Reg. Charity No. 1118894). Incorporating Ahada Bereavement Counselling. Offers free confidential counselling for members of Jewish families affected by loss, bereavement, separation and divorce, economic loss, loss of expectations, and of potential. Counsellors are fully qualified and professionally supervised. Covers Redbridge and neighbouring Boroughs. *Tru.* Dr David Hamilton, Robert Jackson, Rabbi Maurice Michaels, Marc Preston

Finchley Kosher Lunch Service (Meals-on-Wheels for the housebound and disabled)
Covers Edgware, Finchley, Golders Green, Hampstead Garden Suburb, Hendon, Mill Hill.

Hon. T. Ruth Freed, *Tel* 020 8202 8129. *Admin.* by the League of Jewish Women. (*See* p. 77)

Food for the Jewish Poor
To provide (a) food throughout the year; (b) groceries during Passover; (c) special relief for approved emergency cases. (*See* Jewish Care).

Hagadolim Charitable Organisation
(Est. 1950). To provide financial assistance to Homes and charities in England and Israel, and to visit and provide comforts in private homes in the Home Counties. *Ch.* L. Dunitz; *Jt. T.* B. Wallach, R. J. Dunitz; *Sec.* S. Levy, 4 Edgwarebury Court, Edgwarebury Lane, Edgware, Middlesex HA8 8LP *Tel* 020 8958 8558

Hospital Kosher Meals Service
Lanmor House, 370/386 High Road, Wembley, Middlesex HA9 6AX
Tel 020 8795 2058 *Fax* 020 8900 2462
Email hkms@btconnect.com *Website* www.hkms.org.uk
(Reg. Charity No. 1025601). Provides supervised kosher meals to patients in hospitals throughout Greater London. *Ch.* M.G. Freedman, MBA, FCA; *V. Ch.* H. Glyn, BSc, FRICS; *Sec.* G. Calvert; *Admin.* E. Stone; *Hospital Liaison Off.* S. Patashnik

The Industrial Dwellings Society (1885) Ltd
Head Office Ockway House, 41 Stamford Hill, London N16 5SR
Tel 020 8800 9606*Fax* 020 8800 5990
Email housing@ids.org.uk *Website* www.ids.org.uk
(Industrial & Provident Society Reg. No. 14044; Homes and Communities Agency Reg. No. L0266). IDS is a housing association founded by the Rothschild family and other Jewish philanthropists. Direct applications can be made for sheltered housing schemes including Ajex House where priority is given to Jewish Ex-service men and women and their dependents. *Ch.* Jonathan Davies; *Chief Exec.* Paul Westbrook

Jewish Aged Needy Pension Society
(Est. 1829. Reg. Charity No. 206262). Provides pensions for members of the Jewish community aged 60 or over, who have known better times and who, in their old age, find themselves in reduced circumstances. Also supplements income provided from statutory sources. Services to the middle-class of society who find themselves in greater financial need and who do not seem to fall within the purview of any other charitable organisations. *Pres.* M.E.G. Prince; *T.* A.H.E. Prince; *Hon. S.* G. B. Rigal; *Sec./Admin.* Sheila A. Taylor 34 Dalkeith Grove, Stanmore, Middlesex HA7 4EG *Tel* 020 8958 5390 *Fax* 020 8958 8046

Jewish Bereavement Counselling Service (JBCS)
c/o Martin B. Cohen Centre, Deansbrook Road, Edgware, Middlesex HA8 9BG
Tel 020 8951 3881
Email enquiries@jbcs.org.uk *Website* jbcs.org.uk
(Est. 1980. Reg. Charity No. 1047473). The Jewish Bereavement Counselling has for over 30 years offered confidential counselling to individuals, couples, families and children in the Jewish Community who are experiencing loss. Bereavement counselling and support is offered on a one to one basis by trained and experienced volunteer counsellors in the client's own home or in designated venue. Group counselling may also be offered where available. JBCS also has two support groups, Butterflies (support group of mums and dads (of young children) who have lost a parent) and Aftershock (support group for young adults (18-30 year olds) who have lost a parent). JBCS is an Independent organisation, which relies on donations and bequests. *Ch.* Keith Simons; *Man.* Trisha Curtis; *Admin.* Barbara Freed

Jewish Blind & Disabled
35 Langstone Way, Mill Hill East, NW7 1GT
Tel 020 8371 6611 *Fax* 020 8371 4225
Email info@jbd.org
(Est. 1969. Reg. Charity No. 259480). Jewish Blind & Disabled is the only Jewish charity providing mobility apartments for people of all ages with physical disabilities or impaired vision. Tenants range from their early 20's, and encompass a wide spectrum of disabilities. Whatever their individual circumstances, the life of each tenant is transformed by being

enabled to live independently with the safety net of knowing that support is always on hand 24/7 if required. *Ch.* John Joseph; *Pres.* Malcolm Ozin; *Chief Exec.* Hazel Kaye

Jewish Blind & Disabled Projects
Assisted Living Schemes: Fairacres, 164 East End Road, Finchley, N2 0RR; Cherry Tree Court, Roe Green, Kingsbury, NW9; Milne Court, Churchfields, South Woodford, E18; Hilary Dennis Court, Sylvan Road, Wanstead, E11 1QX; Aztec House, 163 Tomswood Hill, Ilford, IG6; Frances and Dick James Court, Mill Hill, NW7; and new development, opened in November 2012, in Bushey Heath.

Jewish Care
Amélie House, Maurice & Viviene Wohl Campus, 221 Golders Green Road, London NW11 9DQ *Tel* 020 8922 2000
Jewish Care Direct (helpline) *Tel* 020 8922 2222 *Fax* 020 8201 3897
Email jcdirect@jcare.org *Website* www.jewishcare.org
(Est. 1990. Reg. Charity No. 802559).
Services managed by Jewish Care:
    Care Homes – Clore Manor, Hendon; Ella & Ridley Jacobs House, Hendon; Hyman Fine House, Brighton; Lady Sarah Cohen House, Friern Barnet; Otto Schiff, Golders Green; The Princess Alexandra Home, Stanmore; Raymond House, Southend on Sea; Rela Goldhill Lodge, Golders Green; Rosetrees, Friern Barnet; Rubens House, Finchley; Vi & John Rubens House, Redbridge
    Community Centres – Brenner Community Centre at Raine House, Stamford Hill; Redbridge Jewish Community Centre (formerly Sinclair House), Redbridge; Southend and Westcliff Community Centre, Southend and Westcliff; Michael Sobell Community Centre, Golders Green.
    Connect@centres – connect@kenton (Monday); connect@southgate (Tuesday); connect@southend (Thursday)
    Day Centres – Edgware & Harrow Jewish Day Centre, Edgware; Stepney Jewish Day Care Centre, Stepney.
    Centres for people living with Dementia – The Dennis Centre, Redbridge; Leonard Sainer Centre, Edgware; Sam Beckman Centre, Hendon.
    Mental Health Wellbeing Centres – Kadimah Centre for Wellbeing, Stamford Hill; Mitkadem Centre for Wellbeing, Redbridge; Martin B. Cohen Centre for Wellbeing, Edgware.
    Mental Health Residential Homes – Jack Gardener House (ages 18-50), Golders Green; Sidney Corob (ages 50+), Hampstead.
    Other Services – Holocaust Survivors' Centre & Shalvata, Hendon; Various Support and social groups, The Karten CTEC Centre, Golders Green & Stamford Hill; The KC Shasha Centre for Talking News & Books, Golders Green; Tay Sachs Screenings; Homecare; Community support and social work services.
    Independent Living Apartments – Selig Court, Golders Green
    Sheltered Housing – Shebson Lodge, Westcliff on Sea.
    Youth Services – Redbridge Jewish Community Centre (formerly **Sinclair House**).

Jewish Children's Holidays Fund (formerly **Jewish Branch of the Children's Country Holidays Fund**)
JCHF, P.O. Box 1206, Enfield, EN1 9SH
Tel 020 7100 5097
Email secretary@jchf.org *Website* www. jchf.org
(Est. 1888. Reg. Charity No. 295361). *Pres.* Joyce Kemble, JP; *Ch.* Ian Donoff; *Sec.* Nicole Conway, JCHF, P.O. Box 1206, Enfield, EN1 9SH *Tel* 020 7100 5097

Jewish Community Housing Association
Harmony Close, Princes Park Avenue NW11 0JJ
Tel 020 8381 4901 *Fax* 020 8458 1772
Website www.jcha.org.uk
Ch. B. Reback; *Chief Exec.* S. Clarke. The Association owns and manages sheltered housing in London, Hertfordshire and Kent. Supported housing for people with special needs is managed on the Association's behalf by Jewish Care and Norwood. Short-term accommodation for students is located in Golders Green.

Jewish Crisis Help Line Miyad

Tel 0800 652 9249

Website www.jewishhelpline.co.uk

Confidential listening service for those experiencing stress in their lives. Open Sunday-Thursday noon-midnight; Friday noon-3pm (winter), 6pm (summer). To help assist, please email jewishhl@googlemail.com

Jewish Deaf Association

Julius Newman House, Woodside Park Road, London N12 8RP

Tel 020 8446 0502 (voice), 020 8446 4037 (text) *Fax* 020 8445 7451

Website www.jewishdeaf.org.uk

(Reg. Charity No. 1105845). Full range of information and support services for people with all levels of hearing loss and hearing people living/working with deaf and hard of hearing people. Includes professional guidance on coping with hearing loss, Tinnitus management, weekly Hear to Help aid maintenance service, impartial information on audiology in the NHS and private sector. Vibrant programme of discussion groups enabling participants to become more socially active, more confident and thereby more connected to those around them. Deaf awareness training courses and lip-reading classes also available. Technology and Information Centre features wide range of latest specialist equipment and aids to facilitate independence. *Tel* 020 8446 0214 for appointments or email info@hearingconnect.org.uk. *Pres.* E. Gee, JP; *Ch.* Trudy King; *Exec. Dir.* Susan Cipin

Jews' Temporary Shelter

Amelie House, 221 Golders Green Road, London NW11 9DQ

Tel 07546 519 043

(Reg. Charity No. 1098798). *Admin.* R. Lewis

Kinneret Trust

127-129 Clapton Common, E5 9AB

Tel 020 8809 4844

Email ginaabrahams1@hotmail.com

Supporting the Aden Jews community of the Stamford Hill area. *Ch.* G. Abrahams; *Cttee.* G. Mahalla, G. Nissim, N. Mansoor

Kisharon Services (For Head Office and Administration *See* p. 179)

Asher Loftus Business Centre - comprising the **Print Shop** and **Bus Stop Bikes**

27-31 Church Road, Hendon NW4 4EB

Tel 020 8202 3936 *Fax* 020 8203 6071

Email raymond.bonham@kisharon.org.uk

Hackney Community Inclusion Project

(Women) Brenner Community Centre, 91-93 Stamford Hill, London N16 5TP *Tel* 020 3393 0164

(Men) 9 Amhurst Park, N165DH (Scheme Address) *Tel* 020 3393 0164

For more details contact Head Office at 54 Parson Street NW4 1TP

Email aviva.braunold@kisharon.org.uk

The Hackney Community Inclusion Project was established in collaboration with Hackney Local Authority and provides young people with learning difficulties with an opportunity to develop independence skills within their own community. The people supported are encouraged to become self-supporting in accessing local facilities, travelling, shopping and cooking.

The project is in the heart of the Stamford Hill community and comprises separate male and female sites. Work opportunities in the community are actively sourced for both groups. Home industries have also been developed and Kisharon runs a horticulture business as well as a toy library with several new projects underway

Residential Services

Hanna Schwalbe Residential Home

48 Leeside Crescent, Golders Green NW11 0LA

Tel 020 8458 3810

Email petrona.johnson@kisharon.org.uk

Kisharon Residential and Supported Living Services
Contact Hadassa Kesler *Tel* 020 3393 0167 *Email* hadassa.kessler@kisharon.org.uk

Necessitous Ladies' Fund
(Reg. Charity No. 266921 A3L1). Founded by the Union of Jewish Women. For the relief of Jewish women who are in need, hardship or distress *Ch. J.* Nathan; *H. Admin.* H. Davis, c/o 1 Martlett Lodge, Oakhill Park, London NW3 7LE *Email* admin@nelf.wanadoo.co.uk

Nightingale Hammerson
Nightingale House, 105 Nightingale Lane, SW12 8NB
Tel 020 8673 3495
Email info@nightingalehammerson.org *Website* www.nightingalehammerson.org
Hammerson House, 50A The Bishops Avenue, N2 0BE
Tel 020 8458 4523
Email info@nightingalehammerson.org *Website* www.nightingalehammerson.org
(Est. 1840. Reg. Charity No. 207316). Nightingale Hammerson runs two care homes, Nightingale House, in Clapham, South West London and Hammerson House in North West London. It provides quality care for older members of the Jewish community on both sites, and it offers residential, nursing and respite care in both of its homes. Nightingale House also offers dementia care. All rooms in both homes have private facilities, in addition to which there are numerous lounges and other facilities. Aid Societies, NW London; SW London; Literary Lunch Cttee.; Dinner Cttee.;The Young Nightingales; Business Group; Youth Cttee. *Life Patrons* Dame Vivien Duffield DBE; Sue Hammerson CBE; *Pres.* G. Lipton MBE; *V. Pres.* Patricia Beecham; *Ch.* Harvey Rosenblatt; *Dep. Ch.* David Winton; *Chief Exec.* Leon Smith.

Norwood
Broadway House, 80/82, The Broadway, Stanmore, HA7 4HB
Tel 020 8809 8809
Email info@norwood.org.uk *Website* www.norwood.org.uk
(Est. 1795. Reg. Charity No.1059050). Norwood is a leading UK charity which each year supports over 7,000 people with learning disabilities and children and families in need. It provides a wide range of Family Services and Learning and Disability Services which help people to live the life they choose and reach their full potential. Delivered by 1,200 staff, and supported by 800 dedicated volunteers, these vital services are provided to the Jewish and wider communities in London and the South East as follows: *Family Services*: family centres, children and family support, social work, an inclusive nursery, adoption. *Learning and Disability Services*: education, after-school clubs and holiday schemes, short breaks, transition, supported living, residential care, work skills and employment, life skills and learning, leisure, health and wellbeing. *Patron* Her Majesty The Queen; *Pres.* Richard Desmond; *Ch.* Bernie Myers; *Chief Exec.* Elaine Kerr

Norwood Drugsline Drop-In Centre
The Kennedy Leigh Centre, Edgworth Close, Hendon, London NW4 4HJ
Email drugsline@norwood.org.uk *Website* www.norwood.org.uk/drugsline
(Reg. Charity No. 1067573). Drugsline is an independent crisis, information and support charity that provides free and confidential information and support for people with drugs, alcohol and addiction issues, their families and friends. Thursday 6-8pm. No appointment necessary. *Exec. Dir.* Rabbi Aryeh Sufrin, MBE

Raphael - The Jewish Counselling Service
P.O. Box 172, Stanmore HA7 3WB
Tel 0800 234 6236 (24 hour)
Email info@raphaeljewishcounselling.org *Website* www.raphaeljewishcounselling.org
(Reg. Charity No. 278522). London and Essex based professional Jewish Counsellors provide confidential counselling for individuals and couples. Donations, grants and bequests enable us to continue this important work in the community and to further professional training.

Rishon Multiple Sclerosis Aid Group
20 Heathside Court, High Road, Bushey Heath, Herts WD23 1EN
Tel 020 8950 9212

Email bibrings@sky.com
(Est. 1966. Reg. Charity No. 252359). Affiliated to the Multiple Sclerosis Society. Provides social and cultural activities, help and welfare, for Jewish persons, diagnosed with MS. Funds are raised for this objective as well as contributing on behalf of Anglo-Jewry to the MS Society's Research Fund, which underwrites research into the causes and search for a cure of MS. *Life Pres.* H. Bibring; *Ch.* Frances Anthony 20 Greenhalgh Walk, London N2 0DJ *Tel* 020 8455 9579

Sunridge Housing Association Ltd
76 The Ridgeway, NW11 8PT
Tel 020 8458 3389
Ch. Linda Stone; *Hon. S.* Richard Levy. *Man.* P. Peterkin

Westlon Housing Association
850 Finchley Road, NW11 6BB
Tel 020 8201 8484 *Fax* 020 8731 8847
Providers of affordable housing for the elderly. *Ch.* Joan Ansell; *Chief Exec.* J.W. Silverman **Annette White Lodge**, 287/289 High Road, N2 8HB; **Deborah Rayne House**, 33b Sunningfields Road, NW4 4QX; **The Woodville**, 1a Woodville Road, W5 2SE Applications to 020 8201 8484

Yad Voezer
9 Amhurst Park, London N16 5DH
Tel 020 8809 4303/9060 *Fax* 020 8809 9061
Email enquiries@yadvoezer.com *Website* www.yadvoezer.com
(Est. 1975. Reg. Charity No. 1032490). Residential care and support for people with learning disabilities, mental health problems and their families. *Ch.* Rabbi E. Landau; *Chief Exec.* Z. Landau

Clubs and Cultural Societies

See also under Synagogues and Organisations concerned with Jewish Youth

London Jewish Forum
6 Park End, NW3 2SE
Tel 020 7317 8814
Email info@londonjewishforum.org.uk *Website* www.londonjewishforum.org.uk
The London Jewish Forum is an advocate for the Capital's Jewish Community, campaigning and influencing change in the public institutions that make decisions which affect Jewish lives. Rooted within Jewish Values, London Jewish Forum works across the Community regardless of religious, cultural or political affiliations or beliefs, and with our neighbours. It works to identify the issues and concerns of London's Jewish community and ensure that City Hall and Town Halls understand and are responsive to them. These are often the same issues and concerns of London's wider community. Our wellbeing is tied to that of our neighbours, so working with communities across the city, the London Jewish Forum strives to deliver a cohesive, inclusive and tolerant London that all communities can enjoy. *Ch.* Adrian Cohen; *Exec. Dir.* Peter Mason

Alyth Choral Society
North Western Reform Synagogue, Alyth Gardens, NW11 7EN
Tel 020 8455 6763
Website www.alythchoralsociety.org
(Est. 1983). *Musical Dir.* Michael Etherton; *Ch.* Lucille Sher; *Sec.* Ms L. Perez

Association of Jewish Friendship Clubs *See under* Representative Organisations

Centre for Jewish Life
Media House, 4 Stratford Place, W1C 1AT
Tel 020 7495 6089 *Fax* 020 7495 6099
Email info@thecjl.org *Website* www.thecjl.org
(Est. 2008). The Centre is dedicated to providing social, educational and business events for young unaffiliated Jews of all backgrounds and nationalities, enabling them to connect with

each other and their heritage. *Hon. Pres.* Dr. Sam Peltz; *Ch.* Rabbi F. Vogel; Advisory Bd. Eduardo Azar, Keith Breslauer, Colin Gershinson, Dennis Levine, Edward Mishrahi, Conrad Morris, Martin Moshal, Alan Samson

Chabad Lubavitch Centres of North East London and Essex
395 Eastern Avenue, Ilford, Essex IG2 6LR
Tel 020 8554 1624 *Fax* 020 8518 2126
Email rabbisufrin@chabadilford.co.uk *Website* www.chabadilford.co.uk
(Est. 1986. Reg. Charity No. 1123001). *Exec. Dir.* Rabbi A.M. Sufrin, MBE; *Asst. Dir.* Rabbi M. Muller

Chabad Wimbledon
42 St. George's Road, Wimbledon, SW19 4ED
Tel 020 8944 7770
Email rabbi@dubov.org *Website* www.chabadwimbledon.com
(Est. 1988. Reg. Charity No. 227638). Chabad Hebrew School, Adult Jewish education, Chabad Shul, library, food and bookshop, mailings, mikvah, Bar/Bat Mitzvah, tuition, Mitzva campaigns, youth activities, mothers and toddlers groups and camps. *Dir.* Rabbi Nissan Dubov

Friends of Jewish Youth *See under* Organisations concerned with Jewish Youth

Jewish Appreciation Group Tours
32 Anworth Close, Woodford Green, Essex IG8 0DR
Tel 020 8504 9159
(Est. 1960). Full history tours of the Jewish East End, the Jews in England from 1066 etc. Historic walks and tours throughout the year. *Tours Org.* Adam Joseph

Jewish Association of Cultural Societies (J.A.C.S.)
Edgware Synagogue, Parnell Close, Edgware, Middlesex HA8 9YE
Tel 020 8958 7508 *Fax* 020 8905 4449
Email office@edgwareu.com
(Est. 1978). Twenty-three clubs located throughout the Greater London area, with two in Surrey, one in Brighton, one in Westcliff-on-Sea, providing weekly meetings for the 65+, embracing cultural and social programmes. *H. Pres.* Cyril Gordon; *H. Nat. Ch.* Harold Newman MBE; *Nat. Sec.* Sheila Levitt; *Hon. S. S.* Pizer

JHSE Essex Branch
Email jhseessex1@aol.com *Website* www.jhse.org
Lectures will start at 8.15pm at the King Solomon High School.
Contact S. Lassman *Tel* 020 8554 9921

KabbalahUK.com
42 St George's Road Wimbledon SW19 4ED
Tel 020 8944 7770
Email rabbi@dubov.org
(Est. 2005). To disseminate Kabbalistic and Chassidic teaching in the UK. *Dir.* Rabbi N.D. Dubov

Kadimah Youth Club *See under* Organisations concerned with Jewish Youth

London Jewish Male Choir
c/o 29b The Burroughs, London NW4 4AR
Tel 07889 465 417
Email info@ljmc.org.uk *Website* www.ljmc.org.uk
For over 85 years, The London Jewish Male Choir has entertained audiences throughout the world with high quality performances of a broad range of Jewish Music, encompassing Liturgical music through to Broadway and Yiddish. Regular rehearsals on Thursday evenings, and new members welcome, especially those with sight reading ability. *Mus. Dir.* Joseph Finlay; *Ch.* David Renton; *T.* Tony Margolis

Lubavitch of Edgware
230 Hale Lane, Edgware, Middlesex HA8 9PZ
Tel 020 8905 4141 *Fax* 020 8958 1169
Email rabbi@lubavitchofedgware.com *Website* www.lubavitchofedgware.com

(Est. 1986). Pioneers in Street Youth Work programmes: Kindergarten, Synagogue (affiliated to the Union of Orthodox Hebrew Congregations), Gan Israel Day Camp, Library, Tel Torah: telephone learning service. *Dir* Rabbi L. and F. Sudak. *Publ.* Central, *Ed.* F. Sudak

The Maccabaeans

(Est. 1891). Consisting primarily of those engaged in professional pursuits, its aims being to provide 'social intercourse and co-operation among its members with a view to the promotion of the interests of Jews, including the support of any professional or learned body and charities'. *Pres.* Prof. D. Latchman; *Hon. T.* R. Michaelson; *Hon. S.* L. Slowe 4 Corringway, NW11 7ED

Museum of Immigration and Diversity

19 Princelet Street, E1 6QH

Tel 020 7247 5352

Email office@19princeletstreet.org.uk *Website* www.19princeletstreet.org.uk

(Reg. Charity 287279). Grade II* heritage building incorporating a Victorian synagogue. Occasional public openings are held in celebration of immigration and diversity; private tours for educational groups by advance arrangement.

Redbridge Jewish Cultural Society

(Est. 1965). Meetings held at South West Essex & Settlement Reform Synagogue Oaks Lane, Newbury Park. *Contact* Isabel Morris *Tel* 020 8599 1746. Monthly meetings on Sunday evenings 8pm. Call for further details.

Redbridge Jewish Community Centre

Sinclair House, Woodford Bridge Road, Ilford, Essex, IG4 5LN

Tel 020 8551 0017 *Fax* 020 8551 9027

(Reg. Charity No. 3013185). *Ch.* P. Leigh; *Centre Man.* R. Shone. Redbridge JCC, home of the Redbridge Jewish Community Centre, meets the social, educational and welfare needs of all sections of the Redbridge and District Jewish Community. More than 2,500 people make use of the Centre's facilities each week. The Redbridge Jewish Day Centre provides a high level of essential care for over 350 elderly and disabled people. A Meals-on-Wheels service provides approx. 250 kosher meals each week. There are programmes and services for young people, including those with special needs. There are also social, educational, welfare and active sports programmes for the young and adults alike. The Centre is also the base for the Community Shlicha, Clayhall Synagogue, Ackerman Resource Centre, and many communal events and activities. The Redbridge Jewish Community Centre is part of Jewish Care.

Stepney Jewish Community Centre

2-8 Beaumont Grove, E1 4NQ

Tel 020 7790 6441 *Fax* 020 7265 8342

Administered by **Jewish Care**. Community Centre for the Elderly; Special care centre for physically and mentally frail; Kosher Meals on Wheels; outreach and support services; and Friendship Clubs. *Centre Man.* Philippa Paine

Tribe (Young United Synagogue) *See under* Organisations concerned with Jewish Youth

Western Charitable Foundation

32 Great Cumberland Place, W1H 7TN

Tel 020 7724 7702

Ch. Harold Pasha; *V. Ch.* David I. Winton; *T.* Anthony H. Yadgaroff; *Exec. Sec.* S. Garcia

Zemel Choir

Contact Anthony Cohen

Tel 07770 345 679

Email marketing@zemelchoir.org *Website* www.zemelchoir.org

(Reg. Charity No. 252572/ACL). The UK's leading mixed voice Jewish Choir performing a varied repertoire, with an emphasis on Hebrew, Yiddish, Israeli and liturgical music, and contemporary compositions of Jewish interest. Overseas tours, prestige concerts in London and provinces, recordings, and social events. Zemel welcomes enthusiastic and committed singers with some experience of reading music. Rehearsals most Mondays 8-10.30pm. North London. *Musical Dir.* Benjamin Wolf

Miscellaneous Organisations

ALL ABOARD SHOPS LIMITED
(Reg. Charity No. 1125462). All Aboard operate Charity Shops for the benefit of UK-based Jewish Charities. All Aboard welcome donations of clothing, bric-a-brac etc, and welcome volunteers to assist in the shops and at Head Office. *Life V. Pres.* Stella Lucas; *Ch. of Tru.* Howard Brecker; *T.* Michael Green, Alan Millet, Brian Finch, Jeffrey Pinnick; *CEO* Carol Marks, Flo Kaufmann, Robert Lipson, Harvey Rose, Michael Wernicke
Tel 020 8381 1717 *Fax* 020 8381 1718
Email admin@allaboardshops.com *Website* www.allaboardshops.com
Head Office Stella Lucas House, 105 High Street, Edgware, Middlesex HA8 7DB
Shops located at **Barnet** 67 High Street, EN5 5UR; **Borehamwood** 120 Shenley Road WD6 1EF; **East Finchley** 124 High Road, N2 9ED; **Edgware** Unit 1, Boot Parade, 88 High Street, HA8 7HE, 224 Station Road, HA8 7AU; **Finchley Central** 102 Ballards Lane, N3 2DN; **Finchley Road** 150 Finchley Road NW3 5HS; **North Finchley** 369 Ballards Lane, N12 8LJ; **Golders Green** 616 Finchley Road NW11 7RR *and* 125 Golders Green Road NW11 8HR; **Hendon** 98 Brent Street NW4 2HH; **Manchester** Unit 10, The Longfield Centre, Prestwich MA25 5AY; **Mill Hill** 51 The Broadway NW7 3DA; **Paddington** 12 Spring Street W2 3RA; **Stamford Hill** 2a Regent Parade, Amhurst Park N16 5LP; **Streatham** 83 Streatham High Road SW16 1PH; **Temple Fortune** 1111 Finchley Road NW11 0QB; **West Hampstead** 224 West End Lane NW6 1UU

JEWISH POLICE ASSOCIATION
Non Charter Mail, Peel Centre, Aerodrome Road, Hendon, London NW9 5JE
Tel 07770 492 782
Email info@jewishpoliceassociation.org.uk *Website* www.jewishpoliceassociation.org.uk
(Est. 2001). Provides a network for support and advice of Jewish staff within the Metropolitan Police Service; to promote understanding of the Jewish faith within the Police Service; and to act as a resource reference for Police Services regarding religious and cultural issues, in particular those that affect front-line policing. *Ch.* Tim Williams; *Dep. Ch.* Michael Loebenberg; *T.* Sara Levene; *Sec.* Danny Phillips; *Youth Officer*, Daniel Morris; *Chaplains* Rabbi Geoffrey Shisler, Dr. Rabbi Jonathan Romain

JEWISH VISITING
Admin. United Synagogue Visitation Committee, 305 Ballards Lane, London N12 8GB
Tel 020 8343 6238
Email admin@jvisit.org.uk
The Visitation Committee, while under the administration of the United Synagogue, includes Hospital Visiting and Prison Chaplaincy services for anyone Jewish, irrespective of synagogue affiliation. The Committee is recognised by the National Health Service as the provider of hospital chaplaincy for Jewish patients, servicing hospitals within London and the Home Counties. Visits by chaplains and lay visitors are made in those hospitals where there is a regular intake of Jewish patients, and information is given to other hospitals for emergency situations and occasional visits. The Jewish Prison Chaplaincy department, is officially recognised by the Ministery of Justice as the sole provider for religious, spiritual and pastoral needs of all Jewish prisoners throughout England and Wales. Its director is the Jewish Faith Advisor to HM Prison Service.
Ch. Keith D. Simons; *Snr. Hospital Chaplain*, Rabbi Zorach Meir Salasnik; *Dir. of Jewish Prison Chaplaincy* Rev. Michael Binstock MBE
   Bereavement Counselling Service (*See* p.184).

LONDON JEWISH MEDICAL SOCIETY
The Medical Society of London, P.O. Box 382, Wembley, Middlesex HA9 9FA
Tel 07929 633 108
(Est. 1928). A learned society for doctors, senior medical students and members of allied professions. *Pres.* Prof. L. Spitz; *Hon. S. B.* Jacobs

LONDON SOCIETY OF JEWS AND CHRISTIANS
21 Maple Street, London W1T 4BE
Tel 020 7580 1663
Email m.solomon@liberaljudaism.org

(Est. 1927). The oldest interfaith organisation of its kind in the UK. It was established to give an opportunity to Jews and Christians to confer together on the basis of their common ideals and with mutual respect for differences of religion. *Jt. Pres.* Rabbi Dr. D.J. Goldberg OBE, Revd. Dr. A. Harvey; *Jt. Ch.* Rabbi M. L. Solomon, Rev. Dr. N. Sagovsky; *Hon. S.* Paula Flynn

THE REGIONS

There are disused cemeteries at a number of towns in the British Isles, including Bath, Canterbury, Dover, Falmouth, Ipswich, Kings Lynn, Penzance, Sheerness, and Yarmouth. General enquiries about these and other locations should be addressed to the Board's Community Issues Division, or to Jewish Heritage (*See* page 325–328).

Mikvaot are maintained in the following towns: Birmingham, Bournemouth, Brighton, Cardiff, Edinburgh, Gateshead, Leeds, Leicester, Liverpool, Manchester, Newcastle, Sheffield, Southend, Southport, Sunderland and Glasgow.

Memorials Large stone/slate memorial in Aberdovey Town Centre Park, West Wales, to No.3 Jewish Troop, No.10 Commando – plaque opposite on sea wall explains the Jewish refugee make-up of the troop; Clifford's Tower, York; Lincoln Cathedral.

BASILDON (Essex)
Merged with Southend.
Burials arranged through Southend & Westcliff Hebrew Congregation at their cemetery in Southend.

BATH
The last synagogue closed in 1910. Services are currently being revived under the auspices of the Bristol and West Progressive Jewish Congregation (*See* p.199) at The Friends' Meeting House, York Street.

BEXHILL-ON-SEA
Bexhill and District
Jewish Friends, P.O. Box 198, TN40 9BG *Ch.* G. Lee; *T.* R. Caidan; *Sec* J. Caidan; *Asst. Sec.* M. Phillips *See also under* Hastings

BIRMINGHAM
This Jewish community is one of the oldest in the provinces, dating from 1730, if not earlier. Birmingham manufacturing attracted early Jewish settlers. In the Anglo-Jewish economy Birmingham's position was similar to a port, a centre from which Jewish pedlars covered the surrounding country week by week, returning to their homes for the Sabbath. The first synagogue of which there is any record was in The Froggery in 1780. But there was a Jewish cemetery in the same neighbourhood in 1730, and Moses Aaron is said to have been born in Birmingham in 1718. The history of the Birmingham community has been investigated by the Birmingham Jewish History Research Group under the leadership of the late Zoë Josephs.

REPRESENTATIVE BODIES
Representative Council of Birmingham and West Midland Jewry
Email jewishbirmingham@talktalk.net *Website* www.jewishbirmingham.org
(Est. 1937). *Pres.* Sir B. Zissman; *Ch.* R. Jacobs; *Hon. S.* Leonard Jacobs *Tel* 0121 236 1801; *Admin. c/o* BHC, Singers Hill, Ellis Street, Birmingham, B1 1HL *Tel* 07768 761 930
SYNAGOGUES
Birmingham Central Synagogue
4 Speedwell Road, B5 7PA
Tel 0121 440 4044 *Fax* 0121 440 5405
Email office@central-shul.com *Website* www.centralshul.com
M. Rabbi C. Atlas; *Sec.* C. Jennings
Birmingham Hebrew Congregation
Singers Hill, Ellis Street, B1 1HL
Tel 0121 643 0884 Fax 0121 643 2273
Email office@singershill.freeserve.co.uk *Website* www.singershill.com
The present synagogue was consecrated on September 24, 1856 and celebrated its 150th anniversary in 2006. *M.* Rabbi Y. Jacobs; *Admin.* B. Gingold

Birmingham Progressive Synagogue (LJ)
Bishopsgate Street, 1 Roseland Way, B15 1HD
Tel 0121 634 3888
Email office@bps-pro-syn.co.uk *Website* www. bpsjudaism.com
Hon. S. Yvonne Stollard *Tel* 01905 775 972; *M.* Rabbi Dr. Margaret Jacobi

CEMETERIES
Brandwood End Cemetery
(Entrance Broad Lane) Woodthorpe Road, Kings Heath, Birmingham, West Midlands B14
6EQ Enquiries to Hebrew Congregation *Tel* 0121 643 0884
Witton Cemetery
Warren Road, B44 8QH
The Ridgeway, College Road, Erdington *Tel* 0121 382 9900

EDUCATIONAL
King David School
244 Alcester Road, B13 8EY
Tel 0121 449 3364
Email enquiry@kingdavidschool.co.uk
Hd. S. Langford

RELIGIOUS ORGANISATIONS
Birmingham Rabbinic Board
Ch. Rabbi Y. Jacobs *Tel* 0121 643 0884 *Email* rabbinicboard@gmail.com
Lubavitch Centre & Bookshop
95 Willows Road, B12 9QF
Tel 0121 440 6673 *Fax* 0121 446 4299
M. Rabbi S. Arkush. Also at this address: Operation Judaism (*See* p. 140).
Midlands Centre for Liberal Judaism
c/o Birmingham Progressive Synagogue, Bishopsgate Street, Roseland Way, B15 1HD
Mikveh
at Central Synagogue, For appointments *Tel* 0794 664 2265

SOCIAL, CULTURAL & INTERFAITH
Jewish Historical Society
(Branch Est. 1968). *Ch.* Dr A. P. Joseph
Midlands Israel Information Centre
c/o Birmingham Progressive Synagogue, 1 Roseland Way, B15 1HD
Email iicmids@talktalk.net
Dir. Ruth Jacobs *Tel* 0121 643 2688

WELFARE
Birmingham Jewish Community Care
Bill Steiner Suite, Riverbrook Drive, B30 2SH
Tel 0121 459 3819 *Fax* 0121 459 1487
Email admin@bhamjcc.co.uk *Website* www.bhamjcc.co.uk
Pres. Dr B. Roseman; *Dir.* I. Myers
Care Home with Residential, Nursing, and Respite Care
Andrew Cohen House, Riverbrook Drive, Stirchley, B30 2SH
Tel 0121 458 5000
Email admin@bhamjcc.co.uk

YOUTH & STUDENTS
Birmingham Union of Jewish Students
c/o Hillel House, 26 Somerset Road, Edgbaston, B15 2QD
Tel 0121 454 5684
Email ujs@ujs.org.uk

Hillel House
26 Somerset Road, Edgbaston, B15 2QD
Tel 0121 454 5684
Email birminghamhillel@hotmail.co.uk
Website www.ujshillel.co.uk/hillel-facilities/accomodation/midlands/birmingham
Applications for admission to Bella Lupasco, 10 East Drive, Edgbaston, Birmingham, B5 7RX
Tel 0121 471 4370

BLACKPOOL
SYNAGOGUES
United Hebrew Congregation
Leamington Road, FY1 4HD
(Consecrated 1916). Services were first held in the 1890s in a private house. Later a synagogue was built in Springfield Road. *Pres.* F. H. Freeman *Tel* 01253 393 767; *Sec.* B. Goodstone *Tel* 01253 764 275
Blackpool Reform Jewish Congregation
40 Raikes Parade, FY1 4EX
Tel 01253 623 687
A constituent of the Movement for Reform Judaism. Services: Erev Shabbat 8pm, Shabbat morning 11am.

SOCIAL, CULTURAL & INTERFAITH
Fylde League of Jewish Women
Hon. S. A. Poston, Flat 16, The Royals, 11 Links Gate, Lytham St Annes, Lancashire FY8 3LJ
Tel 01253 711 078 *Email* abposton123@btinternet.com

BOGNOR REGIS
Hebrew Congregation
Elm Lodge, Sylvan Way, PO21 2RS
Hon. S. J. S. Jacobs, *Tel* 01243 823 006 *Email* jackneve@talktalk.net

BOURNEMOUTH
The Bournemouth Hebrew Congregation was established in 1905 and met in the Assembly Rooms, where the Bournemouth Pavilion now stands. A synagogue, built in Wootton Gardens in 1911, was rebuilt in 1961 to seat some 950 congregants. The Menorah suite was added in 1974, and a mikveh in 1976.

Bournemouth Reform Synagogue was started by a small band of enthusiasts in 1947. Ten years later the congregation was large enough to build the present synagogue building at 53 Christchurch Road. It was extended in 1980 and now has a membership of over 700, with a voluntary mixed choir, an active Cheder, and many social activities. It is host to the Jewish Day Centre every Monday.

Chabad Lubavitch has been an integral part of Bournemouth Jewish community for the past twenty years. In 2009 they opened their million pound centre which houses a shul, library, classrooms and catering facilities. They have Shabbos and weekday minyanim and hold numerous events throughout the year.

Bournemouth is the religious and social centre for the fast growing community in Dorset, West Hampshire and Wiltshire.

REPRESENTATIVE BODIES
Bournemouth Jewish Representative Council (incorporating Southampton)
Website www.masorti-bournemouth.co.uk

SYNAGOGUES
Bournemouth Masorti Group
Tel 07810 854 673
Email masortibmth@btinternet.com
Website www.masorti-bournemouth-masorti.co.uk

Bournemouth Hebrew Congregation
Synagogue Chambers, Wootton Gardens, Dorset BH1 1PW
Tel 01202 557 433 *Fax* 01202 557 578
Tel 07984 427 375 (Ladies Mikveh)
Email office1@bhcshul.co.uk
Website www.bhcshul.co.uk
M. Rabbi Adrian Jesner

Reform Syngagogue
53 Christchurch Road, BH1 3PA
Postal address P O Box 8, BH1 3PN
Tel 01202 557 736
Website www.bournemouthreform.org
(Est. 1947). A Constituent of the Reform Movement. It now has a membership of over 400, with an active Cheder, art group, Bridge club, educational classes and many social activities. *V. Ch.* Irving Mindel; *Hon. T.* Mark Chaloner; *Ch.* Ruth Reed; *H. Ch.* Ron Rosenfeld; *Hon. S.* Laura Mellins; *Principal Rabbi* Rabbi N. Amswych; *Associate Rabbi* Jenny Goldfried Amswych

CEMETERIES
Kinson Cemetery (used by both the Hebrew Congregation and the Reform Synagogue)
Boscombe Cemetery (used by old established members Hebrew Congregation)
Throop Cemetery (Hebrew Congregation)

EDUCATIONAL
Yavneh Kindergarten
Gertrude Preston Hall, Wootton Gardens, BH1 3PW
Tel 07831 530 216
Email yavnehkindergarten@gmail.com
Facebook yavenehkindergarten
Princ. Jan Knapp, Hayley Bun

RELIGIOUS ORGANISATIONS
Bournemouth Sephardi Association
69 Orchard Avenue, Poole, BH14 8AH
Tel 01202 745 168 after 8pm
Ch. Simon Tammam; *T.* David Kalfon

Lubavitch Centre
Chabad House, 20 Lansdowne Road, BH1 1SD
Tel 01202 555 367

Mikva Gertrude Preston Hall, Wootton Gardens Rebbetzin Jesner *Tel* 07984 427 375

SOCIAL, CULTURAL & INTERFAITH
Wessex Jewish News (6 issues a year)
3 De Lisle Road, BH3 7NF
Email edwin@onetel.com

WELFARE
Home for Aged
Hannah Levy House, 15 Poole Road, Dorset
Tel 01202 765 361
Email hlhtrust@btconnect.com

YOUTH & STUDENTS
Bournemouth University Jewish Society
Wallisdown Road, Poole
Tel 01202 524 111

BRADFORD

Jews of German birth, who began settling in Bradford in the first half of the nineteenth century, were in a large measure responsible for the development of its wool yarns and fabrics exports to all parts of the world. Jewish services, first held in the 1830s in private houses, were held in 1873, on Reform lines, in a public hall. About the same period saw the beginnings of the Orthodox community.

SYNAGOGUE

Bradford Synagogue
7a, Bowland Street, Bradford, BD1 3BW
Website www.bradfordsynagogue.co.uk
(Est. 1880). A constituent of the Reform Movement. Ad hoc Shabbat and morning services about once a month. R. Leavor, 76 Heaton Park Drive, BD9 5QE *Tel* 01274 544 198 *Email* leavor@onetel.com

CEMETERIES
Scholemoor, Necropolis Road, Cemetery Road, Bradford (both Orthodox and Reform).

WELFARE
Jewish Benevolent Society
Contact 1 Fern Chase, Scarcroft, Leeds LS14 3JL
Pres. A. A. Waxman; *Hon. T.* W. Behrend

BRIGHTON & HOVE

There were Jews living in Brighton in the second half of the eighteenth century, and by the beginning of the nineteenth century there was an organised community (The earliest synagogue was founded in Jew Street in 1792).

REPRESENTATIVE BODIES
Sussex Jewish Representative Council
Tel 07789 491 279
Email info@sussexjewishrepresentativecouncil.org
Website www.sussexjewishrepresentativecouncil.org
Nearly every synagogue, charitable organisation, social and cultural institution, as well as the communities in Eastbourne, Hastings, Bexhill and Worthing, are affiliated to this Council, and meetings are held quarterly. *Pres.* Beryl Sharpe; *Sec.* Jessica Rosenthal *Corr.* P.O. Box 2178, Hove, BN3 3SZ

SYNAGOGUES
Brighton & Hove Hebrew Congregation
West Hove Synagogue: 29-31 New Church Road, Hove BN3 4AD /66 Middle Street, BN1 1AL
Tel 01273 888 855
Email office@bhhc-shul.org *Website* www.bhhc-shul.org
(Reg. Charity No. 1115092). Open monthly Sundays for viewing; contact Admin for details. *M.* Rabbi H. Rader
Brighton & Hove Progressive Synagogue (LJ)
6 Lansdowne Road, Hove, BN3 1FF
Tel 01273 737 223
Email bhps@freenetname.co.uk
(Est. 1935). *M.* Rabbi Elizabeth Tikvah Sarah; *Admin* Chandra Wishart
Brighton & Hove Reform Synagogue
Palmeira Avenue, Hove, BN3 3GE
Tel 01273 735 343
Email accounts@bh-rs.org
(Est. 1955). *Admin.* L. Shaw
Hove Hebrew Congregation
79 Holland Road, Hove, BN3 1JN
Tel 01273 732 035

Email hollandroadshul@btconnect.com *Website* www.hollandroadshul.com
Ch. Stanley Cohen; *T.* Michele Cohen; *M.* Rabbi V. Silverman

CEMETERIES
Cemetery (Orthodox) Meadow View Cemetery, Bear Road
Contact Rabbi P. Efune *Tel* 01273 321 919
Cemetery (Non-Orthodox) Old Shoreham Road
Contact either the Reform or Progressive Synagogues.

EDUCATIONAL
Torah Nursery
29 New Church Road, Hove BN3 4AD
Tel 01273 328 675
Centre for German-Jewish Studies
University of Sussex, Sussex House, BN1 9RH

RELIGIOUS
Joint Kashrut Board
Contact Rabbi H Rader *Tel* 01273 888 855 or Rabbi V. Silverman *Tel* 01273 732 035
Lubavitch Brighton
15 The Upper Drive, East Sussex BN3 6GR
Email rabbiefune@lubavitchbrighton.com
Rabbi P. Efune *Tel* 01273 321 919

SOCIAL, CULTURAL & INTERFAITH
AJEX
Ch. Aubrey Cole, 61 Langdale Road, Hove BN3 4HR
Tel 01273 737 417
Ben Gurion University Foundation
Ch. & Delegate Sam Barsam 47 Woodruff Avenue, Hove BN3 6LH *Contact Tel* 01273 508 323
Email sambarsam@hotmail.com
Brighton & Hove Interfaith Contact Group IFCG
c/o Community Base, 113 Queens Road, BN1 3XG
Website www.interfaithcontactgroup.com
Contact Charlotte Gravestock *Email* mail@jcgravestock.plus.com
Brighton & Hove Jewish Centre
Ralli Hall, 81 Denmark Villas, Hove BN3 3TH
Tel 01273 202 254
Email rallihall@tiscali.co.uk
(Reg. Charity No. 269474). Incorporating Ralli Hall Lunch and Social Club, Film Club, Ralli
Hall Israeli Dance Group, Jewish Arts Society, SARID (Holocaust Survivors Group). *Man.*
Norina Duke; *Ch.* Roger Abrahams.
Meeting centre for various senior clubs, mother & baby club, youth clubs and communal
groups. Facilities include committee rooms, theatre facilities, library/reading room, cafeteria,
etc. Kosher kitchen (lunch available on Tuesdays and Thursdays). Function rooms and
Ballrooms for hire.
JACS (Jewish Association of Cultural Societies)
Social group for over 50s. *Ch.* Nina Taylor *Tel* 01273 720 390; *Delegate* Joan Levene 11
Gainsborough House, Eaton Gardens, Hove BN3 3UA *Tel* 01273 722 926
JAS - Jewish Arts Society
Ch. Rochelle Oberman 23 Hove Park Road, Hove BN3 6LA
Sussex Jewish Golfing Society
Pres. Roland Moss *Tel* 01273 502 221; *T.* Michael Marks 9 Woodlands, Hove BN3 6TJ
Tel 01273 541 299 *Email* michael@marksand.co.uk
Sussex WIZO-Ziona
Ch. Claire Barsam 47 Hove Park Road, Hove BN3 6LH *Tel* 01273 508 323
Email sambarsam@hotmail.com

Youth Aliyah
Ch. Elizabeth Posner 18 Baltimore Court, 74 The Drive, Hove BN3 3PR Tel 01273 776 671
Email liz.posner@orchidserve.com

WELFARE
Brighton & Hove Jewish Day Centre - See Brighton & Hove Jewish Centre at Ralli Halll
Brighton & Hove Jewish Welfare Board
Tel 07952 479 111
Contact, Ch. Fiona Sharpe Email sussexjwb@googlemail.com
Helping Hands
3/80 Langdale Road, Hove BN3 4HP
Email helping-hands@helping-hands.org Website www.helping-hands.org
(Reg. Charity No. 1117001). Provide care and assistance both in practical and emotional
terms for all members across the community. ie visiting or phoning someone who is lonely,
shopping for house bound transport for medical appointments and much more.
Hyman Fine House (Jewish Care residential home)
20 Burlington Street, Brighton BN2 1AU
Website www.jewishcare.org
Hd. of Home, Natasha Carson Tel 01273 688 226 Email ncarson@jcare.org
Sussex Tikvah (Home for Jewish adults with learning difficulties)
25 Chatsworth Road BN1 5DB
Tel 01273 564 021
Man. Joanne Osbaldiston Email manager@sussextikvah.org.uk

YOUTH & STUDENTS
Hillel House
18 Harrington Road, Brighton BN1 6RE
Tel 01273 503 450
Ch. & Delegate Aileen Hill 2/9 Adelaide Crescent, Hove BN3 2JH Tel 01273 727 979
Brighton Union of Jewish Students
Adam Email jsoc@ussu.sussex.ac.uk

BRISTOL
Bristol was one of the principal Jewish centres of medieval England. Even after the
Expulsion from England in 1290 there were occasional Jewish residents or visitors. A community of Marranos lived here during the Tudor period. There had been a Jewish community in the City before 1754 and the original Bristol Hebrew Congregation Synagogue
opened in 1786. The present building dates from 1871 and was renovated in 1981-83 and
again in 2008-09. It was listed in 2012.
    Bristol & West Progressive Jewish Congregation was founded in 1961; its present
Synagogue in Easton in Bristol was consecrated in 1971, extended in 1988, and again in 2003.
    A residential house for Jewish students at the independent school in Bristol, Clifton
College, called Polack's House after its first Housemaster, was founded in 1878 and closed
in 2007. Many Jewish students attend the University of Bristol. There is also a Chabad
House.

SYNAGOGUES
Bristol Hebrew Congregation (I)
9 Park Row, BS1 5LP
Tel 07503 886 790
Email info@bristolhebrewcongregation.co.uk Website www.bristolhebrewcongregation.co.uk
Chabad Contact Email bristolchabad@gmail.com
Bristol & West Progressive Jewish Congregation (LJ)
43-47 Bannerman Road, Easton BS5 0RR
Email bwpjc@bwpjc.org Website www.bwpjc.org
(Reg. Charity No. 73879). Ch. Gary Webber, Rabbi Monique Mayer

CEMETERIES
Oakdene Avenue, Fishponds, Bristol BS5 6QQ
Memorial Woodlands, Earthcott Green, Alveston, Bristol, BS35 3TA
Canford, Canford Lane, Westbury-on-Trym, Bristol, BS9 3PQ
South Bristol, Bridgewater Road, Bedminster Down, Bristol, BS13 7AS

EDUCATIONAL
Davar
Suite 413, 179 Whiteladies Road, Clifton BS8 2AG
See under Educational and Cultural Organisations chapter

YOUTH & STUDENTS
Bristol University Jewish Society (JSoc)
Website www.bristoljsoc.co.uk
Pres. Natasha Isaac *Email* chair@bristoljsoc.org.uk
Hillel
The Ark & Dove, 36 Oakfield Road, Clifton, BS8 2BA

CAMBRIDGE

The present congregation was founded in 1888, but an organised community was present from 1774. There is extensive Jewish life in Cambridge. The Cambridge Jewish Residents Association (CJRA) was the original resident organisation set up in 1940-41 following the influx of evacuees and refugees into Cambridge and the need for a Jewish Burial Ground. The Jewish section of the Newmarket Road City Cemetery dates from this time.
A variety of religious services are held on a regular basis, there are also extensive cultural and educational programmes held across and for the whole community. The School of Divinity also has a regular programme of activities and there is extensive Interfaith work carried out in the Woolf Institute.

SYNAGOGUES
Cambridge Traditional Jewish Congregation
3 Thompson's Lane, CB5 8AQ
Tel 01223 501 916
(Est. 1937. Reg. Charity No. 282849). *Ch.* Prof. S. Goldhill
Email sdg1001@cam.ac.uk *Website* www.ctjc.org.uk
Beth Shalom Reform Synagogue
Email info@beth-shalom.org.uk *Website* www.beth-shalom.org.uk
(Est. 1978). Services, cheder, pre-cheder, adult education and welfare programmes. *Ch.* Mike Frankl

RELIGIOUS
Cambridge & Suffolk Jewish Community (Hama'ayan)
Correspondence, Sec. D. Gilinsky 101 Perse Way, Cambridge, CB4 3SB
Email info@jewishcambridge.org.uk *Website* www.jewishcambridge.org.uk
(Reg. Charity No. 1111197). Mikveh and children's nursery at 268 Milton Road, CB4 1LQ
Cambridge Commmunity Mikveh Charitable Trust (CCMC)
(Reg. Charity No. 1067075). *Enquiries* D. Gilinsky 101 Perseway, Cambridge CB4 3SB
Chabad of Cambridge
37a Castle Street, CB3 0AH
Email info@cuchabad.org.uk *Website* www.cuchabad.org
Tel/Fax 01223 354 603
Rabbi Reuven Leigh; *Dir.* Rochel Leigh

SOCIAL, CULTURAL & INTERFAITH
Cambridge Jewish Residents' Association (CJRA)
Email admin@cambridgejewishresidents.org *Website* www.cambridgejewishresidents.org
(Est. 1940. Reg. Charity No. 289724). The CJRA acts as an umbrella group for the whole

community, concentrating on social, educational, cultural and welfare activities that encompass Jews of all persuasions in Cambridge. Membership is open to all Jews, irrespective of their Jewish religious affiliation. Non-Jewish partners are encouraged to join in all activities. In September 2011 the CJRA celebrated its 70th anniversary with a special event and tea at Girton College at which the Chief Rabbi, Lord Sacks, gave an address.

Cambridge Jewish Cultural Association
The Cambridge Jewish Cultural Association is an offshoot of the CJRA and the cross communal welfare group (Cambridge Jewish Community Support) and meets on a monthly basis on a Monday afternoon.

YOUTH & STUDENTS
Cambridge University Jewish Society
3 Thompsons Lane, CB5 8AQ
Website www.cujs.org

CANTERBURY & DISTRICT
The history of the Canterbury community, 'The Jews of Canterbury, 1760–1931' by Dan Cohn-Sherbok, was published in 1984.

SOCIAL, CULTURAL & INTERFAITH
Canterbury and District Jewish Community
c/o 10 Durnford Close, Canterbury, Kent CT2 7RY
(Est. 1974). To provide social and cultural events for Jewish people in East Kent. *Ch.* Cedric Rebuck *Email* cedric.rebuck@btinternet.com; *T.* Ian Smiler *Tel* 07798 555 391

CHATHAM
There was an organised Jewish community in Chatham from the first half of the eighteenth century. The present synagogue was erected in 1869 in memory of Captain Lazarus Simon Magnus, by his father, Simon Magnus. It is on the site of its predecessor, erected about 1740. It is an independent traditional orthodox congregation holding regular services and events. A Centenary Hall and Mid-Kent Jewish Youth Centre was consecrated in 1972. Instigated 'Jewish Kent', Social organisation, incorporating all Jewish communities in Kent. The old cemetery, dating back to about 1790, is behind the synagogue.

Chatham Memorial Synagogue
366 High Street, Rochester ME1 1DJ
Website www.chathamshul.org.uk
Enquiries David Herling *Email* d.a.herling@city.ac.uk

CHELMSFORD
Jewish Community
Suite 6, Springfield Lyons House, Springfield Lyon Approach CM2 5LB
Tel 07961 838 560
Email info@jewishcommunitychelmsford.co.uk *Website* wwjewishcommunitychelmsford.co.uk
(Est. in 1974. Reg. Charity No. 281498). The community holds regular services, religion classes and social activities. It has burial arrangements through the Jewish Joint Burial Society.

CHELTENHAM
The congregation was established in 1823 and the cemetery in Elm Street was consecrated the following year. The present synagogue in St. James's Square opened in 1839. The furniture, Ark and Bimah came from the New Synagogue, Leadenhall Street, London, when it relocated to Great St Helen's in 1837. The furniture is thus the oldest extant Ashkenazi synagogue furniture in the country. The Community dwindled and the synagogue closed in 1903. Evacuees and Refugees helped the few residents to re-open the synagogue in 1939. *The History of the Community of Cheltenham, Gloucester and Stroud* by Rev Brian Torode was issued in 1989, reprinted in 1999 and again in 2011.

Hebrew Congregation
The Synagogue, Synagogue Lane, St James's Square, Cheltenham GL50 3PU
Email info@cheltenhamsynagogue.org.uk *Website* www.cheltenhamsynagogue.org.uk
(Reg. Charity No. 1135352). *Contact* J. Silverston *Email* chair@cheltenhamsynagogue.org.uk

CHESHAM
South Bucks Jewish Community (LJ)
P.O. Box 826, Amersham, HP6 9GA
Tel 0845 644 2370
Email info@sbjc.org.uk *Website* www.sbjc.org.uk
Eruv Shabbat services every week in Amersham; monthly Shabbat morning services;
High Holy days and festivals; Cheder; adult education services; Rosh Chodesh Group.
M. Rabbi R. Benjamin. Cemetery: *See* Edgwarebury Cemetery

CHESTER
Jewish Congregation
Ian and Lesley Daniels Porthouse, 6 South Crescent Road, Queens Park, CH4 7AU
Tel 01244 677 776

COLCHESTER
Colchester and District Jewish Community
The Synagogue, Fennings Chase, Priory Street, CO1 2QG
Tel 01206 860 0107 (not always manned)
(Est. 1969. Reg. Charity No. 237240). An independent shul, serving North Essex and Suffolk.
The community has close links with the University of Essex. Services are held on Friday
nights at 8pm and are conducted by a lay readers as the shul has no Rabbi. For information
about services, cheder and social events, please contact the Honorary Secretary Anna
Molen *Tel* 01255 679 919 *Email* colchester22@gmail.com or *Co. V. Ch.* Michael Cohen
Tel 07869 089 801

COVENTRY
There were Jews settled in and around Coventry from at least 1775. The watch making
industry was instrumental in the growth of the community in the late 1800's.
The synagogue was built in 1870 and has been in (almost) continual use to the present day.
The Reform community started in 1993.
SYNAGOGUES
Synagogue
Barras Lane, Coventry CV1 3AF *Pres.* Russel Starr; *T.* Adrian Berger

SOCIAL, CULTURAL & INTERFAITH
Coventry Reform Jewish Community
24 Nightingale Lane, Coventry CV5 6AY
Sec. Ros Johnson *Tel* 02476 672 027 *Email* rosjohnson@gmail.com

CRAWLEY
Jewish Community (LJ)
Ch. Lynda Bloom *Tel* 01293 534 294; *T.* Joyce de Ath *Tel* 01444 811 825; *Sec.* Shirley
Livingstone *Tel* 01403 791 753

DARLINGTON
CEMETERIES
Contained in a consecrated section of: The West Cemetery, Carmel Road, Darlington DL3 8RY

SOCIAL, CULTURAL & INTERFAITH
Hebrew Congregation (Movement for Reform)
13 Bloomfield Road, DL3 6RZ
(Est. 1904). *Ch.* P. Freitag, 237 Parkside, DL1 5TG *Tel* 01325 468 812

EAST GRINSTEAD AND DISTRICT
Jewish Community
(Est. 1978. Reg. Charity No. 288189). *M.* Rev. M. Weisman, MA; *Warden* E. Godfrey, East Grinstead JC, 7 Jefferies Way, Crowborough, Sussex TN6 2UH *Tel* 01892 653 949; *Correspondence* M. Beevor, East Grinstead JC, 6 Court Close, East Grinstead, West Sussex RH19 3YQ *Tel* 01342 312 148

EASTBOURNE
SYNAGOGUES
Hebrew Congregation
22 Susans Road, BN21 3TJ
Hon. S. Tel 01323 484 135
Services every Saturday at 10am and on festivals.

CEMETERIES
Eastbourne Borough Cemetery
A part is set aside for the community in conjunction with the Brighton Chevra Kadisha.

SOCIAL, CULTURAL & INTERFAITH
Eastbourne Liberal Jewish Community
c/o 'Jaybirds', 39 Mountbatten Drive, Langney Point, BN23 6AX
Enquiries Tel 01323 725 650/07258 155 135
Website www.eljc.org.uk
(Reg Charity No. 1115670). Please call for information on services. *Ch.* Suzanne King *Email* malka.seltzer@gmail.com; *V. Ch.* Yvonne Greene *Email* aviva.greene@gmail.com; *Admin./Hon. S.* Angela Jay *Email* eljcommunity@gmail.com

EXETER
Before the expulsion, Exeter was an important Jewish centre. The cemetery in Magdalen Road dates from 1757. The Synagogue off Mary Arches Street, was built in 1763 and is celebrating its 250th Anniversary throughout 2014. Jews are known however to have lived in Exeter 30 years earlier and the community is said to have been founded as early as 1728. The community greatly decreased during the 19th century, but has revived in recent years. Regular Traditional and Progressive services. Active parents and toddlers group, Dreidl Dribblers and Cheder Adult education and cultural activities.

Hebrew Congregation Synagogue
Synagogue Place, Mary Arches Street, EX4 3BA
Tel 01392 251 529
Email mail@exetersynagogue.org.uk *Website* www.exetersynagogue.org.uk
Pres. Tony Reese

CEMETERIES
Historic cemetery at Bull Meadow (off Magdalen Road)
Exwick Cemetery (municipal) has a part set aside for Jewish Burials.

GATESHEAD
SYNAGOGUES
Beis Hatalmud
1 Ashgrove Terrace, NE8 1RL
Princ. Rabbi S. Steinhaus *Tel* 0191 478 4352

Kolel Synagogue
22 Claremont Place, NE8 1TL
Constituent of the Union of Orthodox Hebrew Congregations. *Sec.* S. Ehrentreu *Tel* 0191 477 2189
Gateshead Hebrew Congregation
180 Bewick Road, NE8 1UF
Tel 0191 477 3552 (Mikveh) *Rabbi*, Rabbi S. Zimmerman

EDUCATIONAL
Gateshead Girls High School
6 Gladstone Terrace, NE8 4DY
Tel 0191 477 3471
Princ. Rabbi D. Bowden; *Sec.* R. Dunner
Gateshead Jewish Boarding School
10 Rydal Street, Gateshead NE8 1HG
Tel 0191 477 1431 *Fax* 0191 477 1432
Email admin@gjbs.gateshead.sch.uk
(Reg. Charity No. 527371)
Institute for Higher Rabbinical Studies (Kolel Harabbonim)
22 Claremont Place, NE8 1TL
Sec. S. Ehrentreu *Tel* 0191 477 2189
Jewish Primary School
18 Gladstone Terrace, NE8 4EA
Tel 0191 477 2154 *Fax* 0191 478 7554
(Reg. Charity No. 527372). *Hon. S.* C. Rabinowitz
Ohel Rivka Kindergarten
Alexandra Road, NE8 1RB
Tel 0191 478 3723
Hon. S. Esofsky, 13 Grasmere Street *Tel* 0191 477 4102
Sunderland Kolel – Centre for Advanced Rabbinical Studies
139 Prince Consort Road, NE8 1LR
Tel 0191 477 5690
Princ. Dayan Ch. Ehrentreu
Sunderland Talmudical College and Yeshiva
Prince Consort Road, NE8 4DS
Tel 0191 490 0195 (Office); 0191 490 0193 (Students)
Princ. Rabbi J. Ehrentreu
Yeshiva
88 Windermere Street, NE8 1UB
Tel 0191 477 2616 *Fax* 0191 490 0480
Email talmudical@btopenworld.com
Students, 179 Bewick Road *Tel* 0191 478 3048/1351 *Sec.* S. Esofsky
Yeshiva Lezeirim
36-38 Gladstone Terrace, NE8 4EF
(Office) *Tel* 0191 477 1317 *Fax* 0191 381 0250
Email yltyuk@yahoo.co.uk
(Reg. Charity No. 514963). *Princ.* Rabbi E. Jaffe *Tel* 0191 477 0744

GLOUCESTER
Gloucestershire Liberal Jewish Community
1 Norwood House, 6 Lansdown Crescent, Cheltenham, GL50 2JY
Tel 01242 521 468
Email gljc@btinternet.com *Website* www.gljc.org.uk
(Est. 2008). To provide an egalitarian form of Judaism for the people of Gloucestershire.
Ch. David Naydorf; *Hon. S.* Allison Hyman; *Hon. T.* Maggie Conu; *Cheder* Chaya Douglas; *Burial Off.* Benny Goodman; *Event and Fund-raising* Jill Rosenheim.

GRIMSBY

There are records of Jews living here prior to 1290 and a community of sorts existed in the early 1800s. Mass immigration came from Eastern Europe when Grimsby, like so many East coast ports, was the first landfall for these 'escapees' from persecution. It saw many passing through *en route* for the larger northern cities and even further onward to Canada and the United States. A fair number remained, though and a proper community was created. The synagogue and cemetery were consecrated in 1885. The community reached its numerical peak in the 1930s, when it numbered between 450/500, but its gradual decline began in the immediate post-war years. The history of the community has been published: D. and L. Gerlis, 'The Story of the Grimsby Jewish Community', 1986. Regular services are held every Friday evening at 7pm, and also on all the major festivals and holidays.

SYNAGOGUES
Sir Moses Montefiore Synagogue
Holme Hill, Heneage Road, DN32 9DZ
Pres. L. Solomon *Tel* 01472 824 463; *T.* H. S. Kalson; *Hon. S.* M. Saunders 29 Manor Drive, Waltham DN37 ONS

CEMETERIES
Chevra Kadisha First Avenue, Nunsthorpe, Grimsby
Sec. R. Resner, 14 Welholme Avenue, DN32 0EA *Tel* 01472 342 521; *T.* H. Kalson, 12A Welholme Avenue, DN32 0HP

GUILDFORD

In 1995 archaeologists from Guildford Museum discovered an unusual stone chamber beneath a High Street shop that may have been a medieval synagogue. Built in the late 12th century and demolished in the late 13th century, the chamber has features that fit in with what is known about medieval synagogues. The only object found in the building, was a coin depicting Henry III. It was of a type minted about 1272 and taken out of circulation in 1279.

Although there is no definitive proof that the chamber was a synagogue, Jews were known to have lived in Guildford before their expulsion from England in 1290.

Further information about the Medieval and Contemporary Guildford Jewish Community can be seen at www.guildfordjewish.com

SYNAGOGUES
Guildford and District Hebrew Congregation (1979)
York Road, GU1 4DR
The community has grown up since the Second World War. Regular services, Cheder and social activities. *Ch.* Prof. R. Spier *Tel* 01483 560 074; Cheder, Silke Goldberg *Tel* 07809 200 255; *Contact* B. Gould *Tel* 01483 576 470

CEMETERIES
Cemetery: Consecrated section of municipal cemetery.

YOUTH & STUDENTS
University of Surrey Jewish Society and Chaplaincy
Senate House, University of Surrey, Guildford GU2 7XN
Alex Goldberg *Tel* 07939 594 212 *Email* a.goldberg@surrey.ac.uk

HARLOW
Jewish Community
Harberts Road, Hare Street, Essex CM19 4DT
Tel 01279 432 503
Movement for Reform. *Life Pres.* C. Jackson; *Ch.* Ms H. Garnelas, Rabbi I. Shillor; *Sec.* S. Pollack

HARROGATE

'The History of the Harrogate Jewish Community' by Rosalyn Livshin was published in 1995.

SYNAGOGUES

Harrogate Hebrew Congregation
St. Mary's Walk, HG2 0LW
Website www.harrogatehebrewcongregation.co.uk
(Est. 1918). Services every Shabbat at 10am, Kiddush every week. All festivals have services, details on application. Visitors very welcome. *Sec.* P.E. Morris *Tel* 01423 871 713 *Email* morris.philip2@gmail.com; *Warden* L. Shrago *Tel* 01423 886 713 *Email* l.shrago@ntlworld.com

HASTINGS

Hastings and District Jewish Society
Hon S. Sheila Stanley 55a Sea Road, Bexhill-on-Sea, East Sussex TN40 1JJ
Tel 077 4399 2295
(Reg. Charity No. 273806). Regular meetings of the Society, including a short service are held on the first Friday of the month in Bexhill, at 7pm.

HEMEL HEMPSTEAD

SYNAGOGUES

Hebrew Congregation (affiliated to US)
Lady Sarah Cohen Community Centre, Midland Road, Hemel Hempstead, Herts HD1 1RP
(Est. 1956). *Hon. S.* H. Nathan *Tel* 01923 32007

WELFARE

Morton House (Jewish Care residential home)
Midland Road, HP2 5BJ

HITCHIN

Yeshivas Toras Chessed
Wellbury House, Great Offley, Hitchin, Herts SG5 3BP
Rab. A. S. Stern *Tel* 01462 768 698

HOVE (*See* Brighton & Hove)

HULL

In Hull, as in many English port towns, a community was formed earlier than in inland areas. The first recorded resident was in 1766. The first synagogue was used in 1780, which is about when the first cemetery was acquired. After London, Hull was the principal port of entry for Jews from Continental Europe. Of the 2.2 million immigrants who came through Hull between 1850 and 1914, 0.5 million were Jews. Today there are 130 in the Orthodox congregation and 70 in the Reform.

REPRESENTATIVE BODIES

Hull Jewish Representative Council
Pres. Judah Rose *Tel* 01482 655 367; *Hon. S.* Prof. J. Friend 9 Allanhall Way, Kirk Ella, HU10 7QU *Tel* 01482 658 930 *Email* j.friend@cj2f.karoo.co.uk

SYNAGOGUES

Hull Hebrew Congregation
30 Pryme Street, Anlaby HU10 6SH
Website www.hullhebrewcongregation.co.uk
(Reg. Charity No. 1035451). *Hon. S.* D. Lewis; *M.* Rabbi N. Lifschitz (part time) *Tel* 07917 468 659

Reform Synagogue
Great Gutter Lane, Willerby HU10 7JT

Constituent of RSGB. *Hon. S.* Joanne Kearsley 29 Copse Road, Ashby, Scunthorpe DN16 3JA
Tel 01724 340 506

SOCIAL, CULTURAL & INTERFAITH
Mikveh, Cemeteries, Jewish Archive, Kosher food
Contact Hull Hebrew Congregation.

WELFARE
Hull Jewish Community Care
Menorah House, 331-337 Anlaby Road, HU3 2SA
Ch. H. Flasher *Tel* 07766 416 605; *Hon. S.* D. Lewis *Tel* 01482 650 282
(Est. 1880).

ISLE OF WIGHT
Isle of Wight Jewish Society
IWJS, Flat 5 Appley Sands, Appley Rise, Ryde, PO33 1LE
Tel 01983 568 970
Email lo@gleet2.plus.com
(Est. 2005). Encourages Jewish people living on the island to enjoy their Jewish heritage,
to socialise with each other and to establish and maintain contact with other Jewish
Communities. *Tru.* Henry Harris; *Sec.* Leonard Osterman

KENT
Kent Liberal Jewish Community
Correspondence c/o Liberal Judaism, The Montagu Centre, 21 Maple Street, London
W1T 4BE
Tel 07952 242 432
Email kljc@liberaljudaism.org *Website* http://tinyurl.com/kentljc
Monthly Shabbat morning services in Maidstone, High Holyday services, Seder, social events.

LANCASTER
Lancaster and Lakes Jewish Community
Covering North Lancashire and Cumbria up to the Scottish border, we are open to all
who are Jewish, have Jewish connections, or who wish to learn about Judaism and the
Jewish way of life. There are services in the synagogue room at Lancaster University
on festivals and occasionally on Shabbat. Our Havurah group meets monthly and there
are other social and cultural events. We also work closely with the Lancaster University
Jewish Society, which runs regular Friday night meals and bagel brunches.
Ch. Prof. Stanley Henig *Email* stanhenig@googlemail.com; *Sec.* Fiona Frank *Tel* 07778 737 681
Email fionafrank@googlemail.com; *M.* Rev Malcolm Weisman (also Chaplain for the
Lancaster University Jewish Society).
Lancaster University Jewish Society
Chaplain, Rev Malcolm Weisman *Email* jsoc@lancaster.ac.uk

LEEDS
Leeds has the third largest Jewish community in Britain. Jews have lived in Leeds at least
from the middle of the eighteenth century, but it was only in 1840 that a Jewish cemetery
was acquired. The first so-called synagogue was a converted room in Bridge Street, where
services were held up to 1846. Thereafter the place of worship was transferred to the Back
Rockingham Street Synagogue, which was replaced by the Belgrave Street Synagogue built
in 1860. Another synagogue was built in 1877, but this closed in 1983.
   The Leeds Jewish community is mainly the product of the persecution of Russian
Jewry in the latter half of the nineteenth century. The bulk of the immigrants settled in
Leeds between 1881 and 1905, enhancing the growth of the clothing industry which
developed from woollen and worsted manufacturing in the West Riding of Yorkshire.
This industry was made world famous by John Barran, a non-Jew, and his Jewish
associate Herman Friend, who were responsible for introducing the division of labour into

the clothing industry. While the Sweating system existed in Leeds, both wages and working conditions were better than in London or Manchester. Trade unionism was successful and the first recorded strike by Jewish industrial workers took place spontaneously in Leeds in 1885.

During the early decades of this century the old Leylands area where most of the immigrants lived, began to break up. The main move of the Jewish people was to northern districts of Leeds, first to Chapeltown, which flourished in the 1940s, and then to the Moortown and Alwoodley suburbs. The Leeds Representative Council republished in 1985 the late Louis Saipe's 'A History of the Jews of Leeds'.

Today, this well-organised, strong community of over 8,000 provides Leeds Jews with over 100 organisations which are affiliated to the Leeds Jewish Representative Council, the official spokesman of the Leeds Jewish community.

REPRESENTATIVE BODIES

Leeds Jewish Representative Council
Marjorie & Arnold Ziff Community Centre, 311 Stonegate Road, LS17 6AZ
Tel 0113 269 7520
Website www.leedsjewishcommunity.com
Nearly every synagogue, charitable organisation, social and cultural instititution and Zionist Society is affiliated to this council and on its executive committee. Serves ex-officio all local Jewish magistrates, public reps. and BoD members. *Pres.* Simon Jackson; *V. Pres.* Alan Dunwell, Abigail Levin; *Hon. T.* Keith Ackerman; *Hon. S. (acting)* Jonathan Rose

SYNAGOGUES

Beth Hamidrash Hagadol Synagogue
399 Street Lane, LS17 6HQ
Email office@bhhs.co.uk *Website* www.bhhs.co.uk
(Est. 1874). *M.* Rabbi J. Kleiman, Rabbi M. Sufrin; *Exec. Off.* Wendy Tobias *Tel* 0113 269 2181

Chassidishe Synagogue
Donisthorpe Hall, Shadwell Lane, LS17 6AW
(Est. 1897).

Etz Chaim Synagogue
411 Harrogate Road, LS17 7BY
Email admin@etzchaim.co.uk
Rab. Rabbi S. Kupperman; *R.* Rabbi A. Gilbert; *Sec.* Sandhill Parade, 584 Harrogate Road, LS17 8DP
Tel 0113 266 2214 *Fax* 0113 237 1183

Leeds Masorti
Contact Eva Frojmovic *Email* e.frojmovic@leeds.ac.uk w.e.kunin@leeds.ac.uk

Queenshill Synagogue
Contact Hon. S. 49 Queenshill Drive, Moortown, LS17 6BG

Shomrei Hadass Congregation
368 Harrogate Road, LS17 6QB
Tel 0113 268 1461/7611
M. Dayan Y. Refson

Sinai Synagogue
Roman Avenue, Street Lane, LS8 2AN
Tel 0113 266 5256
Email info@sinaisynagogue.org.uk *Website* www.sinaisynagogue.org.uk
(Est. 1944). Reform Judaism. Rabbi I. Morris; *Hon. S.* Pippa Brook; *Admin/Bookkeeper* Heidi Sizer. Monday-Friday 9.30am-2pm.

United Hebrew Congregation
151 Shadwell Lane, LS17 8DW
Tel/Fax 0113 269 6141
Email office@uhcleeds.com *Website* www.uhcleeds.com
(Reg. Charity No. 515316). *M.* Rabbi D. Levy. *Tel* 0113 266 4772

EDUCATIONAL

Brodetsky Jewish Primary School
Wentworth Avenue, LS17 7TN
Hd. Jeremy Dunford, School *Tel* 01132 930 578; Deborah Taylor Nursery. *Tel* 0113 293 0579

Leeds Jewish Education Authority (Talmud Torah)
(Est. 1879). Providing top quality education for children, teens and adults. In addition, providing assemblies in local non-Jewish schools. *Pres.* Rabbi Anthony Gilbert, BA Hons *Tel* 0113 268 5657; *Ch. of Education*, Rabbi Daniel Levy, BA Hons, MA *Tel* 0113 266 4772

Makor–Jewish Resource Centre and Israel Information Centre (JPMP)
311 Stonegate Road, LS17 6AZ
Tel 0113 268 0899

Leeds Menorah School
399 Street Lane, LS17 6HQ
Tel 0113 237 0360 *Fax* 0113 320 0770
Independent school for boys and girls aged from 3 to 16. *Co-Dir.* Rabbi Yehuda Refson, Ettel Refson; *Teacher*, Rabbi Chaim Bell, Rabbi Menachem Mendel Sufrin, S. Angyalfi

Reform Hebrew Classes
Sinai Synagogue, 22 Roman Avenue, LS8 2AN
Tel 0113 266 5256

RELIGIOUS

Beth Din
Tel 0113 269 6902 *M.* Dayan Y. Refson; Rev. A. Gilbert, BA

Chevra Kadisha: Reform
Convenors Rabbi Morris, Maxine Brown *Tel* 0113 266 5256

Leeds Joint Chevra Kadisha
Admin./Co-ord. Linda Schulman 21 Linton Rise, LS17 8QW
Tel 0113 237 0159 *Mobile* 0771 387 9759 *Email* leedsjointchevrakadisha@gmail.com
   Voluntary service for Leeds Jewish community On Sundays and Bank-Holidays, the on call registrar can be contacted via the Leeds Joint Chevra Kadisha on the numbers above.

Mikveh
411 Harrogate Road, LS17 7BY
M. Morris *Tel* 0113 269 4377

SOCIAL, CULTURAL & INTERFAITH

AJEX *Ch.* Leonard Fineberg; *Hon. S.* Leonard Cohen, 72 High Ash Drive, LS17 8RB

Emunah
  Shoshanah
  Ch. Sylvia Baum, Lynda Gilmore; *Hon. S.* Cynthia Myerson 37 Primley Park Road, LS17 7HR
  Tel 0113 268 6984
  Tzfia Goren
  Ch. Maureen Brooke, Monica Gay; *Hon. S.* Margaret Gothelf 37 Primley Park Crescent, LS17 7HY *Tel* 0113 268 2374

Makor Leeds Jewish Resource and Cultural Centre
311 Stonegate Road, LS17 6AZ
Tel 0113 268 0899 *Fax* 0113 268 8419

M.B. Sender Programmes
12 Plantation Gardens, LS17 8RY
Tel 0113 318 6403
Email msender@talktalk.com
Jt. Sec. Anita Buxbaum, Peter Brostet; *Jt. T.* Gerald Leonard, Murray Winer

Jewish Telegraph
The Gatehouse Business Centre, Mansion Gate, Chapel Allerton LS7 4RF
Tel 0113 295 6000 *Fax* 0113 262 2384
Email leeds@jewishtelegraph.com

Leeds Council of Christians and Jews
(Reg. Charity No. 238005). *Ch.* A. M. Conway *Tel* 0113 268 0444; *Hon. S.* Rabbi Morris, S. Crowther *Tel* 0113 256 1407

Leeds Zionist Federation
311 Stonegate Road, LS17 6AZ
Tel 0113 218 5865 *Fax* 0113 218 5880
District Org. S. Cohen

Porton Collection
The Information Centre, Central Library, Calverley Street, LS1 3AB (*See* p.134)
Tel 0113 247 8282 *Fax* 0113 395 1833

UJIA Office
Balfour House, 299 Street Lane, LS17 6HQ
Tel 0113 269 3136 *Fax* 0113 269 3961

Women's International Zionist Organisation (WIZOuk)
311 Stonegate Road, LS17 6AZ
Tel 0113 268 4773
Admin. Shelley Peel

WELFARE
Leeds Jewish Welfare Board
Marjorie & Arnold Ziff Community Centre, 311 Stonegate Road, LS17 6AZ
Tel 0113 268 4211
Pres. E. Ziff; *Chief Exec.* R. Weinberg

Care Home for the Elderly
Donisthorpe Hall, Shadwell Lane, LS17 6AW
Tel 0113 268 4248
Website www.donisthorpehall.org
(Est. 1923). *CEO* Carol Whitehead

YOUTH & STUDENTS
Chaplaincy Board–Yorkshire & Humberside
Tel 0113 278 9597
Hon. Ch. Ivan Green *Tel* 0113 269 6610

Community Shaliach
311 Stonegate Road, LS17 6AZ
Tel 0113 268 0899 *Fax* 0113 266 8419

Jewish Students' Association
Hillel House, 2 Springfield Mount, LS2 9NE
Tel 0113 243 3211
(Est. 1912). *Sec.* c/o Leeds University Union, LS2

LEICESTER
There have been Jewish communities in Leicester since the Middle Ages, but the first record of a Synagogue appears in the 1861 Leicester Directory and the first marriages were consecrated in 1875. The present synagogue dates from 1897.

SYNAGOGUES
Synagogue
Highfield Street, P.O. Box 6836, LE2 1WZ
Website www.Jewishleicester.org
M. Rabbi S. Pink *Email* rabbipink@btinternet.com *Tel* 0116 270 6622; *Hon. S.* David May *Tel* 0116 270 4333 For synagogue tours, contact Dana Simons *Tel* 0116 288 4887

Leicester Progressive Jewish Synagogue (LJ)
24 Avenue Road, LE2 3EA
(Est. 1950). *Ch.* R. King *Email* robcking@aol.com

CEMETERIES
Leicester Hebrew Congregation uses a section of the Gilroes Cemetery, Groby Road LE3 9QG

Contact Rabbi S. Pink *Tel* 0116 270 6622. The Progressive congregation uses a section of the Loughborough Municipal Council

EDUCATIONAL
Jewish Library
Communal Centre, 39 Highfield Street, LE2 1AD
Tel 0116 254 0477

RELIGIOUS
Mikva
Synagogue Building, Highfield Street LE2 1AB
Contact Rivie Pink *Tel* 07515 422 072

SOCIAL, CULTURAL & INTERFAITH
Communal Centre
39 Highfield Street, LE2 1AD
Tel 0116 254 0477

Maccabi Association
Communal Centre, 39 Highfield Street, LE2 1AD
Tel 0116 254 0477

YOUTH & STUDENTS
Jewish Students' Society
c/o The Union, Leicester University, LE1 7RH
Email leicesterjsoc@yahoo.co.uk

LINCOLN
Lincolnshire Jewish Community (Affiliated to LJ)
Email ljc@liberaljudaism.org
Sec. Allan Levene *Tel* 01427 628 958

LIVERPOOL
Liverpool, for centuries an important port, first for Ireland, later also for America, had a natural attraction for Jews looking for a place in which to start their new lives. There is evidence of an organised community before 1750. It appears to have had a burial ground attached. Little is known of this early community. It declined, but about 1770 was rein-forced by a new wave of settlers chiefly from Europe, who worshipped in a house in Frederick Street, near the river front, with a Mikveh and a cemetery. In 1807 a synagogue of some size was built in Seel Street, the parent of the present synagogue in Princes Road, one of the handsomest in the country. At this time Liverpool was already one of the four leading regional communities. The site for the Seel Street Synagogue was a gift from the Liverpool Corporation.

REPRESENTATIVE BODIES
Merseyside Jewish Representative Council
433 Smithdown Road, L15 3JL
Tel 0151 733 2292 *Fax* 0151 734 0212
Email repcouncil@mjccshifrin.co.uk *Website* www.liverpooljewish.com
(Reg. Charity No. 1140569). *Pres.* Prof. Julian Verbov, JP; *Ch. of the Council* Ian S. Cohen; *Hon. S.* S. Sprince *Publ.* Year Book

SYNAGOGUES
Allerton Hebrew Congregation
207 Mather Avenue, L18 9UB
Tel 0151 427 4811
Email allerton.syn@virgin.net
M. Rabbi Daniel Lieberman; *Admin.* D. A. Coleman
Childwall Synagogue
Dunbabin Road, L15 6XL

Email rabbi@theshul.co.uk *Website* www.theshul.co.uk
Tel 0151 722 2079
(Est. 1935. Consecrated 1938). *M.* Rabbi M. Wollenberg; *Admin.* A. Reuben
Liverpool Old Hebrew Congregation
Synagogue Chambers, Princes Road, L8 1TG
Tel 0151 709 3431 *Fax* 0151 709 4187
Email lohc1@aol.com *Website* www.princesroad.org
(Congregation founded c. 1780; Synagogue consecrated 1874). *Admin.* P. Nevitt
Liverpool Progressive Synagogue & Cheder
28 Church Road North, L15 6TF
Tel 0151 733 5871
(Est. 1928). Affiliated to the Movement for Reform Judaism. *M.* Rabbi M. Mayer; *Hon. S.* E. Kearney

CEMETERIES
Springwood; Lowerhouse Lane; Broad Green; Long Lane

EDUCATIONAL
King David and Harold House Foundation
King David Campus, 120 Childwall Road, LI5 6WU
Tel 0151 235 1584 *Fax* 0151 737 1752
Email admin@kdf.org.uk
Pres. M. Fraenkel; *Clerk* S. Heaps
King David High School
Childwall Road, L15 6WU
Tel 0151 235 1428
Clerk to Govs. King David High School - Jean McMeakin
King David Kindergarten
King David Campus, Childwall Road, L15 6WU
Email kdk@kdf.org.uk
Teacher-in-charge R. Shiffman *Tel* 0151 235 1586 *Fax* 0151 737 1752
King David Primary School
Childwall Road, L15 6WU
Tel 0151 7235 1420
Clerk to Govs. Jean McMeakin King David Campus, Childwall Road, L15 6WU *Tel* 0151 235 1428 *Fax* 0151 737 1752
Hon. T. Rachel Rick, MA (Ed), NPQH
Merseyside Amalgamated Talmud Torah
Cheder Etz Chayim, Harold House
Ch. M. Levitt

RELIGIOUS
Liverpool Kashrut Commission
c/o Shifrin House, 433 Smithdown Road, L15 3JL
Tel 0151 733 2292 *Fax* 0151 734 0212
Rab. Under the Liverpool Rabbonim
Mikveh
Childwall Synagogue
Ch. Rebbetzin Wollenberg *Tel* 07794 907 284

SOCIAL, CULTURAL & INTERFAITH
Jewish Telegraph
Harold House, Dunbabin Road, L15 6XL
Tel 0151 475 6666 *Fax* 0151 475 2222
Email liverpool@jewishtelegraph.com
Liverpool Jewish Historical Society
(Branch). *Ch.* A. Lewis, 61 Menlove Avenue, L18 2EH

Tel 0151 722 5021
Email arnoldslewis@gmail.com
Liverpool Jewish Resource Centre
King David Campus, Childwall Road, L15 6WU
Tel 0151 235 1594
Email ljrc@btconnect.com
Monday and Thursday 1-4pm, Tuesday and Wednesday 11am-5pm. *Dir.* A. Lewis

WELFARE
Merseyside Jewish Community Care
Shifrin House, 433 Smithdown Road, L15 3JL
Tel 0151 733 2292 *Fax* 0151 734 0212
Email info@mjccshifrin.co.uk *Website* www.merseysidejewishcommunitycare.co.uk
(Est. 1875). *Chief Exec.* L. Dolan
Merseyside Jewish Women's Welfare Society
433 Smithdown Road, L15 3JL
Tel 0151 733 2292
Email info@mjccshifrin.co.uk
Hon. S. P. Talisman
Stapely Jewish Residential and Nursing Home
North Mossley Hill Road, L18 8BR
Admin. Tel 0151 724 3260; 0151 724 4548 (Hospital wing)

YOUTH & STUDENTS
Hillel House
101 Ullet Road, L17 2AB
Applications to *Tel* 0151 280 0551 (office hours)
Chaplain Rabbi Y. Y. Rubinstein *Tel* 0151 721 4066
Jewish Community Centre
King david Campus, 118-120 Childwall Road, L15 6XL
Tel 0151 235 1587
University Jewish Students' Society
101 Ullet Road, L17 2AB
Email liverpool.jsoc@hotmail.co.uk *Website* www.liverpooljsoc.org
Co-Ch. Stuart Lesser, Naomi Kudren

LUTON, DUNSTABLE & DISTRICT

SYNAGOGUES
Bedfordshire Progressive Synagogue (Rodef Shalom) (LJ)
c/o Liberal Judaism, The Montagu Centre, 21 Maple Street, W1T 4BE
Tel 01234 218 387
Email info@bedsps.org.uk *Website* www.bedfordshire-ps.org.uk
(Reg. Charity No. XN22769). Based in Luton and Bedford. Friday night services and twice monthly Shabbat morning services. *Ch.* David Young; *T.* Rosie Comb; *Sec.* Hilary Fox
Luton United Synagogue
656 Dunstable Road, Luton, Bedfordshire LU4 8SE
Email info@lutonhebrew.co.uk *Website* www.lutonhebrew.co.uk
M. Rabbi Y. Schwei

MAIDENHEAD
Maidenhead started in 1940 as an evacuee congregation during the Blitz. It experienced a rapid growth in the 1980s as younger families moved out of London, obliging it to move into larger premises in 2001. Its membership now covers a wide area of Berks and Bucks, numbering 800 households, with regular services and a religious school.

SYNAGOGUES
Synagogue
Grenfell Lodge, Ray Park Road, SL6 8QX
Tel 01628 673012
Email admin@maidenheadsynagogue.org.uk   *Website* www.maidenheadsynagogue.org.uk
Reform. *M.* Rabbi Dr. J. A. Romain *Tel* 01628 671058

CEMETERIES
Braywick Cemetery, Maidenhead.

MANCHESTER

The Jewish community of Greater Manchester is the largest community outside London numbering approximately 30,000 and, in contrast with other communities in the UK, is still growing. The greater part of the community lives to the north of the city in Salford, Broughton Park, Prestwich, Whitefield and Bury, and to the south of the city in Altrincham, Cheadle, Gatley, Hale and Sale.

The community is very diverse: there are more than 44 congregations, of which four are Sephardi, three Reform, and one Liberal.

There are more than 400 different communal organisations, including yeshivot, schools, charities, and welfare, Zionist, social and youth groups.

The strictly observant and large Charedi community is centred on Broughton Park, Salford, and is the fastest-growing part of the community. The Charedi community is very well-served by its own network of charities and gemachs.

The Jewish Representative Council of Greater Manchester and Region (JRC) acts as the umbrella representative body of the community; each year it publishes a Year Book, which is a valuable guide to communal infrastructure and organisations. The JRC forges links with local councils, other faith communities, hospital trusts and other bodies in order to protect and defend the Jewish community and its interests. It coordinates its efforts with the Board of Deputies of British Jews and the Jewish Leadership Council.

Manchester's Jewish community is staunchly Zionist; over the years many members of the community have made aliyah. Manchester-based charities raise funds to purchase ambulances and support hospitals in Israel; and to support needy families and children with special needs. Other groups work to promote bilateral trade between Israel and the UK, and to promote collaboration between Israeli and British universities.

Manchester Jewish Museum
The history of Manchester's Jewish community from its earliest beginnings has been meticulously researched and documented by Bill Williams in his book The Making of Manchester Jewry 1740–1875 (Manchester: Manchester University Press, 1985), and subsequent works. Bill's scholarship and vision were the foundation upon which Manchester Jewish Museum was created by converting the Spanish and Portuguese Synagogue, which has been beautifully restored and is now a Grade II* listed building.

In 1865 there were 4,500 Jewish Mancunians. The rapid and great increase came between 1883 and 1905, a consequence of the intensified persecution of the Jews in Russia. Newcomers to England in the eighteenth century were encouraged by their co-religionists in London to go farther afield. This they did, as pedlars in the countryside, generally financed by their longer-settled fellow Jews in London. As these newcomers prospered they settled in the ports, for their part sending out a wave of later arrivals similarly supplied with stock to peddle in the inland towns and villages, where this new wave ultimately settled. Thus was laid the foundation of the Jewish community of Manchester.

The middle of the 1780s saw the first signs of an organised community, when two pedlar brothers, Jacob and Lemon Nathan, opened small shops in the centre of Manchester. In 1794 a plot for Jewish burials was rented just outside the city, and in 1796 a large warehouse was hired for public worship. This period coincided with Manchester's development as a major centre of industry and commerce, and Manchester Jewry steadily increased in number, attracting many enterprising settlers, including merchants and men of substance from the European mainland. Among these was Nathan Mayer Rothschild, the first of that family to settle in England.

A later influx was from North Africa and the Levant, lands closely connected with the cotton industry of which Manchester was then the centre. This was the origin of the Sephardi community still prominent in Manchester. The last two decades of the nineteenth century saw the mass immigration to Manchester of Eastern European Jews, fleeing from poverty and persecution. By the end of the century Manchester had the largest Jewish population in the provinces, reaching a peak of 35,000 just before the First World War.

REPRESENTATIVE BODIES

Jewish Representative Council of Greater Manchester and Region (Incorporating the Trades Advisory Council). The Representative body for the Jewish community of Manchester, Salford and the surrounding region, including Stoke, Blackpool and St Annes. Made up of representatives from all synagogues and other organisationss, local Jewish MPs and MEPs, local members of the Board of Deputies, magistrates and town councillors.
Office Jewish Community Centre, Bury Old Road, M7 4QY
Tel 0161 720 8721
Email office@jewishmanchester.org *Website* www.jewishmanchester.org
Pres. Frank Baigel BA B Dent Sc; *V. Pres.* Sharon A. Bannister, Jacky Buchsbaum BSc ACA CTA; *Hon. T.* Philip A. Langer; *Hon. S.* Filis Rosenberg, Ray Cook BA(Hons); Ex-officio, Lucille M. Cohen MA; *H. Media Analyst*, Frank R. Baigel. *Publ.* Year Book, Newsletter *RepPresents*

SYNAGOGUES

Adass Yeshurun Synagogue
Cheltenham Crescent, Salford, M7 4FE
Tel/Fax 0161 740 3935
Adath Yisrael Synagogue (formerly **Kahal Chassidim Synagogue**)
Upper Park Road, Salford M7 0HL
(present building opened in 1957) *Tel* 0161 740 3905
Beis Hamedrash Chanichei Hayeshivos Eitz Chaim
106 Kings Road, Prestwich, M25 0FY
Tel 0161 773 5932
Beis Hamedrash Shaarei Mordechai
80 Bury New Road, Prestwich M25 0JA
Tel 0161 798 7374
Beis Mordechai
90 Kings Road, Prestwich M25 0FY
Bury Hebrew Congregation
Sunnybank Road, Bury, BL9 8ET
Tel/Fax 0161 796 5062
Email m.rappaport.bhc@hotmail.co.uk *Website* buryhc.org.uk
M. Rabbi B. Singer; *Admin.* M. Wilson, M. Rappaport
Chaim v'Tikvah (Independent Reform)
Chaim v'Tikvah is a small, independent Progressive congregation with traditional values. It has a high percentage of attendance at all its services.
For further information, please contact the Chairman, Jay *Email* chaimvtikvah@onetel.com
Tel 07767 478349
Cheetham Hebrew Congregation
Jewish Cultural Centre, Bury Old Road M7 4QY
Tel 0161 740 7788
Pres. B. M. Stone. *M.* Rabbi Y. Abenson
Cheshire Reform Congregation
Menorah Synagogue, 198 Altrincham Road, M22 4RZ
Tel 0161 428 7746 *Fax* 0161 428 0937
Email office@menorah.org.uk *Website* www.menorah.org.uk
(Est. 1964. Reg. Charity No. 1124560). A constituent of MRJ. *M.* Rabbi Chaim Shalom;
Hon. S. J. Krell; *Ch.* Gita Conn

Chortkov Beis Hamedrash
42 Broom Lane, Salford M7 4FJ
Tel 0161 792 7870
Damesek Eliezer Synagogue
Prestwich Beth Hamedrash, 74 Kings Road, Prestwich M25 0JG
Tel 0161 798 9298
Hale and District Hebrew Congregation
Shay Lane, Hale Barns, Cheshire WA15 8NZ
Tel 0161 980 8846
Email admin@hale-community.org.uk
(Est. 1976). *M.* Rabbi J. Portnoy; *Hon. S.* J. Steinberg
Heaton Park Hebrew Congregation
Ashdown, 84 Middleton Road, M8 4JX
Tel 0161 740 4766
Email corinne@hphc.org.uk
M. Rabbi D. Walker
Higher Crumpsall and Higher Broughton Hebrew Congregation
Bury Old Road, Salford, M7 4PX
Tel 0161 740 1210
M. Emer. Rabbi A. Saunders, Rev. A. Hillman *Tel* 0161 740 4179; *Admin.* E. Somers *Tel* 0161 740 8155
Higher Prestwich Hebrew Congregation
445 Bury Old Road, Prestwich M25 1QP
Tel 0161 773 4800
Email hphc@btinternet.com
M. Rabbi A. Z. Herman; *Pres.* L.B. Finley; *Sec.* B. Task
Hillock Hebrew Congregation
Beverley Close, Ribble Drive, Whitefield, M45 8LB
Email hillock.shul@ntlworld.com
Hon. S. R. Walker, 13 Mersey Close, Whitefield, M45 8LB *Tel* 0161 959 5663
Holy Law South Broughton Congregation
Bury Old Road, Prestwich M25 0EX
Tel 0161 740 1634 *Fax* 0161 720 6623
Email admin@holylaw.org.uk
(Est. 1865, present building opened 1935, merged with South Broughton Synagogue, 1978).
M. Rabbi Y. Chazan *Tel* 0161 792 6349 (Study 0161 721 4705); *Admin.* N. Bor
Burial Bd. Tel 0161 740 1289
Kahal Chassidim Lubavitch Synagogue
62 Singleton Road, Salford M7 4LU
M. Rabbi A. Jaffe *Tel* 0161 740 3632; *Sec.* D. Lipsidge *Tel* 0161 740 1629
Kol Rinoh Horodenka
64 Waterpark Road, Salford M7 4JL
Tel 0161 720 6659
Machon Levi Yitschok
Tel 0161 795 4000
Machzikei Hadass Communities
17 Northumberland Street, Salford M7 4RP
Tel 0161 792 1313 *Fax* 0161 792 8592
Email admin@mhmanchester.org.uk
Kashrus, Burial Board, Shul, Kolel, Mikvah, Beis Hoiroel, charity vouchers *Rov.* Rabbi M. M. Schneebalg; *Dayonim* Rabbi A. Grinfeld *Tel* 0161 792 7731; Rabbi M. Mehler *Tel* 0161 792 1563; Rabbi D. Orzel *Tel* 0161 792 7295; Rabbi P. Weiss *Tel* 0161 740 2923; Rabbi C. M. Zahn *Tel* 0161 740 7239

   Manchester & District Mikva Sedgley Park Road, Prestwich *Tel* 0161 773 1537/795 2852/ 708 8989 (facilities for the disabled available)

Manchester Congregation of Spanish and Portuguese Jews - KK Sha'are Tefilla
18 Moor Lane, Salford, M7 3WX
Tel 0161 792 4168
Email synagogue@moorlane.org *Website* www.moorlane.org
(Est. 1873). *M.* Rabbi N. Nadav; *Pres.* A.N. Bitton

Manchester Great New and Central Synagogue
'Stenecourt', Holden Road, Salford, M7 4LN
Email shul@stenecourt.com *Website* www.stenecourt.com
(Est. 1740). *M.* Rabbi J. Rubinstein *Tel* 0161 740 7762; Pres. Mr D. Caplan *Tel* 0161 792 8399
Monday-Friday 9.30am-12.30pm

Manchester Liberal Jewish Community (LJ)
c/o Cross Street Chapel, Cross Street, M2 1NL
Email mljc@mljc.org.uk *Website* www.mljc.org.uk
(Reg. Charity No. 1120548). We actively seek to include those who have experienced
exclusion and discrimination on account of their gender, sexuality, disability or Halakhic
status (interfaith, marriage, adoption, patrilineal descent etc). Based on the central Jewish
values of truth (Emet), Social Justice (Tzedek) and loving kindness (Chesed). *Ch.* Len Alden;
Rabbi Mark Solomon *Email* m.solomon@liberaljudaism.org

Manchester Reform Synagogue (Reform)
Jackson's Row, M2 5NH
Tel 0161 834 0415
Email admin@jacksonsrow.org
(Est. 1856). Former synagogue in Park Place was destroyed by enemy action in 1941; present
premises occupied since 1953. 150 Years of Reform Judaism in the Heart of Manchester. *M.*
Rabbi Dr. R. Silverman; *Sec.* Mandy Bornhardt *Tel* 0161 834 0415

Meade Hill Shul (formerly United Synagogue Manchester)
88 Meade Hill Road, M8 4LP
Tel 0161 740 9586
Website www.meadehillshul.co.uk
Pres. Col. Martin Newman; *Sec.* Lance Bookatz

North Salford Synagogue
2 Vine Street, Kersal, Salford M7 0NX
c/o *Tel* 0161 720 8721

Ohel Torah Synagogue
132 Leicester Road, Salford M7 0ES
Tel 0161 792 3442

Ohr Yerushalayim Synagogue
470 Bury New Road, Manchester M7 4NU
Tel 0161 705 0625
Website www.ohryerushalayim.org.uk
Daily services held. *Pres.* A. Stern

Prestwich Hebrew Congregation
Bury New Road, Prestwich M25 9WN
Tel 0161 773 1978
Email office@shrubberies.org.uk
Rev. Rabbi D. Eisenberg; *Chazan* A. Caplan; *Admin.* W. Cohen-Wilks

Sale and District Hebrew Congregation
12a Hesketh Road, Sale, Cheshire M33 5AA
Tel 0161 973 2172
M. Rev N. Fagelman; *Sec.* M. Clyne *Tel* 0161 973 4565

Satmar Cultural Centre
Tel 0161 792 9421

Sedgley Park Synagogue (Shomrei Hadass)
Parkview Road, Prestwich M25 5FA
Email shomreihadass@googlemail.com *Website* www.shomreihadass.com

Tel 0161 773 4828
Rabbi, Rabbi D. Kestenbaum; *Pres.* Steven Baddiel
Sephardi Congregation of South Manchester
8 Queenston Road, West Didsbury M20 2WZ
Tel 0161 445 1943 *Fax* 0161 438 0571
Email shaarehayim@clara.co.uk
(Reg. Charity No. 1067759). (Shaare Hayim). Amalgamated with the former Sha'are Sedek
Synagogue. *M.* Rabbi S. Ellituv *Tel* 0161 434 6903
Sephardi Congregation Zichron Yitzchak
2 New Hall Road, Salford M7 4EL
Tel 0161 795 0822
Sha'arei Shalom North Manchester Reform Congregation
Elms Street, Whitefield, M45 8GQ
Tel 0161 796 6736
Email office@shaareishalom.org.uk *Website* www.shaareishalom.org.uk
(Est. 1977. Reg. Charity No. 506117). A Constituent of the Movement for Reform Judaism.
Shaarei Shamayim (Sephardi)
Tel 0161 773 3233 *Fax* 0161 773 3381
Email achocron@freenet.co.uk
Shaarei Tefillah
Tel 0161 772 0484
South Manchester Synagogue
The Firs, Bowdon, Altrincham, WA14 2TE
Tel 0161 928 2050 *Fax* 0161 924 0344
Email info@southmanchestersynagogue.org.uk
(Est. 1872. Reg. Charity No. 1124507). *M.* Rabbi D.Y. Lewis MA; *Admin.* T. Hyams, J. Samuels
Talmud Torah Chinuch N'orim Synagogue
11 Wellington Street, East, Salford M7 2AU
Tel 0161 792 9292
Constituent of the Union of Orthodox Hebrew Congregations. *M.* Rev. P. Koppenheim; *Hon.*
S. J. Waldman
Whitefield Hebrew Congregation
Park Lane, M45 7PB
Tel 0161 766 3732 *Fax* 0161 767 9453
Email mail@whitefieldshul.co.uk
(Est. 1959). *M.* Rabbi J. Guttentag, BA Hons; *C.* Chazan Y. Muller
Yeshurun Hebrew Congregation
Coniston Road, Gatley, Cheadle, Cheshire SK8 4AP
Tel 0161 428 8242 *Fax* 0161 491 5265
Email office@yeshurun.org.uk
(Reg. Charity No. XN10469A). *M.* Rabbi Ch. Kanterovitz; *Admin.* M. Pawlowski
Zerei Agudas Israel Synagogue
35 Northumberland Street, Salford M7 0DQ
Tel 0161 795 4000

CEMETERIES

Agecroft Cemetery *Tel* 0161 736 5552 Admin. Stenecourt Synagogue Burial Board *Tel* 0161
792 8399

Agecroft Liberal Cemetery *Tel* 0870 991 7327 Admin. Manchester Liberal Community

Blackley Cemetery *Tel* 0161 740 2317 Admin. Stenecourt Synagogue Burial Board *Tel* 0161
792 8399

Cheadle Cemetery *Tel* 0161 428 8242 Admin. Yeshurun Synagogue Burial Board Tel 0161
428 8815

Crumpsall Cemetery Admin. Stenecourt Synagogue Burial Board *Tel* 0161 792 8399

Dunham Lawn Cemetery Admin. Hale and District Hebrew Congregation Burial Board
Tel 0161 980 8846

Failsworth Cemetery Admin. Holy Law South Broughton Burial Board *Tel* 07974 268 565
Great Synagogue Cemetery Bury New Road, Prestwich (historic).
Mill Lane Cemetery Tel 0161 428 7746 Admin. Menorah Synagogue Burial Board and
Manchester Reform Synagogue Burial Board.
Philips Park Cemetery *Tel* 0161 766 2065 Admin. United Synagogue Burial Board *Tel* 0161
740 9586; Whitefield Synagogue Burial Board *Tel* 0161 766 3732; Machzikei Hadass
Communities Burial Board *Tel* 0161 792 1313
Rainsough Cemetery *Tel* 0161 773 2641Admin. Rainsough Joint Burial Board - Central and
North Manchester Synagogue, Higher Crumpsall and Higher Broughton Synagogue,
Manchester Communal Burial Board *Tel* 0161 740 9711
Southern Cemetery *Tel* 0161 881 2208 Admin. South Manchester Synagogue *Tel* 0161 928
2050; Shaare Hayim Synagogue *Tel* 0161 445 1943; Manchester Reform Congregation
Tel 0161 834 0415
Urmston Cemetery *Tel* 01706 840 642 Admin. Stenecourt Synagogue Burial Board *Tel* 0161
792 8399; Whitefield Synagogue Burial Board *Tel* 0161 766 3732
Whitefield Cemetery *Tel* 0161 834 0415 Admin. Manchester Reform Congregation

EDUCATIONAL
Academy for Rabbinical Research (Manchester Kollel)
134 Leicester Road, Salford M7 4DA
Tel 0161 740 1960
(Reg. Charity No. 526665). *Princ.* Rabbi W. Kaufman; *Sec.* D. Cohen
Beis Yaakov High School
Hubert Jewish High School for Girls, 69 Broom Lane, Salford, M7 4FF
Tel 0161 708 8220 *Fax* 0161 708 9968
Princ. Rabbi Y. Goldblatt, MA (Oxon), PGCE
Bnos Yisroel School - Fayge Sufrin Kindergarten
Leicester Road, Salford, M7 4DA
Tel 0161 792 3896
Infant, Junior and Senior
Broughton Jewish Cassel Fox Primary School
Legh Road, Salford M7 4RT
Tel 0161 921 2500 *Fax* 0161 921 2510
Email admin@bjps.net
Nursery *Tel* 0161 921 2512; Kindergarten *Tel* 0161 921 2513
Acting Hd. S. Caplan; *Princ.* Rabbi Y. Pearlman; *Ch.* D Black
Bury & Whitefield Jewish Primary School
Parr Lane, Bury, Lancs BL9 8JT
Tel 0161 766 2888
Email bwjp@bury.gov.uk
Hd. Claire Simon; *Ch. of Govs.* Rabbi A. J. Jaffe; *Hd. Jewish Studies* B. Z. Lewis *Tel* 0161
796 3341
Private Nursery School, Parr Lane, Bury, Lancs
Tel 0161 767 9390 (from birth upwards). *Hd.* Miri Weisz
Jewish Senior Boys School - Kesser Torah
Hubert House, 4 New Hall Road, Salford M7 4EL
Tel 0161 708 9175
King David Schools (Est. 1838. Reg. Charity No. 526631)
King David Schools, Administration Centre
Eaton Road, Crumpsall, M8 5DY
Tel 0161 740 3181 *Fax* 0161 741 5081
Campus Bursar D. Rose
King David High School
Eaton Road, Crumpsall, M8 5DY
Tel 0161 740 7248 *Fax* 0161 740 0790

Email admin@kingdavidhigh.manchester.sch.uk *Website* www.kdhs.org.uk
Hd. B. N. Levy, BEd; *H. Yavneh Girls* Rabbi R. Cohen; *Yavneh Boys Ramim* Rabbi P. Cohen, Rabbi Y. Joseph, Rabbi C. Kanterovitz, Rabbi S. Schwalbe
King David Primary School
Wilton Polygon, Bury Old Road, Crumpsall, M8 6DR
Tel 0161 741 5090
Hd. M. Macklin
King David Private Nursery & Crèche
Wilton Polygon, Bury Old Road, Crumpsall, M8 6DR
Tel 0161 740 3481
Man. L. Balaban
Lubavitch Yeshiva
Lubavitch House, 62 Singleton Road, Salford M7 4LU
Email manchesty@aol.com
Dean Rabbi A. Cohen; *Admin*. S. Weiss *Tel* 0161 740 4243
Manchester Mesivta
Beechwood, Charlton Avenue, Prestwich M25 0PH
Tel 0161 773 1789 *Fax* 0161 772 9170
Email mesivta@bury.gov.uk
Princ. Rabbi B. Sulzbacher
Mechinah L'Yeshiva
13 Upper Park Road, Salford M7 0HY
Tel 0161 795 9275
North Cheshire Jewish Primary School
St. Anns Road North, Heald Green, Cheadle, Cheshire SK8 4RZ
Tel 0161 282 4500 *Fax* 0161 282 4501
Hd. Joseph Kelly
Seed Manchester
5 Knoll Street, Salford M7 2EQ
Tel 0161 792 4457 *Fax* 0161 210 2995
Website www.seed.uk.net
(Reg. Charity No. 281307).
Talmud Torah Chinuch N'orim
11/13 Wellington Street, East, Salford M7 2AU
Tel 0161 792 9292
Ch. Bd. of Govs. J. Waldman
Whitefield Community Kollel
c/o Whitefield Hebrew Congregation, Park Lane, Whitefield, M45 7PB
Admin. B. Woolfstein *Tel* 0161 766 2150
The forum runs a wide selection of programmes for adults and youth
Yeshiva Kollel
Saul Rosenberg House, Seymour Road, Higher Crumpsall, M8 5BQ
Tel 0161 740 0214
(Est. 1911). *Princ*. Rabbi Y. Ehrentreu; *Sec*. Rev. G. Brodie
Yesoiday HaTorah School
Sedgley Park Road, off Bury New Road, Prestwich M25 0JW
Tel 0161 773 6364 *Fax* 0161 773 3914
Yocheved Segal Kindergarten
Sedgley Park Road, Prestwich M25 0JW
Tel 0161 773 8413

RELIGIOUS
Communal Mikveh (under Beth Din authority)
Broom Holme, Tetlow Lane, Salford, M7 0BU
Appointments Tel 0161 740 4071/5199 (ladies) *Tel* 0161 792 3970 (during opening hours)

Council of Synagogues (Orthodox)
8 Castlefield Avenue, Salford M7 4GQ
Ch. S. Lopian *Tel* 0161 832 8721 *Email* sal@lopiangb.co.uk; *Sec. M.* Green *Tel* 0161 792 2275 Sunday-Friday 9am-12.30pm

Hershel Weiss Children and Family Centre (inc. Aguda Community Services)
35 Northumberland Street, Salford M7 4DQ
Tel 0161 778 0700/0071
Sure Start childrens centre services, Citizens Advice Bureau and health services

Lubavitch Foundation
62 Singleton Road, Salford M7 4LU
Tel/Fax 0161 720 9514
(Reg. Charity No. 1101651). *M.* Rabbi L. Wineberg

Manchester Beth Din
Jewish Community Centre, Bury Old Road, M7 4QY
Tel 0161 740 9711 *Fax* 0161 721 4249
Email info@mbd.org.uk *Website* www.mbd.org.uk
Dayan I. Berger; Dayan G. Krausz; Dayan Y. O. Steiner. *Registrar* Rabbi Y. Brodie, BA (Hons)

MBD Shechita Services Ltd and MBD Kosher Certification Services Ltd
Jewish Community Centre, Bury Old Road, M7 4QY
Tel 0161 740 9711 *Fax* 0161 721 4249
Email info@mbd.org.uk *Website* www.mbd.org.uk
Pres. J. Nussbaum; *Chief Exec.* Rabbi Y. Brodie, BA (Hons)

Naomi Greenberg South Manchester Mikveh
Shay Lane, Hale Barns, Altrincham, Cheshire
By Appointment Tel 0161 904 8296
Under Beth Din Authority

Tevilas Leilim Mikveh Tel 0161 795 2272

Whitefield Hebrew Congregation Mikveh
By appointment only *Tel* 0161 796 1054

Whitefield Keilim Mikveh
Park Lane, M45 7PB
By arrangement with Shul office *Tel* 0161 766 3732

SOCIAL, CULTURAL & INTERFAITH

B'Nai Brith Lodge (Whitefield, Prestwich, Salford, Higher Crumpsall)
Email office@bnaibrithuk.org
Sec. Leila Yesner *Tel* 0161 796 9906; *Email* leilayesner@hotmail.com

Israel Information Centre
85 Middleton Road, Manchester M8 4JY
Tel 0161 721 4344
Email iicmcr@clara.co.uk
Information and public relations on behalf of Israel. *Dir.* Doreen Gerson

Jewish Agency Aliyah Dept
Consultant, Eitan Sadeh *Tel* 0161 773 9733 *Email* eitansa@jafi.org

Jewish Telegraph
11 Park Hill, Bury Old Road, Prestwich M25 0HH
Tel 0161 740 9321 *Fax* 0161 740 9325
Email manchester@jewishtelegraph.com *Website* www.jewishtelegraph.com

Jewish National Fund
JNF Regional Dir. Jo Krasner *Tel* 07711 390 145 *Email* jo@jnf.co.uk

Manchester Jewish Community Centre
Jubilee School, Bury Old Road, M7 4QY
Tel 0161 795 4000 *Fax* 0161 720 6222
(Reg. Charity No. 1089467). *Admin.* M. Allweis

Manchester Jewish Museum (MJM)
190 Cheetham Hill Road, M8 8LW
Tel 0161 834 9879
Website www.manchesterjewishmuseum.com
Facebook www.facebook.com/manchesterjewishmuseum *Twitter* @manjewishmuseum
(Est. 1984 Reg. Charity No. 508278). MJM is for Jewish and non-Jewish people offering a unique experience as both a social history museum and as a resource for learning.
The museum tells the story of Manchester's Jewish community from the 1780s to the present day. It has over 30,000 items in its collections, and explores the cultural and religious evolution of Manchester's Jewish community - the largest Jewish community in the UK (outside London). The museum galleries reveal the political and industrial legacies of this community on a local, regional, national and international scale. MJM is the only UK museum housed in an original synagogue and, built in 1874, it is Manchester's oldest surviving synagogue building. The building provides a unique and powerful learning space for all ages. From schoolchildren to adult learners, the museum helps over 15,000 people a year discover, explore and celebrate Jewish faith and culture.
The museum is situated in a spectacular Grade II* listed building and through its displays, exhibitions and event programme it offers an experience that will inspire, inform and educate everyone. Opening hours Sunday-Thursday 10am-4pm Friday 10am-1pm. Admission charges apply.

UJIA
P.O. Box 800, Altrincham WA15 5GD
Tel 0161 740 1825
Pres. J Rowe, D Hamburger

WIZO
Suite 7, Sulaw House, 1 Chapel Street, Bury New Road, Prestwich M25 1AE
Hon. Life Pres. J Woolfe MBE *Tel* 0161 425 5018 *Email* manchester@wizouk.org

Zionist Central Council of Greater Manchester
C/o Bnei Akiva, 72 Singelton Road, Salford M74LU
Email zcc.man@zen.co.uk *Website* www.zcc.org.uk
Dir. Karen Solomon *Tel* 0161 740 8835

WELFARE

Brookvale
Simister Lane, Prestwich, M25 2SF
Tel 0161 653 1767 *Fax* 0161 655 3635
Email admin@brookvale.org
(Reg. Charity No. 526086). Under supervision of Manchester Beth Din. Caring for People with Special Needs. *Exec. Dir.* L. Richmond; *Fin. Dir.* M. Walters

Delamere Charitable Trust
132-134 Great Ancoats Street, M4 6DE
Tel 0161 773 2580
Email charity@delamereschool.org.uk *Website* www.delamereschool.org.uk
(Reg Charity No. 1117339). For Jewish children with special needs. *Ch. of Dir.* M. Joels; *Admin.* P.W. Reed

The Fed
The Federation of Jewish Services (formerly **The Fed** and **Heathlands Village**)
Head Office Heathlands Village, Heathlands Drive, Prestwich, M25 9SB
Tel 0161 772 4800 *Fax* 0161 772 4934
Email info@thefed.org.uk *Website* www.thefed.org.uk
South Manchester Branch 207a Ashley Road, Hale, Cheshire WA15 9SQ
Tel 0161 941 4442 *Fax* 0161 941 5039
Email southside@thefed.org.uk
(Reg. Charity No. 1117126). *Ch.* Mark Adlestone; *V. Ch.* Dr Simon Jenkins, MBE; *Chief Exec.* Karen Phillips MBE, DL. The Fed is the leading social care agency for the Greater Manchester Jewish Community, serving people of all ages. Its services are based at its

main multigenerational centre at Heathlands Village in North Manchester and its South Manchester branch office. It looks after over 1,000 people at any one time offering among other things: residential, nursing, dementia, end-of-life, and respite care supported living and day services for older people, mental health, carer and volunteer support, social work assessment and support, and respite for children with special needs

Jewish Soup Kitchen (Meals-on-Wheels Service)
Rita Glickman House, Ravensway, Prestwich M25 0EX
Tel 0161 795 4930
(Reg. Charity No. 226424). *Hon. S. H.* Amdurer *Tel* 0161 773 5229

Manchester Jewish Community Care (The Nicky Alliance Day Centre)
85 Middleton Road, M8 4JY
Tel 0161 740 0111 *Fax* 0161 721 4273
Email info@mjcc.org.uk *Website* www.mjcc.org.uk
(Reg. Charity No. 257238). Provides day care for those with visual impairment, physical disability, elderly, frail, lonely or suffering from dementia-related illness. *Pres.* N. Alliance OBE; *Ch.* R. Levene; *Chief Exec.* M. Wiseman

Morris Feinmann Home (Care Home for older people)
178 Palatine Road, Didsbury, M20 2YW
Tel 0161 445 3533
Website www.morrisfeinmannhome.com
Ch. A. Wilkins *Email* heather@morrisfeinmannhome.com; *Gen. Man.* H. Naylor.

Outreach Community & Residential Services
Redbank House, 4 St Chads Street, Cheetham, Manchester M8 8QA
Tel 0161 740 3456 *Fax* 0161 740 5678
Email jennifer@outreach.co.uk *Website* www.outreach.co.uk
(Reg. Charity No. 509119). *Chief Exec.* A. Akinola; *Ch.* P. Elton

YOUTH & STUDENTS

Bnei Akiva Northern Youth Centre
72 Singleton Road, Salford M7 4LU
Tel 0161 740 1621
Email north@bauk.org *Website* www.bauk.org
Correspondence Daniel Gillis

Hillel House
Greenheys Lane, M15 6LR
Tel 0161 226 1139 (Warden); *Tel* 0161 226 1061(Residents)

Jerusalem Academy Study Groups
43 Stanley Road, Salford M7 4FR
Tel 0161 740 2506
Ch. Rev. G. Brodie

The Forum/Whitefield Community Kollel
C/o Whitefield Hebrew Congregation, Park Lane, Manchester M45 7PB
Tel 0161 766 2150 *Email* info@theforumwck.org
Tru. Rabbi J Guttentag (*Ch.*), Rabbi M Kupetz, G. Nussbaum
Whitefield Community Kollel: Academy of higher Jewish Learning and rabbinical training college; The Forum: Informal Jewish education and outreach for the community.

MARGATE

SYNAGOGUES

Margate Hebrew Congregation
Synagogue, Albion Road, Cliftonville, CT9 2HP
(Est. 1904; new synagogue consecrated 1929; Reg. Charity No. 273506). *Pres.* Dr N. Jacobs. Enquiries to *Hon. S.* David Gradus, 11 Dalmeny Avenue, CT9 3NL *Tel* 01843 226 983

CEMETERIES

For Margate Hebrew Congregation & Thanet Reform at Manston Road, Margate.

MIDDLESBROUGH
Linthorpe Cemetery, Ayresome Green Lane, Middlesbrough TS5 5AP

MILTON KEYNES & DISTRICT
Reform Synagogue (Beit Echud) (Movement for Reform)
1 Hainault Avenue, Giffard Park, MK14 5PQ
Tel 01908 617 790
Email info@mkdrs.org.uk *Website* www.mkdrs.org.uk
(Est. 1978. Reg. Charity No. 1058193) Rabbi Shulamit Ambalu *Email* rabbi@mkdrs.org.uk;
T. S. Friedman *Tel* 01908 560 714

NEWCASTLE UPON TYNE
The community was established in the 1820s, when services were held and a Shochet employed. A cemetery was acquired in 1831. Jews, however, had been resident in Newcastle since before 1775. In the Middle Ages Jews are known to have been established in Newcastle in 1176.

REPRESENTATIVE BODIES
Representative Council of North East Jewry
Email repcouncilpresident@northeastjewish.co.uk *Website* www.northeastjewish.org.uk
(Reg. Charity No. 1071515). *Co-Pres.* B. Mark *Tel* 0191 284 2808, E. Joseph *Tel* 0191 285 7654;
Hon. S. B. Joseph 21 Church Avenue, Newcastle upon Tyne NE3 1AN *Tel* 0191 285 7654;
PR, c/o E. Joseph *Tel* 0191 285 7654; *Hon. T.* W. Knoblauch *Email* walter@total-accounting.com

SYNAGOGUES
United Hebrew Congregation
The Synagogue, Graham Park Road, Gosforth NE3 4BH
Tel 0191 284 0959
(Est. 1973). *Pres.* V. Gallant; *M.* Rabbi A. Lipsey; *Sec.* M. Conway. Mikva on premises.
> **Burial Committee** *Ch.* P. Gold *Tel* 0191 285 1680

Newcastle Reform Synagogue
The Croft, off Kenton Road, Gosforth, NE3 4RF
Tel 0191 284 8621
Email admin@nertamid.org.uk *Website* www.nertamid.org.uk
(Est. 1963). A Constituent of Movement for Reform Judaism. *Ch.* Bill Fleming
> **Burial Committee** *Ch.* P. Gold *Tel* 0191 285 1680

CEMETERIES
Hazelrigg and Heaton (UHC)
North Shields (Reform)

SOCIAL, CULTURAL & INTERFAITH
AJEX
Tel 01661 824 819
Ch. J. Fox *Tel* 0191 213 0304; *Sec.* Mr. Topez *Tel* 01661 824 819
North East Council Of Christians and Jews
Contact D. Van der Velde *Tel* 0191 285 1253 *Email* clivando@hotmail.com
Newcastle Jewish Leisure Group
(Founded in 1981) A senior citizen's group, which meets in the Marion Abrahams Hall two afternoons every month except July and August. There is a varied programme of entertainment, talks, bingo, and bus outings during the summer. Tea is provided as well as transport facilities.
Newcastle WIZO
Co-Ch. Pam Peterson *Tel* 0191 285 4302 and Monica Stern *Tel* 0191 284 2502
Email monica@sternmail.co.uk
North East Jewish Recorder (communal journal published by the Representative Council).
Contact Louise Karker *Tel* 07917 733 781 *Email* recorderofficers@northeastjewish.co.uk

WELFARE
North East Jewish Community Services
NEJCS offers a wide range of services to those who are in need and live in the North East. Counselling, meals-on-wheels, voluntary visiting and work with the voluntary and statutory sector are the key components. *P/T Community Worker* Pamela Muscat *Tel* 0191 285 7698; *Ch.* Henry Ross *Tel* 0191 285 4043 *Email* henry.ross@dsl.pipex.com
Philip Cussins House (Residential Care for Jewish Aged in the North East)
33/35 Linden Road, Gosforth NE3 4EY
Tel 0191 213 5353 *Fax* 0191 213 5354
Email christine@philipcussinshouse.co.uk *Website* www.philipcussinshouse.co.uk

YOUTH & STUDENTS
Education and Youth Committee
c/o United Hebrew Congregation
Ch. D. Sadlik
Jewish Students' Society and Hillel House
Ilford Road, Gosforth
Email info@newcastlejsoc.com *Website* www.newcastlejewish.co.uk
Pres. Tamma; *T.* Jack; *Sec.* Jo

NORTHAMPTON
The community marked its centenary in 1988. For a history of the medieval and modern settlement in the town See *A Short History of the Jews of Northampton, 1159–1996* (1996), by M. Jolles.

SYNAGOGUES
Northampton Hebrew Congregation
Overstone Road, Northampton, NN1 3JW
Website www.northantshc.org
Sec. G. Goldcrown *Tel* 01604 633 345

CEMETERIES
Towcester Road Cemetery

NORWICH
There has been a Jewish presence in Norwich during the 11th and 12th century up to the expulsion in 1290. The first known community in Norwich after the re-settlement was in 1759 and the first small synagogue was in 1828. A new larger synagogue was consecrated in 1849 and was destroyed in an air raid in 1942. A temporary Synagogue opened in 1948 and the present Synagogue was consecrated by the late Chief Rabbi, Dr I Jacobovitz in 1969. The congregation serves a large area, having members in Great Yarmouth, Lowestoft and Sheringham.

SYNAGOGUES
Norwich Hebrew Congregation Synagogue
3a Earlham Road, NR2 3RA
Tel 01603 623 948
Email enquiries@norwichsynagogue.org.uk
M. A. Bennett *Tel* 01263 710 726; *H. Pres.* M. Leveton *Tel* 01603 749 706; *Hon. S.* F. Cadywould *Tel* 01603 502 084

SOCIAL, CULTURAL & INTERFAITH
Chevra Kadisha 3a Earlham Road, NR2 3RA *Pres.* B. Leveton *Tel* 01603 749 706
Jewish Ladies' Society
3a Earlham Road, NR2 3RA
Jt. Pres. P. Simons, F. Cadywould *Tel* 01362 850 515
Norfolk and Norwich Branch of the Council of Christians and Jews
(Est. 1991). *Sec.* Jill Gower *Tel* 01508 491 770 *Email* jill@jill495.orangehome.co.uk

Norwich Israel Social Society (NISS)
Tel 01603 623 948
Email enquiries@norwichsynagogue.org.uk
Ch. Jo Cummin Tel 01603 613 922
Progressive Jewish Community of East Anglia (Norwich)
Website www.pjcea.org.uk
Affiliated to the LJ. Regular services at The Old Meeting House, Colegate, Norwich NR3 1BN.
Enquiries to Hon. S. Steven Pruner Publ. PJCEA Newsletter.

NOTTINGHAM

A small community has lived in Nottingham since the early 19th century, and in 1890, with a community increased by immigrants to some 100 families, the Hebrew Congregation built its first synagogue in Chaucer St. During the Second World War, there was a sharp growth in the community, and the congregation acquired its present synagogue in 1954. With the closure of the Derby synagogue in 1986, many of its members joined the Nottingham Hebrew Congregation. The Progressive Jewish Congregation was established in 1959.

SYNAGOGUES
Nottingham Hebrew Congregation
Shakespeare Villas, NG1 4FQ
Tel 0115 947 2004
Email info@officenhc.co.uk Website www.nottinghamsynagogue.co.uk
Pres. L.N. Goodman
Progressive Jewish Congregation (LJ)
Lloyd Street, NG5 4BP
Tel 0115 962 4761
Email npjc@liberaljudaism.org Website www.npjc@org.uk
Ch. Kathy Sylvester, David Leigh

WELFARE
Nottingham Jewish Women's Benevolent Society
c/o 4 Levens Close, West Bridgford, NG2 6SN
Ch. Natalie Bogod Tel 0115 945 2170 Email natalie@bogod.eu

YOUTH & STUDENTS
University of Nottingham Jewish and Israel Society
c/o The University of Nottingham, NG7 2RD

OXFORD

An important centre in the medieval period – see www.oxfordjewishheritage.co.uk for the history of the Jews in Oxford. The modern community was established in 1842 and in 1974 the Oxford Jewish Centre was built on the site of the earlier synagogue. The Centre underwent a major refurbishment and extension in 2004. It serves a resident community of some 400 families, with a fluctuating number of University students, graduates and visitors. The Centre is available for Orthodox, Masorti and Liberal forms of worship. The following are available to all members (including students who are honorary members during their time in Oxford):: Mikveh; Oxford WIZO; Marriage and Burial Services; Playshul (0-5) Cheder (5+) and Barmitzvah preparation; Mosaic Adult Education Programme including Hebrew, lectures and films; Friendship club (over 60's); Midweek Lunch club (over 60's) and midweek social and cultural activities; Counselling services (BLESS); Oxford Shir Choir; Helping Hand; Oxford Jewish Heritage Group; Oxford Social Action Group; Oxford CCJ; shop and Kosher Cafe (Sunday mornings in termtime). For information on all of these, please contact Oxford Jewish Congregation.

SYNAGOGUES
Oxford Jewish Congregation
The Oxford Jewish Centre, 21 Richmond Road, OX1 2JL

Tel 01865 514 356
Email connections@ojc-online.org *Website* www.ojc-online.org
Oxford Orthodox
(under the auspices of the United Synagogue). Services Friday evenings, Saturday mornings, and daily morning minyan, plus all festivals. *Contact* Barry Freilich *Tel* 01865 559 899
Oxford Masorti Group
The Synagogue, 21 Richmond Road, Oxford OX1 2JL
Email connections@ojc-online.org *Website* www.ojc-online.org
Services usually held once a month on Shabbat morning at the Oxford Jewish Centre, usually on the last Shabbat of the (secular) month. The service follows the Sacks Siddur. Families can sit together and women and men lead the services. Visitors are welcome to attend and participate. Please email for further information. *Contact* Wendy Fidler
Oxford Progressive
Email progressive@ojc-online.org *Website* www.ojc-online.org
Contact Katherine Shock *Tel* 01865 515 584
Services usually held on the second Shabbat of each month, monthly Friday night services and some festivals.

EDUCATIONAL
University Jewish Societies (Oxford University and Oxford Brookes University)
(Est. 1903). *Snr. Member* J Getzler, St Hugh's *Tel* 01865 557 058/375 942; *JSoc Pres. Email* presidents@oxfordjsoc.co.uk; *Student Chaplains* Rabbi Daniel, Hannah Braune Friedman

PETERBOROUGH

SYNAGOGUES
Hebrew Congregation (Affiliated to the US)
142 Cobden Avenue, PE1 2NU
Tel 01733 264151
(Congregation Est. 1940. Synagogue opened 1954). *Admin.* C. Salmon Services Kabbalat Shabbat 7pm.

SOCIAL, CULTURAL & INTERFAITH
Liberal Jewish Community (LJ)
c/o The Montagu Centre, 21 Maple Street, London W1T 4BE
Enquiries Elisabeth Walker *Tel* 020 7580 1663

PLYMOUTH

The Plymouth community was founded in 1745, when a cemetery was opened. Jews lived in the city even earlier. The synagogue, built in 1762, is the oldest Ashkenazi house of worship still standing in the English-speaking world, still in regular use, with services every Erev Shabbat, Shabbat morning and all festivals. Its 250th anniversary in May 2012 was marked by a service conducted by Reverend Elkan Levy in the presence of the Chief Rabbi Lord Sacks, representatives of the United Synagogue, the Board of Deputies and the Civic Authorities. In the early 19th century, Plymouth was one of the four most important provincial centres of Anglo-Jewry. The history of the community, 'The Plymouth Synagogue 1761–1961' by Doris Black, was published in 1961.
Plymouth Hebrew Congregation
Catherine Street, Synagogue Chambers, Devon PL1 2AD
Tel 01752 263 162
Email imannahi@hotmail.com *Website* www.plymouthsynagogue.com
(Est. 1762. Reg. Charity No. 220010). *Hon. S.* A. Kelly *Tel* 01822 614 203

PORTSMOUTH

The community was established in 1746 and opened a synagogue in Oyster Row, later to move to a building in White's Row, off Queen St. which was occupied for over 150 years. The present synagogue was built in 1936. The cemetery was acquired in 1749 and is the oldest in the Regions still in use. It is situated in Fawcett Road, which was known for more than 200 years as Jews' Lane. By 1815 Portsmouth was one of the four main Jewish centres outside London, the others being Plymouth, Liverpool and Birmingham. Portsmouth's prosperity declined after the Napoleonic Wars. For South Hampshire Reform Jewish Community *See under* Southampton.

SYNAGOGUES

Portsmouth & Southsea Hebrew Congregation Synagogue
The Thicket, Elm Grove, Southsea PO5 2AA
Tel 023 9282 1494
(Reg. Charity No. X50585). Officers of the Board of Guardians (Est. 1804), the Chevra Kadisha, Friendship Club, and the Jewish Ladies' Benevolent Society (Est. 1770) may be contacted through the synagogue. *M.* Rabbi D. Katanka

CEMETERIES
Fawcett Road, Kingston, New Road; Catherington

PRESTON
Synagogue established 1882, now closed.

RAMSGATE
SYNAGOGUES
Sir Moses Montefiore Synagogue
Honeysuckle Road, Ramsgate, Kent CT11 8AA
Website www.montefioreendowment.org.uk
Thanet and District Reform Synagogue
293A Margate Road, Ramsgate, Kent CT12 6TE
Tel 01843 851 164
Website www.tdrs.org.uk

READING
The community began in 1886 with the settlement of a number of tailors from London. They attracted the help of such personages as Lord Swaythling, Claude Montefiore, Sir Hermann Gollancz and Lady Lucas to build and support a synagogue in 1900, and the synagogue has been in continuous use ever since. This flourishes today as the centre of the Reading Hebrew Congregation, and is the only Orthodox congregation in Berkshire. The Sir Hermann Gollancz Hall next to the synagogue is the venue of many social groups. The Progressive Community was founded in 1979 and attracts membership from across the Thames Valley. (*See also under* Maidenhead).

REPRESENTATIVE BODIES
Berkshire Jewish Representative Council
(Est. 1995). Representing Maidenhead Synagogue, Reading Hebrew Congregation and Reading Liberal Jewish Community. *Contact,* Myer Daniels *Email* mdaniels@globalnet.co.uk
SYNAGOGUES
Reading Hebrew Congregation Synagogue
Goldsmid Road, RG1 7YB
Tel 0118 957 3954
Website www.rhc.org.uk *Email* secretary@rhc.org.uk
(Reg. Charity No. 220098). *M.* Rabbi Z. Solomons

SOCIAL, CULTURAL & INTERFAITH
Reading Liberal Jewish Community (LJ)
2 Church Street, Reading RG1 2SB
Email rljcl@liberaljudaism *Website* www.rljc.org
(Est. 1979). For details of services, religious/social events, please contact Gill Switler
Tel 0118 375 3422

YOUTH & STUDENTS
University Jewish Society
c/o Hebrew Congregation.

ST ANNE'S ON SEA
SYNAGOGUES
Hebrew Congregation
Orchard Road, FY8 1PJ
Tel 01253 721 831
(Charity No. 66492). *Pres.* R. Pinkus; *Warden*, M. Harris; *Hon. T.* J. Hecht

CEMETERIES
Consecrated section of municipal cemetery at Regents Avenue, Lytham and consecrated section of municipal cemetery at Carleton Blackpool.

SHEFFIELD
The earliest records of an organised Jewish community in Sheffield date from 1850, but the congregation had already been in existence for some time and Jews are known to have been living in the city from the eighteenth century. At its peak in the 1960s, the community numbered over 2,000. A study of the community, 'Sheffield Jewry' by Armin Krausz, was published in 1980. In 2000, the Orthodox congregation moved from the large Wilson Road synagogue (built 1929) into a new and smaller synagogue within the grounds of the Jewish Centre which was consecrated by the Chief Rabbi in 2000. The Reform congregation was founded in 1989 and was admitted as a full constituent member of the RSGB in 2000. Though now a smaller community, Sheffield has an exceptional range of societies and groups, covering all varieties of Jewish interests.

SYNAGOGUES
Sheffield Jewish Congregation and Centre (Orthodox)
Kingfield Synagogue, 3 Brincliffe Crescent, S11 9AW
Tel 0114 255 2296 (synagogue) 0114 281 7459 (home)
Email ycgolomb@gmail.com *Website* www.jewishsheffield.org.uk
(Reg. Charity No. 250281). *M.* Rabbi Y. Golomb; *Pres.* E. Patnick. Mikvah on premises.

EDUCATIONAL
Sheffield Jewish Education Organization
Sheffield Jewish Community Centre, 3 Brincliffe Crescent, S11 9AW
(Reg. Charity No. 529362). *Pres.* Dr A. Anderson *Tel* 0114 235 1041

SOCIAL, CULTURAL & INTERFAITH
Sheffield & District Reform Jewish Congregation
For information contact P.O. Box 675, SW PDO, S11 8TE
Email enquiries@shef-ref.co.uk *Website* www.shef-ref.co.uk
Ch. Mrs Kay *Tel* 07719 209 259

WELFARE
Sheffield Jewish Welfare Organisation in association with SJCC
Pres. A. Kaddish *Tel* 0114 236 7958 *Email* tony.kaddish@talktalk.net

YOUTH & STUDENTS
Hillel House
1 Guest Road, S11 8UJ
Office Tel/Fax 0114 268 7638/0845 108 0109
Email jss@netheredgelaw.co.uk
(Reg. Charity No. 529385). *Pres.* Jeffrey Shaw

SOLIHULL
The community began in 1962. The synagogue was built in 1977. Its close proximity to

Birmingham means that many of the facilities of the Birmingham community are shared by Solihull.

SYNAGOGUES
Solihull & District Hebrew Congregation
Solihull Jewish Community Centre, 3 Monastery Drive, Solihull, West Midlands B91 1DW
Tel/Fax 0121 706 8736
Email rabbi@solihullshul.org *Website* www.solihullshul.org
M. Rabbi Y. Pink *Tel* 0121 706 8736; *Pres.* S. Fisher; *Admin.* H. Woolf

EDUCATIONAL
Solihull & District Cheder
Hon. T. Rabbi Y. Pink *Tel* 0121 706 8736

SOCIAL, CULTURAL & INTERFAITH
Hakol – Community Magazine
3 Monastery Drive, B91 1DW
Email rabbi@solihullshul.org
Mother and Toddler's Group
Solihull Jewish Community Centre, 3 Monastery Drive, Solihull, West Midlands B91 1DW
Email dinapink@gmail.com *Website* www.solihullshul.org
Every Monday 11am-1pm. Dina Pink *Tel* 0121 706 8736
Stanley Middleburgh Library
3 Monastery Drive, B91 1DW
Email rabbi@solihullshul.org
Open Thursday 11am-2pm, Sunday 9.30am–1pm or by appointment.

WELFARE
The Thursday Club
Solihull Jewish Community Centre, 3 Monastery Drive, Solihull, West Midlands B91 1DW
Website www.solihullshul.org
For the over 60s. Every Thursday 11am-2pm. *Co-ord.* Ruth Abrahams *Tel* 0121 705 5287

SOUTH SHIELDS
Cemetery: Consecrated section of the municipal cemetery.

SOUTHAMPTON
The orthodox congregation dates from 1833 when the first synagogue in East Street was founded. The synagogue built in 1864 in Albion Place was demolished in 1963, when the present one was consecrated. There were Jewish residents in Southampton in 1786. Since 1838, when Abraham Abraham was elected to the Town Council, they have shared in civic affairs. The South Hampshire Reform Jewish Community was formed in 1983.

SYNAGOGUES
Orthodox Synagogue
Mordaunt Road, Inner Avenue, SO14 6GP
Tel 023 8022 0129
Website www.sotonhebrew.org.uk
Pres. M. Rose
South Hampshire Reform Jewish Community
Email shrj2@hotmail.com *Website* www.southhantsreform.wordpress.com
(Est. 1983; Reg. Charity No. 1040109). For Hampshire and the Isle of Wight. *Pres.* I. Elia
Tel 02380 220 034; *Sec.* J. Badley *Tel* 01489 783 385

CEMETERIES
Cemetery: Consecrated section at the municipal Hollybrook cemetery.

SOCIAL, CULTURAL & INTERFAITH
Hartley Library
University of Southampton, Highfield, houses the Anglo-Jewish Archives and Parkes
Library (See p. 131).

SOUTHEND, WESTCLIFF & LEIGH-ON-SEA
Jewish families settled in the Southend area in the late nineteenth century, mainly from
London's East End. In 1906 the first temporary synagogue was built of wood in Station
Road, Westcliff. In 1912 a synagogue was built in Alexandra Road, which served the
community until February 2001 when it was sold. A second synagogue was built in Ceylon
Road, Westcliff, in 1928, but when a new synagogue was built in Finchley Road, the Ceylon
Road premises were converted into a youth centre. The Ceylon Road premises have now
been sold and a new youth centre has been opened at the Talmud Torah premises.

SYNAGOGUES
Southend and District Reform Synagogue
851 London Road, Westcliff-on-Sea SS0 9SZ
Tel 01702 711 663 (answerphone)
Email mail@southendreform.co.uk *Website* www.southendreform.co.uk
M. Rabbi Warren Elf *Email* rabbielf@southendreform.co.uk; *Ch.* D. Carr; *Hon. T.* K.
Phillips; *Hon. S.* S. Levitas
Southend and Westcliff Hebrew Congregation
Finchley Road, Westcliff-on-Sea, Essex SS0 8AD
Email swhc@hotmail.co.uk *Website* www.swhc.org.uk
Pres. S. Salt; *M.* Rabbi Bar *Tel* 01702 344 900 *Fax* 01702 391 131
Gen. Man. Janice Steel *Email* swhcmanager@hotmail.co.uk; *Admin.* Pamela Freedman
Email swhc@hotmail.com

CEMETERIES
Orthodox Jewish Cemetery, Sutton Road, Southend SS2 5PX (Entrance Stock Road)
Tel 01702 344 900
Reform Jewish Cemetery, Sutton Road, Southend SS2 5PX (Entrance Stock Road)

EDUCATIONAL
Coleman & Lilian Levene Talmud Torah (Orthodox)
Finchley Road, Westcliff-on-Sea SS0 8AD
Tel 01702 344 900
Princ. Rabbi B. Bar
Hebrew Education Board
Ch. Paul Winston (Synagogue)
Talmud Torah (Reform)
851 London Road, Westcliff, SS0 9SZ *Princ.* B. Barber *Tel* 01702 297 238

RELIGIOUS
Kashrut Commission
Ch. M.Nelkin
Mikveh
44 Genesta Road, Westcliff-on-Sea SS0 8DA
Tel 01702 344 900
Supt. R. Samuel

SOCIAL, CULTURAL & INTERFAITH
Council of Christians and Jews
Terry Mendoza *Tel* 01702 478 789; Jack De Metz *Tel* 01702 391 535
Myers Communal Hall
Finchley Road, Westcliff-on-Sea, Essex SS0 8AD
Tel 01702 344 900

Southend & District AJEX

An active branch of the Association of Jewish Ex-Servicemen and Women. For more information contact Sid Barnett, Jeffrey Barcon via the Shul office *Tel* 01702 344 900 or visit the national website www.ajex.org.uk

Tuesday Nighters

For the over 55s. For more information, contact Lewis Herllitz *Tel* 01702 715 676

WIZO

A local branch of national organisation. *Ch.* Jackie Kalms *Tel* 01702 437 801
Email jackiekalms@live.co.uk or central@wizouk.org

WELFARE
Kosher Meals-on-Wheels Service

Delivery to Jewish residents in Southend. For more information contact Tony Rubin *Tel* 01702 345 568 (24 hours)

Raymond House

7 Clifton Terrace, SS1 1DT
Man. Tel 01702 352 956

Southend Aid Society

Jewish Care's support group in Southend, working closely with Raymond House, a Jewish Care residential home for the elderly, Shebson Lodge, Jewish Care's warden assisted flats and the community centre. *Ch.* Norman Zetter; *Sec.* Janice Linden *Tel* 01702 478 375

Southend & Westcliff Community Centre

1 Cobham Road, Westcliff-on-Sea, SS0 8EG (a Jewish Care Community Centre)
Tel 01702 334 655
Website www.jewishcare.org
Man. G. Freeman *Email* gfreeman@jcare.org

YOUTH & STUDENTS
The Buzz Youth Club (Orthodox)

Finchley Road, Westcliff-on-Sea SS0 9SZ *Tel* 01702 432 067
Email sjyc.thebuzz@gmail.com
Youth Co.-Ord. Paul Winston

SOUTHPORT

The first Synagogue was consecrated in 1893 and the congregation moved to Arnside Road, in 1924. The New Synagogue (Reform) was established in 1948. The community grew between and during the First and Second World Wars, but is now decreasing.

REPRESENTATIVE BODIES
Jewish Representative Council

Pres. Sonia Abrahamson 65 Beach Priory Gardens, PR8 2SA *Tel* 01704 540 704;
Hon. S. R. Jackson 33 The Chesters, 17-19 Argyle Road PR9 9LG *Tel* 01704 532 696

SYNAGOGUES
Southport Hebrew Congregation

Arnside Road, PR9 0QX
Tel 01704 532 964
(Est. 1893). *Ch.* R. Roukin; *Snr. Warden* Adrian Fletcher; *Sec.* Susan Dutch

Southport Reform Synagogue

Princes Street, PR8 1EG
Tel 01704 535 950
Email southportsynagog@btconnect.com
Office Hours Tuesday, Thursday, Friday 10am-1pm. *Office Admin.* Lisa Sachs

RELIGIOUS
Mikveh

Arnside Road, PR9 0QX
Tel 01704 532 964

SOCIAL, CULTURAL & INTERFAITH
Southport Hebrew Philanthropic Society
(Est. 1897). *Sec.* M.P. Braham *Tel* 01704 563 665

WELFARE
Southport Rest Home
81 Albert Road, PR9 9LN
Tel 01704 531 975 (office); 01704 530 207 (visitors)
Email office@sjah.freeserve.co.uk
Ch. B. King
Manchester House
83 Albert Road, Southport, PR9 9LN
Tel 01704 534 920 (office); 01704 530 436 (visitors)

STOKE-ON-TRENT AND NORTH STAFFORDSHIRE
Hebrew Congregation
London Road, Newcastle, Staffs, ST5 1LZ
(Est. 1873. Reg. Charity No. 232104).
Pres. H. S. Morris, MBE 27 The Avenue, Basford, Newcastle, ST5 0ND *Tel* 01782 616 417;
Jt. Hon. T. M.D. Morris, R. Elias *Tel* 01782 318 110 *Email* martin@mmorris01wanadoo.co.uk

SUFFOLK
Suffolk Jewish Community (LJ)
Suffolk Jewish Community is a very small and friendly community. We try to meet once a month in Ipswich (generally last Friday of the month), and have a few Shabbatons throughout the year. We meet in people's houses, or local village halls, but at present, do not have a fixed base. We hold a communal Seder service, and services for Erev Rosh Hashanah and other festivals. We are affiliated to LJ. *Enquiries* Beverley Levy *Tel* 01473 250 797 *Email* sjc@liberaljudaism.org

SUNDERLAND
The first Jewish settlement was in 1755. The first congregation was established about 1768; it was the first regional community to be represented at the BoD. A synagogue was erected in Moor Street in 1862; rebuilt in 1900; and in 1928 the congregation moved to Ryhope Road, The Beth Hamedrash, which was established in Villiers St. in 1899, and moved to Mowbray Road in 1938, closed in December 1984. Arnold Levy published a 'History of the Sunderland Jewish Community' in 1956. There is also a history of the Beth Din Hamedrash, written by Derek Taylor and Harold Davis (2010).

CEMETERIES
Bishopwearmouth Cemetery, Hylton Road, Sunderland.

SWINDON
The community formed by Second World War evacuees has dispersed, but a community was re-formed in 1983.
Swindon Jewish Community (Associated Community of the Movement for Reform Judaism)
c/o Reform Judaism, Sternberg Centre, 80 East End Road, London N3 2SY *Tel* 020 8349 5643
(Est.1983). *Contact Tel* 01793 831 335

TORQUAY (TORBAY)
SYNAGOGUES
Synagogue
Old Town Hall, Abbey Road
The synagogue was closed at the end of 2000 and the congregation dissolved.

RELIGIOUS
Chevra Kadisha Cemetery, Colley End Road, Paignton, Torbay TQ3 3QX *Ch.* E. Freed
11 Kestor Drive, Paignton TQ3 1AP *Tel* 01803 553 781

TOTNES
Totnes Jewish Community (Movement for Reform)
We are a small, open-hearted community representing a diverse range of Jewish expression, and offering regular spiritual, social and cultural events. For all enquiries contact Marc Frank *Tel* 07508 806 770 *Email* marcfrank12@googlemail.com

TRURO
Kehilllat Kernow
Website www.kehillatkernow.com
(Est. 1999 Reg. Charity No. 1090562). Kehillat Kernow is a thriving Jewish community in Cornwall which has recently celebrated its tenth anniversary. Kehillat Kernow is a growing congregation of over 50 families who live all over Cornwall. We meet fortnightly for Shabbat Services and cheder followed by a kiddush lunch at Three Bridges School in Blackwater near Truro. We also celebrate all major holidays and festivals together including a very popular and delicious communal seder. Holiday makers and visitors are warmly welcome. For service dates, times and directions please refer to our website.
Ch. Harvey Kurzfield Owl Cottage, Mill Road, Penponds, Cornwall *Tel* 01209 719 672 *Email* hkurzfield@yahoo.co.uk; *T.* Leslie Lipert *Tel* 01736 762 675 ; *Sec.* Rachel Brown *Tel* 01872 862 665 *Email* brownierus@lineone.net

WALLASEY
Hebrew Congregation
28 Grant Road, Wirral, Merseyside, L46 2RY
Tel 0161 638 6945
(Est. 1911). *Pres.* D. Daniels; *T.* D. J. Waldman; *Hon. S.* L.S. Goldman

WELWYN GARDEN CITY
Synagogue (Affiliated to US)
Barn Close, Handside Lane, Herts AL8 6ST
Tel 01707 322 443
Email info@wgcshul.org.uk
M. Rabbi H. Gruber; *Hon. S.* H. Rosenberg

WORTHING
Worthing & District Jewish Community
The Friends Meeting House, 34 Mill Road, Worthing BN11 5DR
Meet for social and cultural events. *Outreach Chaplain*, Rev. Malcolm Wiseman. *Ch.* Ian Gordon *Tel* 01903 779 720 *Email* barbaraian@talktalk.net

YORK
A memorial stone was consecrated at Clifford's Tower, York Castle, in 1978 in memory of the York Jewish community massacred there in 1190. A small community resettled and continued to live in York until the 1290 expulsion. There is now a small community in the city and a Jewish Society at York University.
York Hebrew Congregation
Aldwalk Road
Contact A. S. Burton *Tel* 01423 330 537

WALES

CARDIFF
Jews settled in Cardiff about the year 1787. The present community was founded in 1840.

REPRESENTATIVE BODIES

The Interfaith Council for Wales
c/o Cytun, 58 Richmond Road, Cardiff CF24 3UR
Emaill info@interfaithwales.org *Website* www.interfaithwales.org
Sec. Rev Aled Edwards OBE *Tel* 02920 464 204; *Ch.* Rev Alan Bayes

South Wales Jewish Representative Council
9 Holmwood Close, Cyncoed, Cardiff CF23 6BT
Tel 029 2048 8198
Email swjewishrepcouncil@gmail.com
Ch. Stanley Soffa; *Hon. S.* Ruth Levene *Tel* 07920 585 848

SYNAGOGUES

Cardiff United Synagogue
Cyncoed Gardens, Cyncoed Road, Penylan, CF23 5SL
Tel 029 2047 3728
Website www.cardiffshul.org
Rabbi R. Rose *Email* rabbi@cardiffshul.org
   Mikveh Appointments *Tel* 07928 669 536

Cardiff Reform Synagogue (Movement for Reform)
Moira Terrace, CF24 0EJ (opposite Howard Gardens)
Tel 029 2049 1689
Email info@cardiffreformsyn.org.uk *Website* www.cardiffreformsyn.org.uk
Ch. M. Odey; *Sec.* J. Golten

Cathedral Road Synagogue
(Opened 1871). Closed 1997. *Tel* 01633 810 013 *Ch.* A. Davidson *Email* abd321@onetel.com

CEMETERIES
Old Cemetery – High Fields Road, Roath Park
New Cemetery – Greenfarm Road, Ely
Reform: at Cowbridge Road Entrance, Ely Cemetery

RELIGIOUS

Kashrus Commission
Cyncoed Gardens, Cyncoed Road, Penylan, CF23 5SL
Tel 029 2047 3728

SOCIAL, CULTURAL & INTERFAITH

Bimah (Three issues annually)
18 St Edeyrns Road, Cyncoed, Cardiff CF23 6TB
Tel 0292 076 2689
(Est. 1994). The Platform of Welsh Jewry. *Ed.* Barbara Michaels
Email barbara.michaels@btopenworld.com

Israel Information Centre Wales & the West of England
P.O.B. 98, CF2 6XN
Tel/Fax 02920 461 780
Dir. Jean A. Evans

WELFARE

Cardiff Jewish Helpline (formerly **Cardiff Jewish Board of Guardians**)
23 Solva Avenue, CF14 0NP
Tel 029 2075 0990
Ch. A. Schwartz

Penylan House, Jewish Residential and Nursing Home
Penylan Road, CF23 5YG
Tel 029 2048 5327 *Fax* 029 2045 8409
Nursing Office 029 2049 2574
Email penylanhouse@aol.com
Dir. Paul Evans; *Pres.* Judy Cotsen; *Matron/Nursing Man.* Geraldine Paterson

YOUTH & STUDENTS
Hillel House
89 Crwys Road, Cardiff CF24 4NF
Applications for admission: L. Gerson *Email* lisa.gerson@gmail.com
Hillel House is located in the heart of Cardiff's student area, amongst many local shops including a large supermarket. It is within walking distance from Cardiff University and Cardiff City Centre and is close to Medical School, UWIC campuses and Atrium and accesses major bus, rail and road routes with roadside resident parking. Each room is spacious and comes complete with its own kitchenette and ensuite shower facilities. Additionally the house has a large living room with flat screen tv and is the meeting place of the JSoc where Friday night meals are regularly held.

Union of Jewish Students
c/o Hillel House
Website www.groups.cardiffstudents.com/jewish/about/ *Facebook* Cardiff Jewish Society

LLANDUDNO AND COLWYN BAY
Hebrew Congregation
28 Church Walks, Llandudno LL30 2HL
(Est. 1905). Llandudno serves as the centre for the communities of North Wales, including Bangor, Rhyl, Colwyn Bay and Caernarvon.

MERTHYR TYDFIL
The synagogue is now closed. The community was established before 1850. The cemetery is still being maintained. Apply to the Cardiff Jewish Representative Council.

NEWPORT (Gwent)
CEMETERIES
Cemetery: Risca Road, Newport

RELIGIOUS
Burial Society c/o Cardiff United Synagogue, Penylan, Cardiff

SOCIAL, CULTURE & INTERFAITH
Synagogue (opened 1871). Now closed.
Tel 01633 810 013
Ch. A. Davidson *Email* abd321@onetel.com

SWANSEA
The Jewish community dates at the latest from 1768, when the Corporation granted a plot of land for use as a cemetery. In 1780 a synagogue was built. Probably its history is even older, for Jews are known to have been living in the town from about 1730. The synagogue in Goat Street was destroyed in an air raid in Feb. 1941, but another was erected in the Ffynone district. The former Llanelli congregation is now part of the Swansea community.

SYNAGOGUES
Swansea Hebrew Congregation
(Est. 1780). Synagogue, Ffynone. *Sec.* J. Arron *Tel* 01792 473 333

CEMETERIES
There are cemeteries at Oystermouth and Townhill.

RELIGIOUS
Chevra Kadisha
S. Franks 4 The Causeway, Parc Wern Road, Sketty, Swansea SA2 0SX *Tel* 01792 205 298

WELSHPOOL
Welshpool Jewish Group
c/o M. and S. Michaels, 10 Corndon Drive, Montgomery, Powys SY15 6RE
Tel 01686 668977
Email markjmichaels@googlemail.com

SCOTLAND

REPRESENTATIVE BODIES
Scottish Council of Jewish Communities (SCoJeC)
Jewish Community Centre, 222 Fenwick Road, Giffnock, Glasgow G46 6UE
Tel 0141 638 6411 *Mobile* 07887 488 100 *Fax* 0141 577 8208
Email scojec@scojec.org *Website* www.scojec.org
(Est. 1987 as the Standing Committee of Scottish Jewry. Charity SCO 29438). A Democratic umbrella body representing all the Jewish Communities in Scotland to the Scottish Parliament and Executive churches and other faith communities, educational, health and welfare organisations. An educational charity to promote understanding of the Jewish religion and community *Ch.* H. Rifkind; *V. Ch.* Gillian Raab; *Dir.* Ephraim Borowski; *Deputy Dir.* Leah Granat *Tel* 07887 488 100

SOCIAL, CULTURAL & INTERFAITH
The Scottish Jewish Archives Centre
Garnethill Synagogue, 129 Hill Street, Glasgow G3 6UB
Tel/Fax 0141 332 4911
Email info@sjac.org.uk *Website* www.sjac.org.uk
(Est. 1987). Aims to: collect, catalogue, preserve and exhibit records of communal interest, stimulate study of the history of the Jews of Scotland, heighten awareness, in the Jewish communities of Scotland, of their cultural and religious heritage. Exhibition on Jewish history in Scotland. *Ch.* Dr Kenneth Collins, PhD; *Hon. T.* Fiona L. Brodie BSc; *Dir.* Harvey L. Kaplan, MA; *Hon. S.* D. Wolfson

ABERDEEN
Refurbished synagogue and community centre opened in 1983.

Hebrew Congregation
74 Dee Street, AB11 6DS
Tel 07810 024 456
www.aberdeenhebrew.org.uk
(Est. 1893. Reg. Charity No. SC002901). *Hon. S.* Esther Shoshan *Tel* 01224 642 749

DUNDEE

Hebrew Congregation
9 St. Mary Place, DD1 5RB
Email jewsdundee@gmail.com
(Est. 1874. New synagogue opened 1978). *Ch.* Bill Shackman. In an emergency, the Scottish Council of Jewish Communities can be contacted on our behalf *Tel* 0141 638 6411
Dundee University Jewish Society is centred at the synagogue.

EDINBURGH

The Edinburgh Town Council and Burgess Roll, Minutes of 1691 and 1717, record applications by Jews for permission to reside and trade in Edinburgh. Local directories of the eighteenth century contain Jewish names. There is some reason to believe that there was an organised Jewish community in 1780 but no cemetery, and in 1817 it removed to Richmond Ct. where there was also for a time a rival congregation. In 1795, the Town Council sold a plot of ground on the Calton Hill to Herman Lyon, a Jewish dentist, to provide a burying place for himself and members of his family. In 1816, when a synagogue was opened, a cemetery was also acquired. The present synagogue in Salisbury Road was consecrated in 1932 and renovated in 1980.

SYNAGOGUES

Edinburgh Hebrew Congregation
Synagogue Chambers, 4 Salisbury Road, EH16 5AB
Website www.ehcong.com
(Est. 1816, Present Synagogue built 1932). *Ch. of the Board of Management*, Raymond Taylor *Tel* 0131 447 7386 *Email* ray.taylor@blueyonder.co.uk; *M.* Rabbi D. Rose; *Sec./Admin.* Jackie Taylor Email secretary@ehcong.com
   Board of Guardians *Hon. S.* I. Shein c/o 4 Salisbury Road, EH16 5AB

RELIGIOUS

Edinburgh Jewish Burial Friendly Society
Tel 0131 447 2947
Pres. Sylvia Donne 11/4 The Steils, Glenlockhart Road, EH10 5XD *Email* jsdonne@o2.co.uk

SOCIAL, CULTURAL & INTERFAITH

The Edinburgh Star (2 times a year)
31/3 Rattray Grove, EH10 5TL
Email michelinebrannan@msn.com
Community Journal. *Ed.* M. Brannan

Jewish Literary Society
c/o Hebrew Congregation, 4 Salisbury Road, EH16 5AB
Pres. A. Meiksin; *Hon. S.* A. Gilbert *Tel* 0131 667 4266

Ladies' Guild
37 Cluny Drive, Edinburgh EH10 6DU
Tel 0131 447 7386
Pres. H. Rifkind *Email* h.riffkind@blueyonder.co.uk

Wizo
Synagogue Chambers, 4 Salisbury Road, EH16 5AB
Co-Ch. K. Goodwin, S. Donne

YOUTH & STUDENTS

University Jewish Society
c/o Societies' Centre, Room 6, 21 Hill Place, EH8 9DP
Pres. S. Hyman

GLASGOW AND WEST OF SCOTLAND

The Glasgow Jewish community was founded in 1823 although there are records of Jewish activity in the city for many years prior to that. The first Jewish cemetery was opened in the prestigious Glasgow Necropolis in 1831 and the community was housed in a variety of synagogues in the city centre for many years. The community grew in the 1870s and the Garnethill Synagogue, the oldest Jewish building in Scotland and home of the Scottish Jewish Archives Centre, was opened in 1879. At the same time Jews began settling in the Gorbals district, just south of the River Clyde, where there was a substantial Jewish community with many synagogues and Jewish shops and communal institutions until the 1950s. None of these now remain. In more recent years the community has been centred in the southern suburbs, such as Giffnock and Newton Mearns, where most Jewish institutions are now situated.

Details of Jewish history in Glasgow in the early days (1790–1919) can be found in 'Second City Jewry' and 'Scotland's Jews' by Dr. Kenneth Collins, available from the Glasgow Jewish Representative Council.

REPRESENTATIVE BODIES

Glasgow Jewish Representative Council
Jewish Community Centre, 222 Fenwick Road, Giffnock, Glasgow G46 6UE
Tel 0141 577 8200 *Fax* 0141 577 8202
Email office@glasgowjewishrepcouncil.org *Website* www.glasgowjewishrepcouncil.org
Pres. Paul H. Morron; *Admin.* Julia Tatarenko; *Hon. S.* Fiona L. Brodie

SYNAGOGUES

Garnethill Synagogue
129 Hill Street, G3 6UB
Tel 0141 332 4151
Email greenhillm@btinternet.com
(Est. 1875). *Ch.* Bernard Goodman; *Hon. S.* Suzanne Dover; *Corres. Sec.* Dr. M.D. Greenhill

Giffnock and Newlands Synagogue
222 Fenwick Road, Giffnock G46 6UE
Tel 0141 577 8250
Email admin@giffnockshul.co.uk *Website* www.giffnockshul.co.uk
M. Rabbi A.M. Rubin; *Ch.* N. Allon; *Admin.* H. Livingstone

Glasgow Masorti Synagogue
Call for venue
Tel 0141 423 3384/07815 731 484
Contact Warren Bader

Glasgow Reform Synagogue - Or Chadash
147 Ayr Road, Newton Mearns G77 6RE
Tel 0141 639 4083
Email shul@grs.org.uk *Website* www.grs.org.uk
Ch. Eileen Carroll; *V. Ch.* Jonathan Green

Langside Hebrew Congregation
125 Niddrie Road, G42 8QA
Tel 0141 649 2962
M. Ch. J. Levingstone; *Hon. S.* N. Barnes

Newton Mearns Synagogue
14 Larchfield Court, G77 5PL
Tel 0141 639 4000
Email office@nmhc.org.uk *Website* www.nmhc.org
Ch. B. Fox; *Hon. S.* G. Winston

Shul in the Park (Lubavitch)
Tel 0141 638 5613
Email lubofscot@aol.com *Website* www.lubofscot.co.uk
Founder M. Rabbi Mendel Jacobs

EDUCATIONAL

Calderwood Lodge Jewish Primary School
28 Calderwood Road, G43 2RU
Tel 0141 570 7070
Hd. V. Thomson

RELIGIOUS

Hebrew Burial Society (as Representative Council)
Tel 0141 577 8226 For burial arrangements *Tel* 07748 676 429
Email hebrewburialsociety@gmail.com
Ch. B. Cooper; *Enquiries* A. Levy

Mikveh
Giffnock & Newlands Synagogue, Maryville Avenue, Giffnock G46 7NE
Mikveh appointments: Margalit Borowski *Tel* 07831 104 110 (between mid-August and last week of June). Synagogue office *Tel* 0141 577 8250 *Email* office@giffnockshul.co.uk (between end of June and approx 12th August).

West Scotland Kashrut Commission
Tel 0141 221 1827
Ch. M. Livingstone

SOCIAL, CULTURAL & INTERFAITH

Chaim Bermant Library
222 Fenwick Road, Giffnock G46 6UE

Glasgow Zionist Federation
222 Fenwick Road, Giffnock G46 6UE

Israel Scottish Information Service
Jewish Community Centre, 222 Fenwick Road, Giffnock, G46 6UE

Jewish Telegraph
May Terrace, Giffnock G46 6LD
Tel 0141 621 4422 (classified ads) *Tel* 0141 621 4433 (Newsdesk) 0141 621 4455 (Display Ads)
Email glasgow@jewishtelegraph.com *Website* www.jewishtelegraph.com

Lubavitch of Scotland
8 Orchard Drive, Giffnock G46 7NR
Tel 0141 638 6116
Email lubofscot@aol.com *Website* www.lubofscot.co.uk
Dir. Rabbi Chaim Jacobs, Sora Jacobs

Maccabi GB Scotland
May Terrace, Giffnock, G46 6LD
Tel 0141 638 6177
Email info@maccabigbscotland.org *Website* www.maccabiscotland.com
Ch. D. Shenkin; *Operations Man.* Sue Faber

UJIA (incorporating Glasgow Jewish Continuity)
Jewish Community Centre, 222 Fenwick Road, Giffnock, G46 6UE
Tel 0141 577 8210. Renewal *Tel* 0141 577 8220 *Fax* 0141 577 8212
Dir. Alex Steen; *Renewal Dir.* Joanna Hyman

WELFARE

Arklet Housing Association
Barrland Court, Barrland Drive, Giffnock, G46 7QD
Tel 0141 620 1890 *Fax* 0141 620 3044
Email arklet@arklet.org.uk *Website* www.arklet.org.uk
Dir. Maureen Patterson

Cosgrove Care
May Terrace, Giffnock, G46 6LD
Tel 0141 620 2500 *Fax* 0141 620 2501
Email info@cosgrovecare.org.uk *Website* www.cosgrovecare.org.uk
Ch. J. Dover; *Exec. Off.* W. Hecht; *Hon. S.* M. Goldman

Jewish Blind Society (Scotland)
Walton Community Care Centre, May Terrace, Giffnock, G46 6LD
Tel 0141 620 3339 *Fax* 0141 620 2405
Email jbs@jcarescot.org.uk
(Reg. Charity No. SCO11789). *Ch.* L. Sellyn; *Sec.* C. Blake

Jewish Care Scotland
May Terrace Giffnock, G46 6DL
Tel 0141 620 1800 *Fax* 0141 620 2409
Email admin@jcarescot.org.uk *Website* www.jcarescot.org.uk

(Caring for 1858. Reg. Charity No. SCO 05267). Jewish Care Scotland is Scotland's largest welfare charity dedicated to providing an extensive range of support and care services for Jewish people in need throughout Scotland. Professional staff and volunteers working in partnership offer Social Work support, specialist help for people with mental health problems, Welfare Rights advice, Registered Day Care, Meals on Wheels, befriending and Social Clubs for older people and those with long term physical illnesses and disabilities. Please contact for services, volunteering or how to support their work. *Ch.* Maureen Solomons. *Chief Exec.* Suzanne Neville

Newark Care
32 Burnfield Road, Giffnock, G46 7PZ
Tel 0141 621 2560 *Fax* 0141 621 2569
Email info@newarkcare.org.uk
Provides residential and nursing care within a Jewish environment for those no longer able to continue in their homes. *Ch.* M. Jackson; *Chief Exec.* B. Elder

YOUTH & STUDENTS
Jewish Youth Forum (UJIA Scotland)
Based at UJIA, Jewish Community Centre, 222 Fenwick Road, Giffnock, Glasgow, G46 6UE
(Reg. Charity No. Sc039181) *Tel* 0141 530 5340
Scottish Programmes Dir. Joanna Hyman *Tel* 0141 530 5343 *Email* Joanna.hyman@ujia.org
Scottish Youth Worker Jared Ross *Tel* 0141 530 5344 *Email* jared.ross@ujia.org
Northern Region Chaplaincy
Chaplain Rabbi Gary Wayland *Tel* 0141 638 9403

HIGHLANDS
Jewish Network of Argyll and The Highlands (JNAH)
Contact Willow Brae, Lochaline, Morvern PA80 5XT
Tel 01967 421 662/07801 382 584
Volunteering Ambassador, Linda Martin *Email* linda@scojec.org

NORTHERN IRELAND

BELFAST
There was a Jewish community in Belfast about the year 1771, but the present community was founded in 1865.

SYNAGOGUES
Hebrew Congregation
49 Somerton Road, BT15 3LH
(Est. 1872; Synagogue erected at Annesley Street, 1904, present building consecrated, 1964). *M.* Rabbi M. Brackman *Tel* 028 9077 5013

SOCIAL, CULTURAL & INTERFAITH
Belfast Jewish Record (quarterly)
42 Glandore Avenue, BT15 3FD
Tel 028 9077 9491
(Est. 1953). *Hon. S.* Noma Simon *Email* norma@paran42.plus.com
Jewish Community Centre
49 Somerton Road, BT15 3LH
Tel 028 9077 7974

ISLE OF MAN

CEMETERIES
Consecrated section of the Douglas Cemetery, Glencrutchery Road IM2

SOCIAL, CULTURAL & INTERFAITH

Hebrew Congregation
Contact Carol Jempson, 8 Mountain View, Douglas IM2 5HU; *Visiting M.* Rev. Malcolm Weisman OBE, MA (Oxon)

CHANNEL ISLANDS

JERSEY
A synagogue existed in St. Helier, the capital of the island, from 1843 until about 1870. The present community was founded in 1962.

Jersey Jewish Congregation
La Petite Route des Mielles, St Brelade, JE3 8FY
Tel 01534 44946
Pres. S. J. Regal; *Hon. S.* M. Morton, 16 La Rocquaise, La Route des Genets, St Brelade, JE3 8HY *Tel* 01534 742819; *Hon. T.* M. Kalman; *Visiting M.* Rev. M. Weisman, OBE, MA. Seven families of the Jersey congregation live in Guernsey.

OTHER COUNTRIES

AFGHANISTAN

Jews have lived in Afghanistan since antiquity. Just over 100 years ago they reportedly numbered 40,000. Since 1948 there has been a mass emigration to Israel. Zebulon Simantov is believed to be the sole remaining Afghan Jew in Afghanistan since 2005. There is an old synagogue on Flower Street, in Kabul.

ALBANIA

There have been Jews living in the area, now known as Albania, since Roman times, and there are remains in Dardania, in the north, of an ancient synagogue. The community was re-established by Jews from Iberia escaping the Spanish Inquisition in the fifteenth and early sixteenth centuries.

By 1930, the Jewish population had grown to 200, but was soon augmented by refugees escaping the Nazis. Most Jews were helped to hide from Italian occupiers, and then from the Nazis.

Post–war communism isolated Jews until the regime fell. In 1991 almost the entire community, about 300, was airlifted to Israel. The few Jews who remained in Albania live in the capital Tirana.

Albania Israel Friendship Society
Contact Refik Veseli
Rruga Barriskatave 226, Tirana
Tel +355 (4) 222 611

ALGERIA

It is believed that there were Jews in Algeria as early as the fourth century, BCE. The fortunes of the community varied under the Turkish regime, which began in 1519. After the French conquered Algeria the community was reorganised and, in 1870, most Jews were granted French citizenship. However, there have been anti-Jewish excesses even in the present century. After Algeria's bitter fight for independence, the Jews, like other French nationals, lost their possessions when they left the country. About 120,000 at Independence in 1962, there remain less than 50 today: almost all fled to France.
Contact Mme L. Meller-Saïd, 12 Ave Louis Pasteur, 92220 Bagneux France
Email linemeller@wanadoo.fr

Jewish Community Office and Synagogue
6 Rue Hassena Ahmed, Algiers
Tel +213 (2) 62 85 72
Pres. Maitre Roger Said *Tel* +213 (3) 49 26 57 *Fax* +213 (2) 64 55 36

ANDORRA

Andorra, which is governed by two co-princes – the Bishop of Urgel in Spain and the President of France – does not have a Jewish history. There are currently, however, around 15 Jewish families.

A synagogue was established in 1997 in Escaldes and is the first in Andorra's 1,100 year history. While its liturgy leans towards Sephardism, it is also influenced by its Ashkenazi members. There is a community centre in Escaldes.

CONTACT INFORMATION
Francesco B.P. 244, Andorra la Vella
Dr. David ben-Chayil or Dr. David Bezold *Tel* +376 333 567
For visits to the synagogue, contact Isaac Benisty *Tel* +376 860 758
Noga Lewerstein *Email* aciv.ad@gmail.com

ANTIGUA AND BARBUDA (West Indies)

A few Jewish residents live permanently on the island.
Correspondence B. Rabinowitz, Cedar Valley, P.O.B. 399 *Tel* +268 461 4150

ARGENTINA

The early Jewish settlers in Argentina were Marranos, who were gradually absorbed in the general population. The present community grew through immigration (beginning in 1862) from Germany, the Balkans, and North Africa. Immigrants began to arrive from Eastern Europe in 1889, many of them going to the agricultural settlements established by the Jewish Colonization Association. The community is estimated to number 300,000, including 60,000 Sephardim, who have their own separate institutions, according to D.A.I.A., the representative organisation of Argentine Jews. The Jewish population of Greater Buenos Aires is estimated at 220,000. A survey conducted by the Hebrew University of Jerusalem however estimates the Jewish population at 240,000, of whom 210,000 are Ashkenazim and 30,000 are Sephardim.

There are nine other major communities in Parana, Rosario, Cordoba, Bahia Blanca, Posadas, Resistencia, Tucuman, Mendoza and La Plata. There is a small but very active community in Mar del Plata, south of Buenos Aires. Very few Jewish families remain on the former J.C.A. settlements. There are about 100 synagogues (80 Orthodox, one Reform, the rest Conservative or Liberal), and a well-organised network of communal and educational institutes. There are community offices in **Cordoba** at Alvear 254, and in **Rosario** at Paraguay 1152.

BUENOS AIRES
Congreso Judio Latinoamericano
Larrea 744, 1030
Tel +54 (11) 4962 5028 *Fax* +54 (11) 4963 7056
Representative Organisation of Argentine Jews
DAIA, Pasteur 633, 5th floor
Argentine Jewish Community (AMIA)
Pasteur 633, C1028AAM
Tel +54 (11) 4959 8800
Email amia@amia.org.ar *Website* webamia@amia.org.ar
(Est. 1894) A victim of terrorism in 1994, the reconstructed Community Centre has now re-opened in the service of the life and culture of the Jewish community of Argentina
Central Sephardi Community
FESERA, Las Heras 1646

ARMENIA

Jews have lived in Armenia for over 2,000 years and the various communities were spread around different parts of the country. There was a synagogue in Yerevan, but in the 1930s it was destroyed. Nowadays, nearly all the Armenian Jews live in Yerevan, with only a few families living in Vanadzor (Kirovakan) and Gjumri (Leninakan). Others are scattered in some small towns and villages. When 'perestroika' was introduced in 1989, the Jewish community organised itself and in 1991 was registered as a non-formal organisation. Perestroika opened the doors, so that a large number of the population emigrated to Israel. In 1991 a Jewish Sunday school was opened both for children and adults. In 1992 the Israeli embassy in Moscow financed the school. Over 60 per cent of the population is over 60 years of age and there are about 40 children below the age of 16.
CONTACT INFORMATION
Pres. Willi Weiner *Tel* +374 (1) 525 882; *Dir. of Educ.* Dr. George Fajvush *Tel* +374 (1) 735 852; *Rabbi* Gersh-Meir Burchstein *Tel* +374 (1) 271 115
Chabad Lubavitch of Yerevan Synagogue
23 Nar-Dosa Street, Yerevan, Armenia 375018 *Tel* +374 (1) 571 677

ARUBA

Today, the Jewish community has about 85 members, and 150 Overseas Members. Due to its small size, and the intimate, close-knit nature of the community, one joint organization was formed, blending the Sephardic with the Ashkenazic traditions,

respecting their common culture, and enjoying the differences. The Jewish Community of Aruba publishes a monthly newsletter, *Chadashot Beth Israel*, that is mailed to local and overseas members. It portrays significant events in the life of the community, and connects all members.
Beth Israel Synagogue (Independent Conservative/Reform)
A. Laclé Blvd. #2, P.O. Box 655, Oranjestad
Tel +297 582 3272 *Fax* +297 886 264
Rabbi Mario Gurevich *Email* rabbi.aruba@yahoo.com
The synagogue of Aruba is an independent Conservative/Reform style congregation.
CEMETERY
There is an Old Jewish Cemetery in Oranjestad, on Petronia Street, which contains eight gravestones dating back to 1563. The cemetery did not begin to be utilized by Jewish settlers regularly until 1837. These gravestones are the only indication of a Jewish presence on the island in the past centuries.

AUSTRALIA

The earliest organisation of Jews in Australia was in 1817 when 20 Jews in New South Wales formed a burial society. In 1828 a congregation was formed in Sydney and the first specially erected synagogue was opened in 1844. The first Jewish service was held in Melbourne in 1839, four years after the beginning of the colonisation on the banks of the River Yarra. A synagogue was opened in 1847. A permanent congregation was formed in Adelaide in 1848. Congregations were established at Ballarat (1853) and Geelong (1854) in South Australia. A congregation in Brisbane was established in 1865. In Western Australia the first congregation (now ended) was formed at Fremantle in 1887, and the present Perth congregation established in 1892, with Kalgoorlie in 1895. In Tasmania a synagogue was opened in Hobart in 1845 and another at Launceston in 1846. Organised Jewish communities were established in other States a few years later.

In Australia's public life Jews have played a distinguished part. Many have risen to high office in the Federation and State Parliaments or on the Judicial bench. Two Governors-General of Australia have been Jews; The late Sir Zelman Cowen and the late Sir Isaac Isaacs. Sir John Monash, the Commander of the Australian Expeditionary Forces in the First World War, was a Jew. The Exec. Council of Australian Jewry represents the central Jewish organisations in each State. The Australian census has an optional question on religious affiliation. In 2001, 88,993 people declared themselves Jews by religion. If a proportionate number of 'no religion/religion not stated' replies are regarded as Jewish, the number of Jews rises to 105,000. Recent demographic res. indicated that there are probably about 92,000 people in Australia who are religiously or ethnically Jewish. The main Jewish coms. are in Melbourne; Sydney; Perth; Brisbane; Adelaide; The Gold Coast, Queensland; Canberra and Hobart.
KASHRUT CONTACTS
Kosher Australia
P.O. Box 2247 Caulfield Junction, 3161, Victoria
Tel +61 (3) 8317 2555 *Fax* +61 (3) 9527 5665
Email info@kosher.org.au *Website* www.kosher.org.au
The Kashrut Authority
Office hours Monday to Thursday 9am-5pm, Friday 9am-2pm
Tel +61 (2) 9365 2933 *Fax* +61 (2) 9365 0933
Email office@ka.org.au *Website* www.ka.org.au

MAIN JEWISH ORGANISATIONS
Australasian Union of Jewish Students
306 Hawthorn Road, Caulfield, Victoria 3162
Tel +61 (3) 9272 5622 *Fax* +61 (3) 9272 5620
Australia/Israel and Jewish Affairs Council (AIJAC)
See under International Organisations
B'nai B'rith Australia/New Zealand
P.O. Box 443, Kings Cross, Sydney, NSW 1340

Tel +61 (2) 9361 3875 *Fax* +61 (2) 9331 3131
Email bbozdist@ozemail.com.au
Pres. James Altman
Jewish Community Council of Victoria
306 Hawthorn Road, South Caulfield, Victoria 3162
Email community@jccv.org.au *Website* www.jccv.org.au
Pres. John Searle *Tel* +61 (3) 9272 5566
NSW Jewish Board of Deputies
146 Darlinghurst Road, Darlinghurst, NSW 2010
Tel +61 (2) 9360 1600 *Fax* +61 (2) 9331 4712
Pres. Yair Miller
Sephardi Federation of Australian Jewry
40-42 Fletcher Street, Bondi Junction, NSW 2022
Tel +61 (2) 9130 3192 *Fax* +61 (2) 9365 3856
Pres. A. Gubbay
Union for Progressive Judaism (Australia, New Zealand, Asia)
Email upj@upj.org.au *Website* www.upj.org.au
Victorian Office P.O. Box 347, Balaclava, Victoria 3183
Tel +61 (3) 9533 8587 *Fax* +61 (3) 9529 1229
NSW Office *Tel* +61 (2) 9328 7644 *Fax* +61 (2) 9327 8715

MAIN SYNAGOGUES AND COMMUNAL CENTRES

ADELAIDE
See B.K. Hyams, *Surviving: A History of The Institutions and Organisations of the Adelaide Jewish Community* (1998).
Beit Shalom Synagogue
41 Hackney Road, P.O. Box 47, Stepney, SA 5069
Tel +61 (8) 8362 8281 *Fax* +61 (8) 8362 4406
Email info@bshalomadel.com
Admin. L. Willis
Hebrew Congregation
13 Flemington Street, P.O. Box 320, Glenside, SA 5065
Tel +61 (8) 8338 2922 *Fax* +61 (8) 9379 0142
Email office@adelaidehebrew.com

BRISBANE
Brisbane Hebrew Congregation (Orthodox)
98 Margaret Street, Brisbane, Qld. 4000
Tel +61 (7) 3229 3412 *Fax* +61 (7) 3366 8311
Email pgt_levy@world.net
Beit Knesset Shalom (Liberal)
15 Koolatah Street, Camp Hill, Qld. 4152
Tel +61 (7) 398 8843
Email info@bks.org.au

MELBOURNE
Melbourne Hebrew Congregation (Orthodox)
One Toorak Road, South Yarra, Victoria 3141
Tel +61 (3) 9866 2255
Email mhc@melbournesynagogue.org.au
Temple Beth Israel (Liberal)
76 Alma Road, St. Kilda, Victoria 3182
Tel +61 (3) 9510 1488 *Fax* +61 (3) 9521 1229
Email info@tbi.org.au

PERTH
Chabad of Western Australia (Inc) (Orthodox)
395 Alexander Drive, Noranda, WA 6062

M. Rabbi Mordi Gutnick; *Contact* Max Green *Tel* +61 (8) 9375 13770
Email info@chabadwa.org
Perth Hebrew Congregation
Corner Plantation Street and Freedman Road, Menora, WA 6050
Tel +61 (8) 9271 0539
Email phc@theperthshule.asn.au *Website* www.theperthshule.asn.au
Mikvah on premises. *Pres.* K. Blitz; *M.* Rabbi D. Freilich
Temple David Congregation (Progressive)
34 Clifton Crescent, Mount Lawley, 6050
Tel +61 (8) 9271 1485 *Fax* +61 (8) 9272 2827
Email admin@templedavid.org.au
SYDNEY
Central Synagogue (Orthodox)
15 Bon Accord Avenue, Bondi Junction, NSW 2022
Tel +61 (2) 9389 5622 *Fax* +61 (2) 9389 5418
Email central@centralsynagogue.com.au
TASMANIA
Hobart Hebrew Congregation (Orthodox and Progressive)
59 Argyle Street, 7000
Tel +61 (3) 6234 4720
Email shule@hobart.org *Website* www.hobartsynagogue.org
The synagogue is the oldest in Australia, having been consecrated in July 1845. *See* H.
Fixel, 'Hobart Hebrew Congregation: 150 Years of Survival Against All Odds' (1999);
P. and A. Elias, 'A Few from Afar: Jewish Lives in Tasmania from 1804' (2003).

AUSTRIA

Jews arrived in this area of Europe more than one thousand years ago. The community was
expelled from Austria between 1420 and 1421, but Jews were allowed to return in 1451. The
Jews were granted their own quarter of Vienna in 1624, but were expelled again in 1670. The
economy declined after the expulsion and so they were asked to come back.
It was not until 1782 that the situation became more stable, when Joseph II began lifting the
anti-Jewish decrees that his mother, Maria Theresa, had imposed on her Jewish subjects. The
Jews received equal rights in 1848 and, in 1867, legal and other prohibitions were lifted.
Anti-semitism did continue, however, and many influential anti-semitic publications were
available in Vienna and were keenly read by many people, including the young Adolf Hitler.
After the First World War Austria lost its empire (which included Czech lands and Galicia,
which had a very large Jewish community), and the Jewish population fell accordingly. At the
time of the Nazi take-over in 1938, 200,000 Jews lived in the country. Some 70,000 were killed
in the Holocaust, the rest escaped or were hidden.
Today there are several synagogues in Vienna. The city has an active Ultra-Orthodox community and kosher food is available. There are prayer rooms in some provincial cities.
Visitors to Vienna should not miss the new Jewish Museum opened in 2001. It combines
Rachel Whiteread's memorial, the Museum of Medieval Jewish Life and details of the exca-
vation of a medieval synagogue built around the middle of the thirteenth century.

VIENNA
Chief Rabbi Rabbi Paul Chaim Eisenberg *Tel* +43 (1) 5310 4111
Jewish Community Centre
Israelitische Kulturgemeinde, Seitenstettengasse 4, 1010 Vienna
Tel +43 (1) 5310 4104 *Fax* +43 (1) 5310 4108
Pres. Dr. A. Muzicant; *Sec. Gen.* R. Fastenbauer, F. Herzog
Jewish Welcome Service
A-1010 Vienna, Stephansplatz 10
Tel +43 (1) 533 2730 *Fax* +43 (1) 533 4098
Dir. Dr. L. Zelman

The Viennese Yeshiva
College for Jewish social occupations & Boarding School.
Offers three year courses for 14 to 16 year olds.
1020 Vienna, Grosse Mohrengasse 19
Tel +43 (1) 216 06 79
Rabbi Chayim Stern

MAIN SYNAGOGUES
Baden Synagogue, Grabengasse 14, Baden 2500 (Modern Orthodox); **Bet Hamidrash Torah Etz-Chayim**, Grosse Schiffgasse 8, Vienna (Orthodox); **Khal Israel**, Tempelgasse 3, 1020 (Orthodox); **Machsike Hadass**, Grosse Mohrengasse 19, 1020 (Orthodox); **Ohel Moshe**, Lilienbrunngasse 19, 1020 (Orthodox); **Or Chaddasch Congregation** (Reform), Robertgasse 2, 1020 **Stadttempel**, Seitenstettengasse 4 (Traditional)

AZERBAIJAN

Azerbaijan has a remarkable Jewish history, which can be better explored now that the country is independent from the former Soviet Union. The Tats (mountain Jews) believe that their ancestors arrived in Azerbaijan at the time of Nebuchadnezzar. They lived in several mountain villages and adopted the customs of their non-Jewish neighbours. They spoke a north Iranian language known as Judeo-Tat, to which they added some Hebrew words. The Soviets clamped down on their way of life after 1928, changing the alphabet of their language from Hebrew to Latin, and then in 1938, to Cyrillic. Some of their synagogues were also closed down. Zionist feeling is high, with almost 30,000 emigrating to Israel since 1989.
The other strand in Azerbaijan's Jewish population are the Ashkenazis who arrived in the nineteenth century from Poland and other countries to the west.
The largest synagogue in Baku is the Tat synagogue, but there are also Ashkenazi and Georgian synagogues. Synagogues are found in other towns as well.

BAKU
Mountain Jews Synagogue
Dmitrova Street 39 370014
Tel +994 (12) 892 232 8867
Chabad Lubavitch Synagogue
18 D. Alieva str. apt. 6, C. Mustafayev kuc., dalan 4 ev 1, Baku 370014
Tel +994 (12) 4945297

KUBA
Kuba Synagogue
Kolkhoznaya Street 46

BAHAMAS

Luis de Torres, the official interpreter for Columbus, was the first Jew in the Bahamas, as well as being one of the first Europeans there. He was a *converso*. The British arrived in 1620 and eventually gained control of the islands. Although there was a Jewish Attorney-General and Chief Justice in the islands in the eighteenth century, few Jews settled there until the twentieth century. They came from Eastern Europe and the UK after the First World War, and settled in the capital Nassau.
There are approximately 300 Jewish residents in the Bahamas. However, it is estimated that about 350,000 Jews visit the islands each year as tourists. There are congregations in Nassau and Freeport. Both cities have Jewish cemeteries, that in Nassau being the more historic.

Luis de Torres Synagogue
East Sunrise Highway, P.O. Box F-41761, Freeport Grand Bahama
Tel +1242 373 2008 Please contact for times of services.
Pres. Anthony Gee *Tel* +1242 373 8994 *Email* goldylocks@coralwave.com
Sec. Jean Berlind *Tel* +1242 373 9457 *Email* jberlind@coralwave.com

BARBADOS

Jewish history in Barbados starts in 1628, a year after the British first settled there. Jewish settlers came from Brazil, Suriname, England and Germany, and were mainly Sephardi. The first synagogue was established in the capital, Bridgetown, in 1654. Early settlers were engaged in cultivating sugar and coffee.

The Jewish population was well treated. In 1831 Barbados was the first British possession in which Jews were granted full political emancipation. Despite a largely favourable climate the community suffered losses from hurricanes, which destroyed sugar plantations, and the Jewish population fell to 70 by 1848. In 1925 no Jews remained, but a new influx (30 families escaping Nazism) came shortly after.

The synagogue was restored in 1987, and postage stamps were produced which commemorated its restoration. The Jewish population remains small, but it was a group of Barbadian Jews who founded the Caribbean Jewish Congress. The Jewish cemetery, one of the oldest in the Americas, is now back in use.

Jewish Community Council
P.O.B. 256, Bridgetown
Tel +1246 809 432 0840 *Fax* +1246 426 4768
Contact Benny Gilbert

BELARUS

For the adventurous traveller who has a keen interest in Jewish history, Belarus (also known as White Russia) makes an interesting and unusual destination. Situated on the western side of the former Soviet Union, this largely flat country borders Poland and Lithuania to the west, Ukraine to the south and Russia to the east. Belarus finally achieved independence in 1991, and within its present borders are many towns and villages of Jewish interest, such as Minsk, Pinsk and Grodno. One of the most famous villages in Belarus is Lubavitch, a hamlet in the far east of the country, near the Russian border, where the worldwide Lubavitch movement had its origins.

During WWII over 800,000 Belarusian Jews were massacred, and in the following years emigration to Israel was very high. However, the community has slowly started to rebuild itself and in the late 1980s an Ulpan (class to study Hebrew) and a Jewish Sunday School were opened. In 1992 the first Rabbi to Belarus arrived and the community continued to flourish with the publication of the first Jewish newspaper and openings of the first Kindergarten, Secondary school and an Israeli Embassy.

Religious Union for Orthodox Judaism in Belarus
Tel/Fax +375 (17) 334 5612
Pres. Yuri Dorn; Chief Rabbi Avraam Benenson
Email iro@open.by
Religious Union for Progressive/Reform Judaism in Belarus
Internationalnya 16, 220050 Minsk
Tel +375 (17) 206 5850
Email roopi@mail.ru
Rabbi Grigory Abramovich

BELGIUM

Jewish settlement in the area now called Belgium dates back to the thirteenth century, and suffered a similar fate to other medieval European Jewish communities, taking the blame for the Black Death and suffering expulsions. The Sephardim were the first to resettle in Belgium, mainly in Antwerp. After independence in 1830, conditions for the Jews improved and more Jews began to settle there. The diamond centre of Antwerp later developed rapidly, attracting many Jews from Eastern Europe.

By 1939 the Jewish population had grown to 100,000, a large proportion of whom were refugees hoping to escape to America. Some succeeded, but many became trapped after the German invasion. Some 25,000 Belgian Jews were deported and killed in the Holocaust.

A national monument listing the names of the victims stands in Anderlecht in Brussels. The present Jewish population includes a large Hassidic community in Antwerp, where there are some 30 synagogues. There are also more than ten synagogues in Brussels. There are Jewish schools and newspapers in Antwerp and Brussels.

International Jewish Center of Belgium
Avenue Louise 149, 1050 Brussels
Tel +32 477 281 678
Email info@ijc.be Website www.ijc.be
(Est. 2003) The IJS is Belgium's only liberal, English-speaking reform Jewish community. It has more than 150 members. Rabbi Nathan Alfred. A Belgian ASBL/VZW non-profit organization. Officially recognised by the World Union of Progressive Judaism.
Each Sunday there is a Talmud Torah, Shabbat services twice a month, regular Shabbat dinners are held and all major Jewish holidays are celebrated. A Rosh Chodesh woman's group meets every month. Many Jewish cultural events are hosted here.

ANTWERP
Central Jewish Welfare Organisation
Jacob Jacobsstr. 2, 2018 Antwerpen
Tel +32 (3) 232 3890
Machsike Hadass (Orthodox)
Jacob Jacobstr. 22. Main synagogue: Oostenstr. 42-44, 2018 Antwerpen
Sephardi Synagogue
Hovenierstr. 31, 2018 Antwerpen
Shomre Hadas
Israëlitische Gemeente van Antwerpen, Terliststraat 35, 2018 Antwerpen
Tel +32 (3) 232 0187 Fax +32 (3) 226 3123
Email info@shomre-hadas.be Website www.shomre-hadas.be

BRUSSELS
Centre Communautaire Laic Juif
52 Rue Hotel des Monnaies, 1060 Brussels
Comité de Coordination des Organisations Juives de Belgique (C.C.O.J.B.)
Av. Ducpétiaux 68, 1060 Brussels
Tel +32 (2) 537 1691 Fax +32 (2) 539 2295
Email ccojb@scarlet.be
Consistoire Central Israélite de Belgique
2 rue Joseph Dupont, 1000 Brussels
Tel +32 (3) 512 2190
Machzikei Haddass
Rabbinat Av. St. Augustin 40, 1190 Bruxelles
Tel +32 (2) 345 4518 Fax +32 (2) 347 5222
Email info@ciob.be Website www.ciob.be

BERMUDA

The small community of 120 members, has just opened the first Jewish Community Centre ever in Bermuda, at 75 St. Johns Road, Pembroke. Friday night services are held once a month and there is also an active Hebrew school and some adult education classes. A visiting Rabbi has conducted High Holy day services for the last 10 years.

Jewish Community of Bermuda
P.O. Box HM 1793, Hamilton, HMHX Bermuda
Tel +1441 291 1785
Website www.jewishbermuda.com

BOLIVIA

The history of the Jews of Bolivia dates back to the Spanish colonial period. Conversos came with the Spaniards in the seventeenth century.

The main influx of Jews occurred in 1905 with immigrants from Eastern Europe, but the number entering Bolivia was much smaller than that going to other South American countries. In 1933 there were only some 30 Jewish families. At the end of the decade, however, there was a small increase in Jewish immigration as German and Austrian Jews fled from Europe. Ironically, the Jewish community did not grow that much, even though the government granted every Jew an entry visa.

Many Jews started to leave Bolivia in the 1950s because of political instability and the apparent lack of educational opportunities. The present-day community has a central organisation known as the Circulo Israelita de Bolivia in La Paz.

COCHABAMBA
Asociación Israelita de Cochabamba
P.O.B. 349, Calle Valdivieso
Pres. Ronald Golan
Synagogue Calle Junin y Calle Colombia, Casilla 349

LA PAZ
Comunidad Israelita Synagogue
Calle Canada Stronguest 1846, P.O.B. 2198
Tel +591 (2) 232 5925 *Fax* + 591 (2) 234 2738
Israel Tourist Information Office
Centro Shalom, Calle Canada Stronguest 1846, La Paz Country Club, Quinta J.K.G. Obrajes. Calle 1, esquina calle Hector Ormachea Casilla 1545, La Paz
Synagogue
Circulo Israelita de Bolivia, Casilla 1545 *Tel* +591 (2) 278 5083 Calle Landaeta 346, P.O.B. 1545 Services Saturday morning only. *Pres.* Dr Miguel

SANTA CRUZ
Circulo Israelita de Santa Cruz
P.O.B. 7087, WIZO, Casilla 3409 *Tel* +591 (3) 3435848 *Pres.* Sra Guicha Schwartz

BOSNIA AND HERZEGOVINA
Sephardi Jews were the first to arrive in the area in the late sixteenth century. They established a Jewish quarter in Sarajevo, and this was home for the poorer Jews until the Austrians conquered the area in 1878. It was the Turks, however, who emancipated the Jews in the nineteenth century when Bosnia and Herzegovina was under Ottoman rule.

When Bosnia and Herzegovina became part of the newly formed Yugoslavia, after the First World War, the community maintained its Sephardi heritage and joined the all-Yugoslav Federation of Jewish Religious Communities. The Jewish population numbered 14,000 in 1941. This number dropped sharply after the Germans conquered Yugoslavia.

After the war the survivors were joined by many who had decided to return. The Sephardi and Ashkenazi communities became unified. La Benevolencija, founded 100 years ago, is a humanitarian organisation which ameliorated the plight of the community and became well known in the early 1990s at the time of the civil war. After the Yugoslav civil war, many made aliyah to Israel, reducing the community still further.

Sarajevo Jewish Community
Hamdije Kresevljakovica 59, Sarajevo, Bosnia, 71000
Tel +387 (33) 229 666 *Fax* +387 (33) 229 667

BRAZIL
The first Jewish settlers in Brazil came with the Portuguese in 1500. They were mainly *Conversos* escaping persecution in Portugal, and initially worked on the sugar plantations. In due course they played important roles as traders, artisans and plantation owners. The huge area which is called Brazil today was in the process of being conquered by the Dutch and the Portuguese. Two synagogues were opened in Recife during the 1640s when many Jews came from Holland. When the Dutch left Brazil in 1654 one of the terms of surrender allowed the Jews who had been on their side to emigrate. Many fled and some went on to found the first

Jewish community in New York, then known as New Amsterdam. A seventeenth-century Mikveh was discovered in 2000 in the basement of the Tsur Israel Synagogue in Recife. With Brazilian independence in 1822, conditions became more favourable for Jews and many came from North Africa and Europe. The majority of Jews in Brazil today, however, originate from the immigration of East European Jews in the early twentieth century. From about 6,000 Jews in 1914, the community grew to 30,000 in 1930. After 1937 Brazil refused to allow Jewish immigrants into the country, but some limited immigration managed to continue despite the restrictions.

A central organisation was established in 1951 (the CONIB), and this includes 200 various Jewish organisations. Brazilian Jews live in an atmosphere of tolerance and prosperity, and assimilation is widespread.

There are synagogues in all the major cities.

RIO DE JANEIRO
Congrecão Beth El
Rua Barata Ribeiro 489 (Sephardi)
Federacão Israelita & Fundo Communitario
R. Buenos Aires 68, AN15
Orthodox Rabbinate
R. Pompeu Loureiro No.40
Tel/Fax +55 (21) 236 0249

SYNAGOGUES
Agudat Israel, Rua Nascimento Silva, 109 Beth Aron, Rua Gado Coutinho, 63 Kehilat Yaacov Copacabana, Rua Capelao Alvares da Silva 15; Templo Uniao Israel, Rua Jose Higino, 375-381

SÃO PAULO
Escola Beit Yaacov
Av Marques de São Vicente, 1748 Cep 01139-002
Tel +55 (11) 361 1060
Federacao Israelita do Estado de São Paulo
Av. Paulista 726, 2nd floor
Tel +55 (11) 288 6411

SYNGOGUES AND RELIGIOUS CENTRES
Centro Judaico Religioso de Sao Paulo (Orthodox)
Tel 220 5642; Beit Chabad, Rua Chabad 56/60; Communidade Israelita Sefaradi, Rua da Abolicao 457; Congregacão Israelita Paulista, "Einheitsgemeinde" (Liberal), Rua Antonico Carlos 653. Sinagoga Beit Yaacov (Congregação e Beneficência Sefardi Paulista) Rua Dr. Veiga Filho, 547 Cep 01229-000 São Paulo *Tel* +55 (11) 366 2215

BULGARIA

Dating back to the Byzantine conquest, the community in Bulgaria was established by Greek Jews in Serdica (Sofia, the capital). The Jewish community grew when the Bulgarian state was founded in 681. Czar Ivan Alexander (1331–71) had a Jewish wife who converted to Christianity.

The community has included eminent rabbinic commentators, such as Rabbi Dosa Ajevani and Joseph Caro, the codifier of the Shulchan Aruch, who escaped to Bulgaria after the expulsion from Spain. The various Jewish groups joined to form a unified Sephardi community in the late seventeenth century.

About 50,000 Jews lived in Bulgaria in 1939. Bulgaria joined the war on the side of Germany but, despite much pressure from the Nazis, the government and general population refused to allow Bulgarian Jews to be deported. Only Jews from Macedonia and Thrace, then occupied by Bulgaria, were deported. Despite being saved, most of the community emigrated to Israel after the war. The 10 per cent who remained were then under the control of the communists and had little contact with the outside world.

Since the fall of communism, the community has been reconstituted and now has synagogues in Sofia and Plovdiv. The community is ageing, although 100 children attend a Sunday school run by the Shalom Organisation, the central Jewish organisation for Bulgaria.

Central Jewish Religious Council and Synagogue
16 Exarch Joseph Street, Sofia 1000
Tel +359 (2) 983 1273
Pres. Robat Djerassi

Beit Ha'am
50 Stambolijski
Tel +359 (2) 926 5301 *Fax* +359 (2) 981 1139

Organization of the Jews in Bulgaria
"Shalom", 50 Al. Stambolijski Street, Sofia 130
Tel/Fax +359 (2) 4006 301 *Pres.* Dr. Maxim Benvenisti. Publishes newspaper "Evrejski Vesti" and research compendium "Annual". Jewish museum in the Synagogue: Sofia, 16 Exarch Joseph St. Joseph. Caro permanent exhibition in the city. Museum and a memorial stone in the town of Nikopol. Publishing house "Shalom", Jewish Sunday School, Jewish Resource Centre, Memorial stone dedicated to the Salvation of the Bulgarian Jews near the Parliament, B'nai Brith, Maccabi and other Jewish organizations.

BURMA (Myanmar)

The first Jews came to Myanmar in the early eighteenth century from Iraq and other Middle Eastern countries. A synagogue was built in 1896. In the first years of the twentieth century Rangoon and Bassein both had Jewish mayors. The Jewish population swelled to 2,000 before 1939, but most of these fled to Britain and India before the Japanese invasion in the Second World War. Only a few hundred more returned after the war, and the community began to decline through intermarriage and conversion. The handful of remaining Jews are elderly and services are held only on the High Holy Days, when a minyan is made up with help from the Israeli embassy.
There is also a tribe of Jews in the north of the country (the Karens), who have their own prayer houses and who believe that they are descended from the tribe of Menassah.

YANGON
Israel Embassy
15 KhaBaung Street, Hlaing Township, Yangon
Tel +95 (1) 515 115 *Fax* +95 (1) 515 116
Email info@yangon.mfa.gov.il

Musmeah Yeshua Synagogue
85 26th Street, P.O. Box 45, Yangon
(Est. 1896). *Man. Tr.* Moses Samuels *Email* samuels@mptmail.net.mm

CANADA

Jews were prohibited by law from living in Canada as long as it remained a French possession. Nevertheless, Jews from Bordeaux – David Gradis, a wealthy merchant and shipowner, and his son Abraham Gradis, in particular – had a large share in the commercial development of the colony.
Jews played some part in the British occupation of Canada. Half a dozen Jewish officers, were suppliers to the expeditionary force which occupied Quebec. They included Aaron Hart, and their descendants played important roles in Jewish and Canadian life for several generations.
A number of Jews settled at an early date in Montreal, where the Spanish and Portuguese Synagogue, Shearith Israel (still flourishing), was established in the 1770s. A congregation of 'German, Polish and English' Jews was granted a charter in 1846. A burial society was formed in Toronto in 1849. Montreal Jews were also among the fur traders in the Indian territories.
In the 19th century, Jewish immigrants arrived in Canada in some numbers, and in 1832 – a

quarter of a century earlier than in Britain – the Lower Canada Jews received full civil rights. A fresh era in the history of Canadian Jewry opened at the close of the century, when emigration on a large scale from Eastern Europe began. Montreal, Toronto, and, to a lesser degree, Winnipeg became the seats of Jewish communities of some importance.

On the history of the Jews in Canada generally, *See* A. D. Hart, *The Jew in Canada*, 1926; L. Rosenberg, *Canada's Jews*, 1939; B. G. Sack, *The History of the Jews in Canada*, 1945; and I.M. Abella, *A Coat of Many Colours: Two Centuries of Jewish Life in Canada*, 1990. The early colonial period in North America is covered in Sheldon and Judith Godfrey, *Search Out the Land*, 1995.

Association for Canadian Jewish Studies
c/o Dept of Religion, Concordia University, 1455 De Maisonneuve Blvd West, Montreal H3G 1MP
Tel +1 (514) 848 2424/2074 *Fax* +1 (514) 848 4541
Contact Dr. I. Robinson *Email* robinson@alcor.concordia.ca *Website* www www.acjs-aejc.ca

Canada-Israel Committee
130 Slater Street, Suite 630, Ottawa K1P 6E2
Exec. Dir. Shimon Fogel *Tel* +1 (613) 234 8271
Ontario Office 2221 Yonge Street #502, Toronto M4S 2B4 *Tel* +1 (416) 489 8889

Canadian Zionist Federation
5250 Decarie Boulevard #550, Montreal, H3X 2H9
Tel +1 (514) 486 9526
(Est. 1967).

NATIONAL INSTITUTIONS
Canadian Jewish Congress
(Est. 1919. reorganised 1934)
National Office 100 Sparks Street, Suite 650, Ottawa, Ontario K1P 5B7
Tel +1 (613) 233 8703 *Fax* +1 (613) 233 8748
Email canadianjewishcongress@cjc.ca *Website* www.cjc.ca
Nat. Co-Pres. Rabbi Dr. Reuven Bulka and Sylvain Abitobol
Chief Exec. Bernie M. Farher 4600 Bathurst Street Fourth Floor, Toronto Ontario M2R 3V2
Tel +1 (416) 635 2883 ext. 5186 *Fax* +1 (416) 635 1408 *Email* bfarber@on.cjc.ca
Dir. of Operations Joshua Rotblatt National Office address *Email* joshr@cjc.ca
Nat. Gen. Counsel Jonathan Schwartz 4600 Bathurst Street, 4th Floor, Toronto Ontario M2R 3V2 *Tel* +1 (416) 635 2883 ext. 5265 *Fax* +1 (416) 635 1408 *Email* jschwartz@on.cjc.ca
Nat. Archives Janice Rosen. Archives Director, Canadian Jewish Congress Charities Committee, 1590 Avenue Doctor Penfield, Montreal, Quebec H3G 1C5 *Tel* +1 (514) 931 7531 ext. 271 *Fax* +1 (514) 931 0548 *Email* janicer@cjccc.ca

CJC Atlantic Region
Tel +1 (902) 422 7491 *Fax* +1 (902) 422 7372
Reg. Dir Jon M. Goldberg *Email* jgoldberg@theajc.ns.ca

CJC Ontario Region
Tel +1 (416) 638 1991 ext. 5147
Regional Dir. Len Rudner *Email* lrudner@cjc.ca

CJC Pacific Region
Tel +1 (604) 622 4240 *Fax* +1 (604) 622 4244
Regional Dir. Romy Ritter *Email* rritter@cjc.ca

CJC Quebec Region
Tel +1 (514) 345 6411 ext. 3162 *Fax* +1 (514) 345 6412
Regional Director/Directeur général Daniel Amar Email damar@cjq-qjc.ca

CJC Saskatchewan Region - North
Tel +1 (306) 343 7023 *Fax* +1 (306) 343 1244
June Aviva *Email* ajavivi@shaw.ca

CJC Saskatchewan Region-South
Tel +1 (306) 569 8166 *Fax* +1 (306) 569 8166

CAYMAN ISLANDS

There are approx. 60 Jewish residents in the 3 Cayman Islands, nearly all living on Grand Cayman. They are joined by about 40 others who are regular visitors. Services in private homes. *Contact* Harvey De Souza P.O. Box 72, Grand Cayman, KY1 1102

The Jewish Community of the Cayman Islands (JCCI)
P.O. Box 292, Grand Cayman KY1-1104
Tel +345 526 0572
Email info@jccicayman.org *Website* www.jccicayman.org

CHILE

The original Jewish settlers in Chile were *Conversos*. Rodrigo de Organos, a *Converso*, was the first European to enter the country in 1535. The Inquisition, however, curtailed the growth of the community.
The first legal Jewish immigration, albeit small, occurred only after Chile's independence in 1810. In 1914 the Jewish community numbered some 500, but this increased in the late 1930s with those refugees from Nazism who were able to avoid the strict immigration laws. Antisemitism, however, also grew, and the *Comite Representativo* was formed to respond to it. There is an umbrella organisation and a large Zionist body in Chile. Most of the community is not religious, but some keep kosher and there are several synagogues in the capital Santiago and a few kosher shops. There are two Jewish schools, and several Jewish newspapers are published.

SANTIAGO
B'nai Brith
Ricardo Lyon 1933 *Tel* +56 (2) 274 2006 *Fax* +56 (2) 225 2039
Comunidad Israelita de Santiago
Tarapaca 870 (Ashkenazi)
Tel +56 (2) 633 1436 *Fax* +56 (2) 638 2076
Comunidad Israelita de Santiago Congregacion Jafetz Jayim
Miguel Claro 196 (Orthodox)
Tel +56 (2) 274 5389
Comunidad Israelita Sefaradi de Chile
R. Lyon 812
Tel +56 (2) 209 8086 *Fax* +56 (2) 204 7382
Comité Representativo de las Entidades Judias de Chile (CREJ)
Miguel Claro 196
Tel +56 (2) 235 8669 *Fax* +56 (2) 235 0754

CHINA

In recent years, Jewish tourists from a number of countries, including Britain and the United States, have visited the ancient city of Kaifeng, 300 miles south of Peking. There they met people who claim descent from a sizeable community which lived there for centuries and dispersed in the 19th century. Some experts believe the Kaifeng Jews to have originated from Persia or Yemen. Few are left of the communities formed by other immigrants from Asia at the end of the 19th century and by the Russian and German refugees of the First and Second World Wars.
 A comprehensive bibliography on the Jews of China was published in 1998: *Jews and Judaism in Traditional China: A Comprehensive Bibliography*, Donald Daniel Leslie (Sankt Petersburg: Steyler Verlag, 1998) (Monumenta serica, XLIV).

HONG KONG
Although there were some Jewish merchants trading out of Hong Kong over the centuries, the first permanent community consisted of Jews who came from Baghdad in the early nineteenth century. The first synagogue was not established until 1901, the early settlers preferring to organise communal events from their homes. The majority of the community were Sephardi, but Nazi persecution led to more Ashkenazi settlers arriving in Hong Kong, via Shanghai. Since

the Second World War many Chinese Jews have emigrated through Hong Kong to Australia and the USA, although some have remained in Hong Kong. Following the reversion to Chinese control in mid-1997, the Jewish community is still thriving, and the mood is optimistic.

The Jews have contributed greatly to the building of the infrastructure of Hong Kong and, since the 1960s, many Western Jews, attracted by the success of this major financial centre, have made their homes there. The first communal hall was founded in 1905, but a new, multipurpose complex (the Jewish Community Centre) has recently been opened, which is one of the most luxurious in the world. The Centre includes everything from a library and a strictly kosher restaurant to a swimming pool and sauna.

Chabad of Hong Kong
Hoover Court 1/F 7-9 Macdonnell Road, Midlevels, Hong Kong
Tel +852 2523 9770 *Fax* +852 2845 2772
Website www.chabadasia.com
Rabbi Mordechai Avtzon
Chabad-Lubavitch in the Far East
Email chabadhk@netvigator.com *Website* www.chabadhk.org
Israel Consulate-General
Admiralty Centre, Tower II, Room 701, 18 Harcourt Road
Tel +852 2529 6091 *Fax* +852 2865 0220
The Jewish Community Centre
1 Robinson Place, 70 Robinson Road, Mid-levels
Tel +852 2868 0828, (Information)*Tel* +852 2801 5440 *Fax* +852 2877 0917
Website www.jcc.org.hk
Gen. Man. Michael Sheppard
Mikvah
Contact Revital Ben Yishai *Tel* +852 2140 6475
Shanghai Jewish Centre
Shang-Mira Garden Villa #1, 89 South Shui Cheng Road, Shanghai, 200336
Tel +862 6278 0225 *Fax* + 862 6278 0223
Email info@chinajewish.org *Website* www.chinajewish.org
Rabbi Shalom Greenberg
The United Jewish Congregation of Hong Kong
1 Robinson Place, 70 Robinson Road, Mid-levels
Tel +852 2523 2985 *Fax* +852 2523 3961
Email ujc@ujc.org.hk *Website* www.ujc.org.hk
(Liberal/Reform) (Est. 1991). Rabbi L. Diamond

COLOMBIA

The first Jews in Colombia were *Conversos*, as was common in South America. However, they were soon discovered by the Inquisition when it was established in Colombia.

The next influx of Jews came in the nineteenth century, followed by mass immigration from Eastern Europe and the Middle East after 1918. Jews were banned from entering after 1939, but this restriction was eased after 1950.

The present community is a mix of Ashkenazi and Sephardi elements, each having their own commununal organisations. There are also Youth and Zionist organisations. There is a central organisation for Colombian Jewry in the capital Bogota. There are also Jewish schools and synagogues, and Jewish publications and radio programmes.

Centro Israelita de Bogota
Carrera 29 No. 126, Bogota or: Apartado Aereo 12.372
Santa Fe de Bogota
Tel +011 (571) 626 4367, +011 (571) 625 4377 *Fax* +011 (571) 274 9069
Email centrocib@tutopia.com
Kosher Meals available by calling Rabbi Goldschmidt *Tel* +011 (571) 218 2500
Embassy of Israel in Bogota
Edificio Caxdac, Calle 35, No. 7-25 14 Piso, Bogota

Tel +011 (571) 287 7962 or +011 (571) 232 0764 *Fax* +011 (571) 287 7783
Email Bogota@israel.org

CONGO, DEMOCRATIC REPUBLIC (Formerly Zaire)

Today, Congo has approximately 320 Jews living predominately in Lubumbashi. Most of the Jews are of Sephardic descent and speak Ladino, a Spanish-Jewish dialect. There is a synagogue in Lubumbashi that is served by a rabbi. There is also a small Jewish community in Kinshasa called Congregation Israelite. The Jewish community in Congo is represented by the Communaute Israelite du Shaba. There is a Jewish cemetery under the control of the Chief Rabbi of Zaire, Rabbi Levy.

Chief Rabbi of Zaire
Rabbi Moishe Levy 50 W. Churchill Avenue, Box 15, 1180 Brussels, Belgium
Chabad-Lubavitch of Central Africa
251 Avenue de la Mission, Kinshasa
Tel +243 999 770 *Fax* +212 504 2621
Exec. Dir. Rabbi Shlomo Bentolila; *Co-Dir.* Miriam Bentolila
Embassy of Israel
12 Avenue des Aviateurs, P.O. Box 8343 KIN 1, Kinshasa
Tel +243 122 1955 *Fax* +243 884 5055
Synagogue
Congregation Israelite, Baite Postale No. 931, Kinshasa

COSTA RICA

The first Jews arrived in Costa Rica in the nineteenth century from nearby islands in the Caribbean, such as Jamaica. The next wave of immigrants came from Eastern Europe in the 1920s. Thereafter Costa Rica did not welcome new Jewish immigrants, and passed laws against foreign merchants and foreign land ownership. However, the Jewish community in Costa Rica established a communal organisation in 1930. There is a monthly newsletter, and a synagogue in San Jose. Most Jewish children attend the Haim Weizmann School, which has both primary and secondary classes.

It is interesting to note that the Costa Rican embassy in Israel is in Jerusalem and not Tel Aviv, where most other embassies are situated.

Centro Israelita Sionista de Costa Rica
Orthodox Commmunity Carretera a Pavas, San Jose 1007
Tel +506 2520 1013 *Fax* +506 2520 1951
Website www.centroisraelita.com
Pres. S. Aizenman; *Exec. Dir.* Guita Grynspan *Email* ggrynspan@centroisraelita.com; *Chief Rabbi* Rabbi Gershon; *Sec.* M. Froimzon

CROATIA (Formerly constituent republic of Yugoslavia)

Jews were in the land now known as Croatia before the Croats themselves. The Croats arrived in the seventh century, the Jews some centuries before with the Romans: there are the remains of a third-century Jewish cemetery in Solin (near Split).

The first Jewish communites were involved in trade with Italy across the Adriatic Sea, and also in trade along the River Danube. Their success was brief, however, and they were expelled in 1456, only returning more than 300 years later. The area became part of the newly formed Yugoslavia after the First World War, and the Jewish community became part of the Federation of Jewish Communities in Yugoslavia.

The Croatian Jews suffered greatly under the German occupation in the Second World War when the local *Ustashe* (Croatian Fascists) assisted the Germans. Despite their efforts some Jews survived and even decided to rebuild their community when peace returned.

Today, after the civil war, there are synagogues in towns across the country. There are some Hebrew classes and newsletters are published. There are also many places of historical interest, such as Ulicia Zudioska (Jewish Street) in Dubrovnik. This street has recently been renamed Jewish Street.

There is an impressive monument to Jewish victims of the Holocaust in the Jewish cemetery of Mirogoj and a monument to Jewish soldiers who fell in the First World War.
There is a plaque in Praška Street 7 on the site of the pre-war Central synagogue of Zagreb.
Before 1941 the community numbered over 12,000 Jews. Today there are 1,500 members.

DUBROVNIK
Jewish Community and Synagogue
Zudioska Street 3 (Jewish Street)
Tel +385 (20) 321 028
This is the second oldest synagogue in Europe, dating back to the 14th century. It was damaged in the 1991-2 war. There are 47 Jews in the city and services are held on Jewish holidays. *Pres.* S. Horovic

ZAGREB
Bet Israel Jewish Community of Croatia and Synagogue
Židovska Vjerska Zajednica Bet Israel u Hrvatskoj, Mažuranićev trg 6, 10 000 Zagreb, Hrvatska
Tel +385 (1) 4851 008   *Fax* +385 (1) 4851 376
office Email ured@bet-israel.com   *Website* www.bet-israel.com

CEUTA
Ceuta Kashrut Information and Synagogue
Calle Sargento Coriat 8

CUBA

The first Jew to set foot in Cuba (1492) was Luis de Torres. Although hundreds arrived following the Spanish Inquisition, they were prohibited from practising their religion. This changed in 1898 following Cuba's liberation from Spain. With the end of Spanish colonial rule in that year, Jews from nearby areas, such as Jamaica and Florida, and Jewish veterans of the Spanish American War, began to settle in Cuba. A congregation was established in 1904. Later, Turkish Sephardim formed their own synagogue. The community was then augmented by immigrants from eastern Europe who had decided to stay in Cuba, which was being used as a transit camp for those seeking to enter America. A central committee was established for all Jewish groups in the 1930s. Cuba imposed severe restrictions on immigration at that time, and the story of the German ship St Louis (full of Jewish refugees), which was refused entry into Cuba, is well known.
About 12,000 Jews lived on the island in 1952. Havana had by far the largest community, and 75 per cent of the Cuban community was Ashkenazi. Although the Cuban revolution did not target Jews, religious affiliations were initially discouraged and many Jews emigrated (as did many non-Jews). The remaining community has synagogues and a Sunday school. Kosher food and Judaica are imported, mainly from Canada and Panama. Cuba broke off diplomatic relations with Israel in 1973, although in 1998/99 a number of Jews were allowed to emigrate to Israel.

Cuban Jewish Community - Comunidad Hebrea de Cuba
Calle 1, #259, Esquina 13, Vedado, Ciudad de la Habana 10400
Tel +53 (7) 832 8953
Email beth_shalom@enet.cu or patronato_ort@enet.cu
Website www.chcuba.org/english/index.thm
Pres. Dr Jose Miller; *V. Pres.* Adela Dworin

CYPRUS

During the Roman Empire, Jewish merchants made their home on Cyprus. However, after a revolt that destroyed the town of Salamis, they were expelled. In medieval times small Jewish communities were established in Nicosia, Limassol and other towns, but the community was never large.
It is interesting to note that Cyprus was seen as a possible 'Jewish Homeland' by the early Zionists. Agricultural settlements were established at the end of the nineteenth century, but they were not successful. Herzl himself tried to persuade the British government to allow Jewish

rule over Cyprus in 1902, but met with failure.

Some German Jews managed to escape to Cyprus in the early 1930s. After the war, many Holocaust survivors who had tried to enter Palestine illegally were deported to special camps on the island. Some 50,000 European Jews were held there. Since the establishment of the state of Israel, the Jewish community on the island has become small; the Israeli embassy serves as a centre for community activities.

CJCC - Cyprus Jewish Community Centre
Diogenous 7b, Larnaca, 6020 Cyprus
Tel +357 (24) 828 770/1
Website www.koshercyprus.com
A full list of kosher products in Cyprus, as well as details for the mikveh, synagogue services and the Jewish school can be found on the chabad Cyprus website. There is also a list of recommended hotels within walking distance of the synagogue and chabad centre.
Rabbi Arie Zeev and Sheindel Raskin

CZECH REPUBLIC

Prague, the capital of this small central European country, has become a major tourist attraction. It is one of the few cities to actively promote its Jewish heritage, which dates from early medieval times. The oldest (still functioning) synagogue in Europe is there (the Altneuschul), as well as other interesting Jewish sites.

After the arrival of the first Jews in the country in the tenth century, they suffered similar tragedies to those of other medieval Jewish communities; forced baptism by the Crusaders and expulsions, although occasionally there was some tolerance. Full emancipation was reached in 1867 under the Habsburgs. The celebrated Jewish writer, Franz Kafka, lived in Prague and did not neglect his Judaism, unlike many other Czech Jews who assimilated and intermarried. The German occupation led to 85 per cent of the community (80,000 people) perishing in the Holocaust. Further difficulties were faced in the Communist period after the war, but since the 1989 'Velvet Revolution', Judaism is being rediscovered. The community (mostly elderly) has several synagogues around the country, a kindergarten and a journal, and there are kosher restaurants in the old Jewish Quarter in Prague.

CONTACT INFORMATION
Federation of Jewish Communities in the Czech Republic
Maiselova 18, 110 01, Prague
Tel +420 (2) 2480 0824 *Fax* +420 (2) 2481 0912
Email sekretariat@fzo.cz *Website* www.fzo.cz
Sec. JuDr. Tomas Kraus
Orthodox
Chabad Prague, Parizska 3, Praha 1 (just steps from the Old Town Square)
Tel +420 (2) 2232 0200/0192 *Fax* +420 (2) 2232 0200
Email jewishprague@gmail.com *Website* http://www.chabadprague.cz/
Dir. Rabbi Manis Barash *Email* chabadprague@gmail.com
Liberal
BEJT SIMCHA, Maiselova 4, 110 00 Praha 1
Tel +420 (7) 2402 7929
Website http://www.bejtsimcha.cz
Jewish Museum
U Staré školy 1, 110 00 Prague 1
Tel +420 (2) 2171 1511 *Fax* +420 (2) 2274 9300
Email office@jewishmuseum.cz
Please email for information on the Jewish museum, the Jewish cemetery, and any research activities.

DENMARK

Jews were allowed to settle in Denmark in 1622, earlier than in any other Scandinavian country. Thereafter the community grew, with immigration largely from Germany. The Danish

King allowed the foundation of the unified Jewish community of Copenhagen in 1684, and the Jews were granted full citizenship in 1849.

In the early part of the twentieth century many refugees arrived from eastern Europe, and Denmark welcomed refugees from Nazi Germany. When the Germans conquered Denmark and ordered the Jews to be handed over, the Danish resistance managed to save 7,200 (90% of the community) by arranging boats to take them to neutral Sweden. Some Jews did, however, stay behind and were taken to the transit ghetto of Theresienstadt (Terezin), where many died. After the war most of the Jews returned, and there is now a central Jewish organisation based in Copenhagen. There are also homes for the elderly, synagogues and a mikveh.

COPENHAGEN
Chief Rabbi Rabbi Bent Lexner Bomhusvej, 18, DK 2100
Tel +45 3929 9520 *Fax* +45 3929 2517
Email bent@lexner.dk Private Oestbanegade 9, DK 2100 *Tel* +45 3526 3540
Det Mosaiske Troessamfund i Kobenhavn (Jewish Congregation of Copenhagen)
Ny Kongensgade 6, DK 1472
Tel +45 3312 8868 *Fax* +45 3312 3357
Email mt@mosaiske.dk *Website* www.mosaiske.dk
Great Synagogue
Krystalgade 12, DK 1172
Tel +45 3312 8868
Progressive Judiasm of Denmark
Website http://www.shirhatzafon.dk/

DOMINICAN REPUBLIC

Jewish settlement in the Dominican Republic was comparatively late; the oldest Jewish grave dates back to 1826. Descended from central European Jews, the community was not religious and many married Christians. President Francisco Henriquez y Carvajal (1916) traced his ancestry back to the early Jewish settlers.

In 1938 the republic decided to accept refugees from Nazism (one of the very few countries of the world that did so freely), and even provided areas where they could settle. As a result, there were 1,000 Jews living there in 1943. This number declined as, once again, the Jewish community assimilated and married the local non-Jewish population. Despite this, many non-Jewish husbands, wives and children take part in Jewish events.

Two synagogues and a rabbi who divides his time between them, are features of Jewish life. There is also a Sunday school in Santo Domingo and a bi-monthly magazine is produced. There is a small Jewish museum in Sosua.

Chabad Lubavitch of Dominican Republic
Avenida Sarasota 71 Apt # 702, Santo Domingo
Chabad House *Tel* +1 (809) 533 8770 *U.S. Tel* 718 504 1990
Email ChabadDominican@gmail.com *Website* http://www.chabadominican.com/
Dir. Rabbi Shimon Pelman

SANTO DOMINGO
Centro Israelita de la República Dominicana
Avenida Sarasota #21, (between Av. Lincoln & Av. Churchill)
Tel +1 (809) 535 6042 La Julia, Santo Domingo.

ECUADOR

As in most Latin American countries, *Conversos* comprised the earliest Jewish settlers in Ecuador. It was not until 1904 that Eastern European Jews began to arrive, and numbers increased further following the Nazi take-over in Germany, as Ecuador granted refuge to more Jews than other neighbouring countries. About 3,000 Jews entered Ecuador in the 1930s. The Jewish population peaked in 1950 at 4,000, but this number declined owing to emigration. In recent years, some Jews have moved to Ecuador from elsewhere in South America. There are no Jewish schools, but children do have access to Jewish education.

Comunidad Judia del Ecuador
Calle Roberto Andrade OE3-580 y Jaime Roldos, Urbanizacion Einstein, P.O. Box 17-03-800
Tel +593 (2) 483 800/927 *Fax* +593 (2) 486 755
Email aiq@cje-ec.com *Website* www.cje-ec.com

Beit Jabad del Ecuador
Chabad of Ecuador, Los Cabildos #135, Edif. Paola Apt. 2 y Afganistan Quito
Telfax +1 (593) 2243 3481 *U.S. Tel* +1 (770) 884 6113 *Mobile* +1 59392 666 954
Email jabadecuador@gmail.com *Website* www.jabad.org.ec

EGYPT

The history of the Jewish community in Egypt goes back to Biblical times. Following the establishment of the State of Israel in 1948 and the subsequent wars, only about 200 Jews remain, about 150 in Cairo and 50 in Alexandria. Services are conducted in Shaar Hashamayim Synagogue during the High Holy Days.

ALEXANDRIA
Great Synagogue Eliahu HaNabi
69 rue Nebi Daniel, Ramla Station
Pres. Dr. Max Salama

CAIRO
Jewish Community Headquarters
13 rue Sebil el Khazendar, Midan el Gueish, Abbasiya
Tel +20 (2) 2482 4613
Email bassatine@yahoo.com *Website* www.bassatine.news
Pres. C. Weinstein *Tel* +20 (2) 2393 5896

EL SALVADOR

The Jewish connection to El Salvador is not a strong one. It is believed that some Portuguese *Conversos* crossed the country a few hundred years ago. After that, some Sephardis from France moved to Chaluchuapa. Other Jews came from Europe, but in smaller numbers than those settling in other Latin American countries. There were only 370 Jews in 1976, a number reduced during the civil war, when many emigrated. Some returned, however, when the war was over.
An official community was set up in 1944 and a synagogue was opened in 1950. El Salvador is one of the few countries to have an embassy in Jerusalem, rather than Tel Aviv.

Israelite Community of El Salvador (Conservative)
Boulevard del Hipodromo 626 # 1, Colonia San Benito, San Salvador
Telefax +503 2263 8074
Email cisraelita@integra.com.sv *Website* http://www.comunidadisraelitadeelsalvador.org/

ERITREA

There is one last native Jew left in Eritrea, Sami Cohen, who attends to the Asmara Synagogue and cemetery.

ASMARA
Asmara Jewish Community
P.O. Box 1475, 34 Serae Street
Tel +291 (1) 120 084/480 *Fax* +291 (1) 120 340
Email samico@gemel.com.er

ESTONIA

Despite being the only country officially declared 'Judenrein' (free of Jews) at the Wannsee conference in 1942, there is a Jewish community today. The community has always been small, and is believed to have begun in the fourteenth century. However, most Jews arrived in the nineteenth century, when Czar Alexander II allowed certain groups of Jews into the area.

The first community was established in Tallinn in 1830. By 1939, the community had grown to 4,500 and was free from restraints. After the Soviet and Nazi occupations in the Second World War the Jews returned, mainly from the Soviet Union. Now that Estonia is independent, the Jewish community is able to practise its religion freely.

TALLINN
Jewish Community of Estonia
16 Karu Street
Tel/Fax +372 (6) 644 370
Email rabbi@ejc.ee Website www.ejc.ee
Contact Cilja Laud P.O.B. 3576 Tallinn 10507
Jewish Cultural Centre and Synagogue
16 Karu Street
Tel +372 (6) 662 3050

ETHIOPIA

The indigenous Jews of Ethiopia, known as Falashas, have probably lived in the country for about 2,000 years. Their origin is obscure but they are believed to be the descendants of members of the Agau tribe who accepted pre-Talmudic Judaism brought into Ethiopia (Abyssinia) from Jewish settlements in Egypt, such as that at Elephantine (Aswan). They were estimated to number half-a-million in the 17th century but by the 1970s the population had shrunk to less than 30,000. In 1975 the Israel Government recognised their right to enter under the Law of Return. Towards the end of 1984 the Israel Government undertook Operation Moses which entailed transporting about 8,000 Ethiopian Jews from refugee camps in Sudan to Israel. It is estimated that approximately 3,000 died from famine and disease before they could reach Israel. A further dramatic mass emigration to Israel was completed in 1991 and very few remain. A useful book on the subject is Emanuela Trevisan-Semi's *Jacques Faitlovitch and the Jews of Ethiopia*, obtainable from Vallentine Mitchell Publishers.
Jewish Community
P.O.B. 50 Addis Ababa

FIJI

Many Jews, mostly from Britain and some from Australia, settled in the islands in the 19th and early 20th centuries. About 12 Jewish families now live in Suva.
Correspondence K.R. Fleischman, GPO Box 905, Suva or Cherry Schneider, P.O.B 882, Suva

FINLAND

When Finland was occupied by Russia in the nineteenth century, many Jewish conscripts in the Russian army settled in Finland after their discharge. They were still subject to restrictions, but these ended after Finland's independence in 1917. In addition to these *'Cantonists'*, as they were known, immigrants came to Finland from eastern Europe. Finland proved a safe haven, as the government refused to hand over Finnish Jews to the Nazis, despite being allied to Germany in its war with Soviet Russia.

The community is keen to preserve a sense of Jewish identity among the young generation, who are encouraged to experience Jewish life in Israel. The community is also keen to help other Jews in the newly independent Baltic states across the sea to the south of the country. There is a central body for Jewish communities, and kosher food is available. There are also synagogues and a school.

Synagogue and Communal Centre
Malminkatu 26, 00100 Helsinki 10
Tel +358 (09) 586 0310 *Fax* +358 (09) 694 8916
Email srk@jchelsinki.fi *Website* www.jchelsinki.fi
Chabad Lubavitch of Finland
Ilmarinkatu 10b Suite 66, Helsinki, 00100 Finland

Tel +358 (9) 278 1770 *Fax* +358 (9) 278 1770
Email rabbi@lubavitch.fi *Website* http://www.lubavitch.fi/
Co-Dir. Rabbi Benyamin Wolff & Fruma Ita Wolff

FRANCE

France now boasts the largest Jewish community in Europe. The Jewish connection with France is a long one: it dates back over 1,000 years as there is evidence of Jewish settlement in several towns in the first few centuries of the Jewish Diaspora. The community grew in early medieval times, and contributed to the economy of the region. Two great Jewish commentators, Rashi and Rabenu Tam, both lived in France. However, French Jewry suffered both from the Crusaders and from other anti-semitic outbursts in the medieval period.

Napoleon's reign heralded the emancipation of French Jewry and, as his armies conquered Europe, the emancipation of other communities began. Despite this, later incidents, such as the Dreyfus Affair, highlighted the fact that anti-semitism was not yet dead. The worst case of anti-semitism in France occurred under the German occupation, when some 70,000 Jews were deported from the community of 300,000. After the war, France became a centre for Jewish immigration, beginning with 80,000 from eastern Europe, and then many thousands from North Africa, which eventually swelled the Jewish population to nearly 700,000.

The community is well served with organisations. Paris alone has 380,000 Jews, more than in the whole of the UK. There are many kosher restaurants, synagogues in many towns throughout the country, newspapers, radio programmes and schools in several cities. In Carpentras and Cavaillon there are synagogues which are considered to be national monuments.

PARIS

Consistoire Central The principal Jewish religious organisation in France. It administers the
Union des Communautés Juives de France
19 rue St. Georges, 75009
Tel +33 (01) 49 70 88 00 *Fax* +33 (01) 42 81 03 66
Website www.consistoire.org
Pres. Joël Mergui; *Dir. Gen.* F. Attali

Chief Rabbi of France
Rabbi Gilles Bernheim, Consistoire Central, 19 rue Saint-Georges, 75009
Tel +33 (01) 49 70 88 00 *Fax* +33 (01) 40 16 06 11

Communauté Israélite de la Stricte Observance
10 rue Cadet, 75009
Tel +33 (01) 42 46 36 47

Conseil Représentatif du Judaisme Traditionaliste
c/o Eric Schieber 6 rue Albert Camus, le Montigny 75010 Paris 16¡.
Tel +33 (01) 45 04 94 00
Representative organisation of Orthodox Jewry.
Pres. I. Frankforter; *Sec. Gen.* E. Schieber

Jeunesse Loubavitch
8 Rue Lamartine, 75009
Tel +33 (01) 45 26 87 60 *Fax* +33 (01) 45 26 24 37

Mouvement Juif Libéral de France (MJLF)
11 Rue Gaston de Caillavet, 75015
Tel +33 (01) 44 37 48 48 *Fax* +33 (01) 44 37 48 50
Affiliated to World Union of Progressive Judaism. *Pres.* Félix Mosbacher; *Rabbis* Daniel and Gabriel Farhi

Mouvement Loubavitch
8 rue Lamartine 9°
Tel +33 (01) 45 26 87 60

Union Libérale Israélite
24 rue Copernic, 75116 Organisation of LJ.
Pres. C Bloch. *Tel* +33 (01) 47 04 37 27 *Fax* +33 (01) 47 27 81 02

SYNAGOGUES
Orthodox Synagogues
10 rue Cadet, 9°; 31 rue de Montévidéo, 16°; 10 rue Pavee, 4°; 6 rue Ambroise Thomas, 9°; 3 rue Saulnier, 9°; 32 rue Basfroi, H°; 25 rue des Rosiers, 4°; 17 rue des Rosiers, 4°; 24 rue de Bourg Tibourg, 4°; 80 rue Doudeauville, 18°; 5 rue Duc, 18°; 18 rue des Ecouffes, 4°
Conservative Synagogue
Adath Shalom, 22 bis, rue des Belles Feuilles, 75116 Paris
Tel +33 (01) 45 53 84 09
Liberal Synagogues
24 rue Copernic, 16°; 11 rue Gaston de Caillavet 15°
There are also many synagogues in the Paris suburbs and in the Provinces.

AVIGNON
Avignon Synagogue
2 Place J'rusalem, 84 000 Avignon
Tel +33 (04) 90 85 21 24

BORDEAUX
CONTACT INFORMATION
Rue du Grand-Rabbin-Joseph-choen, Bordeaux
Tel +33 (05) 56917939

LYON
Grande Synagogue
13 qui Tilsitt, Lyon
Tel +33 (04) 78 37 13 43 *Fax* +33 (04) 78 38 26 57
Email aci@9online.fr *Website* http://www.consistoiredelyon.fr/

MARSEILLE
Consistoire Israélite de Marseille
117-119 rue breteuil, 13006 Marseille
Tel +33 (04) 91 37 49 64, +33 (04) 91 81 13 57 *Fax* +33 (04) 91 37 83 90
Email consistoiremarseille@yahoo.fr *Website* http://www.consistoiremarseille.com/
Dayan Rabbi Hai Amram, Dayan of kashrus *Email* ravamram@yahoo.fr

NICE
Bet Yossef Synagogue (Sephardic, Orthodox)
16 rue alexis Mossa, 06000 Nice
Tel +33 (04) 97 07 18 89
Email betyossef@hotmail.fr

GEORGIA

The Jews of Georgia are divided into two groups; the native Georgian-speaking Jews, who have a history going back 1,500 years, (some claim much longer), and the Ashkenazi Jews who came to Georgia following its annexation by Russia at the beginning of the nineteenth century. The Jewish population of Georgia has declined over the last 35 years due to emigration, mostly to Israel. Once numbering as many as 100,000, today the Georgian Jewish population is approximately 13,000. Tiblisi has the largest Jewish population at 11,000. Jewish communities are also located in Kutaisi, Batumi, Oni, Achaltische, Ahalkalaki, Surami, Kareli, and Gori, and synagogues are located in most of these cities.

The Georgian Synagogue
45-47 Leselidze Street, Tbilisi
Tbilisi Hillel
c/o JDC Office, Galaktion Tabidze st. 5/3 Rm. 48, Tbilisi
Tel +995 (32) 517 7185

GERMANY

It may be a surprise to many that Germany comes immediately after France and the UK in the population table of Western European Jews. German Jews have contributed much to the culture of European Jews in general since their arrival, in what is now Germany, in the fourth century. The massive Jewish presence in Poland and other east European states stemmed from German Jews escaping persecution in the late Middle Ages. They took the early Medieval German language with them, which formed Yiddish, the old *lingua franca* of European Jews.

The Jews who stayed behind in Germany contributed much towards Jewish and German culture, with the Reform movement starting in nineteenth-century Germany, and Heine and Mendelssohn contributing to German poetry and music respectively. The Enlightenment Torah Im Derech Eretz and the Masorti also began in Germany.

The rise of Nazism destroyed the belief that the German Jews were more German than Jewish. Most managed to escape before 1939, but 180,000 were killed in the Holocaust (of the 503,000 who lived in Germany when Hitler came to power). Following the events of 1933–45, it seems incredible that any Jew should want to live in Germany again. However, the community began to re-form, mainly with immigrants from Eastern Europe, especially Russia. Now there are again Jewish shops in Berlin, and kosher food is once more available. There are many old synagogues which have been restored, and several concentration camps have been kept as monuments. There is also a great interest in Jewish matters among some of the non-Jewish younger generation.

Visitors to Berlin should try to visit the new Jewish Museum (officially opened in September 2001). It covers the history of German Jewry through the Middle Ages and up to the present. It revives the tradition of an earlier museum opened in 1933 before the Nazis came to power.

Allgemeine Rabbinerkonferenz
Rabbiner Dr. Henry G. Brandt. c/o Israeliische Kultusgemeinde Schwaben-Augsburg, Hunoldsgraben 28, 86150 Augsburg

B'nai B'rith Lodges
Berlin, Cologne, Düsseldorf, Frankfurt a.Main Hamburg, Munich and Saarbrücken

Bundesverband Jüd. Studenten
Oranienburger Str. 29-31, D-10117 Berlin
Tel +39 (30) 885 5304
Email info@bjsd.de
Also at Jewish Student Organisations at Aachen, Cologne, Frankfurt, Stuttgart, Hanover, Hamburg, Heidelberg and Munich

Chabad Berlin
Tel +49 (30) 2128 0830
Email service@jg-berlin.org *Website* www.jg-berlin.org
Rabbi Tiechtel

Israelitischen Kultusgemeinde Munchen und Oberbayern
Tel +49 (89) 2024 0021
Email rabbinate@ikg-m.de *Website* www.ikg-m.de
Rabbi Steven Langnas

Jewish Agency for Israel
Hebelstr. 6,D- 60318 Frankfurt
Tel +49 (69) 943 3340 *Fax* +49 (69) 9433 3420
Email jafi.frankfurt@t-online.de

INFORMATION REGARDING SYNAGOGUES, SERVICES AND KASHRUT
Orthodoxe Rabbinerkonferenz in Deutschland
c/o Synagogen-Gemeinde köln, Roonstr., 50674 Koln
Email info@ordonline.de *Website* www.ordonline.de

The Union of Progressive Jews in Germany, Austria & Switzerland
Herman-Hummel-Str. 18, D-82166 Graäfelfing
Tel +49 8980 9373
Email info@liberale-juden.de

Zentralarchiv zur Erforschung der Geschichte der Juden in Deutschland
Bienenstr. 5, D-69117 Heidelberg
Tel +49 (62) 2116 4141 *Fax* +49 (62) 2118 1049
Website www.zentralarchiv.uni-hd.de

Zentralrat der Juden in Deutschland (Central Council of Jews in Germany)
Tucholskystr. 9, D-10117 Berlin
Tel +49 (30) 244 4560 *Fax* +49 (30) 2844 5613
Email info@zentralrat derjuden.de *Website* www.zentralratderjuden.de

GIBRALTAR

In 1473 there was a suggestion that the promontory should be reserved for Marranos (*See* D. Lamelas, *The Sale of Gibraltar in 1474*, 1992). The present Jewish community was formed of immigrants from North Africa shortly after the British annexation in 1704, but Jews had no legal right to settle in the city until 1749, by which year however, the Jewish residents numbered about 600, a third of the total number of residents, and had two synagogues.
During the siege of 1779 to 1783 the size of the Jewish population was reduced, a large proportion removing to England. After the siege the numbers rose again, being at their highest in the middle of the nineteenth century, when they rose above two thousand. (For the history of the Jews of Gibraltar, *See* A. B. M. Serfaty, *The Jews of Gibraltar under British Rule*, 1933.)
  Following the period of decline, the last ten to fifteen years has seen a marked increase in the Jewish numbers, with a large number of Gibraltarians returning from study and residence abroad. This has created a young and vibrant Community.
Managing Board of the Jewish Community
91 Irish Town
Tel +350 (200) 72606 *Fax* +350 (200) 40487
Pres. H. J. M. Levy *Fax* +350 (200) 40487 *Admin.* S. Levy *Email* mbjc@gibtelecom.net
Gibraltar Jewish Community
10 Bomb House Lane, Gibraltar; *Tel* +350 (200) 72606

For more information on Jewish life in Gibraltar including kosher restaurants, visit http://www.haruth.com/jw/JewsGibraltar.html

GREECE

After the Hellenistic occupation of Israel (the Jewish revolt during this occupation is commemorated in the festival of Hanukah), some Jews were led into slavery in Greece, beginning the first recorded Jewish presence in the country. The next significant Jewish immigration occurred after the Inquisition, when many Spanish Jews moved to Salonika, which was a flourishing Jewish centre until the German occupation in the Second World War. In 1832 Jews were granted the same equal rights as all other Greek citizens.
By the early 1940s, the Jewish population had grown to over 70,000, with 45,000 living in Salonika. The country was occupied in July 1941 and split among the Axis (German, Italian and Bulgarian) forces. During the occupation a relatively large number of Jews joined the Partisans. Many local Christians did protect their Jewish neighbours in Athens. After the war many of the survivors emigrated to Israel.
Today there are Sephardi synagogues in Greece and, in Athens, a community centre and a Jewish museum. There are Jewish publications and a library in the community centre. In Aegina, Corfu and other Greek islands; ancient synagogues may be visited.

ATHENS
B'nai B'rith
15 Paparigopoulou Street, 105 61
Tel +30 (210) 323 0405
Central Board of Jewish Communities
36 Voulis Street, GR 105 57
Email hhkis@ath.forthnet.gr *Website* www.kis.gr
Pres. Moissis Constantinis *Tel* +30 (210) 324 4315 *Fax* +30 (210) 331 3852
Beth Shalom Synagogue
5 Melidoni Street, 105 53
M. Rabbi Jakob Arar *Tel* +30 (210) 325 2773

THESSALONIKI
Jewish Community Office
26 Vasileos Irakliou Street, 54624
Tel +30 (2310) 275 701 *Fax* +30 (2310) 229 063
Monastirioton Synagogue
35 Sigrou Street, 54630
Tel +30 (2310) 524 968

OTHER COMMUNITIES
Corfu Jewish Community
25 Agias Sofias Street, GR-491 00, Corfu
Pres. Moisis Velelis *Tel/Fax* +30 (2661) 037 713
Halkis Jewish Community
5 Papingi Street, 34100
Pres. M. Maissis *Tel* +30 (2221) 060 111 *Fax* +30 (2221) 083 781
Ioannina Jewish Community
18 Joseph Eliyia Str. GR 452 21
Pres. M. Elisaf *Tel* +30 (2651) 025 195
Larissa Jewish Community
Platia Evreon Martiron, 29 Kentavron Street, GR 412 22
Pres. M. Magrizos *Tel* +30 (2410) 532 965
Rodos Jewish Community
5 Polidorou Str. GR 85100
Tel +30 (2241) 022 364 *Fax* +30 (2241) 073 039
Email jcrhodes@otenet.gr
Pres. Bella Angel-Restis
Trikala Jewish Community
11 Sokratous Street, GR-421 00
Pres. Ovadias Sabas *Tel* +30 (2431) 021 623/025 834
Volos Jewish Community
51 Hatziargyuri Street, GR 383 33
Email jcvol@otenet.gr *Website* www.atlantis.gr/kis/volos.html
Pres. M. Solomon *Tel/Fax* +30 (2421) 025 302

GUADELOUPE
GOSIER
Gosier Synagogue
Bas du Fort, Lot 1
Tel +590 909 909
The community centre and restaurant/kosher store are also located here.

GUATEMALA
Conversos were the first recorded Jews in the country, but a few centuries later, the next Jewish immigration occurred with the arrival of German Jews in 1848. Later, some East European Jews arrived but Guatemala was not keen to accept refugees from Nazism, and, as a result, passed some laws which, although not mentioning Jews directly, were aimed against Jewish refugees.
Even though these laws were in place, in 1939 there were 800 Jews in Guatemala. An Ashkenazi community centre was built in 1965, but despite accepting some Jewish Cuban refugees, the community is shrinking owing to assimilation and intermarriage.
Most Jews live in Guatemala City, and others in Quetzaltenango and San Marcos. There is a Jewish school and kindergarten.

GUATEMALA CITY
Centro Hebreo (East European Jews)
7a. Av. 13-51 Zona 9

Tel +502 (2) 331 1975
Pres. Boris Barac
Comunidad Judia Guatemalteca
7a. Av. 13-51 Zona 9, Guatemala City, C.A.
Tel +502 (2) 560 1509 *Fax* +502 (2) 560 1589
Email comjugua@guaweb.net
Pres. T. Rybar
Consejo Central Sionista de la Comunidad Judia de Guatemala
Apto. Postal 502, Guatemala, C.A.
Pres. Mano Permuth
Maguen David (Sephardi)
7a. Avenida 3-80 Zona 2
Tel +502 (2) 232 0932 *Fax* +502 (2) 360 1589
Pres. Moises Beer

HAITI

Christopher Columbus brought the first Jew to Haiti–his interpreter, Luis de Torres, a *Converso* who had been baptised before the voyage. Thereafter more Jews settled, but the community was destroyed in an anti-European revolt by Toussaint L'Ouverture in 1804. A hundred or so years later, Jews from the Middle East and some refugees from the Nazis settled in Haiti, but many subsequently emigrated to Israel.
The remaining community has benefited from the help of the Israeli embassy, and services are held in the embassy or in private homes. The community is too small to support other Jewish facilities.
The Jewish Community Of Haiti
The Honorary Consul, Gilbert Bigio, P.O. Box 687, Port-au-Prince
Tel 509 1 20 638
Email info@promointer.net

HONDURAS

During the Spanish colonial period, some *Conversos* did live in Honduras, but it was only in the nineteenth century that any significant Jewish immigration occurred. In the early twentieth century refugees from Nazism followed a handful of immigrants from eastern Europe. Honduras was one of the small number of countries to aid refugees from Nazism, and many Jews owe their lives to the help of Honduran consulates which issued visas in wartime Europe. The capital Tegucigalpa contains the largest Jewish population, but the only synagogue in the country is in San Pedro Sula (services are held in private homes in Tegucigalpa).

San Pedro Sula Synagogue and Community Centre
Sec. M. Weizenblut *Tel* +504 552 8136 *Fax* +504 557 5244
Comunidad hebrea de Tegucigalpa
P.O. Box U 8914, Tegucigalpa
Tel 504 238 5114 *Fax* 504 236 7776

HUNGARY

There were Jews living in Hungary in Roman times, even before the arrival of the Magyars (ancestors of the present-day Hungarians). The Jews suffered during the Middle Ages when there was a good deal of anti-semitism, but conditions improved under Austro-Hungarian rule, and Judaism was recognised as being on a legal par with Christianity in 1896.
Hungary lost a considerable amount of territory after the First World War and, as a result, many of its original Jewish communities (such as Szatmar) found themselves within other countries. Anti-semitism reached a peak in March 1944, when, during the German occupation, most Jewish communities began to be transported to Auschwitz. A number of those who were deported survived when Auschwitz was liberated by the Red Army in January 1945.
After the war Hungary had the largest Jewish community in central Europe. Inevitably the community dwindled through emigration (especially after the 1956 uprising) and assimilation.

Communism in Hungary was far more lenient than in other Warsaw Pact countries, and synagogues were allowed to operate. Since 1989, religious interest has increased, and the government has recently renovated the Dohany Synagogue, the second biggest synagogue in the world and the largest in Europe. The Jewish population is still the largest in the region, although most are not very observant. The Hungarian national tourist office has published 'Shalom', an excellent guide to Jewish Hungary.

BUDAPEST
Central Rabbinate
Budapest VII Sip utca 12
Dir. Robert Deutsch, Chief Rabbi
The Budapest Jewish Community
1075 Budapest VII Sip utca 12
Tel +36 (1) 413 5569 *Fax* +36 (1) 342 1790
Man. Dir. Gusztav Zoltai; *Dir. Foreign Rel.* Ernö Lazarovits
Main Synagogue (Conservative)
The Dohány Street Synagogue (Dohány utcai zsinagóga)
Pest, VII. district, Budapest, Dohány utca 2
Tel +36 (1) 342 8949
Email info@bpjewmus.hu *Website* http://www.bpjewmus.hu/
There are 20 other synagogues and prayer houses in Budapest. The main provincial communities are at Debrecen, Miskolc, Szeged, Pécs, Györ

INDIA
The Jewish population of India can be divided into three components: the Cochin Jews, the Bene Israel and the Baghdadi Jews. The Cochin Jews are based in the south of India in Kerala. This community can be further divided into Black (believing themselves to be the original settlers) and White (of European or Middle Eastern origin), and the Paradesi. Most of the community has emigrated, but there is still a synagogue in Cochin that is a major tourist attraction.

The Bene Israel believe they are descended from Jewish survivors of a ship wrecked on its voyage from ancient Israel during the period of King Solomon. No reliable documentary evidence, however, exists to support this claim. More reliable evidence dates settlement to around the tenth century. The Bene Israel follow only certain Jewish practices, such as kosher food and Shabbat, and also adhere to certain Muslim and Hindu beliefs; for example, they abstain from eating beef. In the eighteenth century, they settled in Bombay and now form the largest group of Indian Jews.

Baghdadi Jews, immigrants from Iraq and the other Middle Eastern countries, arrived in India in the late eighteenth century, and followed British Colonial rather than local custom. Many emigrated to Israel in the 1950s and 1960s.

During the Indo-Pakistan war of 1972, the leading Indian military figure was General Samuels. In 1999 Lt-Gen J.F.R. Jacob was appointed Governor of Punjab State.

There is a central Council of Indian Jewry, based in Mumbai, where most of the Indian Jews live. Kosher food is available, and there are three Jewish schools in the city. Relations with Israel have recently improved and it is now a major trading partner.

Council of Indian Jewry
c/o The Jewish Club, Jeroo Building, 2nd Floor, 137 Mahatma Gandhi Road, Bombay, 400023
Tel +91 271 628
Pres. N. Talkar *Tel* +91 515 195/861 941; *V. Pres.* A. Talegawkar, A. Samson; *Sec.* J. Bhattacharya *Tel* +91 632 0589
Ohel David Synagogue
9 Dr. Ambedkar Road, Pune 411 001, Maharashtra
Tel +91 (20) 261 32 048
Email dsoloman2002@yahoo.com

INDONESIA

After World War II, many Jews left Indonesia because they had lost their homes and possessions during the war, but several families remained. By the 1950s, the Jewish communities were beginning to thrive again, especially in Surabaya. In the early 1960s, with the rise of nationalist and anti-Dutch sentiments among the people of Indonesia, many Jews emigrated to the United States, Australia, and Israel. By 1970, most of the thriving Jewish communities of Indonesia had almost vanished, leaving only a scattering of Jews behind. Today, about 20 Jews live in Indonesia, and Judaism is not recognized as a religion.

The local Jewish cemetery is frequently vandalized. Of the seventy graves with marble tablets, many are illegible.

Synagogue Kajoon (Orthodox)
Rivka Sayers, Jalan Kajoon #6, Surbaya, Jawa Timur
Tel +62 (315) 777 770 or +62 (315) 455 2815

IRAN

Jews have lived in the country at least since the time of the Persian King Cyrus in the sixth century BCE. Many of the tombs of Jewish prophets, such as Daniel, Habakuk, Esther and Mordechai, are located in the cities of Iran. These holy places are respected by both Jews and Muslims. From the beginning of the twentieth century, the Iranian Jewish population has been under 70,000. Today it is in the region of 20,000. There are some legal differences between the majority and minority religions in Iran. Jews have been free to maintain their religious affairs and ceremonies, and culture training of Jewish students since the Islamic Revolution of 1979. There has been a Jewish representative in every Islamic parliament in the modern period. Iranian Jews live in Tehran, Shiraz, Isfahan, Kerman, and Kermanshah.

TEHRAN
Synagogues
Yousef-abad, 15th Street, Seyed Jama-leddin Assad-abadi Avenue; Abrishami, 4th Street, North Felestin Avenue *Chief Rabbi* Rabbi Yousef Haim Hamedani Cohen.

Tehran Jewish Committee
223 Sheikh-Hadi Street, Jomhuri Avenue, 11397 3 3317
Tel +98 6670 2556 *Fax* +98 6671 6429
Email iranjewish@iranjewish.com

IRAQ

From 1949 to 1951, 104,000 Jews were evacuated from Iraq. In 2004, approximately 35 Jews were living in Baghdad, but by 2008, the once-thriving community of Jews living in the capital dwindled to below 10, not enough to hold a minyan (the requisite 10 men needed for most religious rituals), and a handful more in the Kurdish-controlled northern parts of Iraq. The community still lives in fear, scared even to publicize the exact numbers of Jews remaining in Baghdad, but the Jewish Agency estimates it at about seven.

The one synagogue, the Meir Taweig Synagogue, was closed in 2003, after it became too dangerous to gather out in the open.

IRELAND, REPUBLIC OF

Jews lived in Ireland in the Middle Ages, and a Sephardi community was established in Dublin in 1660, four years after the Resettlement in England. In the eighteenth century there was also a community in Cork. The Dublin congregation declined in the reign of George III, and was dissolved in 1791, but was revived in 1822. The community received its largest influx of members around 1900, the immigrants coming from Eastern Europe; Lithuania in particular. There are now some 1,300 Jews in the country. (*See* Hyman: *The Jews of Ireland*, 1972, repr. 1996.)

Chief Rabbi
Office Herzog House, 1 Zion Road, Dublin 6

Tel +353 (1) 492 37 51 *Fax* +353 (1) 492 08 88
Email irishcom@iol.ie
Jewish Community Office
Herzog House, 1 Zion Road, Dublin 6
Tel +353 (1) 492 3751 *Fax* +353 (1) 492 0888
Email irishcom@iol.ie *Website* jewishireland.org
Sec. Stewart Barling
Also located at **Herzog House**
Chief Rabbi's Office
Tel +353 (1) 492 3751
Irish-Jewish Museum (Est. 1984).
3-4 Walworth Road, Portobello, Dublin 8
Tel +353 (1) 453 1797
Museum contains memorabilia of the Irish-Jewish Community and houses a former synagogue.
Jewish Representative Council of Ireland
Email jrcisec@gmail.com
Ch. Leonard Abrahamson; *Pres.* Stephen Molins

CORK
Hebrew Congregation
10 South Terrace
(Est. 1880). *Ch. of Tru.* F. Rosehill 7 Beverly, Ovens, Co. Cork *Tel* +353 (021) 487 0413
Email rosehill@iol.ie

DUBLIN
Dublin Hebrew Congregation
(Merged with Terenure Hebrew Congregation in 2004)
Rathfarnham Road, Terenure, Dublin 6
Email dhebc@eircom.net
Tel +353 (1) 490 59 69
Dublin Jewish Progressive Congregation
Pres. Malcolm Lewis
Tel +353 872 303 435
Email djpc@liberaljudaism.org
For further information please contact the secretary.

SYNAGOGUES
Knesset Orach Chayim (Dublin Jewish Progressive Congregation)
7 Leicester Avenue, Rathgar, Dublin 6   *Correspondence* P.O. Box 3059, Rathgar, Dublin 6
Tel +353 (1) 285 6241 *Email* djpc@liberaljudaism.org
(Est. 1946). *M.* Rabbi C. Middleburgh; *Hon. S.* J. Solomon *Tel* +353 (1) 285 6241

ISRAEL

Palestine was administered until May 14, 1948, by Great Britain under a Mandate approved by the Council of the League of Nations, the preamble to which incorporated the Balfour Declaration. On November 20, 1947, the Assembly of the United Nations recommended that Palestine should be reorganised as two States, one Jewish, the other Arab, together with an internationalised Jerusalem and district, combined in an economic union. On the surrender of the Mandate by Britain on May 14, 1948, the Jewish territory, with a Jewish pop. of 655,000, took the name of Israel and set up a Provisional Government, with Dr. Chaim Weizmann as President and David Ben-Gurion as PM. On July 5, 1950, the 'Law of Return' was proclaimed, conferring on every Jew the right to live in Israel.

The signing of a declaration of a set of principles by Israel and the PLO under the leadership of Yasser Arafat on September 13, 1993, concluded an era of forty-five years of strife between Israel and her Arab neighbours and recognised the aspirations of Palestinian Arabs for territory proposed for them by the UN in 1947. A peace treaty with Jordan was agreed in 1994. PM Rabin was assassinated in November 1995.

Key events in this history include:

The invasion of the Jewish state by the Arab armies in 1948 concluded by a series of armistices in 1949 and the recognition of Israel by the UN on May 11, 1949; the annexation of Arab Palestine by Jordan in 1950; the absorption by Israel of Jews from Arab lands. The establishment of Palestinian refugee camps in the Arab states; seizure by Egypt of the Suez Canal Zone and the (Franco-British and Israeli) Sinai-Suez campaign of 1956; Egypt's closure of the Straits of Tiran in May 1967 which provoked the Six-Day War of June 1967 and saw the Israeli capture of Jerusalem and occupation of Gaza, Sinai, the Golan and the West Bank and the first Nat. Unity Coalition (1967–70); the Yom Kippur War of October 1973 and the ensuing negotiations leading to partial Israeli withdrawals in Sinai and the Golan; the Likud election victory of 1977 and the visit to Israel by Egyptian President Anwar Sadat in November 1977 which led to the Camp David Agreement of March 26, 1979, the establishment of diplomatic relations between Egypt and Israel, and the Israeli withdrawal from the whole of Sinai in April 1982; Israel's 'Operation peace for Galilee' in Lebanon in June 1982 and withdrawal in 1985, a war which caused great divisions in Israel; the Intifada of the Palestinians in Gaza and the West Bank starting in 1988; the US-inspired five-point peace plan of 1989 and its failure in 1990; the Gulf War (January 1991) following the Iraqi invasion of Kuwait, when the PLO supported Iraq and Israel sustained scud missile attacks without retaliation; the launching of negotiations for a comprehensive Middle East 'peace settlement' between Israel, the Arabs, and representatives of the Palestinians at a meeting in Madrid in October 1991.

It is these negotiations that came to fruition on the eve of the New Year 5754. The continuing 'Peace Process' was repeatedly put in jeopardy through the actions of terrorists intent on destabilizing any progress towards détente and under protest at the consolidation of Israeli settlements. President Clinton endeavoured to broker a new agreement between PM Barak and the PLO, but this failed and Mr. Barak resigned. Nonetheless Mr. Barak's achievement in securing withdrawal of Israeli forces from southern Lebanon indicated positive efforts to reconcile neighbourly relations. The new *Intifada* broke out in 2000 and Israel's predicament has been exacerbated by the aftermath of the terror of September 2001, the American war against the Taliban of Afghanistan and the Anglo-American war of 2003 against Saddam Hussein's Iraq. Interventions by President Bush and the promulgation of a 'Road Map' for reviving the peace process have faltered. Ariel Sharon saw through the construction of a barrier-wall to deflect continuing bombing raids from Gaza into Israel but broke with his Likud government in 2005 when he also forced through the withdrawal from Gaza. With the establishment of his Kadima Party he indicated some prospect of withdrawals also from parts of the West Bank.

The death of Yasser Arafat and the election of Mahmoud Abbas as PLO President were followed by Palestinian elections at the beginning of 2006. These were won by Hamas who, in government, have not rescinded their policy towards the destruction of Israel. Ariel Sharon suffered a stroke ahead of the scheduled elections in Israel and, while Kadima secured power at these elections, the new government found itself at increased risk from continuing militancy in Gaza and a new embroilment in Lebanon, which was provoked by the rise and belligerency of the Hizbollah, turning northern Israel into a war-zone. Following UN Resolution 1701 on the cease-fire in southern Lebanon, and the monitoring of the withdrawal of Hizbollah under UN control, a tentative measure of peace has been restored. Against this, the increasing stridency of Iranian rhetoric and her unabashed pursuit of nuclear power leave Israel exposed to untold dangers.

Government

The Provisional Government of Israel was replaced by a permanent one after the election of the First **Knesset** (Parl.) in January, 1949.

Israel's Basic Law provides that elections must be 'universal, nationwide, equal, secret and proportional'. A general election must be held at least every four years. The Knesset is elected by a form of proportional representation in which members are selected in strict proportion to the votes cast for each party. Any candidate who obtains one per cent of the total votes cast is assured of a Knesset seat.

Mainly as a result of the voting system, no single party has so far been able to form a government on the basis of its own Knesset majority. Until the election in 1977, the dominant political force was a coalition of the Left, which formed governments with the help of various smaller parties, usually those with a religious programme. In the elections of 1977 and 1981 an alliance of the Right was able to form an administration with the help of religious parties. One feature of the political situation has been that the religious parties, in particular, have been able to exercise an influence out of proportion to their members.

Within recent years, however, there has been a marked polarisation of attitudes among sections of Israeli society and this was reflected by the proliferation of small parties which contested the 1984 election. The 1984 election produced an inconclusive result, with only three seats separating the two big party blocs. The two big parties formed Israel's second Nat. Unity Government to cope with the urgent economic and other problems. The office of PM was held in rotation, first by Shimon Peres, the Labour Alignment leader, and then by Yitzhak Shamir, the Likud leader. The 1988 election was also inconclusive and was followed by another Coalition Government, with Mr. Shamir continuing as PM and Mr. Peres as V. Premier. The Nat. unity government broke up in March 1990 when the Likud declined to go along with a U.S. plan to promote peace talks. Mr. Shamir constructed a centre-right religious government, supported by 66% of the 120 members of the Knesset. The elections of 1992 produced a Labour coalition led by Yitzhak Rabin. Demographic changes brought about by the influx of settlers from Eastern Europe and political and economic pressures, contributed in large part to this outcome. The Knesset elections of 1996 were the first at which there was also direct voting for the position of PM. Following the resignation of Mr. Barak in 2001, Ariel Sharon was elected PM while the 15th Knesset remained in session. While political power rests constitutionally in the Knesset, the President of Israel, essentially a symbolic and representational figure, can in certain circumstances exercise a degree of de facto power based on his prestige. In particular, he can emerge as the voice of the nation's conscience. The President is elected for a five-year period, renewable only once. Moshe Katsav was elected President in 2000, but was obliged to stand down in 2007.

The results of the March 2006 election gave Mr. Olmert the opportunity to form a Centrist government with Labour support in a coalition of 73 seats. He resigned in August 2008 and Foreign Sec., Tzipi Livni won the Kadima vote to succeed him in negotiations for a new coalition. This failed to materialise and new elections were held in February 2009.

Elections to the 18th Knesset were held in February 2009. Party votes were as follows:

Kadima	28	(-1)	United Arab List-Ta-al	4	(-)
Labour	13	(-6)	National Union	4	([A])
Shas	11	(-1)	The Jewish Home	3	([B])
Likud	27	(+15)	United Torah Judaism	5	(-1)
Yisrael Beitenu	15	(+4)	New Movement-Meretz	3	(-2)
Hadash	4	(+1)	Balad	3	(-)

A The four parties making up National Union had six seats in the previous elections in the combined National Union–National Religious Party slate. The Ahi party (2 seats) left the National Union and joined the Likud.
B The Jewish Home (formerly the National Religious Party) had three seats in the combined National Union–National Religious Party slate. The two parties together won 7 seats in this election for a net loss of 2.

The Presidents of Israel Chaim Weizmann 1949–52; Yitzhak Ben Zvi 1952–63; Zalman Shazar 1963–73; Prof. Ephraim Katzir 1973–78; Yitzhak Navon 1978–83; Chaim Herzog 1983–93; Ezer Weizman 1993–2000; Moshe Katsav 2000–07; **Shimon Peres** 2007–

The Prime Ministers of Israel David Ben-Gurion 1948–53 and Nov. 1955–63; Moshe Sharett Dec. 1953–55; Levi Eshkol 1963–69; Golda Meir 1969–74; Yitzhak Rabin 1974–77 and 1992–95; Menachem Begin 1977–83; Yitzhak Shamir Oct. 1983–Sept. 1984, Oct. 1986–June 1992; Shimon Peres Sept. 1984–Oct. 1986, Nov. 1995–May 1996; Benjamin Netanyahu, May 1996–99; Ehud Barak, May 1999–Feb. 2001; Ariel Sharon, Feb. 2001–06; Ehud Olmert (Apr. 2006–09); Benjamin Netanyahu (2009-)

Judiciary The *Pres.* appoints judges on the recommendation of an independent committee.

Defence Forces Unified command of Army, Navy and Air Force. Small regular force;

compulsory military service for men and women aged between 18 and 29 followed by annual service in the Reserve.

Area Following 1949 armistice agreements – approx. 20,750 sq. km. Following withdrawal from Sinai in April 1982, approx. 28,161 sq. km. (including Golan Heights, West Bank and Gaza).

Neighbouring countries Egypt, Jordan, Syria, Lebanon.

Population Sept. 1998: 4,850,000. These figures include 17,000 Druse on the Golan Heights but not the other territories occupied in the Six-Day War (Est. at 1,381,000).

Main Towns Jerusalem (the capital), Tel Aviv, Haifa, Ramat Gan, Petach Tikvah, Netanya, Holon, Bnei Brak, Rehovot, Hadera, Nazareth, Rishon le-Zion, Beersheba, Ashkelon, Ashdod, Bat Yam, Tiberias, Eilat.

Industry Main products: Cement, fertilisers, metal products, polished diamonds, ceramics, tyres and tubes, plywood, textiles, clothing and footwear, citrus by-products, electrical and electronic applicances, micro-electronics, chemicals, canned fruit, military equipment.

Agricultural Products Citrus, fruit, vegetables, eggs, milk, wheat, barley, tobacco, groundnuts, cotton, sugarbeet, beef, fish, flowers, wine.

Minerals Potash and bromine, magnesium, phosphate, petroleum, salt, glass, sand, clay, gypsum, granite, copper, iron, oil, natural gas.

With the exception of Jerusalem and Haifa, the country's largest port, the main centres of population are concentrated in the flat and fertile western coastal plain. Tel Aviv, the centre of Israel's largest metropolitan area, is the chief commercial and industrial centre. Beersheba is the capital of the arid northern Negev, while Eilat, the country's southernmost port, has become a bustling Red Sea township linked to the northern centres by a modern highway and giving access now to Jordan as well. In the north lies the largely Arab centre of Nazareth, the popular health resort of Tiberias, and Safad. Round Tel Aviv are clustered a number of towns, including Ramat Gan, Holon and Bnei Brak.

Pres. of State Shimon Peres; *Knesset Speaker* Dalia Itsik

ISRAELI EMBASSIES AND LEGATIONS

Israel now enjoys diplomatic relations with 160 countries and many of these ties have come into being or have been renewed following the peace agreements of 1993. For more information and a full list of Israeli embassies around the world, please visit http://www.mfa.gov.il/MFA/

Main Political Parties

ISRAEL LABOUR PARTY

Established 1968 by the merger of Mapai, Achdut Avoda and Rafi. Its programme: 'To attain nat., social and pioneering aims, in the spirit of the heritage of the Jewish People, the vision of socialist Zionism and the values of the Labour movement'.
Ch. Amir Peretz 1 Urim Street, Tel Aviv *Tel* +972 689 9444

KADIMA ('Forward')

Website www.kadimahsharon.co.il
A new party that defines itself as a broad popular movement which works to ensure the future of Israel as a Jewish democratic state. The party, formed by Ariel Sharon in November 2005 following the Israeli withdrawal from Gaza which split the Likud alliance, has adopted a 'centrist and liberal' platform designed to uphold a moderate political agenda.
Ch. Tsipi Livni, Petah Tikva *Tel* +972 (3) 978 8000 ext.157 *Fax* +972 (3) 978 8009

LIKUD PARTY

Email webmaster@likud.org.il
Conservative Political Party. Dedicated to the principles of a free-market economy and the attainment of peace with security while preserving Israel's national interests.
Ch. B. Netanyahu Metsudat Ze'ev, 38 King George Street, Tel Aviv *Tel* +972 (03) 621 0666

MERETZ-YACHAD

Website www.meretz.org.il
Meretz-Yachad was formed in 1992 by a merger of 'Ratz', 'Mapam' and the then 'Shinui'.

It was led by Shulamit Aloni. The party disbanded in 2003 and joined Yossi Belin's 'Shahar' party which renamed itself 'Yachad' but the original name re-emerged in 2005 under Belin's chairmanship. Meretz-Yachad defines itself as a Zionist Green left wing social democratic party. It has inherited Meretz's membership in the Socialist International.
Ch. Yossi Belin
GIL (Pensioners' Party)
Founded 2005, by Rafi Eitan to fight the Knesset Elections, committed to support for pensioners.

NATIONAL RELIGIOUS PARTY
Tel +972 (02) 537 727
Created through the merger of Mizrachi and Hapoel Hamizrachi in 1956. Its motto 'The People of Israel in the Land of Israel, according to the Torah of Israel'. *Ch.* Binyamin Elon

SHINUI ('Change' in English)
Established 1971. A reformist and liberal party. Maintains that the rights of the individual are supreme and that all legislation must be measured against that principle. A democratic, secular, liberal, Zionist, peace-seeking party.
Ch. R. Levinthal 100 Hashmona'im Street, P.O. Box 20533, Tel Aviv 61200 *Tel* +972 (03) 562 0118

AGUDAT ISRAEL
Founded in 1912 in Katowice, Poland. Its principle is that only the Torah unites the Jewish people. *Political Sec.* M. Porush *Central Office* Haherut Sq., Jerusalem *Tel* +972 (02) 384 357 and 5 Bardechefsky Street, Tel Aviv *Tel* +972 (02) 561 7844

SHAS
Founded in 1984 as representing Haredi Sephardi Judaism. The party was formed under the leadership of Rabbi Ovadia Yosef (former Israeli Chief Rabbi), who remains its spiritual leader today. *Ch.* Eli Yishai

YISRAEL BEYTENU
Website www.beytenu.org.il
A right-wing party formed by Avigdor Liberman in 1997 to create a platform for Russian immigrants who support a hard line in negotiations with the Palestinian Authority.

HISTADRUT – GENERAL FEDERATION OF LABOUR IN ISRAEL
93 Arlozoroff Street, Tel Aviv. 62098
Tel +972 (03) 692 1513 *Fax* +972 (03) 692 1512 *Email* histint@netvision.net.il
Ch. Amir Peretz, MK
Histadrut, the largest labour organisation in Israel, is a democratic organisation. It strives to ensure the welfare, social security and rights of working people, to protect them and act for their professional advancement. It endeavours to reduce the gaps in society to achieve a more just society. The executive body of Histadrut is separate from the elected body and the legislative body. The legislative and regulatory body, the Histadrut Assembly, represents the relative strengths of the different political groups of Israel.

Membership is voluntary, and open to all men and women of 18 years of age and above who live on the earnings of their own labour without exploiting the work of others. Membership totals over 600,000, including workers from all spheres, housewives, self-employed and professionals as well as the unemployed, students and pensioners. Workers' interests are protected through a number of occupational and professional unions affiliated to the Histadrut. The Histadrut operates courses for trade unionists and new immigrants and apprenticeship classes. It maintains an Institute for Social and Economic Issues and the International Institute, one of the largest centres of leadership training in Israel, for students from Africa, Asia, Latin America and Eastern Europe. The institute includes the Levinson Centre for Adult Education and the Jewish–Arab Institute for Regional Cooperation. Attached to the Histadrut is a women's organisation, 'Na'amat'. This promotes changes in legislation, operates a network of legal service bureaux and vocational training courses, and runs counselling centres for the treatment and prevention of domestic violence, etc.

Selected Educational and Research Institutions

BAR-ILAN UNIVERSITY
Correspondence BIU, Ramat Gan, Israel 52900
Tel +972 (03) 531 8111 *Student information Tel* +972 (03) 531 8274 *Fax* +972 (03) 535 1522
Website www.biu.ac.il
Since its founding in 1955, Bar-Ilan has grown to become Israel's second-largest university, with a modern 70-acre campus in Ramat Gan, outside Tel Aviv and five regional colleges across Israel. Over 6,000 courses are taught in the faculties of Exact Sciences, Life and Social Sciences, Humanities, Jewish Studies and Law, by 1,300 academic faculty to 25,000 students. Today, Israel's largest schools of educational and social work and the premier Jewish studies faculty operate at Bar-Ilan. Additionally, the university is home to world-class scientific research institutes in Physics, Med. Chemistry, Mathematics, Brain Research, Economics, Strategic Studies, Developmental Psychology, Musicology, Archaeology, Bible, Jewish Law and Philosophy, and more. Some 40 prominent universities around the world maintain academic cooperation agreements with Bar-Ilan. Every day, Israelis of widely varying backgrounds and religious beliefs work and study together in harmony at Bar Ilan. *Chancellor* Rabbi Prof. Emanuel Rackman; *Pres.* Prof. Moshe Kaveh; *Rector* Prof. J. Menis

BEN GURION UNIVERSITY OF THE NEGEV, BEERSHEVA
Founded 1969, the university includes the following faculties: Humanities and Social Sciences, Natural Sciences, Engineering Sciences, Health Sciences, School of Man., the Kreitman School of Advanced Graduate Studies and the Jacob Blaustein Institute for Desert Research. *Pres.* Prof. R. Carmi P.O. Box 653, BeerSheva, 84105 *Tel* +972 (08) 646 1279

CENTER FOR JEWISH ART
Hebrew University of Jerusalem, Mount Scopus, Humanities Building, Jerusalem 91905
Tel +972 (02) 588 2281 *Fax* +972 (02) 540 0105
Email cja@vms.huji.ac.il *Website* http://.lcja.huji.ac.il
Dir. Dr. R. Talgam; *Acad. Ch.* Prof. R. Elior

HAIFA UNIVERSITY
Mount Carmel, Haifa 31905
Tel +972 (04) 824 011 *Fax* +972 (04) 828 8110
Email webmaster@univhaifa.ac.il *Website* www.haifa.ac.il
Established in 1963, Haifa is one of the seven accredited research universities in Israel. Academic instruction is conducted in the framework of the six Faculties (Humanities, Social Science, Law, Social Welfare and Health, Education, Sciences). Most of the 59 departments and schools offer bachelor, master and Ph.D. degrees. Research activity is carried out in the framework of research institute and centres. The Research Authority encourages and coordinates research at the University. *Pres.* A. Ben-Ze'ev; *Rector* Y. Ben-Artzi

HEBREW UNIVERSITY OF JERUSALEM
Mount Scopus, Jerusalem, 91905
Tel +972 (02) 588 2811 *Fax* +972 (02) 588 0058
Website www.huji.ac.il
Founded in 1918 and opened in 1925 on Mount Scopus. When, contrary to the provisions of the Armistice Agreement after the War of Independence in 1949, access to Mount Scopus was denied by Jordan, the University functioned in scattered temporary quarters until a new campus was built on Givat Ram, and a med campus in Ein Kerem, both in Jerusalem. After the Six-Day War of June 1967, the Mount Scopus campus was rebuilt and expanded. Today the University serves some 24,000 students in its seven faculties: Humanities, Social Sciences, Science, Law, Med, Dental Med and Agricultural, Food and Environmental Quality Sciences (the latter located in Rehovot). There are 11 Schools: Education, Business Administration, Nutritional Sciences, Nursing, Occupational Therapy, Pharmacy, Public Health, Social Work, Veterinary Medicine, Library, Archive and Information Studies, and the Rothberg International School. The Jewish National and

University Library is on the Givat Ram campus and there are about 100 research centres. The Magnes Press/Hebrew University publishes scientific and academic works. Five graduates and faculty have received Nobel prizes since 2001. *Ch. Bd. of Govs.* Charles H. Goodman; *Pres.* Prof. Menachem Magidor; *Rector* Prof. Haim Rabinowitch

ISRAEL NATURE AND PARKS AUTHORITY
3 Am Ve'Olamo Stret, Givat Shaul, Jerusalem 95463
Tel 972 (02) 500 5444 *Fax* +972 (02) 652 9232 *Website* www.parks.org.il
The Authority is the result of a merger in 1968 of two bodies, one of which was in charge of the Israeli nature reserves and the other of national parks and heritage sites in Israel.

ISRAEL OCEANOGRAPHIC AND LIMNOLOGICAL RESEARCH
(Est. 1967) To develop knowledge and technology for sustainable use of marine and fresh water resources. *Dir. Gen.* Prof. Barak Herut, Tel Shikmona, P.O.B. 8030, Haifa 31080
Tel +972 (04) 856 5200 *Fax* +972 (04) 851 1911 *Email* barak@ocean.org.il

JERUSALEM ACADEMY OF JEWISH STUDIES - Yeshivat Dvar Yerushalayim
53 Katzenellenbogen Street, Har Nof, P.O.B. 34580, Jerusalem 91344 *Tel* +972 (02) 652 2817 *Fax* +972 (02) 652 287 *Email* dvar@dvar.org.il *Website* www.dvar.org.il
Courses for students without a background in Jewish Learning and more advanced courses. The student body comes from many countries. Students can take part in the Academy's community educational projects. Special features include: Classes in English, Hebrew, Russian, German, French, part-time and summer courses; Kollel and research department; recognised Ulpan; tours of historic sites; and college credits. A special one-year programme, accredited by Touro and other U.S. colleges, for post high school graduates and post 6th formers. *Dean* Rabbi B. Horovitz, MA; UK office (Reg. Charity No. 262716), 1007 Finchley Road, London NW11 7HB *Ch.* A. Maslo *Tel/Fax* 020 8458 8563 *Student Off.* Rabbi Taubman *Tel* 020 8203 0333/07957 650 325 (*See* p. 105)

JERUSALEM COLLEGE OF TECHNOLOGY
Established in 1969 to train engineers and applied scientists within a religious framework. The College has a men's campus in Jerusalem-Machon Lev and Machon Naveh, and 2 campuses for women Machon Tal in Jerusalem and Machon Lustig in Ramat Gan. These have departments in Electro-Optics and Applied Physics, Medical Engineering, Electronic Engineering, Computer Sciences, Technology Management and Marketing, Software Engineering, Teacher Training and Registered Nursing. The men's Jerusalem complex and a Bet Midrash for Jewish studies; a one year yeshiva academic programme for English-speaking students. The women's programmes also include religious studies.
Pres. Prof. J. Bodenheimer; *Rector* Prof. M. Steiner 21 Havaad Haleumi Street, Jerusalem
Tel +972 (02) 675 1111 *Fax* +972 (02) 642 2075 *Email* pr@mail.jct.ac.il

THE LOUIS GUTTMAN ISRAEL INSTITUTE OF APPLIED SOCIAL RESEARCH
Founded in 1946 to advise governmental, public and private bodies on research in social psychology, sociology, psychology and related disciplines. *Scientific Dir.* Professor S. Kugelmass *Tel* +972 (02) 231 421

MIKVEH ISRAEL AGRICULTURAL SCHOOL
Mikveh Israel, Doar Holon, 58910
Tel +972 (03) 842 050
The first agricultural school in Israel, it was founded by Charles Netter of the Alliance Israelite Universelle in 1870. The curriculum, in addition to training in agriculture, comprises instruction in the humanities, Jewish subjects, science, etc.

ORT ISRAEL NETWORK
Head office, 39 King David Boulevard, Tel Aviv 61160 *Tel* +972 (03) 520 3275
Email zvikap@admin.ort.org.il *Website* www.ort.org.il
(Est. 1949) ORT Israel manages Scientific and Tech. Colleges and schools for around 100,000 young and adult students yearly. *Dir. Gen.* Z. Peleg

TECHNION-ISRAEL INSTITUTE OF TECHNOLOGY
Tel +972 (04) 829 4986 *Fax* +972 (04) 823 5195
Website www.technion.ac.il
Established in 1924 as a small technology institute, it now has more than 12,500 students, making it the largest full-service university wholly dedicated to science and technology in Israel. The institute has 19 faculties and department including: Aerospace, Biomedical, Chemical, Civil, Electrical and Industrial Engineering and Architecture, Chemistry, Computer Science and Management, Medicine and Physics. The Technion is located on Mount Carmel. The main buildings include the Winston Churchill Auditorium and the Shine Student Union. It also has a graduate school, a school for continuing education and a Research & Development Foundation. *Pres.* Prof. Y. Apeloig, Technion City, Mount Carmel, Haifa 32000

TEL AVIV UNIVERSITY
Ramat Aviv, Tel Aviv
Tel +972 (03) 545 0111
The university sponsors studies and research in all the arts and sciences and includes, among its faculties, a department of space and planetary sciences. Its observatory, at Mitzpe Ramon in the Negev, was the first in Israel. A science based industry utilising the university's manpower and equipment has been established. Its Graduate School of Business Administration was the first established in the country. There is a one year course which prepares new immigrants for entry into Israeli universities. *Pres.* Prof. Joseph Klafter; *Rector* Prof. Aron Shai

WEITZ CENTER FOR DEVELOPMENT STUDIES
P.O.B. 12 Rehovot, 76100
Tel +972 (08) 947 4111 *Fax* +972 (08) 947 5884
Email training@netvision.net.il *Website* www.ort.org.il
Founded in Rehovot in 1963, its main object is interdisciplinary research & training activities related to regional development in Israel and the developing world.

WEIZMANN INSTITUTE OF SCIENCE
P.O.B. 26, Rehovot 76100
Tel +972 (08) 934 3111 *Fax* +972 (08) 934 107
Website www.weizmann.ac.il
The Institute engages in research in Mathematical Sciences, Chemistry, Physics, Biology, Biochemistry and Science Teaching. *Pres.* Prof. D. Zajfman; *V. Pres.* Prof. H. Garty

THE ZINMAN COLLEGE OF PHYSICAL EDUCATION AND SPORTS SCIENCES AT THE WINGATE INSTITUTE
P.E. College at Wingate Institute, Netanya, Israel 42902
Tel +972 (09) 863 922 *Fax* +972 (09) 865 0960
Email zinman@wincol.macam98.ac.il *Website* www.zin.macam98.ac.il
(Est. 1944) Teachers College for Physical Educators. Offers a four-year Bachelor of Education course, including Teachers' Diploma. Specializes in early childhood, special education, sports for the disabled, posture cultivation, cardiac rehabilitation, physical activity for the elderly, public health, behaviour analysis, dance and movement, leisure and recreation education, nautical education, scouting education and sports media. Joint M.A. programme with Haifa University. Faculty of 200, student body of 900 full-time students, 1,500 in part-time in-service courses.

Selected Commercial Organisations
BANK OF ISRAEL
Email webmaster@bankisrael.gov.il
Set up by the Knesset in 1954. Its functions include those usually discharged by central banks. It issues the currency and acts as Government banker, and manages the official gold and foreign reserves. The governor is chief economic advisor to the Government, Rechov Eliezer Kaplan, Kiryat Ben-Gurion, Jerusalem, 9100 *Tel* +972 (02) 655 2211 *Fax* +972 (02) 652 8805

ISRAEL-AMERICA CHAMBER OF COMMERCE AND INDUSTRY
35 Shaul Hamelech Boulevard, Tel Aviv
Tel +972 (03) 695 2341 *Fax* +972 (03) 695 1272
Email amcham@amcham.co.il *Website* http://amcham.co.il
Exec. Dir. Tamar Guy

ISRAEL-BRITISH CHAMBER OF COMMERCE
29 Hamered Street, P.O. Box 50321, Tel Aviv 61502
Tel +972 (03) 510 9424 *Fax* +972 (03) 510 9540
Email isrbrit@bezeqint.co.il *Website* www.ibcc.co.il
(Est. 1951). *Ch.* L. Judes, *Exec. Dir.* F. Kipper

MANUFACTURERS' ASSOCIATION OF ISRAEL
29 Hamered Street, Tel Aviv 68125
Tel +972 (03) 519 8787 *Fax* +972 (03) 510 3154
Email trade@industry.org.il
Pres. S. Brosh

Other Selected Organisations

ASSOCIATION FOR THE WELLBEING OF ISRAEL'S SOLDIERS
Head Office P.O. Box 21707, Tel Aviv 61217
Overseas Dept 60 Weizman Street, Tel Aviv 62155
Tel +972 (03) 546 5135 *Fax* +972 (03) 546 5145
Email awis@awis.co.il
(Ha'aguda Lemaan Hechayal. Charity No. 580004307) The Association for the
Wellbeing of Israel's Soldiers was founded in 1942, during the Second World War, at a
time when the young men of pre-state Israel were being drafted into the allied armies
and the Jewish Brigade. The slogan back then was 'The Heart of the People is with its
Soldiers', and this sentiment continues to guide the Association's activity today.

BETH HATEFUTSOTH
Tel Aviv University Campus, Ramat-Aviv, P.O.B. 39359, Tel Aviv 61392
Tel +972 (03) 745 7800 *Fax* +972 (03) 745 7891
Email bhwebmas@post.tau.ac.il *Website* www.bh.org.il
The Nahum Goldmann Museum of the Jewish Diaspora, which opened in Tel Aviv in 1978,
tells the story of the Jewish people from the time of their expulsion from the Land of Israel
2,500 years ago to the present. History, tradition and the heritage of Jewish life in all parts
of the world are brought to life in murals, reconstructions, dioramas, audio-visual displays,
documentary films and interactive multi-media presentation. *Dir.* Hasia Israeli

CHIEF RABBINATE
Beit Yahav, 80 Yirmiyahu Street, P.O.B. 36016, Jerusalem 91360
Tel +972 (02) 5313191/531 3190 *Fax* +972 (02) 537 7872
The Chief Rabbinate consists of two joint Chief Rabbis and the Chief Rabbinical Council of
16. *Chief Rabbis* Rabbi Israel Yona Metzger (Ashkenazi) and Rabbi Shlomo Amar (Rishon
Lezion, Sephardi). There are District Rabbinical Courts (Batei Din) in Jerusalem, Haifa,
Petach Tikvah, Rehovot, Tiberias-Safad, Beersheba and Ashkelon.

ISRAEL MOVEMENT FOR PROGRESSIVE JUDAISM (IMPJ)
13 King David Street, Jerusalem 94101
Tel +972 (02) 620 3448
Email info@reform.org.il *Website* www.reform.org.il
The Israel Movement for Progressive Judaism (IMPJ) is Israels liberal Jewish religious
movement, and a constituent member of the World Union for Progressive Judaism.

THE ISRAEL MUSEUM
Ruppin Boulevard, Jerusalem, P.O. Box 71117, Jerusalem 91710
Tel +972 (02) 670 8811 *Fax* +972 (02) 563 1833
Website www.imj.org.il
Israel's leading cultural institute and a museum of world-class status. Its 20-acre campus
houses an encyclopaedic collection of art and archaeology, with special emphasis on the

culture of the Land of Israel and the Jewish people. The Museum has the world's most extensive collections of the archaeology of the Holy Land, Judaica and the ethnography of the Jewish world. It also has significant and extensive holdings in the Fine Arts, ranging from Old Masters to Contemporary Art. There are separate departments for Asian Art, the Arts of Africa and Oceania, Prints and Drawings, Photography, and Architecture and Design. The campus also includes the Shrine of the Book, which houses the Dead Sea Scrolls, the Billy Rose Art Garden and a Youth Wing. *Dir.* James Snyder

JEWISH AGENCY FOR ISRAEL
Tel +972 (02) 620 2080 *Fax* +972 (02) 625 2352
Email zeevik@jafi.org *Website* www.Jewishagency.org
Founded 1929; Reconstituted 1971. Constituents are the World Zionist Organisation, United Israel Appeal, Inc. (USA), and Keren Hayesod. By reasons of its record and world-wide organisation, the Jewish Agency has come to be widely regarded as the representative organisation of Jews the world over, particularly in regard to the development of Israel and immigration to it. The governing bodies of the Jewish Agency are: the Assembly, which lays down basic policy, the Board of Governors, which manages its affairs between annual Assembly meetings, and the Executive, responsible for day-to-day operations. *Ch. Exec.* Ze'ev Bielski; *Ch. Bd.* R. L. Pearlstone; *Dir. Gen.* M. Vigdor; *Sec.-Gen.* J. Schwarcz P.O. Box 92, Jerusalem 91000

KEREN KAYEMETH LEISRAEL (Jewish National Fund)
P.O. Box 283, Jerusalem 91002 *World Ch.* Yehiel Leket; *Dir. Division of Resource and Dev.* Avi Dickstein. (Est. 1901) A non-profit organisation dedicated to the development of Israel through improvement of the quality of life, through afforestation, water conservation, ecology and educational activities.

SHAMIR - ASSOCIATION OF JEWISH RELIGIOUS PROFESSIONALS FROM THE FORMER SOVIET UNION AND EASTERN EUROPE
6 David Yellin Street, P.O.B. 5749, Jerusalem
Tel +972 (02) 538 5384 *Fax* +972 (02) 538 5118
Email shamirbooks@bezeqint.net *Website* www.shamirbooks.org.il
Sec. Bayla Granovsky

STANDWITHUS ISRAEL
King George 58, Jerusalem, Israel 91073
Tel +972 (02) 636 0200 *Fax* +972 (02) 624 0558
Email israel@standwithus.com *Website* www.standwithus.co.il
The international office of StandWithUs. A leader in Israel advocacy with offices and chapters in the United States, Canada, Israel, the UK and Australia. StandWithUs hosts speakers and conferences, offers website resources and creates brochures and materials about Israel that are distributed globally. *Dir.* Michael Dickson

WOMEN'S INTERNATIONAL ZIONIST ORGANISATION (Wizo)
38 David Hamelech Boulevard, Tel Aviv 64237
Tel +972 (03) 692 3717 *Fax* +972 (03) 695 8267
(Reg. Charity No. 580057321). 250,000 women, 100,000 of them in Israel, are members of this organisation which maintains 800 institutions and services in Israel. *World Wizo Pres.* Helena Glaser; *Ch. World Wizo Exec.* Tova Ben-Dov

WORLD ZIONIST ORGANISATION
P.O. Box 92, Jerusalem 91000
Tel +972 (02) 602 2080 *Fax* +972 (02) 625 2352
Founded by Theodor Herzl at the First Zionist Congress in Basle in 1897, it was the moving spirit in the events leading up to the establishment of the State of Israel in 1948. The 'Jerusalem Programme', adopted by the 27th Zionist Congress in Jerusalem in 1968, reformulated the aims of the Zionist Movement as: the unity of the Jewish people and the centrality of the State of Israel in its life. The ingathering of the exiles in the historic Jewish homeland by aliya. The strengthening of the State of Israel, which is founded on the

prophetic ideals of justice and peace. Preserving the uniqueness of the Jewish people by promoting Jewish and Hebrew education and upholding Jewish spiritual and cultural values. Defending the rights of Jews wherever they live. The supreme body of the WZO is the Zionist Congress, to which delegates are elected by members of Zionist Federations abroad and by the Zionist parties in Israel. The two gov. bodies elected by the Congress are: the Executive, and the Zionist General Council to which the Executive is responsible and which decides Zionist policy between Congresses. *Ch. of Exec.* S. Meridor *Email* sallaim@jazo.org.il

YAD VASHEM
Har Hazikaron (Mount of Remembrance), Jerusalem
Tel +972 (02) 644 3400 *Fax* +972 (02) 644 3443
P.O.B. 3477, Jerusalem 91034
Email general.information@yadvashem.org.il *Website* www.yadvashem.org
The Holocaust Martyrs' and Heroes' Authority, Archives, Library, International School for Holocaust Studies, International Institute for Holocaust Research, Holocaust Museum, Art Museum, Hall of Remembrance, Hall of Names, Children's Memorial, Memorial to the Deportees, Avenue and Garden of the Righteous Among the Nations, Valley of the Communities, Visual Centre, Synagogue.

UJIA Israel (incorporating the British Olim Society)
Head Office 76 Ibn Gvirol Street, P.O.B. 16266, Tel Aviv 61162
Tel +972 (03) 696 5244 *Fax* +972 (03) 696 8696
Email israel@ujia.org.il
There are branches in Jerusalem and Karmiel. UJIA Israel is the official representative of the United Jewish Israel Appeal of Great Britain & Northern Ireland, form. known as the British Olim Society (Est. 1949 in order to assist and support new immigrants from the UK settling in Israel).

UJIA Israel represents UJIA UK on all campaign and renewal-related activities and aims at strengthening the ties between British Jewry and Israel, through projects, guests, missions and Israel Experience youth programmes.

UJIA Israel provides comprehensive absorption services to immigrants from the UK, Australia and Scandinavia and promotes the absorption needs of new immigrants in Israel.

During 1990, the BOS Charitable Trust was established as a funding conduit for new immigrant activities and programmes in Israel, essentially aimed at helping the disadvantaged and less fortunate.

Israel English Speaking Legal Experts
P.O. Box 2828, Jerusalem
Tel +972 (02) 582 0126 *Fax* +972 (02) 623 2742
Provides legal advice and representation.

Israel, Britain and the Commonwealth Association (IBCA)
Industry House, 29 Hamored Street, Tel Aviv 68125
Fax +972 (03) 510 4646
Branches in Haifa and Jerusalem. The main aims of the Association are to encourage, develop, and extend social, cultural and economic relations between Israel and the British Commonwealth. *Ch.* L. Harris; *V. Ch.* Dr. A. Lerner; *Hon. S.* Madelaine Mordecai; *Contact* Freida Peled

ITALY

Italy has an ancient connection with the Jews, and was home to one of the earliest Diaspora communities. Before the Roman invasion of ancient Israel, Judah Maccabee had a representative in Rome, and one of the reasons for the invasion was the Romans' desire to access the salt supply from the Dead Sea. There were Jewish communities in Italy after the destruction of the Second Temple, as Italy was the trading hub of the Roman empire. After Christianity became the official religion in 313CE, restrictions began to be placed on the Jewish population, forcing the community to migrate from town to town across the country.

In the medieval period there was a brief flourishing of learning, but the Spanish conquered southern Italy in the fifteenth century, expelling the Jews from Sicily, Sardinia and, eventually, Naples. The first ever ghetto was established in Venice in 1516. Later in the century descendants of those expelled from Spain and Portugal arrived. Conquest by Napoleon led to the emancipation of Italian Jewry, and full equal rights were granted in 1870.

Ironically, the Italian Fascist party contained some Jewish members, as Mussolini was not anti-semitic and, even under pressure from Hitler, did not instigate any major anti-semitic policy. The situation changed after Germany's occupation of the north in 1943. Eventually almost 8,000 Italian Jews were killed in Auschwitz, although the local population hid many of those who survived.

Today there is a central organisation which provides services for Italian Jews. There are kosher restaurants in Rome, Milan and other towns. There are also Jewish schools.

ROME
Central organisation
Unione delle Comunità Ebraiche Italiane, 00153 Roma, Lungotevere Sanzio 9
Tel +39 (06) 4554 2200 *Fax* +39 (06) 589 9569 *Pres.* R. Gattegna
Chief Rabbinate of Rome
Comunita Ebraica di Roma, Lungotevere Cenci, Tempio, 00186
Tel +39 (06) 687 5051/2/3 *Fax* +39 (06) 684 00684
Email segretaria@romacer.org *Website* www.romacer.org
Chief Rabbi Dr. Riccardo Shmuel Di Segni

MILAN
Comunita Ebraica di Milano
Chief Rabbi Alfonso Arbib
Tel +39 (02) 4831 10225
Email direttore@mosaico-cem.it *Website* www.mosaico-cem.it
For more info on synagogues and Jewish travel around Italy, please visit the website http://www.jewisheurope.org/city.asp?City=Milan

JAMAICA
During the time of Spanish colonisation, Jamaica witnessed many *Conversos* arriving from Portugal. After the British took over in 1655 many of these could again practise Judaism openly. Soon other Jews, mainly Sephardim, followed from Brazil and other near-by countries. The community received full equality in 1831 (before a similar step was taken in England).

The Jews played an important role in Jamaican life, and in 1849 the House of Assembly did not meet on Yom Kippur! However, assimilation and intermarriage took their toll and in 1921 the Ashkenazi and Sephardi synagogues combined. There is now only one synagogue on the island, but there are remains of old synagogues in Kingston, Port Royal and other towns.

Community life includes WIZO, B'nai B'rith and a school (the Hillel Academy). The community lost members after the Cuban revolution, because many feared a similar revolution in Jamaica.

United Congregation of Israelites
92 Duke Street, Kingston (walk-in entrance on Charles Street or drive in from John's Lane)
Tel +876 922 5931
Email ChabadOfJamaica@gmail.com *Website* www.ucija.org
United Congregation of Israelites, Synagogue Shaare Shalom
Duke Street (Synagogue built 1885, rebuilt 1911)
Acting Spiritual Leader Stephen C. Henriques *Tel* +1 (809) 924 2451

JAPAN
After Japan became open to Western ideas and Westerners in the mid-nineteenth century, a trickle of Jewish immigrants from the Russian Empire, the UK and the USA began to make their homes there. The first Jewish community at Yokohama was founded in 1860. Many were escaping anti-semitism and by 1918 there were several thousand in the country.

Individual Japanese, despite being allied to Nazi Germany, did not adopt the anti-Semitic attitude of the Nazis, and Chiune Sagihara, the Japanese consul in Kovno, Lithuania, even helped the Mir Yeshivah escape from occupied Europe in 1940.

The post-war American occupation of the country brought many Jewish servicemen, and the community was also augmented by Jews escaping unrest in China. In recent years, there have been some Jewish 'gaijin' (foreign workers).

In Tokyo, there is a synagogue which provides meals on Shabbat, a Sunday school, and offices for the Executive Board of the Jewish Community of Japan, which is the central body.

Jewish Community of Japan
8-8 Hiroo 3-chome, Shibuya-Ku, Tokyo 150-0012
Tel +81 (03) 3400 2559 *Fax* +81 (03) 3400 1827
Email office@jccjapan.orjp
M. Rabbi Henri Noach; Kosher meals available on Shabbat and during the week. Please say in advance if you would like to come.

KAZAKHSTAN

The Jews of Kazakhstan are predominately Russian-speaking Ashkenazim and identify with Russian culture. Many arrived only in the 1940s, fleeing the Nazis or 'exiled' by Stalin. There are a number of Bukharian Jews and Tat (Caucasian Mountain Jews). Some 7,000 Jews now remain in the country. Almaty is the main Jewish centre. Smaller Jewish communities are spread out across this large country, in Karaganda, Chimkent, Astana, Semiplatinsk, Kokchetav, Dzhambul, Uralsk, Aktyubinsk, Petropavlovsk and several villages.

Association of Jewish Communities of Kazakhstan
66/120 Buhar-zhirau Street, Almaty 480057
Tel/Fax +7 (3272) 45 00 43

KENYA

Jewish settlement in East Africa dating from 1903, when the British Government offered the Zionist Organisation a territory in the present Kenya for an autonomous Jewish settlement. The offer was refused but not unanimously and shortly afterwards a few Jews settled in the colony. Later, a number of Central European Jewish refugees settled here. The Jewish population today is about 100 families, most of whom are Israelis, together with others employed in the diplomatic services and NGOs. *See Jews of Nairobi 1903–1962*, by Julius Carlebach. The community marked its centenary with a new history by Cynthia Salvadori 'Glimpses of the Jews of Kenya: the Centennial History of the Nairobi Hebrew Congregation 1904–2004, 5664–5764.

Nairobi Hebrew Congregation
P.O. Box 40990, 00100
Tel +254 (20) 222-770 and 219-703,
Email info@nhc.co.ke *Website* www.nhc.co.ke
(Est. 1904) *Rosh Kehilla* Dr. D. Silverstein; *Hon. T.* M. Abbema; *Hon. S.* Ms A. Zola

KYRGYZSTAN

This central Asian ex-Soviet republic has only a short history of Jewish settlement. The community originated from migrants after the Russian Revolution and evacuees from the German advance into the Soviet Union in the Second World War. As a result, community members are almost all Russian speakers and are assimilated into the Russian minority of the country. Before the collapse of the Soviet Union there was no organised community. There has been a synagogue in the capital Bishkek since 1991, where there is also a Jewish library and an Aish Ha Torah centre. The main umbrella group is the Menorah Society of Jewish Culture.

Jewish Community of Bishkek
Karpinskogo str. 193, Bishkek, Kyrgyzstan 720000
Tel +99 (312) 681 966

LATVIA

The Jews in the medieval principalities of Courland and Livonia represent the earliest Jewish settlement in Latvia. Tombstones from the fourteenth century have been found. After the Russian take-over Jews were only allowed to live in the area if they were considered 'useful', or had lived there before the Russians took control, because the area was outside the 'Pale of Settlement' that the Russian Empire had designated for the Jews.

The Jews contributed much to Latvia's development, but this was never recognised by the government, which tried to restrict their influence in business matters. Religious Jewish life, however, was strong. When the Nazis invaded Latvia, 90 per cent of the 85,000 Jews were systematically murdered by them and their Latvian collaborators.

The bulk of today's community originates from immigration into Latvia after the war, although 3,000 Holocaust survivors did return to the country. Before the collapse of communism there was much Jewish dissident activity. There is a Jewish school and a Jewish hospital. There are some Holocaust memorial sites in the capital Riga, and also in the Bierkernieki Forest, where 46,000 Holocaust victims were shot.

Chabad Lubavitch Community of Latvia
Lachplesha str. 141, Riga, Latvia LV1003
Tel +371 720 4022
http://www.chabadcenters.com/riga

Jewish Community Centre, Museum and Library (LOEK)
6 Skolas Street 226050
Tel +371 6728 9580
Com. Leader A, Suharenko

The Riga Synagogue
Lachplesha str. 141, Riga, Latvia LV1003
Tel +371 720 5313

LEBANON

During the civil war, which broke out in 1975, most of the 2,000 Jews left the country. About 100 remain in Beirut.

LIBYA

About the time that Libya became an independent State in 1951 there was a mass emigration of most of its 37,000 Jews to Israel, and only very few remain in Tripoli.

LITHUANIA

The history of Lithuanian Jewry is as old as the state of Lithuania itself. There were Jews in the country in the fourteenth century, when Grand Duke Gedeyminus founded the state. The community eventually grew, and produced many famous yeshivas and great commentators, such as the Vilna Gaon. The community began to emigrate (particularly to South Africa) at the beginning of the nineteenth century; even so, in 1941 there were still 160,000 Jews in the country. Ninety-five per cent of these were murdered in the Holocaust by the local population as well as the Nazis.

The remaining post-war community included some who had hidden or had managed to survive by other means, and some Jews from other parts of the Soviet Union. Interestingly, the Lithuanian Soviet Socialist Republic was more tolerant of Jewish activity than some of the neighbouring republics, such as Latvia. Now that Lithuania is independent, Jewish life is free once again.

The Lubavitch movement is present, and there are synagogues in the capital Vilnius (known to many as Vilna) and Kaunas. There is also a school and it is possible to study Yiddish. There are tours available to show the old Jewish life in Lithuania. The grave of the Vilna Gaon can be visited, as well as Paneriai, otherwise known as Ponary, where thousands of Jews were shot during the Holocaust.

Jewish Community of Lithuania
Pylimo Street 4, 01117 Vilnius

Tel +370 (521) 613 003
Email office@litjews.org or jewishcom@post.5ci.lt
There are also communities in Druskininkai, Klaipeda, Panevezys and Shiauliai.

LUXEMBOURG

The small community in Luxembourg faced massacres and expulsions during medieval times, and Jews only began to resettle here several hundred years later. Napoleon heralded the rebirth of the community when he annexed Luxembourg, and by 1823 a synagogue had been built but the community remained small, although in 1899 another synagogue was built. Later, many refugees from the Nazis arrived in the country, bringing the number of Jews to nearly 4,000. After the Nazi take-over 750 Luxembourg Jews were killed, but many others were saved by the local population.

The present community is generally prosperous and assimilated. The Consistoire Israelite, established by Napoleon, is recognised by the government as the representative of the community, and is also financed by the government. The Orthodox synagogue is situated fairly centrally in Luxembourg City.

Chief Rabbi
Joseph Sayagh, 45, Ave Montery
Ch. M. Bulz *Tel* +352 452 314
Or Chadash Liberal Jewish Community (affiliated to LJ)
Correspondence 29 rue Leandre Lacoix, 1-1913
Tel +352 316 594
Email lljc@liberaljudaism.org
Ch. Erica Peresman
Chabad Lubavitch du Luxembourg
Rav Mendel Edelman
6 rue Albert 1er, L-1117 Luxembourg
Tel +352 2625 9316
Email info@lubavitch.lu *Website* www.lubavitch.lu

MACEDONIA (Republic)

The Jewish presence in Macedonia (form. Yugoslavia) dates back to the 6th century B.C.E. with a considerable influx during the Roman Second-Temple period. The largest migration of Jews to Macedonia took place in the early Ottoman period following the expulsions from Spain and Portugal. In such cities as Bitola, Shtip and Skopje, Jews came to prosper in med. law and trade, as well as more traditionally in agriculture. By 1910 there were more than 90,000 Jews in Macedonia, mostly in Salonika (now Greek Thessaloniki, q.v.), by which time Ladino was widely spoken in that city, and the Shabbat was widely observed throughout all sectors. When Greece took over the city in 1912, prohibitions on residence were brought in and a mass emigration to other parts of Europe and to North America began. Nonetheless, even in 1941 there were over 100,000 living in Macedonia when the effects of the Nazi-domination of Europe and the pressures of the Holocaust took their toll. Those who survived Auschwitz and Treblinka mostly settled in Israel and few returned to Macedonia. Today's community is mainly based in the capital Skopje, but there is little access to Jewish life. However, the community does have contact with Jews in Serbia and Greece.

The Macedonian Jewish Community after a long period of 60 years, has a new native Rabbi born in Macedonia, Avi M. Kozma (27 years old), a student of the Chief Rabbi of the Jewish Community in Serbia Isak Asiel, who was also Rabbi of Macedonia. Rabbi Kozma, was inaugurated on 5 May 2008 at the Macedonian Synagogue "Beth Yaakov".

SKOPJE
Jewish Community of the Republic of Macedonia
Borka Talevski Street, No. 24, 1000
Tel +389 (2) 321 4799 *Fax* +389 (2) 321 4880
ezrm *Pres.* Z. Sami; *Gen. Sec.* Z. Mucheva

Synagogue "Beth Ya'akov"
Borka Talevski Street, No. 24, 1000
Tel +389 (2) 323 7543
Chief Rabbi Rabbi A.M. Kozma (2008-)

MALTA

There have been Jews in Malta since pre-Roman times and, just before the Spanish-directed expulsion in 1492, one-third of the population of the then capital city, Mdina, was Jewish. After the coming of the Knights of St John, the only Jews in Malta became their captives and slaves, held for ransom. This situation persisted until Napoleon overthrew the Knights and released all their prisoners. Following the defeat of the French by the British, a small Jewish community was established early in the nineteenth century which has survived until the present day. There were never more than about 20 families with a normal total of under 100 people, and it was financially unable to build a synagogue. However, following a successful appeal, launched in 1998, local and international donations enabled the acquisition and conversion of premises into a Jewish Centre and Synagogue. The Malta Jewish Community now, once again, owns its own property, after a gap of over 500 years.

Jewish Community of Malta
182/2 St. Ursula Street, Valletta, P.O. Box 42, Birkirkara
Tel +356 676 926 *Fax* +356 676 926
Email jewsofmalta@digigate.net

MARTINIQUE

SCHOELCHER
Kenafe Haarets A.C.I.M.
12 rue de l'Ecole Hoteliere 97233
Tel +596 616 672
There is a Community, which supplies kosher food, plus a kosher meat restaurant.

MAURITIUS

There is no permanent Jewish community. The Jewish cemetery contains the graves of 125 refugees from Europe. They were part of a group of 1,700 Jews denied entry to Palestine and interned on the island during 1940-1945.
Corres. P. M. Birger P.O. Box 209, Port Louis, Mauritius *Tel* +230 202 0200 *Fax* +230 208 3391

MEXICO

Conversos were the first Jews in the country, and some achieved high positions in early Spanish colonial Mexico. As the Inquisition was still functioning there some 200 years after the sixteenth century, the number of Jewish immigrants was small. When Mexico became independent Jews gradually began to enter the country, coming from German and other European communities.

It was during the twentieth century that most Jewish immigrants entered Mexico. There were both Ashkenazim and Sephardim, and they settled throughout the country. The communities grew parallel, rather than together, with two languages, Yiddish and Ladino.

The current community is largely middle class, and all the various factions come under the Comite Central Israelita. There are numerous synagogues and there are also kosher restaurants. The community is well equipped with Jewish schools and yeshivas.

MEXICO CITY
Central Committee of the Jewish Community in Mexico
Cofre de Perote 115, Col. Lomas Barrilaco, 11010 Mexico DF
Tel +52 (55) 209 393 *Fax* +52 (55) 403 050
Exec. Dir. Mauricio Lulka *Email* comitecentral@prodigy.net.mx

CANCUN
Chabad-Lubavitch of Cancun
Cancun, 77500 Mexico
Co-Dir. Rabbi Mendel Druk
Tel +51 (998) 219 5601

MOLDOVA

Chisinau, the capital of the republic of Moldova, was part of the former Soviet Union and became a flourishing Jewish centre in the 18th century when a growing economy presented new commercial and industrial opportunities.

By the turn of the century, there were 16 Jewish schools with 2,100 students and 70 synagogues.

In 1903, 49 Jews were massacred by frenzied mobs. Hundreds were seriously injured; thousands were left homeless and property damage was measured in millions of gold rubles. In 1905 a second pogrom claimed the lives of another 19 Jews. A flood of emigration began, which continued through the interim war years.

The devastation of the Jewish community of Chisinau was completed by the Nazis who killed 53,000 of the 65,000 Jewish inhabitants of the city. Communism brought more restrictions to the remaining Jews. In 1964, all synagogues were closed, except one - the one which is used today.

Towns with Jewish populations include: Baltsy, Bendery, Dubossary, Chisinau, Orxey, Rybnitsa, Rezina, Soroky and Tiraspol.

CHISINAU
Federation of the Jewish Communities
Str. Alecsandri, 125 apt. 2, Chisinau, Moldova 2012
Tel +373 (22) 541 023 *Fax* +373 (22) 541 020
Website www.moldova.org
Chief Rabbi of Kishinev and Moldova Rabbi Zalman Abelsky *Email* Rabbiabelsky@kishinev.org

MONACO

Some French Jews lived in Monaco before 1939, and the government issued them with false papers during the war, thus saving them from the Nazis. This tiny country has also attracted retired people from France, North Africa and the UK.

There is an official Jewish body, the Association Culturelle Israelite de Monaco, and there is a synagogue, a school and a kosher food shop. Half of the total Jewish population are Ashkenazi and the other half are Sephardi. 60 per cent of the community is retired.

The Jewish Community of Monte Carlo
Association Culturelle Israelite de Monaco
15 Avenue de la Costa, 98000 Monte Carlo

MOROCCO

There were Jews in Morocco before it became a Roman province (they first arrived after the destruction of the Temple in 587 BCE). Since the first century, the Jewish population settled in Morocco has increased steadily, owing to several waves of immigration from Spain and Portugal following the expulsion of Jews by the Inquisition in 1492.

Under Moslem rule, the Jews experienced a general climate of tolerance, although they did suffer some persecution. During the Vichy period in the Second World War, Sultan Mohammed V protected the community. Almost 250,000 Jews have emigrated to Israel, Canada, France, Spain and Latin America, but they maintain strong links with the Kingdom. Since ancient times the Jewish community has succeeded in cohabiting harmoniously with the Berber and then with the Arab community. Today the present Jewish population is an active community, playing a significant role in Moroccan society, although they have declined in number.

CASABLANCA
Community Offices
12 rue Abou Abdallah Al Mahassibi
Tel +212 (2) 222 2861 *Fax* +212 (2) 226 6953
There are also communities in Fez, Kenitra, Marrakech, Meknès, Rabat, Tangier, Tetuan, and Agadir.
Chabad Lubavitch au Maroc
10 Rue Washington
Tel +212 (2) 269 037 Fax +212 (2) 201 233

MOZAMBIQUE

The small community in Mozambique originally consisted of South African Jews who were forced out of South Africa by President Kruger for supporting the British at the beginning of the twentieth century. The synagogue was opened in 1926, and there is a cemetery in Alto Maha. The biggest Jewish community is in Maputo.

NAMIBIA

Namibian Jewry began at the time when the country was a German colony before the First World War. The cemetery at Swakopmund dates from that settlement. Keetmanschoop also had a congregation, but this no longer exists. The Windhoek synagogue is still in use, and was founded in 1924. Services are held on Shabbat and festivals. South Africa provides some help for the community, such as a cantor on festivals. The Cape Board of Jewish Education assists with Hebrew education. From approximately 100 Jewish families in the 1920s and 1930s, the number has dwindled.

WINDHOEK
Windhoek Hebrew Congregation
P.O. Box 140, Windhoek
Tel +266 (61) 221 990 *Fax* +264 (62) 226 444

NEPAL

Nepal has no Jewish history. It is however well visited by Israeli and other young Jewish tourists. Each year a large Seder is organised by the Lubavitch movement. In 2000 approximately 1,000 attended at the Radisson Hotel.

KATHMANDU
Chabad House Synagogue
GHA 2-516-4 Thamel 3
Tel +977 (1) 470 0492

NETHERLANDS

Although some historians believe that the first Jews in Holland lived there during Roman times, documentary evidence goes back only to the twelfth century. The contemporary settlement occurred when Portuguese *Marranos* found refuge from the Inquisition in Holland. Religious freedom was advocated in the early seventeenth century and Jews contributed much to the Netherlands' 'golden age' of prosperity and power. The Sephardi community in London was closely associated with Amsterdam.

By the time of Napoleon, the community had grown to 10,000 (the largest in Western Europe), mainly by incoming Jewish traders from Eastern Europe. The Jews were emancipated in 1796, but the community began to decline slowly during the nineteenth century. Of the 140,000 Jews (including 30,000 German Jewish refugees) in Holland in 1939, the Nazis transported 100,000 to various death camps in Poland, but the local Dutch population tended to behave sympathetically towards their Jewish neighbours, hiding many. Anne Frank and her family are the most famous of the hidden Jews from Holland. Amsterdam witnessed a strike in February 1941, called as a protest against the Jewish deportations.

Today there are four Jewish councils in the Netherlands representing the Ashkenazi,

Sephardic, Reform and Orthodox communities. There are many synagogues in Amsterdam, as well as synagogues in other towns. Amsterdam also has many historical sites: Anne Frank House, the Portuguese Synagogue, still lit by candlelight, and the Resistance Museum.

Rabbinate Ashkenazic Community: Amsterdam Chief Rabbi Aryeh L. Ralbag, Dayan Eliezer Wolff, Rabbi Shmuel Katz (secr), Rabbi Zvi Spiero **The Hague** Rabbi Shmuel Katzman, **Rotterdam** Rabbi Raphael Evers, **Other communities** Chief Rabbi Binyomin Jacobs **Rabbinate Sephardic Community** Rabbi Dr. P. Toledano.
Rabbinate Liberal Jewish Congregations Rabbi D. Lilienthal (Amsterdam); Rabbi A. Soetendorp (The Hague); Rabbi Dr E. van Voolen (Arnhem)

AMSTERDAM
Anne Frank House Prinsengracht 267 **Judith Drake Library** at the Liberal Community Centre. There are other small communities are in Amersfoort, Arnhem, Bussum, Eindhoven, Groningen, Haarlem, The Hague, Rotterdam, Utrecht and Zwolle.
Ashkenazi Community Centre and Offices
Van der Boechorststraat 26, 1081 BT
Tel +31 (20) 646 0046 *Fax* +31 (20) 646 4357
Email info@nihs.nl
Liberal Community Centre and Synagogue
J. Soetendorpstraat 8, 1079 *Tel* +31 (20) 642 3562 *Fax* +31 (20) 642 8135
Amsterdam and Dutch Liberal Rabbinate *Tel* +31 (20) 644 2619 *Fax* +31 (20) 642 8135
Sephardi Communal Centre
Visserplein 3, 1011 RD
Tel +31 (20) 624 5351 *Fax* +31 (20) 625 4680
Email info@esnoga.com

NETHERLANDS ANTILLES (West Indies)

CURAÇAO
A Sephardi Jewish settlement was established in 1651, making it the oldest community in the New World. The Mikve Israel-Emanuel Synagogue building, which dates from 1732, is the oldest in continuous use in the Western Hemisphere; there is a small Jewish museum in the synagogue compound. About 350 Jews live in Curaçao. The cemetery (Bet Hayim) at Blenheim (Est. 1659) is the oldest in the Americas.
Synagogue Mikvé Israel-Emanuel
P.O. Box 322, Curaçao
Tel +599 (9) 461 1067 *Fax* +599 (9) 465 4141
Email information@snoa.com *Bd. of Dir.* directiva@snoa.com *Rabbi* rabbi@snoa.com

NEW CALEDONIA
The Jewish community in New Caledonia is predominately located in Noumea. The Jewish community was established in 1987. This relatively new community is composed of 50 Sephardi immigrants from France. Most of the Jews work in commercial businesses or in the state government. There is one synagogue in Noumea and one Jewish community center, Association Culturelle Israelite de Nouvelle Caledonie. Kosher food is imported from Australia.

NEW ZEALAND
The settlement of Jews in New Zealand dates from the establishment of British sovereignty in 1840. In the first emigrant ships were a number of Jews from England. But still earlier a few Jewish wayfarers had settled in the northern part of New Zealand, including John Israel Montefiore, a cousin of Sir Moses Montefiore, who settled at the Bay of Islands in 1831, Joel Samuel Polack, one of the earliest writers on the country, in which he travelled in 1831-37, and David Nathan, who laid the foundations of the Jewish community in Auckland in the early 1840s.

The Wellington Jewish community was founded by Abraham Hort, under the authority of the Chief Rabbi, on January 7, 1843, when the first Jewish service was held. Communities were later established in Christchurch and Dunedin and other parts of the South Island. From the earliest times Jewish settlers have helped to lay the foundation of the commercial and industrial prosperity of the country.

The number of Jews in New Zealand at the census of 2001 was over 8,000. Most live in Auckland and Wellington. There has been recent settlement from the former Soviet Union, South Africa and Israel.

Today the community has six synagogues, four on the North Island and two on the South Island. Auckland and Wellington have Jewish day schools, and the 'Kosher Kiwi Guide' is published in Auckland. There has been recent Jewish immigration from South Africa.

WELLINGTON
Hebrew Congregration
80 Webb Street *Pres.* G. Stone *Tel* +64 (4) 384 5081
Jewish Community Centre
80 Webb Street Moriah Kindergarten open daily.
Progressive Jewish Congregation (Temple Sinai)
P.O. Box 27 176
Tel +64 (04) 385 0720

AUCKLAND
Beth Israel Synagogue
108 Greys Avenue P.O. Box 68 224 *Tel* +64 (9) 373 2908
(Est. 1841).
Beth Shalom
The Auckland Congregation for Progressive Judaism, 180 Manukau Road Epsom
Email bshalom@ihug.co.nz *Website* www.bethshalom.org.nz
Pres. L. Lipman
Hebrew Congregation
Pres. J. Barnett P.O. Box 68 224 *Tel* +64 (9) 373 2908

NORWAY

The only way Jews could enter Norway before the nineteenth century was with a 'Letter of Protection', as Danish control limited the amount of Jewish entry. The situation changed in 1851 when a Norwegian liberal poet, Henrik Wergeland, argued for the admission of Jews into the country, and the parliament eventually agreed. There were only some 650 Jews in the country after emancipation in 1891, mainly in Oslo and Trondheim. By 1920 the community numbered 1,457, and by the time of the Nazi invasion there were 1,800. Despite attempts by the Norwegian resistance to smuggle Jews to Sweden, 767 Jews were transported to Auschwitz, although 930 were able to reach Sweden. The Jewish survivors were joined after the war by Displaced Persons, especially invited by the Norwegian government.

The current situation forbids shechita, but there are no other restrictions on Jewish life. There is a synagogue in Oslo, and a kosher food shop. There is also a Jewish magazine. An old-age home was built in 1988. Trondheim, in the north of the country, has the northernmost synagogue in the world

Chief Rabbi Michael Melchior (Honorary position since he left in 1986 and lives in Israel now.)

Det Mosaiske Trossamfund (Jewish Community)
Bergstien 13 0172 Oslo
Tel +47 (2) 320 5750 *Fax* +47 (2) 320 5781
Website www.dmt.oslo.no
Pres. A. Sender *Email* adam@dmt.oslo.no
Synagogue and Community Centre
Bergstien 13, Oslo 0172 Postbooks 2722, St Hanshaugen, 0131
Synagogue and Community Centre

Ark. Cristiesgt. 1, Trondheim
Tel +47 (7) 352 6568
Pres. R. Abrahamsen

PANAMA

Some Jews, most of them pretending to be Christians, came to Panama during colonial times. Panama was an important crossroads for trade and, as a result, many Jews passed through the country on their journeys in the region.

In 1849 immigrant Sephardi Jews in Panama founded the Hebrew Benevolent Society, the first Jewish congregation in the Isthmus. They came from the pious congregation of the Netherlands Antilles (Curaçao) to settle in Panama.

Jews from Saint-Thomas (Virgin Islands) and Curaçao founded in 1876 the Kol Shearith Israel Synagogue in Panama City, and in 1890 the Kahal Hakadosh Yangacob in Colon.

By the end of the First World War a number of Middle Eastern Jews had settled in the country and founded the Israelite Benevolent Society Shevet Ahim. During the Second World War immigrants from Europe arrived in Panama, establishing Beth-El, the only Ashkenazi community in the country. The majority of the Jewish community is Sephardi (around 80%). There have been two Jewish presidents in Panama, the only country – apart from Israel – where this has happened.

Beth El (Conservative)
Apartado 3087, Panama 3, Panama City
Consejo Central Comunitario Hebreo de Panama
Apartado 55-0882-Paitilla, Panama City
Tel +507 (2) 638 411 *Fax* +507 (2) 647 936
Contact Pres. Sion Harari *Email* sion@plazareg.com
Kol Shearith Israel (Reform)
Apartado 4120, Panama City
Tel +507 (2) 254 100 *Fax* +507 (2) 256 512
There are smaller communities in Colon and David.

PARAGUAY

Jewish settlement in this land-locked country came late for this area of South America. The few who came over from Western Europe at the end of the nineteenth century rapidly assimilated into the general population. The first synagogue was founded early in the twentieth century by Sephardim from Palestine, Turkey and Greece. Ashkenazim arrived in the 1920s and 1930s from Eastern Europe, and some 15,000 came to the country to escape Nazism, intending to move on into Argentina. Some of these settled in Paraguay.

Paraguay, in more recent times, has accepted Jews from Argentina who were fleeing from the military regime.

Today there are three synagogues, a Jewish school and a Jewish museum in Asuncion. There is a high rate of intermarriage, but children of mixed marriages may receive a Jewish education.

Consejo Representativo Israelita del Paraguay (CRIP)
General Diaz 657. Asuncion, P.O.B. 756
Tel +595 (21) 41744

PERU

The first Jews in Peru arrived with the first Europeans, as many *Conversos* were officers in the Spanish army which invaded the country in 1532. After the Inquisition was set up in 1570 the Jews were persecuted, and many were burned alive. From 1870 groups of Jews came over from Europe, but tended to disappear into the general population. In 1880, a group of North African Jews settled in Iquitos and worked in the rubber industry. More Jewish immigration occurred after the First World War and later, refugees from the Nazis entered the country. By the end of the Second World War the Jewish population had reached 6,000, but this subsequently declined.

Almost all of the present Jewish population are Ashkenazi. There are two Jewish newspapers and most Jewish children go to the Colegio Leon Pinelo school, which is well known for its high standards. There is a cemetery at Iquitos built by the nineteenth-century community. The community is shrinking owing to intermarriage and assimilation.

LIMA

Chabad Lubavitch de Peru
Avenue Salaverry 3075, Lima, 27 Peru
Tel +51 (1) 264 6060
Fax +51 (1) 264 5499

Gan Chabad
Ave. Salavemy 3095
Lima, 27 Peru
Tel +51 (1) 422 0082
Fax +51 (1) 221 1628

Synagogue and Communal Centre
Húsares de Junin 163 (Jesus Maria), Lima *Tel* +51 (1) 241 412/312 410

KASHRUT INFORMATION
Chief Rabbi Abraham Benhamu *Email* abenhamu@gmail.com

Union Israelita del Peru (Orthodox Ashkenazi)
210 Carlos Porras Osores, San Isidro
Tel +51 (1) 421 3684
Email unionisraelita@gmail.com *Website* www.kosherperu.com

Kosher Peru
Manuel de la Fuente 676, Barranco, Lima - 04
Tel +51 (1) 251 9628
Website http://www.kosher.pe/

CEMETERY
Bena Vista Cemeterio
Av. O.R. Benavides 2215, Callao
Tel +51 (1) 429 0731
Monday - Thursday 8.30am to 4pm, Friday 8.30am to 12pm, Sunday 8.30am to 1pm

PHILIPPINES

Conversos who came with the Spanish in the sixteenth century were the first Jewish presence in the region. In the late nineteenth century, western European Jews came to trade in the area, and after the Americans occupied the country in 1898 more Jews arrived from a variety of places, including the USA and the Middle East. The first synagogue was built in 1924. The Philippines accepted refugees from Nazism, but the Japanese occupied the islands during the war and the Jewish population was interned. After the war many of the community emigrated. However, a new synagogue opened in 1983, and services are also held in the US Air Force bases around the country.

Jewish Association of the Philippines (Beth Yaakov Synagogue)
110 H.V. de la Costa, crn. Tordesillas West, Salcedo Village, Makati City, Metro Manila 1227
Tel Office +63 (2) 815 0265 Rabbi Eliyhau Azaria *Tel* +63 (2) 815 0263 *Fax* +63 (2) 840 2566
Email jap.manila@gmail.com
Services on Monday and Thursday mornings, Shabbat and all holidays. *Pres.* Paul Rosenberg

POLAND

After just five years of German occupation in the Second World War the thousand-year-old Jewish settlement in Poland, one of the largest Jewish communities in the world, had been almost totally eradicated. Jews came to Poland in order to escape anti-semitism in Germany in the early Middle Ages. They were initially welcomed by the rulers, and Jews became greatly involved in the economy of the country.
Until 1918 most Jews lived in the east and south of the country, under Russian and Austrian

domination, respectively. After 1918 Poland became an independent country once more, with over 3,000,000 Jews (300,000 in Warsaw.) The community continued to flourish before 1939, with Yiddish being the main language of the Jews. The community was destroyed in stages during the war, as Poland became the centre for the Nazi's destruction of European Jewry. After the war, the borders shifted again, and the 100,000 or so survivors mostly tried to emigrate. The few who remained endured several pogroms even after the events of the Holocaust.

Today the community is comparatively small and most of the members are elderly, but there is a functioning synagogue in Warsaw and many Jewish historical sites are scattered throughout the country. The Polish Tourist Board publishes information about the Jewish heritage in Poland.

WARSAW
Secular Organisation
Towarzystwo Spoleczno-Kulturalne Zydów w Polsce (Social and Cultural Association of Jews in Poland), Zarzad Glowny (Central Board), Warsaw, 00-104, Plac. Grzybowski 12/16
Tel +48 (22) 20 05 57/20 05 54
Synagogue and Religious Organisation
Zwiazek Religijny Wyznania Mojzeszowego (Religious Union of Mosaic Faith)
Warsaw 00-105. ul. Twarda 6
Tel +48 (22) 20 43 24/20 06 76

PORTUGAL

Portuguese Jewry had a parallel history to Spanish Jewry until the twelfth century, when the country emerged from Spain's shadow. Jews worked with the Portuguese kings in developing the country. However, they were heavily taxed and had to live in special areas, although they were free to practise their religion as they pleased. As a result the community flourished. Persecution began during the period of the Black Death, and the Church was a key instigator of the riots which broke out against the Jews. After the Inquisition in neighbouring Spain many Jews fled to Portugal, but were expelled in 1497. Many Jews converted in order to remain in the country and help with the economy. These became the Portuguese 'Conversos' and some of their descendants are converting back to Judaism today.

Over the last century and a half Jews have begun to re-enter the country, and many others used it as an escape route to America during the last war. Most of the community are Sephardi, and there is a Sephardi synagogue in Lisbon. There is also a central Jewish organisation which is a unifying force for Jews in the country.

LISBON
Communal Offices
Rua do Monte Olivete, 16 r/c 1200-280 Lisbon
Tel +351 (21) 393 1130 *Fax* +351 (21) 393 1139
Email secretaria@cilisboa.org *Website* www.cilisboa.org
Jewish Centre
Rua Rosa Araujo 10
Tel +351 (21) 357 2041

PUERTO RICO

The Jewish community in Puerto Rico is just over 100 years old, with the first Jews arriving from Cuba in 1898 after the beginning of American rule. During the Second World War, many Jewish American servicemen went to the island, along with refugees from Nazism. The Jewish Community Centre dates from the early war years. After the war the community grew with an influx of Cuban and American Jews.

The capital, San Juan, has the largest Jewish population, and there are two synagogues. There is also a Hebrew school held in the Community Centre. The first Chief Justice of Puerto Rico was Jewish.

Shaare Zedeck Synagogue (Conservative) and **Community Centre**
903 Ponce de León Avenue Santurce, P.R. 00907-3390
Tel +1 (787) 809 724 4110   *Fax* +1 (787) 722 4157
Temple Beth Shalom (Reform)
101 San Jorge & Loiza Street, Santurce, P.R. 00911
Tel +1 (787) 721 6333

ROMANIA

Jews have been resident in the territory that now forms Romania since Roman times. Today they number 10,000, of whom some 4,000 live in Bucharest, and the rest in 160 communities. There are 42 synagogues, three of them in Bucharest, 11 Talmud Torahs and 8 kosher restaurants. A newspaper in Hebrew, Romanian and English, *Realitatea*, with a circulation of 4,500, is published fortnightly. There is a Yiddish theatre in Bucharest, the publishing house Hasefer, a Museum of Jewish History and a Holocaust Exhibit.

BUCHAREST
Federation of Jewish Communities
Centre of Romanian Jewish History Research Mamulari Str., 4, Etaj 1, Apt. 1, Sectorul 3,
Tel/Fax +40 (21) 315 1045
Dir. D. Hîncu

RUSSIA (Russian Federation)

In early Russian history Jews were not allowed to settle, and the few who did were later expelled by various Czars. After 1772, however, Russia acquired a large area of Poland, where lived a significant number of Jews. There were still restrictions against the Jews, but eventually they were allowed to settle in the 'Pale of Settlement', an area in the west of the Russian Empire. Between 1881 and 1914 2,000,000 Jews emigrated from the Empire, escaping from anti-semitism.

Jews were only allowed into Russia itself in the mid-nineteenth century, and by 1890 there were 35,000 Jews in Moscow. Most were expelled the following year. The community grew after the Second World War, drawing Jewish immigration from Belarus and Ukraine to cities such as Moscow and Leningrad. Birobidzhan was a failed experiment to give the Jews their own 'Autonomous District', and those who moved there (in the far east, near China) soon moved away. Under communism both religious practices and emigration were restricted, but since 1991 there has been a revival in Jewish learning. There are synagogues functioning in many cities, and there are now 100 Jewish schools. The major threat is still from anti-semitic right-wing groups, who are unfortunately increasing their activity.

MOSCOW
Rabbinical Alliance of the CiS
Central Office 5A 2nd Vysheslavtzev Pereulok, Moscow, Russia, 127055
Tel +7 (495) 737 8275 *Fax* +7 (495) 783 8471 Rabbi Berel Lazar
Email lazar@jewish.ru *Website* www.fjc.ru
Rabbinical Court of Moscow
Chief Rabbi Pinchas Goldschmidt
Tel +7 (095) 923 4788
Email kasher@post.ru *Website* www.kasher.ru
World Union for Progressive Judaism - Orosir
2 Usevolovsky Pereulot, Entrance 1, Moscow 119034
Email wupj-orosir@yandex.ru
Rabbi Gregory Kotlyar

ST PETERSBURG
Jewish Association 'LEA'
Ryleeva 29-31, 191123
Tel +7 (812) 275 6104 *Fax* +7 (812) 275 6103
Other centres of Jewish population include those of Astrakhan, Berdichev, Berehovo,

Birobidzhan, Irkutsk, Krasnoyarsk, Kuybyshev, Kursk, Malakhavka, Nalchik, Novosibirsk, Ordzhonikidze, Penza, Perm, Rostov, Saratov, Sverdlovsk, Tula.

SERBIA (Republic)

Jews have lived in this territory since Roman times. In 1941 there were about 34,000 Jews in the territory of the former Yugoslavia and some 29,000 perished in the Holocaust.

BELGRADE (BEOGRAD)
Federation of Jewish Communities of Serbia
Ulica Kralja Petra 71a, III, 11000 Belgrade P.O.B. 512 Belgrade
Tel +381 262 1837/291 0363 *Fax* +381 262 6674
Email office@savezscg.org
Pres. A. Nećak; *Sec.* D. Danon
Jewish Community of Belgrade
Ulica Kralja Petra 71a/II
Tel +381 262 2449 *Fax* +381 262 4289
Email jcb@ikomline.net
Pres. Miroslav Herzog *Tel* +381 262 3535/328 1468
Communities also in Kikinda, Novi Sad, Niš, Panševo, Priština, Sombor, Subotica, Zemun and Zrenjanin.

SINGAPORE

As Singapore developed into an important south-east Asian trading centre in the mid-nineteenth century, some Jewish traders from India and Iraq set up a community there in 1841. A synagogue was built in 1878, and another in 1904. By the time of the Japanese occupation in the Second World War the community had grown to 5,000, and included some Eastern European Jews. The Japanese imprisoned the community and took their property. After the war emigration to Australia and the USA reduced numbers, but in recent years Israelis who work in the country and other Jews have moved in. Ninety per cent of the community are Sephardi. David Marshall, who was a POW in Japan, returned to Singapore and in 1955 became Chief Minister.

One of the two synagogues is used regularly, and there is a mikveh and a newsletter. The Sir Manasseh Meyer Community Centre is the hub of Jewish life. The Jewish community today is small and mainly composed of professionals.

Jewish Welfare Board
24/26 Waterloo Street, 187950
Tel +65 (9) 337 2189 *Fax* +65 (9) 336 2127
Tel +65 (9) 731 2181 Rabbi Mordechai Abergel
Pres. Jacob Ballas. *Hon. S.* M. Whelan
Email enquiries@jwb.org.sg *Website* www.singaporejews.com

Synagogue Maghain Aboth
24 Waterloo Street, 187950
Tel +65 337 2189 *Fax* +65 336 2127
Email jewishwb@singnet.com.sg
Open daily except Monday mornings. Mikveh available.
Com. Rabbi Mordechai Abergel *Tel* +65 737 9112 *Email* mordehai@singnet.com.sg

United Hebrew Congregation (Reform)
65 Chulia Street, OCBC Centre #31-00 East Lobby, 049513
Pres. K. Lewis *Tel* +65 536 8300

SLOVAKIA

Slovakia has passed through the control of various countries over the centuries, finally gaining independence after the peaceful splitting of Czechoslovakia in 1992. Before 1918 the region was part of Hungary, and many in southern Slovakia, near the Hungarian border still speak Hungarian.

In 1939 the Jewish population in the Slovak area of Czechoslovakia numbered 150,000, but the Hungarians occupied the south of the country and assisted the Germans in deporting Jews to Auschwitz and other camps. Many survivors emigrated after the war, but some remained and are now rediscovering their Jewish heritage. Since independence, B'nai B'rith and Maccabi have been established, but anti-semitism has re-emerged. There are kosher restaurants in Bratislava and Kosice, and Jewish education is available once more.

BRATISLAVA
Bratislava Jewish Community
Kozia 18, 81103 Bratislava
Tel +421 (2) 5441 6949
Email noba@znoba.sk
Central Union of Jewish Religious Communities (UZZNO)
Hon. Ch. Prof Pavel Traubner, PhD.; *Exec. Ch.* Fero Alexander Kozia 21/II, 81447 Bratislava
Tel +421 (2) 5441 2167 *Fax* +421 (2) 5441 1106
Email uzzno@netax.sk

KOSICE
Jewish Religious Community
Zvonárska 5, 04001 Kosice
Kosher restaurant, Mikveh. *Pres.* Dr P. Sitar *Tel/Fax* +421 (5) 5622 1272

There are Jewish communities in Galanta, Dunajska Streda, Presov, Banska Bystrica, Nove Zamky, Komarno, Zilina, Nitra.

SLOVENIA

Maribor was the centre for medieval Jewish life in what is now Slovenia. Expulsion followed after the Austrian occupation in the late Middle Ages, but in 1867 the Jews in the Austrian empire were emancipated and some returned to Slovenia. The community was never large. During the Second World War the members of the small Jewish community either escaped to Italy, fought with the Yugoslav partisans, or were deported.

After WW2, the Jewish Community of Slovenia was formed and was attached to the Federation of Yugoslav Jewish Communities until Slovenia's secession in 1991. In 1997, the first official Jewish Community office since WW11 was bought and the community activities increased. In 1999 Rabbi Ariel Haddad was inaugurated as the first Chief Rabbi of Slovenia in history.

Today, Slovenian Jews gather for the major Jewish Holidays and Festivals, and there are lectures and dancing classes. A cultural and educational bulletin is published monthly and there is a Youth group, which organises Shabbatot, educational events and outings.

Traces of Jewish history are to be found in Lendava, and there is a restored (but non-functioning) synagogue in Maribor.

Jewish Community of Slovenia
Tržaška, 1000 Ljubljana
Tel/Fax +386 61 221 836
Email judovska.skupnost@siol.net *Website* wwwjewishcommunity.si

SOUTH AFRICA

Although some believe that Jews were present in the country at around the time of the first European settlement in the area in the seventeenth century, the community only really began in the nineteenth century when religious freedom was granted. In 1836 the explorer Nathaniel Isaacs published 'Travels and Adventures in Eastern Africa', an important contemporary account of Zulu life and customs.

The year 1841 saw the first Hebrew Congregation in Cape Town, and the discovery of diamonds in the Transvaal later in the century prompted a wave of Jewish immigration.

The main immigration of Jews into South Africa occurred at the end of the nineteenth century, when many thousands left Eastern Europe, the majority from Lithuania (40,000 had arrived by 1910). Although the country did not officially accept refugees from the Nazis, about

8,000 Jews managed to enter the country after their escape from Europe.
Today the community is affluent and has good relations with the government. There is a South African Board of Deputies, and many international Jewish associations are present in the country. There are kosher hotels and restaurants, and Jewish museums. Kosher wine is produced at the Zaandwijk Winery.

COMMUNAL INSTITUTIONS
Lubavitch Foundation of S.A.
55 Oaklands Road, Orchards 2192 Johannesburg
Tel +27 (11) 640 7561
Mizrachi Organisation of S.A.
P.O. Box 29189, Sandringham 2131
Tel +27 (11) 640 4420
S.A. Jewish Board of Deputies
2 Elray Street, Raedene, 2192, P.O. Box 87557, Houghton 2041
Tel +27 645 2523 *Fax* +27 645 2559
Email sajbod@beyachad.co.za *Website* www.jewishsa.co.za *Nat. Dir.* W. Kahn
S.A. Union for Progressive Judaism
P.O.B. 1190, Houghton 2041
Tel +27 (11) 646 7903 *Fax* +27 (11) 646 7904
Email saupj@worldonline.co.za
Union of Orthodox Synagogues of South Africa
P.O. Box 46559, Orange Grove 2119, Johannesburg
Tel +27 (10) 214 2600 *Fax* +27 (11) 640 7528
Email info@uos.co.za *Website* www.uos.co.za
Incorporating the Johannesburg Beth Din, Kashrut Division, Office of the Chief Rabbi, Jews for Judaism and Jewish Tradition. Rabbi Dr. W. Goldstein, Chief Rabbi of South Africa

CAPE TOWN
Union of Orthodox Synagogues of S.A. and Beth Din
191 Buitenkant Street
Tel +27 (21) 461 6310 *Fax* +27 (21) 461 8320
Exec. Dir. M. Glass

SOUTH KOREA
About 25 Jewish families live in Seoul, the capital.
Religious services are held on Friday evenings at the 8th U.S. Army Religious Retreat Centre. *Tel* +82 7904 4113

SPAIN
Spain has an ancient connection with the Jews, and the term 'Sephardi' originates from the Hebrew word for Spain. Beginning in Roman times the Jews have suffered the usual cycle of acceptance and persecution, with a 'golden age' under the Islamic Moorish occupation which began in 711. Great Jewish figures arose from the Spanish community, such as Ibn Ezra and the Rambam. However, the situation changed when the Christians gained the upper hand, and blood libels began. In 1492, almost 100 years after a particularly violent period of persecution, the Jews were expelled from Spain. Many thousands were baptised but practised Judaism in secret *(the Conversos)*, and thousands were caught doing so and burnt at the stake.

Jewish life began again in the nineteenth century. The Inquisition ended in 1834 and by 1868 Spain had promulgated religious tolerance. Synagogues could be built after 1909, and Spain accepted many thousands of Jewish refugees before and during the Second World War. Angel Sanz-Briz alone helped to save thousands of Hungarian Jews by issuing 'letters of protection' and entry visas.

There has been a recent immigration from North Africa, and the community today has a central body and synagogues in several towns (including Torremolinos and Malaga).

Rambam's ruined synagogue in Cordoba can be visited, and there are several other old synagogues throughout the country.

BARCELONA
Barcelona: Comunidad Israelita de Barcelona
Avenir, 24 08001
Tel +34 (93) 200 8513
Email info@cibonline.org *Website* www.cibonline.org
Chabad Lubavitch de Barcelona
Calle Joan Gamper 27, Barcelona, 08014 Spain
Tel +34 (93) 410 0685 *Fax* + 34 (93) 419 9151
Email Chabad-liber@ctv.es *Website* wwwjabadbarcelona.org
Rabbi Libersohn

MADRID
Comunidad Judía de Madrid
Balmes, 3-28010
Tel +34 (91) 591 3131 *Fax* +34 (91) 594 1517
Email secretaria@comjudiamadrid.org *Website* www.comjudiamadrid.org
Federación de Comunidades Judias de España
Miguel Angel 7, 1˚C 28010 Madrid
Tel +34 (91) 700 1208 *Fax* +34 (91) 391 5717
Email fcje@fcje.org *Website* www.fcje.org
Benidorm Comunidad Judía de Alicante
C/ Berlín Edificio Parque Loix 3500 Benidorm *Contact* Harvey Bourne
Email hbourne@telrefonica.net
Las Palmas de Gran Canaria
Pres. Bendahan, Ap. Correos 2142, Las Palmas 35080
Mallorca: Comunidad Judía de Baleares
Monsenyor Palmer 3 – 07014 – Palma de Mallorca *Contact* Abraham Barchilón
Email a.barchilon@wanadoo.es
Malaga: Comunidad Israelita de Malaga
Duquesa de Parcent, 8, 3º 29001 Alameda Principal, 47, 2ºB. *Pres.* Mr Hayon
Email cimalaga@cimalaga.org
Marbella: Comunidad Judía de Marbella
Jazmines 21 (Urb. El Real) – 29600 – Marbella *Tel* +34 (952) 859 395 *Fax* +34 (952) 765 783
Email cimarbella@yahoo.es *Pres.* Mr. Cohen
Melilla: Comunidad Israelita de Melilla
Duquesa de la Victoria, No19, 52001 *Tel* +34 (952) 674 057
Seville: Comunidad Israelita de Sevilla
41003-Bustos Tavera, 8 *Tel* +34 (95) 427 5517
Email communidadjudiaesevilla@hotmail.com
Valencia: Comunidad Israelita de Valencia
Ingeniero Joaquin Benlloch 29 2ª˜ 46006- Valencia
Email civ@ctv.es
Tenerife
38001-Jewish Community, P. Abecasis, Ap. de Correos 939, Villalba Hervas, Santa Cruz de Tenerife
Torremolinos: Comunidad Israelita de Torremolinos
Av. Palma de Mallorca 55, 29620 *Tel* +34 (952) 602 583
Pres. Mr Stern *Email* rs@yonah-by.info

SRI LANKA
Solid evidence for Jewish settlement was recorded about 1.000 years ago by Muslim travellers. There was a small Jewish community when the Dutch took the island as a colony. This attracted Jews from southern India to the island because of the possibility of trade.
There was a plan put forward when the island came under British rule for mass Jewish immigration. The Chief Justice, Sir Alexander Johnston appeared to consider the idea a serious

one, but the British government did not act on it. A coffee estate was founded in 1841 near Kandy by European Jews.

There is no communal organization on the island. The Sri Lankans appear supportive of Israel, despite the government's official pro-Arab stance. Diplomatic relations with Israel were resumed in May 2000.

Correspondence A. Ranasinghe, 82 Rosmead Place, Colombo 7 *Tel* +94 (11) 269 5642

SURINAM

Surinam is one of the oldest permanent Jewish settlements in the Western Hemisphere. The Sephardi Congregation was established about 1661, but earlier settlements in 1632, 1639 and 1652 have been reported. Some 225 Jews are members of the two synagogues, where Sephardi services are conducted.

Synagogue and Office
Keizerstraat 82 - 84, Paramaribo
Tel +597 472 817
Email isrgem@cq-link.sr

SWEDEN

Sweden was under the influence of the Lutheran church until the late eighteenth century, and was opposed to Jewish settlement. Aaron Isaac from Mecklenburg in Germany, a seal engraver, was the first Jew admitted into the country in 1774. The emancipation of Jews in Sweden was a slow process; Jews had limited rights, as they were designated a 'foreign colony'. After a gradual lifting of restrictions in the nineteenth century Jews were fully emancipated in 1870, although the right to hold ministerial office was closed to them until 1951. The emancipation heralded the growth of the community, and many Eastern European Jews found refuge in Sweden at the beginning of the twentieth century. The initial refusal to accept Jews fleeing the Nazis changed to sympathy as evidence for the Holocaust mounted, and in 1942 many Jews and other refugees were allowed into the country, followed, in 1943, by almost all of Danish Jewry. Sweden also accepted Hungarian, Czechoslovakian and Polish Jews after the war.

There is an Official Council of Jewish Communities in Sweden, and many international Jewish groups are represented. There are three synagogues in Stockholm, including the imposing Great Synagogue built in 1870. There are synagogues in other large towns. Although shechita is forbidden, kosher food is imported, and there are some kosher shops.

Official Council of Jewish Communities in Sweden
Wahrendorffsgatan 3b, 10391 Stockholm
Tel +46 (8) 5878 5800

GÖTEBORG
Judiska Församlingen (Jewish Community)
Östra Larmgatan 12, 411 07
Tel +46 (31) 109 400 *Fax* +46 (31) 711 9360
Email kansli@judiskaforsamlingen.se *Website* www.judiskaforsamlingen.se

MALMÖ
Judiska Församlingen (Jewish Community)
Box 4198,203 13
Tel +46 (40) 611 8460 *Fax* +46 (40) 23 4469
Email jfm@algonet.se

STOCKHOLM
Judiska Församlingen (Jewish Community)
Wahrendorffsgatan 3, Box 7427, 103 91 Stockholm
Tel +46 (8) 5878 5800 *Fax* +46 (8) 5878 5858
Email kansli@jfst.se *Website* www.jfst.se

SWITZERLAND

Swiss Jewry originated in medieval times and their history followed the standard course of medieval European Jewry: working as money-lenders and pedlars, attacked by the local population, who accused them of causing the Black Death, then resettling a few years afterwards, only to be subsequently expelled.

By the late eighteenth century, when the Helvetic Confederation was formed, there were three small communities. Freedom of movement was allowed, and full emancipation was granted in 1866. Theodor Herzl held the first World Zionist Conference in Basle in 1897. Although Switzerland accepted some refugees from Nazism, many were refused, and most of the new refugee Jewish population emigrated soon after the war. The community today has a central body and is made up of various factions, from ultra-Orthodox to Reform. The major towns have synagogues and kosher meat is imported. There are several hotels with kosher facilities. Over half of the community live in the German-speaking area, the French-speaking area has the second largest number, and a small population is found in the southern Italian-speaking area.

Switzerland elected its first Jewish (and first female) president, Ruth Dreifuss in1998. In 2001 it was reported that evidence had been found of an early Jewish presence in the country; a ring bearing images of a menorah and a ram's horn dating from 200CE.

Swiss Federation of Jewish Communities
PO Box 2105, 8027 Zurich
Tel +41 (43) 305 0777 *Fax* +41 (43) 305 0766
Email info@swissjews.org *Website* www.swissjews.org

BASEL
Basel Community Centre
Leimenstrasse 24
Tel +41 (61) 279 9850
Email igb@igb.ch *Website* www.igb.ch

BERNE
Berne Communal Centre and Synagogue
Kapellenstrasse 2
Tel +41 (31) 381 4992
Email info@jgb.ch *Website* www.jgb.ch
M. Rabbi D. Polaner

GENEVA
Geneva Communal Centre
21av. Dumas 1206
Tel +41 (22) 317 8900
Email secretgen@comisra.ch

LAUSANNE
Lausanne Communal Centre
3 Avenue Georgette Case Postale 336, 1001 Lausanne
Tel +41 (21) 341 7240
Email secretariat@cilv.ch *Website* www.cilv.ch

Synagogue
1 Avenue Juste-Oliver (corner Avenue Florimont) *Tel* +41 (21) 311 7168

ZURICH
Zürich Communal Centre
Lavaterstrasse 33, 8002
Tel +41 (44) 283 2299
Email info@icz.org *Website* www.icz.org

SYRIA

The remnants of this historic Jewish community, living in Damascus, Aleppo and Kamishli, have been estimated at 1,500, following recent aliyah.

DAMASCUS

Pres. of Rabbinical Court Rabbi Ibrahim Hamura, Ecole Ben-Maymoun, Kattatib. Al-Ittihad Al-Ahlieh School (Alliance Israélite), rue El Amine

TAHITI (FRENCH POLYNESIA)

The first known Jew in Tahiti was Alexander Salmon, the son of a Rabbi from Hastings (England), who arrived in 1841 and later married the Queen's sister. No community developed however until the 1960s when refugees came from Algeria.

Tahiti Synagogue
121196 Temple Dorette Assael, Rue Morenhout, Quartier Fariipiti, Papeete
Tel +689 437 156 *Fax* +689 433 086
Email sabbherv@mail.pf

TAIWAN

The US Army brought the first Jews to Taiwan in the 1950s, when an American base was set up in the country. In the 1970s some Jewish businessmen began to work on the island, serving two- or three-year contracts with their companies. Most are Americans, although there are some Israelis and other nationalities. Services are held on Shabbat in a hotel, and there is a Jewish community centre.

Taiwan Jewish Community Centre
Information F. Chitayat *Tel* +886 (2) 861 6303 c/o Donald Shapiro, Trade Winds Company, P.O. Box 7-179, Taipei 10602, Taiwan *Tel* +886 (2) 396 0159 *Fax* +886 (2) 396 4022
Email dshapiro@topz.ficnet
Services are held at Landis Hotel, 41 Min Chuan East Road, Sec. 2 Taipei. For details contact Rabbi Dr E. Einhorn at *Tel* +886 (2) 597 1234 *Fax* +886 (2) 596 9223 *Email* einhorn@ttn.net

TAJIKISTAN

One of the former Soviet Republics, Tajikistan has a small Jewish population. After the fall of the Soviet Union, many Jews emigrated to Israel. The community is a mix of 40 per cent Bokharans and 60 per cent Soviet Jews from other parts of the former USSR who migrated to Tajikistan during the Second World War. The Bokharan Jews are believed to be descendants of Persian Jewish exiles. Dushanbe, the capital, and Shakhrisabz are provided with synagogues, and Dushanbe also has a library.

Jewish Community of Dushanbe
Nazima Khikmata Street, 26 Diushanbe 7340001
Tel +7 (372) 217 658

THAILAND

Although the first confirmed presence of Jews in Thailand was in 1890, Thai Jewry really began with Jews escaping Russia and Eastern Europe in the 1920s and 1930s, although most of them emigrated after 1945.

The present community arrived in the post-war period of the 1950s and 1960s. They came from Syria and Lebanon, and also from Europe and America. Some Israelis also came, and jewellery is an important source of trade with Israel. Another relatively large influx came in 1979, as Jews left Iran after the fall of the Shah.

Bangkok has Ashkenazi, Sephardi and Lubavitch synagogues. The community centre is based in the Ashkenazi synagogue. The Lubavitch synagogue offers several communual activities, including Seders at Passover, which have a large attendance.

Jewish Association of Thailand
Beth Elisheva Synagogue, Mikveh and Jewish Centre
121 Soi Sai Nam Thip 2, Sukhumvit 22, Bangkok
Tel +66 (2) 663 0244 *Fax* +66 (2) 663 0245
Email rabbi@jewishthailand.com
Jewish Community of Thailand
121 Soi Sai Nam Thip 2, Sukhumvit Soi 22 Bangkok, Thailand
Tel +66 (2) 663 0244 *Fax* + 66 (2) 663 0245
Email rabbi@jewishthailand.com *Website* www.jewishthailand.com
Rabbi Yosef C Kantor
Ohr Menachem-Chabad
96 Ram Buttri Road, Kaosarn Road, Banglampoo
Tel +66 (2) 629 2770 *Fax* +66 (2) 629 1153
Website www.jewishthailand.com
Daily services. *M.* Rabbi Y. Kantor

TRINIDAD AND TOBAGO

Jewish links go back to 1658 when Portuguese Jews from Livorno and Amsterdam settled there. Most of them left by the end of the 17th century. Portuguese Jews from Venezuela and Curaçao settled in Trinidad in the 19th century. The names of many Catholic families are traceable to 'conversos' of the earlier period. In the mid-1930s some 800 Jews sought temporary refuge in Trinidad and Tobago from Nazi persecution in Germany and Austria and later from other parts of Nazi - occupied Europe. Those with German and Austrian passports were subject to internment between 1940 and 1943. Numbers have dropped since with only a few Jews living there now.
Correspondence Hans Stecher, c/o The Tackle Shop, 176A Western Main Road, Carenago, Trinidad, W.I. (Caribbean) *Tel/Fax* +1 (868) 637 3870

TUNISIA

There is written proof of ancient Jewish settlement in Carthage in the year 200CE, when the region was under Roman control. The community was successful and was left in peace. Under the Byzantine Empire conditions for the Jews worsened, but after the Islamic conquest the 'golden age' of Tunisian Jewry occurred. There was prosperity and many centres of learning were established. This did not continue into the Middle Ages, as successive Arab and Spanish invasions led to discrimination. Emancipation came from the French, but the community suffered under the Nazi-influenced Vichy government. After the war many emigrated to Israel or to France and the community is currently shrinking.
There are several synagogues in the country, together with kindergartens and schools. Tunisia is not as extreme in its attitude towards Israel as some Arab states, and there has been communication between the two countries at a high level. An Israeli Interest Bureau in Tunis acts as an unofficial embassy. The Bardo Museum in Tunis has an exhibition of Jewish ritual objects.

TUNIS
Chabad Lubavitch of Tunisia Website
73 Rue de Palestine, Tunis
Tel +216 (71) 782 536 *Fax* +216 (71) 344 099
Grand Rabbinat de Tunisie
26 Rue Palestine, Tunis
Community Offices, 15 Rue du Cap Vert

TURKEY

There have been Jews in Turkey since at least the fourth century BCE, making Turkey one of the earliest Jewish communities. The fifteenth and sixteenth centuries were periods of major prosperity for the Jews of Turkey.
After the expulsion of the Jews from Spain in 1492, at a time when Jews were not tolerated

in most of the Christian countries of Western Europe, what was then the Ottoman (Turkish) Empire was their principal land of refuge. The Sultan was reported to have said of the Spanish King: 'By expelling the Jews, he has impoverished his country and enriched mine'. During the Second World War Turkey was neutral and accepted those Jews able to enter it.

ISTANBUL
Chief Rabbinate
Yemenici Sok. No. 23 Tünel, Beyoglu
Tel +90 (212) 293 8794/5 *Fax* +90 (212) 244 1980
Chief Rabbi Isak Haleva
Communal Centre
Büyük Hendek Sokak No. 61, Galata
Tel +90 (212) 244 1576 *Fax* +90 (212) 292 0385
There are ten charitable and social institutions, six youth clubs, a high school and an elementary school in Istanbul. Synagogues also in Izmir, Ankara, Bursa and Adane.

TURKMENISTAN
Although some 2,500 Jews lived in Turkmenistan in 1989, many have now emigrated and less than 1,000 remain today, mostly in the capital city, Ashkhabad.

UKRAINE
Federation of Jewish Communities of the CIS Central Office
5A 2nd Vysheslavtzev Pereulok, Moscow, Russia, 127055
Tel +7 (495) 737 8275 *Fax* +7 (495) 783 8471
Website http://www.fjc.ru/communities/communities.asp?aid=80062
KIEV
Association of Jewish Organisations
Kurskaya ul. 6, r. 42 03049
Tel +38 (044) 248 3670
Email vaad-ua@ukr.net
Association of Progressive Jewish Congregations in Ukraine
01023 Kiev-23, P.O.B. 517
Tel +38 (044) 234 2215, *Tel/Fax* +38 (044) 234 8482 *Email* ravdukh@alfacom.net
'Hatikva' Congregation, M. Rabbi A. Dukhovny

Other towns with Jewish centres include Bershad, Chernigor, Chernovtsy, Kharkov,Kremenchug, Lviv, Odessa, Simferopol, Uzhgorod and Zhitomir.

ODESSA
Jewish Community of Odessa
Osipova str. 21, 651125, Odessa
Tel +38 (048) 728 0770
Email odessachabad@gmail.com

UNITED STATES OF AMERICA
The first Jews came to what is now the United States of America in 1654. The ship had come from the West Indies and included 23 Jews from Brazil, attempting to escape the arrival of the Inquisition, following Portugal's recapture of Brazil from the Dutch earlier that year. It is believed they thought they were travelling to Amsterdam in the Netherlands, rather than to New Amsterdam (as New York was then called). Within ten years, however, the community was moribund. The surrender of New Amsterdam to the British in 1664 brought substantial changes to the Jewish settlement, as some restrictions to both civil and religious rights were lifted. In a few colonies they were even granted the right to vote.

Following the English takeover, communities were established along the eastern coast, and by 1700 there were between 200 and 300 Jews in the country. At the time of the Revolution there were between 1,500 and 2,000 Jews and they served both in the Militia (which was compulsory) and as officers and soldiers. In the decades immediately before the Civil War, the Jewish population rose from 15,000 to 150,000 as a result of emigration, mainly from German areas. During that war Jews served on both sides with their respective communities.

Immigration was at its peak between 1880 and 1925 (when free emigration ended) and during this period the Jewish population grew from 280,000 to 4,500,000. Unfortunately, during the 1930s, only a small number of the Jewish refugees trying to escape from Germany were able to enter the USA. America's numerical position in world Jewry has declined, with its population being in 1948 as much as ten times the population of Israel, to its current approaching parity. The largest concentration by far has always been in New York.

Each of the main religious groups has its own association of synagogues and rabbis and, unlike many other countries, there is no central religious organisation. There is therefore no central supervision of kashrut. Instead there are many hashgachot issued by both individual local communal organisations and rabbis, as well as by companies who issue such certificates on a commercial basis. Travellers may always check with a local rabbi to ascertain the appropriate supervisory body in a relevant location.

For general information about the American Jewish Community write to the UJA
UJA - Federation Resource Line 130E 59th Street, New York 10022
Tel +1 (800) 852 3337 *Email* resourceline@ujafedny.org *Website* www.ujafedny.org

REPRESENTATIVE ORGANISATIONS
American Jewish Committee
165 E. 56th Street, New York City, 10022
Email bandlerk@ajc.org
American Jewish Congress
National Headquarters 825 Third Avenue, Suite 18, New York, NY 10022
Tel +1 (212) 879 4500 *Fax* +1 (212) 758 1633
Email contact@ajcongress.org
Conference of Presidents of Major Jewish Organizations
633 Third Avenue, New York, NY 10017
Tel +1 (212) 318 6111
Email info@conferenceofpresidents.org
Consultative Council of Jewish Organizations
15W 16th Street, 6th Floor, New York, NY 10011
Tel +1 (917) 606 8260
Co-ordinating Board of Jewish Organizations
1640 Rhode Island Avenue, N.W. Washington, DC 20036
United Jewish Communities Federations of North America
P.O. Box 30, Old Chelsea Station, New York City, NY 10113
Email info@ujc.com
World Confederation of Jewish Community Centers
15 E. 26th Street New York City, NY 10010
World Jewish Congress
501 Madison Avenue, 17th Floor, New York City, NY 10022
Tel +1 (212) 755 5770

RELIGIOUS ORGANISATIONS
Agudath Israel of America
84 William Street, New York City, 10038
Central Conference of American Rabbis
355 Lexington Avenue, New York City, 10017-6603
Tel +1 (212) 972 3636 (Reform)
Lubavitcher Headquarters
770 Eastern Parkway, Brooklyn, NY 11213 New York
Board of Rabbis, 10 E. 73rd Street, New York City, 10021

Rabbinical Alliance of America (Orthodox)
305 Church Avenue, Brooklyn, NY 11218
Tel +1 (718) 871 4534
Email info@rabbinicalalliance.org

Rabbinical Assembly (Conservative)
3080 Broadway, New York City, 10027
Tel +1 (212) 280 6000
Email info@rabbinicalassembley.org

Rabbinical Council of America (Modern Orthodox)
305 Seventh Avenue, 12th Floor, New York, NY 10001
Tel +1 (212) 807 9000
Email office@rabbis.org

Reconstructionist Rabbinical Association
1299 Church Road, Wyncote, PA 19095
Tel +1 (215) 576 5210 *Fax* +1 (215) 782 8805
Email info@therra.org

Union of American Hebrew Congregations
633 Third Ave, New York City, NY 10017
Tel +1 (212) 650 4000
Email uahc@uahc.org

Union of Orthodox Jewish Congregations
Eleven Broadway, New York, NY 10004
Tel +1 (212) 563 4000
Email info@ou.org

Union of Orthodox Rabbis
235 E. Broadway, New York City, NY 10002

Union of Sephardic Congregations
8 W 70th Street, New York City, NY 10023

United Synagogue of America (Conservative)
820 Second Avenue, New York, NY 10017
Tel +1 (212) 533 7800
Email info@uscj.org

World Union for Progressive Judaism
633 Third Avenue, 6th Floor, New York, NY 10017
Tel +1 (212) 452 6530
Email wupj@urj.org

Jewish National Fund
42 E. 69th Street, New York City, NY 10021
Tel +1 (888) 563 0099
Email communications@jnf.org

World Zionist Organization
American Section, 515 Park Avenue, New York City, NY 10022

EDUCATIONAL AND CULTURAL ORGANISATIONS

Center for Cultural Judaism
80 Eighth Avenue, Suite 206, New York, NY 10011
Tel +1 (212) 564 6711
Website www.culturaljudaism.org

Center for Holocaust Studies
Documentation & Research, 1610 Avenue J., Brooklyn, NY 11230

Center for Jewish History
15 West 16th Street, New York City, NY 10011
Tel +1 (212) 294 6160 *Fax* +1 (212) 294 8302
Website www.cjh.org
The Center has brought together American Jewish Historical Society, American Sephardi

Federation, Leo Baeck Institute, Yeshiva University Museum and YIVO Institute for Jewish Research to create the largest single repository for Jewish history in the Diaspora. It has over 500,000 volumes and over 100 million documents. Tours are available.

Holocaust Museum and Learning Center
12 Milestone Campus Drive 63146, St Louis
Tel +1 (314) 432 0020 *Fax* +1 (314) 432 1277
Website www.hmlc.org
Open 10am to 5.30pm.

URUGUAY

After the *Conversos* in the sixteenth century, there was no known Jewish community in Uruguay until the late nineteenth century when the country served as a stop-over on the way to Argentina. The Jewish population rose in the twentieth century, with immigration from the Middle East and eastern Europe. A synagogue was opened by 1917. Despite restrictive immigration laws imposed against European Jews fleeing Nazism, 2,500 Jews managed to enter the country between 1939 and 1940. Further Jewish immigration followed from Hungary and the Middle East in the post-war period.

There are many Jewish organisations functioning in Uruguay, including Zionist and women's organisations. Kosher restaurants exist in Jewish institutions, and there are a number of synagogues.

There is a Museum of the Holocaust (Museo del Holocausto, Uruguay) which was the first one in South America and the only one until the year 2000. It is situated in the Comunidad Israelita del Uruguay, Canelones 1084 Ground Floor and on its 3rd floor, there is an institution which involves mainly survivors of the Shoa. It is the Centro Recordatorio del Holocausto. There is also a Memorial of the Holocaust in the promenade in Montevideo. There are also communities at Maldonado and Paysandu.

The Jewish Community is vibrant and active in Uruguay. Each community maintains its own synagogues. There are two Jewish schools and an ORT University.

MONTEVIDEO
Comite Central Israelita Del Uruguay (CCIU)
Rio Negro 1308 P5 Esc. 9, 11100 Montevideo
Tel +598 (2) 901 6057/902 9195 *Fax* +598 (2) 900 6562
Email cciu@cciu.org.uy *Website* www.cciu.org.uy

UZBEKISTAN

The ancient Jewish community in this central Asian republic is believed to have originated from Persian exiles in the fifth century. The Jews were subject to harsh treatment under the various rulers of the region, but still managed to become important traders in this area, which straddled the route between Europe and China and the Far East. In the late Middle Ages Jewish weavers and dyers were asked to help in the local cloth industry, and Buhara became a key Jewish city after it became the capital of the country in the 1500s. Once the area had been incorporated into the Russian Empire in 1868, many Jews from the west of the Empire moved into Uzbekistan. A further influx occurred when Uzbekistan was used to shelter Jews during the Nazi invasion of the Soviet Union, and many subsequently set up home there.

The original Bukharan Jews are generally more religious than the Ashkenazim who entered the area in the nineteenth and twentieth centuries. There are Jewish schools in the area, and although there is no central Jewish organisation, there are many Jewish bodies operating on separate levels for the Ashkenazim and the Buharans.

BUHARA
Jewish Community of Buhara
Tcentralnaya str. 20, Buhara, Uzbekistan
Tel +998 (365) 224 2380
Website www.fjc.ru/buhara

Buharian Jewish Community
9 Chkalova Street, Tashkent, 100031 Uzbekistan
Tel +998 (71) 256 6336
Website www.fjc.ru/tashkent

SAMARKAND
3,000 Jews live in Samarkand. Many are Bukharan and live in the special mahala, the quarter designated for Jews.

Synagogue Gumbaz
Gumbaz 2-i Ilyazarov proezd 1, Samarkand, Uzbekistan
Tel +998 (66) 223 6516
Website www.fjc.ru/samarkand

Jewish Community of Samarkand
Respublikanskaya str. 45, Samarkand, 703000 Uzbekistan
Tel +998 (66) 233 1145/236 8392
Website www.fjc.ru/samarkand

TASHKENT
Jewish Community of Tashkent
15/17 2-ya Kunaeva Street, Tashkent, 700015 Uzbekistan
Tel +998 (71) 152 5978 *Fax* +998 (71) 120 6431
Website www.fjc.ru/tashkent
Dir. Rabbi Abba D. Gurevitch

Lubavitch in Uzbekistan & Asia
30 Balakiereva Street (Shohjahon tor –kuchasi), 15 Second Mirobad Street 100100
Tel +998 (71) 253 9640/252 5978 *Fax* +998 (71) 120 6431
Email gurevitchabad@jewishuz.org *Website* www.jewishhuz.com
Central organisation: Lubavitch

Lubavitch in Uzbekistan & Central Asia
30 Shokhzhakhon Street, Tashkent, 100100 Uzbekistan
Tel +998 (71) 152 5978 *Fax* +998 (71) 120 6431
Website www.fjc.ru/tashkent

VENEZUELA

Settlement in Venezuela began in the early nineteenth century from the Caribbean. The Jews were granted freedom early (between 1819 and 1821), which encouraged more settlement. The community at that time was not religious. At the beginning of the twentieth century some Middle Eastern Jewish immigrants organised a central committee for the first time. The powerful influence of the Catholic Church meant few Jews were accepted as immigrants in the pre-war rush to escape Nazi Europe.

After the war however, the community began to expand, with arrivals from Hungary and the Middle East. The successful oil industry and the excellent Jewish education system attracted immigrants from other South American countries.

Today most Jews live in Caracas, the capital. Fifteen synagogues serve the country. The Lubavitch movement is present and maintains a yeshivah. Caracas has a Jewish bookshop and a weekly Jewish newspaper. Venezuela has an expanding Jewish community, in contrast to many of its South American neighbours. The oldest Jewish cemetery in South America, in Coro, with tombstones dating from 1832, is still in use today.

CARACAS
Confederación de Asociaciones Israelitas de Venezuela (CAIV)
Representative organisation of Venezuelan Jewry, Av. Washington (al lado del Hotel Avila), San Bernardino
Tel +58 (2) 551 0368/+58 (2) 550 2454 *Fax* +58 (2) 551 0377/550 1721

Ashkenazi Synagogue and Centre: Unión Israelita de Caracas
Av. Washington, San Bernardino
Tel +58 (2) 551 5253 *Fax* +58 (2) 552 7956 *M.* Rabbi Pynchas Brener

Sephardic Synagogue and Centre: Asociación Israelita de Venezuela
Tiferet Yisrael, Av. Maripérez, Frente al Paseo Colón, Los Caobos
Tel +58 (2) 574 4975/574 8297 *Fax* +58 (2) 577 0259 *M.* Rabbi Isaac Cohén

Chabad Lubavitch
9na. Trans. Altamira final de Ae Luis Roche Altamira
Tel +58 (2) 264 0711 *Fax* +58 (2) 264 7011
Website www.jabadve.com

Chabad Lubavitch
Avenue J Washington QTA Lore No. 8
Tel +58 (2) 552 0044 *Fax* +58 (2) 552 2184

Great Synagogue of Caracas (Ashkenazi)
Avenida Francisco Javier Ustariz, San Bernardino
Tel +58 (2) 511 869

Union Israelita de Caracas Synagogue & Community Centre (Ashkenazi)
Avenida Marques del Toro 9, San Bernardino
Tel +58 (2) 552 8222 *Fax* +58 (2) 552 7628
If notified in advance, kosher lunches can be arranged, a meat snack bar is also open in the evening.

VIETNAM

HO CHI MINH CITY
Chabad House Synagogue
121/137 Le Loi Street, Ben Nghe District 1
Tel +84 (8) 821 8055/+84 090 916 770
Email chabadvietnam@gmail.com

VIRGIN ISLANDS
Jews first began to settle on the island in 1655, taking advantage of liberal Danish rule. They were mainly traders in sugar cane, rum and molasses, and by 1796 a synagogue had been founded. The Jewish population of 400 made up half of the islands' white community in 1850. There have been three Jewish governors. One was Gabriel Milan, the first governor who was appointed by King Christian of Denmark.
The community began to shrink after the Panama Canal was opened in 1914, and by 1942 only 50 Jews remained. Since 1945 the community has expanded again, with families arriving from the U.S. mainland.

Hebrew Congretation of St Thomas (Reform)
P.O.B. 266, St Thomas, 00804-0266
Tel +1 (340) 774 4312 *Fax* +1 (340) 774 3249
Email hebrewcong@islands.vi *Website* www.onepaper.com/synagogue

Jewish Community
Crystal Gade, Charlotte Amalie. *M.* Rabbi A. F. Starr

YEMEN
Since 1948 the vast majority of Yemeni Jews (who then numbered about 50,000) have emigrated to Israel. It is estimated about 1,200 remain in Sa'ana. The bulk of the Jews of Aden, situated in the south of the country in what was known as South Yemen until 1990, left the country prior to Aden attaining independence from Britain in 1967.

ZAMBIA
The Jewish community began in the early twentieth century, with cattle ranching being the main attraction for Jewish immigrants. The community grew, and the copper industry was developed largely by Jewish entrepreneurs. With refugees from Nazism and a post-war economic boom, the Jewish community in the mid-1950s totalled 1,200. The community

declined after independence in 1964.
Today the Council for Zambian Jewry (founded in 1978) fulfils the role of the community's central body.

The Council for Zambia Jewry Ltd
P.O. Box 30020, Lusaka 10101
Tel +260 (211) 229 190 *Fax* +260 (211) 221 428
Ch. M. C. Galaun *Email* ceo@galaunia.co.zm

ZIMBABWE

Jews were among the earliest pioneers in Zimbabwe. The first white child born there (April 1894) was Jewish. The first synagogue in Zimbabwe (formerly Rhodesia) was set up in 1894, in a tent in Bulawayo. In 1897 a Jew was elected as the first mayor of Bulawayo. The first Jews came from Europe (especially Lithuania), and they became involved in trade and managing hotels. They were joined in the 1920s and 1930s by Sephardim from Rhodes. Some senior politicians in the country were Jewish, including one prime minister.

The 1970s saw the turbulent transition to Zimbabwe, and many Jews emigrated to escape the unrest. The community is now mainly Ashkenazi, with an important Sephardi component. Harare has both an Ashkenazi and a Sephardi synagogue; Bulawayo has a Ashkenazi synagogue. There are community centres and schools, in both the towns, although the latter have many local, non-Jewish pupils.

Central African Zionist Organisation
(Head Office) P.O. Box AC 783, Ascot, Bulawayo
Tel +263 (9) 250 443
Email cazobyo@gatorzw.com
Central African Zionist Organisation
(Bulawayo Office) P.O. Box AC 783, Ascot, Bulawayo
Tel +263 (9) 250 443
Email cazobyo@gatorzw.com
Pres. C. Bernstein (Southern Region)

JEWISH STATISTICS

The Jewish population statistics for the United States and rest of the world have been reproduced with kind permission by Ira M. Sheskin and Arnold Dashefsky. Dashefsky, Arnold and Sheskin, Ira M. (Eds), *The American Jewish Year Book 2012*, chapters 5 and 6 (Dordrecht: Springer, 2012). The statistics for England, Wales and Scotland, are from the 2011 Census, Office for National Statistics and the National Records of Scotland.

JEWISH POPULATION BY COUNTRY

Country	Jewish Population [a]
WORLD TOTAL	**13,746,100**
AMERICA TOTAL	**6,183,200**
Canada	375,000
United States	5,425,000
Total North America [b]	**5,800,000**
Bahamas	300
Costa Rica	2,500
Cuba	500
Dominican Republic	100
El Salvador	100
Guatemala	900
Jamaica	200
Mexico	39,200
Netherland Antilles	200
Panama	8,000
Puerto Rico	1,500
Virgin Islands	500
Other	200
Total Central America	**54,200**
Argentina	181,800
Bolivia	500
Brazil	95,300
Chile	18,500

Table 1 continued

Country	Jewish Population [a]
Colombia	2,500
Ecuador	600
Paraguay	900
Peru	1,900
Suriname	200
Uruguay	17,300
Venezuela	9,500
Total South America [b]	**329,000**
EUROPE TOTAL	**1,426,900**
Austria	9,000
Belgium	30,000
Bulgaria	2,000
Czech Republic	3,900
Denmark	6,400
Estonia	1,700
Finland	1,300
France [c]	480,000
Germany	119,000
Greece	4,500
Hungary	48,200
Ireland	1,200
Italy	28,200
Latvia	6,200
Lithuania	3,200
Luxembourg	600
Netherlands	29,900
Poland	3,200
Portugal	600
Romania	9,500
Slovakia	2,600
Slovenia	100
Spain	12,000

Table 1 continued

Country	Jewish Population [a]
Sweden	15,000
United Kingdom [d]	291,000
Other European Union [e]	100
Total European Union	**1,109,400**
Belarus	12,000
Moldova	3,900
Russian Federation [f]	194,000
Ukraine	67,000
Total FSU Republics	**276,900**
[Total FSU in Europe] [g]	**288,000**
Gibraltar	600
Norway	1,300
Switzerland	17,500
Total Other West Europe [b]	**19,400**
Bosnia-Hercegovina	500
Croatia	1,700
Macdeonia	100
Serbia	1,400
Turkey [f]	17,400
Other Balkans	100
Total Bulkans	**21,200**
ASIA TOTAL	**5,941,100**
Israel [h]	5,582,100
West Bank and Gaza [i]	319,000
Total Israel and Palestine	**5,901,100**
Azerbaijan	8,800
Georgia	3,000

Table 1 continued

Country	Jewish Population [a]
Kazakhstan	3,300
Krygzstan	500
Turkmenistan	200
Uzbekistan	4,200
Total FSU in Asia [j]	**20,000**
China [k]	2,500
India	5,000
Iran	10,200
Japan	1,000
Korea, South	100
Philippines	100
Singapore	300
Syria	100
Taiwan	100
Thailand	200
Yemen	200
Other Asia	200
Total Other Asia	**20,000**
AFRICA TOTAL	**75,300**
Egypt	100
Ethiopia	100
Morocco	2,500
Tunisia	900
Total North Africa [b]	**3,600**
Botswana	100
Congo D.R.	100
Kenya	400
Namibia	100
Nigeria	100

Table 1 continued

Country	Jewish Population [a]
South Africa	70,200
Zimbabwe	400
Other Sub-Saharan Africa	300
Total Sub-Saharan Africa [f]	71,700
OCEANIA TOTAL	119,600
Australia	112,000
New Zealand	7,500
Other Oceania	100

[a] Includes all persons, who, when asked, identify themselves as Jews or who are identified as Jews by a respondent in the same household, and do not have another monotheistic religion. It also includes persons of Jewish parentage who claim no current religious or ethnic identity.
[b] Including countries not listed separately.
[c] Including Monaco.
[d] Including Channel Islands and Isle of Man.
[e] Cyprus and Malta.
[f] Including Asian regions.
[g] Including Baltic republics.
[h] Total legal population of Israel, including Jews and non-Jews in East Jerusalem and the Golan Heights and Jews (enlarged definition) in the West Bank, but excluding the Palestinian population in the West Bank and Gaza. 1/1/2012: 7,837,500.
[i] Total Palestinian population on 1/1/2012 in the West Bank (without East Jerusalem): 2,238,500; Gaza: 1,600,000; Total 3,838,500 (our revised estimate).
[j] Including Armenia and Tajikistan with less than 100 Jews each. Not including Asian regions of the Russian Federation.
[k] Including Hong Kong and Macao.
[l] Sudan and Ethiopia included in Northern Africa.

JEWISH POPULATION IN ENGLAND, WALES AND SCOTLAND

Country	Jewish Population
England	261,282
North East	4,503
North West	30,417
Yorkshire and the Humber	9,929
East Midlands	4,254
West Midlands	4,621
East	34,830
London	148,602
South East	17,761
South West	6,365
Wales	2,064
Scotland	5,887

Taken from the 2011 Census, Office for National Statistics and the National Records of Scotland.

There were probably individual Jews in England in Roman and (though less likely) in Anglo-Saxon times, but the historical records of any organised settlement here start after the Norman Conquest of 1066. Jewish immigrants arrived early in the reign of William the Conqueror and important settlements came to be established in London (at a site still known as Old Jewry), Lincoln and many other centres. In 1190 the massacres of Jews occurred in many cities, most notably in York. The medieval settlement was ended by Edward I's expulsion of the Jews in 1290, after which date, with rare and temporary exceptions, only converts to Christianity or secret adherents to Judaism lived here for the next 350 years. The Domus Conversorum, the House for Converted Jews (on the site of the former Public Record Office in Chancery Lane, London) had been established in 1232. Perhaps the most notable Jews in medieval England were the financier, Aaron of Lincoln (d.c. 1186), and Elijah Menahem of London (d. 1284), financier, physician and Talmudist.

After the expulsion of the Jews from Spain in 1492 a secret Marrano community became established in London, but the present Anglo-Jewish community dates in practice from the period of the Commonwealth. In 1650 Menasseh ben Israel, of Amsterdam, began to champion the cause of Jewish readmission to England, and in 1655 he led a mission to London for this purpose. A conference was convened at Whitehall and a petition was presented to Oliver Cromwell. Though no formal decision was then recorded, the conference was advised that there was nothing to stop Jews living in England; the expulsion had been on the personal edict of Edward I and it was not renewed by Edward II. In 1656 the Spanish and Portuguese Congregation in London was organised. Charles II confirmed the resettlement in 1661. The Sephardim were followed towards the end of the seventeenth century by the establishment of an Ashkenazi community, which increased rapidly inside London as well as throwing out offshoots to a number of provincial centres and seaports. The London community, has, however, always been the largest part of British Jewry.

Britain has the distinction of being one of the few countries in Europe where during the course of the past three centuries there has been no serious outbreaks of violence against Jews and in which there has been no ghetto system. In 1753, though, the passage through Parliament of a Bill to facilitate the naturalisation of some foreign-born Jews caused such an outcry that it was soon repealed. A short-lived outbreak of antisemitism in 1772, associated with the so-called 'Chelsea murders' is equally notable for its rarity.

Although Jews in Britain had achieved virtual economic and social emancipation by the early nineteenth century, they had not yet gained 'political emancipation'. Minor Jewish disabilities were then, however, progressively removed and Jews were admitted to municipal rights and began to win distinction in the professions. The movement for the removal of Jewish political disabilities became an issue after the final removal of political disabilities from Protestant dissenters and then Roman Catholics (1829), and a Bill with that object was first introduced into the House of Commons in 1830. Among the advocates of Jewish emancipation were Macaulay, Lord John Russell, Gladstone (from 1847) and Disraeli. The latter, who was a Christian of Jewish birth, entered Parliament in 1837. Jewish MPs were repeatedly elected from 1847 onwards, but were prevented from taking their seats by the wording of the various oaths required from all new members. Owing to the opposition in the House of Lords it was not until 1858 that a Jew (Lionel de Rothschild) was formally admitted to Parliament, this being followed in 1885 by the elevation of his son (Sir Nathaniel de Rothschild) to the Peerage. Meanwhile, in 1835, David Salomons was the first Jew to become Sheriff of London, and in 1855 Lord Mayor of London (Bart. 1869). The first to be a member of the government was Sir George Jessel, who became Solicitor-General in 1871, and the first Jewish Cabinet Minister was Herbert Samuel in 1909.

During the 19th century British Jews spread out from those callings which had hitherto been regarded as characteristic of the community. A further mark of their organisational consolidation can be seen in the growth and strength of many of the communal institutions mentioned elsewhere in this book, such as the Board of Deputies (founded 1760), the Board of Guardians (founded 1859), and the United Synagogue (founded 1870), as well as the development of the office of Chief Rabbi and the longevity of the Jewish Chronicle, which marked its 170th anniversary in 2011. Equally significant, by the middle of the century, was the appearance of a number of newer Jewish communities which had been formed in many of the new industrial centres in the North of England and the Midlands.

There has always been a steady stream of immigration into Britain from Jewish communities in Europe, originally from the Iberian Peninsula and Northern Italy, later from Western and Central Europe. The community was radically transformed by the large influx of refugees which occurred between 1881 and 1914, the result of the intensified persecution of Jews in the Russian Empire. The Jewish population rose from about 25,000 in the middle of the 19th century to nearly 350,000 by 1914. It also became far more dispersed geographically. The last two decades of the nineteenth century saw a substantial growth in the number of communities both in England and in Scotland and, in consequence, the 'provinces' became more significant both in numbers and in their influence upon the community as a whole. The impact of this immigration on the Anglo-Jewish community was intensified because very many of the Jews who left Eastern Europe on their way to North America or South Africa passed through Britain. From 1933 a new emigration of Jews commenced, this time from Nazi persecution, and again many settled in this country. Since the end of the Second World War, and notably since 1956, smaller numbers of refugees have come from Egypt, Iran, Iraq and Hungary. There is, also, a large Israeli 'diaspora' in certain areas.

One of the main features of the years after 1914 was the gradual transfer of the leadership of the community from the representatives of the older established families of Anglo-Jewry to the children and grandchildren of the newer wave of immigrants. Another feature was the growth of Zionist movements, firstly the Chovevei Zion (Lovers of Zion) in the 19th century and later, from the inspiration provided by Theodor Herzl, the English Zionist Federation. The government took soundings from the community and as a result of the comments of the Chief Rabbi and Lord Rothschild issued the historic Balfour Declaration in November 1917. In 1920 the first British High Commissioner in Mandate Palestine was Sir Herbert Samuel. It was after the withdrawal of the British Government from the Mandate that the State of Israel was proclaimed in 1948.

A mark of British Jewry's full participation in public life is reflected in the number of Jewish signatories to the proclamation of accession of Queen Elizabeth II in 1952, which included seven Jewish Privy Counsellors. At the Jubilee there were twenty-one and in 2012 there were 36. In the highest offices of the State, in Parliamentary and municipal life, in the Civil and Armed Services, in the judiciary and the universities. In all professions and occupations, the Jewish subjects of the Crown – both at home and overseas – play their full part as inheritors of the political and civic emancipation that was achieved in the mid-nineteenth century. There were 23 Jewish Members in the House of Commons elected in May, 2010. There are no Jewish members of the Scottish Parliament.

In recent years the religious affiliation of the members of the community has seen substantial change. While the numbers of Reform and Liberal Jews have remained almost unchanged as a proportion of the total community, the ultra-Orthodox Chareidi community has grown substantially. The community remains over 70% Orthodox.

The events marking the celebration of the 350th anniversary of Readmission (1656-2006) culminated in public festivities in Trafalgar Square, a royal reception at St James's Palace and an address by the Prime Minister at Bevis Marks.

In its internal life and organisation, British Jewry has constructed the complex fabric of religious, social and philanthropic institutions enumerated in this book. The Jews in Britain are now estimated to number about 269,000 (see the relevant note in the statistical tables) of whom some 168,000 reside in Greater London and the remainder are spread in some 90 regional communities.

UNITED KINGDOM LEGISLATION CONCERNING JEWS

HISTORICAL BACKGROUND

In the Middle Ages, hostility towards Jews was a common feature in many European countries. In England, during the reign of Edward I (1272–1307), the *Statutum de Judeismo* was passed in 1275. This statute forbade usury and included an order continuing to oblige Jews to wear a distinguishing badge and imposing upon them an annual poll tax.

In 1290, Edward personally decreed the expulsion of Jews from England. During the reign of Charles I (1625–49) the number of Jews in England steadily increased. Menasseh ben Israel (1604–57) of Amsterdam made a direct appeal to Cromwell to authorize readmission. His 'Humble Addresses' presented to the Lord Protector in October 1655 urged the revocation of the edict of 1290 and entreated that the Jews be accorded the right of public worship and the right to trade freely. No formal announcement was ever made of the Jews' 're-admission' but Charles II gave instructions they were to be allowed to live in the country. It also transpired that, as Edward II had not extended the expulsion with his own decree, there had been nothing to stop them living in England since the death of Edward I.

The Religious Disabilities Act 1846 extended to Jews the provisions of the Toleration Act 1688. Under the 1846 Act, British subjects professing the Jewish religion were to be subject to the same laws, in respect of their schools, places for religious worship, education and charitable purposes, and the property held with them, as Protestant dissenters from the Church of England.

UPDATING THE LEGISLATION SECTION OF THE JEWISH YEAR BOOK

(Prepared by His Honour Judge Aron Owen and updated by His Honour Judge Martyn Zeidman and further by Jonathan Arkush and Eleanor F. PLatt QC)

This part of the Year Book, summarising legislation, has in the past been prepared by His Honour Judge Aron Owen z'l who sadly died on 23rd September 2009 - three days after Rosh Hashanah. His elegant explanations are still applicable and there has been very little to report since the last edition. We are very grateful to Judge Owen's son in law, His Honour Judge Martyn Zeidman Q.C. for taking over responsibility for this section and for Jonathan Arkush and Eleanor F. Platt QC who have in 2013 taken over from him.

On 13th January 2010 **The Holocaust (Return of Cultural Objects) Act 2009** came into force and its title summarises the effect of the change. In the past, museums which held items seized by the Nazis were in a legal dilemma: could and should they return the articles to their true Jewish owners, or must the museum hold onto to them as the law seemed to require. A change was necessary. Andrew Dismore proposed the Bill and he explained its purpose:- "the Bill will right a long-standing injustice by giving powers to museums and galleries to return pieces of art and cultural objects taken from their rightful owners during the period of the Nazi regime. Whilst I do not envisage the Act having to be used very frequently, this is an important moral step, to ensure that we can close yet a further chapter on the appalling crimes of the Holocaust." In a rare display of unity, the Bill received cross-party support and the then Culture Minister, Margaret Hodge, observed "For too long, families who had heirlooms stolen from them by the Nazis were unable to reclaim them, although they were the rightful owners. This new Act will restore this possibility for families who suffered so terribly during the Nazi era, to get some justice by getting back their heirlooms.".

Not strictly legislation but the new Supreme Court (which has replaced the Judicial Committee of the House of Lords) in one of its first decisions considered the admissions policy of JFS. The full and profound ruling which has had a drastic effect upon all Jewish schools is reported as **R (on the application of E) (Respondent) v The Governing Body of JFS and the Admissions Appeal Panel of JFS and others (Appellants) [2009] UKSC 15** and it can be read in full on line at www.supremecourt.gov.uk/decided-cases/docs/UKSC_2009_0136_Judgment.pdf

In short, it comes to this:- If over-subscribed, faith schools are permitted to discriminate (select) on grounds of religion but not on the basis of race. It follows that a school may require an entrant to have a certain level of Jewish observance (e.g. attendance at synagogue, observance of Kashrut, or Shabbat) but a school may not require the child to satisfy the Halachic (Jewish legal) definition of a Jew. It follows that a school may not require the child to have a Jewish mother or to have gone through a valid conversion – in the eyes of the court such a requirement amounts to an unlawful racial (rather than a permitted religious) selection. The court emphasised that in reaching its decision no personal criticism was intended. The court's own summary provides that "the judgments of the Court should not be read as criticising the admissions policy of JFS on moral grounds or suggesting that any party to the case could be considered 'racist' in the commonly understood, pejorative, sense. The simple legal question to be determined by the Court was whether, in being denied admission to JFS, M was disadvantaged on grounds of his ethnic origins (or his lack thereof) (paras [9], [54], [124] and [156])." It is argued by some that legislation should be introduced to over-turn the effect of this decision and Parliament most certainly would have the authority to do so, but as yet there is no change. In practice, schools have amended their admission requirements to satisfy the new understanding of the law.

ENGLAND, WALES AND NORTHERN IRELAND

PRESENT POSITION

Today, English Law does not regard Jews as a separate nationality or as different from any other British citizen. They have no special status except in so far as they constitute a dissenting religious denomination.

Provision for that special religious position of Jews has, from time to time, been made in legislation (see, for example, the 1846 Act mentioned above). Various sections of the current edition of Halsbury's Laws contain relevant information on the position of Jews in the 21st Century in the UK.

Some of the various statutory provisions in force today are set out briefly below. Further information and details can be obtained from the Board of Deputies, 6 Bloomsbury Square, London, WC1A 2LP Tel 020 7543 5400). Legal advice should be sought by those wishing to know the impact of specific legislation upon their own particular circumstances.

1. The *Representation of the People Act 1983* (which is a consolidation of several previous Acts) enables a voter in a parliamentary or local election, 'who declares that he is a Jew' and objects on religious grounds to marking the ballot paper on the Jewish Sabbath, to have, if the poll is taken on a Saturday, his vote recorded by the presiding officer. This right does not apply to Jewish Holy-days other than the Sabbath. A person unable by reason of 'religious observance' to go in person to the polling station may apply to be treated as an absent voter and be given a postal vote for a particular parliamentary or local election.

2. The *Education Act 1994* permits Jewish parents to have their children, if they are attending state or state-aided voluntary schools, withdrawn from any period of religious instruction and/or worship where such instruction or worship is not in the Jewish faith. In order to take advantage of these provisions of the Act, a written request must be submitted to the head teacher of the school.

3. The *Oaths Act 1978*. A Jew may take an oath (in England, Wales or Northern Ireland) by holding the Old Testament in his uplifted hand, and saying or repeating after the officer administering the oath, the words: 'I swear by Almighty God that ...' followed by the words of the oath prescribed by law. The officer will administer the oath in that form and manner without question, unless the person about to take the oath voluntarily objects thereto or is physically incapable of so taking the oath.

Any person who objects to being sworn (whether in that way or in the form and manner usually administered in Scotland) is at liberty instead to make a *solemn affirmation* which will have the same force and effect as an oath. The form of the affirmation is as follows: 'I ... do solemnly, sincerely and truly declare and affirm that ...' followed by the words of the oath prescribed by law. The form of affirmation omits any words of imprecation or calling to witness.

4. *Marriage Act 1949*. English law expressly recognizes the validity of marriages by Jews in England if the ceremonies of the Jewish religion have been complied with.

The Secretary of a synagogue has statutory powers and duties in regard to keeping the marriage register books, and the due registration of marriages between persons professing the Jewish religion under the provisions of the Marriage Act 1949. He has no authority unless and until he has been certified, in writing, to be the Secretary of a synagogue in England of persons professing the Jewish religion, by the President of the Board of Deputies.

When the West London Synagogue was established, acting on the advice of the Chief Rabbi and other recognized Jewish ecclesiastical authorities, the President of the Board of Deputies refused to certify the secretary of the new congregation. Accordingly, by the Marriage Act 1949, it is enacted that the Secretary of the West London Synagogue of British Jews, if certified in writing to the Registrar-General by twenty householders being members of that synagogue, shall be entitled to the same privileges as if he had been certified by the President of the Board of Deputies. These privileges are also accorded to a person whom the Secretary of the West London Synagogue certifies in writing to be the secretary of some other synagogue of not less than twenty householders professing the Jewish religion, if it is connected with the West London Synagogue and has been established for not less than one year.

The Marriages (Secretaries of Synagogues) Act 1959 gives similar rights to Liberal Jewish synagogues.

5. *Divorce (Religious Marriages) Act 2002*. This Act, which was passed on 24 February 2002, came into operation on 24 January 2003. It is not retrospective. It amends the Matrimonial Causes Act 1973 by the insertion of a new clause, 10A which enacts important provisions for orthodox Jewish couples seeking a divorce, where a *Get* (Jewish Religious Divorce) is essential.

The relevant wording of the new section 10A reads as follows:

10A Proceedings after decree nisi: religious marriage
(1) This section applies if the decree of divorce has been granted but not made absolute and the parties to the marriage concerned –
   (a) were married in accordance with
      (i) the usage of the Jews ... And
   (b) must co-operate if the marriage is to be dissolved in accordance with those usages.
(2) On the application of either party, the court may order that a decree of divorce is not to be made absolute until a declaration, made by both parties that they have taken such steps as are required to dissolve the marriage, in accordance with those usages, is produced to the court.
(3) An order made under subsection (2) –
   (a) may be made only if the court is satisfied that in all the circumstances of the case it is just and reasonable to do so; and
   (b) may be revoked at any time ...

The effect of the statutory provisions, now in operation, is that where the parties, who have been married in accordance with the usages of Jewish Law (that is *Chuppah* and *Kiddushin*), seek a divorce then, before a Jewish husband and wife would be granted a civil decree absolute of divorce by the English court, they could be required to declare that there had been a *Get*, that is, the Jewish religious divorce. There would thus be a barrier to such a Jewish husband or wife obtaining a civil divorce and being able to remarry, unless and until there has been a prior *Get*.

It is hoped that these new statutory provisions will go some way towards alleviating the plight of an *Agunah*. The usual case of an *Agunah* (literally 'a chained woman') is that of a wife whose husband refuses to give her a *Get*, so that she is unable to remarry in accordance with orthodox Jewish law. Under the above provisions of the Divorce (Religious Marriages) Act 2002, such a husband would himself be unable to obtain a civil divorce and remarry.

To invoke the provisions of section 10A, an application, by either wife or husband, has to be made to the Court. This application must be made in accordance with the Family Proceedings (Amendment) Rules 2003. It is advisable to consult a solicitor (practising, *inter alia*, in Family Law) to ensure that the necessary legal proceedings are carried out correctly.

6. The Marriage (Same Sex Couples) Act 2013 came into force, in part only, on receiving Royal Assent in July 2013. It is stated that it is hoped that the entire act will all be brought into force during 2014. In so far as such marriages between Jews are concerned there has to be an opt-in by the relevant group before such marriages may be performed. At the time of writing it is expected that only Liberal Judaism will opt in, but it is known that Reform Judaism may also do so.

7. *Shechita*. Animals and birds slaughtered by the Jewish method (*shechita*) for the food of Jews, by a Jew duly licensed by the Rabbinical Commission, constituted for the purpose, do not come within the provision of the Slaughterhouses Act 1974 or the Slaughter of Poultry Act 1967, relating to the methods of slaughter of animals and birds. The right to practice *shechita* is thus preserved.

In March 1995 both Acts (the Slaughterhouses Act 1974 and the Slaughter of Poultry Act 1967) were repealed and replaced by secondary legislation in the form of a Statutory Instrument. This implements the European Community's Directive (93/119/EC) on the protection of animals at the time of slaughter. In 2013 the government repealed the Welfare of Animals (Slaughter or Killing) Regulations (WASK) 1995 and replaced them with Welfare of Animals at the Time of Killing Regulations (WATOK) following EU Council Regulation 1099/2009. In keeping with the previous legislation, the requirement for animals and poultry to be stunned before slaughter does not apply in the case of animals subject to methods of slaughter required by certain religious rites. *Shechita* is accordingly safeguarded.

Shechita UK was established in 2003 to promote clarity and understanding of Shechita, the Jewish religious humane method of animal slaughter for food and to counter misinformation and popular misconceptions. It continues to lobby on behalf of the Jewish community in the UK and across Europe for the protection of Shechita.

In addition, The Rabbinical Commission for the Licensing of Shochtim has been retained as the only statutory body with authority for licensing slaughter-men for the purposes of Shechita.

8. The *Sunday Trading Act*, which came into operation on 26 August 1994, has removed many of the difficulties caused by the Shops Act 1950. All shops with a selling and display area of less than 280 square metres may be open at any time on Sundays. Shops with a selling and display area of 280 square metres or more are still subject to some restriction, with an opening time limited to a continuous period of six hours between 10am and 6pm.

There is, however, a special exemption for 'persons observing the Jewish Sabbath' who are occupiers of these 'large' shops. Provided such an individual (and there are parallel conditions for partnerships and companies) gives a signed notice to the Local Authority that he is a person of the Jewish religion and intends to keep the shop closed for the serving of customers on the Jewish Sabbath, he may open it as and when he wishes on a Sunday.

The notice given to the Local Authority must be accompanied by a statement from the minister of the shopkeeper's synagogue, or the secretary for marriages of that synagogue, or a person designated by the President of the Board of Deputies, that the shopkeeper is a person of the Jewish religion. There are severe penalties for any false statements made in connection with this intention to trade.

Large shops which were previously registered under Section 53 of the Shops Act 1950, may continue to trade on Sundays without new notification. But occupiers of food stores and kosher meat shops over 280 square metres who, even if closed on Shabbat, did not previously require exemption, may well have formally to notify their Local Authority that their premises will be closed on Shabbat to enable them to open on Sunday.

Jewish shopkeepers who close their premises for the 25 hours of Shabbat may open after Shabbat.

9. Discrimination against a person on account of his being a Jew is unlawful under the *Equality Act 2010*.

10. *Friendly Societies Act 1974* (which consolidates the Friendly Societies Acts 1896 to 1971 and certain other enactments). A Friendly Society may be registered for the purpose, *inter alia*, of ensuring that money is paid to Jews during *Shiva* (referred to in the Act as 'the period of confined mourning'). Friendly Societies have, since January 2010, become part of the Association of Financial Mutuals. The Jewish Friendly Societies, so useful for help for poor Jews in the 19C and early 20C, have been largely superseded.

11. By the *Places of Worship Registration Act 1855*, as amended by the *Charities Act 1960*, the Registrar-General may certify a synagogue. The effect of Certification is freedom from uninvited interference by the Charity Commissioners and, if exclusively appropriate to public worship, from general and special rates.

12. By the *Juries Act 1870*, the minister of a synagogue who has been certified, was free from liability to serve on a jury, provided he follows no secular occupation except that of a schoolmaster. This provision was retained in the consolidating Act of 1974 but removed by Schedule 33 of the Criminal Justice Act 2003. It follows that any minister, like Judges, are liable for jury service.

THE LAW IN SCOTLAND

(Prepared by Sheriff Sir G. H. Gordon, CBE, QC, LL.D)

There are no records relating to Jews in Scotland prior to the creation of the United Kingdom in 1707, and accordingly no legislation regarding either their expulsion or their re-admission. Jews do not appear in Scots legislation as a unique group, except in relation to United Kingdom statutes which treat them as such, of which the only one still in force is the Representation of the People Act 1983.

European Regulations apply in Scotland as they do in England.

The Education (Scotland) Act 1980 provides by section 9 that every public and grant-aided and self-governing school shall be open to all denominations, and that any pupil may be withdrawn by his parents from instruction in religious subjects and from any religious observance in any such school. It provides further that no pupil shall be placed at any disadvantage with respect to secular instruction by reason of his or his parents denomination or his withdrawal from religious instruction.

Section 10 of that Act provides that where the parents of a boarder in any such school requests permission for the pupil to attend worship on any day exclusively set apart for religious observance by the religious body to which the parent belongs, or to receive religious instruction or practise religious observance in accordance with such tenets, the school shall afford facilities for such observance etc on its premises, provided that does not involve expenditure by the school.

The oath is administered by the judge in Scots courts, and the witness repeats the words (which begin 'I swear by Almighty God') after him with his right hand upraised. No books are used. A Jewish witness is in practice allowed to cover his head if he wishes to do so. Anyone who indicates a wish to affirm is allowed to do so.

Section 8 of the Marriages (Scotland) Act 1977 provides that a religious marriage may be solemnized by the minister or clergyman of any religious body prescribed by Regulations, or by any person recognized by such a body as entitled to solemnize marriages. The bodies prescribed by the Marriage (Prescription of Religious Bodies) (Scotland) (Regulations) 1977 (S.I.No. 1670) include 'The Hebrew Congregation', whatever that denotes. In practice all Rabbis appointed to an established Synagogue or Community (i.e. not necessarily owning premises, e.g. Edinburgh Liberal Jewish Community) are automatically recognised by the Registrar General for Scotland (RG) as being "recognised by the Hebrew Congregation". The RG requires explicit confirmation that all other Rabbis of any persuasion are so recognised before it will recognise a religious marriage "solemnised" by them as also constituting a civil marriage. In practice, the RG contacts the Scottish Council of Jewish Communities (SCoJeC) to ask whether a Rabbi is recognised. SCoJeC enquires of the head office of the relevant brand of Judaism in the relevant country, and, on the basis of information received, informs the RG whether or not the said Rabbi is recognised.

Section 15 of the Family Law (Scotland) Act 2006, which inserted a new clause 3A into the Divorce (Scotland) Act, was included at the specific request of the Jewish community. It comes into effect when

"(2)(a) the applicant is prevented from entering into a religious marriage by virtue of a requirement of the religion of that marriage; and
(2)(b) the other party can act so as to remove, or enable or contribute to the removal of, the impediment which prevents that marriage."

The Scottish legislation looks forward to a situation in which a party to a divorce may be "prevented from entering into a religious marriage by virtue of a requirement of the religion of that marriage" whereas the English legislation looks back to a situation in which the parties to the existing marriage "were married in accordance with the usage of the Jews". The Scottish legislation therefore covers more bases, since, unlike the English legislation, it could be used by a Jewish couple who were married only in a civil ceremony but who would, nonetheless, require a get in order for either party to be able to contract a subsequent religious marriage.

The Law Reform (Miscellaneous Provisions) (Scotland) Act 1980 includes regular ministers of any religious denomination among those persons who, although eligible for jury service, are entitled to be excused therefrom as of right.

The Race Relations Act 1976 (Equalities Act 2010) applies to Scotland, but the Sunday Trading Act 1994 does not, nor does the Places of Worship Registration Act 1855.

'Section 96 of the Crime and Disorder Act 1998 obliges sentencers to take account, as an aggravation, of the fact that any offence has been motivated by ill-will towards members of a group, defined by reference to colour, nationality, or ethnic or national origins ('a racial group'), and section 74 of the Criminal Justice (Scotland) Act 2003 makes similar provision in respect of members of a religious group.'

Marriages registered for civil purposes may be contracted according to the usages of the Jews between persons *both* professing the Jewish religion. This is provided that due notice has been given to the Superintendent Registrar of the local authority register office where the bride and groom live and that certificates for this purpose have been obtained. There is no restriction regarding the hours within which the marriage may be solemnised, nor the place of marriage, which may be a synagogue, private house, or any other building.

The date and place of the intended marriage having been decided, the parties should consult the Minister or Secretary for Marriages of the synagogue through which the marriage is to be solemnised. S/he will explain the necessary preliminary steps and the suitability of the proposed date.

The Registrar's certificates must be handed to the Synagogue Marriage Secretary in advance of the date decided. In the case of a marriage in a building other than a synagogue, care should be taken that these documents contain the words *"both* parties professing the Jewish Religion" following the description of the building.

If the marriage is to be solemnised at or through a synagogue under the jurisdiction of the Chief Rabbi, his Authorisation of Marriage must also be obtained. Enquiries relating to this should be directed to the Marriage Authorisation Office at the Office of the Chief Rabbi (*Tel* 020 8343 6314).

No marriage is valid if solemnised between persons who are within the degrees of kindred of affinity (e.g., between uncle and niece) prohibited by English law, even though such a marriage is permissible by Jewish law.

A marriage between Jews must be registered immediately after the ceremony by the Secretary of Marriages of the synagogue to which the groom must be a member. If he is not already a member he may become one by signing a membership form and paying a membership fee in addition to the marriage charges.

No marriage between Jews should take place without due notice being given to the Superintendent Registrar, and without being registered in the Marriage Register of a synagogue. Marriages in such circumstances are not necessarily valid in English law. (Outside England and Wales other regulations apply and the Minister of the synagogue should be consulted.)

For information on dates when marriages may not be placed, please see page 479.

LISTED SYNAGOGUES, FORMER SYNAGOGUES AND OTHER JEWISH SITES IN THE UK

This list is compiled by **Jewish Heritage UK** (*see* p. 114)
Room 204, Ducie House, 37 Ducie Street, Manchester, M1 2JW
Tel 0161 238 8621 *Email* director@jewish-heritage-uk.org
For regular updates see website www.jewish-heritage-uk.org/
See also *Jewish Heritage in England: An Architectural Guide* (2006, 2nd Edn. 2014) and *The Synagogues of Britain and Ireland* (2011) both by Sharman Kadish.

SYNAGOGUES

LONDON
Grade I
Bevis Marks, EC3 (Joseph Avis 1699–1701)
New West End, St Petersburgh Place, W2 (George Audsley in association with N.S. Joseph 1877–79)

Grade II*
In use as synagogue
Hampstead, Dennington Park Road, NW6 (Delissa Joseph 1892–1901)

Former synagogues
Princelet Street, E1 (Former synagogue 1870 behind Huguenot house 1719. Hudson 1869-70. Remodelled by Lewis Solomon 1893)
Spitalfields Great Synagogue, 59 Brick Lane/Fournier Street, E1 (Former French church 1743. Converted into synagogue 1897-98. Now London Jamia Mosque)

Grade II
In use as synagogues
Golders Green, 41 Dunstan Road, London NW11 (Lewis Solomon & Son [Digby] 1921-22. Enlarged by Messrs. Joseph 1927)
New London, 33 Abbey Road, NW8 (H.H. Collins 1882. Formerly St John's Wood United Synagogue)
New Synagogue, Egerton Road, N16 (Joseph & Smithem 1915. Interior reconstructed from Great St Helen's, Bishopsgate, by John Davies 1837-38)
Sandys Row, E1 (Former chapel 1766. Converted into synagogue 1867. Remodelled by N.S. Joseph 1870)
Spanish & Portuguese, Lauderdale Road, W9 (Davis & Emanuel 1895-96)
West London (Reform), Upper Berkeley Street, W1 (Davis & Emanuel 1869-70)
Western & Marble Arch, 32 Great Cumberland Place, W1 (T. P. Bennett & Son 1960-61. Listed façade)

Former synagogues
Dollis Hill, Parkside, NW2 (Sir Owen Williams 1936-38. Torah Temimah Primary School)
East London, Rectory Square, E1 (Davis & Emanuel 1876-77. Flats)
Hackney, Brenthouse Road, E9 (Delissa Joseph 1897. Enlarged by Cecil J. Eprile 1936. Church)

ENGLISH REGIONS
Grade I
Liverpool, Old Hebrew Congregation, Princes Road, L8 (W. & G. Audsley 1872-74)

Grade II*
In use as synagogues
Birmingham, Singers Hill, Blucher Street, B1 (Henry R. Yeoville Thomason 1855-56)
Bradford Synagogue (Reform), Bowland Street, BD1 (T.H. & F. Healey 1880-81)
Brighton, Middle Street, BN1 (Thomas Lainson 1874-75)

Chatham Memorial Synagogue, High Street, Rochester, ME1 (H.H. Collins 1865-70)
Cheltenham, St James's Square, GL50 (W.H. Knight 1837-39)
Exeter, Mary Arches Street, EX4. (1763-64. Refronted 1835)
Plymouth, Catherine Street, PL1 (1761-62)
Ramsgate, Montefiore Synagogue, Honeysuckle Road, CT11 (David Mocatta 1831-33)

Former synagogues
Liverpool, Greenbank Drive, L17 (E. Alfred Shennan 1936-37)
Manchester, Spanish & Portuguese, 190 Cheetham Hill Road, M8 (Edward Salomons 1873-74. Manchester Jewish Museum)

Grade II
In use as synagogues
Bristol, Park Row, BS1 (H.H. Collins with S. C. Fripp 1870-71)
Coventry, Barras Lane, CV1 (Thomas Naden 1870)
Grimsby, Sir Moses Montefiore Synagogue, Heneage Road, DN32 (B.S. Jacobs 1885-88 and *Mikveh* 1915-16)
Leicester, Highfield Street, LE2 (Arthur Wakerley 1897-98)
Manchester, Withington Spanish & Portuguese, 8 Queenston Road, West Didsbury, M20 (Delissa Joseph 1925-27)
Manchester, Higher Crumpsall, Bury Old Road, Salford, M7 (Pendleton & Dickinson 1928-29)
Manchester, South Manchester, Wilbraham Road, M14 (Joseph Sunlight 1912-13)
Reading, Goldsmid Road, RG1 (W.G. Lewton 1900-01)

Former synagogues
Grade I
Brighton, 26 Brunswick Terrace, Hove, BN3 (Rooftop private synagogue of Philip Salomons *ca.* 1850s)

Grade II
Birmingham, Severn Street, The Athol Masonic Hall, Severn Street, B1 (Richard Tutin 1825-27)
Blackpool, Leamington Road, FY1 (R.B. Mather 1914-16)
Brighton, 38 Devonshire Place, BN2 (Remodelled by David Mocatta 1837-8. Flats)
Canterbury, King Street, CT1 (Hezekiah Marshall 1847-48. King's School Recital Room)
Carmel College Synagogue, Mongewell Park, Crowmarsh, Wallingford, Oxfordshire, OX10 (Thomas Hancock 1961-63)
Falmouth, Smithick Hill, TR11 (1808. Studio)
Hull, The Western Synagogue, Linnaeus Street, HU3 (B.S. Jacobs 1902-03)
Leeds, New Synagogue, Louis Street/Chapeltown Road, LS7 (J. Stanley Wright 1929-32. Northern School of Contemporary Dance)
Newcastle upon Tyne, Leazes Park, NE1 (John Johnstone 1879-80. Flats)
Sheffield, Wilson Road, S11 (Rawcliffe & Ogden 1929-30. Church)
Sunderland, Ryhope Road, SR2 (Marcus K. Glass 1928)

WALES
Grade II
Former synagogues
Cardiff, Cathedral Road, CF11 (Delissa Joseph 1896-97. Demolished behind façade)
Merthyr Tydfil, Bryntirion Road, Thomastown, CF47 (1872-77).

SCOTLAND
Scottish A List
In use as synagogue
Glasgow, Garnethill, 129 Hill Street, G3 (John McLeod in association with N.S. Joseph 1877-79)

Scottish B List
In use as synagogue
Edinburgh, Salisbury Road, Newington, EH16 (James Miller 1929-32)

Former synagogue
Glasgow, Queen's Park, 4 Falloch Road, G42 (Ninian MacWhannel 1925-27. Flats.)

NORTHERN IRELAND
Former synagogue
Belfast, Hebrew Congregation, 4 Annesley Street, BT14 (Young and Mackenzie with B.S. Jacobs 1904. Mater Hospital Physiotherapy Gym)

OTHER LISTED JEWISH BUILDINGS

Grade II
London, Beth Holim, 253 Mile End Road, E1 (Manuel Nunes Costello 1912-13. Flats)
London, Soup Kitchen for the Jewish Poor, Brune Street, E1 (Lewis Solomon 1902. Flats)
London, Stepney Jewish Schools, Stepney Green, E1 (Davis & Emanuel 1906-07)
London, No. 88, Whitechapel High Street, E1: former offices of the *Jewish Daily Post*, with shop signs by Arthur Szyk (*ca*.1935)
London, Whitechapel Drinking Fountain, (King Edward VII Jewish Memorial Drinking Fountain), Whitechapel Road, E1 (opposite Royal London Hospital), (W.S. Frith 1911)
Carmel College, Mongewell Park, Crowmarsh, Wallingford, Oxfordshire, OX10; Julius Gottlieb Gallery & Boathouse (Sir Basil Spence, Bonnington & Collins 1968-70, Grade II*); Amphitheatre (Thomas Hancock 1965)
Belfast, Jaffe Memorial Fountain, Victoria Square, BT1 (1877)

Post-war synagogues currently housed in listed buildings
Grade II*
London, Sukkat Shalom Reform Synagogue, 1 Victory Road, Hermon Hill, E11 (Merchant Seaman's Orphan Asylum at Wanstead Hospital, chapel by George Somers Clarke 1861-63. Contains fixtures and fittings from the synagogue at the former Tottenham Jewish Home & Hospital 1913-18)

Grade II
Elstree Liberal Synagogue, Elstree High Street, Hertfordshire, WD6 (Church of England school house 1882–83. Synagogue 1979)
Nottingham Hebrew Congregation, Shakespeare Street, NG1 (Wesleyan Methodist Chapel by Thomas Simpson 1854. Synagogue 1954. Contains Ark from former Chaucer Street Synagogue 1890)

Medieval sites with possible Jewish associations
Grade I
Bury St Edmunds, Moyses Hall, Cornhill, IP33 (*ca*.1180)
Lincoln: Jews' Court, 2-3 Steep Hill, LN2 (*ca*.1170); Jews' House, 15 The Strait, LN2 (*ca*.1170); Aaron the Jew's House (the Norman House), 47 Steep Hill, LN2 (*ca*.1170)
Norwich, the Music House or Jurnet's House, Wensum Lodge, 167-169 King Street, NR1 (*ca*.1175)

Scheduled Ancient Monuments
Bristol, Jacob's Well, 33 Jacob's Well Road, Bristol BS8 (Possible Medieval *Mikveh ca*.1140)
York, Clifford's Tower, YO1 (Rebuilt)

JEWISH BURIAL GROUNDS, MAUSOLEA AND MEMORIALS

Listed sites (or parts of sites, e.g. boundary walls, screens and gates, buildings or memorials)

LONDON
Grade II
Alderney Road, E1 (Ashkenazi) (1696-97)
Mile End Velho (Sephardi), 253 Mile End Road, E1 (1657)
Mile End Nuevo (Sephardi), Queen Mary University of London Campus, New section (1874, listed boundary walls)
Rothschild Mausoleum (Matthew Digby Wyatt 1866), West Ham Jewish Cemetery, Buckingham Road, E15

ENGLISH REGIONS
Grade II*
Ramsgate, Montefiore Mausoleum, Honeysuckle Road, CT11 (1862)

Grade II
Bath, Greendown Place and 174 Bradford Road, Combe Hill, BA2 (1812)
Birmingham, Granville Street Cemetery Memorial (1876. The whole cemetery (1869-71) is on the *Parks and Gardens Register* - see website)
Birmingham, *Ohel*, Witton New Jewish Cemetery, Warren Road, B44 (Essex & Goodman 1937)
Brighton, Florence Place, Ditchling Road, BN1 (1826, *Ohel* by Lainson & Son 1893)
Brighton, Sassoon Mausoleum, Paston Place, Kemp Town, BN2 (1892)
Bristol, St Philip's Cemetery, Barton Road, BS2 (Oldest tombstone 1762)
Exeter, Magdalen Street, Bull Meadow, EX2 (1757)
Ipswich, Salthouse Lane, off Star Lane, IP4 (1796)
Kings Lynn, Millfleet, Stonegate Street, PE30 (Before 1811)
Liverpool, Deane Road, Fairfield, L7 (1836)
Manchester, Jewish Section, Philips Park Cemetery, M40 (1875. The whole cemetery (1866-67) *Parks and Gardens* – see website)
Penzance, Lestinnick Terrace, TR18 (1791) (Oldest stone)
Ramsgate Jewish Cemetery, *Ohel* and section of boundary wall, Upper Dumpton Park Road, CT11 (1872)
Southampton, *Ohel*, Southampton Old/Common Cemetery, Cemetery Road, SO15 (1854). The whole cemetery (1846) *Parks and Gardens*, Grade II* – see website)
Wolverhampton, Old Jewish Cemetery, Cockshutts Lane, Thomson Avenue, WV2 (1851)

Scheduled Ancient Monument
Falmouth Jews' Burial Ground, Penryn Road, Ponsharden, TR11 (*ca.* 1780)

SCOTLAND
Scottish A List
Glasgow, Jews' Enclosure, Glasgow Necropolis, Cathedral Square, G4 (1836)

Scottish B List
Edinburgh, Sciennes House Place (Braid Place), Causewayside, EH9 (1820)
Edinburgh, Jewish Section, Newington Cemetery, Echobank, EH16 (1867)
Glasgow, Janefield Jewish Cemetery, Eastern Necropolis, Gallowgate, G31 (1856)
Glasgow, Jewish Section, Western Necropolis, Tresta Road, G23 (1882/3, including the *Ohel* 1898)
Greenock Cemetery, Jewish Section, Bow Road, PA16 (1911)

HONOURS LIST 2013

The following members of the Jewish community received honours in 2013.

DBE

Helen Hyde, For services to education. Headmistress of Watford School for Girls.
Janet Wolfson de Botton, For charitable services to the Arts.

CH

Sir Nicholas Serota, For services of national importance (Including overseeing the establishment of the Tate Modern).

KBE

Michael Aron Heller, For charitable services.
Michael Moritz, For promoting British economic interests and philanthropic work.
Prof. Michael Stratton, For services to medical science.

CBE

Claire Bloom, For services to Drama.
Professor Raymond Dwek, For services to UK-Israel scientific collaboration.
David Goldstone, For services to the financial administration of the London 2012 Olympic and Paralympic Games.
Thomas Heatherwick, For services to the Design Industry. Designer of the cauldron to hold the Olympic flame.
Anish Kapoor, For services to visual arts.
Haim Levy, For services to the economy and to the Jewish Community in Gibraltar.
Arlene Phillips, For services to dance and charity
Dr. Leonard Polonsky, For Charitable services. Donated 1.5m to Cambridge University to buy a collection of rare books.
Dr Peter Ruback, For services to council housing reform.
Max Steinberg, For Services to Business and to the Community in Liverpool. A key figure in the City's regeneration.

OBE

Dr Lisa Appignanesi, For services to literature.
Dr. Rodney Berman, For services to local government and the community in Cardiff.
Norma Brier, For services to children and people with learning disabilities (Former Norwood Chief Executive).
Pauline Etkin, For services to music therapy.
Laurence Graff, Jeweller.
Rabbi Herschel Gluck, for services to Interfaith understanding.
David Kustow, For services to film in the UK and his role in achieving the British/Israeli film co-operation treaty.
Leslie Morgan, For services to the pharmaceutical industry and to charity.
David Newman, For services to higher education and promoting academic links between the UK and Israel.

Leslie Rose, For services to children.
Daniel Salbstein, For services promoting UK/Russia mutual understanding.
Professor Penny Ur, For exceptional work in English teaching.
Brett Wigdortz, For Services to Education.

MBE

Gillian Balen, For services to health and the community in west Hertforshire.
Angela Cox, For voluntary service to people affected by Breast Cancer.
Mayer Hersh, For work in the field of Holocaust education.
Judy Ironside, For services to Drama (Founder of the UK Jewish Film Festival).
Dr. Karen Liebreich, For services to education and horticulture in West London.
Joy Moss, For services to charitable giving and disadvantaged children in the UK and abroad.
George Pincus, For services to Education.
Zvi Rabin, For services to libraries. Founder of Lubavitch Lending Library.
Anna Scher, Theatre School founder.
Philip Shapiro, For services to the arts.
Joan Villiers, For charitable services in Yorkshire and Humberside.

BEM

Stanley Coors, For services to the Glasgow community.
Hilary Craft, For charitable services.
Dr. Arnold Phelops, For charitable services.

PRIVY COUNSELLORS, PEERS, MPs, etc

PRIVY COUNSELLORS

Battle, John MP
Barnett, Lord
Bercow, John MP
Brittan, Lord, (QC)
Brown, Lord
Burnton, Sir Stanley, (QC)
Clinton-Davis, Lord
Collins, Lord
Cosgrove, Lady, CBE
Dyson, Lord (Master of the Rolls)
Etherton, Sir Terence (Lord Justice)
   Chancellor of High Court
Freedman, Sir Lawrence
Gilbert, Sir Martin
Goldsmith, Lord, (QC)
Hayman, Baroness
Hodge, Margaret, MP
Hoffman, Lord
Howard, Lord, CH, (QC)
Kaufman, Sir Gerald B., MP
Lawson, Lord
Letwin, Oliver, MP
Leveson, Sir Brian (Lord Justice)
Lewison, Sir Kim, (Lord Justice)
Miliband, David
Miliband, Edward, MP
Millett, Lord
Neuberger, Lord David (President of
   Supreme Court)
Oppenheim-Barnes, Baroness
Phillips, Baron Nicholas
Rifkind, Sir Malcolm, (QC), MP
Rix, Sir Bernard, (QC)
Sedley, Sir Stephen (QC)
Shapps, Grant, MP
Sheldon, Lord Robert E.
Woolf, Lord
Young, Lord

PEERS

Bearsted of Maidstone, 5th Viscount
Finkelstein, Baron of Pinner
Greenhill of Townhead, 3rd Baron, MD
Leigh, Baron of Hurley
Marks of Broughton, 3rd Baron
Mendelsohn, Baron of Finchley
Morris of Kenwood, 3rd Baron
Nathan, 3rd Baron
Rothschild, 4th Baron, OM, FBA, MA
   (Oxon)
Samuel of Mt Carmel & Toxteth, 3rd
   Viscount
Sherbourne, Baron of Didsbury
Swaythling, 5th Baron

LIFE PEERS

Alliance, Baron of Manchester
Barnett, Baron of Heywood & Royton, PC
Beecham, Baron, of Benwell
Brittan, Baron of Spennithorne PC, (QC)
Brown, Baron PC (Justice of Supreme
   Court)
Carlile, Baron, of Berriew, (QC)
Clinton-Davis, Baron of Hackney, PC
Collins, Baron of Mapesbury, PC
Deech, Baroness, of Cumnor, DBE
Dubs, Baron of Battersea
Dyson, Baron, (Master of the Rolls) PC
Ezra, Baron of Horsham, MBE
Feldman, Baron of Elstree
Fink, Baron of Northwood
Glasman, Baron of Stoke Newington &
   Stamford Hill
Gold, Baron of Westcliff-on-Sea
Goldsmith, Baron, of Allerton, PC, (QC)
Grabiner, Baron, of Aldwych, (QC)
Grade, Baron of Yarmouth
Greengross, Baroness, of Notting Hill
Haskel, Baron of Higher Broughton
Hayman, Baroness of Dartmouth Park, PC
Henig, Baroness of Lancaster
Hoffman, Baron of Chedworth PC
Howard, Baron of Lympne, CH, PC, (QC)
Jacobs, Baron of Belgravia
Janner, Baron of Braunstone, (QC)
Joffe, Baron of Liddington
Kalms, Baron of Edgware
Kestenbaum, Baron of Foxcote
King, Baroness of Bow
Kramer, Baroness of Richmond Park
Lawson, Baron of Blaby, PC
Lester, Baron of Herne Hill, (QC)
Levene, Baron of Portsoken
Levy, Baron of Mill Hill
Livingstone, Baron of Parkhead
Marks, Baron of Henley-on-Thames, (QC)
Miller, Baroness of Hendon
Millett, Baron of St Marylebone, PC
Moser, Baron of Regent's Park, FBA
Neuberger, Baron of Abbotsbury PC
   (President of Supreme Court)
Neuberger, Baroness of Primrose Hill, DBE
Oppenheim-Barnes, Baroness of Gloucester,
   PC
Palmer, Baron of Childs Hill
Pannick, Baron of Radlett, QC
Peston, Baron of Mile End
Phillips, Baron of Worth Matravers, PC, (QC)
Puttnam, Baron of Queensgate, CBE
Saatchi, Baron of Staplefield
Sacks, Baron of Aldgate, (Emeritus Chief
   Rabbi)

Sassoon, Baron of Ashley Park
Sheldon, Baron of Ashton-under-Lyne PC
Stern, Baron of Brentford
Sterling, Baron of Plaistow, CBE
Stern, Baroness of Vauxhall
Stone, Baron of Blackheath
Strasburger, Baron of Langridge
Sugar, Baron of Clapton
Triesman, Baron of Tottenham
Turnberg, Baron of Cheadle
Wasserman, Baron of Pimlico
Weidenfeld, Baron of Chelsea
Winston, Baron of Hammersmith
Wolfson, Baron of Aspley Guise
Wolfson, Baron of Sunningdale
Woolf, Baron of Barnes, PC
Young, Baron of Graffham, PC

MEMBERS OF PARLIAMENT

Abrahams, Debbie, (Lab.), Oldham East
and Saddleworth.
Bercow, Rt. Hon John, PC, (Mr Speaker),
Buckingham
Berger, Luciana, (Lab), Liverpool Wavertree
Djanogly, Jonathan S. (C.), Huntingdon
Ellis, Michael (C), Northampton North
Ellman, Louise (Lab.), Liverpool Riverside
Fabrikant, Michael (C.), Lichfield
Featherstone, Lynne (Lib.), Hornsey & Wood
Green
Halfon, Robert, (C), Harlow
Hamilton, Fabian (Lab.), Leeds North East
Harrington, Richard, (C), Watford
Hodge, Rt. Hon Margaret, PC (Lab.), Bark-
ing
Huppert, Julian, (Lib.), Cambridge
Kaufman, Rt. Hon. Sir Gerald, PC (Lab.),
Manchester, Gorton
Letwin, Rt Hon. Oliver, PC (C.), Dorset West
Lewis, Ivan (Lab.), Bury South
Lewis, Dr Julian (C.), New Forest East
Milliband, Rt. Hon Edward, PC, (Lab)
Doncaster North
Newmark, Brooks (C.), Braintree
Rifkind, Rt. Hon. Sir Malcolm, PC, (C.),
Kensington & Chelsea
Scott, Lee (C.), Ilford North
Shapps, Rt. Hon. Grant, PC (C.), Welwyn
and Hatfield
Winnick, David (Lab.), Walsall North

BARONETS

Cahn, Sir Albert Jonas
Jessel, Sir Charles John
Richardson, Sir Anthony Lewis
Tuck, Sir Bruce A. R.
Waley-Cohen, Sir Stephen

KNIGHTS

Arbib, Sir Martyn
Bean, Sir David (the Hon. Mr Justice)
Bean, Sir Michael
Berman, Sir Franklin
Bernstein, Sir Howard
Berry, Sir Michael, FRS
Bindman, Sir Geoffrey
Blank, Sir Victor
Blom-Cooper, Sir Louis
Bodrer, Sir Walter
Burgen, Sir Arnold, FRS
Burnton, Sir Stanley (QC), PC
Burton, Sir Michael (the Hon. Mr Justice)
Callman, Sir Clive (His Honour)
Calne, Sir Roy, FRS
Caro, Sir Anthony, OM
Chinn, Sir Trevor, CVO
Cohen, Sir Edward
Cohen, Sir Ivor Harold
Cohen, Prof. Sir Philip
Cohen, Sir Ronald
Colman, Sir Anthony (the Hon. Mr Justice)
Copisarow, Sir Alcon
Crewe, Sir Ivor
Cunliffe, Sir Jonathon
Djanogly, Sir Harry
Eder, Sir Bernard (Mr Justice)
Elton, Sir Arnold
Epstein, Sir Anthony, FRS
Etherton, Sir Terence (QC) Chancellor of
the High Court
Feldman, Sir Basil
Feldman, Sir Marc
Fersht, Sir Alan, PhD, FRS
Fox, Sir Paul
Freedman, Sir Lawrence, PC
Gainsford, Sir Ian
Garrard, Sir David
Geim, Sir Andre
Gershon, Sir Peter
Gilbert, Sir Martin, CBE, PC
Gillinson, Sir Clive
Globe, Sir Henry Brian (the Hon. Mr Justice)
Goldberg, Prof. Sir David
Goode, Prof. Sir Roy
Gordon, Sir Donald
Gordon, Sir Gerald Henry, CBE, (QC)
Green, Sir Allan, KCB
Green, Sir Philip
Greengross, Sir Alan
Grierson, Sir Ronald
Halpern, Sir Ralph
Harwood, Sir Ronald
Hatter, Sir Maurice
Heller, Sir Michael
Henriques, Sir Richard (the Hon. Mr Justice)

Hirsch, Sir Peter Bernhard, FRS
Hytner, Sir Nicholas
Isaacs, Sir Jeremy
Jacobs, Sir Francis Geoffrey KCMG, (QC)
Jacobsen, Sir George
Japhet, Ernest I., Hon. KBE
Jordan, Sir Gerald
Jowell, Sir Jeffrey, (QC)
Kapoor, Sir Anish
Kaufman, Sir Gerald, PC, MP
Kerzner, Sol
Kingsland, Sir Richard, AO, CBE, DFC
Klug, Sir Aaron, FRS, OM
Kohn, Sir Ralph, FRS
Kornberg, Prof. Sir Hans Leo, FRS
Krusin, Sir Stanley Marks, CB
Lachmann, Prof. Sir Peter, FRS
Landau, Sir Dennis
Lauterpacht, Prof. Sir Elihu
Lawrence, Sir Ivan, (QC)
Leigh, Sir Geoffrey, KCB
Leveson, Sir Brian (Lord Justice) PC
Lewis, Sir Leigh
Lewison, Sir Kim (Lord Justice) PC
Lightman, Sir Gavin, (QC)
Lipton, Sir Stuart
Lipworth, Sir Sydney
Marmot, Prof. Sir Michael
Michels, Sir David
Miller, Sir Jonathan
Moritz, Sir Michael KBE
Ognall, Sir Harry Henry
Oppenheim, Sir Alexander, OBE
Pepper, Sir Michael, FRS
Pepys, Sir Mark
Pomeroy, Sir Brian
Reich, Sir Erich
Rieger, Sir Clarence Oscar, CBE
Rifkind, Sir Malcolm, KCMG, PC, (QC), MP
Ritblat, Sir John
Rix, Sir Bernard, PC, (QC)
Robinson, Sir Albert EP
Rodley, Prof. Sir Nigel
Rosenthal, Sir Norman
Rothschild, Sir Evelyn de
Rubin, Sir Peter
Samuelson, Sir Sydney W., CBE
Sedley, Sir Stephen, PC, (QC)
Serota, Sir Nicholas CH
Shaffer, Sir Peter
Sheinwald, Sir Nigel Elton, KCGM
Sher, Sir Anthony
Sherman, Sir Lou, OBE
Shock, Sir Maurice
Sieff, Sir David
Silber, Sir Stephen (the Hon. Mr Justice)
Smith, Sir David, AK, CVO, AO
Solomon, Sir Harry

Sorrell, Sir Martin
Sternberg, Sir Sigmund, KC*SG
Stoppard, Sir Tom, OM
Stratton, Sir Michael
Supperstone, Sir Michael (the Hon. Lord Justice)
Wald, Sir Nicholas
Walport, Sir Mark
Weinberg, Sir Mark
Wesker, Sir Arnold
Zissman, Sir Bernard
Zunz, Sir Jack

DAMES

Abramsky, Dame Jennifer
Blume, Dame Hilary
Duffield, Dame Vivien
Genn, Dame Hazel
Higgins, Dame Rosalyn, (QC)
Hyde, Dame Helen
Porter, Dame Shirley
Rebuck, Dame Gail
Robins, Dame Ruth, BA
Ronson, Dame Gail
Rose, Dame Vivien (Hon. Mrs Justice)
Suzman, Dame Janet
Waterman, Dame Fanny
Wolfson de Botton, Dame Janet

FELLOWS OF THE ROYAL SOCIETY

Abramsky, Samson
Beloff, Michael, (QC)
Berry, Sir Michael
Born, Prof. Gustav Victor Rudolf
Brenner, Prof. Sydney, CH
Burgen, Sir Arnold
Calne, Sir Roy
Cohen, Prof. Sydney, CBE
Domb, Prof. Cyril
Dunitz, Prof. Jack David
Dwek, Raymond
Epstein, Sir Michael Anthony (Vice-President, 1986–91)
Fersht, Prof. Sir Alan
Glynn, Prof. Ian Michael
Goldstone, Prof. Jeffrey
Grant, Ian Philip
Hirsch, Prof. Sir Peter Bernhard
Horn, Prof. Gabriel
Huppert, Dr Herbert
Ish-Horowicz, David
Josephson, Prof. Brian David
Kalmus, George Ernest
Kennard, Dr Olga, OBE
Klug, Sir Aaron, OM (President 1995–2000)
Kohn, Sir Ralph, FRS
Kornberg, Prof. Sir Hans Leo

Lachmann, Sir Peter Julius
Levitt, Malcolm
Levitt, Michael
Mahler, Prof. Kurt
Mandelstam, Prof. Joel
Mandelstam, Prof. Stanley
Mestel, Prof. Leon
Neumann, Prof. Bernard H.
Orgel, Prof. L. E.
Orowan, Prof. Egon
Pepper, Dr Sir Michael
Pepys, Pepys
Roitt, Prof. Ivan
Sanders, Prof. Jeremy
Segal, Dr Anthony Walter
Sondheimer, Prof. Franz
Wald, Prof. Nicholas
Waldmann, Prof. Herman
Weinberg, Prof. Felix
Weiskrantz, Prof. Lawrence
Woolfson, Prof. Michael Mark

Foreign Members

Calvin, Prof. Melvin
Katzir, Prof. Ephraim, form. President of
　Israel
Kornberg, Prof. Arthur

FELLOWS OF THE BRITISH ACADEMY

Bogdanor, Prof. Vernon, CBE
Cohen, Prof. Gerald Allan
Genn, Prof. Hazel, CBE
Goodman, Prof. Martin
Hajnal, Prof. John
Hobsbawm, Prof. Eric John, CH
Israel, Prof. Jonathan Irvine
Josipovici, Prof. Gabriel David
Lewis, Prof. Bernard
Lukes, Prof. Steven
Marks, Prof. Shula
Moser, Lord, KCB, CBE
Prais, Sigbert J.
Prawer, Prof. Siegbert Salomon
Rothschild, Lord OM, MA
Steiner, Prof. George
Stern, Lord
Supple, Prof. Barry, CBE
Ullendorff, Prof. Edward (Vice-President
　1980–82)
Vermes, Prof. Geza
Yamey, Prof. Basil Selig, CBE

Corresponding Fellows

Blau, Prof. J.
Levi-Strauss, Prof. Claude
Samuelson, Prof. Paul Antony

VICTORIA CROSS

Lieutenant Frank Alexander De Pass
Captain Robert Gee, M.C.
Lance Corporal Leonard Keysor
Acting Corporal Issy Smith
Private Jack White
Lieut.-Cmdr. Thomas William Gould, RNVR
Flt Sgt Arthur Louis Aarons
Co Sgt Major John Kenneally

GEORGE CROSS

Errington, Harry
Lewin, Sgt. Raymond M., RAF
Latutin, Capt. Simmon
Newgass, Lieutenant-Commander Harold
　Reginald, RNVR

ORDER OF MERIT

Caro, Sir Anthony
Freud, Lucian, CH
Klug, Sir Aaron, FRS
Rothschild, Lord
Stoppard, Sir Tom

COMPANIONS OF HONOUR

Brenner, Prof. Sydney, FRS
Freud, Lucian, OM
Hertz, Rabbi Dr Joseph Herman, LL.D
Hobsbawm, Prof. Eric John Ernest, FBA
Pinter, Harold
Serota, Sir Nicholas

NOBEL PRIZE WINNERS

Between 1901 and 2012, Nobel Prizes have
been awarded to more than 800 individuals,
of whom at least 20% were Jews.

Peace

Tobias Asser; Menachem Begin; Rene
Cassin; Alfred Fried; Henry Kissinger;
Shimon Peres; Yitzhak Rabin; Sir Joseph
Rotblat; Elie Wiesel.

Physics

Alexi Abrikosov; Zhores Alferov; Hans
Bethe; Felix Bloch; Aage Bohr; Niels Bohr;
Max Born; Georges Charpak; Claude
Cohen-Tannoudji; Leon Cooper; Albert
Einstein; Francois Englert; Enrico Fermi;
Richard Feynman; James Franck; Ilya
Frank; Jerome Friedman; Dennis Gabor;
Murray Gell-Mann; Vitaly Ginzburg; Don-
ald Glaser; Sheldon Glashow; Roy Glauber;

David Gross; Serge Haroche; Gustav Hertz; Robert Hofstadter; Brian Josephson; Lev Landau; Leon Lederman; David Lee; Gabriel Lippmann; Albert Michelson; Ben Mottelson; Douglas D. Osheroff; Wolfgang Pauli; Saul Pelmutter; Arno Penzias; Martin Perl; H. David Politzer; Isidor Isaac Rabi; Frederick Reines; Burton Richter; Adam Riess; Melvin Schwartz; Julian Schwinger; Emilio Segre; Jack Steinberger; Otto Stern; Igor Tamm; Steven Weinberg; Eugene Wigner.

Chemistry

Sidney Altman; Adolph von Baeyer; Paul Berg; Herbert Brown; Melvin Calvin; Martin Chalfie; Aaron Ciechanover, Walter Gilbert; Fritz Haber; Herbert Hauptman; Dudley Herschebach; Gerhard Herzberg; George de Hevesy; Avraham Hershko; Roald Hoffmann; Jerome Karle; Martin Karplus; Aaron Klug; Walter Kohn; Roger Kornberg; Robert Lefkowitz; Michael Levitt; Rudolf Marcus; Henri Moissan; Max Perutz; Ilya Prigogine; Irwin Rose; Daniel Shechtman; William Stein; Otto Wallach; Arieh Warshel; Richard Willstatter; Ada Yonath.

Medicine

Richard Axel; Julius Axelrod; David Baltimore; Robert Barany; Gary Becker; Baruj Benacerraf; Bruce Beutler; Gunter Blobel; Konrad Bloch; Baruch Blumberg; Sydney Brenner; Michael Brown; Sir Ernst Chain; Stanley Cohen; Gerald Maurice Edelman; Gertrude Eilon; Paul Ehrlich; Joseph Erlanger; Andrew Z. Fire; Edmund H. Fischer; Robert Furchgott; Herbert Gasser; Alfred Gilman; Joseph Goldstein; Paul Greengard; H. Robert Horvitz; Francois Jacob; Eric Kandel; Sir Bernard Katz; Arthur Kornberg; Sir Hans Krebs; Karl Landsteiner; Joshua Lederberg; Rita Levi-Montalcini; Fritz Lipmann; Otto Loewi; Salvador Luria; Andre Lwoff; Elias Metchnikoff; Otto Meyerhoff; Cesar Milstein; Hermann Joseph Muller; David Nathans; Marshall Nirenberg; Andrew Schally; Stanley Prusiner; Tadeus Reichstein; Martin Rodbell; James E. Rothman; Randy W. Schekman; Ralph Steinman; Howard Martin Temin; John Robert Vane; Harold Varmus; Selman Abraham Waksman; George Wald; Otto Warburg; Rosalyn Yalow.

Literature

Shmuel Agnon; Saul Bellow; Henri Bergson; Joseph Brodsky; Elias Canetti; Nadine Gordimer; Paul von Heyse; Imre Kertész; Elfriede Jelinek; Boris Pasternak; Harold Pinter; Nelly Sachs; Jaroslav Seifert; Isaac Bashevis Singer.

Economics

George Akerlof; Kenneth Arrow; Robert Aumann; Gary Becker; Peter Diamond; Robert Fogel; Milton Friedman; John Harsanyi; Leonid Hurwicz; Daniel Kahneman; Leonid Kantorovich; Lawrence Klein; Paul Krugman; Simon Kuznets; Wassily Leontief; Harry Markowitz; Eric Maskin; Merton Miller; Franco Modigliani; Roger Myerson; Alvin E. Roth; Paul Samuelson; Myron Scholes; Reinhard Selten; Herbert Simon; Robert Solow; Joseph Stiglitz.

Who's Who

AARON, Martin, MBA, FAIA, FRSM, FRSA.

b. London, Jan. 25, 1937; m. Jean née Joseph; Vis. Prof. Staffordshire University; Life Fel. Royal Society Medicine; Life Fel. Royal Society of Arts; Hon. T. British Association for the Study of Spirituality (2010-); Pres. B'nai B'rith First-lodge of England (2009-11); M. Advisory Cttee. Chizuk for Mental Health (2006-); Fdr. Ch. National Spirituality and Mental Health (interfaith) Forum (2003–); Adv. M. All-Party Parliamentary Group on Mental Health (2001-); Mem. Advisory Council, Three Faiths Forum (1998-); Fdr. and H. Pres. Jewish Association for the Mental Illness (1989-); Mentor, The Prince's Trust (1995–2006); form. Mem. Concern for the Mentally Ill (1992-98); T. Ravenswood Foundation (1986-90); Mem. Board of Deputies (1979-86); Fdr. Ch. Jewish Society for the Mentally Handicapped (1977-86); form. Mem. Adv. Council, MIND (1976-83); form. Mem. Adv. Council, MENCAP (1975-83); Fdr. Ch. Ravenswood Aid Cttee. (1955-63).

Add c/o JAMI, Olympia House, Armitage Road, London NW11 7RQ

Tel 020 8458 2223/07973 375 170

Email mentalitygb@aol.com

ABRAHAM, Dayan Yonason,

Rabbi, New Hendon Minyan (2006-); Dayan, London Beth Din (2001-); Dayan, Melbourne Beth Din (1997-2001); Rabbi, Caulfield Hebrew Congregation (1995-2001); Rabbinical Consultant, Jewish Association for Business Ethics.

Add The London Beth Din, 305 Ballards Lane, North Finchley, London N12 8GB

Tel 020 8343 6270 *Fax* 020 8343 6257

Email info@bethdin.org.uk *Website* www.theus.org.uk

ABRAMS, Hester,

Dir. Jewish Book Week (2012-); Board of Deputies, Deputy, United Synagogue (2012-); Mem. Commission on Women in Jewish Leadership (2011-12); Board of Deputies Deputy, Brondesbury Park United Synagogue (2009-12); Advisor and Tru. Project Mosaic (2009-12); Mediator, Communications consultant, TV researcher, Facilitator (2004-12); Ed. Reuters Magazine (2000-04); Foreign and Financial correspondent and Ed. Reuters (1988-2004).

Add Jewish Book Week, ORT House, 126 Albert Street, London NW1 7NE

Tel 020 7446 8772

Email hester@jewishbookweek.com *Website* www.jewishbookweek.com

ABRAMSON, Glenda (née Melzer), BA, MA, PhD (Rand), H. D.Litt (HUC).

b. Johannesburg, Nov. 16, 1940; m. David; Academic; Prof. Hebrew and Jewish Studies, University Oxford (2006-); Leverhulme Emer. Fellowship (2009-10); form. Cowley Lecturer Post-Biblical Hebrew, Oxford (1989-2006); Dr. of Humane Letters Honoris Causa HUC-JIR (1998); Ed. Journal of Modern Jewish Studies. Among recent publications: Soldiers' Tales: Two Palestinian Jewish Soldiers in the Ottoman Army during the First World War (2013); Hebrew Writing of the First World War (2008); Ed. with H. Kilpatrick, Religious Perspectives in Modern Hebrew and Islamic Literatures (2006); Ed. Encyclopaedia of Modern Jewish Culture (2005); Modern Jewish Mythologies (2000); The Experienced Soul: Studies in Amichai (1997); The Oxford Book of Hebrew Short Stories (1996); Tradition and Trauma (1995, with D. Patterson); Jewish Education and Learning (1994, with T. Parfitt); Journal of Modern Jewish Studies (Ed.).

Add Oriental Institute, Pusey Lane, Oxford OX1 2LE

Tel 01865 278 093

Email glenda.abramson@stx.ox.ac.uk

ABULAFIA, David Samuel Harvard, MA, PhD, Litt.D, FBA, FRHistS.

b. Twickenham, Dec. 12, 1949; m. Anna née Sapir; Historian; Prof. Mediterranean History, Cambridge; Fel. Gonville and Caius College (1974-); Commendatore dellí Ordine della Stella della Solidarietà Italiana (2003). Among recent publications: The Great Sea (2011); The Discovery of Mankind (2008); Italy in the Central Middle Ages (Ed. 2004); The Mediterranean in History (2003); Medieval Frontiers (Ed. 2002); Mediterranean Encounters

(2000); Cambridge Medieval History, vol. 5, 1198-1300 (Ed. 1999); The Western Mediterranean Kingdoms (1997).

Add Gonville & Caius College, Cambridge CB2 1TA

Tel 01233 332 473

Email dsa1000@hermes.cam.ac.uk

ALBERTI, Sir (Kurt) George Matthew Mayer, MA, BM, BCh, Kt, DPhil, FRCP, FRCPE, FRCPath.

b. Sept. 27, 1937; m. Prof. Stephanie A. Amiel; Ch. Kings College Hospital NHS Foundation Trust, London (2011-); Ch. Diabetes UK (2009-12); Snr. Research Fel. Imperial College, London (2002); Pres. Royal College of Physicians (1997–2002); Prof. of Medicine, University of Newcastle upon Tyne (1985–2002), Dean of Medicine (1995–97); H. DSc: Warwick, Cranfield (2005). Publ.: Author and Ed. of many medical publications.

Add Hambledon Wing, King's College Hospital, NHS Foundation Trust, Denmark Hill, London SE5 9RS

Tel 020 8670 8770

Email george.alberti@ncl.ac.uk

ALDERMAN, Geoffrey, D. Litt (Oxon), MA, D.Phil (Oxon), FRHistS, FRSA, FICPD, MIQA, MCMI.

b. Hampton Court, Feb. 10, 1944; m. Marion née Freed; Prof. Politics Contemporary History University Buckingham (2007-); Guest Prof. Ariel University, Israel (2010-12); Snr. V. Pres. American Intercontinental University, London (2002-06); Snr. V. Pres. Touro College, N.Y. (1999-2002); Pro. V. Ch. and Prof. Middlesex University (1994-99); Visiting Fel. Oxford Centre for Higher Education Policy Studies; form. Prof. of Politics and Contemporary History, Royal Holloway College (London University), Snr. Associate, Oxford Hebrew Centre. Among recent publications: Modern British Jewry; Controversy and Crisis: Studies in the History of the Jews in Modern Britain (2008); The Federation of Synagogues 1887-1987, London Jewry and London Politics, 1889-1986.

Add 172 Colindeep Lane, London NW9 6EA

Email geoffreyalderman@gmail.com *Website* www.geoffreyalderman.com

ALEXANDER-PASSE, Anita,

b. London, July 23, 1931; Speaker; Fundraiser; Initiated exchange of nurses and medical personnel between Homerton Hospital in Hackney and Rambam Medical Centre in Haifa, Israel (2001-); Dir. British Friends of Rambam Medical Centre (1993-); Ch. Operation Wheelchairs Cttee. (1991-); Past Ch. Na'amat/Pioneer Women and WIZO; Correspondent, Jewish Chronicle (1980-90); Volunteer, Miyad (1993-97); Mem. Board of Deputies; JIA; Achdut and Friends of Ben Gurion University. Publ.: A Celebration of Life in Poetry ans Prose (2001).

Add 1 Opal Court, 120 Regents Park Road, London N3 3HY

Tel 020 8371 1500

Email anita@rambamuk.co.uk *Website* www.rambamuk.co.uk

ALONY, Rabbi Dr Dayan Michel Asher, B.A. PhD.

b. Dublin; Mar. 29, 1946; Dayan in Europe, based in Gateshead UK (2005-); Dayan, USA Federation Kashrus Board (1999-2005); Chief Rabbi and Av Beth Din, Helsinki, The Jewish Community of Finland (1996-98); Chief Rabbi and Av Beth Din, The Jewish Community of Estonia (1996-98); Snr. Rabbi, Concord Hotel, New York (1990-96); Dayan, USA The Federation Kashrus Board (1990-96); Rabbi and Dayan Long Island Iggud Harabonim (1988-90); Snr. Lecturer, Ida Crown College, Chicago (1985-88); Rabbinical Advisor to Lord Bishop Cremin of the Catholic Community, Sydney (1982-84); Fdr. Hineni Movement of Australia (1975 -); Chief Min. Central Synagogue Sydney Australia (1975-84); Dayan, the Sydney Beth Din (1975-84); Supervising Rabbi, Liverpool Kashrut Board (1973-75); Rabbi Southport Hebrew Congregation (1968-75); Ch. Council of Christians and Jews (1968-75); Chaplain the Jewish Home for the Blind (1969-75); Co-Fdr. Counterpoint Programmes; Board Mem. Shalom College, University of New South Wales; Presenter N.S.W. Yiddish Programs; Chaplain Merseyside J.L. & G. Brigade, Major.

Add 46 Windermere Street West, Gateshead, Tyne & Wear NE8 1TX

Tel 0191 442 0576/07949 613 613

Email rebmichel@live.co.uk

ALPERT, Michael, MA, PhD.

b. London, Dec. 24, 1935; m. Marie Pradillo Gomez de Acosta; Pres. JHSE (2009-10); Emer. Prof. of Modern and Contemporary History of Spain, University Westminster (1996-2001, Reader, Snr. Lecturer 1966-96). Publ.: The Republican Army in the Spanish Civil War (2013); The Chaste Wife, translated from Elia Karmona's Ladino Novel La Muz'er Onesta, (2009); Secret Judaism and the Spanish Inquisition (2008); A New International History of the Spanish Civil War (1994, 2nd Edition 2004); London 1849 (2004); Two Spanish Picaresque Novels (2nd Edition 2003); Crypto-Judaism and the Spanish Inquisition (2nd Edition 2001).

Add 3 Donaldson Road, London NW6 6NA

Tel 020 7624 9116

Email malpert@onetel.com

ANGIER, Carole (née Brainin), MA (Oxon), MLitt (Cantab), FRSL.

b. London, Oct. 30, 1943; Writer; Associate Lecturer, Creative Writing MA, Oxford Brookes University (2011-12); Tutor in Life Writing, Birkbeck College, London (2005-11); Royal Literary Fund Fel. Oxford Brookes University (2010-11), University Warwick (2008-09, 1999-2003); Fdr. and Tutor, Practice of Biography, University Warwick (2002-03); Tutor, Open University (1975-85). Among recent publications: Jean Rhys: Life and Work and the Double Bond: Primo Levi, A Biography (both reissued, 2011); Life Writing: A Writers' and Artists' Companion (Co-author Sally Cline 2010); See How I Land: Oxford poets and exiled writers (Co-Ed. 2009); Lyla and Majnon by Hasan Bamyani (T. and Ed. 2008); The Story of My Life: Refugees Writing in Oxford (Ed. 2005); The Double Bond: Primo Levi, a Biography (2002); Tongue Pie by Fred Russell (Ed.).

Add 13 High Street, Ascott-under-Wychwood, Oxon OX7 6AW

Tel 01993 830 414

Email carole@cangier.co.uk

ANTICONI, Paul,

Chief Exec. World Jewish Relief (2006-); T. Tree Aid (2006-); Head of International Aid, British Red Cross Society (1999–2006); Leader of Disaster Response Operations, Red Cross (1994-2006).

Add World Jewish Relief, Oscar Joseph House, 54 Crewys Road, London NW2 2AD

Tel 020 8736 1250 *Fax* 020 8736 1259

Email info@wjr.org.uk *Website* www.wjr.org.uk

APPLE, Rabbi Dr Raymond, AO, RFD, MLitt, BA, LLB, Hon LLD, Hon DUniv.

b. Melbourne, Dec. 27, 1935; Jt. Pres. Australian Council of Christians and Jews (1996-); Snr. Rabbi, Australian Defence Force (1988-2006); Dayan and Reg. Sydney Beth Din (1975-2005); Emer. Rabbi, Great Synagogue, Sydney, Snr. Rabbi (1972-2005); Life Rabbinic Gov.; Pres. Association of Rabbis and Ministers of Australia and New Zealand (1988-1992, 1980-4); Pres. Australian Jewish Historical Society (1985-9); M. Bayswater Synagogue (1960-5), Hampstead Synagogue (1965-1972); H. V. Pres. New South Wales Bd. of Jewish Education; Tru. and Emer. Master Mandelbaum House, Sydney University; form. Lecturer, Judaic Studies, Sydney University; Lecturer, Jewish Law, NSW University; Religious Dir. AJY (1959-63). Publ.: Oz Torah: Weekly emails since 1995; Episodes and Eccentrics (2010); Freemasonry: Studies, Speeches and Sensibilities (2009); 'Let's Ask the Rabbi' (2009); To Be Continued: Memoirs and Musings (2009); The Big Shule: A History of the Great Synagogue, Sydney (2008); The Jewish Way: Jews and Judaism in Australia (3rd edition 2002); Francis Lyon Cohen: The Passionate Patriot (1995); The Hampstead Synagogue, 1892-1967 (1967).

Add 20/6 Hatekufah, Jerusalem 92628 Israel

Tel +972 (2) 6794 180

Email rabbiapple@oztorah.com *Website* www.oztorah.com

ARIEL, David, PhD, MA, BA.

    b. New York, USA, June 30, 1949; Pres. Oxford Centre for Hebrew and Jewish Studies (2011-); Pres. Siegal College of Judaic Studies, Cleveland, Ohio, USA (1982-2007). Publ.: Kabbalah: The Mystic Quest in Judaism (2006); Spiritual Judaism (1998); What do Jews Believe? (1995).

    Add Oxford Centre for Hebrew And Jewish Studies, Yarnton Manor, Yarnton Oxford OX5 1PY

ARKUSH, Jonathan,

    b. London, 1954; Barrister and Mediator, 11 Stone Buildings; Deputy Master Chancery Division; V. Pres. Board of Deputies of British Jews (2009-); ADRg Award for services to Mediation (2006); Called to Bar, Middle Temple (1977); Mem. Lincoln's Inn.

    Add 6 Bloomsbury Square, London WC1A 2LP

    Email arkush@11sb.com *Website* www.bod.org.uk www.11sb.com

ARKUSH, Rabbi Shmuel,

    b. May 5, 1951; Rabbi, Birmingham Jewish Community Care (2000-); Chaplain of the Midlands Region Chaplaincy Bd. (1980-85); Dir. Lubavitch in the Midlands; Dir. Operation Judaism; Hd. B.J.E.B. Talmud Torah.

    Add 95 Willows Road, Birmingham B12 9QF

    Tel 0121 440 6673

    Email sarkush@lubavitchuk.com

AUERBACH, Geraldine Yvonne (née Kretzmar), MBE, BA (rand), STC (UCT).

    b. Kimberley, South Africa, to UK 1962; m. Ronnie; Fdr. Dir. Jewish Music Institute, SOAS, University London (1999-2011); Dir. 'Klezimer in the Park', Regents Park (2009-10), 'Simcha on the Square', Trafalgar Square (2006-8); Hon. Fel. SOAS (2008); presented a Day of Jewish Culture, Millennium Dome (2000), many premières including Kaddish for Terezin, Canterbury Cathedral (1986); Sacred Service, St Paul's Cathedral (1995) and York Minster (1990); Fdr. Dir. London Jewish Music Festival (1984-2000); established first full-time Jewish music lectureship at City University (With Professor Malcolm Troup, 1991); initiated a record label for historic or unrecorded Jewish music (1985) and established Jewish Music Distribution.

    Add P.O. Box 232, Harrow, Middlesex HA1 2NN

    Tel 020 8909 2445 *Fax* 020 8909 1030

    Email g.auerbach@jmi.org.uk

AVIDAN, Rabbi Hillel, MA .

    b. London, July 16, 1933, m. Ruth; M. Durban Progressive Jewish Congregation (2005-); First Ch. South African Faith Communities Environment Institute (SAFCEI 2007-08); Ch. Southern African Association Progressive Rabbis (2004-8); M. Bet David Reform Congregation, Johannesburg (1992-2003); Ch. Southern African Association Progressive Rabbis (1995-99); M. Ealing Liberal Synagogue (1986-92); and Ch. ULPS Rabbinic Conference (1990-92); form. M. West Central Liberal Synagogue (1985-92); form. M. Wimbledon and District Reform Synagogue (1974-81), Ch. RSGB Assembly of Rabbis, (1978-80), Teacher Reali High School, Haifa; Libr. Haifa University. Publ.: Feasts and Fasts of Israel, (Contr.) Judaism and Ecology; Renewing the vision.

    Add 28 O'Connor Road, Durban 3629 RSA

    Tel +27 31 266 2792 *Fax* +27 31 209 2429

    Email dpjc@sbsa.com

AZIZ, Alan, BSc., ACCA.

    b. London, Aug. 1, 1968; Chartered Accountant; Dir. Zionist Council Europe (1998-); Exec. Dir. ZF Great Britain and Ireland; Dir. Israel Connect European Training Programme.

    Add Zionist Federation, Box 1948, 116 Ballards Lane, Finchley, London N3 2DN

    Tel 020 8202 0202

    Email alan@zfuk.org

BAIGEL, Frank,

Mem. Jewish Leadership Council; Pres. Jewish Representative Council of Greater Manchester and Region.

Add JRC, Jewish Community Centre, Bury Old Road, Manchester M7 4QY

Tel 0161 720 8721

Email office@jewishmanchester.org *Website* www.jewishmanchester.org

BAKER, Adrienne, PhD, BSc.

b. Manchester, Feb. 15, 1936; UKCP Regd. Psychotherapist; Family Therapist and University Lecturer; Hon. Visiting Fel. School of Psychotherapy, Regent's College, London; Private Clinical Practice. Publ.: The Jewish Woman in Contemporary Society: Transitions and Traditions (1993).

Add 16 Sheldon Avenue, Highgate, London N6 4JT

Tel 020 8340 5970 (home)

Email adriennebaker@hotmail.co.uk *Website* www.highgate-psychotherapy.co.uk

BALFOUR-LYNN, Dr Lionel Peter, MA, MD (Cantab), FRCPCH, DCH.

b. London, May, 4, 1928; m. June Anne née Herbert; Paediatrician; Hon Paediatric Consultant, Hammersmith Hospital. Publ: numerous articles on Paediatric Asthma.

Add 69 Hampstead Way, London NW11 7LG

Tel 020 8455 9063

Email lbl@120harley.co.uk

BARNETT, Rt. Hon. Joel Barnett, Baron of Heywood & Royton, PC, JP.

b. Manchester, Oct. 14, 1923, m. Lilian née Goldstone; Accountant and Ch. and Dirs. of Companies; form. V. Ch. BBC Govs.; Mem. European Union Select Cttee.; Ch. European Union Sub. Cttee. on Finance, Trade and Industry; T. Victoria and Albert Museum; Ch. Education Broadcasting Society Trust; Ch. Public Accounts Cttee. House of Commons (1979-83); MP (Lab.) for Heywood and Royton (1964-83); Mem. of Cabinet (1977-79); Chief Sec. to H.M. Treasury (1974-79); form. Ch. Mem. Public Exp. Cttee.; Hon. Fel. Birkbeck College, London University; H. Doctorate, Strathclyde; Mem. Halle Cttee. Publ.: Inside the Treasury (1982).

Add 7 Hillingdon Road, Whitefield, Manchester M45 7QQ

BARNETT, Sara M., BA (Hons), RGN, RM, PGCE.

b. London, June 22, 1967; m. Dr Benjamin Jacobs; Research Midwife, Imperial College London (2010); Lecturer in Midwifery, City University London (2001); Antenatal and Resuscitation Midwife, The Portland Hospital (1993).

Add 32 Wykeham Road, London NW4 2SU

Tel 020 8203 2241 *Mobile* 07932 730 944

Email sara@smbarnett.com

BARON-COHEN, Gerald, BA, FCA.

b. London, July 13, 1932, m. Daniella née Weiser; Chartered Acct.; Pres. First Lodge of England, B'nai B'rith; National T. B'nai B'rith, District 15; V. Pres. Hillel Foundation; V. Ch. U.J.S.; Ed. Mosaic; Dep. Ed. New Middle East; Ch. Bamah-Forum for Jewish Dialogue (Jewish Unity Working Group).

Add 70 Wildwood Road NW11 6UJ

Email office2gbc@gmail.com

BAUM, Prof. Michael, MB, ChB, ChM, FRCS, FRCR (Hon), MD (Hon).

b. May 31, 1937; m. Judith née Marcus; Prof. Emer. Surgery and Visiting Prof. Medical Humanities, University College London; Prof. Surgery, University College London (1996-2002), Royal Marsden Hospital and Institute of Cancer Research (1990-96), Kings College London (1980-90). Publ.: The Third Tablet of the Holy Covenant (2013); Breast Beating: One man's odyssey in the search for an understanding of breast cancer, the meaning of life and other easy questions (2010); Classic Papers in Breast Disease (2003); Breast Cancer,

The Facts (1981, 3rd edition 1994); multiple publications on breast cancer, cancer therapy, cancer biology and the philosophy of science; Karl Popper Memorial Lecture, LSE 2009. Prizes: Gold Medal, Worshipful Company Apothecaries for Innovation in Therapeutics (2009); Swiss, St. Gallen Award, Breast Cancer Research (2007); Gold medal, International College of Surgeons (1994).

Add 2 Cotman Close, London NW11 6PT

Tel 020 8905 5069

Email michael@mbaum.freeserve.co.uk *Website* www.michaelbaum.co.uk/home.html

BAYFIELD, Rabbi Anthony Michael, CBE, MA (Cantab) DD (Lambeth).

b. Ilford, July 4, 1946; Pres. Movement for Reform Judaism; Lecturer, Personal Theology, Leo Baeck College; Hd. Movement for Reform Judaism (2005-10); Chief Exec. Reform Synagogues of Great Britain (1995-2004); Dir. Sternberg Centre for Judaism (1983-2004); Rabbi, North-West Surrey Synagogue (1972-82); Ch. Assembly of Rabbis, RSGB (1980-1). Publ.: Beyond the Dysfunctional Family: Jews, Christians and Muslims; He Kissed Him and They Wept (Ed. with Sidney Brichto and Eugene Fisher) (2001); Sinai, Law and Responsible Autonomy (1993); Dialogue with a Difference (Ed. with Marcus Braybrooke) (1992); Churban, The Murder of the Jews of Europe (1981).

Add c/o The Sternberg Centre for Judaism, 80 East End Road N3 2SY

BEECHAM, Lord Jeremy Hugh, MA, DCL, DL, H. Fellow, Northumbria University.

b. Leicester, Nov. 11, 1944; m. Brenda Elizabeth née Woolf (dec'd); Solicitor; Opposition Justice Spokesman, House of Lords (2012-); V. Ch. Members Adv. Bd. Harold Hartog School of Government, Tel Aviv University (2009-); Mem. Bd. New Israel Fund (2007-); Newcastle City Councillor (1967-); Ch. Local Govt. Association (1997-04), V. Ch. (2004-10); Ch. Labour Party NEC (2005-06); Ch. Association Metropolitan Authorities (1991-97); Leader Newcastle City Council (1977-84); Com. English Heritage (1983-87).

Add 39 The Drive, Newcastle upon Tyne NE3 4AJ

Email beechamj@parliament.uk

BELLOS, Vivienne, LRAM, ARCM.

b. Southend-on-Sea, Apr. 3, 1951; Musician; Dir. of Music, North Western Reform Synagogue; Musical Dir. Alyth Youth Singers; Artisitic Dir. Alyth Centre for Jewish Music.

Tel 020 8457 8795

Email viv@alyth.org.uk

BENARROCH, Rev. Halfon, BA.

b. Tangiers, Apr. 12, 1939; m. Delia née Sabah; Retired M. Bevis Marks; Emer. Hazan, Spanish and Portuguese Jews' Congregation.

Add 23 Lauderdale Tower, Barbican, London EC2Y 8BY

Tel 020 7638 5100

Email d.h@broch.org.uk

BENEDICTUS, David Henry, BA (Oxon).

b. London, Sept. 16, 1938; author; playwright; theatre Dir.; Hd. Drama, Putney High School; Royal Literary Fund Fel. (2007-08); Ed. Readings BBC Radio (1989-94) plus Radio 3 Drama from 1992; Commissioning Ed. Channel 4 (1984-86); Judith E. Wilson Vis. Fel. Cambridge University (1981-82); Producer 'Something Understood' (with Mark Tully); Berkoff's Macbeth for BBC Radio 4. Among recent publications: The Fourth of June (1962, 2013); Return to the Hundred Acre Wood (2009); Floating Down to Camelot (1985); The Stamp Collector (1984); Local Hero (1983); Who Killed the Prince Consort? (1983); Whose Life is it Anyway? (1981); Lloyd George (1981); A Twentieth Century Man (1978); The Rabbi's Wife (1976); A World of Windows (1971); The Guru and the Golf Club (1969); Hump, or Bone by Bone Alive (1967); This Animal is Mischievous (1965); You're a Big Boy Now (1963).

Add 95D Talfourd Road, London SE15 5NN

Tel 07986 041386

Email davidbenedictus@hotmail.com

BENJAMIN, Bill,

Ch. UJIA (2012-); Mem. Jewish Leadership Council; form. Co-Ch. Assembly of Masorti Synagogues; Tru. JCoSS, Man. Dir. Area Property Partners (UK) Ltd.

Email benjamin@areaprop.com

BENJAMIN, Marc Jonathan (Jon), LLB (Hons) (Manchester).

b. Croydon, Oct. 31, 1964; m. Suzanne née Taylor; Solicitor; Chief Exec. Board of Deputies of British Jews (2005-); form. Chief Exec. British ORT (1999-2004); Ch, Chief Executives' Forum for Jewish Charities; Bd. Mem. World Council of Jewish Communal Service; Mem, Charity Commission's Faiths Advisory Council; Mem. Policy Research Advisory Group, Institute for Jewish Policy Research.

Add Board of Deputies of British Jews, 6 Bloomsbury Square, London WC1A 2LP

Email info@bod.org.uk *Website* www.bod.org.uk

BERCOW, John, BA, MP.

b. Edgware, Jan. 19, 1963; m. Sally née Illman; Public Affairs Consultant; Speaker, House of Commons (2009-); Mem. International Development Select Committee (2004-); MP for Buckingham (1997-); Shadow Sec. of State, International Development (2003-4); Shadow M. Work and Pensions (2002); Shadow Chief Sec. to Treasury (2001-2); Special Adv. to Treasury M. (1995), to National Heritage Secretary (1995-96); Lambeth Councillor (1986-90).

Add House of Commons, London SW1A 0AA

Tel 020 7219 5300

Email bercowj@parliament.uk

BERKOVITCH, Rev. Mordechai, BA (Ed), Dip. Counselling, FIBA.

b. Sunderland, Feb. 15, 1934; H. Vis. M. Nightingale House (1974-2002); Dir. Jewish Studies, Carmel College (1984-92); H. Dir. Welfare Chief Rabbi's Cabinet (1980-1985); M. Kingston, Surbiton and District Synagogue (1972-84), Penylan Synagogue, Cardiff (1968-72), Central Synagogue, Birmingham (1956-68); Jewish Chaplain, Heathrow Airport (1976).

Add POB 2207, 45/3 King David Boulevard, Efrat 90435, Israel

Tel +972 (02) 676 4341 *Fax* +972 (02) 1532 676 4341

Email motisali@012.net.il

BERLINER, Martin,

CEO, Maccabi GB.

Add Shield House, Harmony Way, London NW4 2BZ

Email enquiries@maccabigb.org *Website* www.maccabigb.org

BERNSTEIN, Sir Howard, Kt.

b. Apr. 9, 1953; m. Vanessa; Chief Exec. Manchester City Council (1998-); Ch. ReBlackpool, (2008–10); Mem. Bd. Olympic Delivery Authority (2006–8); Sec. Commonwealth Games Organising Cttee. (1996–2002); Chief Exec. Manchester City Centre Task Force (1996–9).

Add Manchester City Council, Town Hall, Manchester M60 2LA

Tel 0161 234 3006

Email l.bernstein@manchester.gov.uk

BINSTOCK, Dayan Ivan Alan, BSc.

b. London, Oct. 27, 1950; Dayan London Beth Din; Rabbi, St. Johns Wood Synagogue (1996-); M. Golders Green Synagogue (1980-1996), New Synagogue (1978-80), Finsbury Park Synagogue (1974-78), R. South-East London District Synagogue (1972-74); Principal, North West London Jewish Day School.

Add 2 Vale Close, Maida Vale, London W9 1RR

Tel 020 7289 6229

BLACK, Gerald David, LLB, PhD, FRHistS.

b. Montreal, Jan 9, 1928; m. Anita née Abrahams; Mem. of Council of JHSE (1992-), Pres. (1998-2000), Hon. S. (2000-05); T. London Museum of Jewish Life and Jewish Museum (1983-); Ch. Balfour Society for Children (1964-). Among recent publications: Service with a Smile: A History of The league of Jewish Women (2010); Frank's Way: Frank Cass and 50 Years of Publishing (2008); The Joys of Friendship: A History of the Association of Jewish Friendship (2008); Jewish London: an Illustrated History (2003); Lord Rothschild and the Barber (2000); JFS: The History of the Jews' Free School (1997); Living Up West: The Jews of West End (1994).

Add 54 St. Johns Court, Finchley Road, London NW3 6LE

Tel 020 7624 8320 *Fax* 020 7372 9015

Email gblack4455@aol.com

BLACK, Keith,
b. 1959; KB & JB Properties LLP (2009-); T. UJIA National (2005-); Managing Dir. Regatta Ltd (1982-); T. Manchester CST.

Add Regatta Ltd, Risol House, Mercury Way, Urmston, Manchester M41 7RR

BLANK, Sir (Maurice) Victor, MA (Oxon), Hon FRCOG, CIMgt.
b. Manchester, 1942; m. Sylvia Helen née Richford; H. V. Pres. Jewish Leadership Council; form. Ch. Trinity Mirror Plc, Gus Plc and Lloyds Banking; T. Said Business School, Oxford; Adv. Texas Pacific Group; Ch. Rothschild Foundation Europe; Ch. Wellbeing of Women (RCOG Health Research Charity); H. Pres. UK/Israel Britain Business; Gov. Tel Aviv University; Ch. UJS/Hillel; Mem. Advisory Bd. UJIA; Ch. Social Mobility Foundation; Ch. European Adv. Bd. Cheung Kong graduate School of Business; form. British Business Ambassador; form. Council Mem. Oxford University; form. Mem. Financial Reporting Council. Publ.: Weinberg and Blank on Takeovers and Mergers.

Add P.O. Box 57793, London NW11 1HJ

Tel 07747 555 555

Email personalassistant@victorblank.com

BLUE, Rabbi Lionel, OBE, BA, MA, Dr. Div. (Durham) Dr Univ (Open U.).
b. London, Feb. 6, 1930; Broadcaster; Lecturer, Leo Baeck College (1967-); form. Convener Beth Din, RSGB; H. V. Pres. RSGB; V. Ch. Standing Conference Jews, Christians, Moslems in Europe; form. Rel. Dir. (Europe) World Union for Progressive Judaism; Ch. Assembly of Rabbis RSGB; form. M. St George's Settlement Synagogue, Middlesex New Synagogue. Templeton Prize 1993. Among recent publications: The Godseeker's Guide (2010); Best of Blue (2006); Hitchhiking to Heaven (2004); The Little Book of Lionel Blue Thoughts (2001); My Affair with Christianity (1999); Tales of Body and Soul (1995); How to get up when life gets you down (co-author, 1991).

Add 28 Cornwall Avenue, London N3 1LG

BLUMENFELD, Jeffery, OBE, BA (Hons), MA.
b. London, Dec. 1949; m. Judith née Freimark. Ch. Greater Manchester Jewish Mental Health Alliance (2009-); CEO, 'Chizuk' mental health organisation (2003-); Ch. Chief Rabbi's Steering Group on Social and Moral Education (1994-2002); Hd. Jewish Studies, Deputy Hd. Rosh Pinah Primary School (2002-3); Mem. Govt. Adv. Group, Marriage and Relationship Support (1997-2002); Act-Ch. JMC Legal Group (1993-2002); Dir. Jewish Marriage Council (1987-2002); Ed. Resources Bulletin, School Assemblies Council (1978-80); form. Dir. US Youth and Com Services Dept.

Add 41 Holders Hill Crescent, London NW4 1NE

Tel 020 8203 1458

Email jeffery@flowersfield.co.uk

BOGDANOR, Vernon, MA, FBA, CBE, FRSA.
b. London, July 16, 1943; Academic; Emer. Prof. of Government, Oxford University; Research Prof. King's College, London; Gresham Prof. of Law, Gresham College; Hon. Fel. Society for Advanced Legal Studies; Fel. Royal Academy of Social Sciences; Chevalier de la Legion d'Honneur; H. DLitt. University of Kent; Sir Isaiah Berlin Prize, 2008. Publ.: The Coalition and the Constitution (2011); The New British Constitution (2009); Joined-Up Government (2005); Devolution in the UK (1999); The Monarchy and the Constitution (1995); People and the Party System (1981); The British Constitution in the 20th Century.

Add 21 Edmunds Walk, London N2 0HU

Email virginia.preston@kcl.ac.uk

BOLCHOVER, Richard Louis, BA (Hons.), Mlitt. (Oxon).

b. Manchester, Aug. 15, 1960; m. Josephine née Rosenfelder; Fund Manager; Partner, Nimrod Capital LLP; V. Ch. Anglo-Israel Association; Fdr. form. Dir. Close Fund Management Ltd; form. Dir. Jewish Chronicle. Publ.: British Jewry and the Holocaust (1993, 2nd. Edition Littman Library 2004).

Add Nimrod Capital LLP, 3 St Helen's Place, London EC3A 6AB

Email info@nimrodcapital.com *Website* www.nimrodcapital.com

BOROWSKI, Ephraim, MA (Hons)(Glasgow), BPhil (Oxon), MBE.

b. Glasgow, Nov. 19, 1949; m. Margalit; Regional Ch. Board of Deputies (2009-, 2000-06); Dir. Scottish Council of Jewish Communities (1999-); V. Convenor, BEMIS (2004-11); Convenor (2011-); General Teaching Council (M. nominee (2001-11), appointed Lay Mem. (2012); Scottish Qualifications Authority: Principal Assessor for Advanced Higher Philosophy (2000-08); Commission for Racial Equality, Scottish Bd. (2005-07); V. Ch. and Acting Ch. Forum on Scottish Education (2003-07); Glasgow Jewish Representative Council: V. Pres. (2001-04, 1998-2000); Hon. T. Scottish Interfaith Council (2001-03); Pres. Royal Philosophical Society of Glasgow (2000-03); Race Equality Adv. Forum, Scottish executive (1999-2001); Tru. AUT (1993-96); University Glasgow: Lecturer in Philosophy (1976-91); Hd. Dept. (1993-95); Pres. Glasgow AUT (1985-90). Publ.: Scotland's Jews (with Kenneth Collins and Leah Granat, 2008); Collins Dictionary of Mathematics (UK: 1989; 2nd Edition, 2002, rev. Edition 2005, US: 1991, 2nd 2006).

Add 19 Norwood Drive, Glasgow G46 7LS

Tel 0141 638 1214

Email ephraim@scojec.org

BRAIER, Amy,

Dir. The Pears Foundation (2012-), Deputy Dir. (2007-12).

Add The Pears Foundation, Clive House, 2 Old Brewery Mews, Hampstead, London NW3 1PZ

Tel 020 7433 3333 *Fax* 020 7433 3343

Email contact@pearsfoundation.org.uk *Website* www.pearsfoundation.org.uk

BRASS, Laurence Stephen, LL.B.

b. London, July 26, 1947; m. Hilary née Stone; Tribunal Judge; Asylum Appeals Adjudicator (2000-); Mem. Board of Deputies, (1974-), Nat. T. (2009-); Ch. NHS Doctors Disciplinary Appeals Panel; Adviser, Liberal Democrats on Middle-East Affairs; form. V. Ch. Lib Dem Friends of Israel; Ch. Bushey Interfaith Forum; Ch. Board of Deputies 250th Anniversary Cttee.

Add 22 Grange Road, Bushey, Hertfordshire WD23 2LE

Tel 01923 223528 *Fax* 01923 490324

Email l.brass@ntlworld.com

BRAWER, Rabbi Naftali, PhD.

m. Dina; Chief Exec. Spiritual Capital Foundation (2011-); Co-V. Ch. Rabbinical Council of the Unitted Synagogue (2008-11); Rabbi, Borehamwood and Elstree Synagogue (2007-11); Rabbi, Northwood Synagogue (1996-2007); Adv. Rene Cassin Education; Chief Rabbi's Cabinet; Adv. Children of Abraham; Columnist, Jewish Chronicle; Broadcaster, BBC; Honorary research Fel. and Lecturer, LSJS; Author.

Add 7 Welbeck Street, London W1G 9YE

Tel 020 7487 0466

Email nbrawer@spiritual-capital.org *Website* www.spiritual-capital.org

BRICKMAN, Rev. Stanley Ivan,

b. London, Mar. 29, 1939; London Regional V. Pres. Cantorial Council of America (1994-); Cantor, Hampstead Synagogue (1987-2004); Assistant Grand Chaplain, United Grand Lodge of England (2003); Freeman, City of London (2002); Ch. Association of M.

(Chazanim); Cantor: Great Synagogue, Cape Town (1983-86), Singers Hill Synagogue, Birmingham (1971-83), New London Synagogue (1969-71), Ilford Synagogue (1966-69), Great Synagogue, Sheffield (1960-65). Publ.: Friday Evening Service with Zemirot for Children (Birmingham, 1976); Recording: Synagogue Liturgy Music with Singers Hill Choir (1981).

Add 3 Chatsworth Close, Borehamwood, Hertfordshire WD6 1UE

Tel 020 8387 9962

Email sib3432@googlemail.com

BRIER, Norma, OBE, BA (Hons), MSc, CQSW, JP.
b. London, Dec. 23, 1949; Co-Ch. Women in Leadership (May 2013); Interim Exec. Dir. Services, Scope (May-Dec 2012); Independent Consultant (Social Care Sector) Cross-Sector Consultancy (2011-); Tru. JC Trust (2011); Chief Exec. Norwood (1997-2011); Exec. Dir. Ravenswood Foundation (1989-96); Dir. of Com. Services, Ravenswood and Jewish Society for Mental Handicap (1985); Lecturer in Sociology and Social Work/Counselling, Harrow College (1982); Psychiatric Social Worker (1972), Social Worker, Camden (1968). OBE for Services to children and people with learning disabilities.

Add c/o Norwood, Broadway House, 80-82 The Broadway Stanmore, Middlesex HA7 4HB

Tel 020 8809 8809 *Fax* 020 8420 6800

Email normabrier@hotmail.com

BRIER, Sam, PhD, MA.
b. London, July 19, 1946; Dir./Management Consultant, Cross-Sector Consulting Ltd; Snr. Research Associate, Institute for Voluntary Action Research, University of London; form. Chief Exec. KIDS (1999-2005); form. Exec. Dir. (Resources), Norwood Ravenswood (1996-99); form. Exec. Dir. Norwood Childcare (1984-96).

Add IVAR, 25-31 Tavistock Place, London WC1H 9UT

Tel 07939 542 461

Email sambrier@hotmail.com *Website* www.cross-sectorconsulting.co.uk

BRITTAN, Lord Leon, of Spennithorne, PC, QC, MA (Cantab), H. DCL, Newcastle, Durham, H. LLD, Hull, Edinburgh, Bradford, Bath, D.Econ., Korea.
b. London, Sept. 25, 1939; Government trade adviser (2010-11); V. Pres. Commissioner of the European Communities (1989-99); MP (Con) for Richmond, North Yorkshire (1983-88); Sec. of State for Trade and Industry (1985-86); Home Sec. (1983-85); Bencher of the Inner Temple (1983); Chief Sec. to the Treasury (1981-83); MP (Con) for Cleveland and Whitby (1974-83); M. of State, Home Office (1979-81); V. Ch. Employment Cttee. of Parl. Conservative Party (1974-76); Ch. Bow Group (1964-65); Pres. Cambridge Union (1960). Among recent publications: A Diet of Brussels (2000); The 1997 Rede Lecture; European Competition Policy (1992); Europe: the Europe we need (1990); Hersch Lauterpacht Memorial Lectures, University of Cambridge (1990); Discussions on Policy (1989); Europe: Our Sort of Community (1989 Granada Guildhall Lecture); Monetary Union: the issues and the impact (1989).

Add House of Lords, London SW1A 0PW

BRODER, Rabbi Gavin, BA (Hons), MA (London).
b. Uitenhage, South Africa, Apr. 17, 1963; London Region's Jewish University Chaplain; Chief Rabbi of Ireland (1996-2000); form. M. Newbury Park Synagogue (1990-96), Staines Hebrew Congregation (1988-90); form. Governor, Avigdor Primary School.

Tel 07811 286 664

Email rabbibroder@mychaplaincy.co.uk *Website* www.mychaplaincy.co.uk

BRODIE, Rev. Gabriel,
b. Bratislava, July 7, 1924; Snr. M. Emer. Manchester Great New and Central Synagogue; Sec. Manchester Yeshiva; Ch. Jerusalem Academy Study Groups; H. Chaplain, Jewish Meals on Wheels, 45 Aid Society.

Add 43 Stanley Road, Salford M7 4FR

Tel 0161 740 2506

BRODIE, Rabbi Yehuda, BA (Hons).

b. Manchester, Oct. 3, 1950; CEO, MBD Shechita Services Ltd; MBD Kosher Certification Services Ltd; MBD Community Mikveh Ltd; Registrar, Manchester Beth Din; T. Keren L'David Education Trust.

Add Manchester Jewish Community Centre, Jubilee School, Bury Old Road M7 4QY

Tel 0161 740 9711

Email yb@mbd.org.uk *Website* www.mbd.org.uk

BROWN, Malcolm Denis, FSA, MA.

b. Fulwood, Mar. 24, 1936; m. Barbara née Langford; Research historian; V. Pres. JHSE (1999-), Pres. (1996-98); Lecturer, Extra-Mural Dept. University of London (1969-81); Archivist, Anglo-Jewish Archives (1965-66); Assistant Ed. Journal of Warburg and Courtauld Institutes (1962-64); form. Assistant Keeper of Manuscripts, British Museum. Publ.: David Salomons House: Catalogues of Mementos, Commemorative Medals and Ballooniana (1968, 1969 and 1970).

Add c/o The Jewish Historical Society of England, 33 Seymour Place, London W1H 5AP

Tel 020 7723 5852

BRUMMER, Alexander, BSc (Econ), MSc (Business Administration).

b. Brighton, May 25, 1949; m. Patricia Lyndsey née Magrill; City Office; City Ed. Daily Mail (2000-), Consultant Ed. (1999-2000); V. Pres. and Ch. International Division, Board of Deputies, (2012-), V. Ch International Division (2006-12); Guardian (1973-99); Associate Ed. (1998-99); Financial Ed. (1990-8); Foreign Ed. (1989-90); Washington Bureau Chief (1979-89); Financial Correspondent (1973-9); Publ: Britain for Sale (2012); Great Pensions Robbery (2010); The Crunch (2008); Weinstock: Life and Times (1999); Hanson: A Biography (1994); Awards: Overseas Journalist of the Year 1988; Financial Journalist of the Year (1998); Wincott Award (2001); Columnist of the Year (2007); Financial Columnist of the Year (2009); Business Journalist of the Year (2010); Financial Journalist of the Year (2013).

Add Northcliffe House, 2 Derry Street, London W8 5TT

Tel 020 3615 1906

Email alex.brummer@dailymail.co.uk

BURGER, Daniel Richard, BA (Hons).

b. London, Sept. 19, 1975; m. Natalie née Burns; Exec. Dir. Jewish Child's Day (2006-11); Hd. Community Fundraising, Norwood (2003-06); Chief Exec. Magen David Adom UK; Ch. Fundraising Cttee. Young Norwood, Sue Harris Bone Marrow Trust.

Add c/o MDA, Shield House, Harmony Way, London NW4 2BZ

Tel 020 201 5900

Email info@mdauk.org *Website* www.mdauk.org

BURMAN, Michael Alfred, BSc (Hons), PGCE, FRGS.

b. Southport, Sept. 20, 1944; m. Barbara née Schiltzer; form. Dir. Admin. Liberal Jewish Synagogue (2007-11); form. Ch. and T. Masorti; Sec. Masorti Europe; form. Ch. European Masorti Beth Din Man. Cttee.; form. Ch. Gov. Clore Shalom School; T. Akiva School; T. Jewish Community Day School Advisory Board.

Add 71 Longfield Avenue, Mill Hill, London NW7 2SA

Tel 020 8201 7522

Email michael.burman@virgin.net

BURMAN, Rickie Amanda, FRSA, MA (Cantab), MPhil.

b. Liverpool, July 5, 1955, m. Prof. Daniel Miller; Dir. Jewish Museum, London (1995-); Curator, London Museum of Jewish Life (1984-95); Museum Co-ord. Manchester Jewish Museum (1981-84); Res. Fel. in Jewish History; Manchester Polytechnic (1979-84); form. Pres. Assoc. of European Jewish Museum and Bd. Mem. London Jewish Museums Libraries and Archives Council; Visitor (Tru) of Pitt Rivers Museum, University of Oxford. Publ.: on history of Jewish women in England and museum studies; Treasures of Jewish Heritage (Ed. 2006).

Add The Jewish Museum, Raymond Burton House, 129-131 Albert Street, London NW1 7NB

Tel 020 7284 7384

Email rickie.burman@jewishmuseum.org.uk

CALLMAN, His Honour Sir Clive Vernon, Kt. BSc (Econ).

b. June 21, 1927; Gov. Hebrew University of Jerusalem (1992-); Mem. Adv. Cttee. for Magistrates' Courses (1979-); Gov. LSE (1990-2008), Council, AJA (1956); Board of Deputies (1998); Mediator, Court of Appeal (2004); Child and Family Law Q. (1995-2002); Court City University (1991-2001); Mem. Careers Advisory Board (1979-92), Gov. Birkbeck College (1982-2001); Senator, London University (1978-94), Gov. Council (1994-2001); Dep. High Court Judge, Royal Courts of Justice (1975-2000); Circuit Judge, South-Eastern Circuit (1973-2000); Dep. Circuit Judge (2000-02); Ed. Bd. Media Law and Practice (1980-95); Journal of Child Law (1988-94); Council, West London Synagogue (1981-87); Professional Negligence (1985); Ch. St Marylebone Labour Party (1960-62); Exec. Society of Labour Lawyers (1958); Dir. Vallentine Mitchell and Co. Ltd.; T. Jewish Studies Foundation; Knight for services to law, education and charity (2012).

Add 11 Constable Close NW11 6UA

Tel 020 8458 3010

CARLOWE, Melvyn, OBE, B.Soc. Sci. (Hons).

b. Abingdon, Oxon., Apr. 13, 1941; Jewish Community Ombudsman Service (1999-2008); T. Third Sector Trust, North London Hospice (1975-2006); Institute of Jewish Policy Research (2000-05); Mem. Beacon Selection Panel for the office of Deputy PM (2000-04); Mem. King's Fund Inquiry on Care Workers (2000-02); form. Chief Exec. Jewish Care (1990-2000); form. Hon. S. Central Council for Jewish Communal Service (1972-2000); form. Chief Exec. Jewish Welfare Board (1972-89); Jewish Chronicle Trust (2000-11).

Tel 020 8364 6686 *Fax* 020 8364 6686

Email karlatsky@aol.com

CESARANI, David, OBE, D.Phil.

b. London, Nov. 13, 1956; Research Prof. in History, Royal Holloway, University London (2004-); form. Prof. Jewish History and Dir. AHRB Parkes Centre for the Study of Jewish/non-Jewish Relations, University of Southampton (2000-04); Parkes-Wiener Prof. of 20th Century Jewish History and Culture (1996-2000); Dr. Institute of Contemporary History and Wiener Library (1996-2000, 1993-95); Alliance Prof. of Modern Jewish Studies, University Manchester (1995-96); Barnett Shine Snr. Res. Fel. Queen Mary College, University of London, (1986-89). Among recent publications: After the Holocaust: Challenging the Myth of Silence (Co-Ed. 2012); Place and Displacement in Jewish History and Memory (Co-Ed. 2009); Major Farran's Hat: Murder, Scandal and Britain's War against Jewish Terrorism 1945-1948 (Ed. 2008); Jews in Port Cities, 1650-1990 (Co-Ed. 2006); After Eichmann, Collective Memory and the Holocaust Since 1960 (Ed. 2005); Critical Concepts: the Holocaust, (6 volumes, Ed. 2004); Eichmann: His Life and Crimes (2004); Port Jews: Jewish Communities in Cosmopolitan Maritime Trading Centres, 1650-1950 (Ed. 2003); Bystanders to the Holocaust (Co-Ed. 2002).

Add History Dept., Royal Holloway, University of London, Egham, Surrey TW2D 0EX

Tel 01784 443 308

Email david.cesarani@rhul.ac.uk

CHARING, Rabbi Douglas Stephen,

b. London, Nov. 16, 1945; Vis. Rabbi, Southport Reform Synagogue and Bradford Synagogue; Dir. Jewish Education Bureau (1974-), Leeds; Tutor, Geneva Theological College, Adv. Theology and Religious Studies Board; Dir. Concord Multi-Faith/Multi-Cultural Res. Centre (Leeds); Inter-Euro. Com. on Church and School, form. Gov. Centre for Study of Rel. and Education (Salford); M. Sinai Synagogue, Leeds; Lecturer, Leeds University, Manchester Police College Mem. Bd. of Dir. British Friends of the Anne Frank Centre; Exec. M. Council for Religious Freedom. Publ.: Glimpses of Jewish Leeds; Comparative Religions (co-author), The Jewish World Visiting a Synagogue; Modern

Judaism (audio-visual); Jewish Contributor, The Junior R.E. Handbook; World Faiths in Education; Praying Their Faith (contributor); Religion in Leeds (Contr.); A Dictionary of Religious Education In the Beginning (Audio-visual); The Torah; Eyewitness Judaism; Encyclopaedia of Religion (co-author), etc.

Add 8 Westcombe Avenue, Leeds LS8 2BS

Tel 0345 567 4070 *Fax* 0845 003 5370

Email rabbi@jewisheducationbureau.co.uk *Website* www.jewisheducationbureau.co.uk

CHERNETT, Jaclyn, ALCM, MPhil.

b. St. Neots, June 16, 1941; m. Brian Chernett; Exec. Council Cantors Assembly (2011-); Chazan (2006, Academy for Jewish religion, NY); Co Ch. Assembly of Masorti Synagogues (1992-95); Dir. Masorti Association (1984-86); H. Life Pres. Edgware Masorti Synagogue; V. Pres. Assembly of Masorti Synagogues; Past V. Pres. World Council of Synagogues; Fdr. Dir. European Academy for Jewish Liturgy. Publ.: Conference papers.

Add Flat 17, Peter's Lodge, 2 Stonegrove, Edgware, Middlesex HA8 7TY

Tel 020 8958 5090 *Fax* 020 8958 7651

Email jaclyn@eajl.org *Website* www.eajl.org

CHEYETTE, Bryan, PhD.

b. Leicester, Jan. 15, 1959; m. Susan Cooklin; Prof. English Language and Literature University of Reading (2005-); Prof. Twentieth Century Literature, University of Southampton (1999-2005); form. Reader in English & Judaic Studies, Queen Mary College, University of London (1992-99); British Academy Postdoctoral Fel. School of English, University of Leeds (1989-92); Editorial board Jewish Quarterly and Patterns of Prejudice. Publ.: (Ed.), H. G. Wells, 'Tono-Bungay' (1997); Between 'Race' and Culture: Representations of 'the Jew' in English and American Literature (Ed. 1996); Constructions of 'the Jew' in English Literature and Society: Racial Representations, 1875-1945 (1993); published widely on British-Jewish Literature.

Add University of Reading, Whiteknights Campus, Reading RG6 6UR

Tel 0118 378 6500

Email b.h.cheyette@reading.ac.uk

CHINN, Sir Trevor, CVO.

b. London, July 24, 1935; m. Susan née Speelman; Pres. UJIA; Tru. Jewish Leadership Council; Mem. BICOM Exec. Board; Mem. Jewish Community Centre Board; H. V. Pres. Zionist Federation; Pres. Norwood (1996-2006); Snr Adv. CVC Capital Partners; Ch. Lex Service / RAC plc (1973-2003), Man. Dir. (1968-1973); Ch. Tusker.

Add 14 Basil Street, London SW3 1AJ

CLINTON-DAVIS, Stanley, Baron of Hackney, PC, LLB, FRSA.

b. London, Dec. 6, 1928; Solicitor; Hon. Mem. of the Council of Justice (1989-); Min. State for Trade (1997-98); Pres. UK Pilots (Marine) (1991-98); H. D. Polytechnical University of Bucharest (1993); Pres. Association of the Metropolitan Authorities (1992); Order of Leopold II for Services to EC, 1990; Mem. European Commission (1985-89); Pres. British Airline Pilots' Association (BALPA) (1980-2012), H. Life Pres. (2012-); MP (Lab.), Hackney Central (1970-83); Parl. Under Sec. for Companies, Aviation and Shipping, Dept. of Trade (1974-79); Councillor, Hackney Borough (1959-71), Mayor (1968-69); Fel. of Queen Mary and Westfield College and King's College, London University; Fel. Budapest University. Publ.: Good Neighbours? Nicaragua, Central America and the United States (Jt. author).

Add House of Lords, London SW1A 1AA

Tel 020 7219 6203

COCKS, Lady Valerie (née Davis),

b. London, July 10, 1932; m. Michael; Dir. Labour Friends of Israel and Trade Union Friends of Israel (1978-88); Exec. Com. Zionist Federation.

Add 162 South Block, County Hall, London SE1 7GE

Tel 020 7787 2539

COHEN, Adrian,
Fdr. and Ch. London Jewish Forum (2006-); Co-Hd. Partner, Clifford Chance (1998-); Co-ordinator, Canary Wharf Kehilla (2003-08); Ch. UJS (1985-86).
Add London Jewish Forum, 32-36 Loman Street, London SE1 0EH
Email adrian.cohen@cliffordchance.com

COHEN, Daniel, BA Hons (Oxon).
b. London, Jan. 15, 1974; Controller, BBC One (2010-), BBC Three, (2007-10); Hd. of Factual Entertainment and of E4 (2006–07); Hd. of Documentaries, Channel 4 (2004–06); Commissioning Ed. Documentaries, Channel 4 (2001–04).
Email danny.cohen@bbc.co.uk

COHEN, Harry Michael, MP.
b. Dec. 10, 1949; m. Ellen née Hussain; MP (Lab) Leyton and Wanstead (1997-2010) (Leyton, 1983–97); Mem. NATO Parly Assembly (1999-2005) (N Atlantic Assembly, 1992–99) (Rapporteur; Ch. Sub-cttee. for Economic Co-operation and Convergence with Central and Eastern Europe, 1996–2000); Mem. Select Cttee. on Defence (1997–2001); Sec. All-Party Parly Group on Race and Community; Mem. UNISON; V. Pres. Royal College of Midwives.
Add House of Commons, London SW1A 0AA

COHEN, Rabbi Jeffrey M, BA, MPhil, AJC, PhD.
b. Manchester, Feb. 19, 1940; m. Gloria née Goldberg; Scholar-in-Residence, USA (1998); Chaplain to Mayor of Harrow (1994-95); Lecturer, Liturg. Studies, Jews' College (1980-1992); Chief Examiner, Modern Hebrew, Jt. Matric Board (1973-1987); Rabbinical Adv. and Gov. Immanuel College (1990-2012); form. M. Kenton Synagogue; Snr. M. Newton Mearns Synagogue, Glasgow; Lecturer in Hebrew, Glasgow University, Principal Glasgow Hebrew College; Dir. Glasgow Bd. of Jewish Education; Dir. Jew Education, King David Schools, Manchester; Mem. Rev. Cttee. Singers Prayer Book. Among recent publications: Dear Chief Rabbi (Ed.); 1001 Questions and Answers on Pesach; Following the Synagogue Service; 1001 Questions and Answers on Rosh Hashanah and Yom Kippur; Issues of the Day; Abridged Haggadah for Rusty Readers; Let My People Go: Insights into Pesach and the Haggadah; The Bedside Companion for Jewish Patients; 500 Questions and Answers on Chanukah; Torah for Teens: Growing up Spiritually with the weekly Sidrah; Genesis in Poetry; The Siddur in Poetry; the High Holydays Machzor in Poetry; The Haggadah in Poetry.
Add 26 Belvedere Court, 115 Lyttelton Road, London N2 0AH
Tel 020 8457 5849
Email jeffreyandgloria@yahoo.co.uk *Website* www.rabbijeffrey.co.uk

COHEN, Michael, BA, MPhil, PGCE.
b. Oxford, Nov. 3, 1941; Teacher Training Co-ord. (London Borough of Hackney); Principal, MST College; Education Consultant, Stratford College, Dublin, Tiferes Shlomo School, London, American Endowment School (Budapest), Prague Jewish Community; Consultant to Broughton Jewish Cassel Fox Primary School, Manchester (1996-98); Principal of Leibler Yavneh College, Melbourne (1993-95); form. Exec. Dir. US Board of Religious Education, London (1980-92); form. HM Mount Scopus Memorial College, Melbourne (1975-80); form. Dir. Jewish Studies, North-West London Jewish Day School (1969-75).
Add 50 Princes Park Avenue NW11 0JT
Tel 020 8458 4537 *Fax* 020 8201 9396

COHEN, Lieut-Colonel Mordaunt, TD, DL, FRSA.
b. Sunderland, Aug. 6, 1916; Solicitor (1938); Pres. Friends of Jewish Servicemen & Women (2009-); H. Life Pres. Sunderland Hebrew Congregation (1988-); Reg. Ch. Industrial Tribunals (1976-89), Ch. (1974-76); Board of Deputies, (1964-2006); H. Dir. Central Enquiry Desk (1990-2000); Ch. Edgware School (1991-96); form. Mem. Chief Rabbinate Council; T. AJEX; T. AJEX Charitable Foundation; V. Pres. and Nat. Ch. AJEX (1993-95); Dep. Lieut. Tyne & Wear; Ch. Provincial Cttee. Board of Deputies (1985-91); Ch. Mental Health Review

Tribunal (1967-76); Cllr. Tyne & Wear County C. (1973-74); Dep. Ch. Northern Traffic Coms. (1972-74); Alderman Sunderland County Borough Council (1967-74); Ch. Sunderland Education Cttee. (1970-72); Ch. Govs. Sunderland Polytechnic (1969-72); Court, Newcastle upon Tyne University (1968-72); Pres. Sunderland Law Society (1970); War service, RA (1940-46) (dispatches, Burma campaign), TA (1947-55), CO 463 (M) HA A Regt. (1954-55); Territorial Decoration (1954); H. Life Pres. Sunderland AJEX.

Add 1 Peters Lodge, 2 Stonegrove, Edgware, Middlesex HA8 7TY

COHEN, Sir Philip, FRS, FRSE, FFMed.Sci, BSc, PhD.

b. Edgware, Middlesex; m. Patricia née Townsend Wade; Biochemist; Dir. Scottish Inst. for Cell Signalling (2008-12); Dir. MRC Protein Phosphorylation Unit (1990-2012); Royal Society Research Professor (1984-2010). Publ.: Control of Enzyme Activity (1976, 2nd Edition 1993); over 500 research papers and reviews in scientific journals; Honorary DSc Degrees from Abertay, Strathclyde, Linköping, Debrecen and St Andrew's; LLD from Dundee.

Add Inverbay Bramblings, Waterside, Invergowrie, Dundee DD2 5DQ

Tel 01382 562 328 *Fax* 01382 233 778

Email p.cohen@dundee.ac.uk

COHEN, Sir Ronald, MA (Oxon), MBA (Harvard).

b. London, Aug. 1, 1945; m. Sharon Ruth Harel; Businessman; Ch. Commission on Unclaimed Assets (2005-7) and Dir. Social Finance (2008-); Harvard Board of Overseers (2007-); T. British Museum (2005-); Chancellor's Court of Benefactors, Oxford University (2003-); Co-Fdr. and Ch. The Portland Trust (2003-); Ch. Bridges Ventures (2002-); V. Ch. Ben Gurion University (2002-); Hon. Fel. Exeter College, Oxford (2000-); T. International Institute of Strategic Studies (2005-10); Ch. Social Investment Task Force HM Treasury (2000-10); Jewish Leadership Council (2006-09); Mem. Dean's Board of Advisors, Harvard Business School (2003-08); Dir. NASDAQ Europe (2001-05); Co-Fdr. and form. Ch. Apax Partners Worldwide LLP (1972-05). Publ.: The Second Bounce of the Ball: Turning Risk into Opportunity.

Add 42 Portland Place, London W1B 1NB

Tel 020 7182 7801 *Fax* 020 7182 7897

Email ronald.cohen@portlandcap.com

COHEN, Shimon David, FRSA.

b. Cardiff, May 24, 1960; Ch. The PR Office Ltd.; Mem. CIPR; Mem. BAFTA; Mem. Board of Deputies; form. Dir. Bell Pottinger Consultants (1990-2003); form. Exec. Dir. Office of the Chief Rabbi (1983-90).

Email enquiries@theproffice.com *Website* www.theproffice.com

COHN-SHERBOK, Dan, BA, BHL, MA, MLitt, PhD (Cantab), DD.

b. Denver, CO, Feb. 1, 1945; Emer. Prof. University of Wales (2012-); Vis. Prof. York St John University (2011-), St Mary's University College (2008-), University Middlesex (1994-), Charles University Prague (2007), Vilnius (2000), Lampeter (1994-6); Emer. Prof. Judaism, University Wales (Lampeter) (1997-); University Lecturer in Theology, University of Kent (1975-); Vis. Prof. University of Essex (1993-4); H. Research Fel. Heythrop College, University of London (2011-); Ch. Dept. of Theology, University of Kent (1980-2); form. Rabbi in synagogues in the USA, England, S. Africa, Australia (1971-5); H. Prof. Aberystwyth University; H. Fel. Centre of Religions for Peace and Reconciliation, University of Winchester. Among recent publications: The Illustrated History of Judaism (2013); Love, Sex and Marriage (2013); The Palestinian State: A Jewish Justification (2012); Introduction to Zionism and Israel (2011); Judaism Today (2010); The Dictionary of Kabbalah and Kabbalists (2009); The Dictionary of Jewish Biography (2008); Christian Zionism (2006); Kabbalah (2006); The Paradox of Antisemitism (2006); The Politics of Apocalypse (2006); Pursuing the Dream (2005); The Vision of Judaism (2004); Judaism: History, Belief and Practice (2003); Antisemitism (2002); Holocaust Theology: A Reader (2001); Interfaith Theology (2001); The Palestinian–Israeli Conflict (2001); Wisdom of Judaism (2000); Jews, Christians and Religious Pluralism (1999); The Future of Jewish-

Christian Dialogue (Ed. 1999); Understanding the Holocaust (1999); The Jewish Messiah (1997); Fifty Key Jewish Thinkers (1996); The Hebrew Bible (1996); Modern Judaism (1996); Medieval Jewish Philosophy (1996).

Add 89 Winchester Court, Vicarage Gate, London W8 4AF

Email cohnsherbok@googlemail.com

COLLICK, Rabbi Dr Jeremy, COLLICK.

b. London, Aug. 31, 1957; m. Lucinda née Dicks; Rabbi, Edgware Masorti Synagogue (2000-).

Add EMS, Stream Lane, Edgware, Middlesex HA8 7YA

Tel 020 8905 4096

Email rabbi@edgwaremasorti.org

COLLINS, John Morris, MA (Oxon).

b. Leeds, June 25, 1931; Barrister; Doyen, North Eastern Circuit; Hd. of Chambers (1966-2002); Crown Courts Recorder (1980-98); Pres. Beth Hamidrash Hagadol Synagogue, Leeds (1992-95); past Pres. Leeds Lodge, B'nai B'rith; Board of Deputies (1971-93); Dep. Circuit Judge (1970-80); Called to the Bar, Middle Temple (1956); H. Life V. Pres. Leeds Jewish Representative Council (form. Pres. 1986-89); V. Ch. Leeds Kashrut Authority. Publ.: Summary Justice (1963).

Add 14 Sandhill Oval, Leeds LS17 8EA

Tel 0113 268 6008

Email johnmorriscollins@btinternet.com

COLLINS, Dr Kenneth Edward, MBChB, FRCGP, MPhil, PhD.

b. Glasgow, Dec. 23, 1947; Ch. Scottish Council of Jewish Communities (2007-08, 1999-2003); Pres. Glasgow Jewish Representative Council (2004-07, 1995-98); Ch. Scottish Jewish Archives Cttee. Glasgow Board of Jewish Education (1989-93); Vis Prof. Faculty of Medicine, Hebrew University; Ch. Glasgow Yeshiva. Publ.: Moses Maimonides and his Practice of Medicine (Ed. 2013); Scotland's Jews (1999, 2nd edition 2008); Be Well: Jewish Immigrant Health and Welfare in Glasgow (2001); Glasgow Jewry (1994); Second City Jewry (1990); Go and Learn (1988); Aspects of Scottish Jewry (Ed. 1987).

Add 2/2 11 Braidholm Crescent, Giffnock, Glasgow G46 6HH

Tel 0141 404 7488

Email drkcollins@gmail.com

CONWAY, Penelope Lesley (née Lennard), D.O, PGDip, PGCap, FHEA.

b. London; m. Peter; Osteopath; Ch. Association of Jewish Women's Organisations (2010-); UK V. Pres. International Council of Jewish Women (2010-); V. Ch. Ruth Winston Centre (2009-); Pres. League of Jewish Women (2003-2007).

Add Association of Jewish Women's Organisations in UK, 6 Bloomsbury Square, London WC1A 2LP

Tel 020 7242 8300 *Fax* 020 7242 8313

Email contact@ajwo.org *Website* www.ajwo.org

CORREN, Asher, MCMI.

b. Warsaw, Nov. 2, 1932; form. Dir. Central Council Jewish Community Services; form. Exec. Dir. Nightingale House; form. Mem. of Wandsworth Health Authority; form. Mem. of Exec. Cttee. Alzheimer's Society; Mem. of Adv. Cttee. St Wilfrid's Home for Aged, Chelsea; form. Co-T. and form. Mem. Exec. Cttee. Council of Christians and Jews.

Email patricia.corren@virgin.net

COSGROVE, Rt. Hon. Lady Hazel Josephine (née Aronson), CBE, LL.D.

b. Glasgow, Jan. 12, 1946; m. John A. Cosgrove; Senator of the College of Justice, Scotland (1996-2006); Dep. Ch. Boundary Commission for Scotland (1996-2006); Ch. Expert Panel on Sex Offending (1998-2001); Ch. Mental Welfare Commission for Scotland (1991-96); Sheriff of Lothian and Borders at Edinburgh (1983-96); Mem. Parole Bd.; Sheriff of Glasgow and Strathkelvin at Glasgow (1979-83); Privy Counsellor (2001), Queens Counsel

(1991), Advocate (1968-79); Pres. Scottish Friends of Alyn Hospital; H. Fel. Harris Manchester College, Oxford; D. University Stirling (2004); H. LLD, St Andrews University (2003); Glasgow University (2002); Strathclyde University (2002); Napier University (1997).
Add 4 Avenue Mansions, Finchley Road, London NW3 7AU
Tel 020 7435 1236
Email hazelcosgrove@uk2.net

COSGROVE, John Allan, BDS (Glasgow).
b. Carmarthen, S. Wales, Dec. 5, 1943; m. The Rt. Honourable Lady Cosgrove (née Aronson); Dental Surgeon; Warden, St John's Wood Synagogue (2013); Pres. Edinburgh Hebrew Congregation (1986-90), Ch. Scottish Council of Jewish Communities; (2003-07); Scottish representative Chief Rabbinate selection cttee. (1989-91).
Add 4 Avenue Mansions, Finchley Road, London NW3 7AU
Tel 079 7065 7157 *Fax* 0333 344 1236
Email jacosgrove@uk2.net

CREWE, Sir Ivor Martin, Kt., D.Litt (Salford) DU (Essex).
b. Manchester, Dec. 15, 1945; University teacher; Master, University College, Oxford (2008-); V. Chancellor (1995–2007), Pro V. Chancellor (Academic) (1992-95), University of Essex; Pres. Universities UK (2003-5); Ed./Co-Ed. British Journal of Political Science (1984-92, 1977-82); Ch. Dept. of Government (1985-89); Dir. SSRC Data Archive (1974-82); Mem. High Council, European University Institute, Florence; Mem. Council SOAS; University of the Arts, London; Prof. of Government, University of Essex; Hon. Fel. Exeter College, Oxford; Nuffield College, Oxford. Publ.: SDP: The Birth, Life and Death of the Social Democratic Party (1995); Decade of Dealignment (CUP 1983) (1995, with Bo Sarlvik); Survey of Higher Civil Service (HMSO 1969) (with A. H. Halsey), etc.
Add The Master's Lodge, University College, Oxford OX1 4BH
Tel 01865 276 600
Email marion.hawtree@univ.ox.ac.uk

DANAN, Melanie,
Policy and Regeneration officer, Interlink (1999-); Co-ordinator, Chizuk (-1999).
Add Interlink, Lower Ground Floor Offices, 124 Stamford Hill, London N16 6QT
Tel 020 8802 2469 *Fax* 020 8800 5153
Email melanie@interlink-foundation.org.uk

DANGOOR, David Alan Ezra, BSc, ARCS, DL.
b. 1948; Dep. Lieutenant of Greater London; Mem. Jewish Leadership Council (2010-); Pres. Board, Spanish & Portuguese Jews' Congregation (2011-); V. Pres. World Organisation of Jews from Iraq (2008-); Sponsor Gov. Westminster Academy (2006-); T. Jewish Association of Business Ethics (2005-12); Ch. LST Investment Committee (2004-); T. Simon Wiesenthal Centre (UK) (1996-); T. London Sephardi Tru. (1984-); Sephardi Kashrut Authority (1982-); T. The Exilarch's Foundation (1978-); Dir. Carmel College (1997-2010); S&P Mahamad & Gabay (1997-2001).
Add 4 Carlos Place, Mayfair, London W1K 3AW
Email david@dangoor.com *Website* www.dangoor.com

DANGOOR, Dr Naim E, CBE, FRAH.
b. Baghdad, 1914; m. Renée; Company Ch. Property Developer; Editor and Publisher – The Scribe, Journal of Babylonian Jewry; Fdr. and Tru. Exilarch's Foundation; Sponsor, Westminster Academy; Donor, Eliahou Dangoor Scholarships; awarded Professorship by Nanjing University; Fel. Royal Albert Hall; Fel. Birkbeck, University of London.
Add 4 Carlos Place, London W1K 3AW
Email office@dangoor.com *Website* www.dangoor.com

DAVIS, Baruch, BA (Hons) Econ, Semicha, Chief Rabbinate of Israel.
b. London, Feb. 28, 1958; m. Nechama née Lipman; Ch. Rabbinical Council, United Synagogue; Snr. Rabbi, Chigwell & Hainault United Synagogue (1997-); Chief Min. Adelaide

Hebrew Congregation, South Australia (1988-97); Economist Dept of Intl. Affairs; Ministry of Finance, Jerusalem.

Add 5 Mount Pleasant Road, Chigwell, Essex IG7 5EP

Tel 020 8281 9878/07711 231 560

Email baruch.davis@gmail.com

DAVIS, Mick,

b. Port Elizabeth, South Africa, February 15, 1958; m. Barbara née Hyman; Ch. UJIA (2006-); Chief Exec. Xstrata plc (2002-); Ch. Euro Chai of South Africa Trust (2002-); T. Kew Foundation (2009); Chief Exec. Xstrata AG (2001-02); Exec. Ch. Ingwe Coal Corporation (1995-2001); Chief Financial Officer and Exec. Dir. Billiton plc (prev. Gencor) (1994-2001); Exec. Dir. Eskom (1991-94); Mem. Jewish Leadership Council.

Tel 020 7424 6400 *Fax* 020 7424 6401

Email central@ujia.org *Website* www.ujia.org

DE LANGE, Rabbi Nicholas R.M., FBA, MA, DPhil, DD.

b. Nottingham, Aug. 7, 1944; Emer. Prof. of Hebrew and Jewish Studies, Cambridge University; Fel. Wolfson College, Cambridge. Publ.: Penguin Dictionary of Judaism (2008); An Introduction to Judaism (2000); Illustrated History of the Jewish People (1997); Judaism (1986); Atlas of the Jewish World (1984); Apocrypha: Jewish Literature of the Hellenistic Age (1978); various specialised works and literary translations.

Add Wolfson College, Cambridge CB3 9BB

Tel 01223 740 561

Email nrml1@cam.ac.uk

DEECH, Baroness Ruth Lynn (née Fraenkel), DBE, MA (Oxon), MA (Brandeis), H. LLD (Strathclyde, Richmond); H. PhD (Ben Gurion), Barrister, QC (Hon).

b. London, Apr. 29, 1943, m. Dr John Deech; Ch. Bar Standards Board (2009-); Gresham Prof. of Law (2008-12); Ch. Stuart Young Foundation Academic Panel (1991-); Independent Adjudicator for Higher Education (2004-08); Gov. BBC (2002-6); Rhodes Trust (1996-2006); Pro-V. Chancellor, Oxford University (2001-4); Principal, St Anne's College, Oxford (1991-2004); Freeman, Drapers' Co. (2003); Ch. UK Human Fertilisation and Embryology Authority (1994-2002); Governor, Oxford Centre for Hebrew and Jewish Studies (1994-2000); H. Bencher, Inner Temple (1996); Non-executive Dir. Oxon Health Authority (1993-94); V. Principal, St Anne's College (1988-91); Lecturer in Law, Oxford University (1970–91); Governor, Carmel College (1980-90); Snr. Proctor, Oxford University (1985-6). Publ.: From IVF to Immortality (2007).

Add House of Lords, London SW1A OPW

Tel 020 7611 1444 *Fax* 020 7831 9217

Email deechr@parliament.uk

DESMOND, Richard Clive,

b. Dec. 8, 1951; Pres. Norwood (2006–); Proprietor, Express Newspapers (2000-); Ch. Northern and Shell Network (1974-).

Add Northern & Shell Building, Number 10 Lower Thames Street EC3R 6EN

Tel 020 8612 7000

DJANOGLY, Jonathan Simon MP,

b. London, June 3, 1965; m. Rebecca née Silk; Solicitor, SJ Berwin LLP (1990-2009); Parliamentary Under Secretary of State, Ministry of Justice (2010-12); MP Huntingdon (2001-); Shadow M. for Business (2005-10); Shadow Solicitor General (2004-10); form. Councillor, Westminster LBC (1994-2001).

Add House of Commons, London SW1A 0AA

Email jonathan.djanogly.mp@parliament.uk *Website* www.jonathandjanogly.com

DUFFIELD, Dame Vivien, DBE, CBE, MA (Oxon) H. DLitt, H. DPhil, H. RCM.

b. Mar. 26, 1946; Mem. Bd. Clore Leadership Programme (2004–); T. Jewish Community Centre for London (2004–); Dir. South Bank Bd (2002–); Gov. Royal Ballet (2002–); Ch. The

Royal Opera House Endowment Fund; Ch. Clore Duffield Foundation; Bd. Weizmann Institute.

Add c/o Clore Duffield Foundation, 3 Chelsea Manor Studios, Flood Street SW3 5SR

Tel 020 7351 6061

Email info@cloreduffield.org.uk

DWEK, Joseph Claude (Joe), CBE, BSc, BA, AMCT, FTI, H. DSc UMIST.

b. Brussels, May 1, 1940; Mem. North West Development Agency (2004-12) (Ch. Environmental cttee., V. Ch. Business and Innovations Cttee.); Mem. Regional Advisory Cttee. of Forestry Commission; form. Mem. General Assembly, New University Manchester; form. Ch. Environlink; form. Mem. DTI/DEFRA Env. Innovation Adv. Group; Ch. Penmarric Ltd; Dir., form. Ch. and CEO, Bodycode International plc (1972-99); form. Ch. CBI North West; Gov. Manchester High School for Girls; Dir. NW Regional Advisory Cttee. to the Forestry Commission.

Add Penmarric Ltd, Suite One, Courthill House, 66 Water Lane, Wilmslow SK9 5AP

Tel 01625 549 081

Email penjcdwek@aol.com

DWEK, Raymond Allen,

b. Manchester, Nov. 10, 1941; m. Sandra; H. & Dir. Oxford Glycobiology Institute; Advisory Bd. Mem. Oxford University Museum of Natural History; Bd. Mem. The Scripps Korea Antibody Institute (2009-); Emer. Fel. Exeter College, Oxford (2009-); Oxford University Representative – Oxford Philomusica (2009-); Strategic Advisory Bd. Mem. National Institute for Bioprocesssing Research and Training (NIBRT) Dublin (2009-); Institute Prof. The Scripps Research Institute, La Jolla, USA (2008-); Bd. of Govs. Exec. Cttee. & Special Advisor to the President, Ben Gurion University, Israel (2005-); Bd. Scientific Govs. Scripps Research Institute, La Jolla (2003-); Dir. United Therapeutics (2002-), Prof. Glycobiology (1988-); Scientific Advisory Bd. Mem. United Therapeutics (2001-); International Advisory Bd. National Institute for Biotechnology in the Negev (NIBN), Israel (2005); Dir. Penmarric plc (1985).

Add Glycobiology Institute, Department of Biochemistry, University of Oxford, South Parks Road, Oxford OX1 3QU

Tel 01865 275 344 *Fax* 01865 275 771

Email raymond.dwek@exeter.ox.ac.uk

EDER, Prof. Andrew, BDS, MSc, LDS, MFGDP, MRD, FDS, FHEA.

b. London, Apr. 21, 1964, m. Rosina née Saideman; Assoc. V. Provost and Dir. CPD and Short Course Development, UCL Enterprise (2013); Prof. of Restorative Dentistry and Dental Education, UCL Eastman Dental Institute; H. Consultant, Restorative Dentistry, UCLHT Eastman Dental Hospital; Specialist, Restorative Dentistry and Prosthodontics; Exec. and Warden (2010-), Bd. of Management (1997-2010), Stanmore & Canons Park United Synagogue; Medical Advisory Panel, Chai Cancer Care, (2008-); Ch. Alpha Omega London Charitable Trust (2003-); Pres. The British Society for Restorative Dentistry (2005-06); Pres. Odontological Section, The Royal Society of Medicine (2001-02). Publ.: 923 (combination of papers, edited articles, posters, abstracts and press releases); Tooth Surface Loss (A. Eder & R. Ibbetson, 2000).

Add 2nd Floor, 57a Wimpole Street, London W1G 8YP

Tel 020 7486 7180

Email andreweder@restorative-dentistry.co.uk *Website* www.restorative-dentistry.co.uk

EDLIN, Paul Alan,

b. Glasgow, Apr. 25, 1949; Dental Surgeon; V. Pres. Board of Deputies of British Jews (2006-).

Add c/o Board of Deputies, 6 Bloomsbury Square, London WC1A 2LP

EHRENTREU, Dayan Chanoch,

b. Frankfurt-am-Main, Dec. 27, 1932; Av Beth Din, European Beth Din (2008); form. Rosh Beth Din, London Beth Din (1984-2008); Av Beth Din, Manchester Beth Din (1979-84); Principal, Sunderland Kolel (1960-79); Rav, Beth Yisroel Synagogue.

Add 55 Shirehall Park, London NW4 2QN
Tel 020 8202 2364

EIMER, Rabbi Colin, BSc (Econ), MA.
b. London, Mar. 8, 1945; Lecturer, Rabbinic Decision-Making, Leo Baeck College (2008-); Progressive Rabbinic Decision-Making (2008-); M. Sha'arei Tsedek North London Reform Synagogue (1977-); Lecturer, Hebrew, Leo Baeck College (1976-2007); M. Finchley Reform Synagogue (2001-05), Ch. Assembly of Rabbis, RSGB (1999-2001, 1981-83); form. M. Bushey Reform Synagogue (1975-77); Union Liberale Israelite Synagogue, Paris (1971-74).
Add Sha'arei Tsedek, North London Reform Synagogue, 120 Oakleigh Road North, London N20 9EZ
Tel 020 8445 3400
Email colineimer@aol.com

EISENBERG, Neville, BCom, LLB (Wits), LLM (LSE).
b. Cape Town, Apr. 12, 1962; Solicitor; Tru. Tel Aviv Foundation (UK) (2012-); Associate Gov. Hebrew University (2004-); Managing Partner, Berwin Leighton Paisner LLP (1999-); Ch. British Israel Law Association (1996-); Freeman, City of London Solicitors Company; Ch. South African Union of Jewish Students (1982-84); Comptroller, World Union of Jewish Students (1986-89).
Add Adelaide House, London Bridge, London EC4R 9HA
Tel 020 3400 4473
Email neville.eisenberg@blplaw.com *Website* www.blplaw.com

EKER, Rita (née Shapiro), MBE.
b. London, Oct. 15, 1938; Co-Ch. Women's Campaign for Soviet Jewry (the 35s); Tru. of One to One and One to One Treks in Israel.
Add Carradine House, 237 Regents Park Road, London N3 3LF
Tel 020 8343 4156 *Fax* 020 8343 2119
Email rita@one-to-one.org *Website* www.one-to-one.org

ELLMAN, Louise Joyce, BA Hons, MPhil.
b. Nov. 14, 1945; m. Geoffrey David; Ch. Transport Select Cttee (2008–) (Mem. since 2002); Mem. Board of Deputies of British Jews (2008-); Ch. Jewish Labour Movement (2004-); V. Ch. Labour Friends of Israel (2004–); MP (Lab and Co-op), Liverpool Riverside (1997-); Leader, Lancashire County Council (1981-97); Lancs CC (1970–97); V. Pres. All Party Parliamentary Cttee. against Antisemitism; Council Mem. Holocaust Educational Trust; Mem. Holocaust Memorial Day Trust; T. All Party Baha'i Group; V. Ch. All Party Britain-Israel Group.
Add House of Commons, London SW1A 0AA
Email louise.ellman.mp@parliament.uk *Website* www.louiseellman.co.uk

ELTON, Ben, BA.
b. May 3, 1959; m. Sophia Gare; author and performer; Royal Television Society Writers' Award (1989). Publ.: Two Brothers (2013); Meltdown (2010); Blind Faith (2007); Chart Throb (2006); The First Casualty (2005); Past Mortem (2004); High Society (2002); Dead Famous (2001); Inconceivable (1999). Musicals: Love Never Dies (2010); We Will Rock You (2002).
Add c/o Phil McIntyre, 2nd Floor, 35 Soho Square W1D 3QX
Tel 020 7439 2270

EMANUEL, Rabbi Dr Charles, BA, MHL, DD (HUC).
b. New York, Dec. 15, 1944; m. Peduth; Rabbi Emer. North Western Reform Synagogue (2005-), M. (1983-2005); form. Ch. Assembly of Rabbis of the Reform Synagogues of Great Britain (1986-88); form M. Sinai Synagogue, Leeds (1979-83), Temple Beth-El, Huntsville, Alabama (1973-79).
Add North Western Reform Synagogue, Alyth Gardens NW11 7EN
Tel 020 8455 6763 *Fax* 020 8731 8175
Email charles@alyth.org

FABRICANT, Michael Louis David, MP, BA, MSc Systems, CEng.

b. June 12, 1950; Government Whip (2010-); Ch. Royal Marines All Party Parliamentary Group (2005–10) (Jt Ch. 1999–2005); All Party Anglo-German Group (1997–2010); All Party Group on Film Industry (1997–2010); MP (C) Lichfield (1997-2012) (Mid-Staffordshire, 1992–97); V. Ch. All Party Group on Smoking and Health (1997–); Opposition Whip (2005–10); Opposition front-bench spokesman, Trade and Industry (2003–05); Co-Fdr. and Dir. International Broadcast Electronics and Investment Group (1979–91).

Add House of Commons, London SW1A 0AA

Tel 020 7219 5022

Email michael.fabricant.mp@parliament.uk *Website* www.michaelfabricant.mp.co.uk

FARHI, Musa Moris, MBE, FRSL, FRGS.

b. Ankara, July 5, 1935; m. Nina Ruth née Gould (d. 2009); Writer; V. Pres. International PEN (2001-); Ch. International PEN Writers in Prison Cttee. (1997-2000); Ch. English PEN Writers in Prison Cttee. (1994-97); M. Ed. Bd. Jewish Quarterly. Publ.: Songs from Two Continents (2011); A Designated Man (2009); Young Turk (2004); Children of the Rainbow (1999); Journey Through the Wilderness (1989); The Last of Days (1983); The Pleasure of Your Death (1972).

Add 17 Courtenay Gate, Courtenay Terrace, Hove, East Sussex BN3 2WJ

Tel 01273 729 011

Email farhi@clara.net

FARHI, Rabbi Shlomo,

b. Jerusalem, Israel, Mar. 7, 1978; m. Chana née Abihkzer; Rabbi and Dir. Schools Department Aish Hatorah UK; form. Dir and Fdr. Chazak.

Add 379 Hendon Way, London NW4 3LP

FEATHERSTONE, Lynne (née Ryness), MP.

b. London, Dec. 20, 1951; Parliamentary Under Secretary of State (Minister for Equalities) for the Home Office (2010-); MP (Lib Dem) for Hornsey and Wood Green (2005-); Councillor, Haringey (1998-2006); London Assembly (2000-05). Publ.: Marketing and Communication Techniques for Architects (1992).

Add House of Commons, London SW1A 0AA

Tel 020 8340 5459

Email lynne@lynnefeatherstone.org

FEINSTEIN, Elaine (née Cooklin), MA (Cantab), HonD.Litt (Leic.), FRSL.

b. Bootle, Oct. 24, 1930; m. Dr Arnold Feinstein; Writer; Cholmondeley Award for Poetry (1990). Among recent publications: Bride of Ice (2009); The Russian Jerusalem (2008); Talking to the Dead (poems, 2007); Anna of All the Russias: a biography of Anna Akhmatova (2005); Collected Poems and Translations (2002); Ted Hughes: The Life of a Poet (2001); Gold (poems, 2000); Pushkin (biog. 1998); Daylight (poems, 1997); Dreamers (novel, 1996); Lawrence's Women (biog. 1993); Loving Brecht (novel, 1993); All You Need (1991); Survivors (1991); Mother's Girl (1988); A Captive Lion: The Life of Marina Tsvetayeva (1987); Badlands (poems, 1987); Bessie Smith (biog. 1985); The Border (1985); Selected poems.

Add c/o Rogers, Coleridge & White, 20 Powis Mews W11 1JN

Tel 020 8221 3717

FELSENSTEIN, Frank, BA (Hons), PhD.

b. Westminster, July 28, 1944; m. Carole; Prof. Humanities, Ball State University (2002-); Dir. Honors Program, Yeshiva College, NY (1998-2002); form. Reader in English, University of Leeds; Vis. Prof. Vanderbilt University, USA (1989-90). Publ.: Tobias Smollett, Travels through France and Italy (Ed. 2011); John Thelwall: Two Plays (Co-Ed. 2006); English Trader, Indian Maid: Representing Gender, Race and Slavery in the New World (1999); Hebraica and Judaica from the Cecil Roth Collection, exhibition catalogue (Brotherton

Library, 1997); Anti-Semitic Stereotypes: A Paradigm of Otherness in English Popular Culture, 1660-1830 (1995); The Jew as Other: A Century of English Caricature, 1730-1830, exhibition catalogue (Jewish Theological Seminary, New York, 1995); Co-Dir. 'What Middleton Read' Project (www.bsu.edu/libraries/wmr); review work for 'The Jewish Quarterly Review', Journal of Modern Jewish Studies'.

Add 8 Manor Drive, Morristown, NJ 07960-2611, USA

Tel +1 (973) 889 1323

Email felsenstein@bsu.edu

FENTON, Stephen, BSc (Econ), FCA.

b. London, Mar. 26, 1952; m. Susan née Firman; Chartered Accountant; V. Pres. United Synagogue (2011-); T. US (2005-2011); Fin. Representative, Bushey Synagogue (1999-2005).

Add Palladium House, 1-4 Argyll Street, London W1F 7LD

Tel 020 7437 7666

Email Stephenfenton@hazlemsfenton.com *Website* www.theus.org.uk

FERSHT, Sir Alan Roy, MA, PhD, FRS.

b. London, Apr. 21, 1943; m. Marilyn née Persell; Master, Gonville and Caius College (2012-); Group Leader, MRC Laboratory of Molecular Biology; Fel. Gonville and Caius College; Emer. Herchel Smith Prof. Organic Chemistry, Cambridge; Dir. Cambridge Council for Protein Engineering; Prof. Biological Chemistry, Imperial College, London; Wolfson Res. Prof. Royal Society (1978-88); Scientific Staff, MRC Lab. Molecular Biology, Cambridge (1969-77). Publ.: Enzyme Structure and Mechanism; Structure and Mechanism in Protein Science.

Add Gonville and Caius College, Cambridge CB2 1TA

Tel 01223 332 431

Email arf25@cam.ac.uk

FINE, Rabbi Yisroel, BA.

b. Swansea, Nov. 11, 1948; M. Cockfosters and North Southgate Synagogue (1987-), form. M. Wembley Synagogue, United Hebrew Congregation, Newcastle upon Tyne; form. Ch. Rabbinical Council of the US; H. Principal, Wolfson Hillel Primary School; Dir. Cockfosters Learning Centre; Fdr. Rabbi, Hadley Wood Jewish Community.

Add 274 Chase Side, Southgate N14 4PR

Tel 020 8449 1750

Email rabbi.fine@ourshul.co.uk

FINKELSTEIN, Daniel, Baron of Pinner, OBE.

b. London, Aug. 30, 1962; m. Nicola Connor; Journalist; Executive Editor, The Times, form. Associate Ed. and Chief Leader Writer (2008-), Comment Ed. (2004-8), Leader Writer (2001-); Fink Tank column (2002-); form. Conservative Party candidate, Harrow West (2001); Chief Policy Adv. to William Hague (1997-2001); form. Dir. Conservative Party Res. Dept. (1995-97). Awarded the PSA Journalist of the Year Award (2011); Chaim Bermant Journalism Prize (2008).

Add The Times, 1 Pennington Street, London E98 1TT

Email daniel.finkelstein@thetimes.co.uk

FINLAY, Alan Stanley, LL.B.

b. London, Apr. 2, 1950; m. Kathryn née Fine; Solicitor; Pres. Federation of Synagogues (form. Treasurer); Ch. AJY (1984-88); V. Pres. World Confederation of Jewish Community Centres (1984-88); Ch. Jewish Youth Voluntary Service (1974-78).

Add 4 Orchard Close, Edgware, Middlesex HA8 7RE

Tel 020 8952 7517

Email asf@federationofsynagogues.com

FISCHER, John Joseph, BA (Hons).

b. Antwerp, Belgium, Feb. 11, 1937; Banking and Financial Services; Compiler, Calendar entry for The JC (1986-), Calendar section of the Jewish Year Book (1965-); Governor, Henrietta Barnet School, London (1968-1987); Councillor, London Borough of Barnet (Cons) (1968-1974).

Add Flat 2, 39 The Grove, London N3 1QT

Tel 020 8346 7980

FITZSIMONS, Lorna, BA Hons.

b. Aug. 6, 1967; m. Stephen Cooney; CEO, BICOM (2006-12); Lorna Fitzsimons Consulting (2005–06); Snr. Associate Fel. UK Defence Acad. Advanced Res. and Assessment Group (2005); MP (Lab), Rochdale (1997–2005); contested (Lab) same seat (2005); V. Pres. Women's Cttee. Parliamentary Labour Party (2001–05), Ch. (1997–2001); Supporter, Labour Friends of Israel (1997–2005); Parliamentary Private Secretary to Leader of House of Commons (2001–03), to M. of State, FCO (2000–01); Pres. National Union of Students (1992-4).

Email fitzsimonsl@parliament.uk

FIXMAN, Sydney,

b. Manchester, Apr. 5, 1935; Music Lecturer, London University Institute of Education; Fdr. Conductor, Ben Uri Chamber Orchestra, Jewish Youth Orchestra; Music Dir. West London Synagogue; form. Guest Conductor, leading orchestras in Britain and abroad (seasons in Israel: 1976-89); Conductor, BBC (TV and Radio). Publ.: (Ed.) Psaume Tehillim (Markevitch); Recordings, CDs.

Add 5 Bradby House, Hamilton Terrace NW8 9XE

FRANKLIN, Andrew Cecil,

b. London, Mar. 6, 1957; m. Caroline Sarah née Elton; Dir. And Publisher Profile Books Ltd (1996-); Dir. And Publisher Pevsner Books Trust (1996-); Dir. and Publisher Jewish Community Centre UK (2004-10); Dir. And Publisher JCC Ventures Ltd (2010-2012); Dir. Jewish Literary Trust (1991-2010).

Add Profile Books, 3A, Exmouth House, Pine Street, Exmouth Market, London EC1R 0JH

Tel 020 7841 6300 *Fax* 020 7833 3969

Email andrew.franklin@profilebooks.com

FREEDLAND, Jonathan,

b. London, Feb. 25, 1967; m. Sarah née Peters; Journalist; Monthly Columnist, The Jewish Chronicle (1998-); Columnist, The Guardian (1997-); Washington Correspondent, The Guardian (1993-97); Presenter, The Long View (BBC Radio 4). Awards: David Watt Prize for Journalism (2008); Columnist of the Year, What the Papers Say Awards (2002). Publ.: (Fiction, under pseudonym Sam Bourne): Pantheon (2012); The Chosen One (2010); The Final Reckoning (2008); The Last Testament (2007); The Righteous Men (2006); (Non-fiction, under own name): Jacob's Gift (2005); Bring Home the Revolution: The Case for a British Republic (1998).

Add The Guardian, Kings Place, 90 York Way, London N1 9GU

Tel 020 7278 2332

Website www.jonathanfreedland.com

FREEDLAND, Michael Rodney,

b. London, Dec. 18, 1934; Journalist and Broadcaster; contributor to national press; Exec. Ed. and Presenter (BBC and LBC), 'You Don't Have to be Jewish' (1971-94). Among recent publications: Jolson; Andre Previn; Leonard Bernstein: Music Man; Sean Connery: A Biography; All the Way: A Biography of Frank Sinatra; Bob Hope; Bing Crosby; Michael Caine; Doris Day; Some Like it Cool; King of the Road; (with Morecambe and Wise) There's No Answer To That; (with Walter Scharf) Composed and Conducted by Walter Scharf; Confessions of a Serial Biographer; Hollywood on Trial; Witch Hunt in Hollywood;

The Men Who Made Hollywood; Judy Garland: The Other Side of the Rainbow; Elvis Memories; Man on the Rock.

Add 152 Albany, Manor Road, Bournemouth BH1 3EW

Tel 01202 801 787

Email michael.freedland1@talktalk.net

FREEDMAN, Harry, PhD, MA (London), BA.

b. London, 1950; Ch. Exec. The Career Advice Centre; Lecturer, London Jewish Cultural Centre; Tru. Friends of Louis Jacobs; form. Dir. and Lecturer Masorti Academy (1994-2001); form. Chief Exec. Assembly of Masorti Synagogues (1994-2000); European Representative, Masorti; Lay M. Exeter Synagogue (1981-87); Editorial Adv. Cttee. Jewish Bible Quarterly, Judaism Today. Publ.: The Talmud: A Biography (2014); Jerusalem Imperilled (2011); How to get a Job in a Recession (2009); The Gospels' Veiled Agenda (2009); The Halacha in Targum Pseudo-Jonathan (1999).

Add North Gate, Prince Albert Road, London NW8 7EL

Tel 084 5467 4167

Email harry.freedman@btopenworld.com *Website* www.aspera.co.uk

FREEDMAN, Jeromé David, FCA.

b. Brighton, 1935; m. Louise née Hershman; Chartered Accountant; T. Chartered Accountants' Benevolent Association (CABA 1973-2008, Pres. 2003-05); V. Pres. LJ, form. Ch. (1995-2001); form. Hon. T. (1990-95); Past Pres. South London Liberal Synagogue.

Add 5 Thanescroft Gardens, Croydon, Surrey CR0 5JR

Tel 020 8688 2250 *Fax* 020 8680 4631

Email jerome@freedman.org

FREEDMAN, Prof. Sir Lawrence, PC, KCMG, CBE, FBA, FKC.

b. Tynemouth, Dec. 7, 1948; m. Prof. Judith Anne née Hill; Prof. War Studies, King's College London (1982-); V. Principal, (2003-); H. Dir. Centre for Defence Studies (1990–); T. Imperial War Museum (2001–10); Chesney Gold Medal, RUSI (2006). Among recent publications: Strategy: A History (2013); A Choice of Enemies (2008, Lionel Gelber Prize, 2009); The Official History of the Falklands Campaign, Vols. I and II (2005); Deterrence (2004); Superterrorism (Ed. 2002); The Cold War (2001); Kennedy's Wars (2000); The Politics of British Defence (1999).

Add King's College London, James Clerk Maxwell Building, 57 Waterloo Road, London SE1 8WA

Tel 020 7848 3984 *Fax* 020 7848 3668

Email marina.krispel@kcl.ac.uk

FREEDMAN, Vanessa Rosalind (née Gale), MA.

b. Birmingham, July 18, 1969; m. Rabbi Paul; Convenor, Hebraica Libraries Group (2012-); Librarian, Hebrew and Jewish Studies, University College London (2007-); Assistant Librarian, Leo Baeck College (2000-07).

Add UCL Library Services, University College London, Gower Street, London WC1E 6BT

Tel 020 7679 2598 *Fax* 020 7679 7373

Email v.freedman@ucl.ac.uk *Website* www.ucl.ac.uk/library

FREER, Mike,

b. May 29, 1960; Leader, Barnet Council (2006-09, 1990-94); Conservative Member of Parliament, Finchley and Golders Green; Mem. Conservative Friends of Israel; V. Pres. All Party Group Against Anti-Semitism.

Add House of Commons, London SW1A 0AA

Tel 020 7219 7071

Email mike.freer.mp@parliament.uk *Website* www.mikefreer.com

FREI, Saul David, LLB (Hons).

b. Hendon, 1954; m. Aviva Graus; Solicitor; Mem. Board of Deputies Family Law Cttee. (2000-); Gov. Hasmonean High School (1994-2009); United Synagogue Company Sec. and

Dir. of External & Legal Services (2008-); Registrar, London Beth Din (1999-); Solicitor specialising in property litigation (1980-99).

Add 305 Ballards Lane, London N12 8GB

Tel 020 8343 6270 *Fax* 020 8343 6257

Email dfrei@theus.org.uk

FRESHWATER, Benzion,

b. 1948; Ch. and Managing Dir. Daejan Holdings Plc (1980-); T. Mayfair Charities Ltd.

Add Freshwater House 158-162 Shaftesbury Avenue, London WC2H 8HR

FRESHWATER, Rabbi Shlomo,

Rabbi, Sassover Beit Midrash (2003-); Managing Dir. Freshwater Group.

Add Freshwater House 158-162 Shaftesbury Avenue, London WC2H 8HR

FRIEDLANDER, Evelyn (née Philipp), ARCM, Order of Merit (Germany).

b. London, June 22, 1940; Executive Dir. Hidden Legacy Foundation; T. and Ch. Czech Memorial Scrolls Trust. Publ.: Westminster Synagogue: the First 50 Years (2007); The Jews of Devon and Cornwall (2000); Mappot ... The Band of Jewish Tradition (1997, Co-Ed.); Ich Will nach Hause, aber ich war noch nie da (1996).

Add Kent House, Rutland Gardens, London SW7 1BX

Tel 020 7584 2754 *Fax* 020 7581 8012

Email epfriedlander@gmail.com

FRIEDMAN, (Eve) Rosemary (Robert Tibber, Rosemary Tibber, Rosemary Friedman),

b. London, Feb. 5, 1929; Writer. m. Dennis Friedman; Membership: Royal Society of Literature; Society of Authors; Writers Guild of Great Britain; British Academy of Film and Television Arts; Fel. English PEN. Among recent publications: Life is a Joke (2010); A Writer's Commonplace Book (2006); Paris Summer (2004); Intensive Care (2001); The Writing game (1999); Vintage (1996); Golden Boy (1994). Other: An Eligible Man (Stage Play, 2008); Change of Heart (Stage Play, 2004); Home Truths (Stage Play, 1997).

Add Apt. 5, 3 Cambridge Gate, London NW1 4JX

Tel 020 7935 6252 *Fax* 020 7486 2398

Email rosemaryfriedman@hotmail.com *Website* www.rosemary.friedman.co.uk

FRIEND, John, BSc, PhD (Liv), PhD (Cantab), FIBiol, FRSA.

b. Liverpool, May 31, 1931; m. Carol née Loofe; Pres. Hull Jewish Representative Council (1999-2003); Emer. Prof. of Plant Biology, Hull University (Prof. 1969-97); Vis. Fel. Wolfson College, Cambridge (1988); Pro-V. Chancellor, Hull University (1983-87); Vis. Prof. Hebrew University of Jerusalem (1974). Publ.: Recent Advances in the Biochemistry of Fruit and Vegetables (with MJC Rhodes, 1983); Biochemical Aspects of Plant-Parasite Relations (with D. R. Threlfall, 1976).

Add 9 Allanhall Way, Kirkella, Hull HU10 7QU

Tel 01482 658 930

Email j.friend@cj2f.karoo.co.uk

GAFFIN, Jean (née Silver), OBE, JP, HonFRCPCH, MSc, BSc (Econ).

b. London, Aug. 1, 1936; m. Alexander (dec'd); T. St. Luke's Hospice (2007-13); V. Ch. Chronic Pain Policy Coalition (2005-11); Ch. Brent Primary Care NHS Trust (2002-07); Magistrate, Harrow Bench (1981-2006); Mem. Consumer Panel Financial Services Author (1999-2003); Hon. S. Royal Society of Medicine (1997-2001); Exec. Dir. National Hospice Council (1991-98); Chief Exec. Arthritis Care (1988-91); Exec. Sec. British Paediatric Association (1982-87); Organising Sec. Child Accident Prevention Cttee. (1979-82); Lecturer II/Snr. Lecturer, Social Policy and Admin. Polytechnic of the South Bank (1973-79). Publ.: with D. Thoms, Caring and Sharing: the Centenary History of the Co-operative Women's Guild (1983, 2nd edition 1993); The Nurse and the Welfare State (Ed. 1981).

Add 79 Chalet Estate, Hammers Lane, London NW7 4DL

Tel 020 8959 9509

Email jean.gaffin@btopenworld.com

GAINSFORD, Sir Ian, BDS, DDS, FDSRCS Eng, FDSRCS Edin., FRCSEd.H., FICD, FACD, FKC, DDS (Hons) Toronto, FRSA.

b. Twickenham, June 24, 1930; m. Carmel née Liebster; Dental Surgeon; V. Pres. Jerusalem Great Synagogue; H. Pres. British Friends of Magen David Adom (1995-); Regent, Royal College of Surgeons, Edinburgh (2002-9), now Regent Emer.; Pres. Maccabaeans (2000-07); Pres. Western Marble Arch Synagogue (1998-2000); V. Principal, King's College, London (1994-97), now V. Principal Emer.; Dean, King's College School of Medicine and Dentistry (1988-97).

Add Flat 1, 12a Dor Vedorshav, Jerusalem 93117, Israel

Email iandgainsford@aol.com

GALASKO, Prof. Charles Samuel Bernard, MB, BCh. (First Class Hon), MSc (Hon), FRCSEng, FRCSEd, ChM, F.Med.Sci, FCMSA (Hon), FFSEM (Ireland), FFSEM (UK).

b. Johannesburg, South Africa, June 29, 1939; m. Carol; Consultant Orthopaedic Surgeon; Emer. Prof. Orthopaedic Surgery, University of Manchester; Hunterian Prof. Royal College of Surgeons; Inaugural Pres. Intercollegiate Faculty of Sport and Exercise Medicine (UK) (2006-09); Ch. Intercollegiate Academic Board for Sport and Exercise Medicine (2002-05); Member Medical Cttee. British Olympic Association (1988-2003); Pres. British Orthopaedic Association (2000-01), Ch. Academic Board (1998-2002), V. Pres. (1999-2000); V. Pres. Royal College of Surgeons of England (1999-2001), Ch. Hospital Recognition Cttee. (1992-95), Ch. Training Board (1995-99); V. Pres. British Amateur Wrestling Association (1996-2001), Ch. (1989-96); V. Ch. English Olympic Wrestling Association (1988-2001); Ch. Jt. Cttee. of Higher Surgical Training (GB & Ireland) (1997-2000); Sir Arthur Sims Commonwealth Prof. (1998); Pres. International Orthopaedic Research Society (1990-93); Ch. Awards Cttee., International Orthopaedic and Trauma Association (1990-93, 1984-87); V. Pres. Section of Oncology, Royal Society of Medicine (1987); H. Fel. British Orthopaedic Association; H. Fel. South African Orthopaedic Association. Publ.: Imaging Techniques in Orthopaedics (1989); Current Trends in Orthopaedic Surgery (1988); Neuromuscular Problems in Orthopaedics (1987); Recent Developments in Orthopaedic Surgery (1987); Skeletal Metastases (1986); Principles of Fracture Management (1984); Radionuclide Scintigraphy and Orthopaedics (1984); over 250 learned articles in refereed journals or book chapters.

Add 72 Gatley Road, Gatley, Cheshire SK8 4AA

Tel 0161 428 3582 *Fax* 0161 428 4558

Email carolgalasko@aol.com

GELLER, Markham Judah,

b. Corpus Christi, Texas, Jan. 2, 1949; Jewish Chronicle Prof. Dept. of Hebrew and Jewish Studies, University College London; Dir. Institute of Jewish Studies, University College London; on secondment, Gastprofessor für Wissengeschichte, at Freie Universität Berlin until 2015.

Add Dept of Hebrew and Jewish Studies, UCL, Gower Street, London WC1E 6BT

Fax 020 7209 1026

Email m.geller@ucl.ac.uk *Website* www.ucl.ac.uk/hebrew-jewish/ijs

GELLEY, Dayan Menachem,

b. Aug. 23, 1958, Newcastle; m. Devorah Silber; Snr. Dayan, London Beth Din (2007-), Dayan (1993-2006); Rabbi, Ohr Chodosh Community (2004-).

Add London Beth Din, 305 Ballards Lane N12 8GB

Tel 020 8343 6270 *Fax* 020 8343 6257

Email info@bethdin.org.uk

GILBERT, Andrew, BSc.

b. London, May 31, 1959; Managing Dir. Henry Bertrand Silk Fabrics; Ch. UJIA UK Programme Cttee. (2011-); Ch. UJIA Youth Movements Allocations Board (2010-); Tru. London Jewish Forum (2006-); Mem. UJIA UK Programme Cttee. (1997-); HW Fisher Special Award at the Jewish Volunteering Network Awards for Limmud (2010); Mem. MASA Cttee. Bd. Gov. JAFI (2009-10); Fdr. Ch. Limmud International (2006-10); V. Ch.

World Reform Zionist Movement (2006-10); Mem. Education Cttee. Bd. Gov. Jewish Agency for Israel (2001-10); Fdr. Mem. Jewish Leadership Council (2003-05); Ch. RSGB (2002-05); Ch. Israel Experience Policy Group, UJIA (1997-2002); Ch. Jewish Youth Service Partners Group (1994-1998); Ch. Board of Deputies, Education, Youth and Information Cttee. (1994-1997); Exec. Mem. Board of Deputies (1994-97); Ch. Limmud (1990-97); Ch. European Hanhallah, Coalition for the Advancement of Jewish Education of North America (1996).

Add 52 Holmes Road, London NW5 3AB

Tel 020 7424 7000 *Fax* 020 7424 7001

Email alphasilk@gmail.com

GILBERT, Rt. Hon. Sir Martin, CBE, D.Litt, PC.

b. London, Oct. 25, 1936; historian; Official Biographer of Winston Churchill (since 1968); Fel. Merton College, Oxford (1962-99); Vis. Prof. Hebrew University (1995-98, 1980); Vis. Prof. UCL (1995-6); Vis. Prof. Tel Aviv University (1979). Among recent publications: Winston S. Churchill (official biographer of 6 vols., with 11 vols. documents); 85 historical works including 9 Atlases; 9 on Churchill (inc. Churchill, A Life and Churchill, Power of Words); 13 on Twentieth Century History (inc. History of both World Wars); 10 on Holocaust themes (inc. An Atlas of the Holocaust, The Holocaust, The Jewish Tragedy); 7 on Israel (inc. The Story of Israel; Israel, A History); 4 on Jewish themes (inc. Churchill and the Jews and In Ishmael's House: A History of the Jews of the Arab Lands).

Add Merton College, Oxford, Merton Street, Oxford OX1 4JD

Email esthergilbert36@gmail.com *Website* www.martingilbert.com

GINSBURY, Rabbi Mordechai Shlomo,

b. London, May 10, 1960; m. Judy née Burns; Dir. P'eir (Promoting Excellence in Rabbi's), The United Synagogue's In-Service training, Professional development and support facility for its Rabbis and Rebbetzens (2009-); Principal Hasmonean Primary School (2003-); M. Hendon US (1999-); Ch. (2005-08); V. Ch. (2002-05) Rabbinical Council, US; M. Prestwich Hebrew Congregation, Manchester (1985-99); Ch. Rabbinical Council of the Provinces (1997-98).

Add Hendon United Synagogue, 18 Raleigh Close, London NW4 2TA

Tel 020 8202 6924 *Fax* 020 8202 1720

Email rabbiginsbury@hendonus.org.uk

GINSBURY, Rabbi Philip Norman, MA.

b. London, Mar. 26, 1936; form. M. South London Synagogue; M. Streatham District Synagogue, Brixton Synagogue; Ch. South London Rabbinical Council. Publ.: The Phases of Jewish History (2005); Jewish Faith in Action (1995).

Add 146 Downton Avenue, London SW2 3TT

Tel 020 8674 7451

Email rabbi@ginsburyp.co.uk

GLASSER, David,

b. Glasgow, Sept. 10, 1952; m. Susan née DeRose; Freeman, The Company of Arts Scholars (2013-); University Court of the London South Bank University (2012-); Ch. and Chief Exec. (pro bono) of Ben Uri, The London Jewish Museum of Art. (2000-); Northgate Consulting (1990-); Various privately owned companies (1989–1999); Ward White Group plc. (1985-1988); Company Dir. Marks and Spencer plc. (1970-1985). Publ.: Israel and Art: 60 Years through the eyes of Teddy Kollek (2008); contributed to various books on British and European artists of Jewish descent.

Add Ben Uri, 108a Boundary Road, St John's Wood, London NW8 0RH

Tel 020 7604 3991

Email davidg@benuri.org.uk

GLATTER, Robert, FCA.

b. Antwerp, Belgium, Mar. 14, 1937; Chartered Accountant, Non-Exec. Dir. Bank Leumi (UK) plc; Ch. Bank Leumi Pension Fund; Non-Exec. Dir. CP Holdings Ltd; V. Pres. Bnai

Brith Hillel Foundation; H. Life Pres. Maccabi Union GB; form. T. Arbib Lucas Charity; form. V. Pres. Akiva School; Mem. Maccabi World Union; form. Ch. Maccabi Union GB; T. Woolf Institute, Cambridge; form. Council Mem. Weizmann Institute Foundation; T. Maccabi Fd.; form. T. Volcani Fund; form. Gov. T. Carmel College; Ch. NW Reform Synagogue; Ch. RSGB Cttee. for Ed. and Youth; form. Ch. RSGB Israel Action Ct.; form. T. Bd. for Jewish Sport; form. T. Manor House Trustees.

Add 12 York Gate, London NW1 4QS

Email rg@rgconsultancy.co.uk

GLAZER, Ella, MBE.

b. London; m. Stanley; Journalist; H. Exec. Dir. The Celebrities Guild of GB (founded 1977).

Add The Studio, 16 Covert Way EN4 0LT

Tel 020 8449 1234

Email info@celebritiesguild.org.uk

GLINERT, Lewis H, BA (Oxon), PhD.

b. London, June 17, 1950; m. Joan née Abraham; University Lecturer; Prof. of Hebraic Studies and Linguistics, Dartmouth College; form. Prof. of Hebrew, University of London (School of Oriental and African Studies, 1979-97); Dir. Centre for Jewish Studies, SOAS; Vis. Prof. of Hebrew Studies, Chicago University (1987/8); Assistant Prof. of Hebrew Linguistics, Haifa University (1974-77). Publ.: Mamma Dear (1997); Modern Hebrew: An Essential Grammar (1994); Hebrew in Ashkenaz (1993); The Joys of Hebrew (1992); The Grammar of Modern Hebrew (1989).

Add Dartmouth College, 6191 Bartlett Hall, Hanover, N.H 03755, USA

Tel +1 (603) 646 8238 *Fax* +1 (603) 646 3115

Email Lewis.Glinert@Dartmouth.edu *Website* www.dartmouth.edu/~glinert/

GLOBE, Gordon Sherr,

b. Liverpool, Jan. 9, 1950; m. Maxine née Bellman; Property Management Surveyor; Dep. Merseyside Jewish Representative Council (MRJC) Board of Deputies (2011-); Pres. MJRC (2008-12); Ch. MJRC (2008-11); Dir. MJRC Charitable Ltd Company (2010-); Pres. Merseyside Jewish Community Care (MJCC) (2003-6); Dir. MJCC Charitable Ltd Company (2007-); Ch. Wardens of Orthodox Synagogues, Liverpool (1995-98); Pres. and Snr. Warden, Liverpool Greenbank Drive, Hebrew Congregation (1992-4).

Fax 0151 737 1052

Email globe.gordon@gmail.com

GOLD, Trudy,

Chief Exec. London Jewish Cultural Centre; Snr. Lecturer, Jewish History. Publ.: Lessons of the Holocaust (Ed-in-Chief, 1996).

Add LJCC, Ivy House, 94-96 North End Road, London NW11 7SX

Tel 020 8457 5000

Email admin@ljcc.org.uk

GOLDBERG, Rabbi David J, MA (Oxon), DD (Hons), OBE.

b. London, Feb. 25, 1939; Rabbi Emer. Liberal Jewish Synagogue; Co-Pres. London Society of Jews and Christians (2004-); Snr. Rabbi, L.J.S. (1986-2004), Associate Rabbi (1975-86); Interfaith Gold Medallion (1999); Premio Iglesias (1999); Ch. ULPS Rabbinic Conference (1996-98, 1981-83); M. Wembley and District Liberal Synagogue (1971-75). Publ.: This is not the Way: Jews, Judaism and Israel (2012); The Jewish People: Their History and their Religion (with John D. Rayner); To the Promised Land: A History of Zionist Thought; On the Vistula Facing East (Ed.); Progressive Judaism Today (Gen. Ed.); Aspects of LJ (Co-Ed.); The Divided Self: Israel and the Jewish Psyche Today.

Add Liberal Jewish Synagogue, 28 St. John's Wood Road NW8 7HA

Tel 020 7286 5181

GOLDBERG, David Jonathan, MA (Jewish Communal Service) Brandeis; Cert. Youth and Community Studies, London.

b. London, June 27, 1961; Dir. Fundraising, UJIA (2006-); Dir. UJIA Israel Experience (1998-2006); Exec. Dir. Zionist Federation of Great Britain and Ireland (1992-98); H. Ch. Association of Jewish Communal Professionals (1992-98); Snr. Youth and Community Work, Redbridge JYCC (1983-90).

Add 18 Chiltern Avenue, Bushey, Hertfordshire WD23 4QA

Tel 020 8950 0080

Email david.j.goldberg@btinternet.com

GOLDMAN, Alan,

Ch. Crest Nicholson Holdings (2009-11); form. Dir. Heron International Ltd; V. Ch. The Jewish Community Secondary School Trust; form. T. and Jt. Hon. T. Jewish Care.

Add The Jewish Community Secondary School Trust, Palladium House, 1-4 Argyll Street, London W1F 7LD

GOLDMAN, Lawrence Neil, MA, PhD (Cantab), FRHistS.

b. London June 17 1957; m. Madeleine Jean McDonald; University lecturer; Ed. Oxford Dictionary of National Biography (2004-); Fel. and Tutor in Modern History, St. Peter's College, Oxford (1990-). Publ.: Oxford Dictionary of National Biography 2001-04 (1st supplement 2009); Politics and Culture in Victorian Britain: Essays in Memory of Colin Matthew (2006, Ed. with P. Ghosh); Science, Reform and Politics in Victorian Britain (2002); Dons and Workers: Oxford and Adult Education since 1850 (1995); The Blind Victorian: Henry Fawcett and British Liberalism (Ed. 1989).

Add Oxford DNB, OUP, Great Clarendon Street, Oxford OX2 6DP

Tel 01865 278 899

Email lawrence.goldman@spc.ox.ac.uk

GOLDMEIER, Michael,

b. London, Nov. 27, 1946; m. Philippa née Yantian; Solicitor, partner Berwin Leighton Paisner; Immigration Judge (Asylum and Immigration Tribunal) (2001-); Ch. Jewish Care (2002-06); Mem. Bd. Claims Conference (1998-2002); V. Pres. Jewish Care; V. Ch. European Council Jewish Communities (1996-2002).

Add High Liuden, 104 Marsh Lane, Mill Hill, London NW7 4PA

Tel 020 3400 4358

Email michael.goldmeier@blplaw.com

GOLDREIN, Neville Clive, CBE, MA (Cantab.).

b. Hull; m. Dr. Sonia née Sumner; Solicitor; Mem. International Association Jewish Lawyers and Jurists; Mem. BAJS; H. Life Mem. (2008-), Ch. Environment and Energy Cttee. (1993-2006); T. LIPA (2008-); Mem. Port of Liverpool Police Cttee (2000-); Ch. Liverpool Chamber of Commerce (1986-); V. Pres. Crosby MENCAP (1966-); Snr. W. Liverpool Old Hebrew Congregation (2009-10, 1968-71); V. Pres. Southport Jewish Representative Council (2003-09); Mem. Council Liverpool Institute of Performing Arts (LIPA) (2005-08); T. Southport Jewish Representative Council (1999-2006); Ch. Liverpool Royal Court Theatre Foundation (1994-2005); Ch. (Appeals), Crosby Hall Education Trust (1989-91); Board of Deputies (1992-2001, 1965-85); British Association of Chambers of Commerce, Mem. Local and Regional Affiliated Cttee. (1994-97); Leader, Conservative Group (1980-86); form. Dep. Circuit Judge; form. Mem. (Leader, 1980-81, V. Ch. 1977-80) Merseyside County Council (1973-86); Council, Liverpool University (1977-81). Publ.: Life is Too Serious to be Taken Seriously (2010).

Add Torreno, St Andrew's Road, Blundellsands, Liverpool L23 7UR / Rehov Hapalmach 20/7, Jerusalem, Israel

Tel 0151 924 2065 /+972 (02) 563 3085 *Fax* 0151 924 2065

Email goldrein@aol.com

GOLDSMITH, Rabbi Mark, MA (Leo Baeck College).

b. London, July 5, 1963; m. Nicola née Angel; Rabbi, North Western Reform Synagogue (2006-); Ch. Assembly of Reform Rabbis UK (2011-13); Rabbi, Finchley Progressive Synagogue (1999-2006); Ch. Rabbinic Conference, Liberal Judaism (2004-06); Mem. Exec. Cttee. International Interfaith Investment Group (3iG) (2004-); Rabbi, Woodford Progressive Synagogue (1996-99). Publ.: A Passion for Judaism (chapter, 2011); Great Reform lives (chapter, 2009); Aspects of Liberal Judaism (chapter, 2004); My Israel (Michael Goulston Educational Foundation, 1995); My Israel Teacher's Guide (Michael Goulston Educational Foundation, 1995).

Add North Western Reform Synagogue, Alyth Gardens, London NW11 7EN

Tel 020 8457 8791

Email mark@alyth.org.uk *Website* www.alyth.org.uk

GOLDSMITH, Lord Peter Henry, PC, QC, MA (Cantab), LLM (London).

b. Liverpool, Jan. 5, 1950; m. Joy née Elterman; Pres. (2001-), Ch. Bar Pro Bono Unit (1996-2000); European Ch. of Litigation, Devoise and Plimpton LLP; form. H.M. Attorney-General (2001-07); Co-Ch. Human Rights Institute of International Bar Association (1998-2001); Ch. Financial Reporting Review Panel (1997-2000); Ch. Bar of England and Wales (1995). Publ.: contributor to Common Values, Common Law, Common Bond (2000).

Add House of Lords London SW1A

Email phgoldsmith@devoise.com

GOLDSMITH, Walter Kenneth, FCA CiMgt, FRSA.

b. London, Jan. 19, 1938; M. Development Cttee. SOAS (2010-); V. Pres. (2008-), Ch. Jewish Music Institute (2003-08); M. London Jewish Forum (2006-10); V. Pres. (1992-), Ch. (1987-91) British Overseas Trade Group for Israel; Dir. Bank Leumi (UK) plc (1984-2013); Ch. Estates and Management Ltd. (2006-); Ch. ULPS Centenary Cttee. 2002 (1999-02); Co-Fdr. and T. Israel Diaspora Trust (1982-92); Treasurer Leo Baeck College (1987-89); Dir. Gen. Institute of Dirs. (1979-84).

Add 35 Park Lane, London W1K 1RB

Email wg@waltergoldsmith.com

GOLDSTEIN, Rabbi Aaron, BSc, BA, MA.

Snr. Rabbi, Northwood and Pinner Liberal Synagogue (2008-); Mem. JCP Panel (2007-); Hd, Community Dev. for LJ (2002-09); British Steel Strip Products (1993-97).

Add NPLS, Oaklands Gate, Green Lane, Northwood, Middlesex HA6 3AA

Tel 01923 822 592 *Fax* 01923 824 454

Email rabbiaaron@npls.org.uk *Website* www.npls.org.uk

Twitter www.twitter.com/rabbiaaron *Blog* www.thejc.com/users/rabbi-aaron.goldstein

GOLDSTEIN, Rabbi Andrew, PhD.

b. Warwick, Aug. 12, 1943; Pres. Liberal Judaism (2013-); Rabbinic Adv. EUPJ (2012-); M. Northwood and Pinner Liberal Synagogue (1970-2008), Emer. Rabbi (2008-); Ch. LJ Rabbinic Board (Bet Din) (2008-); Liberal Rabbi, Bratislava (2008-); Ch. European Union for Progressive Judaism (2007-); Exec. Bd. ICCJ (2003-11); Ch. ULPS Prayerbook Editorial Cttee. (1990-95); Dir. Kadimah Holiday School, (1970-89); Ch. ULPS Education Cttee. (1970-88); Ch. ULPS Rabbinic Conf. (1979-81). Publ.: Haggadah B'chol Dor Va-Dor (Co-Ed. 2010); High & Holy Days: A Book of Jewish Wisdom (Co-Ed. 2010); Machzor Ruach Chadashah (Co-Ed. 2003).

Add 10 Hallowell Road, Northwood, Middlesex HA6 1DW

Tel 01923 822 818 *Fax* 01923 824 454

Email agoldstein@f2s.com

GOLDSTEIN, Michael Howard, FCA.

b. London, July 7, 1963; m. Lara née Stanton; Chartered Accountant; Partner, BDO LLP (2003-); T. JCC for London (2007-); Ch. Israel Desk (2005-); Ch. Office for Small Communities (2005-); T. UJS Hillel (2003-); V. Ch. UJIA (2003-); Gov. King Solomon High

School (1992-2003); form. Partner, Blick Rothenberg (1990-2003); Chartered Accountant, BDO Stoy Hayward (1988-90).

Add 55 Baker Street, London W1U 7EU

Tel 020 7486 5888 *Fax* 020 7487 3686

Email michael.goldstein@bdo.co.uk

GOLDSTEIN, Rabbi Dr Warren, BA, LLB., PhD, Dayanut-Kollel; Eretz Hemdah.

b. Pretoria, 1971; Chief Rabbi of South Africa, Graduate of the Yeshiva of Johannesburg (1996). Publ.: The Legacy: Teachings for Life from the Great Lithuanian Rabbis (co-author 2012); Sefer Mishpat Tzedek - Halachic work on competition and other Monetary Laws (2011); Defending the Human Spirit: Jewish Law's Vision for a Moral Society (2006); African Soul Talk - When Politics is not Enough (co-author, 2003).

Add Union of Orthodox Synagogues of South Africa, 58 Oaklands Road, Orchards 2192, Johannesburg South Africa

Tel +27 10 214 2603 *Fax* +27 11 485 1497

Email office@chiefrabbi.co.za *Website* www.chiefrabbi.co.za

GOLDSTONE, Barbara D, ALCM, LLAM, Gold Medal LAM, TC, BA (Eng)., M.Ed.

b. Salford, June 24, 1938; Schoolteacher, Tutor of Public Speaking and Drama; Pres. Manchester Bnai Brith (2011-12, 2005, 2003, 2001), Whitefield Bnai Brith (1985); Pres. Jewish Representative Council of Greater Manchester (2007-10); Ch. Prestwich Emunah (1967, 1958); Higher Broughton, Higher Crumpsall Ladies Guild; Ch. Jewish Representative Council Education Cttee.

Add 1 Tower Grange, New Hall Road, Salford M7 4EL

Tel 0161 792 1305

Email barbaradgold@gmail.com *Website* www.jewishmanchester.org

GOODMAN, Martin David, MA, D.Phil, D. Litt (Oxon) FBA.

b. Aug. 1, 1953; m. Sarah Jane née Lock; Prof. of Jewish Studies, University of Oxford; Fel. of the Oxford Centre for Hebrew and Jewish Studies and Wolfson College; Jt. Ed. of Journal of Jewish Studies (1995-99); Sec. European Association for Jewish Studies (1995-98); Reader in Jewish Studies, University of Oxford (1991-96); Pres. British Association for Jewish Studies (1995). Among recent publications: Rabbinic Texts and the History of Late-Roman Palestine (Jt. Ed. 2010); Judaism in the Roman World: Collected Essays (2007); Rome and Jerusalem (2007); Representations of Empire: Rome and the Mediterranean World (Jt. Ed. 2002); The Oxford Handbook of Jewish Studies (Ed. 2002); Apologetics in the Roman Empire (Jt. Ed. 1999); Jews in a Graeco-Roman World (Ed. 1998); The Roman World 44BC-AD180 (1997).

Add Oriental Institute, Pusey Lane, Oxford OX1 2LE

Tel 01865 278 208 *Fax* 01865 278 190

Email martin.goodman@orinst.ox.ac.uk

GOODMAN, Vera (née Appleberg),

b. London; Life V. Pres. Richmond Park Conservative Assoc. (2010); Life V. Pres. (Ch. 1976-9) Richmond Park Conservative Women's Constituent Cttee.; Ch. Richmond Park Women's Conservatives (2005-8); Volunteer Royal Star and Garter Home, Richmond; Volunteer Award for Distinguished Service (2004); Board of Deputies (1973-94), Exec. Cttee. (1985-91), form. Ch. Public Relations Cttee.; Bd. of Elders, Spanish and Portuguese Jews' Congregation (1990-4, 1977-80); Greater London Conservative Women's Gen. Purposes Cttee. (1979-85); V. Ch. Govs. Russell School, Petersham (1974-82); National Council for Soviet Jewry (1977-80); Conservative Representative, National Council of Women (1974-79); form. Central London Council, Conservative Friends of Israel; Representative, Union of Jewish Women at U.N.A.; Central Council, Conservative Party; Conservative Women's National Cttee. Exec.; European Union of Women (British Section); Ch. Sephardi Women's Guild; British Council, World Sephardi Federation.

Add 87 Ashburnham Road, Ham, Richmond, Surrey TW10 7NN

Tel 020 8948 1060

GORDON, Rabbi Jeremy, MA (Hons) Cam Rabbinic Ordination, a Masters in Midrash (Rabbinic Exegesis).

m. Josephine; Rabbi, New London Synagogue (2008-); Rabbi, St Albans Masorti Synagogue (2004-08); Chaplain with the Red Cross in the aftermath of September 11th; active in a number of social action campaigns – relating to refugee issues and international development, convenor of a major interfaith dialogue forum in New York; Teacher, Midrash and contemporary Jewish legal responsa; worked for BBC and a number of independent production companies.

Add 33 Abbey Road, London NW8 0AT

Tel 020 7328 1026

Email rabbi@newlondon.org.uk

GORDON, Lionel Lawrence, BSc (Econ).

b. London, Aug. 31, 1933; form. Market Research Director.; form. Ch. Jewish Chronicle Ltd.; Ch. Jewish Renaissance.

Add The Hyde, 5 Orchard Gate, Esher, Surrey KT10 8HY

Tel 020 8398 5774

Email lionelandjillgordon@talktalk.net

GOULD, MATTHEW, MBE.

b. Aug. 20, 1971; m. Celia née Leaberry; British Ambassador to Israel.

Add 192 Hayarkon Street, Tel Aviv 63405, Tel Aviv, Israel

GOULD, Prof. Samuel Julius, MA (Oxon).

b. Liverpool, Oct. 13, 1924; Bd. of Dir. Centre for Policy Studies (1985-97); Res. Bd. & Policy Planning Group, IJA; BoD (1984-90); Res. Dir. Instit. Political Research (1983-85); Ch. and T. Social Affairs Unit, London (1981-2007); Prof. of Sociology, Nottingham Univ. (1964-82); Reader, Social Inst. London School of Economics and Political Science. Publ.: Dictionary of the Social Sciences (Jt. Ed.); Jewish Life in Modern Britain (Jt. Ed.); The Attack on Higher Education (1977); Jewish Commitment: A study in London (Jt. Ed. 1984).

Add c/o The Reform Club, Pall Mall London SW1

GOULDEN, Simon Charles, BSc (Eng), DMS, CEng, MCMI, MICE.

b. London, Mar. 1, 1949; Education and Management Consultant; Consultant, Jewish Leadership Council (2011-); Consultant, Inst. Professional Development for Jewish Studies (2009-); Principal, Simon Goulden Consultancy (2009-); Education Consultant, United Synagogue (2009-); Mem. Singer's Prayer Book Publication Cttee.; Chief Exec. Agency for Jewish Education (1995-2009); Principal Engineer, London Borough Haringey (1976-1986); form. Exec. Dir. Jews' College (1986-95); Publ.: Medinatenu: the Israel History Book (with M. Binstock, 2002).

Tel 020 8441 0475

Email simongoulden@gmail.com

GRABINER, Michael, CBE, MA (Cantab).

b. St. Albans, Aug. 21, 1950; m. Jane Olivia née Harris; Ch. World Union for Progressive Judaism (2011-); Ch. of Governors, Jewish Community Secondary School (2009-); Ch. Partnership for Schools (2005-12); Bd. Mem. UK Jewish Film Festival (2004-12); Partner, Apax Partners LLP (2002-09); Ch. Movement for Reform Judaism (2005-08); Governor Leo Baeck College (2005-08); Mem. Jewish Leadership Council (2005-08).

Email mike@grabiner.net

GRAHAM, Prof. (Stewart) David, QC, MA, BCL (Oxon), FRSA.

b. Leeds, Feb. 27, 1934; Barrister; form. Ch. Law, Parl. and Gen. Purposes Cttee. Board of Deputies; Vis. Prof. Faculty of Business, Kingston University (2004-); form. Mem. Insolvency Rules Adv. Cttee.; form. Mem. Ch. and Exec. Cttee. of Justice; Snr. Vis. Fel. Centre for Commercial Law Studies, QMW College; form. Mem. Council Insurance Ombudsman Bureau; Associate Mem. British and Irish Ombudsman Association. Publ.: Works on bankruptcy and insolvency.

Add 6 Grosvenor Lodge, Dennis Lane, Stanmore, Middlesex HA7 4JE

Tel 020 8954 3783

GRANT, Linda, BA, MA.

b. Liverpool, Feb. 15, 1951; Writer. Publ.: (fiction) Still Here (2002); When I Lived in Modern Times (2000); The Cast Iron Shore (1996); (non-fiction) We Had It So Good (2011); The Thoughtful Dresser (2009); The Clothes on Their Backs (2008); The People on the Street: A Writer's View of Israel (2006); Remind Me Who I Am Again (1998); Sexing the Millenium: A Political History of the Sexual Revolution (1993).

Add c/o A.P. Watt, Literary Agents, 20 John Street, London WC1N 2DR

Email linda@lindagrant.co.uk *Website* www.lindagrant.co.uk

GREEN, Dr Abigail Frances Floretta, B.A. Oxon 1993 1st class; Certificat en Etudes Européennes, ULB, 1994 Distinction; D.Phil. Cantab 1999.

b. Stoke Newington, May 12, 1971; m. Boaz Brosh; Tutorial Fel. History, Brasenose College, Oxford; CUF Lecturer, University of Oxford (2000-); Research Fel. St John's College, Cambridge (1998-2000). Publ.: Moses Montefiore: Jewish Liberator, Imperial Hero (2010); Fatherlands: State-building and Nationhood in Nineteenth Century Germany (2001).

Add Brasenose College, Oxford OX1 4AJ

Tel 01865 277868

Email abigail.green@bnc.ox.ac.uk

GREEN, Sir Philip, Kt.

b. London, Mar. 15, 1952; m. Tina Green; Retail Exec. Arcadia Group (2002); Bhs (2000); Sears (1999); Shoe Express (1997-98); Mark One (1996); Ch. and Chief Exec. Amber Day (1988–92).

Add Bhs Ltd, Marylebone House, 129–137 Marylebone Road NW1 5QD

GREENBAT, Alan, OBE, JP.

b. London, Apr. 1929; H. Consultant, Office of the Chief Rabbi (1995-2012); Sec. Rabbinical Commission for the Licensing of Shochetim; Pres. Norwood Old Scholars Association; Mem. Inner London Youth Courts (1964-99); V. Pres. AJY (1989-96); V. Pres. London Union of Youth Clubs (1984-94); Exec. Dir. Office of the Chief Rabbi (1990-91); Exec. and V. Ch. National Council of Voluntary Youth Services (1981-91); Dir. Association for Jewish Youth (1980-89); Dir. Victoria Community Centre (1961-80); V. Principal Norwood Home for Jewish Children (1955-61).

Email info@chiefrabbi.org

GREENBERG, Rabbi Philip T, BA, MPhil, FJC.

b. Liverpool, June 28, 1937; Emer. Rabbi, Giffnock and Newlands Synagogue, Glasgow; Ch. Va'ad HaRabbonim, Glasgow; H. Chaplain, Calderwood Lodge Jewish School, Glasgow; Rav, Glasgow Shechita Board (1993-99); Hd. Mishna Stream, Hasmonean Boys' School (1972-81); M. Nottingham Synagogue (1968-72), Highams Park and Chingford Synagogue (1959-68).

Add 72 Bridge Lane, Golders Green, London NW11 0EJ

Tel 020 8455 5685 *Fax* 020 8455 5685

Email phillip_anna@yahoo.co.uk

GREENGROSS, Dr Wendy, MB, BS (Lond), LRCP, MRCS, DObst, RCOG; Dip. Med. Law & Ethics.

b. London, Apr. 29, 1925; Medical Practitioner; Broadcaster; Medical Consultant; Marriage Guidance Council; V. Pres. AJY Fel. Leo Baeck College; T. Leonard Cheshire Foundation; Pres. Ranulf Association; Mem. Govt. Enquiry into human fertilisation and embryology; Ch. Ethics Cttee. Wellington Humana Hospital. Publ.: Living, Loving and Ageing (1989); Jewish and Homosexual (1982); Entitled to Love (1976); The Health of Women (1974); Sex in Early Marriage (1970); Sex in the Middle Years (1969); Marriage, Sex and Arthritis.

Add 35 Regency House, 269 Regent's Park Road, London N3 3JZ

Tel 020 8455 1153

GREENWOOD, Jeffrey Michael, MA, LLM.
b. London, Apr. 21, 1935; Dep. Ch. Jewish Chronicle Ltd (1995-2005); Dir. Bank Leumi (UK) plc (1988-2005); Ch. Jewish Literary Trust (2001-3); Ch. Central Council for Education and Training in Social Work (1993-98); Snr. Partner Nabarro Nathanson (1987-95); Ch. Jewish Welfare Bd. (1985-1990), Jewish Care (1990). V. Pres. Jewish Care; Council, Anglo-Israel Association; M. Council JHSE.
Add 5 Spencer Walk, Hampstead High Street, London NW3 1QZ
Tel 020 7794 5281 *Fax* 020 7794 0094
Email jeff@thegreenwoods.org

GRUNEWALD, Rabbi Jacob Ezekiel, BA.
b. Tel Aviv, Oct. 26, 1945; M. Pinner Synagogue (1976-2010); Youth Rabbi, St John's Wood Synagogue (1971-6); T. Rabbinical Council, US; Mem. Chief Rabbi's Cabinet.
Add 1 Cecil Park, Pinner, Middlesex HA5 5HJ
Tel 020 8868 7204

GRUNFELD, Rabbi Joey,
b. London. Adult education pioneer; Fdr. and Exec. Dir. Project SEED (1980-).
Add 2530 San Pablo Avenue, Suite K, Berkeley, CA 94702-2000 USA
Tel +1 (510) 644 3422 *Fax* +1 (510) 644 0566
Email jgrunfeld@seed.uk.net

GRUNWALD, Henry Cyril, OBE LLB (Hons).
b. London, Aug. 8, 1949; m. Alison née Appleton; Barrister, Queen's Counsel; Pres. National Council of Shechita Boards; Pres. World Jewish Relief (2009-); V. Pres. Council of Christians and Jews (2009-); Adv. Bd. Mem. Community Security Trust (2006-); V. Ch. National Holocaust Memorial Day Trust (2005-); Ch. Shechita UK (2003-); Bencher, H. Society of Gray's Inn (2002-); Mem. Hillel Bd. Dir. (2000-); Tru. The Holocaust Centre (Beth Shalom) (2010); Jt. Ch. Jewish Human Rights Cttee. UK (2008-10); Pres. North London Relate (2007-09); Pres. Board of Deputies (2003-09), Snr. V. Pres. (2000-03), V. Pres. (1997-2000); Ch. Jewish Leadership Council (2003-09); V. Ch. European Jewish Congress (2003-09); Ch. Pikuach Bd. Gov. (2000-09); Warden, Hampstead Synagogue (1997-07); Fel.: UCL (2006); H. Patron, Yad Vashem UK; Patron, Youth Interfaith Trust; Patron, Drugsline.
Add Charter Chambers, 33 John Street WC1N 2AT
Tel 020 7618 4400 *Fax* 020 7618 4401
Email h.grunwald@btinternet.com *Website* www.charterchambers.com

GRUNWALD-SPIER, Agnes (née Grunwald), JP, BScEcon. (Hons, Lond), MA.
b. Budapest July 1944; Magistrate (Bromsgrove Bench 1948-91; Sheffield 1992-2012; Highbury 2012-); Dep. World Jewish Relief (2009-12); Lay M. Architects' Registration Bd. (2008-13); Ch. Women in the Jewish Community Regional Co-ord. Council (1997-2003, Acting Ch. 2006-); T. Holocaust Memorial Day Trust (2004-12); Board of Deputies; Ch. Regional Assembly (2006-09), M. Defence Div. (2003-12), Deputy for Sheffield (1997-2009); Diversity in Public Appointments Ambassador (2009-11); Lay M. Conduct and Registration Cttee. Gen. Social Care Council (2003-11); Lay M. Herbal Medicines Adv. Cttee. (2005-09); Mem. Yorkshire and Humber Faiths Forum (2005-08); Pres. Sheffield and District Jewish Representative Council (1999-2002); M. National Council, World Jewish Relief (1998-2001). Publ.:The Other Schindlers: Why Some People Chose to Save Jews in the Holocaust (2010).
Add 28 Dolphin Court, Woodlands, London NW11 9QY
Tel 07816 196 517
Email agnesgrunwaldspier@gmail.com *Website* www.agnesgrunwaldspier.com

GUBBAY, Lucien Ezra, MA (Oxon), MICE, C.Eng.
b. Buenos Aires, 1931, m. Joyce née Shammah; Consulting Engineer; Ch. Montefiore Endowment; T. and Dir. LSJS; form. Mem. Exec. Jewish Memorial Council; form. Warden

Spanish and Portuguese Synagogue; form. Dir. Industrial Dwellings Society (1885) Ltd; Pres. of the Bd. of Elders, Spanish and Portuguese Jews' Congregation London (1996-2000); Flg. Off. RAF (1952-54). Publ.: A Bath of Wine for the Sabbath (2013); Encyclopaedia of Jews in the Islamic World (contr. 2010); Two Worlds Supplement (2009); Our Glorious Tradition (2007); Two Worlds (2004); Sunlight and Shadow: Jewish Experience of Islam (1999); The Sephardim (1992); You Can Beat Arthritis (1992); Quest for the Messiah (1990); Origins (1989); The Jewish Book of Why and What (1987); Ages of Man (1985).

Add 26 Linden Lea, London N2 0RG

Tel 020 8458 3385

Email lucien@gubbay.co.uk

GUTTENTAG, Rabbi Jonathan, BA (Hons).

b. Newcastle, Nov. 12, 1959, m. Deborah Halle; Jt. Pres. Manchester CCJ (2008-); Mem. Schools Strategic Implementation Group Jewish Leadership Council (2008-); Fdr. National Association Orthodox Jewish Schools (2007-); Mem. Standing Cttee. Conference European Rabbis (2000-); T. Jewish Memorial Council (2006-); Mem. Greater Manchester Faith and Communities Leaders Forum (2001-); Fdr. and T. Whitefield Community Kollel / The Forum (1990-); Rabbi, Whitefield Synagogue Manchester (1987-); Jewish Faith Representative to Metropolitan Borough of Bury Education Cttee. (1990-2003); Rabbi, Southport Hebrew Congregation (1984-87).

Add 1 Park Hill Drive, Whitefield, Manchester M45 7PD

Tel 07980 262 767 *Fax* 0161 280 5452

Email rjg@theforumwck.org *Website* www.theforumwck.org

HALBAN, Martine (née Mizrahi), BA (Hons) Sussex.

b. Alexandria, Dec. 29, 1953; m. Peter Francis Halban; Book Publisher; Dir. Halban Publishers (1992-).

Add Halban Publishers, 22 Golden Square, London W1F 9JW

Tel 020 7437 9300 *Fax* 020 7437 9512

Email books@halbanpublishers.com *Website* www.halbanpublishers.com

HALBAN, Peter Francis, BA (Princeton).

b. New York, June 1 1946; m. Martine neé Mizrahi; Book Publisher; M. Exec. UK Bd. Jerusalem Foundation (2006-), Ch. (2010); T. Woolf Centre for Study of Abrahamic Faiths, Cambridge, (2003-); T. The Humanitarian Trust (1998-); Council European Jewish Publication Society (1994-); Co-Dir. Halban Publishers Ltd. (1986-); T. Jewish Heritage UK (2007-11); Mem. Exec. Institute for Jewish Policy Research (1994-2010).

Add Halban Publishers, 22 Golden Square, London W1F 9JW

Tel 020 7437 9300 *Fax* 020 7437 9512

Email books@halbanpublishers.com *Website* www.halbanpublishers.com

HALPERN, Rabbi Elchonon,

b. Kashau, Slovakia, 1922. Life Pres. Union of Orthodox Hebrew Congregations; Principal, Pardes House School; Rabbi, Beis Medrash Beis Shmuel, Golders Green.

Add 140 Stamford Hill, London N16 6QT

Tel 020 8802 6226

HAMILTON, Fabian, BA, MP.

b. Apr. 12, 1955; m. Rosemary née Ratcliffe; MP, Leeds North-East (1997-); Mem. Foreign Affairs Select Cttee. (2001-10); Leeds City Councillor (1987-98); Ch. Education Cttee. (1996-97); Ch. Economic Development Cttee. (1994-96); Ch. Race Equality Cttee. (1988-94).

Add House of Commons, London SW1A 0AA

Tel 0113 249 6600 (Constituency Office)

Email fabian@leedsne.co.uk *Website* www.leedsne.co.uk

HARRIS, Dr Evan, MP, BA, BM, BS.

b. Sheffield, Oct. 21, 1965; Hon. Assoc. National Secular Society (2000-); Front Bench Science Spokesman (2005-10); MP (Lib. Dem.), Oxford West and Abingdon (1997-2010); Registrar in Public Health Medicine (1994-97).

Add House of Commons, London SW1A 0AA

Tel 020 7219 5128

HARRIS, Rabbi Michael Jacob, MA (Cantab), MA (Jerusalem, PhD (London).

b. London, Feb. 17, 1964; Rabbi, Hampstead Synagogue (1995-), Southend and Westcliff Hebrew Congregation (1992-95); Lecturer in Jewish Law, Jews' College, London (1995-97); Res. Fel. London School of Jewish Studies; Affiliated Lecturer, Faculty of Divinity, University of Cambridge; Mem. Chief Rabbi's Cabinet. Publ.: Radical Responsibility: Celebrating the thought of Chief Rabbi Lord Jonathan Sacks (co.-Ed. 2012); Divine Command Ethics: Jewish and Christian Perspectives (2003).

Add The Hampstead Synagogue, Dennington Park Road, London NW6 1AX

Tel 020 7435 1518 *Fax* 020 7431 8368

Email rabbi.michael@talk21.com

HARTOG, Melvyn Allan,

b. London, Dec. 30, 1947; m. Marilyn née Green; Hd. Burial, United Synagogue; Prison Chaplain (1997-); Royal Navy (1963-71); Mem. Home Office Advisory Board on Burial and Cemeteries.

Add 305 Ballards Lane, London N12 8GB

Tel 020 8343 6283 *Mobile* 07939 110 508 *Fax* 020 8343 6262

HASKEL, Lord Simon,

b. Kaunas, Oct. 9, 1934; m. Carole Lewis; Life Peer; Deputy Speaker, House of Lords (2002-); Pres. Institute for Jewish Policy Research (2002-).

Add House of Lords, London SW1A 0PW

Tel 020 7219 4076

Email haskels@parliament.uk

HASSAN, Judith, OBE, BSc (Hons), Postgrad. Diploma Applied Social Sciences, CQSW.

b. London, Mar. 27, 1946; Special Advisor, Therapeutic Services for Survivors of War Trauma, Jewish Care; Ed. Bd. Kavod (2012-); Dir. of Services for Holocaust Survivors and Refugees, Jewish Care (1990-2011); Fdr. Holocaust Survivors Centre (1993). Awards: Lifetime Achievement in Care, National Care Awards (2007). Publ.: Good Practice in Promoting Recovery and Healing for Abused Adults (chapter, Recovery and Healing in Survivors of the Holocaust); A House Next Door to Trauma: Learning from Holocaust Survivors How to Respond to Atrocity (2003); The Handbook of Psychotherapy: Therapy with Survivors of the Nazi Holocaust (chapter, 1994); Witness and Vision of the Therapist: Counselling with Holocaust Survivors (chapter, 1998); Past Trauma in Later Life: From Victim to Survivor - The Possibility of Healing Aging Survivors of the Nazi Holocaust (chapter, 1997); A Global Perspective on Working with Holocaust Survivors and the Second Generation: Individual Counselling Techniques with Holocaust Survivors and Helping Elderly Survivors cope with Aging (chapters, 1995).

Add Jewish Care, Amelie House, The Wohl Campus, 221 Golders Green Road, London NW11 9DQ

Tel 07769 235 106

Email jhassan@jcare.org

HAYEK, Samuel, LLB.

b. Israel, 1953; Ch. JNF UK (2008-); Fdr. S. Hayek Holding Company (2004); Prop. Arlen Properties plc. (1984); Fdr. The Hayek Contemporary Art Centre, Old Jaffa, Israel.

Add Spring Villa Park, Middlesex HA8 7ED

Tel 020 8732 6100 *Fax* 020 8732 6148

Email info@jnf.co.uk *Website* www.jnf.co.uk

HAYMAN, Baroness Helene (née Middleweek), GBE, PC, MA (Cantab).

b. Wolverhampton, Mar. 26, 1949; m. Martin Hayman. Lord Speaker (2006-11); Ch. Human Tissue Authority (2005-06); Ch. Cancer Research UK (2001-04); Min. State, Agriculture (1999-2001); PPS Dept. of Health (1998-99); Parl. Under Sec. of State, Dept. of Environment, Transport and the Regions (1997-98); Ch. Whittington Hospital (1992-97); Labour Mem. of Parl. (1974-79).

Add House of Lords, London SW1A 0PW

Email haymanh@parliament.uk

HELFGOTT, Ben, MBE, D. Univ (Southampton), D.Litt Inst. Education, University of London.

b. Pabianice, Poland, Nov. 22, 1929; Pres. Holocaust Memorial Day Trust (2012-); Pres. Yad Vashem - UK Foundation (2005-); V. Pres. Claims Conference (2000-); Mem. Holocaust Memorial Day Home Office Steering and Education (1999-); Mem. of Exec. World Confederation of Holocaust Survivor Organisations (1998-); Founding Patron, Mem. Advisory Group of the Permanent Holocaust Exhibition at the Imperial War Museum (1995-); Ch. Polin Institute for Polish Jewish Studies (1994-); Tru. Board of Management, Holocaust Education Trust (1993-); Deputy, Board of Deputies (1982-); Mem. of Exec. Wiener Library (1982-); Ch. '45 Aid Society (1963–); V. Pres. Bnei Brith First Lodge of England (1992-93); Jt. T. Central British Fund - World Jewish Relief (1978-84); Ch. Cttee. Promotion of Yiddish and Yiddish Culture; Council, Jewish Youth Fund. Awards - Jewish News Lifetime Achievement Award (2011); Commander's Cross, Order of Merit, Poland (2005); Knight's Cross, Order of Merit, Poland (1994); British Weightlifting Champion and Record Holder; competed in Olympic Games (1960, 1956); Bronze Medal, Commonwealth Games (1958); Gold Medals, Maccabiah (1957, 1953, 1950); Lifetime Achievement Award, Jewish News.

Add 46 Amery Road, Harrow, Middlesex HA1 3UG

Tel 020 8422 1512

Email benhelfgott@talktalk.net

HELLER, Sir Michael Aron, MA, FCA.

b. London, m. Morven née Livingstone; Company Chairman; Ch. London & Associated Properties plc; Ch. Bisichi Mining plc; Ch. Electronic Data Processing plc; Dep. Ch. Centre for Policy Studies; Fel. Commoner of St. Catherine's College, Cambridge; H. Doctor, Technion, Haifa, Israel; H. Doctor, Sheffield Hallam University; H. Fel. University College London.

Add 24 Bruton Place, London W1J 6NE

Tel 020 7415 5000

Email m.heller@lap.co.uk

HELLNER, Rabbi Frank, BA, BHL, MA, DD (Hon).

b. Philadelphia, PA, Jan. 1, 1935; Emer. Rabbi Finchley Progressive Synagogue; Exec. Barnet Com. Rel. Council; form. Gov. Akiva School; Mem. Jewish Community Day School Adv. Bd.; T. Jewish Community Schools Adv. Bd.; V. Pres. Finchley CCJ; Mem. Leo Baeck College Co.; Extra-Mural Lecturer Birkbeck College (Pt.-time); Chaplain to Mayor of L. B. Barnet (1993-94); Ed. ULPS News (1978-86); Ch. ULPS Rabbinic Conference (1970-71). Publ.: I Promise I Will Try not to Kick My Sister and Other Sermons (1987).

Add Finchley Progressive Synagogue, 54 Hutton Grove N12 8DR

Tel 020 8446 4063

Email f.hellner@dsl.pipex.com

HENIG, Baroness Ruth,

b. Leicester, Nov. 10, 1943; m. Jack Johnstone; Life Peer; Historian and Lecturer; Ch. Security Industry Authority (2007-); Ch. and Pres. Association of Police Authorities (1997-). Publ.: A History of the League of Nations (2010); Women and Political Power (with Simon Henig, 2000); The Weimar Republic (1998); Europe 1870-1945 (with Chris Culpin, 1997); Origins of the First World War (1987); Origins of the Second World War (1985); Versailles and After (1984); The League of Nations (Ed. 1973).

Add House of Lords, London SW1A 0PW

Tel 020 7219 5133

Email ruthhenig@gmail.com

HILL, Brad Sabin, AB, FRAS.

b. New York, Nov. 2, 1953; Curator, Kiev Judaica Collection, George Washington University, Washington DC; Snr. Assoc. Oxford Centre for Hebrew and Jewish Studies; form. Dean of the Library, Snr. Res. Librarian, Yivo Institute for Jewish Research, NY (2002-07); form. Librarian and Fel. in Hebrew Bibliography, Oxford Centre for Hebrew and Jewish Studies (1996-2001); form. Hd. Hebrew Section, The British Library (1989-96); Curator of Rare Hebraica, National Library of Canada, Ottawa (1979-89). Publ.: Miscellanea Hebraica Bibliographica (Ed. 1995); Hebraica from the Valmadonna Trust (1989); Incunabula, Hebraica and Judaica (1981).

Add 35 Thackley End, 119 Banbury Road, Oxford OX2 6LB

Email hebraica@gwu.edu

HILTON, Rabbi Michael, MA(Oxon), MA (London), D.Phil (Oxon), PGCE (London).

b. London, Feb. 27, 1951; M. Kol Chai Hatch End Jewish Community (2001-); Lecturer, Leo Baeck College (2008); Hon. Res. Fel. Centre for Jewish Studies, University of Manchester (1998-); Lecturer, Three Faiths Summer School, Ammerdown Centre (1991-); M. North London Progressive Synagogue (1999-2001); M. Cheshire Reform Congregation (1987-98). Publ.: Bar Mitzvah: A History (2014); The Christian Effect on Jewish Life (1994); The Gospels and Rabbinic Judaism (with G. Marshall, 1988).

Add Hatch End Jewish Community, 434 Uxbridge Road, Pinner, Middlesex HA5 4RG

Tel 020 8906 8241

Email rabbiM@kolchai.org *Website* www.rabbim.co.uk

HIRSH, David, BSc, MA, PhD.

b. Sep. 29, 1967; Lecturer, Goldsmiths, University of London; Founding Ed. Engage website (2005-); Sociological Review Fel. (2001-02). Many publications, including: Anti-Zionism and Antisemitism (2007); Law against Genocide (2003).

Add Goldsmiths, University of London, New Cross, London SE14 6NW

Tel 020 7919 7730

Email d.hirsh@gold.ac.uk

HOCHHAUSER, Prof. Daniel, MA, D.Phil, FRCP.

b. London, July 18, 1957; m. Joanne née Garland; Kathleen Ferrier Prof. and Consultant in Medical Oncology, University College London and UCLH Trust. Publ.: articles on treatment of gastrointestinal cancer and new agents for treating cancer.

Add UCL Cancer Institute, 72 Huntley Street, London WC1E 6BT

Tel 020 7679 6006

Email d.hochhauser@ucl.ac.uk

HOCHHAUSER, Victor, CBE.

b. Kosice, Czechoslovakia, Mar. 27, 1923; m. Lillian; Impresario for international artists, orchestras, ballet companies, etc; arrived in London, 1939 as a refugee.

Add 4 Oak Hill Way NW3 7LR

Tel 020 7794 0987 *Fax* 020 7431 2531

Email admin@victorhochhauser.co.uk *Website* www.victorhochhauser.co.uk

HODGE, Rt. Hon. Margaret (Eve) (née Oppenheimer), BSc, MBE, PC.

b. Sept. 8, 1944; m. Henry Egar Garfield Hodge; MP (Lab), Barking (1994-); Ch. Public Accounts Cttee. of the House of Commons (2010-); Min. of State, DCMS (2007–08); DTI (2006-07); DWP (2005–06); M. for Children (2003-05); Higher Education M. (2001-03). Publ.: Elected Mayors and Democracy (1997); Beyond the Town Hall (1994); Quality, Equality and Democracy (1991).

Add c/o House of Commons, London SW1A 0AA

Email hodgem@parliament.uk *Website* margaret-hodge.co.uk

HOFFMAN, Eva Alfreda (née Wydra), PhD, FRSL.

b. Cracow, July 1, 1945; Writer; Distinguished Writer, Kingston University (2010-); Vis. Prof. Hunter College, CUNY (2006-), MIT (1990-05); Ed. New York Times (1980-90). Publ.: Time: Big Ideas, Small Books (2010); Illuminations (2008); After such Knowledge (2004); The Secret (2001); Shtetl (1997); Exit into History (1994); Lost in Translation (1989).

Add 18 Goldhurst Terrace, London NW6 3HU

Tel 020 7625 8771 *Fax* 020 7625 8771

HOROVITZ, Michael, OBE, MA (Oxon).

b. Frankfurt am Main, Apr. 4, 1935; Writer, Artist, Singer, Musician, Publisher; Ed. New Departures, Dir. Poetry Olympics (www.poetryolympics.com); H. C. Creative Britons Award (2000); Poetry Book Society V. C. Recommendation (1986); Arts Council Translator's Award (1983); Arts Council Writer's Award (1976). Publ.: A New Waste-Land (2007); Lost Office Campaign Poem (2005); The POT! Anthology (2005); Jeff Nuttall's Wake on Paper (2004); The Pom! Anthology (2001); The POP! Anthology (2000); The POW! Anthology (1996); Wordsounds and Sightlines: New and Selected Poems (1994); Midsummer Morning Jog Log (1986); A Celebration for Frances Horovitz (1984); Growing Up: Selected Poems and Pictures, 1951-1979 (1979); A Contemplation (1978); Love Poems (1971).

Add New Departures/Poetry Olympics, P.O. Box 9819, London W11 2GQ

Tel 020 7229 7850 *Fax* 020 7229 7850

Email michael.horovitz@btinternet.com

HOWARD, Alan,

Fdr. Alan Howard Charitable Foundation (1982-); Fdr. Brevan Howard; form. Hd. of Proprietary Training, Credit Suisse First Boston.

Add Brevan Howard, Ground and First Floor, 55 Baker Street, London W1U 8EW

Tel 020 7022 6200

HOWARD, Michael, Baron of Lympne, CH, PC, QC.

b. Gorseinon, Wales, July 7, 1941; MP (Con.) for Folkestone and Hythe (1983-2010); Leader of the Opposition (2003-05); Shadow Chancellor (2001-03); form. Home Sec. (1993-97); Sec. of State for the Environment (1992-93); Sec. of State for Employment (1990-92); Ch. Conservative Bow Group (1970-71); form. Pres. Cambridge Union.

Add House of Lords, London SW1A 0PW

HUDSON, Lucian J.,

Mem. Jewish Leadership Council; Ch. Liberal Judaism; Gov. Leo Baeck College.

Add Liberal Judaism, The Montagu Centre, 21 Maple Street, London N1T 4BE

Tel 020 7580 1663

Email montagu@liberaljudaism.org *Website* www.liberaljudaism.org

HYMAN, Barry S,

b. Scotland, June 24, 1941, m. Judith; Broadcaster, Writer; Pres. Radlett and Bushey Reform Synagogue (2011-), H. V. Pres. (2000-11); PR consultant and newsletter Ed. to Movement for Reform Judaism (1995-2002); Mem. of the Institute of Public Relations (1987-2002); Board of Deputies Public Relations Cttee. (1988-97); Hd. of Corporate Affairs, Media Relations, Community Affairs and Company Archive, Marks and Spencer (1984-94). Publ.: Reform Judaism News (Ed. 1996-2002); A Job for a Jewish Girl ... or Boy? The Rabbinate as a Career (2000); Young in Herts (1996), a history of the Radlett and Bushey Reform Synagogue; Retail Revolutionary - The Story of Lord Marks of Broughton, Ch. of Marks and Spencer 1916-64 (co-author).

Add Radlett & Bushey Reform Synagogue, 118 Watling Street, Radlett, Hertfordshire WD7 7AA

Tel 01923 856 110 *Fax* 01923 818 444

Email bsh@hypeople.co.uk

IRONSIDE, Judy (neé Mazzier),

b. Brighton, Mar. 1946; Fdr. and Dir. UK Jewish Film Festival (1997-); T. The Forgiveness

Project; form. Mem. British Association of Drama Therapists.

Add UK JFF 5.09 Clerkenwell Workshops, 27-31 Clerkenwell Close, London EC1R 0AT

Tel 020 3176 0048

Email judy.ironside@ukjewishfilm.org *Website* www.ukjff.org.uk

ISAACS, Sir Jeremy (Israel), MA, Kt.

b. Sept. 28, 1932; m. Gillian Mary Widdicombe; Ch. Sky Arts; Chief Exec. Jeremy Isaacs Productions (1998–2008); General Dir. Royal Opera House (1988-97); Chief Exec. Channel Four TV Co. (1981–87).

Add 8 Shelton Street, London WC2H 9SR

Tel 020 7253 8898

Email jlp@jlp.co.uk

JACKSON, Bernard Stuart, LLB (Hons), D.Phil, LLD, DHL (h.c.).

b. Liverpool, Nov. 16, 1944; Barrister; (part-time) Professor of Law and Jewish Studies, Liverpool Hope University (2009-); Ch. The Jewish Law Association, (2008-); Sec. Jewish Law Publ. Fund (1980-2012); Alliance Prof. of Modern Jewish Studies, Co-Dir. Centre for Jewish Studies, University Manchester (1997-2009); Ed. Jewish Law Annual (1978-97); Pres. BAJS (1993); Hd. of Academic Research; TAG Institute for Jewish Social Values (2010-11). Among major publications: Theft in Early Jewish Law; Essays in Jewish and Comparative Legal History; Semiotics and Legal Theory; Law, Fact and Narrative Coherence; Making Sense in Law; Making Sense in Jurisprudence; Studies in the Semiotics of Biblical Law; Wisdom-Laws: a study of the Mishpatim of Exodus 21:1-22:16; Essays in Halakhah in the New Testament; Agunah, The Manchester Analysis; (Ed.) Studies in Jewish Legal History in Honour of David Daube; Modern Research in Jewish Law, Jewish Law in Legal History and the Modern World; An Introduction to the History and Sources of Jewish Law.

Add Department of Theology, Liverpool Hope University, Hope Park, Taggart Avenue, Liverpool L16 9JD

Email bsj@legaltheory.demon.co.uk

Website http://www.hope.ac.uk/staffindex/staffmembers/name,2883,en.html

JACOBS, David,

b. Manchester, 1951; m. Hannah Rose née Noorden; Ch. JHSE (2009-); Dir. of Synagogue Partnership, Movement for Reform Judaism (1992-); Dir. Victoria Community Centre (1988-91); Co-Fdr. London Museum of Jewish Life (1983); RSGB Youth Development Officer (1975-9); Co-Fdr. Jewish East End Project (1977); V. Pres. Jewish Genealogical Society of GB (1996-); Ch. WP on Jewish Monuments in the UK and Ireland. Publ.: A History of Our Time; Rabbi and Teachers Buried at Hoop Lane Cemetery (2006, with J. Epstein).

Add The Sternberg Centre, 80 East End Road, London N3 2SY

Tel 020 8349 5643

Email david.jacobs@reformjudaism.org.uk

JACOBS, David Michael,

b. Bristol, June 4, 1930, m. Marion née Davis; Exec. (form. Gen. Sec.), AJA; form. Exec. Dir. Likud-Herut GB; Ch. Jewish Affiliates of the United Nations Association; form. Ch. Guild of Jewish Journalists; form. Ch. Beds.-Herts. Progressive Jewish Congregation; form. Board of Deputies, Press Officer; British Zionist Federation. Publ.: Research and writing for Jewish Communities of the World (Ed. A. Lerman, 1989); Israel (World in Colour series) 1968.

Add 56 Normandy Road, St. Albans, Hertfordshire AL3 5PW

Tel 01727 858 454

Email davidmjacobs@waitrose.com

JACOBS, Jeremy,

Chief Exec. US (2008-); Ch. Tribe (2002-8); V. Ch. University Chaplaincy Bd. (2002-06); Treasurer, US (1996-2002); Bd. of Man. Financial Representative and Warden, Belmont Synagogue (1980s and 1990s).

Add 305 Ballards Lane N12 8GB

Tel 020 8343 8989 *Fax* 020 343 6236

Email info@theus.org.uk *Website* www.theus.org.uk

JACOBS, June Ruth (née Caller),

b. London, June 1, 1930; Professional Volunteer; V. Ch. NAWO UK (National Council of Women's Organisations); Past Pres. International Council of Jewish Women; Patron, Jewish Council for Racial Equality and Jewish Black Asian Forum; Life Mem. League of Jewish Women; Life Pres. Jewish Child's Day; Mem. International Council of the New Israel Fund and their grants cttee.; Exec Mem. Memorial Foundation for Jewish Culture; Ch. Nahum Goldmann Fel.; Mem. Bd. Paideia, European Institute of Jewish Studies in Sweden; Found. Mem. Jewish Forum for Justice and Human Rights.

Add 13 Modbury Gardens, London NW5 3QE

Tel 020 7485 6027

Email juneruth@tiscali.co.uk

JACOBSON, Howard, MA (Cantab).

b. Manchester, Aug. 25, 1942; Novelist and critic; JQ/Wingate Prize for Fiction, 2001, 2007; Snr. Lecturer, Wolverhampton Polytechnic (1974-80); Supervisor in English Studies, Selwyn College (1968-72); Lecturer, English Literature, University of Sydney (1965-67); Fel. Royal Society of Lit.; H. Fel. Downing College, Cambridge; Vis. Prof. English Lit, New College of the Humanities. Among recent publications: Zoo Time (2012); Whatever It Is, I Don't Like It (2011); The Finkler Question (2010) - Winner of the Man Booker Prize; The Act of Love (2008); Kalooki Nights (2006); The Making of Henry (2004); Who's Sorry Now? (2002); The Mighty Walzer (1999); No More Mister Nice Guy (1998); Seriously Funny: An Argument for Comedy (1996); Roots Schmoots (1993). Recent films: Creation (Ch. 4, 2010) - Winner, The Sandford St. Martin Award; Jesus the Jew (Ch. 4, 2009).

Add c/o Curtis Brown, Haymarket House, 28-29 Haymarket, London SW17 4SP

Tel 020 7393 4400

JANNER, Greville, Baron of Braunstone, MA Hons. (Cantab), H. PhD (Haifa), H. LLD (De Montfort), QC.

b. Cardiff, July 11, 1928; Barrister-at-law; Pres. Association Jewish Ex-Servicemen and Women (2009-); Jt. Fdr and Pres. Coexistence Trust (2006-); Ch. All-Party Parl. Industrial Safety Group (1975-97); form. MP (Lab.) for Leicester West (1970-97); Ch. Select Cttee. on Employment (1993-96); Exec. Lab. Friends of Israel; Pres. Board of Deputies (1979-85); Pres. Commonwealth Jewish Council; Ch. Holocaust Educational Trust; Ch. British Israel Parl. Group; Hon. S. All-Party Parl. War Crimes Group; Cttee Against Antisemitism; V. Ch. All-Party Parl. Morocco Group; Pres. All-Party Parliament India Group; V. Ch. All-Party Parl. Jordan Group; V. Pres. AJY; Bd. Dirs. UJIA; Mem. NUJ; form. Pres. WJC (Europe); form. Dir. Jewish Chronicle; form. Pres. National Council for Soviet Jewry; H. V. Pres. WJC; Fdr. and V. Ch. All-Party Parl. Cttee. for Jews from the FSU; form. Pres. Jewish Museum; form. Pres. Maimonides Foundation; Pres. ret. Execs. Action Group (REACH); T. Elsie and Barnett Janner Trust; H. Mem. National Union Mineworkers (Leicester BR); Mem. Magic Circle and International Brotherhood of Magicians; form. Pres. Cambridge Union, Fdr. and Ch. The Bridge in Britain; Ch. Cambridge University Lab. Club; form. Ch. Brady Boys, Club. Lecturer, contributor and author of 70 books.

Add House of Lords, London SW1A 0PW

JANNER-KLAUSNER, Rabbi Laura (née Janner), BA, MA.

b. London, Aug. 1, 1963; m. Dr David Janner-Klausner; Rabbi, Movement for Reform Judaism (2012-); Rabbi, Alyth Synagogue (2004-2012). Publ.: Great Refom Lives (chapter on Leopald Zunz, 2010); DIY Rituals - A Guide to Creating Your Own Jewish Rituals; God, Doubt and Dawkins (chapter); Woodland burial (Teshuvot with Rabbi Paul Freedman); Status of second night sedarim (Teshuvot with Rabbi Paul Freedman); European Judaism. 'Education Within Our Faith Communities (Keynote, Bendorf JCM, 2001); Neshama Hadasha (A New Life) - An Anthology of New Jewish Birth Celebrations; Sources of Jerusalem history of Jerusalem (used as a text book for the 1996 international Bible Quiz).

Add Sternberg Centre, 80 East End Road, London N2 0AD

Tel 020 8349 5658

Email rabbilaura@reformjudaism.org.uk *Website* www.reformjudaism.org.uk

Twitter @LauraJanklaus

JEUDA, Basil Simon,

b. Manchester, Sept. 17, 1938; m. Laura née Madden; Chartered Accountant; Ch. NHS Pensions Agency Special Health Authority (2004-06); Ch. Macclesfield Museums Trust (2002-05); T. Manchester Jewish Museum (1998-2004); Ch. Mersey Regional Ambulance Service, NHS Trust (1999-2003); form. Leader, Cheshire County Council (1981-85). Publ.: History of Churnet Valley Railway, 1849-1999; History of Rudyard Lake, 1797-1997; The Knotty: An Illustrated History of the North Staffordshire Railway; North Staffordshire Railway in LMS Days, Vols I and II; History of Sha'are Sedek Synagogue, South Manchester.

Add 47 Sandringham Road, Macclesfield SK10 1QB

Tel 01625 426 740

Email basil@jeuda.co.uk

JOFFE, Joel Goodman, Baron of Liddington, CBE, BCom, LLB (Witwatersrand).

b. May 12, 1932; m. Vanetta; Lawyer; T. and Patron of various voluntary organisations including Ch. OXFAM (T. 1997-01); Ch. Thamesdown Voluntary Services Council (1974-2000); Ch. Swindon and Marlborough NHT (1993-95); Ch. Swindon Health Authority (1988-93); Fdr. T. Action on Disability and Dev.; Fdr. T. Ch. Allied Dunbar Charitable Trust (1974-93); Dep. Ch. Allied Dunbar Assurance (1971-91); Ch. Swindon Private Hospital plc (1982-87); Solicitor in Johannesburg appearing for the defence in a number of trials including that of Nelson Mandela (1952-65).

Add House of Lords, London SW1A 0PW

Email joel@lidmanor.co.uk

JOLLES, Michael Adam, MB BS MRCGP FRHistS.

b. Northampton, Apr. 4, 1951; General Practitioner; Council Mem. Jewish Historical Society of England (1999-); form. Ed. JHSE Newsletter. The Rabbi Dr Bernard Susser Annual Award (Jewish Genealogical Society of Great Britain), 2001. Publ.: The Palgrave Dictionary of Anglo-Jewish History (with W.D. Rubinstein & H.L. Rubinstein, 2011); Jews and the Carlton Club, with notes on Benjamin Disraeli, Henri Louis Bischoffsheim and Saul Isaac, M.P. (2002); A Directory of Distinguished British Jews, 1830-1930, with selected compilations from 1830 to 2000 (1999; 2002); The Chatham Hebrew Society Synagogue Ledger 1836-1865 (2000); Samuel Isaac, Saul Isaac and Nathaniel Isaacs (1998); A Short History of the Jews of Northampton 1159-1996 (1996); The Northampton Jewish Cemetery (1994).

Add 78 Greenfield Gardens, London NW2 1HY

Tel 020 8458 3193

JOSEPH, Dr Anthony Peter, MBBChir (Cantab), MRCGP, FSG.

b. Birmingham, Apr. 23, 1937; form. GP; Pres. Jewish Genealogical Society of Great Britain (1997-2013), Emer. Pres. (2013-); Ch. Birmingham Branch of JHSE (1969-); Corresponding Mem. for Great Britain, Australian Jewish Historical Society (1965-); Dir. International Association Jewish Genealogical Societies (2000-04); form. Pres. JHSE (1994-96); UK representative of Society of Australian Genealogists (1965-95); Post-graduate tutor in paediatrics, University of Birmingham (1986-91); Mem. Bd. Governors Institute for Jewish Genealogy. Contributor on Jewish Genealogy to Blackwell Companion to Jewish Culture; Author of papers in many different genealogical publications, including JHSE.

Add 3 Edgbaston Road, Smethwick, West Midlands B66 4LA

Tel 0121 555 6165 *Mobile* 07710 448 897 *Fax* 0121 555 5975

JOSEPH, John Michael,

b. London, Feb. 11, 1939; voluntary Ch. Jewish Blind and Disabled (1994-); Ch. GET Group (1995-2006).

Add 35 Langstone Way, Mill Hill East, London NW7 1GT
Email info@jbd.org *Website* www.jbd.org

JOSIPOVICI, Prof. Gabriel David, FRSL, FBA.

b. Nice, France, Oct. 8, 1940; Writer; University Teacher; Res. Prof. Graduate School of Humanities, University of Sussex; Prof. (1985-98), Reader in English (1973-85), Lecturer in English (1965-73), Assistant Lecturer in English (1963-5) School of European Studies, University of Sussex; Lord Weidenfeld Vis. Prof. Oxford (1996-97), FRL, FBA. Among recent publications: Infinity: The Story of Movement; The Big Glass; In a Hotel Garden; Moo Pak; Now; The Book of God; Touch; On Trust; A Life; Goldberg Variations; Only Joking; The Singer on the Shore; Everything Passes; After; Making Mistakes; What Ever Happened to Modernism?.

Add 60 Prince Edward's Road, Lewes, Sussex BN7 1BH
Email gabriel@josipovici.plus.com *Website* www.gabrieljosipovici.org

JULIUS, Brigadier (Retd.) Allan Aubrey,

b. June 30, 1928; Brigadier, British Embassy (Rome) (1979-83); Most Senior Jewish Officer, British Armed Forces (1947-1983); Dep. Chief Engineer HQ BAOR, Colonel (1975-78); Commander Waterloo Company, Royal Military Academy, Sandhurst (1969-70); 9 Parachute Squadron RE, UK (1959-61); 22 Special Air Service Regiment, serving in Malaysia (1956-59); Royal Engineers (1948); Duke of Cornwall's Light Infantry (1947); Staff Off. NATO, Naples, Special Force Planning; Defence (attaché).

Add c/o 7 Grasmere Court, Holders Hill Road London NW4
Tel 020 8346 1992

JULIUS, Anthony Robert, MA (Cantab), PhD (London), PhD (H., Haifa).

b. London, July 16, 1956; Solicitor; Ch. Jewish Chronicle (2011-); Partner, Mishcon de Reya (1984-98), Hd. Litigation (1988-98); Dep. Ch. (2009-); Vis. Prof. Birkbeck College (2005-); V. Pres. Diana, Princess of Wales Mem. Fund (2002-), T. (1997-2002), Ch. (1997-99); Ch. Law Panel, IJPR (1997-), reporting on Holocaust Denial Legislation; Ch. London Consortium (2005-10); Ch. Management Bd. Centre for Cultural Analysis, Theory and History, University of Leeds (2001-05); Mem. Appeals Cttee. Dermatrust (1999-2004). Publ.: Trials of the Diaspora (2010); T.S. Eliot, Antisemitism and Literary Form (1995, 2nd Edition 2003); Transgressions: The Offences of Art (2002); Idolizing Pictures (2001).

Add Mishcon de Reya, Summit House, 12 Red Lion Square London WC1R
Tel 020 7440 7000
Email anthonyjulius@mishcon.com

KADISH, Sharman, BA (London), D.Phil. (Oxon), FSA, FRHist.S.

b. London, Sept. 21, 1959; m. Sydney Greenberg. Dir. Jewish Heritage UK; has lectured and held research fellowships at the universities of London and Manchester. Publ.: The Synagogues of Britain and Ireland (2011); Jewish Heritage in Gibraltar: An Architectural Guide (2007); Jewish Heritage in England: An Architectural Guide (2006); Bevis Marks Synagogue 1701-2001 (2001); Synagogues (in the Heinemann Library Places of Worship series for children 1998); Building Jerusalem: Jewish Architecture in Britain (1996 Ed.); A Good Jew and A Good Englishman: The Jewish Lads' and Girls' Brigade 1895-1995 (1995); Bolsheviks and British Jews (1992).

Add Jewish Heritage UK, Room 204, Ducie House, 37 Ducie Street, Manchester M1 2JW
Tel 0161 238 8621
Email director@jewish-heritage-uk.org *Website* www.jewish-heritage-uk.org

KAHN-HARRIS, Rabbi Dr Deborah (née Myers-Weinstein),

b. Oklahoma, USA, May 28, 1968; m. Dr Keith; Princ. Leo Baeck College, London (2011-); PhD, University of Sheffield Department of Biblical studies (completed 2011); Co-V. Ch. Assembly of Reform Rabbis (2009-2010); Lecturer, Leo Baeck College (2005-); Teaching Fel. in Judaism, SOAS, University of London (2008-2009); Associate Rabbi, Sha'arei Tsedek North London Reform Synagogue (2005-2011); Dir. Student and Young Adult Work, RSGB

(2000-2001). Among recent publications: A Hammer for Shattering Rock: Employing Classical Rabbinic Hermeneutics to Fashion Contemporary Feminist Commentary on the Bible (PhD, completed 2011); Who Are We: An Exploration of Voice in Lam 5:19-22 (Keynote Lecture at 40th International Jewish-Christian Bible Week at Haus Ohrbeck, Osnabruck, Germany, published on line).

Add Leo Baeck College, Sternberg Centre for Judaism, 80 East End Road, London N3 2SY

Tel 020 8349 5600

Email deborah.kahn-harris@lbc.ac.uk

KALMS, Lady Pamela, MBE.

b. London, July 29, 1931; T. Chai Cancer Care (current); form. Vol. Services Co-ordinator, Edgware General Hospital; form. Deputy Ch. form. NHS Wellhouse Trust (Barnet and Edgware General Hospitals); form. Mem. Exec. Jewish Marriage Council; T. and Dir. Ravenswood Foundation.

Add 39-40 St James's Place, London SW1A 1NS

Tel 020 7491 1301 *Fax* 020 7499 3436

Email pkalms@o2.co.uk

KALMS, Lord Stanley, H. FCGI (1991), H. D.Litt CNAA/ University of London (1991), H. D. University North London (1994), H. Fellow London Business School (1995), H. D. Econ. Richmond (1996), H. D.Litt, Sheffield (2002), H. Degree, Buckingham (2002).

b. London, Nov. 21, 1931; m. Pamela née Jimack; Life Pres. Dixons Group (2002-); Vis. Prof. Business School, University of North London (1991-); Ch. Henry Jackson Society (2011); Hon. Fel. Shalom Hartman Institute (2005); T. Conservative Party (2001-03); Dir. Business for Sterling (1998-2002); Dir. Centre for Policy Studies (1991-2002); Ch. Dixons Group plc (1948-2002); Non-Exec. Dir. British Gas (1987-97); Ch. King's Healthcare NHS Trust (1993-96); T. The Economic Education Trust (1993); form. Ch. Jewish Education Dev. Trust (1978-89) and Jews' College (1983-89); Fdr. and Sponsor of Centre for Applied Jewish Ethics in Business and the Professions, Jerusalem; Fdr. of Stanley Kalms Foundation; Co-Fdr. and Sponsor of Immanuel College. Publ.: A Time for Change (1992).

Add 39-40 St James's Place, London SW1A 1NS

Tel 020 7499 3494

Email stanley.kalms@btinternet.com

KAPLAN, David, MA LLB.

b. Edinburgh, 1971; Dir. University Jewish Chaplaincy (2009-); Dir. US Community Services (2006-); Man. Dir. Tribe (2000-); form. Exec. Dir. British Friends of Laniado (2000-03); form. Exec. Dir. UJIA Renewal Scotland (1996-99); form. Ch. UJS (1994-95). Publ.: 60 Days for 60 Years - Israel (2008); 60 Days for 60 Years (2005); 50 Days for 50 Years (1995).

Add 305 Ballards Lane, London N12 8GB

Tel 020 8343 8989

Email dkaplan@theus.org.uk

KAPLAN, Harvey, MA.

b. Glasgow, Dec. 6, 1955; Civil Servant; Dir. Scottish Jewish Archives Centre (1987-). Publ.: The Gorbals Jewish Community in 1901 (2006).

Add Scottish Jewish Archives Centre, Garnethill Synagogue, 129 Hill Street, Glasgow G3 6UB

Tel 0141 332 4911

Email rvlkaplan@googlemail.com

KATTEN, Brenda (née Rosenblit),

b. London, Sept. 8, 1936; Co-Ch. Europeans for Israel (Israel) (2010-); Ch. World WIZO Pub. Rel. Dept. (2008-); Exec Mem. Israel, Britain and Commonwealth Association (2009); form. Ch. Israel, Britain and Commonwealth Association (2006-09); form. Ch. Public Affairs and NGO Dept. World WIZO [Israel] (2000-08); form. Ch. Bnai Brith Hillel Fd; (1994-98); Ch. UK National Cttee. Jerusalem 3000 (1995-96); form. Mem. JC Trust Ltd; H. V. Pres.

Zionist Federation of Great Britain and Ireland (Ch. 1990-94); Jt. H. Pres. WIZO.uk (Ch. 1981-87).

Add c/o World WIZO, 38 David Hamelech Blvd, Tel Aviv 64237, Israel

Tel +972 (03) 692 3729 *Fax* +972 (03) 695 8267

Email brendak@wizo.org *Website* www.wizo.org

KATZ, Dovid, BA (Columbia), PhD (London).

b. New York, May 9, 1956; Yiddish linguist, author, educator, cultural historian, Holocaust scholar and activist; Awards including Guggenheim Fel. (2001-02); Leverhulme Trust Research Award (1999-2001); British Academy Research Award (1998). Yiddish culture awards include: Leyb Rubinlicht (Tel Aviv, 2006); Y.Y. Sigal (Montreal, 1999); Manger Prize (Tel Aviv, 1997); Hirsh Rosenfeld (Montreal, 1994). Co-Fdr. Research Dir. Vilnius Yiddish Institute (2001-10); Prof. Yiddish Language, Literature and Culture, Vilnius University (1999-2010); Fdr. Dir. Center for Stateless Cultures, Vilnius University (1999-2001); Vis. Prof. Yale University (1998-9); Fel. St Antony's College Oxford (1986-97); Fdr. Yiddish Studies at Oxford University (taught 1978-1996). Among recent publications: Lithuanian Jewish Culture (2004, 2010); Seven Kingdoms of the Litvaks (2009); Windows to a Lost Jewish Past (2008); Words on Fire: The Unfinished Story of Yiddish (2004, 2007). Columnist, Algemeyner Zhurnal (1997-); Yiddish Forward (1991-2002). Yiddish fiction under the name Heershadovid Menkes includes Eldra Don (1992); The Flat Peak (1993); Tales of the Misnagdim of Vilna Province (1996). Books on Litvak culture include: Lithuanian Jewish Culture (2010); Seven Kingdoms of the Litvaks (2009); Vilna Yiddish Book Stamps (2008). From 2008, leader in Campaign Against Holocaust Obfuscation and the 'Prague Declaration'; articles in the Jewish Chronicle, Jewish News, Guardian, Irish Times, Washington Jewish Week, Tablet etc.; Fdr-Ed. defendinghistory.com (form. holocaustinthebaltics.com).

Add c/o Jewish Community of Lithuania, Pylimo 4, Vilnius, Lithuania

Email dovidkatz7@yahoo.com *Website* www.dovidkatz.net

KATZ, Rabbi Steven Anthony, BA (Hons).

b. London, Dec. 18, 1948; M. Hendon Reform Synagogue; Hon. S. RSGB Assembly of Rabbis; Chaplain, University College Hospital, London.

Add Hendon Reform Synagogue, Danescroft Avenue NW4 2NA

Tel 020 8203 4168

KAUFMAN, Rt. Hon. Sir Gerald Bernard, KB, PC, MA, MP.

b. Leeds, June 21, 1930; Journalist; Ch. House of Commons Culture, Media and Sport Cttee. (1997-2005); Ch. House of Commons National Heritage Cttee. (1992-97); Mem. National Exec. Cttee. of the Labour Party (1991-1992); Opposition Spokesman for Foreign Affairs (1987-92); Labour Party Parl. Cttee. (1980-92); Opposition Spokesman for Home Affairs (1983-87); Opposition Spokesman for Environment (1980-83); MP (Lab.) for Gorton, Manchester (since 1983), Ardwick (1970-83); form. Min. of State, Dept of Industry; Parl. Under-Sec. Industry; Parl. Under-Sec. Environment. Publ.: How to be a Minister; To Build the Promised Land; How to live under Labour (co-author); My Life in the Silver Screen; Inside the Promised Land; Meet me in St Louis; The Left (Ed.); Renewal (Ed.).

Add 87 Charlbert Ct., Eamont St., London NW8 7DA

Tel 020 7219 5145 *Fax* 020 7219 6825

KAUFMANN, Flo (née Israel), JP, BA.

b. Berkhamsted, Aug. 3, 1942, m. Aubrey Kaufmann; Rotary Club of London Council (2010-); Ch. Commonwealth Jewish Council and Trust (2009-); Ch. Haifa Foundation UK (2009-); V. Pres. World Jewish Congress (2009-); V. Pres. (2007-); Ch. Council, European Jewish Congress (2007-); Ch. Valuation Tribunal of England (1996-2010); V. Pres. Board of Deputies British Jews (2003-09); Ch. International Div. Israel Cttee. (2003-09), Ch. Finance and Organisation Div. (1997-2003), T. H. Off. (1997-2003), Ch. (1994-97), V. Ch. (1989-94); Hon. T. Magistrates' Association (2001-06).

Email flokaufmann@btinternet.com *Website* www.gowiththeflo.co.uk

KEDOURIE, Sylvia (née Haim), MA, PhD (Edin).

b. Baghdad, Iraq; Independent scholar; Ed. Middle Eastern Studies. Publ.: Elie Kedourie's Approach to History and Political Thought (2006); Elie Kedourie CBE, FBA (1926-1992): History, Philosophy, Politics (1998); Arab Nationalism: An Anthology (1962, 1967, 1975).

Add 75 Lawn Road, London NW3 2XB

KEMPNER GLASMAN, Sheila (née Goldstein),

UK V. Pres. International Council of Jewish Women (2001-); Business Advisor Young Enterprise (2007); Ch. Board of Deputies Women's Issues Action Group (1995-99); Mem. Thames Customer Service Cttee. OFWAT (1993-96); Mem. Women's National Commission (1990-94); Mem. Hillingdon District Health Authority (1983-87); V. Ch. Hillingdon Community Health Council (1974-82); form. Pres. League of Jewish Women.

Add 10 Ashurst Close, Northwood, Middlesex HA6 1EL

KENDLER, Maureen (nee Rose), BA Dip.Ed, MA.

b. London, 1956; m. Dr Hayden Kendler; Hd. Educational Programming, London School of Jewish Studies; Hd. Jewish Literacy, UJIA (2004-07); Educational Officer, JCORE (2002-04); Teacher, North London Collegiate School (1995-2002).

Add Schaller House, London School of Jewish Studies, Wohl Campus for Jewish Education, 44a Albert Road, London NW4 2SJ

Tel 020 8203 6427 *Fax* 020 8203 6420

Email maureen.Kendler@lsjs.ac.uk *Website* www.lsjs.ac.uk

KERNER, Brian Philip, MRPharms.

b. London, Nov. 21, 1934; m. Sylvia Evelyne née Goldstein; Bd. Mem. JLC (2007-); V. Ch. Britain, Israel Communications and Research Centre (BICOM, 2001-11); Pres. UJIA (2000-); form. Gov. Jewish Agency for Israel; Co-Ch. priority Regions Sub Cttee. of Jewish Agency; form. Exec. Mem. and T. Keren Hayesod; Co-Ch. Cross Community Co-ordinating Group (CCG); Co-Ch. Fair Play Campaign Group (FPCG); T. Haifa Fund.

Add 4 Greenaway Gardens, London NW3 7DJ

Tel 020 7435 2494 *Fax* 020 7435 2180

Email bpkerner@googlemail.com

KERSHEN, Anne Jacqueline (née Rothenberg), BA, MPhil, PhD, FRHistS, FRSA.

b. London, June 8, 1942; Historian; H. Snr. Res. Associate, Bartlett School of Graduate Studies, UCL (2012-); H. Snr. Res. Fel. QMUL (2011-). Among recent publications: There was a Priest, A Rabbi and a Immman: Material Religion (with Laura Vaughn, Vol. 9, Issue 1 2013); Strangers, Aliens and Asians: Huguenots, Jews and Bangladeshis in Spitalfields, 1660-2000 (2005); Food in the Migrant Experience (2002); Language, Labour and Migration (2000); A Question of Identity (1998); London, the Promised Land? (1997); (with Jonathan Romain) Tradition and Change: The History of Reform Judaism in Britain, 1840-1995 (1995); Uniting the Tailors.

Add c/o School of International Relations and Politics, QMUL, Mile End Road E1 4NS

Tel 020 7882 8600

Email a.kershen@qmul.ac.uk *Website* www.QMUL.ac.uk/politics/staff

KESSLER, Dr Edward, BA Hons. (Leeds), MTS (Harvard), MBA (Stirling), PhD (Cantab), MBE.

b. London, May 3, 1963; m. Tricia née Oakley; Exec. Dir. The Woolf Institute; Fdr. Centre for Public Education, CPE (2006); Centre for the Study of Muslim-Jewish Relations, CMJR (2006); Centre for the Study of Jewish-Christian Relations (CJCR) (1998). Publ.: Jews, Christians and Muslims, Perceptions of the 'Other' (2013); An Introduction to Jewish Christian Relations (2010); What Do Jews Believe? (2006); A Dictionary of Jewish-Christian Relations (2005); A Reader of LJ: Israel Abrahams, Claude Montefiore, Israel Mattuck and Lily Montagu (2004); Aspects of LJ: Essays in Honour of John D Rayner on the occasion of his 80th Birthday (2004, Eds. E Kessler and D J Goldberg); Bound by the Bible: Jews and the Sacrifice of Isaac (2004); An English Jew: The Life and Writings of Claude Montefiore (1989, 2nd edition 2002); Jews and Christians in Conversation: crossing cultures and generations (2002, Eds. E. Kessler, JT Pawlikowski and J Banki).

Tel 01223 741 834

Email edk21@cam.ac.uk *Website* wwwwoolf.cam.ac.uk

KESTENBAUM, Lord Jonathan Andrew, BA, MA, MBA.

b. Tokyo, Japan, Aug. 5, 1959; m. Deborah Jane; COO, RIT Capital Partners PLC (2011-); Ch. Five Arrows Ltd (2010-); Non-Exec. Mem. Profero Ltd. (2008-); Chief Exec. Nesta (2005-10); (Ch. Apax Partners Ltd) and Chief Exec. The Portland Trust (-2005); Chief Exec. Office of the Chief Rabbi (1991-96); Dir. Bd TSB; Tru. Rowley Lane Recreational Trust, RSC; Chief of Staff to Sir Ronald Cohen; Chief Exec. UJIA; Tru. Yoni Jesner Foundation.

Add RIT Capital Partners PLC, 27 St James Place, London SW1A 1NR

Tel 020 7647 8565

KETT, Russell, FIH, FHOSPA.

b. Workington, May 24, 1953; m. Melinda née Sackheim; Hotel Consultant; Ch. HVS London (2012-); V. Pres. and T. United Synagogue (2011-); T. British Friends of Reuth (2009-); Man. Dir. HVS (global hotel consultancy) (1995-2011); Gov. JFS School (1995-2011), Ch. of Gov. (2003-09); T. JFS Charitable Trust, Development Trust, School Fund (2003-9); Warden, Belmont United Synagogue (1992-5).

Add 7-10 Chandos Street, London W1G 9DQ

Tel 020 7878 7701 *Fax* 020 7878 7799

Email rkett@hvs.com *Website* www.hvs.com

KHALILI, Nasser David,

b. Iran, Dec. 18, 1945; m. Marion née Easton; Prof. and Businessman; Fdr. The Khalili Collections; Co-Fdr. The Maimonides Foundation. Publ.: The Nasser D. Khalili Collection of Islamic Art. Awards: Goodwill Ambassador, UNESCO (2012); High Sheriff of London Award for cultural contribution to London (2007); Tru. City of Jerusalem; Knight Commander, Royal Order of St Francis I (KCFO); Knight of the Pontifical Equestrian Order of St Sylvester (KSS) (honoured by Pope John Paul II); Knight Commander in the said order (KCSS) for his work in the pursuit of peace, education and culture amongst nations (honoured by Pope Benedict XVI).

Add c/o Sue Bond Public Relations, Hollow Lane Farmhouse, Hollow Lane, Thurston, Bury St. Edmunds, Suffolk IP31 3RQ

Website www.khalili.org

KIENWALD, Dr Eli,

b. Rome, Italy, Sept. 28, 1947; m. Denise née Wassing; Architect; Chief Exec. Federation of Synagogues (2008-).

Add Federation of Synagogues, 65 Watford Way, London NW4 3AQ

Tel 020 8202 2263 *Fax* 020 8203 0610

Email eli.kienwald@federationofsynagogues.com

KIRSCH, Rabbi Danny, Dip F.M.

b. Letchworth, May 28, 1959; m. Jacqueline née Goschalk; Dir. JLE; form. Jt Ch. National Jewish Youth Council (1979); Mem. Board of Deputies (1979); form. London Student Chaplain; form. Organiser, National Jewish Youth Study Groups.

Add JLE, 152-154 Golders Green Road, London NW11 8HE

Tel 020 8458 4588 *Fax* 020 8458 4587

Email rabbikirsch@jle.org.uk *Website* wwwjle.org.uk

KLASS, Melanie,

b. Aug. 31, 1969; Exec. Dir. Jewish Child's Day (2011-); Exec Dir. Hazon Yeshaya UK (2010-11); Fundraiser JNF (2009); Man. Dir. Loot Ltd (2007), Commercial Dir. (2002-07); Associated Newspapers (1990-2002).

Add Jewish Child's Day, 707 High Road, London N12 0BT

Tel 020 8446 8804

Email melanie.klass@jcd.uk.com *Website* www.jcd.uk.com

KLINER, Stephen Ivor, MA, LLB, NP.

b. Glasgow, Apr. 15, 1953; m. Barbara née Mitchell; Solicitor (Partner), Vallance Kliner and Associates, Glasgow; V. Ch. Cosgrove Care (2006-); Ch. National Habonim-Dror (2003-09); Ch. Scottish Council Jewish Communities (2007-08); Pres. Glasgow Jewish Representative Council (2001-04); V. Pres. National Executive Habonim-Dror (1993-2003); Ch. Habonim-Dror Glasgow (1990-2002); Hon. S. Giffnock and Newlands Hebrew Congregation (1995-98).

Add 1d Whitecraigs Court, Whitecraigs, Glasgow G46 6SY

Tel 0141 258 6873

Email stephen.kliner@gmail.com

KLUG, Sir Aaron, OM, ScD, FRS.

b. Aug. 11, 1926, m. Liebe née Bobrow; Pres. Royal Society (1995-2000); Dir. Laboratory of Molecular Biology, Cambridge (1986-96); Nobel Prize in Chemistry (1982); Hon. Fel. Peterhouse, Cambridge; form. Nuffield Fel. Birkbeck Col. London; Lecturer, Cambridge University, Cape Town University. Publ.: Papers in scientific journals.

Add MRC Laboratory of Molecular Biology Cambridge CB2 2QH

KLUG, Brian, MA (London), PhD (Chicago).

b. London, Jan. 15, 1949; University Teacher; Mem. Faculty of Philosophy, University of Oxford (2003-); Hon. Fel. Parkes Institute, University Southampton (2002-); Snr. Res. Fel. St Benet's Hall, Oxford (2001-); Assoc. Ed. Patterns of Prejudice. Publ.: Being Jewish and Doing Justice: Bringing Argument to Life (2010); Offence: The Jewish Case (2009); A Time to Speak Out: Independent Jewish Voices on Israel, Zionism and Jewish Identity (2008, Co-Ed. with A. Karpf, J. Rose, B. Rosebaum); Children as Equals: Exploring the Rights of the Child (2002, Co-Ed. with K. Alaimo); Ethics, Value and Reality: Selected Papers of Aurel Kolnai (1977, Co-Ed. with F. Dunlop).

Add St. Benet's Hall, 38 St. Giles, Oxford OX1 3LN

Email brian.klug@stb.ox.ac.uk *Website* www.philosophy.ox.ac.uk/members/brian_klug

KNAPP, Alexander Victor, MA, MusB, PhD (Cantab); Hon ARAM, LRAM, ARCM.

b. London, May 13, 1945; sometime Joe Loss Lecturer in Jewish Music, SOAS (1999-2006); City University (1992-99); Vis. Scholar Wolfson College, Cambridge (1983-86); Assistant Dir. of Studies, Royal College of Music, London (1977-83). Publ.: Anthology of Essays on Jewish Music (in Chinese) (1998); Four Sephardi Songs (1993). CDs: Di Sheyne Milnerin (Nimbus 2012); Yiddish Winterreise (Naxos 2010).

Add 234 Rayners Lane, Harrow, Middlesex HA2 9TZ

Tel 020 8429 9374

Email alexknapp@waitrose.com *Website* www.yiddishwinterreise.com

KNOBIL, Henry Eric, FTI, Hon. Doctorate, Bar Ilan University.

b. Vienna, Nov. 27, 1932; Ch. UK Friends Bar Ilan University; form. Ch. Jewish Marriage Council; form. Pres. British-Israel Chamber of Commerce; form. Bd. Gov. Immanuel College; form. Pres. Western Marble Arch Synagogue; form. Bd. Govs. Carmel College (1980-87).

Add Garden Flat, 31 Belsize Park, London NW3 4DX

Tel 020 7691 0934 *Fax* 020 7224 0875

Email henry@knobil.freeserve.co.uk

KOHN, Sir Ralph, FRS, FMedSci, DSc, FRCP (Hon), MAE, FRAM, DMus.

b. Leipzig, Germany, Dec. 9, 1927; m. Zahava née Kanarek; Ch. Harley Street Holdings (1998-); H. DMus (Manchester 2010); Hon. Fel. British Pharmacological Society (2008); H. Fel. Royal Society (2006); Man. Dir. UK subsidiary of Robapharm AG (1965-71); T. The Kohn Foundation; Snr. Exec. Research and Development Division, Smith Kline & French of Philadelphia, USA; H. Mem. European Academy of Sciences; Fel. Royal Society of Medicine; H. Fel. Academy of Medical Sciences; H. Fel. Royal College of Physicians; Hon. T. Monteverdi Choir and Orchestra; H. Fel. Royal Academy of Music; International

Governor, Israel Philharmonic Orchestra; Knighthood citation of Services to Science, Music and Charity. Numerous recitals and performances in the UK and abroad; numerous recordings; lectures on medical, scientific and musical topics.

Add 14 Harley Street, London W1G 9PQ

Tel 020 7436 6001 *Fax* 020 7255 1168

Email rkohn@harleystreetholdings.com *Website* www.ralphkohn.com

KOPELOWITZ, Lionel, MA (Cantab), MRCS, LRCP, MRCGP, JP.

b. Newcastle upon Tyne, Dec. 9, 1926; V. Pres. Council of Christians and Jews (2009-); Council Initiation Society (1993-); Ch. St Marylebone Division BMA (1992-); Exec. Cttee. British Friends of Hebrew University (1998-2008); Ch. London Regional Council, BMA (2001-04); Council, Royal College of General Practitioners (1995-99); Council, United Synagogue (1991-96); Mem. General Medical Council (1984-94); Council, BMA (1982-94), Fel. (1980); Mem. General Optical Council (1979-1994); Pres. Old Cliftonian Society (1991-93); V. Pres. Conference on Jewish Material Claims against Germany (1985-92); Pres. EJC (1988-91); World Exec. WJC (1988-91); Pres. Board of Deputies (1985-91), now 'Father' of the Board (first elected June 1951); Pres. National Council for Soviet Jewry (1985-91); First Pres. United Hebrew Congregation Newcastle (1973-76); Life Pres. (Pres. 1964-74), Newcastle Jewish Welfare Board; Pres. Rep. Council, Newcastle Jewry (1967-73); Pres. Jesmond Hebrew Congregation, Newcastle (1963-67); V. Pres. Trades Advisory Council; Council, AJA; V. Pres. British Friends Shaare Zedek Hospital Medical Centre; Mem. Bd. of Governors, Clifton College, Bristol; V. Pres. Association of Baltic Jews.

Add 10 Cumberland House, Clifton Gardens, London W9 1DX

Tel 020 7289 6375

KOSMIN, Barry A, BA, MA, PhD.

b. London, 1946; m. Helen; Res. in Public Policy; Prof.; Exec. Dir. JPR (2000-05); Dir. of Research, Council of Jewish Federations, NY (1986-96); Founding Dir. North American Jewish Data Bank, The Graduate School and University Center of The City University of New York (1986-96); Dir. CJF 1990 US National Jewish Population Survey (1990); Exec. Dir. Research Unit, Board of Deputies of British Jews (1974-86); Fel. Institute for Advanced Studies, Hebrew University (1980-81).

Add Trinity College, 300 Summit Street, Hartford, Conn 06106-3100, USA

Tel +1 (860) 297 2388

Email isssc@trincoll.edu

KRAIS, Anthony, JP.

b. London, May 3, 1938; General Commissioner of Taxes (1997-2008); Mem. The Appeals Service (1998-2006); Dep. Ch. Resources for Autism (1997-2004); Associate Ch. Exec. Jewish Care (1990-97); Exec. Dir. Jewish Blind Society (1980-89); Ch. British Friends of Israel Guide Dog Centre for the Blind.

Add 14 Mayflower Lodge, Regents Park Road, London N3 3HU

Tel 020 8349 0337

Email ajkrais@gmail.com

KRAMER, Baroness Susan Veronica, BA PPE, MA, MBA.

b. July. 22, 1950; m. John Davis Kramer; Dir. Infrastructure Capital Partners Ltd (1999-); MP (Lib Dem) Richmond Park (2005-10); Mem. Bd. Transport for London (2000–05); Dir. Speciality Scanners plc (2001); London Mayoral candidate (2000); V. Pres. Corporate Finance, Citibank/Citicorp, USA (1988–92).

Add 53 Riverview Gardens, London SW13 8QZ

Email info@susankramer.org.uk

KRAUSZ, Ernest, MSc, PhD.

b. Romania, Aug. 13, 1931; Prof. School of Behavioural Science, Netanya (2000-); Prof. Bar-Ilan University (1973-), Rector (1985-89), Prof. Emer. (1999-); Ed. Studies of Israeli Society (1979-2000); Visiting Prof. LSE (1981-82). Publ.: Exploring Reality and its Uncertainties (2010); The Limits of Science (2000), Starting the XXIst Century (2002).

Add Dept. of Sociology Bar-Ilan University, Ramat Gan 52900, Israel
Tel +972 (03) 531 7892 *Fax* +972 (03) 635 0422
Email krauszm@netvision.net.il

KRIKLER, Douglas Henry, MA.
b. London, Nov. 3, 1965; m. Tali née Zetuni; Hd. High Net Worth Business Development, Investec; Fdr. Co-Ch. UK Task Force on issues relating to Arab Citizens of Israel (2010-); School Gov. Campsbourne School (2003-08); Fdr. Dir. Jewish Leadership Council (2003-05); Exec. Dir. CST (2000-04); Fdr. Dir. Maimonides Foundation (1994-2000); Fdr. Dir. British Jewish Yemeni Cultural Society (1991-94); Mem. New Leadership Network; National Olympic Cttee. (NOC) Assistant for London 2012; Chief Exec. UJIA.
Add Investec, 2 Gresham Street, London EC2V 7QP
Tel 020 7424 6400 *Fax* 020 7424 6401

KUSHNER, Tony, PhD.
b. Manchester, May 30, 1960; Marcus Sieff Prof. Dept of History; Dir. Parkes Institute for the Study of Jewish/Non-Jewish Relations, University of Southampton; T. Jewish Heritage UK (2007-); Pres. BAJS (2002); Historian at Manchester Jewish Museum (1985-86). Among recent publications: The Battle of Britishness, Migrant Journeys 1685 to the Present (2012); Anglo-Jewry Since 1066 (2009); Remembering Refugees: Then and Now (2006); The Holocaust: Critical Historical Approaches (2005); Philosemitism, Antisemitism and the Jews (Jt. Ed. 2004); We Europeans (2004); Disraeli's Jewishness (Jt. Ed. 2002); Refugees in an Age of Genocide (1999); Remembering Cable Street (Jt. Ed. 1999); Cultures of Ambivalence and Contempt (Jt. Ed. 1998); Belsen in History and Memory (1997).
Add Dept. of History, University of Southampton, Southampton SO17 1BJ
Tel 0238 059 2233 *Fax* 0238 059 2211

KYTE, David,
Co-Fdr. London Maccabi Recreational Trust; Fdr. and Dir. The Kyte Group Ltd (1985); Tru. Maccabi London Brady Recreational Trust; Tru. Maccabi Foundation; Bd. Mem. Maccabi World Union; Fdr. Partner, Hamilton Court FX.
Add Business Design Centre, 52 Upper Street, London N1 0QH
Tel 020 7390 7777 *Fax* 020 7390 7778
Email david.kyte@kyteinvestments.com

LASSERSON, Rachel, BA (Hons).
b. London, Dec. 11, 1968; m. James Rossiter; Ed. Jewish Quarterly (2007-); Dir. Contraband Productions Ltd. (1993-2003). Publ.: Adam International Review (Ed. 2005).
Tel 020 7267 9442
Email editor@jewishquarterly.org *Website* www.jewishquarterly.org

LATCHMAN, David Seymour, CBE, MA (Cantab.), PhD, DSc (London), FRCPath, FRSA.
b. London, Jan. 22, 1956; m. Hannah née Garson; Master of Birkbeck College (2003-); Prof. of Genetics, University of London (1999-); Dean, Institute Child Health, UCL (1999-2002); Prof. of Molecular Biology, UCL (1991-99); Pres. The Maccabaeans; Ch. T. Maurice Wohl Charitable Foundation; form. Mem. Council, US; Bd. Man. Golders Green Synagogue; form. Mem. Board of Deputies, Council JHSE. Publ.: Gene Control (6th edition Gene Regulation, 2010); Eukaryotic Transcription Factors (1991, 5th edition, 2008); Gene Regulation (1990, 5th edition 2005); Viral Vectors for Treating Diseases of the Nervous System (2003, Ed.); Stress Proteins (1999, Ed.); Landmarks in Gene Regulation (1997, Ed.).
Add Master, Birkbeck University of London, Professor of Genetics, Birkbeck & University College London, Malet Street, London WC1E 7HX
Tel 020 7631 6274 *Fax* 020 7631 6259
Email master@bbk.ac.uk

LAWRENCE, Sir Ivan, MA (Oxon), Dr of Laws (Honoris Causa) (LLD) (Hon); University of Buckingham (2013), QC.
b. Brighton, Dec. 24, 1936; Barrister; Mem. of Board of Deputies (1979-), representing NW Surrey Reform Synagogue; Recorder of the Crown Courts (1983-2002); form. MP

(C.) for Burton (1974-97); Bencher, Inner Temple (1990); T. Holocaust Educational Trust; Mem. of Commonwealth Jewish Council; Vis. Prof. of Law, University Buckingham; Exec. Mem. Society of Conservative Lawyers; form. Ch. and V. Ch. Conservative Friends of Israel; form. Mem. of Policy Planning Group of IJA; form. V. Ch. Inter-Parl. Cttee. for the Release of Soviet Jewry; Knighted for Political Service (1992). Publ.: My Life of Crime.

Add Dunally Cottage, Walton Lane, Shepperton, Middlesex TW17 8LH

Email sirilawrenceqc@aol.com

LAWSON, Arthur Abraham, MBE.

b. Glasgow, April 19, 1922; m. Toby Green née Sagman; Ret. Consulting Engineer; Ch. City of Westminster Branch AJEX (2011-);V. Pres. AJEX (National Ch. 2002-2004); Hon. S. AJEX Housing Association Ltd (1997-2006); Hon. S. Monash Branch, Royal British Legion (1998- 2006); V. Pres. Glasgow Jewish Representative Council (Pres. 1964-68); form. Ch. Glasgow Branch, AJEX and Glasgow Jewish Branch, Royal British Legion Scotland; Mem. Jewish Committee for H.M. Forces; form. Hon. T. Glasgow Maccabi; Co-opted Mem. University of Strathclyde Gen. Convocation; Mem. Children's Panel for Glasgow and Strathclyde (1971-82); Jt. Ch. Scottish Committee for Jewish Christian Relations (1964-68); form. National Ch. Combined Heat & Power Association.

Add 21 Woronzow Road, London NW8 6BA

Tel 020 7722 5405

Email arthurlawson422@btintemet.com

LAWTON, Clive Allen, JP, BA, MA, MEd, MSc, Cert. Ed., ADB (Ed).

b. London, July 14, 1951; Education and organisational consultant; form. UJIA Fel. in Jewish Education, SOAS (2001-5); form. Ch. Exec. Jewish Continuity (1993-96); Snr. Consultant Limmud; Scholar-in-Residence, London Jewish Cultural Centre; Independent Mem. Metropolitan Police Authority; form. Ch. North Middlesex University Hospital NHS Trust; T. Jewish Community Centre for London; form. Ch. Tzedek; Patron, Jewish AIDS Trust; form Mem. Home Office Racial Equality Adv. Panel; form. V. Ch. Anne Frank Educational Trust; form. Ch. Shap Working Party on World Religions in Education; Ed. Shap Calendar of World Rel. Festivals; Fdr. Limmud Conference; form. HM, King David High School, Liverpool; Exec. Dir. Central Jewish Lecturer and Information Cttee. and Education Off, Board of Deputies; Co-ordinator, Vietnam Working Party; Educational Off. Yad Vashem Cttee. Exec. Council CCJ; form. V. Ch. IUJF. Publ.: Passport to Israel; Religion Through Festivals; Celebrating Cultures: Islam; Ethics in Six Traditions; The Story of the Holocaust; The Web of Insights; Auschwitz; Hiroshima.

Add 363 Alexandra Road, London N10 2ET

Email clive@clivelawton.co.uk

LAYTON, Nigel Graham, BSc (Hons).

b. London, Mar. 23, 1963; m. Sarah née Nelson; Managing Dir. Quest Ltd.; Ch. Leadership Excellence And Development Centre (LEAD), Jewish Leadership Council (2011-), Mem. (2005-); Ch. World Jewish Relief (2002-11).

Add World Jewish Relief, Oscar Joseph House, 54 Crewys Road, London NW2 2AD

Tel 020 8736 1250 *Fax* 020 8736 1259

Email nlayton@quest.co.uk

LEBRECHT, Norman,

b. London, July 11, 1948; m. Elbie née Spivack; Writer; assistant Ed. Evening Standard (2002-09); Whitbread First Novel Award 2003 (Song of Names); Presenter of Lebrecht Interview, BBC Radio3; The Record Doctor, WNYC. Publ.: Why Mahler? (2010); The Game of Opposites (2009); Maestros, Masterpieces and Madness (2007); Covent Garden: the Untold Story : Dispatches from the English Culture War, 1945-2000 (2000); When the Music Stops (1996); The Maestro Myth (1991).

Email norman@normanlebrecht.com *Website* www.norman.lebrecht.com

LEIBLER, Isi Joseph, AO, CBE, BA (Hons); D.Litt (Hon), Deakin University.

b. Antwerp, Belgium, Oct. 9, 1934; m. Naomi née Porush; Ch. Diaspora-Israel Relations Cttee. Jerusalem Centre for Public Affairs (2005-); Ch. and Chief Exec. Leibler Investments

Ltd. (1997-); Bd. of Gov. Tel Aviv University (1990-); Snr. V. Pres. World Jewish Congress (2001-04), Ch. Gov. Bd. (1997-2001); Ch. Australian Institute of Jewish Affairs (1983-2003); Pres. Asia Pacific Region, World Jewish Congress (1981-2001); Fdr. Ch. and Chief Exec. Jetset Tours Pty Ltd. (1965-2000); Bd. of Gov. Memorial Foundation for Jewish Culture (1979-95); Dir. and Mem. Exec. Cttee. Conference on Jewish Claims Against Germany (1979-95). Among recent publications: Is the Dream Ending? Post Zionism and Its Discontents (2001); The Israel-Diaspora Identity Crisis: A Looming Disaster (1994); Jewish Religious Extremism: A Threat to the Future of the Jewish People (1991). Weekly columnist: Jerusalem Post, Yisrael Hayom.

Add 8 Ahad Ha'am Street, 92151 Jerusalem, Israel

Tel +972 (02) 561 2241 *Fax* +972 (02) 561 2243

Email ileibler@leibler.com *Website* www.wordfromjerusalem.com

LEIGH, Howard D, BSc., FCA, ACTI.

b. London, Apr. 3, 1959; m. Jennifer née Peach; Investment Banker; Jewish Leadership Council (2010-); Pres. Westminster Synagogue (2010-), Ch. (2000-10); Exec. Board, Conservative Friends of Israel (2004-); Snr. T. Conservative Party (2001-); Ch. Jewish Care Breakfast Group (1998-); T. Jerusalem Foundation (1995-); Mem. Exec. Board Jewish Care (2004-06).

Add 40 Portland Place, London W1B 1NB

Tel 020 7908 6000 *Fax* 020 7908 6008

Email hleigh@cavendish.com

LENGA, Paul Oliver,

b. London, May 22, 1953; m. Sharon née Miller; Solicitor (England & Wales); Advocate, (Israel); Partner, Epstein Chomsky Osnat & Co & Gilat Knoller & Co Law Offices, Tel Aviv (2009–); Exec. Bd. Mem. Israel-British Chamber of Commerce (2007-); Dir. Confederation House Cultural Centre, Jerusalem (2005-); Fdr and Exec. Bd. Mem. ATID - International Partnership of Pluralistic Youth Movements (1996–); V. Pres. World Confederation of United Zionists (1995–) ; Notary Public (1989–); Life Pres. Federation of Zionist Youth of Great Britain (1984–); Mem. Israel Bar Association (1984-); Exec. Mem. Zionist General Council, World Zionist Organization (1984-2000); Mem. Law Society (1978-); Asst. Hon. S. Zionist Federation of Great Britain & Ireland (1978-1980); Solicitor of the Supreme Court of England & Wales (1977–); V.-Ch. Federation of Zionist Youth (1977), (Co-Ch. 1975). Publ.: Privatization of the Beersheva Prison: Impingement on the Freedom of the Individual or a Restriction on BOT Projects in Israel? (2010).

Add Rubinstein House, 9th Floor, 20 Lincoln Street, Tel Aviv 67134, Israel

Tel +972 (3) 561 4777 *Fax* +972 (3) 561 4776

Email lenga@ecglaw.com *Website* www.egclaw.com

LERMAN, Antony, BA Hons.

b. London, Mar. 11, 1946; Writer, Tru. The Humanitarian Trust; Mem. Bd. Directors, Paideia, European Institute for Jewish Studies, Stockholm; Hon. Fel. Parkes Inst. for Study of Jewish/Non-Jewish Relations, University of Southampton; Mem. Steering Group, Independent Jewish Voices; Exec Dir. Institute for Jewish Policy Research (2006-09; previously 1991-99); Chief Exec. Hanadiv Charitable Foundation (2000-06); Dir. European Programmes, Yad Hanadiv (1999-2000); Mem. Runnymede Trust Commission on the Future of Multi-Ethnic Britain (1998-2000); Mem. Jewish Memorial Foundation Think-Tank on the Holocaust (1996-99); Ch. Jewish Council for Community Relations (1992-94); Mem. Imperial War Museum Holocaust Exhibition Adv. Cttee. Publ.: The Making and Unmaking of a Zionist: A Personal and Political Journey (2012); Patterns of Prejudice (Ed. 1983-95, Jt. Ed. 1995-99); Antisemitism World Report (Jt. Gen. Ed. 1992-98); The Jewish Communities of the World (Ed. 1989), Survey of Jewish Affairs 1982-92 (Asst. Ed.); Jewish Quarterly (Ed. 1985-6).

Add 29 St. George's Avenue, London N7 0HB

Tel 07968 162 579

Email tonylerman@gmail.com *Website* www.antonylerman.com

LETWIN, Rt. Hon. Dr Oliver, PC.

b. London, May 19, 1956; m. Isabel Grace née Davidson; Minister for Government Policy (2010-); Ch. Conservative Party Policy Review (2006-); MP (Dorset West 1997-); Shadow Sec. State for Environment (2005-06); Shadow Chancellor (2003-05); Shadow Home Sec. (2001-03); Shadow Chief Sec. to the Treasury (1999-2001); Shadow Financial Sec. (1998-99). Publ.: The Purpose of Politics (1999); Privatising the World (1989); Ethics, Emotion and the Unity of Self (1987).

Add House of Commons, London SW1A 0AA

LEVENBERG, Fayge (née Schwab), BA (Hons), MA.

b. Gateshead, Dec. 10, 1949; m. Rabbi Yechiel Levenberg; Teacher; Additional Inspector, Independent and Faith Schools (2004-); External assessor, GTP and RTP Students (2001-); Hd. of Jewish Studies, Dep. Hd. Naima Jewish Preparatory School (1997-); Pikuach Inspector (1997-); OFSTED Inspector (1996-); form. Lecturer, Jews' college (1984-95); Inspector/Adv. US Bd. Rel. Education (1990-93), Education Off. (1988-93).

Add 76 Princes Park Avenue, London NW11 0JX

Tel 020 8381 4227 *Fax* 020 8455 0769

Email levenberg@totalise.co.uk

LEVIN, Rabbi Shlomo,

Rabbi, South Hampstead Synagogue; Rabbi, US (1983-).

Add 21/22 Eton Villas, Eton Road, London NW3 4SG

Tel 020 7722 1807 *Fax* 020 7586 3459

Email shlomo.levin@southhampstead.org

LEVY, Rabbi Abraham, Knight Commander (Encomienda) Order of Civil Merit (Spain), OBE, BA, PhD, FJC.

b. Gibraltar, July 16, 1939; m. Estelle née Nahum; Chaplain, Lord Mayor of London, Michael Bear (2010); Jewish Faith Advisor to Ministry of Defence (2010); H. Chaplain, Lord Mayor of London (1998-9); Pres. Union Anglo-Jewish Preachers (1973-75); Com. Rabbi, Spiritual Head, Spanish and Portuguese Jews Congregation, London (1980-2012), Emer. Spiritual Hd. (2012-); M. Lauderdale Road Synagogue; Jt. Ecclesiastical Authority (with the Chief Rabbi) of Board of Deputies; Dep. Pres. LSJS; V. Ch. Rabbinical Commission for the Licensing of Shochtim; Fdr. and Dir. The Sephardi Centre; form. Dir. Young Jewish Leadership Institute; Fdr. and H. Principal, Naima Jewish Preparatory School; H. Chaplain, Jewish Lads' and Girls' Brigade; Patron, Jewish Medical Association (UK); Mem. Standing Cttee. Conference of European Rabbis; V. Pres. British Friends Hebrew University; Hospital Kosher Meals Service, Jewish Care, Norwood; Pres. Jewish Child's Day; V. Pres. AJA, JHSE; Pres. Council of Christians and Jews; H. Principal Montefiore College and T. Montefiore Endowment; H. Fel. Queen Mary University London (2012-). Publ.: The Sephardim – A Problem of Survival; Ages of Man (Jt. author); The Sephardim (Jt. author).

Add 2 Ashworth Road, London W9 1JY

Tel 020 7289 2573 *Fax* 020 7289 5957

Email scadmin@spsyn.org.uk

LEVY, Dan,

Ed. Jewish Tribune; M. Enfield Synagogue. Presenter: Spectrum Radio; LBC.

Add Jewish Tribune, 97 Stamford Hill, London N16 5DN

Tel 020 8800 6688

Email info@jewishtribune.com

LEVY, Daniel, BA.

b. Feb. 8, 1962; Ch. Tottenham Hotspur (2001-); Managing Dir. ENIC International Ltd.

Add c/o Tottenham Hotspur, Bill Nicholson Way, 748 High Road, Tottenham N17 0AP

LEVY, Elkan David, BA (Hons), MHL.

b. Preston, Lancs, Mar. 29, 1943; m. Celia née Fisher (dec'd 2012); Solicitor; Ed. Jewish Year Book (2010-); M. Radlett United Synagogue (2010-11, 2005); Dir. Office of Small

Communities (2004-10); Pres. United Synagogue and Ch. Chief Rabbinate Council (1996-99); Ch. US Burial Society (1992-96); Warden, Stanmore Synagogue (1988-90); M. Belmont Synagogue (1969-73, 1991-92); Ch. Singers Prayer Book Publication Cttee.; form. Jt. Ch. Working Party on Monuments in the UK; form. Mem. Religious Advisory Committee to the Armed Forces; Freemason.

Add 14/14 Rechov Hamapilim, Netanya 42264, Israel

Tel 020 8150 6117

Email elkan.levy@gmail.com

LEVY, Rabbi Emanuel, BA (Hons).

b. Manchester, July 31, 1948; m. Myriam née Blum; Ch. Rabbinical Council of the Provinces (1986-8); F.P. Southend Community Relations Council, (1986-8); form. Chaplain to Mayor of Southend (1981-2, 1983-4); M. Palmers Green and Southgate Synagogue; form. V. Ch. Rabbinical Council of the US; Mem. Borough of Enfield Education Cttee.; Chaplain to Whittington Hospital; form. H. Principal, Herzlia Jewish Day School, Westcliff-on-Sea; form. Rabbi, Southend and Westcliff Hebrew Congregation; Chief Rabbi's Cabinet, Regional Affairs, to Chief Rabbi's Cabinet Education Portfolio; Jewish Representative to Standing Adv. Council for Religious Education (SACRE) for Borough of Enfield; form. Rabbi, Langside Hebrew Congregation, Glasgow; Rabbi, South Broughton Synagogue, Manchester. Publ.: Pninei Kahal (2005).

Add 11 Morton Crescent, Southgate, London N14 7AH

Tel 020 8882 2943

Email rabbilevy@rabbilevy.org

LEVY, Rabbi Joel Gideon, M.A. (Cantab).

b. Birmingham, 1965; m. Susanna Cohen; Rabbi, Kol Nefesh Masorti Synagogue, Edgware (2001-); Dir. NOAM (1991-94). Rabbinic ordination - The Shalom Hartman Institute; Congregational Rabbi and Talmud teacher; Dir. Conservative Yeshiva, Jerusalem; Mem. European Masorti Bet Din.

Add c/o Cohen, 3 Lawrence Court, Mill Hill, London NW7 3QP

Tel 07762 901 197

Email joelglevy@gmail.com

LEVY, John David Ashley, BA (Hon) Sociology.

b. London, Sept. 10, 1947; Dir. Friends of Israel Education Fund; Exec. Dir. Academic Study Group on Israel and Middle East; Tru. UK Society for the Protection of Nature in Israel; form. Information Dir. Zionist Federation; Social Worker, London Borough of Lambeth.

Add POB 42763, London N2 0YJ

Tel 020 8444 0777 *Fax* 020 8444 0681

Email info@foi-asg.org *Website* www.foi-asg.org

LEVY, Rabbi Joshua Benjamin Israel, BA (Oxon), MA, MSc.

b. Manchester, 1974; m. Judith née Green; Rabbi, North Western Reform Synagogue (Alyth) (2008-).

Add North Western Reform Synagogue, Alyth Gardens, London NW11 7EN

Tel 020 8457 8799

Email josh@alyth.org.uk

LEVY, Michael Abraham, Baron of Mill Hill, FCA, HonD (Middx).

b. London, July 11, 1944; Patron, Etz Chaim Jewish Primary School (2011-); Tru. Jewish Leadership Council (2006-10); Pres. Jewish Lads' and Girls' Brigade (2006); Pres. Specialist Schools and Academies Trust (2005-08); Israel Policy Forum Recognition Award (2003); H. Patron, Cambridge University Jewish Society (2002-); Patron, Simon Marks Jewish Primary School Trust (2002-); Pres. JFS School (2001-); Mem. Exec. Cttee. Chai-Lifeline (2001-02); Mem. H. Cttee. Israel, Britain and the Commonwealth Association (2000-); Patron, Save a Child's Heart Foundation (2000-); Ch. Bd. Trustees of New Policy Network Fund (2000-07); Mem. Community Legal Service Champions Panel (1999-); Patron of Friends of Israel

Education Trust (1998-); Pres. CSV (Community Service Volunteers) (1998-); Pres. Jewish Care (1998-); T. Holocaust Educational Trust (1998-2007); Scopus Award Friends of the Hebrew University (1998); Mem. National Council for Voluntary Organisations Adv. Cttee. (1998-2011); Patron, Prostate Cancer Charitable Trust (1997-); Mem. of World Commission on Israel-Diaspora Relations (1995-); Patron of the British Music Industry Awards (1995-); V. Ch. Central Council for Jewish Social Services (1994-2006); B'nai B'rith First Lodge Award (1994); H. Pres. UJIA; Ch. Fdr. for Education (1993-); Ch. Chief Rabbinate Awards for Excellence (1992-2007); Patron, Mathilda Marks-Kennedy Jewish Primary School.

Add House of Lords, London SW1A 0PW

Email ml@lordlevy.com

LEVY, Peter Lawrence, OBE, BSc, FRICS.

b. London, Nov. 10, 1939; Chartered Surveyor; V. Ch. JIA (1979-81); Professional Div. JIA (1977-79); Ch. Young Leadership JIA (1973-77); V. Pres. IJPR; H. V. Pres. Reform Judaism; T. Dementia UK; Tru. Akiva School; V. Pres. Cystic Fibrosis Trust; V. Pres. London Youth.

Add 52 Springfield Road NW8 0QN

Tel 020 7328 6109 *Fax* 020 7372 7424

Email peterllevy@btinternet.com

LEWIN, Sylvia Rose (née Goldschmidt), BA (Log), (Rand), RSA Dip.Sp.L.D.

b. Johannesburg; Speech and Dyslexia Therapist; H. Life Pres. (National Pres. 1988, 1982-86) Bnai Brith UK; Ch. Leadership Training and Dev. B'nai B'rith, UK; V. Pres. Jewish Music Institute; past Ch. Jewish Music Heritage Trust.

Add White Gables, 156 Totteridge Lane N20 8JJ

Tel 020 8446 0404

Email sylvialewin@btinternet.com

LEWIS, D. Jerry, BA (Econ) (Hons, Manchester).

b. Surrey, June 12, 1949; Parl. Lobby Journalist and Broadcaster; V. Pres. Board of Deputies (2009, 2000-03), Snr. V. Pres. (2003-06), Ch. Community Issues Div. (2009–, 2000-06); Mem. Board of Deputies Exec. (2009-, 1985-2006); form. Mem. Defence Div. (2006-09) and Intl. Div. (1997-2000); Exec. (1985-2006), V. Ch. Law, Parl. and General Purposes Cttee. and Board of Deputies Constitution Standing Cttee. (1994-97), Constitution Standing Cttee. (1981-97) etc.; Mem. Exec. Cttee. ZF, National Council for Soviet Jewry; Mem. Foreign Press Association; London correspondent Israel Radio, Yediot Ahronot; Political and diplomatic Correspondence: Jewish Telegraph; contributor BBC World TV, BBC News 24, BBC World Service, BBC Radio 5 Live, Sky News, etc.

Add 9 Weech Hall, Fortune Green Road, London NW6 1DJ

Tel 020 7794 0044 *Mobile* 07956 968 265

Email attnjerrylewis@aol.com

LEWIS, Ivan,

b. Manchester, Mar. 4, 1967; Shadow Sec. State, International Development; Shadow Sec. State for Culture, Media and Sport (2010-11); T. Minister of State - Foreign Office (2009-10); Parl. Under Sec. for Health (2006-07); T. Holocaust Educational Trust (1998-); DFID (2008-09); Adult Skills (2001-05), Young People Learning (2001-2), Adult Learning and Skills (2002), Young People and Adult Skills (2002-03), Skills and Vocational Education (2003-5); Economic Sec. to Treasury (2005-06); PPS Sec. State of Trade and Industry (1999-2001); Mem. Exec. Cttee. of the Commonwealth Jewish Council (1998-2001); V. Ch. Inter-Parliamentary Council Against Antisemitism (1998-2001); V. Ch. Labour Friends of Israel (1998-2001); Ch. All-Party Parliamentary Group for Parenting (1999); Mem. Health Select Cttee. (1998-99); MP (Lab.), Bury South (1997); Chief Exec. Jewish Social Services, Greater Manchester (1992-97); Co-ordinator, Contact Community Care Group (1986-89).

Add House of Commons, London SW1A 0AA

Tel 0161 773 5500

Email ivanlewis@burysouth.fsnet.co.uk *Website* www.ivanlewis.co.uk

LEWIS, Jonathan Malcolm, MA (Law) (Cantab).

b. London, Mar. 27, 1946; m. Rosemary Anne née Mays; Solicitor; Freeman of the City of London; Designated Immigration Judge, Deputy District Judge; Mem. Board of Deputies (Pinner, 1995-2009), Ch. Constitution Cttee. Exec. Cttee. (1997-03); Ch. UK Association of Jewish Lawyers and Jurists (2002-07); Authorised insolvency practitioner (1986-2000). Publ.: Insolvency in Jewish Law (1996).

Add Taylor House, 88 Rosebery Avenue, London EC1R 4QU

Tel 0845 6000 877

Email lewisjandr2004@yahoo.co.uk

LEWIS, Dr Julian Murray,

b. Swansea, Sept. 26, 1951; Historian, researcher and campaigner; MP (Con.), New Forest East (1997-); Dir. Policy Research Associates (1985-); Shadow Defence M. (2005-10, 2002-04), Shadow Min. for the Cabinet Office (2004-05), Opposition Whip (2001-2); Mem. Intelligence and Security Cttee. (2010-); Mem. Select Cttee. on Defence (2000-1); V. Ch. Cons. Parl. Foreign Affairs and Europe Committees (2000-1); Mem. Select Cttee. on Welsh Affairs (1998-2001); Jt. Sec. Cons Parl. Defence Cttee. (1997-2001); Dep. Dir. Conservative Research Dept. (1990-96); Research Dir. and Dir. Coalition for Peace Through Security (1981-85). Publ.: Racing Ace: The Fights and Flights of 'Kink' Kinkead DSO DSC* DFC* (2011); Changing Direction: British Military Planning for Post-War Strategic Defence, 1942-1947 (1988, 2nd edition, 2003, University pbk. edition, 2008); What's Liberal? Liberal Democrat Quotations and Facts (1996); Who's Left? An Index of Labour MPs and Left-wing Causes, 1985-1992 (1992).

Add House of Commons, London SW1A 0AA

Tel 020 7219 4179

Website www.julianlewis.net

LEWIS, Leonie Rachelle (née Merkel), BA (Hons), MSc, MBA.

b. London, Dec. 1955; m. Howard Lewis; Dir. Jewish Volunteering Network (2008-); Co-Ch. Faith Forum for London (2012-); Exec. Mem. London Jewish Forum (2006-); Exec. Mem. JLC Women's Commission (2012-); Tru. Faith Based Regeneration Network (2000-); Adv. Children's Aid Cttee. (2003-); Project Dir. Office of the Chief Rabbi (2007-08); Dir. Communities, US (1995-2007). Publ.: Ten out of Ten: Perspectives on Community Development.

Add 659 Uxbridge Road, Pinner, Middlesex HA5 3LW

Tel 020 8866 9239

Email leonie@jun.org.uk *Website* www.jun.org.uk

LEWIS, Steven,

Mem. Jewish Leadership Council; New Leadership Network; Ch. Jewish Care.

Add JLC, 6 Bloomsbury Square, London WC1A 2LP

Email stevenlewisandpartners.com *Website* www.lewisandpartners.com

LIBESKIND, Daniel, B.Arch, MA, BDA.

b. Lodz, May 12, 1946; m. Nina née Lewis; Architect; Principal, Studio Daniel Libeskind (1989-); Prof. Hochschule fur Gestaltung, Karlsruhe; Cret Ch. of Architecture, University of Pennsylvania; Frank O. Grety Ch. University of Toronto. Recent architectural projects include: Danish Jewish Museum (Copenhagen, 2003); Maurice Wohl Convention Centre (Bar Ilan University, 2003); University of North London Graduate School (2003); Imperial War Museum North (Manchester, 2002); Jewish Museum (Berlin, 2001). Among recent publications: The Space of Encounter (2001); Fishing from the Pavement (1997); Radix: Matrix: Works and Writings (1997).

Add Studio Daniel Libeskind, Windscheidstr. 18, 10627 Berlin, Germany

Tel +49 (30) 327 7820 *Fax* +49 (30) 3277 8299

Email info@daniel-libeskind.com

LIBSON, James,

Ch. World Jewish Relief; Tru. Jewish Leadership Council; New Leadership Network; Exec. Partner, Mishcon de Reya Solicitors, London.

Add Mishcon De Reya, 12 Red Lion Square, London WC1R 4QD

Email james.libson@mishcon.com *Website* www.mishcon.com

LIGHTMAN, Sir Gavin Anthony,

b. London, Dec. 20, 1939; Patron, UK LFI (2012-), The Hammerson Home (1995-2012) and British Fulbright Scholars Association (2009-); Ch. Commonwealth Jewish Association (1999-2006); Ch. Sainer Legal Fund (1999-); Association of Jewish Lawyers and Jurists (2011-); V. Pres. Hillel (1994-), Ch. Education Cttee. (1992-94); V. Pres. AJA (1994-), Ch. Education Cttee. (1988-94); Deputy Pres. (1986-92); Pres. Gemme (European Assoc. of Judges for Mediation) (2009-12); Ch. Investment Cttee. Harbour Litigation Funding (2010-); T. Lincolns Inn (2008); Justice of the High Court, Chancery Division (1994-08); Fel. University College London (2002); Ch. Legal Friends of University Haifa (1986-2002); QC (1980-94); Bencher of Lincolns Inn (1987). Publ.: (with G. Moss) Law of Admin. and Receivers of Companies (5th edition 2011); (with G. Battersby) Cases and Statutes on the Law of Real Property (1965).

Add Serle Chambers, 6 New Square, Lincoln Inn London WC2

Tel 020 7242 6105

Email gavinlightman@yahoo.co.uk

LIGHTMAN, Sidney, FCIL.

b. London, Apr. 5, 1924; journalist, translator; Foreign News Dept. Jewish Chronicle (1963-96); Asst. Foreign Ed. Jewish Chronicle (1981-89); form. Ed. Jewish Travel Guide (1966-89); Ed. Dept. Jewish Observer and Middle East Review (1959-63); Asst. Ed. Israel and Middle East (Tel Aviv) (1951-4); Sec. British and European Machal Association.

Add 5 West Heath Court, North End Road, London NW11 7RE

Tel 020 8455 1673 *Fax* 020 8455 1673

Email lightmantranslations@talktalk.net

LIND, Eleanor Frances (née Platt), QC, LLB (London).

b. May 6, 1938; m. Frederick (Freddy) M. Lind; Barrister, Gray's Inn 1960, QC. (1982); Mem. Panel Jewish Genealogy and Ethics (2011-); Ch. 'Get' Cttee./FamLaw Working group (1999-); Legal assessor GMC (1995-); V. Pres. and Ch. Defence and Group Relations, Board of Deputies (2003-6), Mem. (1984-); Jt. H. 1 Garden Court Family Law Chambers (1990-2007); Pres. Medico-Legal Society. (2002-04); Deputy High Court Judge, Family Division (1987-2004); Recorder Crown Court (1982-2004); Ch. New London Synagogue (1994-9); Act. Ch. Family Law Bar Association (1995), T. (1990-5); Ch. Law, Parliamentary Gen. Purposes Cttee. (1988-94).

Add 1 Garden Court, Temple, London EC4Y 9BJ

Tel 020 7797 7900

Email platt@1gc.com

LIPMAN, Maureen Diane, CBE, H. D.Litt.

b. Hull, May 10, 1946; Actress/Writer. Theatre: Re:Joyce; Lost in Yonkers; The Cabinet M.; See How they Run (Olivier Award for Best Comedy Performance, 1985); Peggy For You; Oklahoma; Aladdin; Glorious. TV: Agony; About Face; The Knowledge: Eskimo Day; In Search of Style - Art Deco; Dr Who; Sensitive Skin; He Kills Coppers; Casualty; Skins. Film: The Pianist. Publ.: 7 books of anecdotes published by Robson Books. Regular column in Guardian; Good Housekeeping.

Add c/o Conway Van Gelder, 18/21 Jermyn Street SW1Y 6HP

Tel 020 7287 0077

LIPTON, Sir Stuart (Anthony), Kt.

b. Nov. 9, 1942; m. Ruth Kathryn neé Marks; Deputy Ch. Chelsfield LLP (2006-); Mem. Royal Opera House (1998–2006); Ch. (2003–06), Chief Exec. (1995–2003), Stanhope PLC; Ch. CABE (1999–2004).

Add 53 Grosvenor Street W1K 3HU

Email slipton@chelsfield.com

LIPWORTH, Sir (Maurice) Sydney, BCom, LLD, Kt, QC.

b. May 13, 1931; m. Rosa neé Liwarek; T. Philharmonic Orchestra (1982–); T. International Accounting Standards Cttee. Foundation (2000–06); Ch. Financial Reporting Council (1993–2001); Ch. Monopolies and Mergers Commn (1988–93); Dir. Allied Dunbar Assurance plc (form. Hambro Life Assurance) (1971–88).

Add International Accounting Standards Board, 30 Cannon Street EC4M 6XH

LIVINGSTON, Edward Colin, MBE, MB, BS (London), JP.

b. London, Mar. 22, 1925; Med. Practitioner; Barrister; Ch. Austrian Fund Com. AJR Agudas; Ch. Emergency Fund; Ch. H.S.C. Adv. Cttee. form. Ombudsman, Central Council for Jewish Community Services; Medical Examiner, Medical Fund for Care of Victims of Torture; P/T Ch. Social Sec. Appeal Tribunal, Harrow; V. Pres. Harrow Community Trust; Liveryman. Society of Apothecaries; Freeman, City of London; form. P/T Ch. Disability Appeal Tribunal, South East Region; Flt./Lieut (Med. Br.) RAFVR (1948-50).

Add Wyck Cottage, Barrow Point Lane, Pinner, Middlesex HA5 3DJ

LOBENSTEIN, Josef H, MBE.

b. Hanover, Apr. 27, 1927; m. Bella neé Mosbacher; Mayor, London Borough of Hackney (1997-2001); Conservative Opposition Leader, London Borough of Hackney (1974-97); Councillor, Metropolitan Borough of Stoke Newington (1962-65); H. Freeman, London Borough of Hackney; Pres. Adath Yisroel Synagogue and Burial Society; Ch. North London Jewish Liaison Cttee.; V. Pres. Union of Orthodox Hebrew Congregations and Ch. External Affairs Cttee.; V. Ch. Agudath Israel of Great Britain; Mem. Editorial Bd. Jewish Tribune; V. Pres. National Shechita Council; Exec. Shechita UK; Ch. and Bd. Gov. Yesode Hatorah Snr. Girls' School; Bd. Gov. Homerton University Hospital; Pres. Hackney Conservative Association; form. Gen. Sec. Agudath Israel of Great Britain; Mem. Board of Deputies; T. Jewish Secondary School Movement; H. Pres. Hackney and Tower Hamlets Chamber of Commerce; Gov. Avigdor Primary School, Craven Park Primary School.

Add 27 Fairholt Road, London N16 5EW

Tel 020 8800 4746 *Mobile* 07976 724 081 *Fax* 020 7502 0985

LUCAS, Stella, MBE, JP.

b. London, July 30, 1916; née Waldman; Pres. First Women's Lodge B'nai B'rith (1975-77); V. Pres. (Ch. 1978-84), Frs. of Hebrew University (Women's Group); Pres. Dollis Hill Ladies' Guild; Ch. Union of Jewish Women (1966-72); Exec. Off. International Council of Jewish Women (1963-66); Ch. Women Frs. of Jews' Coll. (1957-66); V. Pres. Jewish Care; Ch. Stepney Girls' Club and Settlement; V. Pres. Assn. of US Women; Central Council for Jewish Social Services; Board of Deputies; Ch. Brodie Institute; Convenor, Board of Deputies Central Enquiry Desk; Fdr. 'All Aboard Shops'.

Add 51 Wellington Court, Wellington Road NW8 9TB

Tel 020 7586 3030

LUSTIGMAN, Stuart,

Pres. European Maccabi Confederation; V. Pres. Maccabi GB; Pres. Faithfold FC; Exec. Mem. Maccabi World Union; Mem. European Jewish Parliament (MEJP); Mem. International Sports Committee, 19th Maccabiah; Pres. Maccabi Junior Football League; Ch. Maccabi Masters Football League.

Tel 020 8958 8893

Email stuartlustigman@aol.com

MAGONET, Rabbi Prof. Dr Jonathan David, MB, BS, PhD (Heid.), FRSA.

b. London, Aug. 2, 1942; Research Prof. Seinan Gakuin University, Fukuoka, Japan (2010-13); Theologische Hochschule Wuppertal (2004-10); Schalom Ben Chorim Prof. Jewish Studies, University Würzburg and Augsburg (2008); Principal, Leo Baeck College (1985-2005), form. Emer. Prof. of Bible; Guest Prof. University Lucerne (2004), University Oldenberg (1999); V. Pres. Movement for Reform Judaism. Among recent publications:

Netsuke Nation: Tales from Another Japan (2013); A Rabbi who reads the Torah (2013); Seder Ha-t'fillot Forms of Prayer: Daily and Sabbath (Ed. 8th edition 2008); Einführung in Judentum (2004); Talking to the Other: Interfaith Dialogue with Christians and Muslims (2003); Abraham-Jesus-Mohammed: Interreligioser Dialog aus Jüdischer Perspektiv (2000); Rabbino Seishokaishak: Yudaiyakkuo to Kiristokuo No Taiwa (Japanese Rabbinic Bible Commentary, Jewish Christian Dialogue) (2012); Ed. European Judaism (2005-), Co-Ed. (1992-2005).

Add 22 Avenue Mansion, Finchley Road, London NW3 7AX

Tel 020 7209 0911

Email jonathan.magonet@gmail.com *Website* www.jonathanmagonet.co.uk

MANN, John, BA.

b. Jan. 10, 1960; m. Joanna White; MP (Lab) Bassetlaw (2001-); Mem. Editorial Advisory Panel, People Management (2005–9); Liaison Officer, National Trade Union and Lab Party (1995–2000); Hd of Res. and Education, AEU (1988–90); Mem. (Lab), Lambeth BC (1986–90); Ch. Parliamentary Cttee. against Antisemitism; commissioned the All-Party Parliamentary Inquiry into Antisemitism.

Add House of Commons, London SW1A 0AA

Tel 020 7219 8345

Email mannj@parliament.uk *Website* www.johnmannmp.com

MARANTZ, Jason,

Chief Exec. London School of Jewish Studies.

Add Schaller House, Wohl Campus for Jewish Education, 44a Albert Road, London NW4 2SJ

Tel 020 8203 6427 *Fax* 020 8203 6420

Email info@lsjs.ac.uk *Website* www.lsjs.ac.uk

MARCUS, Rabbi Barry, BA (Hons), PGCE.

b. Cape Town, Oct. 28, 1949; Patron, Yad Vashem UK (2005-); T. Holocaust Memorial Day Trust (2004-); Rabbi, Central Synagogue (1995-); Pioneer of the one-day educational visits to Auschwitz-Birkenau. Publ.: You Are Witnesses (1999); Father and son (1986).

Add 40 Hallam Street, London W1W 6NW

Tel 020 7580 1355 *Fax* 020 7636 3831

Email administrator@centralsynagogue.org.uk *Website* www.centralsynagogue.org.uk

MARCUS, Daniel,

b. London, July 9, 1973; m. Deborah née Saville; Chief Exec. UJS Hillel (2007-); form. Exec. Dir. John Hopkins University Hillel (2005-07).

Add 4 Greenland Place, London NW1 0AP

Tel 020 7388 0801 *Fax* 020 7424 3288

Email danielm@ujs.org.uk

MARCUS, Mark Hyman, BA (Com).

b. Manchester, Feb. 22, 1933; form. Exec. Dir. B'nai B'rith UK (1984-98); form. Ch. B'nai B'rith London Bureau of International Affairs; Dir. Provincial and London Divisions, UJIA.

Add B'nai B'rith UK, ORT House, 126 Albert Street, London NW1 7NE

MARGOLYES, Miriam, BA (Cantab), LGSM&D.

b. Oxford, May 18, 1941; Actress. BAFTA Best Supporting Actress (1993); Sony Radio Award, Best Actress on Radio (1993); Best Supporting Actress, LA Critics Circle Awards (1989). Major film credits include: Cold Comfort Farm; Magnolia; The Life and Death of Peter Sellers; Modigliani; Professor Sprout in the Harry Potter films and many more. TV credits include: Blackadder; The Girls of Slender Means; Oliver Twist; The History Man; Vanity Fair; Supply & Demand. Frannie's Turn; BBC TV documentary series about Charles Dickens. Stage credits include: Dickens' Women (world tour 2012); Endgame; WICKED (London and Broadway, Blithe Spirit (Melbourne Theatre Company); The Vagina Monologues; Romeo & Juliet (Los Angeles production), She Stoops to Conquer; Orpheus

Descending (London). Many audio book recordings, including: Oliver Twist; Great Expectations; Matilda; Pinnocchio; The Worst Witch series; The Queen & I; The Little White Horse; The Sea; Troy; Wise Child.

Add c/o Lindy King, United Agents, 12-26 Lexington Street, London W1F 0LE

Tel 020 3214 0800 *Fax* 020 3214 0803

Email lking@unitedagents.co.uk *Website* www.miriammargolyes.com

MARINER, Rabbi Rodney John, BA (Hons), Dip. Ed.

b. Melbourne, Australia, May 29, 1941; m. Susan; Emer. Rabbi, Belsize Square Synagogue; Convener, Beth Din, Reform Judaism (Ret. 2013); Associate M. Edgware and District Reform Synagogue (1979-82); Assistant M. North Western Reform Synagogue (1976-79). Publ.: Prayers For All The Year: Part 1, Shabbat; Part 2, Festivals; Part 3, New Year; Part 4, Atonement; Part 5, Evening Prayers.

Add 92 North Road, London N6 4A A

Tel 020 8347 5306

Email rodmariner@aol.com

MARKS, Laura,

Snr. V. Pres. Board of Deputies.

Add Board Of Deputies, 6 Bloomsbury Square, London WC1A 2LP

Tel 020 7543 5400 *Fax* 020 7543 0010

Email info@bod.org.uk *Website* www.bod.org.uk

MARKS, Shula Eta (née Winokur), Emer. Prof, SOAS, OBE, FBA, BA (UCT), PhD (London), H. DLitt (UCT), H. D.Soc.Sci. (Natal), H. DLitt (University of Johannesburg; Distinguished Africanist Award, African Studies Assoc. (UK) (2002); Distinguished Res. Fel. SAS, London; H. Fel., SOAS (2005-); H. Prof., UCT (2005-).

b. Cape Town, Oct. 14, 1936; m. Isaac Meyer Marks; Historian; Emer. Prof. History of Southern Africa, SOAS (2001-), Prof. (1993-2001); Ch. International Records Management Trust (1995-2004); Ch. Council for Assisting Refugee Academics, (CARA) (1993-2004); Mem. Council (1983-); Mem. Arts and Humanities Research Bd. (1998-2000); Dir. Institute of Commonwealth Studies, University of London (1983-93). Publ.: Divided Sisterhood: Class, Race and Gender in the South African Nursing Profession (1994); Not Either an Experimental Doll: The Separate Lives of Three South African Women (1987); In Defence of Learning: The Plight, Persecution and Placement of Academic Refugees, 1933-80 (with Paul Weindling and Laura Wintour).

Add 43 Dulwich Common, London SE21 7EU

Email shulamarks@yahoo.co.uk

MARKS-WOLDMAN, Olivia,

Chief Exec. Holocaust Memorial Day Trust.

Add PO Box 61074, London SE1P 5BX

Tel 020 7785 7029

Email enquiries@hmd.org.uk *Website* www.hmd.org.uk

MARMUR, Rabbi Dow,

b. Sosnowiec, Poland, Feb. 24, 1935; Rabbi Emer. Holy Blossom Temple, Toronto; form. Pres. Toronto Board of Rabbis; form. Ch. Council of Reform and Lib. Rabbis; M. North Western Reform Synagogue (1969-83); South-West Essex Reform Synagogue (1962-69). Publ.: Beyond Survival; The Star of Return; Walking Toward Elijah; On being a Jew; Six Lives: a Memoir; Reform Judaism (Ed.); A Genuine Search (Ed.); Choose Life.

Add 1950 Bathurst Street, Toronto, Ontario, M5P 3K9, Canada

Tel 416 789 3291 *Fax* 416 789 9697

Email dmarmur@hotmail.com

MASSIL, Stephen W, BA, Dip. Lib, FLA, FSA, FRAS.

b. Eynsham, Oxon, Sept. 21, 1941; m. Brenda Goldstein; Librarian; posts at the Garrick Club (2006-); National Trust (2006-); Sir John Soane's Museum (2002-6); University College

London (2002-3); Warburg Institute (1999/2002); Cambridge (1996-2000); London University (1977-96); University of Birmingham (1966-77); consultant for Unesco, the British Council and other international organisations; V. Pres. JHSE (2006-), Pres. (2004-6); T. Jewish Literary Trust, Ed. Jewish Book News and Reviews (1986-); Ed. Jewish Year Book (Vallentine Mitchell, 1994-2009, JC 1989-93); Convenor, Hebraica Libraries Group (1991-2007); Ed. Jewish Travel Guide (1991-4). Publ.: Anglo-Jewish Bibliography, 1971-90 (Co-Ed. 1992); Facsimile edition of 'Jewish Year Book, 1896' (Ed.); articles and conference papers on library history, bibliography; consultancy reports for Unesco and the British Council.

Add JHSE, 33 Seymour Place, London W1H 5AP

MICHAELS, Leslie David, FCA, MBA.

b. London, July 14, 1943; m. Lesley née Stern; Dir. Time Products Ltd; T. Cecil Roth Memorial Trust; Ch. North Western Reform Synagogue, Israel Support Group; form. Ch. Ben Uri Art Gallery and Society; Movement of Reform Judaism, Israel Cttee.

Add 34, Dover Street, London W15 4NG

Tel 020 7343 7200

Email lmichaels@timeproducts.co.uk

MICHAELS, Rabbi Maurice Arnold, M.A.

b. Woolmer's Park, Herts., Aug. 31, 1941; Rabbi, North Western Reform Synagogue; Hd. Vocational Studies and Lecturer, Leo Baeck College; Lecturer, Gregorian University, Rome; V. Pres. Movement for Reform Judaism; H. Life V. Pres. Leo Baeck College; T. Interfaith Network UK; Gov. Chlore Tikva School; Patron, Haven House Children's Hospice; Patron, Waging Peace; form. Ch. and V. Pres. RSGB; Ch. Leo Baeck College; Ch. Assembly of Reform Rabbis; Ch. SW Essex Reform Synagogue; Ch. of Govs. Clore Tikva School; Ch. Redbridge Business Education Partnership; Ch. and T. Ahada Bereavement Counselling; T. Empathy Counselling; Gov. Redbridge College; Gov. Akiva School; Gov. Jewish Jt. Burial Society; T. Redbridge Racial Equality Council; T. Limmud; Council Mem. Redbridge Campaign Against Racism and Fascism; Dir. Harlow Enterprise Agency; V. Ch. Harlow and District Employers' Group; Dir. Refugee and Migrant Forum of East London; Man. Cttee. Redbridge Faith Forum; Patron, St Francis Hospice; Chaplian London 2012.

Add 19 Moray Close, Rise Park, Essex RM1 4YJ

Tel 020 8554 2812

Email ramaby@ntlworld.com

MIDDLEBURGH, Rabbi Charles H, BA Hons, PhD, FZS.

b. Hove, Oct. 2, 1956; Rabbi, Cardiff Reform Synagogue (2005-), Dublin Jewish Progressive Congregation (2002-11), Shir HaTzaphon, Copenhagen (2002-05), Harrow and Wembley Progressive Synagogue (1983-97); Dir. Jewish Studies, Leo Baeck College (2011-), Snr. Lecturer Rabbinics (2004-), Lecturer Aramaic, Practical Rabbinics (2002); Co-Ed. Mahzor Ruach Chadashah (1996-2003); Exec. Dir. Union of Liberal and Progressive Synagogues (1997-2002); Fel. Zoological Society, London; Publ.: High and Holy Days: A Book of Jewish Wisdom (with Rabbi Dr. A. Goldstein, 2010); Tefillot ve-Tachanunim (with A. Goldstein, 2006).

Add Leo Baeck College, 80 East End Road, London N3 2SY

Tel 020 8349 5615 *Fax* 020 8349 5619

Email charles.middleburgh@lbc.ac.uk

MILIBAND, Rt. Hon. David (Wright), BA, MSC.

b. July. 15, 1965; m. Louise neé Shackelton; MP (Lab) South Shields (2001-13); Shadow Foreign Sec. (2010); Sec. of State for Foreign and Commonwealth Affairs (2007-10); Sec. of State for Environment, Food and Rural Affairs (2006–07); Cabinet Office (2004–05); M. of State: DfES (2002–04); Hd. PM's Policy Unit (1998–2001).

Add IRC UK, 3 Bloomsbury Place, London WC1A 2QL

Email Bernadette.McGee@rescue.org *Website* www.davidmiliband.net

MILIBAND, Rt. Hon. Edward, BA, MSc.

b. Dec. 24, 1969; m. Justine née Thornton; Leader of Labour Party (2010-); MP (Lab) Doncaster North (2005-); Sec. of State for Energy and Climate Change (2008-10);

Chancellor of the Duchy of Lancaster and M. for the Cabinet Office (2007–08); Parly Sec. Cabinet Office (2006–07); Council of Econ. Advs. HM Treasury (2004–05); Special Adv. to Chancellor of the Exchequer (1997–2002).

Add House of Commons, London SW1A 0AA

MILLER, Helena, Cert Ed., Adv. Dip. Ed., MA, PhD Jewish Education (London).

b. London, Oct. 27, 1955; m. Steve Miller; Research Dir. UJIA; Dir. of Research and Education, Dir. Community Israel Engagement, UJIA (2007-); Ch. Pikuach Schools Inspection Service (2006-); Dir. of Education, Leo Baeck College (2001-07); Awarded Max Fisher Prize for Contribution to Jewish Education in the Diaspora (2012). Publ.: Four Years On: A Review of Inspections of Jewish Schools 2007-11 (2012); The International Handbook of Jewish Education (2011); Beyond the Community: Jewish Day School Education in Britain (2009); Meeting the Challenge: the Jewish Schooling Phenomenon in the UK (2001); The Magic Box (1995); Craft in Action (1981).

Add 37 Kentish Town Road, London NW1 8NX

Tel 020 7424 6400 *Fax* 020 7424 6401

Email helena.miller@ujia.org *Website* www.ujia.org

MILLER, Jonathan,

V. Pres. United Synagogue (2011-); form. Ch. Hendon Synagogue; form. Fin. Rep. St John's Wood Synagogue, form. Ch. Gov. Hasmonean Primary School.

Add United Synagogue, 305 Ballard's Lane, London N12 8GB

Tel 020 343 8989

Website www.theus.org.uk

MILLER, Jonathan Moss, BSc (Hons), ARCS, PGCE, MA, NPQH.

m. Hannah née Babad; Hd. JFS (2008-).

Add JFS, The Mall, Kenton, Harrow, Middlesex HA3 9TE

Tel 020 8206 3100 *Fax* 020 8206 3101

Email admin@jfs.brent.sch.uk *Website* www.jfs.brent.sch.uk

MILLETT, Rt. Hon. Lord Peter, Baron of St. Marylebone, PC, MA (Cantab), H. DLL (University London).

b. London, June 23, 1932; m. Anne Mireille Harris; Hon. Fel. Queen Mary College, London (2013); Hon. LLD London University (2008); Non-Permanent Judge, Court of Final Appeal, Hong Kong (2000-); T. Lincoln's Inn (2004); Lord of Appeal in Ordinary (1998-2004); Mem. Court of Appeal (1994-8); Pres. West London Synagogue (1991-5); Hon. Fel. Trinity Hall (1994); Judge of the High Court Chancery Div. (1986-94); form. Ch. Lewis Hammerson Home (1981-91); QC (1973-86), Mem. Insolvency Law Review Cttee. (1976-82); Standing Jnr. Counsel, Trade and Industry Dept. (1967-73); Bencher, Lincoln's Inn; Called to Bar, Middle Temple. Publ.: (Contr.) Halsbury's Law of England; Editor-in-Chief: Encyclopaedia of Forms and Precedents.

Add 18 Portman Close, London W1H 6BR

Tel 020 7935 1152

MILSTON, Michael, BA (London).

b. June 7, 1949; m. Helen Esther née Moss; Freelance journalist; Radio Producer, Tikkun Spectrum; Lecturer, English as a Foreign Language; Lecturer, Magen Ohel Avraham Shiur; Lay Preacher, Fieldgate Street Great Synagogue; Ch. Friends of East London Orthodox Association of Synagogues (2001-). Publ.: A Critical Review (2nd Edition 2003).

Add 6 Elmfield House, 77 Carlton Hill, London NW8 9XB

Tel 020 7624 8183 *Fax* 020 7624 8183

Email francamil@talk21.com

MIRVIS, Rabbi Ephraim, BA, Education and Classical Hebrew, University of South Africa.

b. 1956, Cape Town, South Africa; m. Valerie née Kaplan; Chief Rabbi-Elect, United Hebrew Congregations of the Commonwealth (Sept 2013-); Snr. Rabbi, Finchley United Synagogue (1996-); Ch. Rabbinical Council of the United Synagogue (1999-2002);

arranged and led the first group visit by United Synagogue rabbis to the United States (2001); Religious Adv. Jewish Marriage Council (1997-); Mem. Chief Rabbi's Cabinet (1996-); Rabbi, Western Marble Arch Synagogue (1992-6); Pres. Irish Council of Christians and Jews (1985-92); Ch. of the Board of Governors, Stratford Jewish Schools, Dublin (1984-92); Rabbi, Adelaide Road Synagogue, Dublin (1982); Chief Rabbi of Ireland, (1985-92); first United Synagogue rabbi to host an address by an imam, Dr. Mohammed Essam El-Din Fahim, in his synagogue; Fdr Rabbi and Hon. Princ. Morasha Jewish Primary School; Fdr and Pres. Kinloss Community Kollel; learned at Machon Ariel, Jerusalem, where he received his rabbinic ordination (1978-80), Yeshivat Har Etzion (1976-8), Yeshivat Kerem B'Yavneh (1973-6).

Add Finchley Synagogue, Kinloss Gardens, London N3 3DU

Tel 020 8346 8551 *Fax* 020 8349 1579

Email rabbi@kinloss.org.uk *Website* www.kinloss.org.uk

MIRVIS, Chief Rabbi Ephraim Yitzchak, BA.

b. Johannesburg, Sept. 7, 1956; m. Valerie née Kaplan; Chief Rabbi of the United Hebrew Congregations of the Commonwealth (2013-); Rabbi, Finchley Synagogue (1996-2013); Chaplain to the Mayor, London Borough of Barnet (2006-07); Chaplain to the Mayor, London Borough of Redbridge (2004-05); Mem. Chief Rabbi's Cabinet; Ed. Daf Hashavua (2001-06); Ch. Rabbinical Council of the US (1999-2002); M. Western Marble Arch Synagogue (1992-96); form. Chief Rabbi, Jewish Communities of Ireland (1984-92); M. Dublin Hebrew Congregation (1982-84); Lecturer Machon Meir, Jerusalem (1980-82); Mem. Standing Cttee. of Conference of European Rabbis; Religious Adv. to the Jewish Marriage Council; Dir. Kinloss Learning Centre; Dir. Kinloss Kollel; H. Princ. Morasha Jewish Primary School.

Add Office of the Chief Rabbi, 305 Ballards Lane, London N12 8GB

Tel 020 8343 6301 *Fax* 020 8343 6310

Email info@chiefrabbi.org *Website* www.chiefrabbi.org

MITCHELL, Lord Parry Andrew, (Baron Mitchell of Hampstead), B.Sc. (London), MBA (Columbia).

b. London, May 6, 1943; m. Hannah née Lowy; Ch. Coexistence Trust (2008-); Ch. eLearning Foundation (2006-); Ch. Weizmann UK (2006-); Mem. House of Lords Select Cttee. for Science and Technology; T. Genesis Research Trust; T. Lowy Mitchell Foundation.

Add House of Lords, London SW1A 0PW

Tel 020 7433 3238

Email parrym@mac.com

MOONMAN, Eric, OBE, FRSA, M.Sc.

b. Liverpool, Apr. 29, 1929; m. Gillian Louise née Mayer; Adv. IRN Counter-Terrorism; Snr. Fel. Inter-University Centre for Terrorism, Washington, USA; Pres. Zionist Federation (2001-); Ch. Academic Response to Racism and Antisemitism (1994-2005); Ch. Friends Natural History Museum (2007-11); Ch. ERG Group of Radio Stations (1991-2002); (seconded) Ch. WJC Europe Branch Cttee. on Antisemitism (1998-2002, 1985-92); V. Pres. Board of Deputies (1994-2000), Snr. V. Pres. (1985-91); Ch. National Aliyah and Volunteers Council (1975-99); CRE Award for Multi-Racial Service (1996); Ch. Community Research Unit, (1985-96); Hon. Pres. Friends of Union of Jewish Students (1990-95); Dir. Natural History Museum Dev. Trust (1989-91); MP (Lab.) for Basildon (1974-9), for Billericay (1966-70); Ch. Media Network; Prof. Health Management, City University, London; T. Balfour Trust; Tru. Everton Former Players Foundation. Publ.: Learning to Live with the Violent Society (2004); The Alternative Government; The Manager and the Organisation; Reluctant Partnership; European Science and Technology, etc.

Add 1 Beacon Hill N7 9LY

MORGENSTERN, Philip Louis, BA.

b. London, Jan. 15, 1932; m. Estelle Pamela née Erenberg; Solicitor; Ch. Institute of Jewish Studies (1999-2013, Emer. Pres. 2013-); Dir. Jewish Law Publication Fund (1990-2012);

Dir. Kessler Foundation 1993-2011); Partner, Nicholson Graham & Jones (1962-95); Freeman, City of London.

Add 7 Princes Close, Edgware, Middlesex HA8 7QB

Tel 020 3271 0035

Email plmorgen@gmail.com

MORRIS, Henry,

b. London, Mar. 5, 1921; Pres. Jewish Military Museum; form. Ch. Jewish Defence and Group Relations Cttee. Jewish Board of Deputies; V. Pres. (National. Ch. 1979-81), AJEX. Publ.: We Will Remember Them (1989, Addendum 1994, 2nd Edition 2011); The AJEX Chronicles: A History of the Association (2000).

Add 4 Ashbrook, Stonegrove, Edgware, Middlesex HA8 7SU

Tel 020 8958 7154

MORRIS, Simon, CQSW (Certificate of qualification in Social Work), BA Hons Sociology and Applied Social Studies (Keele University), MBA (Henley/Brunel).

b. June 4, 1960; m. Lucille née Balcombe; Chief Exec. Jewish Care; form. Dir. of Community Services, Jewish Care (1999-2003); Assistant Dir. Community Services, Jewish Care (1996-99); London Borough of Hounslow, Commissions Manager Adult Services (1994-96), Team Manager Community (1988-94).

Add Jewish Care, Amélie House, Maurice and Vivienne Wohl Campus, 221 Golders Green Road, London NW11 9DQ

Tel 020 8922 2000 *Fax* 020 8458 7802

Email smorris@jcare.org

MOSES, Jennifer,

Est. ARK children's charity (2002); form. Special Adv. British PM; form. Chief Exec. Centreforum (think tank); Gov. King Solomon Academy; Acland Burghley School; JCC.

Add ARK, 15 Adam Street, London WC2N 6AH

Tel 020 7395 2050

Email info@arkonline.org

MOSS, Stephen David, CBE, LLB, MBA.

b. London, September 13, 1952; m. Joy Rochelle née Berger; read Law at King's College, London, Gray's Inn and MBA at London Business School; Ch. Grosvenor Securities; Ch. Bonasystems Europe; Fdr. and Ch. Springboard Charity; T. People 1st, the Sector Skills Council for hospitality, leisure travel and tourism; Tru. Institute of Jewish Policy Research; T. Jewish Child's Day; Tru. JCOSS; Ch. (2002-05); Pres. West London Synagogue (2011-); Ch. (2008-11), Jt. T. (2005-), Reform Judaism.

Add 28 Bolton Street, London W1J 8BP

Email stephen@stephenmoss.co.uk *Website* www.stephenmoss.co.uk

MYERS, Bernie,

b. Apr. 2, 1944; m. Sandra; Mem. Jewish Leadership Council; Ch. Norwood; Dir. Rothschild Group companies; form. Dir. Moss Bros Group PLC; Dir. Industrial Dwellings Society (1885) Ltd; form. V. Ch. British Friends of the Hebrew University; form. Ch. Harrow Citizens Advice Bureau; T. Grief Encounter.

Add Norwood, Broadway House, 80/82 The Broadway, Stanmore, Middlesex HA7 4HB

Email bernie.myers@rothschild.com

NAGLER, Neville Anthony, OBE, MA (Cantab).

b. London, Jan. 2, 1945; m. Judy née Mordant; Exec. Dir. Taxation Disciplinary Bd. (2007-); form. Dir. Gen. Board of Deputies (1991-2005); Certificate in Public Services Management (2000); form. Assistant Sec. Home Office (1980-91); Fin. Representative and Warden, Pinner Synagogue (1979-91); Ch. Council of Europe Drug Co-op Group (1984-88); UK Representative to UN Narcotics Commission, (1983-88); Haldane Essay Prize (1979); Pte. Sec. Chancellor of Exchequer (1971); Lord Chancellor's Adv. Cttee. for Justices of the Peace for West London; V. Ch. Investigation Cttee. CIMA (Chartered Inst. of Management

Accountants); form. Dir. Sternberg Fund; form. V. Ch. Inter-Faith Network; Principal H.M. Treasury.

Add 24 Dawlish Drive, Pinner HA5 5LN

Tel 020 8868 3103

Email n.nagler@btinternet.com

NATHAN, Clemens Neumann, CTexFTI, FRAI, Officers' Cross, Austria; Cavalieri, al Merito della Repub. Italiana.

b. Hamburg, Aug. 24, 1933; Company Dir.; Society of Heshaim, Spanish and Portuguese Jews Congregation, London (1979-), Bd. of Elders (1977-83); Companionship of the Textile Institute (2007); form. Ch. Centre for Christian–Jewish Studies, Cambridge (1998-2004); V. Pres. Anglo-Jewish Association (Pres. 1983-9, T. 1965-71); CCJ, Fdr. Mem. International Cttee. for Human Rights in Soviet Union (1966); Jt. Ch. Consultant Council of Jewish Organisations (Non-Govt. Organisation at United Nations); Hon. Fel. Shenkar College, Israel; Pres. Centre for German-Jewish Studies, Sussex; Hon. Fel. SSEES, University London; Dir. Sephardi Centre; Textile Institute Medal for services to the Industry and Institute. Publ.: The Changing Face of Religion and Human Rights (2009); Technological, Marketing and Human Rights Works.

Add Flat 10, 3 Cambridge Terrace, London NW1 4JL

Tel 020 7034 1980

NEUBERGER, Lord David Edmund, Baron of Abbotsbury,, P.C. MA.

b. January 10, 1948, m. Angela Holdsworth; Lawyer; Pres. Supreme Court (2012-); Master of the Rolls (2009-12); Ch. Schizophrenia Trust (2003-); Ch. Adv. Cttee. on Spoliation of Art during the Holocaust (1999-2012); Gov. University of the Arts London (2000-10); Lord of Appeal in Ordinary (2007-09); Lord Justice of Appeal (2004-07); Supervisory Chancery Judge, Midland Wales and Chester (2001-04); High Court Judge, Chancery Division (1996); Recorder (1990-96); Queen's Counsel (1987); Called to Bar, Lincolns Inn (1974); Mem. Privy Council.

Add Supreme Court of the United Kingdom, Parliament Square, London SW1P 3BD

Email jackie.sears@supremecourt.gsi.gov.uk *Website* www.supremecourt.gov.uk

NEUBERGER, Rabbi Dame Julia Babette Sarah (née Schwab), Baroness, DBE, MA (Cantab), H. Doctorates University Humberside, Ulster, City, Stirling, Oxford Brookes, Teesside, Nottingham, Open University, Queens Belfast, Sheffield Hallam, Aberdeen, Liverpool, London, Southampton.

b. London, Feb. 27, 1950; m. Anthony; Ch. Review of the Liverpool Care Pathway (2013-); Tru. Van Leer Foundation (2012-); Snr. Rabbi, West London Synagogue (2011-); Ch. One Housing Group (2009-12); Ch. Responsible Gambling Strategy Bd. (2009-11); T. Booker Prize Foundation (2003-10); T. New Philanthropy Capital (2007-11); T. Jewish Care (2009-11, 2005-07); Ch. Adv. Panel on Judicial Diversity (2009-10); Vis. Prof. Bloomberg Ch. Harvard (2006); T. Imperial War Museum (1999-2006); Chief Exec. The King's Fund (1997-2004); Civil Service Commissioner (2001-2); Chancellor, University Ulster (1994-2000); Rabbi, S. London Liberal Synagogue (1977-89); Lecturer, Leo Baeck College; Hon. Fel. Roy College Physicians; Hon. Fel. Royal College GPs, Royal College Psychiatrists. Among recent publications: Is That All There Is? (2011); Not Dead Yet: a Manifesto for Old Age (2008); The Moral State We're In (2005); Caring for Dying Patients of Different Faiths (3rd edition 2004); Dying Well: A Guide to Enabling a Good Death (2nd ed, 2004); Hidden Assets: Decision Making in the NHS (Jt. Ed. 2002); (Jt. Ed. with Canon John White, 1995), On Being Jewish (1995).

Add West London Synagogue, 33 Seymour Place, London

Tel 020 7535 0255

Email julia.neuberger@wls.org.uk *Website* www.wls.org.uk

NEUFELD, Edgar, OBE, BSc, PhD, CPhys, FBCS, CEng, FRSA.

b. Vienna, Apr. 18, 1933; m. Sue Robinson; Ch. Governing Body, Park View Academy (1999-2006); H. Doctorate, Middlesex University (2003), Pro. Chancellor (2000), Ch. Bd. of Governors (1991-96); Ch. Haringey Employment Commission Report (1997); Group Dir.

IBM Europe (1987-89), IBM UK (1961-89); Ch. Governors, Haringey Sixth Form Centre; T. and V. Ch. Shelter; Founding Ch. North London Cultural Diversity Forum; T. Finsbury Park Community Trust.

Add 32 Bancroft Avenue, London N2 0AS

Email neufeld@blueyonder.co.uk

NEWMAN, Aubrey Norris, MA (Glasgow), MA, D.Phil (Oxon), FRHistS.

b. London, Dec. 14, 1927; m. Bernice Freda née Gould; Prof. (Emer.) of History, Leicester University; Pres. Jewish Historical Society (1977-79, 1992-93); form. Pres. Leicester Hebrew Congregation. Publ.: Jewish Migration to South Africa (Jt. Ed. 2006); The Holocaust (2002); Patterns of Migration, 1850-1914 (Jt Ed. 1996); The History of the Board of Deputies (1985); The Jewish East End, 1840-1939 (Ed. 1981); The US, 1870-1970 (1977); Provincial Jewry in Victorian Britain (Ed. 1975); Migration and Settlement (Ed. 1970); The Stanhopes of Chevening (1970).

Add 33 Stanley Road, Stoneygate, Leicester LE2 1RF

Tel 0116 270 4065 (home) *Fax* 0116 252 3986

Email new@le.ac.uk

NEWMAN, Eddy,

b. Liverpool, May 14, 1953. Councillor Woodhouse Park (Lab); Manchester City Councillor (1979-85, 2002-); Mem. of the European Parliament's Delegation for Relations with Israel and the Knesset (1994-99); Labour MEP for Greater Manchester Central (1984-99); Ch. European Parliament Cttee. on Petitions (1994-97); V. Ch. Cttee. on Petitions (1997-99); V. Ch. European Parliament Regional Policy and Regional Planning Cttee (1984-87); Ch. Wythenshaw Community Housing Group; Ch. Manchester City Council's Health Scrutiny Cttee. Publ.: Contributor to 'The European Ombudsmen' (2005).

Add 234 Ryebank Road, Manchester M21 9LU

Tel 0161 881 8147

Website cllr.e.newman

NEWMAN, Rabbi Jeffrey, MA (Oxon.).

b. Reading, Dec. 26, 1941; m. Bracha; Emer. form Rabbi, Finchley Reform Synagogue (1973-2001); Ed. Living Judaism (1969-73); Dir. Earth Charter UK; form. Ch. Rabbinic In-service training, Leo Baeck Rabbinical College (LBC); form. Ch. Pastoral Skills and Counselling Department LBC; form. Ch. of Tru. Israel Palestine Centre for Research and Information; Lecturer in Heimler Training; contributor to various journals on Judaism, psychology, spirituality and Earthcharter.

Add 46 Torrington Park, London N12 9TP

Email jeffrey@jnewman.org.uk

NEWMAN, Dr Joanna Frances, BA (hons), MA in Jewish History (UCL), PhD (Southampton).

b. London; m. Uwe Westphal; Dir. UK Higher Education International and Europe Unit, Universities UK (2011-); Civil Servant; Hon. S. JHSE (2007-); Hd. Higher Education, British Library (2007-11); Exec. Dir. Arts and Education, London Jewish Cultural Centre (2002-2006); Bd. Mem. Artsdepot; V. Ch. Centre for German-Jewish Studies, University Sussex; Hon. Fel. University Southampton; Postdoctoral Fel. Institute of Commonwealth Studies; Mem. Council, Wiener Library; Parkes Fel. (Southampton). Publ.: (Ed. with Toby Haggith) Holocaust and the Moving Image: Representation in Film and Television Since 1993 (2005).

Add The British Library, 96 Euston Road, London NW1 2DB

Email info@Universitiesuk.ac.uk

NEWMAN, Lotte Therese, CBE, MB, BS, LRCP, MRCS, FRCGP FRNZCGP.

b. Frankfurt am Main, Jan. 22, 1929; m. Norman Aronsohn, 1959; form. posts held General Practitioner; Ch. of Circumcision Working Group (1999-2005); Mem. Board of Deputies (1999-2005); Mem. Hampstead Synagogue Board of Management (1999-2005); Medical Adv. St John Ambulance (1999-2003); Pres. London Jewish Medical Society (1998-99); Gov. PPP Medical Trust (1996-99); Ch. Registration Cttee. General Medical Council (1997-98); Mem. GMC (1984-98); Pres. Royal College General Practitioners (1994-97); Freeman,

City of London; Mem. Defence Group Relations Cttee. Publ.: Papers on Medicine, health and medical training issues especially relating to women doctors, and 'medicine and the Jews'.

Add The White House, 1 Ardwick Road, London NW2 2BX

Tel 020 7436 6630 *Fax* 020 7435 6672

Email JH44@dial.pipex.com

NEWMAN, Colonel Martin, DL, FCIPR.

b. Prestbury, Sept. 26, 1947; m. Lisa Chernin; Public relations consultant; Pres. United Synagogue, Manchester, Mead Hill Shul (2012-); Colonel Cmdt Gibraltar Cadet Force (2012-); Dept. Lieutenant of Greater Manchester (2009); Mem. Management and Trustees Cttee. Fusiliers Museum Lancashire (2007-); Tru. and V. Pres. Friends of Jewish Servicemen and Women (2006-); Ch. Jewish Committee, HM Forces (2007-); Colonel Special Advisor MOD Youth Policy Unit (2002-09); Lt. Col. CO ACF PR Unit (1994-2002); NW Regional Ch. Inst. of Public Relations (1994-96); Major TA Pool of Public Information Officers (1986-2004); Commissioned TA Gen List (ACF) 1975; Ed. Menorah magazine.

Add 12 Conisborough Place, Whitefield, Manchester M45 6EJ

Email martin.newman@armymail.mod.uk

NEWMARK, Brooks Philip Victor, MP.

b. Norwalk, Connecticut, May 8, 1958; m. Lucy née Keegan; Businessman; Govt. Whip (Office of the Deputy Prime Minister and Dept. for International Development (2011-12)); Dir. Fdr. 'A Partner in Education' (2010-); Business, Innovation and Skills, Wales Office (2010-11); Opposition Whip (Foreign Affairs 2009-10, Treasury 2007-09); Co-Ch. Conservative Party 'Women2Win' (2006-); Dir. Harvard University Alumni Association (2005-); MP (Cons.), for Braintree (2005-); Mem. Treasury Sect Cttee. (2006-07, 2012-); Mem. Science and Technology Sect Cttee. (2005-07); Partner, Apollo LP (1998-05); Ch. Southwark and Bermondsey Conservative Association (1990-93). Publ.: The Price of Irresponsibility (CPS, 2008); Simply Red: The True State of the Public Finances (CPS, 2006); Direct Democracy: an Agenda for a New Model Party (2005).

Add House of Commons, London SW1A 0AA

Tel 020 7219 3464

Website www.brooksnewmark.com

NEWMARK, Jeremy, MCIPR.

b. Hertfordshire, Sept. 19, 1972; m. Hilary née Cawson; Mem. Steering Group and Ch. Global Coalition for Israel (2010-); Tru. Ebor Eruv Trust (2010-); Ch. 'Salute to Israel' Group (2008-); Mem. JLC School's Strategy Implementation Group (2008-); Mem. Bd. Directors, European Institute for the Study of Antisemitism (2007-); Mem. Government Interdepartmental Task Force on Antisemitism (2007-); Chief Exec. Jewish Leadership Council (2006-13); Mem. BBC Standing Conference on Religions and Faith (2010); Dir. Antisemitism Co-ordination Unit (2004-06); Mem. Gov. Review Panel - 'Working with Faith Communities' (2003-04); Director of Communications, Office of the Chief Rabbi (1999-2004); Chief Media Officer, Israel 50 (UK) (1999); International Affairs Officer, Board of Deputies (1997-99); Campaigns Organiser, UJS (1995-96); Man. Council Fair Play Campaign Group; Jt. Hd. Stop the Boycott; form. T. Anglo-Israel Association; form. Man. Council, Searchlight Education Trust.

Email info@eboreruv.org

NOE, Leo,

T. Kisharon; T. Seed; Ch. F&C; REIT Asset Management; V. Pres. and Tru. Jewish Leadership Council; Ch. Board of Deputies; Jt. Ch. Joint Liaison Group; Fdr. Lee Baron Commercial Limited, property consultants; Chief Exec. Bourne End Properties PLC 1989-97).

Add c/o 6 Bloomsbury Square, London WC1A 2LP

Tel 020 7242 9734 *Fax* 020 7099 5897

Email info@thejlc.org

OPPENHEIM-BARNES, Sally, Baroness of Gloucester, PC.
b. Dublin, July 26, 1930; Non-Exec. Dir. HFC Bank (1989-98); Dir. (non-exec.) Robert Fleming (1989-97); Non-Exec. Dir. Boots (1983-94); Ch. National Consumer Council (1987-89); MP (Conservative) for Gloucester (1970-87); M. of State, Consumer Affairs (1979-83); Mem. Shadow Cabinet (1974-79); form. Ch. Conservative Party Parl. Prices and Consumer Protection Cttee.; form. National V. Pres. National Union of Townswomen's Guilds; form. National V. Pres. ROSPA.
Add House of Lords, London SW1 0AA

OPPENHEIMER, Peter Morris, MA.
b. London, Apr. 16, 1938; Pres. Oxford Centre for Hebrew and Jewish Studies (2000-8); Dir. Jewish Chronicle Ltd (1986-2006), Ch. (2001-4); Delbanco, Meyer and Co. Ltd. (1987-2001); Dir. Dixons plc (1987-93); Chief Economist, Shell International Petroleum Co. (1985-6); Student (Fel.) Emer. Christ Church Oxford.
Add Christ Church, Oxford OX1 1DP
Tel 01865 558 226 *Fax* 01865 516 834
Email peter.oppenheimer@chch.ox.ac.uk

OZIN, Malcolm John, MBE.
b. London, Nov. 14, 1934; Pres. Jewish Blind and Disabled; T. Cecil Rosen Foundation; Hon. S. Cavendish Housing Trust Ltd.
Add 35 Langstone Way, London NW7 1GT
Tel 020 8371 6611 *Fax* 020 8371 4225
Email mjo@manninggroup.co.uk

PACK, Stephen Howard John, MSc (Finance), BSc.
b. London, Apr. 26, 1950; m. Cheryl née Klyne; Chartered Accountant; Pres. United Synagogue (July 2011-); Tru. United Synagogue (2002-); Ch. Remuneration; Pres. Hadley Wood Association (2001-); Partner, Price Waterhouse (1984-), Dir. I/C operations for the audit practice and London office, Head of Risk and Quality for the UK firm; US Rep. JLE cttee. dealing with Jewish Education; T. Chief Rabbinate Trust; Life Pres. Hadley Wood Jewish Community; form. Ch. Cockfosters Shul.
Add United Synagogue, 305 Ballard's Lane, London N12 8GB
Tel 020 343 8989
Email president@theus.org.uk *Website* www.theus.org.uk

PADWA, Rabbi Ephraim,
Hd. Beth Din of the Union of Orthodox Hebrew Congregations.
Add Union of Orthodox Hebrew Congregations, 140 Stamford Hill, London N16 6QT
Tel 020 8802 6226

PADWA, Joseph,
Dayan, Beth Din of the Union of Orthodox Hebrew Congregations (2000-).
Add UOHC, 140 Stamford Hill N16 6QT
Tel 020 8802 6226

PAISNER, Harold Michael, BA (Oxon).
b. London, June 4, 1939; m. Judith née Rechtman; Solicitor; Snr. Partner of Berwin Leighton Paisner LLP; Mem. of the Paris Bar pursuant to European Directive 98/5/CE; H. Mem. of the Lithuanian Bar; form. UK National Pres. Union Internationale des Avocats; Mem. International Issues Cttee. the Law Society, the International Bar Association, the British Baltic Lawyers Association and the American Bar Association; Directorships, Interface, Inc.; Puma High Income VCT plc.; Ch. The Institute of Jewish Policy Research and Ben Gurion University Foundation; Gov. Ben Gurion University of the Negev.
Add 16 Ilchester Place, London W14 8AA
Email Harold.paisner@blplaw.com

PAISNER, Martin David, CBE, MA (Oxon), LLM (Ann Arbor, Michigan).

b. Windsor, Berks., Sept. 1, 1943; m. Susan Sarah née Spence; Solicitor; Partner, Berwin Leighton Paisner Solicitors; Ch. The Jerusalem Foundation (1997-2010); Ch. Weizmann UK; Ch. Myers JDC Brookdale Institute; Bd. Mem. – The American Jewish Joint Distribution Cttee. Inc; Oxford Centre for Hebrew and Jewish Studies, Shaare Zedek UK; Holocaust Educational Trust; Ovarian Cancer Action; The Royal Free Cancerkin Breast Cancer Trust, British Library Trust; Governor, Weizmann Institute of Science; Hon. Fel. Queen Mary, University of London; Worcester College; Oxford; King's College, London and IDC Herzliya; H. Doctorate, University of Glasgow; Hon. PhD Weizmann (2011).

Add 4 Heath Drive, Hampstead, London NW3 7SY

PANNICK, Lord David, QC, MA, BCL.

b. London, Mar. 7, 1956; m. Nathalie née Trager-Lewis; Barrister; Mem. House of Lords (2008-); QC 1992; Deputy High Court Judge (1998); Recorder, South Eastern Circuit (1995); Queen's Counsel (1992); Junior Counsel to the Crown in Common Law (1988-92); called to the Bar, Gray's Inn (1979). Publ.: Human Rights Law and Practice (3rd edition, 2009).

Add Blackstone Chambers, Blackstone House, Temple, London EC4Y 9BW

Tel 020 7583 1770

Email davidpannick@blackstonechambers.com

PASCAL, Julia, BA (Hons) (London), M.Phil (University of York).

m. Alain Carpentier; Playwright/Theatre Director; Dir. Pascal Theatre Co.; Leverhulme writer-in-Residence, Wiener Library (2007-); Artistic Dir. Pascal Theatre Co. (1983-2009); Nesta Dream Time Fellowship (2006); Theatre Dir. National Theatre (1978); Prima Ballerina Assoluta in Virago's 'Truth, Dare or Promise' and Boxtree's 'Memoirs of a Jewish Childhood'. Plays include: Nineveh (2013); Honeypot (2011); The Merchant of Venice (2007); Crossing Jerusalem (2003); The Golem (2002); Woman in the Moon (2001); 20/20 for Amici Dance Theatre (2000); London Continental (2000); The Yiddish Queen Lear (1999); Elegy for Amici Dance Theatre Co. Other publ. include: Political Plays (2013); The Shylock Play (2007); Crossing Jerusalem (2002); The Holocaust Trilogy (2000).

Add c/o United Agents, 120, Lexington Street, London W1F 0LE

Tel 020 3214 0800 *Fax* 020 3214 0801

Email juliapascal7@gmail.com *Website* www.juliapascal.org

PAUL, Geoffrey D, OBE, FRSA.

b. Liverpool, Mar. 26, 1929; Dir. Anglo-Israel Association (2001-3); American Affairs Ed. Jewish Chronicle (1991-96), Ed. (1977-90).

Add 1 Carlton Close, West Heath Road NW3 7UA

Tel 020 8458 6948

Email infoman@btinternet.com

PEPPER, Sir Michael, Kt., BSc, MA, PhD, ScD, Hon D.Sc, FREng, FRS.

b. London, Aug. 10, 1942, m. Jeannette; Prof. Nanoelectronics, University College London; Emer. Physics Prof. Cambridge University; Fel. Trinity College; Warren Research Fel. Royal Society (1978-86); Vis. Prof. Bar-Ilan University (1984).

Email michael.pepper@ucl.ac.uk

PEPYS, Prof., Sir Mark Brian, Kt, MD, PhD, FRCP, FRCPath, FRS, FMedSci.

b. Sept. 18, 1944; m. Dr Elizabeth Olga Winternitz; Fdr. National Health Service National Amyloidosis Centre; Emer. Prof. of Medicine, University College London; Dir. Wolfson Drug Discovery Unit; H. Consultant Physician, Royal Free Hospital, London; form. Hd. Division of Medicine, Royal Free Campus, UCL (1999-2011); International Society for Amyloidosis: Mandema Memorial Lecturer (2012); UCL Business Award (2011); Dundee University: Adam Neville Lecture (2010); Medical Research Society: Gordon Cumming Memorial Lecturer (2010); Michael Feiwel Lecturer (2010); Academy of Medical Sciences: Keynote Lecturer (2009); Royal Society of Medicine: Richard Kovacs Lecturer (2009); Imperial College: Ernst Chain Prize and Lecture (2008); Royal Society of London:

GlaxoSmithKline Prize and Lecture (2007); Royal College of Physicians: Harveian Orator (2007); Israel Society for Rheumatology: Gerald Loewi Memorial Lecturer (2004); Fel. Imperial College Faculty of Medicine (2004), UCL (2003); American Society of Nephrology: State of the Art Lecturer (2003); British Society for Rheumatology: Heberden Medallist and Orator (2002); Renal Association: Chandos Lecturer (2000); Prof. of Immunological Medicine, Royal Postgraduate School (1984-99).

Add 22 Wildwood Road, London NW11 6TE

Tel 020 8455 9387

Email mbpepys@aol.com *Website* www.ucl.ac.uk/medicine/amyloidosis

PERL, Benjamin, MBE.

b. Jan. 27, 1945; m. Dr. Shoshana Perl; Ch. The Huntingdon Foundation (2008-); H. Pres. Yavneh College, Borehamwood; Morasha Primary School, Finchley; Beis Yaakov Primary School, Colindale; BNOS Primary School, Kingsbury; T. JNF; Founding Mem. Beth Jacob Primary School, Colindale; Moriah Primary School, Pinner; Nancy Rubin Primary School, Hendon; Torah Vodaath Primary School, Golders Green; Morasha Primary School, Finchley; Noam Primary School, Wembley; Hertsmere Primary School, Borehamwood.

Add 35-37 Brent Street, Hendon, London NW4 2EF

Email bperl@sixtrees.co.uk

PERLMAN, Suzanne,

Prize winning artist; Officer of the Royal Order of Oranje Nassau; Hon. Fel. Israel Museum; Patron, Hebrew University, Jerusalem; Ch. Women's Group; British Friends of Hebrew University; WIZO International Rebecca Sieff Prize, Israel; Freeman of the City of London. Works of Art - Permanent Collections: London, England, Museum of London; House of Lords; Ben Uri Gallery; House of Orange Nassau, The Netherlands; Mikve Israel Jewish Cultural Historical Museum, Curacao; Museum of Fine Arts, Willemstad, Netherlands Antilles; Galleria Bellas Artes and Instituto Bolkivariana, Caracas, Venezuela; Joods Historisch Museum, Amsterdam, The Netherlands; Jewish Museum, Budapest, Hungary.

Add Chancery House, 53-64 Chancery Lane, London WC2A 1QS

PERSOFF, Dr Meir, JP, MA, PhD, FRHistS, FRSA.

b. Letchworth, Aug. 25, 1941; Jewish Chronicle, Judaism Ed. Saleroom Ed. (1981-2000), Features Ed. (1976-90), Arts Ed. (1980-85), News Ed. (1974-76); Pres. Israel-Judaica Philatelic Society; form. Publ. Cttee. Jewish Marriage Council; Silver Medallist, international philatelic exhibitions, Jerusalem, London, Stockholm, Pretoria, Paris, Madrid. Among recent Publications: Hats in the Ring: Choosing Britain's Chief Rabbis from Adler to Sacks (2013); Another Way, Another Time: Religious Inclusivism and the Sacks Chief Rabbinate (2010); Faith Against Reason: Religious Reform and the British Chief Rabbinate, 1840-1990 (2008); Immanuel Jakobovits: a Prophet in Israel (2002) etc.

Add 14 Hanassi Str., P.O. Box 4130, Jerusalem 91041, Israel

Tel +972 (02) 623 5834

Email meir-per@013.net

PESTON, Robert,

b. Apr. 25, 1960; m. Sian Busby (dec'd 2012); Business Ed. BBC News (2006-); Fdr. Speakers for Schools (2011); City Ed. The Sunday Telegraph (2002-05); Political, Financial Ed. Financial Times (1991-2000); Journalist, The Independent (1986-90); Investors Chronicle (1983-86). Awards: Harold Wincott Snr. Financial Journalist of the Year Award (2005); Royal Television Society Scoop of the Year (2007); Broadcasting Press Guild, Best Performer in Non-Acting Role (2008); Royal Television Society Journalist of the Year, Specialist Journalist of the Year, Scoop of the Year (2008); London Press Club: Business Journalist of the Year (2008). Publ.: How Do We Fix This Mess (2012); Who Runs Britain? (2008); Brown's Britain (2005).

Add Rm 4220, Television Centre, Wood Lane W12 7RJ

Tel 020 8576 4433

Email peston@gmail.com *Website* www.bbc.co.uk/robertpeston

PHILLIPS, Karen, MBE, DL.

b. Aug. 15, 1951; Chief Exec. The Fed (2009-) (The Federation of Jewish Services, 1997-2009); Dir. Manchester Jewish Social Services (1995-97), Social Services Manager (1993-95); Probation Off. Salford Probation Service (1987-93); Area Manager, Trafford and South Manchester, Chest, Heart and Stroke Association (1980-87).

Add The Fed, Heathland Village, Heathland Drive, Prestwich, Manchester M25 9SB

Tel 0161 772 4800 *Fax* 0161 772 4934

Email info@thefed.org.uk *Website* www.thefed.org.uk

PHILLIPS, Melanie, BA.

b. June 4, 1951; m. Joshua Rufus Rozenberg; Pulbisher and Ed-in-Chief, emBooks; Columnist, Daily Mail (2001-), Sunday Times (1998–2001), Observer (1993–98); News Ed. Guardian (1984–87), Leader Writer (1980–84), Social Services Corres. (1978–80), Reporter (1977). Publ.: Guardian Angel: My Story, My Britain (2013); The World Turned Upside Down: The Global Battle Over God, Truth and Power (2010); Londonistan (2007); The Ascent of Woman (2003); All Must Have Prizes (1996).

Add c/o Daily Mail, Northcliffe House, 2 Derry Street W8 5TT

Tel 020 7938 6000

Email melanie@embooks.com *Website* www.embooks.com

PINNICK, Jeffrey, FCA.

b. London, Dec. 6, 1935; H. Tru. All Aboard Shops (1987-), H. Ch. (2008-12), Hon. T. (1987-2008); H. Ch. Yad Vashem UK Foundation (2004-09); H. Ch. British Friends of Boys Town, Jerusalem (2000-08); Hon. T. Board of Deputies (1985-91).

Add Stella Lucas House, 105 High Street, Edgware HA8 7DB

Tel 020 8381 1717

Email community@allaboardshops.com *Website* www.allaboardshops.com

PINTER, Rabbi Abraham (Avraham),

b. Jan. 21, 1949; m. Rachel; Dean, Beer Miriam Seminary (2008-); Ch. Chizuk (1996-); Principal, Yesodey Hatorah Schools (1994-); T. Union of Orthodox Hebrew Congregations (1990-); Mem. (Lab) Hackney BC (1982–90); V. Ch. Ezer Leyoldos (Children and Families).

Add 6 Northdene Gardens N15 6LX

Tel 020 8826 5500 *Fax* 020 8826 5505

Email yeshatorah@aol.com

PLANCEY, Rabbi Alan,

b. Edinburgh, Oct. 30, 1941; Herts County Councillor (2009-); Associate Jewish Chaplain, London Luton Airport; M. Northwood US (2007-9); Borehamwood and Elstree Synagogue (1976-2007); Ch. Rabbinical Council US (1987-94); Youth M. Hampstead Garden Suburb Synagogue (1970-6); M. Luton Synagogue (1965-9); Mem. Chief Rabbi's Cabinet; H. V. Pres. and Rel. Adv. Jewish Care; Area Chaplain Herts. Police; H. Chaplain JLGB; H. Chaplain Jewish Scouting Adv. Cttee.; Freeman of the City of London.

Add 98 Anthony Road, Borehamwood, Hertfordshire WD6 4NB

Tel 020 8207 3759 *Mobile* 07768 906 627 *Fax* 020 8207 0568

Email alan.plancey@lineone.net

PLASKOW, Rev. Michael Lionel, MBE, LTSC, ALCM.

b. Israel, July 8, 1936; form. Chaplain, Jewish Deaf Association, England; Emer. Chazan, Woodside Park Synagogue; Life Pres. Central Foundation School, Jewish Old Boys Group; Chaplain to the Mayor of Barnet (1999-2000); Freeman City of London (1994); Norman B. Spencer Award for research into Freemasonry (1992). Publ.: The Story of a Community: Woodside Park 1937-1987.

Add 4/4 Nitza Boulevard, 42262 Netanya, Israel

Tel +972 (09) 832 9592

Email michaelplaskow@hotmail.com

PLEN, Matt,

b. London, July 7, 1972; m. Atira née Winchester; Chief Exec. Masorti Judaism (2008-); Founding Gov. Alma Primary School (2012-); Tru. London Citizens (2011-12); Teacher/Lecturer, Conservative Yeshiva and Masorti High School, Jerusalem (2004-8); Snr Educator, Melitz (2000-4).

Add Alexander House, 3 Shakespeare Road, London N3 1XE

Tel 020 8349 6656

Email matt@masorti.org.uk *Website* www.mattplen.blogspot.org.uk

POLAK, Stuart,

Dir. Conservative Friends of Israel (1989-); Education Dir. Board of Deputies (1985); Youth and Community Worker, Edgware (1984); Fdr. Ch. European Friends of Israel; T. Langdon Foundation; T. Yavneh College; Bd. Mem. Europe Near East Forum.

Tel 020 7262 2493 *Fax* 020 7224 8941

POLLOCK, Karen,

Mem. JC Power 100 Panel (2007-); Chief Exec. Holocaust Educational Trust (2002-); Mem. Jewish Human Rights Coalition UK.

Add BCM Box 7892, London WC1N 3XX

Fax 020 7233 0161

Website www.het.org.uk

POLONSKY, Antony, BA (Rand), MA, D.Phil (Oxon), Doc h.c. (Vars), Officer's Cross of the Order of Merit, Poland, Officer's Cross of the Order of Merit of Independent Lithuania.

b. Johannesburg, Sept. 23, 1940, m. Arlene née Glickman; Albert Abramson Prof. of Holocaust Studies at the United States Holocaust Memorial Museum and Brandeis University; V. Pres. Institute for Polish-Jewish Studies, Oxford; V. Pres. American Association for Polish-Jewish Studies, Cambridge, MA. Among recent publications: The Jews in Poland and Russia, Vol III: 1914-2008 (2012), Vol. II: 1881-1914 (2010), Vol. I: 1350-1881 (2010); The Neighbours Respond: the Controversy Over the Jedwabne Massacre (2004); Contemporary Jewish Writing in Poland (Ed. 2001); The Jews in Old Poland (Ed. 1992); The Jews of Warsaw (Ed. 1991); Polish Paradoxes (Ed. 1990); Recent Polish Debates about the Holocaust (1990).

Add 322 Harvard Street, Cambridge, MA 02139 USA

Tel +1 (617) 492 9788 *Fax* +1 (617) 736 2070

Email polonsky@brandeis.edu

POSEN, Felix, BA (John Hopkins University), D.Phil. (H., Hebrew University, Tel Aviv University), H. Fel. (Hebrew University).

b. Berlin, Oct. 24, 1928; m. Jane née Levy; Gov. Emer. and Hon. Fel. Oxford Centre for Hebrew and Jewish Studies; Gov. Hebrew University; T. Institute of Archaeo-metallurgical Studies, University of London; Fdr. Posen Foundation.

Add Flat 6, 7 Sheffield Terrace, London W8 7NG

Tel 020 7313 9521

Email felix@nesop.co.uk *Website* www.posenfoundation.com

POSEN, Michael,

Mem. JC Power 100 Panel (2007); Man. Agudas Israel Community Services; Cttee. and T. Interlink Foundation and Chizuk.

Add 46 Riverside Road, London N15 6DA

Tel 020 8800 6688 *Fax* 020 3240 0110

Email mposen@agudas.org.uk

PRAIS, Sigbert J, M.Com, PhD, ScD (Cantab), H. D.Litt (City), FBA, Hon D.Sc (Birmingham).

b. Frankfurt am Main, Dec. 19, 1928; Economist; Snr. Res. Fel. National Institute of Economic and Social Res. London; form. Ed. Adv. Bd. Jewish Journal of Sociology; Vis. Prof. of Econometrics, City University; form. Hd. Consultant, Board of Deputies Statistical and Demographic Res. Unit; Economist, International Monetary Fund; Adv. on Statistics, Govt. of Israel; Lecturer, Cambridge University. Publ.: Productivity and Industrial Structure; The Evolution of Giant Firms; Analysis of Family Budgets; Productivity, Education and Training, etc.

Add 83 West Heath Road NW3 7TN

Tel 020 8458 4428

PRESTON, Rosalind (née Morris), OBE.

b. London, Dec. 29, 1935; Professional Volunteer; Ch. Jewish Human Rights Coalition UK (2010-); Adv. Bd. Olive Tree Trust (2009-); Pres. Jewish Volunteering Network (2009-); T. Jewish Chronicle (2000-); Ch. Nightingale House (1999-2007, T. 1999-); H. V. Pres. WIZO UK (1993-); Jt. Hon. S. CCJ (1997-2005); form. Pres. The National Council of Women of Great Britain (1988-90); form. Co-Ch. Interfaith Network, UK; form. V. Pres. Board of Deputies.

Add 7 Woodside Close, Stanmore, Middlesex HA7 3AJ

Tel 020 8954 1411 *Fax* 020 8954 6898

Email rpreston@f2s.com

PROSOR, Ron, MA.

b. 1958; m. Hadas; Israeli Ambassador to the United Nations (2011-); Ambassador of Israel to the Court of St. James's (2007-11); Dir. Gen. Israeli Foreign Ministry (2004-2007); Snr. Deputy Dir. Gen. Foreign Ministry (2004), Chief of Staff to the Foreign Minister (2003-04); Deputy Dir. Gen. for Strategic Affairs, Counter-Terrorism and Nuclear Disarmament (2003); M. Counsellor, Political Affairs, Israeli Embassy, Washington DC (1998-2002); Spokesman, Israeli Embassy, London (1995-98); Dir. Operations Center, Foreign Ministry (1993-95); Deputy Dir. European Division, Foreign Ministry (1992-93); Spokesman, Israeli Embassy, Bonn (1988-92).

Add c/o Embassy of Israel, 2 Palace Green, Kensington, London W8 4QB

Email club-sec@london.mfa.gov.il

PULZER, Peter George Julius, MA, B.Sc.(Econ.), PhD.

b. Vienna, May 20, 1929; Grosses Silbernes Ehrenzeichen, Republic Austria (2008);Bundesverdienst Kreuz, Rep. of Germany (2004); Gladstone Prof. Government and Publ. Admin. Fel. All Souls, Oxford (1985-96); Official Student (Fel.) in Politics, Christ Church, Oxford (1962-84). Publ.: The Rise of Political Antisemitism in Germany and Austria; Political Representation and Elections in Britain; Jews and the German State: The Political History of a Minority (1848-1933); German Politics 1945-1995; Germany 1870-1945: Politics, State Formation and War; contributor German Jewish History in Modern Times (Ed. M. Meyer).

Add All Souls College, Oxford OX1 4AL

Tel 01865 559 347 *Fax* 01865 279299

Email peter.pulzer@ntlworld.com

RABINOWITZ, Rabbi Lippa,

b. Manchester, Nov. 15, 1930; Rav, Vine St Synagogue, Manchester; Principal, Manchester Jewish Grammar School; form. Principal, Judith Lady Montefiore College, Ramsgate; Lecturer, Etz Haim Yeshiva, Tangier. Publ.: Eleph Lamateh Chidushim on Sugioth (Israel).

Add 57 Waterpark Road, Salford

RAJAK, Tessa (née Goldsmith), MA, D.Phil(Oxon).

b. London, Aug. 2, 1946, m. Harry Rajak; Classicist and Jewish Historian; Emer. Prof. Ancient History, University Reading; Res. Fel. Somerville College, Oxford; Hon. Vis. Prof. University College, London. Publ.: Translation and Survival: The Greek Bible and the Ancient Jewish Diaspora (2009); The Jewish Dialogue with Greece and Rome; Josephus: the Historian and His Society; Jewish Perspectives on Hellenistic Rulers; Philosophy and Power; The Jews among Pagans and Christians in the Roman Empire.

Add 64 Talbot Road, London N6 4RA

Email tessa.rajak@orinst.ox.ac.uk

RAPHAEL, Frederic Michael, MA (Cantab), FRSL.

b. Chicago, Aug. 14, 1931; Writer. Among recent publications: Non-fiction: Byron; Somerset Maugham; Cracks in the Ice; Of Gods and Men; France: the Four Seasons; The Necessity of Antisemitism; Popper: Historicism and its Poverty; Eyes Wide Open; The Benefits of Doubt (essays), A Spoilt Boy (autobiography); Some Talk of Alexander; Josephus and his Kind; Distant Intimacy (with Joseph Epstein); J. Robert Oppenheimer, For example. Published Screenplays and Drama: Two for the Road; Darling, Oxbridge Blues; Eyes Wide Shut (with Stanley Kubrick). Novels: The Limits of Love; Lindmann; The Glittering Prizes; Fame and Fortune; Final Demands: Short Stories; Sleeps Six; Uxbridge Blues; Think of England. Notebooks: Personal Terms, Rough Copy, Cuts and Bruises; Ifs and Buts; There and Then. Translations: The Satyrica of Petronius; The Poems of Catullus (with Kenneth McLeish); The Plays of Aeschylus; Sophocles' Aias; Euripides' Medea; Bacchae and Hippolytus.

Add Ed Victor Ltd., 6 Bayley Street, London WC1B 3HE

RECHTSCHAFFEN, Shlomo, LLB, LLM, MBA.

b. Israel, Aug. 10, 1975; Solicitor; Co-Fdr. Pantheon India and Pantheon Bond (2010); Bd. Mem. Ramat-Gan Foundation in the UK (2010-); Chief Exec. British Friends of Bar Ilan (2009-); Lectures, Corporate and Commercial Law, University of London (2004-); leading Israeli law firm S. Horowitz & Co. (2001-03) and GKH Law (2001-02); Mem. Israeli Bar and the Law Society of England & Wales (2000-).

Add 109 Baker Street, London W1U 6RP

Tel 020 7486 7394 *Fax* 020 7935 1192

Email shlomo@bfbiu.org

REIF, Stefan, BA, PhD (London), LittD (Cantab).

b. Edinburgh, Jan. 21, 1944; m. Shulamit, d. 2010; Pres. Cambridge Theological Society (2002-04); Pres. British Association for Jewish Studies (1992); Pres. JHSE (1991-92); Fdr. Dir. Taylor-Schechter Genizah Research Unit, Cambridge University Library; Emer. Prof. of Medieval Hebrew Studies Cambridge University; Fel. St John's College, Cambridge; Hon. Fel. Mekize Nirdamim Society, Jerusalem; Adv. Panel, International Society for the Study of Deuteronomical and Cognate Literature; T. Cambridge Traditional Jewish Congregation. Among recent publications: The History and Religious Heritage of Old Cairo (2013); Death in Jewish Life: Burial and Mourning Customs among the Jews in Europe (2013); A Jewish Archive from Old Cairo; Why Medieval Hebrew Studies?; Problems with Prayers; (Ed.) Interpreting the Hebrew Bible; Genizah Research after Ninety Years; The Cambridge Genizah Collections; Cambridge University Library Genizah Series; Charles Taylor and the Genizah.

Add Genizah Research Unit, University Library, Cambridge CB3 9DR

Tel 01223 766 370 *Fax* 01223 333 160

Email scr3@cam.ac.uk

REUBEN, David,

b. Sept. 14, 1938; m. Debra; T. Reuben Brothers Foundation (2002-); Jt. Chief Exec. Officer, Reuben Brothers Ltd (1988-); Ch. Trans World Metals Group (1977–2000).

Add Millbank Tower, 21-24 Millbank, London SW1P 4PQ

Website www.reubenfoundation.com

REUBEN, Simon,

m. Joyce Nounou; T. Reuben Foundation (2002-); Jt. Chief Exec. Officer, Reuben Brothers Ltd (1988-); Dir. and Jt. Principal, Trans-World Metals Group (1977–2000).

Add c/o Reuben Foundation, Millbank Tower, 21-24 Millbank, London SW1P 4PQ

Website www.reubenbrothers.com

RICH, Ben,

b. London, Mar. 29, 1966; m. Rachael Reeves; Communications Consultant for Jewish and other faith organisations; Gov. Avanti House School Harrow.

Add 69 Cecil Park, Pinner, Middlesex HA5 5HL
Email ben.rich@reformjudaism.org.uk *Website* www.reformjudaism.org.uk
Twitter @BenRichMRJ

RICH, Rabbi Danny, BA (Hons) Dip. Crim.

b. London, Mar. 7, 1961; Emer. Rabbi, Kingston Liberal Synagogue (2005-), Rabbi (1989-2005); Founding Ch. Royal Borough of Kingston Interfaith Forum (2005-); Chief Exec. LJ (2005); Dir. Kadimah Summer Camp (1990-2005); Jewish Chaplain to HMP Highdown, Coldingley, Kingston Hospital and Surrey and Borders NHS Trust; Founding Ch. Dittons Council of Christians and Jews. Publ.: Co-author, Zionism: A Jewish Communal Response from the UK (2010); LJ and Mixed Marriage (2004).

Add The Montagu Centre, 21 Maple Street, London W1T 4BE

Tel 020 7631 9830 *Fax* 020 7631 9838

Email d.rich@liberaljudaism.org *Website* www.liberaljudaism.org

RIFKIND, Rt. Hon. Sir Malcolm, MP, QC, PC.

b. Edinburgh, June 21, 1946; MP, Kensington (2010-); Ch. Intelligence and Security Cttee. (2010-); Ch. Standards and Privileges Cttee. (2009-10); MP, Kensington and Chelsea (Con.) (2005-10); form. MP for Edinburgh, Pentlands (Con.) (1974-97); Foreign Secretary (1995-97), Min. of Defence (1992-95), Min. of Transport (1990-92); Sec. of State for Scotland (1986-90), Min. of State Foreign and Commonwealth Office (1983-86); Parl. Under-Sec. of State, FCO (1982-83); Select Cttee. on Overseas Dev. (1978-79); Hon. S. Conservative Friends of Israel Parl. Group (1974-79); Opposition Spokesman on Scottish Affairs (1975-76); Edinburgh Town Council (1970-74).

Add House of Commons, London SW1 0AA

Tel 020 7219 5683 *Fax* 020 7219 4213

RIGAL, Margaret H. (née Lazarus),

b. London, Nov. 28, 1932; Co-Ch. Women's Campaign for Soviet Jewry (the 35s); Pres. Jewish Aged Needy Pension Society; Ch. Jewish Aid Cttee.; Hon. S. London Society of Jews and Christians.

Add 31 St. John's Wood Ct., St. John's Wood Road, London NW8 8QR

Tel 020 7286 4404

Email Margaret.Rigal@gmail.com

RITBLAT, Sir John (Henry), Kt, FRICS, Hon. DLitt London Metropolitan, Hon. DLitt University of Buckingham.

b. Oct. 3, 1935; m. Jillian Rosemary Zilkha; Colliers International (UK) Ltd (2010-12); V. Pres. Seafarers UK (2010), (Hon. Surveyor, 1979-); H. Pres. The British Land Company PLC (2007), (Ch. 1970-2006), (Man. Dir. 1970–2004); Tru. Tate Gallery (2006–); Ch. and Tru. Wallace Collection (2005–); Colliers Conrad Ritblat Erdman (2000–); Ch. Conrad Ritblat Group plc (1993–97); Prince of Wales' Royal Parks Tree Appeal Cttee. (1987–); Mem. Council, Business in the Community (1987–); Olympic Appeal Cttee. 1984, 1988, 1996 and 2000; British Olympic Assoc. (1979); Commander, Crown Estate Paving Commission (1969–), now Commander Emeritus; Fdr. Partner, Conrad Ritblat & Co., Consultant Surveyors and Valuers (1958); Articles with West End firm of Surveyors and Valuers (1952–58).

Add Lansdowne House, Berkeley Square, London W1J 6ER

ROBERG, Rabbi Meir, BA (Hons), MPhil, DipEd.

b. Wurzburg, Germany, June 25, 1937; Dean, Lauder Midrasha, Berlin; Education Consultant to Jewish Schools and Colleges in the CIS and England; Reporting Inspector of Schools in Pikuach; Pres. Association of Head Teachers of Orthodox Schools; form. HM, Hasmonean; Ch. Academic Cttee. Massoret Institute; Dep. HM, Yavneh Grammar School.

Add 19 Sorotzkin Street Jerusalem, Israel

Tel 020 538 6020

Email hineni@zahav.net.il

ROBSON, Jeremy,

b. Llandudno, Sept. 5, 1939; Publisher, J. R. Books Ltd. Publ.: 33 Poems, In Focus (poetry); Poetry anthologies, incl. The Young British Poets (Ed.); Poems from Poetry and Jazz in Concert (Ed.).

Add J.R. Books, 10 Greenland Street, London NW1 0NO

Email jeremyr@jrbooks.com

RODEN, Claudia,

Cookery writer; Contributor, The Jewish Princess; Patron, The Food Chain Charity. Publ.: Arabesque—Sumptuous Food from Morocco, Turkey and Lebanon (2005); The New Book of Middle Eastern Food (2000); The Book of Jewish Food (1997); A Book of Middle Eastern Food (1968).

Add The Food Chain, New North House, 202–208 New North Road, London N1 7BJ

Website www.foodchain.org.uk

RODRIGUES-PEREIRA, Miriam, BA.

b. Manchester, July 4, 1922; Retired Civil Servant; Hon. Archivist, Spanish & Portuguese Jews Congregation, London (1985-). Publ.: Bevis Marks Records (on Genealogy and History) (parts iv 1991, v 1993, vi 1997, co-author/ed.).

Add 22 Latymer Court, Hammersmith Road, London W6 7JD

Tel 020 8748 6298

ROMAIN, Rabbi Jonathan Anidjar, MBE, BA; PhD.

b. London, Aug. 24, 1954; m. Sybil Sheridan; M. Maidenhead Synagogue; Ch. Assembly of Rabbis (2007-09); Ch. Youth Association of Synagogues in Great Britain (1972-74); Dir. Jewish Information and Media Service; Chaplain, Jewish Police Association; form. M. Barkingside Progressive Synagogue. Among recent publications: Tradition and Change, Till Faith Us Do Part, Renewing the Vision, Your God Shall Be My God, Reform Judaism and Modernity; God, Doubt, and Dawkins; Really Useful Prayers; Great Reform Lives; A Passion for Judaism; Signs and Wonders; Royal Jews; The Jews of England.

Add Grenfell Lodge, Ray Park Road, Maidenhead, Berks SL6 8QX

Tel 01628 671 058

RONSON, Dame Gail (née Cohen), DBE.

b. July. 3, 1946; m. Gerald Maurice Ronson; Dep. Pres. (2010-), Dep. Ch (2002-), Bd. Mem. (1992-), Jewish Care; Dep. Ch. Gerald Ronson Foundation (2005–); Dir. Royal Opera House (2001-); Co-Ch. Association for Research into Stammering in Childhood (1991–); T. Royal Opera House Trust (1985–); St Mary's Hospital Save the Baby Fund (1985–96); T. Ronson Foundations (1980–95); T. Home Farm Develt Trust (1991–94); Jt Ch. Council for a Beautiful Israel (1987–94).

Add 4 Bentinck Street, London W1U 2EF

Email gailronson@heron.co.uk

RONSON, Gerald Maurice, CBE, H. PhD (Northumbria).

b. London, May 27, 1939; m. Dame Gail née Cohen; H. Fel. College of Estate (2012); Pres. JCOSS; Fdr. Mem. JLC (2004); Fdr. Mem. Cancer Research Campaign/Imperial Cancer Research Fund, Appeal Cabinet Mem. (2001-); Ch. Liaison Cttee. Office of the Chief Rabbi (2001-); Fdr. Ch. Community Security Trust (1995-); Mem. Major Gift Board Prince's Trust (1986-); Patron, Philip Green Memorial Trust (1985-); Fdr. Ch. Group Relations Educational Trust (1978-); Ch. Trustees, Gerald Ronson Foundation (2005); Gov. London Academy (2004); Patron, Princess Royal Trust for Carers (2003); Ch. Development Council of the Roundhouse (2000); V. Pres. Joint Israel Appeal (1984); V. Pres. NSPCC (1984). Previous positions: Fdr. Ch. of Trustees, The Ronson Foundation; Co-Ch. Chindit Memorial Appeal; V. Pres. Jewish Educational Trust (1976-); Co-Ch. Israel Bonds in the UK (1988-93); Mem. Councils of British Olympic Appeals (1992, 1988); T. Natural History Museum (1987-91); Fdr. Mem. One Per cent Club (1986); Ch. SNAX 24 Corporation Ltd (1996); Fdr. Heron Group (1956). Awards: City AM Personality of the Year Award (2011); Variety Club 'Props' Lifetime Achievement Award (2011); Property Week - Lifetime Achievement Award (2010);

Encomienda de Numero, Order of Civil Merit for services to Spain (2009); H. Doctorate, Northumbria University (2009); Norwood Lifetime Achievement Award (2008); Property Industry Award (2007); Property awards, personality of the Year (2002/2001 and 2000); Variety Club of Great Britain, Entrepreneur of the Year (2000); Hambros Businessman of the Year (1984); "The Director" Award for Excellence (1984); The Inaugural estates Gazette Architecture Award.

Add 4 Bentinck Street, London W1U 2EF

RONSON, Mark Daniel,

b. Sept. 4, 1975; British music producer, artist; Co-Fdr. Allido Records (2004-); BRIT Award Winner (2008); Grammy Award Winner (2008).

Add 19 Mercer Street, 5th Floor New York, NY 10013, USA

Tel +1 (212) 226 7320? *Fax* +1 (212) 226 7346

Website www.markronson.co.uk

ROSE, Aubrey, OBE, CBE, D. University (Hon), FRSA.

b. London, Nov. 1, 1926; Solicitor; Snr. V. Pres. Board of Deputies (1994, 1991); Pres. Indian Jewish Association UK; Pres. Royal British Nurses Assoc.; Commissioner and Dep. Ch. Commission for Racial Equality (CRE); Dep. Ch. British Caribbean Association; T. Project Fullemploy; T. Commonwealth Human Rights Initiative; Mem. Working Group Commonwealth Jewish Council; form. Ch. Defence and Group Rel. Cttee. Board of Deputies; Ch. Working Group on Environment Board of Deputies. Publ.: Sea Olympics (2012); Arieh Handler: Modest Jewish Hero (2010); Jewish Communities in the Commonwealth (CJT); Letters to my Wife (2007); The Rainbow Never Ends (2005); From Bitter Came Sweet (2004, Ed.); The Story of Vera (2001, Ed.); Brief Encounters of a Legal Kind (1997); Journey into Immortality, the Story of David Rose (1997); Judaism and Ecology (1992).

Add 14 Pagitts Grove, Hadley Wood, Hertfordshire EN4 0NT

Tel 020 8449 2166 *Fax* 020 8449 1469

Website www.aubreyrose.co.uk

ROSE, Dinah, QC, BA (Hons) Oxon, Diploma in Law with distinction.

Barrister of the Year, The Lawyer Awards (2009); City University Barrister of the Year (2009); Human Rights Lawyer of the Year, Liberty and Justice Human Rights Awards (2009); Appointed to Silk (2006); Called to Bar, Gray's Inn (1989); Mem. Treasury "A" Panel; Mem. New North London Synagogue; T. Responsibility; Regular lecturer on public law, human rights and employment law.

Add Blackstone Chambers, Blackstone House, Temple, London EC4Y 9BW

Tel 020 7583 1770 *Fax* 020 7822 7350

ROSE, Harvey John,

b. London, June 10, 1946; m. Sandra née Dudack; Chartered Accountant; Ch. Zionist Federation of Great Britain and Ireland (2010-); Tru. Save a Child's Heart UK (2007-).

Add 7 Arkenside Road, London NW3 5RA

Tel 020 7794 5636

ROSEN, Clive H, FCOptom., FSMC, Dip. Sports Vision.

b. London, Apr. 15, 1938; Ch. Palmers Green and Southgate Synagogue (2011-), Mem. Bd. of Management, (2008-); H. Pres. Broomfield House-owners and Residents Association (2002-); Hon. Officer. ZF (2002-08, 1994-98); Cttee. Mem. Sports Vision Association (1997-2006); Consultant to Leyton Orient FC (1997-2003); Hon. T. East London and City Health Authority L.O.C. (1994-2002); Ch. Israel-Judaica Stamp Club (1990-2010); Ed. The Israel-Judaica Stamp Club Journal (1990-2010); Zionist Federation National Council (1989-2010); H. Off. JNF (1983-90, 1979-81); Dir. David Elliott (Opticians) Ltd. (1965-2003); Freeman, City of London (1964).

Add 152 Morton Way, London N14 7AL

Tel 020 8886 9331 *Fax* 020 8886 5116

Email clive@cliverosen.co.uk *Website* www.israeljudaica.co.uk

ROSEN, Rabbi Jeremy, MA (Cantab), PhD.

b. Sept. 11, 1942; Currently Scholar-in-residence, JCC Manhattan; Rabbi, Persian Jewish Community, New York (2009-); Prof. Jewish Studies F.V.G. Antwerp. (1991-); Dir. Yakar Foundation (1999-2009); Rabbi, Western Marble Arch Synagogue (1991-92); Rabbi, Western Synagogue (1985-91); Chief Rabbi's Cabinet adv. Interfaith (1987-90); T. Yakar Foundation; Principal, Carmel College (1971-84); Rabbi, Giffnock and Newlands Synagogue Glasgow (1968-71). Publ.: Deborah (2010); Mad Messiah (2010); Wallingford (2009); Kabbalah Inspirations (2005); Understanding Judaism (2003); Exploding Myths that Jews Believe (2001).

Add 1965 Broadway, New York, NY 10023, USA

Email jeremyrosen@msn.com *Website* www.jeremyrosen.com

ROSENBERG, Rosita (née Gould),

b. London, Sept. 2, 1933; V. Pres. form. Exec. Dir. Liberal Judaism. Publ.: Liberal Judaism: the First Hundred Years (Jt. author, 2004).

Add The Montagu Centre, 21 Maple Street W1T 4BE

Tel 020 7580 1663 *Fax* 020 7631 9838

ROSENBLATT, Harvey,

Ch. Nightingale Hammerson; Mem. Jewish Leadership Council.

Add Nightingale House, 105 Nightingale Lane, London SW12 8NB

Tel 020 8673 3495

Email info@nightingalehammerson.org *Website* www.nightingalehammerson.org

ROTHSCHILD, Sir Evelyn de,

b. Aug. 29, 1931; Merchant Banker; Ch. EL Rothschild Ltd; Ch. ERANDA Foundation; Gov. Emer. London School of Economics and Political Science; Fel. Imperial College London; H. Life Pres. Norwood and Ravenswood Children's Charity; Ch. and CEO, NM Rothschild and Sons Ltd (1976-2003); Ch. Economist Newspaper (1972-89); Ch. United Racecourse Ltd (1977-94); British Merchant Banking and Securities Houses Assoc. (form. Accepting Houses Cttee.) (1985-89); Bd. Dir. De Beers and IBM UK; Dep. Ch. Milton Keynes Development Corporation; Ch. St Mary's Hospital Medical School; Mem. Council of Shakespeare Globe Trust; Pres. The Evelina Children's Hospital Appeal.

Add 31 Tite Street, London SW3 4JP

Tel 020 7376 5271

ROTHSCHILD, Lord Nathaniel Charles Jacob,

b. Cambridge, Apr. 29, 1936; Ch. RIT Capital Partners plc, J. Rothschild Capital Management plc and Five Arrows Ltd; Sir Winston Churchill Award, Technion (2004); Pres. IJPR (1992-2002); Commonwealth Council Award (2001); Ch. Trustees of the National Heritage Memorial Fund (1992-98); Ch. Trustees of the National Gallery (1985-91); Weizmann Award (1977); Ch. Yad Hanadiv; Ch. Rothschild Foundation; T. Weizmann Institute; Hon. Fel. City of Jerusalem; Hon Fel. Israel Museum.

Add 14 St James's Place SW1A 1NP

Tel 020 7493 8111 *Fax* 020 7647 8585

ROTHSCHILD, Rabbi Sylvia Helen Fay, BSc.

b. Bradford, West Yorkshire, Nov. 21, 1957; m. Martin Fischer; M. Wimbledon Synagogue (2002-); Ch. Assembly of Rabbis (2000-2003), Co-Ch. (1998-2000); M. Bromley and District Reform Synagogue (1987-2002). Publ.: Co-Ed. Taking up the Timbrel (2000).

Add c/o Wimbledon Synagogue, 1 Queensmere Road, Parkside, London SW19 5QD

Email rabbirothschild@wimshul.org

ROWE, Joshua, MBE, LLB Hons Bar.

Ch. of Governors, Manchester King David School; Jt. Pres. Manchester UJIA.

Add KDHS, Eaton Road, Manchester M8 5DY

ROZENBERG, Joshua Rufus, MA (Oxon).

b. London, May 30, 1950; m. Melanie Phillips; Freelance legal commentator (2009-); Legal Ed. Daily Telegraph (2000-08); H. Bencher, Gray's Inn (2003); BBC News (1975-2000) (Legal and Constitutional Affairs Corr. 1997-2000, Legal Affairs Corr. 1985-97); Solicitor (1976). Publ.: Privacy and the Press (2004); Trial of Strength (1997); The Search for Justice (1994); The Case for the Crown (1987); Your Rights and the Law (with N. Watkins, 1986).

Add BCM Rozenberg, London WC1N 3XX

Email joshua@rozenberg.net *Website* www.rozenberg.net

RUBEN, David-Hillel, BA, PhD.

b. Chicago, July 25, 1943; Emer. Prof. Philosophy, University of London; Dir. Arcadia University, London (2012-13); Prof. Philosophy, Birkbeck College (2004-11); Dir. New York University in London (2000-11); form. Dir. London School of Jewish Studies (1998-99); Prof. of Philosophy, London School of Economics (1984-97); The City University, London, Snr. Lecturer in Philosophy (1979-84); University of Essex, Lecturer in Philosophy (1975-79); University of Glasgow, Lecturer in Philosophy (1970-75). Publ.: Action and Its Explanation (2003); Explaining Explanation (1990); The Metaphysics of the Social World (1985); Marxism and Materialism (1979).

Add 29 Sunny Gardens Road, London NW4 1SL

Tel 07799 694 103 *Fax* 020 8922 7410

Email d.ruben@bbk.ac.uk or david.ruben1@yahoo.co.uk

Website http://www.bbc.ac.uk/philosophy/our-staff/visiting-professors/ruben

RUBENS, Kenneth David, OBE, FRICS, FRSA.

b. London, Oct. 10, 1929; Chartered Surveyor; V. Pres. Jewish Museum, London; L. Elder, Spanish and Portuguese Jews Congregation; Past Ch. Council World Jewish Relief; Past Master, Worshipful Company, Painter-Stainers.; H. Life Mem. British Property Federation.

Add Flat 20, Westfield, 15 Kidderpore Avenue, London NW3 7SF

Tel 020 7794 7259

Email kenneth@rubens.org

RUBENSTEIN, Alan, JP.

b. London, 1943; m. Beryl née Brand; Managing Dir. Jewish Chronicle.

Add 25 Furnival Street, London EC4A 1JT

Tel 020 7415 1500 *Fax* 020 7415 1577

Email alanrubenstein@thejc.com

RUBIN, Stephen, OBE.

Hon. Ch. International Jewish Sports Hall of Fame (1992-); Ch. Pentland Group (1969-); Pres. World Federation of the Sporting Goods Industry (1995–2001); World Ch. Textile Institute (1994-96).

Add The Pentland Centre, Lakeside, Squires Lane, Finchley, London N3 2QL

RUBINSTEIN, William David, BA, PhD, FAHA, FASSA, FRHistS.

b. New York, Aug. 12, 1946; m. Hilary L. Rubinstein; Pres. JHSE (2002-04), Mem. Council (1996-); ret. Prof. of History, The University of Wales, Aberystwyth, now Emer.; Ed. Journal of the Australian Jewish Historical Society (1988-95); Prof. of Social and Economic History, Deakin University, Australia (1987-95); Mem. Cttee. of Management, Executive Council of Australian Jewry (1983-95); Pres. Australian Association for Jewish Studies (1989-91). Among recent publications: Shadow Pasts (2008); Genocide: a History (2004); Twentieth Century Britain: A Political History (2003); The Jews in the Modern World: A History since 1750 (co-author, 2002); Philosemitism: Admiration and Support in the English-speaking World for Jews 1840-1939 (with Hilary L. Rubinstein, 1999); Britain's Century: A Political and Social History 1815-1905 (1998); The Myth of Rescue (1997); A History of the Jews in the English-Speaking World: Great Britain (1996).

Add 4/1 Frederick Street, Caulfield South, Victoria 3162, Australia

Email wdr@aber.ac.uk

RUDMAN, Michael Edward, MA (Oxon), BA (Oberlin College).

b. Tyler, Texas, USA, Feb. 14, 1939; Artistic Director, Sheffield Theatres (1992-94); Dir. Chichester Festival Theatre (1989-90); Associate Dir. National Theatre, (1979-88); Dir. Lyttelton Theatre (1979-81), Bd. Dirs. Art. Director, Hampstead Theatre (1973-78); Art. Dir. Traverse Theatre Club (1970-73).

Add c/o Peter Murphy, Curtis Brown Group, 4th Floor, 28/29 Haymarket, London SW1Y 4SP *Tel* 020 7396 6600 *Fax* 020 7396 0110

RUDOLF, Anthony, BA (Cantab), Chevalier de l'Ordre des Arts et des Lettres, FRSL, FEA.

b. London, Sept. 6, 1942; Writer, Publisher, Translator. Royal Literary Fund Fel. University Hertfordshire and Westminster (2002-8); Publ.: Silent Conversations: A Readers Life (2013); A Vanished Hand (2013); ZigZag (2010); Claude Vigée's Songs of Absence (2007); Piotr Rawicz and Blood from the Sky (2007, 1996); Kitaj (2001); The Arithmetic of Memory (1999); The Diary of Jerzy Urman (1991, rev. ed. 2013); Primo Levi's War against Oblivion (1990); After the Dream (1979).

Add 8 The Oaks, Woodside Avenue N12 8AR

Email anthony.rudolf@virgin.net

SACERDOTI, Cesare David Salomone,

b. Florence, Feb. 24, 1938; m. Judith née Margulies; Publisher, Company Director; Dir. Sephardi Centre Ltd (1997-); T. Winnicott Clinic of Psychotherapy Charitable Trust (1999-2009); Publications Dir. International Psychoanalytical Association (2002-08); Pres. Bd. of Elders, Spanish and Portuguese Jews' Congregation (2000-04), Thesoureiro (2000-03), V. Pres. (1996-2000), Parnas Heshaim (1995-2000); Man. Dir. H. Karnac (Books) Ltd (1984-99); 'Associate of the British Psychoanalytical Society' awarded 2011; 'Premio Cesare Musatti' awarded 2003 by the Societa' Psicoanalitica Italiana.

Add 25 Manor House Drive, London NW6 7DE

Tel 020 8459 2012 *Fax* 020 8451 8829

Email cesare@sacerdoti.com

SACKS, Rabbi, Lord Jonathan Henry, MA (Cantab), PhD, DD (Lambeth), H. DD (Cambridge), H. DD (King's College, London), H. D. University (Middx.), H. D. University (Glasgow).

b. London, Mar. 8, 1948; m. Elaine née Taylor; Associate Pres. Conference European Rabbis (1999-2013); Hon. Fel. Gonville and Caius College Cambridge (1993-); Ch. Rabbi of the United Hebrew Congregations of the Commonwealth (1991-2013); BBC Reith Lecturer (1990); Vis. Prof. Philosophy, University Essex (1989-90); Ed. L'Eylah (1984-1990); form. Principal, Jews College and holder of the Lord Jakobovits Ch. (1984-1990); M. Marble Arch Synagogue (1983-1990); M. Golders Green Synagogue (1978-1982); Vis. Prof. Philosophy Hebrew University; Vis. Prof. Theology and Religious Studies, King's College, London. Publ.: Koren Sacks Pesah Mahzor (2013); Koren Sacks Yom Kippur Mahzor (2012); Koren Sacks Rosh Hashanah Mahzor (2011); The Great Partnership (2011); Future tense (2009); The KorenSacks Siddur (2009); Authorised Daily Prayer Book (4th edition New translation and commentary, 2007); The Home We Will Build Together (2007); To Heal a Fractured World (2005); From Optimism to Hope (2004); The Passover Haggadah (2003); The Dignity of Difference (2002); A Letter in the Scroll (2000); Celebrating Life (2000); Radical Then, Radical Now (2000); Morals and Markets (1999); The Politics of Hope (1997); Community of Faith (1995); Faith in the Future (1995); Will We Have Jewish Grandchildren? (1994); One People: Tradition Modernity and Jewish Unity (1993); Crisis and Covenant (1992); Arguments for the Sake of Heaven (1991); Orthodoxy Confronts Modernity (1991); The Persistence of Faith (1991); Tradition in an Untraditional Age (1990); Traditional Alternatives (1989); Torah Studies (1986); Tradition and Transition (1986).

Email joanna@rabbisacks.org

SAIDEMAN, Seymour Geoffrey, FCA.

b. London, Apr. 5, 1939; m. Shirley née Lewis; Elder, Stanmore and Canons Park Synagogue; H. Life Pres. B'nai B'rith Europe; Mem. B'nai B'rith International Advisory Council and Delegate, 36th Zionist Congress of the World Zionist Organisation; form. Snr.

V. Pres. B'nai B'rith International (2006-09); form. Pres. B'nai B'rith Europe (1999-2003); form. National Pres. B'nai B'rith District 15 of Great Britain and Ireland (1997-9); form. Ch. Chief Rabbinate Council (1992-6); form. Pres. US (1992-6); form. Ch. Governors JFS Comprehensive School (1984-7); form. Ch. London Bd. of Jewish Rel. Education (1984-7).

Add 10 Oak Lodge Close, Stanmore HA7 4QB

SALAMON, Rabbi Thomas,

b. Kosice, May 10, 1948; m. Renée née Heffes; Rabbi/Solicitor; M. Westminster Synagogue (1997-); M. Hampstead Reform Jewish Com. (1988-90); M. Hertsmere Progressive Synagogue (1980-88); Exec. Dir. Norwood Child Care (1975-80); Associate M. West London Synagogue (1972-75).

Add Westminster Synagogue, Kent House, Rutland Gardens London SW7

Tel 020 7584 3953 *Fax* 020 7581 8012

Email thomas@westminstersynagogue.org *Website* www.westminstersynagogue.org

SALASNIK, Rabbi Eli,

b. Old City of Jerusalem; Rav in London since 1950; District Rav, London Bd. for Shechita.

Add 8 The Lindens, Prospect Hill, Waltham Forest, London E17 3EJ

SALASNIK, Rabbi Zorach Meir, BA, FJC.

b. London, July 29, 1951; M. Bushey and District Synagogue (1979-); Ch. Rabbinical Council, US (2002-05); Sec. Chief Rabbi's Cabinet; Snr. Jewish Hospital Chaplain; Cttee. Multi Faith Group for Health Care Chaplaincy; Rabbinic representative, Jewish Emergency Support Service; Hertfordshire SACRE; Chaplain, Rishon Multiple Sclerosis Aid Group; form. Gov. Agency for Jewish Education; form. M. Notting Hill Synagogue, Leytonstone and Wanstead Synagogue.

Add 8 Richfield Road, Bushey Heath, Hertfordshire WD23 4LQ

Tel 07961 366 689

Email zm@salasnik.net

SAMUELSON, Sir Sydney Wylie, CBE, H. D. Sheffield Hallam Uni.

b. Paddington, London, Dec. 7, 1925, m. Doris née Magen; first recipient, The Friese-Greene Award for Outstanding Career in Cinema (2011); Mem. Pres. Council (2002-); Pres. (2002-) Projected Picture Trust; F. T. (1977-2008), British Academy of Film and Television Arts, T. (1973-2008), Fel. (1993), Ch. of Council (1973-6); Fel. British Film Institute (1997); First British Film Commissioner (1991-7); Patron (1997), Fdr. Ch. and Chief Exec. Samuelson Group PLC (1954-1990); Pres. (1980-81), Cinema and Television Veterans, Mem. (1970); British Kinematograph Sound and Television Society, Hon. Fel. (1970); Pres. (1985-), Israel Association for the Mentally Handicapped (AKIM); Guild of British Camera Technicians; Mem. Beth Hatefutsoth, Tel Aviv; Founding Pres. Hon. Life Patron, UK Jewish Film.

Add 31 West Heath Avenue NW11 7QJ

Tel 020 8455 6696 *Fax* 020 8458 1957

Email sydney.samuelson@zen.co.uk

SANDERS, Jeremy Keith Morris, ScD., FRS, FRSC, CChem.

b. London, May 3, 1948; m. Louise Sanders née Applebaum; Research Chemist and Academic; University of Cambridge: Pro-V. Chancellor for Institutional Affairs (2011-), Prof. (1996-), Hd. of School of Physical Sciences (2009-11), Deputy V. Chancellor (2006-10), Hd. of Dept. (2000-06), Reader (1992-96), Lecturer in chemistry (1973-92). Publ.: Modern NMR Spectroscopy (with B.K. Hunter, 1987, 2nd edition 1993).

Add University Chemical Laboratory, Lensfield Road, Cambridge CB2 1EW

Tel 01223 336 411 *Fax* 01223 336 017

Email jkms@cam.ac.uk *Website* http:/www-sanders.ch.cam.ac.uk

SAPERSTEIN, Prof. Marc Eli, AB (Harvard), MA (H.U.), MA (Hebrew Union C.), PhD (Harvard).

b. Brooklyn, NY, Sept. 5, 1944; m. Tamar de Vries Winter; Academic; Council, JHSE (2008–); Vis. Prof. Harvard (Spring 2012); Prof. Jewish Studies, Kings College London

(2008-); Principal, Leo Baeck College, London (2006-11); Prof. Jewish History, George Washington University (1997-2006); Prof. Jewish History and Thought, Washington University, St. Louis (1986-97); Associate Prof. Jewish Studies, Harvard Divinity School (1983-86). Among recent publications: Edited volumes and contributed articles in Jewish history, literature and thought. Books: Jewish Preaching in Times of War 1800-2001 (2008); Exile in Amsterdam: Saul Levi Morteira's Sermons to a Congregation of 'New Jews' (2005); 'Your Voice Like a Ram's Horn': Themes and Texts in Traditional Jewish Preaching (1996); Jewish Preaching 1200-1800 (1989); Moments of Crisis in Jewish-Christian Relations (1989); Decoding the Rabbis (1980).

Add 21 Owlstone Road, Cambridge CB3 9JH

Tel 01223 312 082

Email msaper@gwu.edu

SARAH, Rabbi Elizabeth Tikvah, BSc (Soc.).

b. 1955; Semichah Leo Baeck College (1989); Associate Jewish Chaplain, University Sussex (2008-), Brighton University (2003-); Rabbi, Brighton and Hove Progressive Synagogue (2001-); Mem. Editorial Bd. MANNA (1994-); Ch. Rabbinic In-Service Training, Leo Baeck College (1996-2002); Rabbi, Leicester Progressive Jewish Congregation (1998-2000); Pt. time Lecturer Leo Baeck College (1997); Dep. Dir. Sternberg Centre (1994-97); Rabbi, Buckhurst Hill Reform Synagogue (1989-94); Dir. Programmes RSGB. Among recent publications: Trouble-Making Judaism (2011); Compelling Commitments (2007); Aspects of LJ (2004); Machzor Ruach Chadashah (2003); Lesbian Rabbis - the First Generation (2001); Taking up the Timbrel (2000); Renewing the Vision (1996); Contributions to Jewish Explorations of Sexuality (1995).

Add Brighton & Hove Progressive Synagogue, 6 Lansdowne Road BN3 1FF

Tel 01273 737 223

Email bhps@freenetname.co.uk

SAXTON, Robert Louis Alfred, MA (Cantab), BMus (Oxon), DMus (Oxon), FGSM.

b. London, Oct. 10, 1953; Composer and University Lecturer; Prof. of Composition, Oxford (2008-); Fel. and Tutor in Music, Worcester College, Oxford (1999-); Hd. Composition, RAM (1998-99); Hd. Composition, GSMD (1991-97). Publ.: Over 50 compositions; 20 commercial recordings; articles.

Add Worcester College, Oxford OX1 2HB

Email robert.saxton@music.ox.ac.uk

SCHAMA, Simon Michael, CBE, PhD.

b. London, Feb. 13, 1945; m. Virginia Papaioannou; Writer and Broadcaster; University Prof. Columbia University. Presented BBC TV series: A History of Britain. Publ.: Patriots and Liberators: Revolution in the Netherlands, 1780-1813 (1977); Two Rothschilds and the Land of Israel (1978); The Embarrassment of Riches: An Interpretation of Dutch Culture in the Golden Age (1987); Citizens: A Chronicle of the French Revolution (1989); Dead Certainties: Unwarranted Speculations (1991); Landscape and Memory (1995); Rembrandt's Eyes (1999); A History of Britain (3 vols, 2000-2).

Add Columbia University, 1180 Amsterdam Avenue, MC 2533, New York NY 10027

SCHIFF, Rabbi Naftali,

Exec. Dir. Aish UK (1999-); Fdr. GIFT (Give It Forward Today); Fdr. Dir. JRoots; Dir. Forum for Jewish Leadership; Dir. Chazon UK; Dir. JLink; Common Denominator; Chazak; The Danny Frei Jerusalem Fellowship.

Add Aish, 79 Hendon Way, London NW4 3LP

Tel 020 8457 4444 *Fax* 020 8457 4445

Email n.schiff@jewish-leadership.com

SCHMOOL, Marlena (née Lee), BSoc. Sc.

b. Leeds, 1941; Social Res. Consultant; Dir. Community Issues Divison, Board of Deputies (1999-2003); Tru. Jewish Journal of Sociology; Action for Childrens Arts. Publ.: Reflections on the 2011 Census of England and Wales (2011); Jews in Britain: a Snapshot from the 2001

Census (with D. Graham and S. Waterman, 2007); The Relaxation of Community? (2003); A Profile of British Jewry (with F. Cohen) (1998); Women in the British Jewish Community (with S.H. Miller) (1994); various statistical publications.

SCHNEIDER, Prof. Michael,

Hd. National Heart and Lung Institute (2009-11), Hd. Cardiovascular Science (2007-); Prof. of Medicine, Molecular and Cellular Biology, Molecular Physiology and Biophysics, Dir. Center for Cardiovascular Dev. Baylor College of Medicine, Texas (1984-2007); Dir. British Heart Foundation Centre at Imperial College London; Mem. MRC Council. Recipient, Medical Futures Cardiovascular Innovation Award (2008).

Add BHF Centre, Imperial College London, South Kensington Campus, London SW7 2AZ

Tel 020 7589 5111

Email m.d.schneider@imperial.ac.uk

SCHOCHET, Rabbi Yitzchak, M.A.

b. Canada; Rabbi, Mill Hill Synagogue (1993-), Richmond Synagogue (1991-93); Principal, Rosh Pinah Primary School, Edgware; Columnist, Jewish News; Diary Rabbi, Guardian; Mem. Chief Rabbi's Cabinet.

Add 305 Ballards Lane, London N12 8GB

SCHONFIELD, Jeremy Joseph, BA (East Anglia), PhD (Cantab).

b. London, July 11, 1951; m. Tamar née Rahmani; Research Fel. Oxford Centre for Hebrew and Jewish Studies (2011-), Mason Lecturer (1989-); Thesoureiro do Heshaim (2004-); Lecturer, Leo Baeck College (1995-); Ed. Jewish Historical Society of England (1981-); Transactions, Vols 27-35; Jewish Historical Studies, Vols 36-44; Assistant Dir. Israel Diaspora Trust (1988-2002); Editorial team (1982-99), Bulletin of the Anglo-Israel Archaeological Society, Jt. Founding Ed. (1982). Among recent publications: Megillat Esther (Ed. 2007); Undercurrents of Jewish Prayer (2006); The North French Miscellany (Ed. 2003); The Rothschild Haggadah (Ed. 2000); Perek Shirah (Ed. 1996); Me'ah Berakhot (Ed. 1994).

Add 71 Woodland Rise, London N10 3UN

Tel 020 8365 3226

Email jeremy.schonfield@blueyonder.co.uk

SCHREIER, Sir Bernard, Kt.

Mechanical engineer; Dir. CP Holdings Ltd; Pres. IIC Industries Inc; Ch. Danubius Hotels. Jubilee Award, Israel (1998); Officer's Cross, Order of Hungarian Republic (1998).

Add CP Holdings Ltd, CP House, Otterspool Way, Watford, Hertfordshire WD25 8JP

SCOTT, Lee, M.P.

b. London, Apr. 6, 1956; m. Estelle née Dombey; Consultant; MP (Con.) for Ilford North (2005-); Council Redbridge (1998-2006); Scott Associates Consultancy on Regeneration.

Add House of Commons, London SW1A 0AA

Tel 020 7219 8326

Email scottle@parliament.uk *Website* www.leescott.co.uk

SEAL, Gail (née Lew),

b. London, Oct. 29, 1948; m. Michael Seal; form. Mem. Jewish Leadership Council; Adv. Bd. LJCC; T. Tel Aviv Found.; Bd. Latrun, Israel; T. UK Friends of OR; Fdr. Mem. and Co-Ch. Communal Liaison Group; V. Pres. Zionist Federation; Bd. Mem. BICOM; JNF (Pres. 1995-2007, Deputy Pres. 1993, Education Officer, 1987).

Add c/o Zionist Federation of GB and Ireland, BM Box 1948, London WC1N 3XX

SECHER, Paul, LLB, Chartered MCIPD.

b. Whitehaven, Mar. 1, 1951; Man. Dir. JSB Group (Management Development,Training and Consulting); Mem. Employment Tribunal; V. Pres. Commonwealth Jewish Council. Author/contributor, books and articles on employment law, communication and management; Ed. Employment Lawletter.

Add Dove House, Arcadia Avenue, London N3 2JU

Tel 020 8371 7000 *Fax* 020 8371 7001

Email paul.secher@jsbonline.com *Website* www.jsbonline.com

SEFTON, Kevin,

T. Moishe House, Ch. Limmud (2012-), T. (2009-11); Ch. Limmud Conference (2007); Mem. JC Power 100 Panel (2007); Fdr. NuMa - Creative space for new Jewish ideas including the Jewish Bee Project hosted by the JCC for London.

Tel 020 8816 7895

Email kevin.sefton@4000rpm.co.uk

SEGAL, Anthony Walter, MB, ChB, MD, MSc, PhD, DSc, FRCP, FMedSci, FRS.

b. Johannesburg, Feb. 24, 1944; Charles Dent Prof. of Med. London University; attached University College and Middlesex Hospital Medical School.

Add The Rayne Institute, Centre for Molecular Medicine, 5 University Street, London WC1E 6JF

Tel 020 7679 6175

Email t.segal@ucl.ac.uk

SEROTA, Sir Nicholas (Andrew), CH, Kt, BA, MA.

b. Apr. 27, 1946; m. Teresa neé Gleadowe; Mem. Olympic Delivery Authority (2006-12); Dir. Tate Gallery (1988-); Dir. Whitechapel Gallery (1976-88); Dir. Museum of Modern Art, Oxford (1973-6). Publ.: Experience or Interpretation: The Dilemma of Museums of Modern Art (1996).

Add Tate Gallery, Millbank SW1P 4RG

Tel 020 7887 8003

SHAERF, Paul Simon, MA (Cantab).

b. London, Mar. 4, 1950; m. Judith née Tunkel; Judicial officeholder; Ombudsman (2001-).

Add Board of Deputies, 6 Bloomsbury Square, London WC1A 2LP

Tel 020 7543 0105 *Fax* 020 7543 0010

Email ombudsman@bod.org.uk

SHAPPS, Grant,

b. Watford, Sept. 14, 1968; m. Belinda neé Goldstone; M. of State for Housing & Local Government (2010-); Shadow Housing M. (2007–10); MP (Cons), Welwyn Hatfield (2005-); Fdr. and Ch. Printhouse Corporation (1990-2007); V. Ch. (Campaigning), Conservative Party (2005–07).

Add House of Commons, London SW1A 0AA

Tel 020 7219 8497 *Fax* 020 7219 0659

Email grant@shapps.com

SHAW, Rabbi Andrew Clive, BEng. (Hons), MA.

b. London, Sept. 18, 1971; m. Gila née Zamir; United Synagogue Dir. Living and Learning; Community Development Rabbi, Stanmore and Canons Park Synagogue; Exec. Dir. Tribe (2003-13); Consultant, Facilitator, Jewish Association for Business Ethics (2000-12); Chaplain, Mayor of Harrow (2006-7); Dir. Youth New Hempstead Synagogue, NY (1998-2000); form. National Education Co-ordinator, UJS (1994-95). Publ.: 60 Days for 60 Years: Israel (gen. Ed. 2008); 60 Days for 60 Years (Ed. 2005); 50 Days for 50 Years (Ed. 1995).

Tel 020 8343 5693

Email rabbishaw@theus.org.uk *Website* www.theus.org.uk

SHAW, Martin, BA.

b. London, Aug. 16, 1949; Fundraising and Management Consultant (2002-), Gen. Man. Variety Club, GB (2001-2); Ch. Haringey Shed (2001-); Ch. Jubilee Waterside Centre (1998-2008); Snr. Consultant, Charity Recruitment (1999-2001); Independent Consultant, Action Planning (1995-99); Exec. Dir. Association for Jewish Youth (1989-95); Snr. Youth Off.

London Borough of Ealing (1986-89). Publ.: Young People and Decision; Putting the Fun into Fundraising.

Add 64 The Grove, Edgware, Middlesex HA8 9QB

Tel 020 8958 6885

Email mshaw@dircon.co.uk

SHEFF, Sylvia Claire (née Glickman), MBE, JP, BA.

b. Manchester, Nov. 9, 1935; Ret. Teacher (1958-77); Exec. Cttee. Mem. Jewish Representative Council of Greater Manchester and Region (2009-); Fdr. Dir. Organisation of Jewish Lawyers (2009-); Concert and events promoter (2002-); Mem. UK Assoc. Jewish Lawyers & Jurists (2001-); Del. Board of Deputies (1987-); Pres. (1980-), Manchester 35 Group Women's Campaign for Soviet Jewry, Fdr. Ch. (1972-80); Associate Dir. Jewish Cultural and Leisure Centre (1990-93); International Co-ord. Yeled Yafeh Fel. of Children of Chernobyl (1990-94); Fdr. and Dir. Friendship with Israel, Group (European Parl.) (1979-90); Hon. S. National Council for Soviet Jewry (1987-89); Asst. Nat. Dir. Conservative Friends of Israel (1985-89); Fdr. Mem. Bury Family Conciliation Service Management Cttee. (1985-87); Nat. Projects Dir. Conservative Friends of Israel (1974-85); Magistrate (1976).

Add 6 The Meadows, Old Hall Lane, Whitefield, Manchester M45 7RZ

Tel 0161 766 4391 *Fax* 0161 766 4391

Email sylvia@sheff.fsbusiness.co.uk

SHELDON, Peter, OBE, JP, FCA.

b. Chesterfield, June 11, 1941; m. Judith Marion née Grunberger; International Business Consultant; Ch. Kardan N.V. (2012-); Ch. Chief Rabbinate Trust (2010-, 2003-05), T. (2005-10); T. The Jerusalem Foundation UK (2010-); T. Finchley Jewish Primary School Trust (2007-); Dep. Board of Deputies (2006-13); Ch. North West London Eruv Cttee. (2001-12); Ch. BATM Advanced Communications Ltd (1999-); T. Hadassah Medical Relief Association UK (2006-11); British Israel Chamber of Commerce (2006-2010); Pres. United Synagogue (1999-2005), H. Officer (1996-99); Ch. Kashrut Division London Beth Din (1996-99); Ch. Kerem Schools (1976-88).

Add 8 Denver Court, 132 Hendon Lane, Finchley N3 3RH

Tel 020 8346 5155

Email sheldp@btinternet.com

SHELLEY, Ronald Charles, MBE.

b. London, Mar. 27, 1929; V. Pres. AJEX; form. National Ch. AJEX (2004-06, 1975-77); T. Board of Deputies (1991-97); Ch. AJEX Housing Association (1987-91); Ch. Jewish Military Museum; Ch. AJEX Charitable Foundation; Winner, LB of Barnet Civic Award 2010.

Add AJEX Charitable Foundation, Shield House, Harmony Way, Hendon NW4 2BZ

Tel 020 7323 6626 *Fax* 020 7255 1203

SHERIDAN, Rabbi Sybil Ann, MA (Cantab).

b. Bolton, Lancs., Sept. 27, 1953; m. Rabbi Dr Jonathan Romain; M. Wimbledon and District Reform Synagogue (2003-); form. M. Thames Valley Jewish Community (1994-2003), Ealing Liberal Synagogue; Chaplain, Roehampton University. Publ.: Shirei Hatefilla (Ed. 2012); Abraham's Children: Jews, Christians and Muslims in Conversation (Contr. 2006); Feminist Perspectives on History and Religion (Contr. 2001); Taking up the Timbrel (Ed. 2000); Stories from the Jewish World (1987, 1998); Renewing the Vision (Contr. 1996); Creating the Old Testament (Contr. 1994); Hear Our Voice (Ed. 1994).

Add 1 Queensmere Road, Wimbledon, London SW19 5QD

Tel 020 8946 4836 *Fax* 020 8944 7790

Email rabbisheridan@wimshul.org

SHINDLER, Colin, BSc, MSc DipEd (Further Education), PhD.

b. Hackney, London, Sept. 3, 1946; Founding Ch. European Association of Israeli Studies (2009-13); Prof. Israeli Studies (2008-11); Emer. Prof. (2011-), Centre for Jewish Studies (2006-10), SOAS; Dir. European Jewish Publication Society (1995-2010); Ed. Judaism Today

(1994-2000); Ed. Jewish Quarterly (1985-94); Associate Lecturer in Chemistry, Open University. Among recent publications: Israel and the European Left (2012); History of Modern Israel (2008, 2013); What do Zionists Believe? (2007); The Triumph of Military Zionism (2005); The Land Beyond Promise (2002); Israel, Likud and the Zionist Dream (1995).

Add SOAS, Thornhaugh Street, Russell Square, London WC1H 0XG

Tel 020 7898 4358

Email cs52@soas.ac.uk

SHINDLER, Rabbi Julian, MSc, PhD.

b. London, Jan 9, 1950; m. Rosalyn née Brysh; Programmes Dir. PEIR (2010-); Exec. Dir. Rabbinical Council of the US (1999-); Dir. Marriage Authorisation Office, Office of the Chief Rabbi (1987-); Rabbi, Muswell Hill Synagogue (1987-99); UJS London Region Student Chaplain (1986-7); Kalms Fel. (1983-86); Hd. Science, Menorah Grammar School (1980-84); Chief Rabbi's Cabinet (Rabbinic Liaison).

Add 305 Ballards Lane, London N12 8GB

Email rabbi.shindler@chiefrabbi.org

SHIRE, Rabbi Dr Michael, BA (Hons) UCL, MA, PhD (Hebrew Union College LA); MA, Hon Doctorate, Jewish Religious Education (2008), Jewish Religious Education; Hon Fel. Leo Baeck College (2012); Rabbinic Ordination at Leo Baeck College (1996).

b. 1957; Dean and Prof. of Jewish Education, Hebrew College Boston (2011-); V. Principal, Leo Baeck College (2001-2011); Dir. Centre for Jewish Education (1988-2001); Dir. of Education, Temple Beth Hillel, Hollywood (1983-88). Publ.: Mazal Tov (2003); The Jewish Prophet (2002); L'Chaim! (2000); The Illuminated Haggadah (1998); Ed. Cons. Illustrated Atlas of Jewish Civilization.

Add Hebrew College, 160 Herrick Road, Newton Centre, MA 12459, USA

Tel +1 (617) 559 8617

Email mshire@hebrewcollege.edu

SILKIN, Yitzchok, MA (Cantab), MSc (London).

b. London, Feb. 26, 1947; m. Sylvia née Wieselberg BA; CEO, Agudas Israel Great Britain (2009-); Seminars Dir. Seed (1984-2009).

Add 97-99 Stamford Hill, London N16 5DN

Tel 020 8800 6688

Email ysilkin@agudas.org.uk

SILVERMAN, Rabbi Robert (Reuven), BA, PhD, DD, FLBC, MBACP, Adv. Dip. Counselling.

b. Oxford, July 26, 1947; m. Dr Isobel Braidman; Ch. Assembly of Rabbis, RSGB (1991-93); M. Manchester Reform Synagogue; Hon. Fel. Middle Eastern Studies Dept. and Centre for Jewish Studies, University Manchester; Anglo-Israel Friendship League, Manchester; Chaplain, Progressive Jewish Students, Manchester; form. Second M. Edgware Reform Synagogue; M. Mikve Israel Emanuel, Curacao. Publ.: Baruch Spinoza.

Add 26 Daylesford Road, Cheadle, Cheshire SK8 1LF

Tel 0161 834 0514 *Fax* 0161 834 0415

Email rabbi@jacksonsrow.org

SIMONS, Dayan Shmuel,

b. London, Jun 3, 1963; m. Miriam née Zucker; Dayan, London Beth Din; Principal (Rosh Kolel), London Academy Jewish Studies (1998-06). Publ.: Sefer Meil Shmuel (Jerusalem 1994).

Add 15 Elmcroft Crescent, London NW11 9TB

Tel 07974 837 456

SINCLAIR, Clive John, BA, PhD (East Anglia University), FRSL.

b. London, Feb 19, 1948; British Library Penguin Writers Fel. (1996); Writer-in-Residence, Uppsala University (1988); form. Lit. Ed. Jewish Chronicle. Prizes: Jewish Quarterly Award for Fiction (1997); PEN Silver Pen for Fiction (1997); Somerset Maugham Award (1981).

Publ.: Death and Texas; The Brothers Singer; Bedbugs; Hearts of Gold; Bibliosexuality; Blood Libels; Diaspora Blues; Cosmetic Effects; Augustus Rex; The Lady with the Laptop; A Soap Opera from Hell; Meet the Wife; Clive Sinclair's True Tales of the Wild West.

Add 16 Canonbury Grove, London N1 2HR

SINCLAIR, Rabbi Dr Daniel Bernard, LLB, LLM, LLD.

b. London, June 30, 1950; Prof. Jewish Law and Comparative Biomedical Law, Striks Law School, CMAS, Israel; Prof. in Jewish Law, Fordham University, NY; Lecturer in Jewish Law and Comparative Biomedical Law, Tel Aviv University (1988-); Snr. Research Fel. Institute for Research in Jewish Law, Jerusalem (1987-); Principal, Jews' College (1994-97); Lecturer in Jewish and Comparative Bioethics, Hebrew University, Jerusalem (1991); Assistant Ed. Jewish Law Annual (1990); Lecturer in Jewish Law and Philosophy of Halakhah, Pardes Institute, Jerusalem (1988-90); Jacob Herzog Memorial Prize (1980). Publ.: End of Life: Oxford Handbook of Jewish Ethics (2012); Jewish Biomedical Law: Legal and Extra-Legal Dimensions (2003); Law, Judicial Policy and Jewish Identity in the State of Israel (2000); Selected Topics in Jewish Law, vols. 4-5 (1994); Tradition and the Biological Revolution (1989).

Add 3/21 Ben Tabbai Street, Jerusalem 93591, Israel

Tel +972 (02) 678 4268

Email dsinclair@law.fordham.edu

SINCLAIR, Dr Michael J,

b. London, Dec. 20, 1942, m. Penny; Ch. Sinclair Montrose Trust Ltd.; Ch. Laniado UK; Ch. and Exec. Bd. World Council of Torah Educ.; Ch. of Management Cttee. Sidney and Ruza Last Foundation Home; V. Ch. JNF; Bd. Mem. British Friends of Arad; T. Jewish Outreach Network; Exec. Ch. Care Capital.

Add 6th Floor, 54 Baker Street, London W14 7BU

Tel 020 7034 1949 *Fax* 020 7034 1941

Email msinclair@carecapital.co.uk

SINGER, Malcolm John,

b. London, July 13, 1953; m. Sara née Nathan; Composer and Conductor; Director of Music, Yehudi Menuhin School (1998-).

Add Yehudi Menuhin School, Stoke D'Abernon, Cobham, Surrey KT11 3QQ

Tel 01932 584 402

Email malcolmsinger@yehudimenuhinschool.co.uk

SINGER, Norbert, CBE, BSc, PhD, H. DSc (Greenwich), C.Chem., FRSC.

b. Vienna, May 3, 1931; Physical Chemist; Fel. Queen Mary and Westfield College; Fel. Nene College; Ch. Gov. St. Peter's CE Primary School (2004-11); Vis. Prof. University Westminster (1996-2001); Ch. Oxleas NHS Trust (1994-2001); Ch. Rose Bruford College Gov. Body (1994-9); Ch. Bexley District Health Authority (1993-4); Mem. of C.N.A.A. and Cttees. (1982-93); V. Chancellor, University Greenwich [form. Thames Polytechnic] (1978-92); Assistant then Dep. Dir. Polytechnic of North London (1974-8); Res. Chemist, Morgan Crucibles Co. Ltd. (1954-7).

Add Croft Lodge, Bayhall Road, Tunbridge Wells, Kent TN2 4TP

Tel 01892 523 821

Email n.singer@greenwich.ac.uk

SKEAPING, Lucie (née Finch),

b. London, Dec. 30, 1951; m. Rodrick Mursell Skeaping; Musician; Writer on early and traditional music; Columnist for BBC Music Magazine (2005-); BBC Broadcaster; Presenter 'The Early Music Show' BBC Radio 3 (1999-); Dir. The Burning Bush, Klezmer/Sephardi Music (1990-). Publ.: Broadside Ballads (Faber Music 2005); Let's Make Tudor Music (2000). CDs include: The English State Jig (2008); Penny Merriments (2005); Music of the Old Jewish World (2003); Best of Yiddish, Klezmer and Sephardic Music (1996); Raisins and Almonds (1990).

Add 19 Patshull Road, London NW5 2JX

Email lucieskeaping@hotmail.com *Website* www.lucieskeaping.co.uk and www.theburningbush.co.uk

SKELKER, Philip David, MA (Oxon).

b. Sept. 7, 1946; HM, Immanuel College (2000-12); Educ. Leadership Dir. UJIA (1998-2000); English Master, Eton College (1997-98); HM, Carmel College (1984-97); HM, King David High School, Liverpool (1981-84).

Add 4 Broadhurst Avenue, Edgware, Middlesex HA8 8TR

Tel 020 8950 0604 *Fax* 020 8950 8687

Email pdskelker@gmail.com

SKLAN, Alexander, BSc, Soc. Sci, MSc Econ, CQSW.

b. London Jan. 13, 1947; Dir. of Clinical Services, Medical Foundation for Care of Victims of Torture (1997-); Jt. Ch. Assembly of Masorti Synagogues (1996-2000); Dir. of Social Services, Jewish Care (1990-96); Dir. of Quality Assurance; Dir. of Social Services, Jewish Welfare Bd. (1979-90).

Add 111 Isledon Road, London N7 7JW

Tel 020 7697 7777 *Fax* 020 7697 7799

Email asklan@torturecare.org.uk

SMITH, Rabbi Amnon Daniel, MA.

b. Hadera, Israel, Oct. 10, 1949; Snr. M. Edgware and District Reform Synagogue; form. Ch. RSGB Assembly of Rabbis; form. M. Wimbledon and District Synagogue; form. Associate M. West London Synagogue; Fdr. Ch. Raphael Centre – a Jewish counselling service.

Add 118 Stonegrove, Edgware, Middlesex HA8 8AB

SMITH, Leon Adrian,

b. Bristol, July 17, 1950; m. Claude née Cohen; Charity Director; Chief Exec. Nightingale Hammerson (1998-); various management roles, Nightingale House (1973-1997); Dir. English Community Care Association; Mem. Board of Deputies.

Add Nightingale House, 105 Nightingale Lane, London SW12 8NB

Tel 020 8673 3495

Email info@nightingalehammerson.org *Website* www.nightingalehammerson.org

SMITH, Stephen, MBE.

b. April 15, 1967; Exec. Dir. USC Shoah Foundation Institute (2009-); Ch. Holocaust Memorial Day Trust (2004-); Executive Dir. Shoah Foundation (2009); Co-Fdr. Aegis Trust (2000); Co-Fdr. Beth Shalom Holocaust Centre (1995). Publ.: Forgotten Places: The Holocaust and the Remnants of Destruction (2001); The Holocaust and the Christian World (Co-Ed.) (2000); Making Memory: Creating Britain's First Holocaust Centre (1999).

Add The Holocaust Centre, Beth Shalom, Laxton, Newark, Notts NG22 0PA

Tel 01623 836 627 *Fax* 01623 836 647

Email office@holocaustcentre.net *Website* www.holocaustcentre.net

SOBER, Phillip, FCA, FRSA.

b. London, Apr. 1, 1931; m. Vivien; Chartered Accountant; form. Dir. Capital Shopping Centres plc (Ch. Audit Cttee.) (1994-2006); form. Dir. Capital and Counties plc (1993-2002); Mem. Finance Cttee, University of London (1999); Mem. Council, University of London (1998); form. Mem. Council, University of Arts, London (1997); form Gov. and Ch. of Audit Cttee. London Institute of Higher Education Corporation (1994); Pres. Norwood Child Care (1989-94); Crown Estate Commissioner (1983-94); T. Royal Opera House Trust (1985-91); Consultant, BDO Stoy Hayward, Chartered Accountants (1990); Partner, Stoy Hayward, Chartered Accountants (1958-90); form. Dir. Liberty International plc; form. T. Jewish Association of Business Ethics; form. Ch. Central Council for Jewish Community Services; form. Jt. T. Ravenswood. Publ.: Articles in professional press on various subjects but primarily on property company accounting.

Add 5 Sheffield Terrace, London W8 7NG

Tel 020 3220 0165

Email viviphil@aol.com

SOLOMON, Sir Harry, KB, FRCP (Hon).

b. Middlesbrough, Mar. 20, 1937; m. Judy; Non-Exec. Dir. Hillsdown Holdings plc (1993-97), Fdr. Ch. (1975-1993); Fel. Royal College of Physicians (H.).

Add Hillsdown House, 32 Hampstead High Street, London NW3 1QD

Tel 020 7431 7739

SOLOMON, Rabbi Norman, PhD (Manc), MA (Cantab.), BMus (London).

b. Cardiff, May 31, 1933; Fel. Oxford Centre for Hebrew and Jewish Studies (1995-2001); Pres. BAJS (1994); Ed. Christian Jewish Relations (1986-91); form. Lecturer, Faculty of Theology, University Oxford; form. Dir. Centre for Study of Judaism and Jewish Christian Relations, Selly Oak College; form. M. Birmingham Central Synagogue, Hampstead Synagogue, London, Greenbank Drive Synagogue, Liverpool, Whitefield Hebrew Congregation, Manchester. Publ.: Torah From Heaven (2012); The Talmud: Selections (2009); Ed. Abraham's Children (2006); Historical Dictionary of Judaism (1998); A Very Short Introduction to Judaism (1996); The Analytic Movement (1993); Judaism and World Religion (1991).

Add The Oriental Institute, Pusey Lane, Oxford OX1 2LE

Tel 01865 278 200

Website www.normansolomon.info

SPIRO, Nitza (née Lieberman), M.Phil. (Oxon).

b. Jerusalem, Nov., 1937; m. Robin; Chief Exec. Dir. Spiro Institute (1983-98); Chief Exec. Spiro Ark (1998-2013); Lecturer in Hebrew and Hebrew Literature, University Oxford (1976-83); Deputy Dir. Ulpan Akiva Netanya, Israel (1959-68); Organiser, national and international Jewish tours and cultural events; teaching of Hebrew on English radio. Publ.: Hebrew Correspondence Course (1987); Hebrew Accelerated Learning Course (Suggestopedia course co-author); weekly Hebrew column, London Jewish News; Organiser of Children's Intensive Ulpanim.

Add The Spiro Ark, 788-790 Finchley Road, London NW11 7TJ

Tel 020 7289 6321

Email education@spiroark.org *Website* www.spiroark.org

SPIRO, Robin Myer, MA (Oxon), M.Phil (Oxon), FCA.

b. London, Feb. 9, 1931; m. Nitza née Lieberman; Jt. Developer, Anglo-Jewish Heritage Trail (2006-); Jt. Founding Dir. and part time Lecturer in Jewish History, Spiro Institute (1978-98), Spiro Ark (1998-); Dir. Property Companies (1961-78); Creator and developer of St Christopher's Place, off London's Oxford St. (W1); Part time lecturer, Jewish History at Florida Atlantic University, Boca Raton, USA (1984-93); organiser and contributor, The Jewish Enigma (Open University, BBC 1994).

Add 80 St. John's Wood Court, St. John's Wood Road, London NW8 8QS

Tel 020 7289 6321

Email rspiro@ukpt.co.uk *Website* www.spiroark.org

STANTON, Prof. Stuart Lawrence Richard, MB, BS, FRCS, FRCSE, FRCOG.

b. Oct. 24, 1938; m. Julia Heller; Pres. British Society of Urogynaecology (2003–); form. Ch. Hadassah UK (2010-11); Pres. Obstetric and Gynaecological Section of the Royal Society of Medicine (2003-4); Prof. of Pelvic Surgery and Urogynaecology, St George's Hospital Medical School (1997–2003), now Emer. Prof.; Consultant Gynaecologist; Dir. of tru. Boys Town Jerusalem; Urogynaecology Unit, St George's Hospital (1984–2003); H. FRANZCOG (2000); V. Ch. and T. Patron, British Friends Hebrew University; Tru. Jewish Music Institute. Publ.: Pelvic Floor Re-education and Practice (2008); Gynaecology (2003); Female Pelvic Reconstructive Surgery (2002); Urinary Tract Infection in the Female (2000); (Co-Ed.) Clinical Urogynaecology (1999).

Add Flat 10, 43 Wimpole Street W1G 8AE

Tel 020 7486 0677

Email stuartstanton@hotmail.co.uk *Website* www.stuartstanton.com

STEPHENS, Judge Martin, QC, MA (Oxon).

b. Swansea, June 26, 1939; Circuit Judge (1986-2012); Bencher, Middle Temple (2004); Mem. Main Board, Judicial St. Board (1997-2000); Mem. Parole Board (1995-2000, 2011-); form. Ch. Cardiff Jewish Representative Council (1986-95); Recorder (1979-86).

Add c/o Central Criminal Court, City of London, London EC4M 7EH

STERLING, Jeffrey Maurice, Baron of Plaistow, GCVO, CBE; H. DBA (Nottingham Trent University); H. DCL (Durham), Kt., Order of St John.

b. Dec. 27, 1934; m. Dorothy Ann née Smith; V. Pres. British ORT (1978-); Ch. Sterling Guarantee Trust plc (1969-) (merging with P&O 1985); Ch. P&O (1983-2005); Ch. Queen's Golden Jubilee Weekend Trust (2002); Ch. P&O Princess Cruises (2000); Gov. Royal Ballet (1986-99); Ch. Govs. Royal Ballet School (1983-99); H. Fel. Research Institute of Naval Architects (1997); Fel. of the ISVA (1995); Pres. European Community Shipowners' Associations (1992-94); Hon. Fel. Institute of Chartered Shipbrokers (1992); Elder Brother, Trinity House (1991); H. Captain, Royal Naval Reserve (1991); Hon. Fel. Institute of Marine Engineers (1991); Spl Adv. to Sec. of State for Trade and Industry (1983-90) and to Sec. of State for Industry (1982-83); Dep. Ch. and Hon. T. London Celebrations Cttee. Queen's Silver Jubilee (1975-83); Freeman of the City of London.

Add 15 St. James's Place, London SW1A 1NP (Office

Tel 020 7409 2345

STERNBERG, Lady Hazel, DSS, DFO, JP, BA (London School of Economics).

b. Dec. 13, 1927; m. Sir Sigmund Sternberg; Cruse Bereavement counsellor (1989-90 supporting victims of Kings Cross fire and Marchioness disaster); Relate counsellor; Fdr. and Ch. Highgate Bereavement Services; Tru. Sternberg Charitable Foundation and Manor House Centre in Psychotherapy and Counselling; Dame of the Order of St Sylvester (1999); St Robert Bellarmine Medal by Gregoriana Pontifical University Rome (jointly awarded, 2002); Dame of the Order of Francis I – Constantinian Order (2006).

Add Star House, 104 Grafton Road. London NW5 4BA

STERNBERG, Sir Sigmund, KC*SG, JP, DU: Essex; H. LLD Leicester; H. Fellow UCL; DUniv Open; Hon DHLitt Richmond American Internat; Hon DHLitt Hebrew Union College.

b. Hungary, June 2, 1921; m. Hazel née Everett Jones; Life Pres. Movement for Reform Judaism (2011-); Snr. Life V. Pres. Royal College Speech and Language Therapists (2002-); Religious Adv. World Economic Forum (2002-); Life Pres. Sternberg Centre for Judaism (1996-); Pres. Movement for Reform (1998-2011); Alawite Officer Wissam (Morocco) (2009); St. Mellitus Medal (2008); The FIRST Lifetime Achievement Award (2008); LL.D. (Leic, 2007); Order Pentru Merit (Romania, 2007); Knight Grand Cross, Royal Order of Francis I (2005); Patron, Board of Deputies (2005); Hungarian Jewry Award (2004); Miranda Award (Venezuela, 2004); Order of Merit (Hungary, 2004); Off. Legion d' Honneur (2003); Order of Merit (Portugal, 2002); Order of Ukraine for Public Services (2001); Order of Bernardo O'Higgins Gran Cruz (Chile, 1999); Order of Commandatore of the Italian Republic (Italy) (1999); The Commander's Cross with a Star of the Order of Merit (Poland) (1999); Templeton Prize for Progress in Religion (1998); Wilhelm Leuschner Medal (Wiesbaden) (1998); Commander, Royal Order of Polar Star (Sweden) (1997); Patron, International Council of Christians and Jews; Gov. Hebrew University of Jerusalem; Co-Fdr. Three Faiths Forum; Fel. Leo Baeck College; Commander Order of Honour (Greece); Commander's Cross Order of Merit (Germany).

Add Star House, 104-108 Grafton Road NW5 4BA

Tel 020 7485 2538 *Fax* 020 7485 4512

Email sternberg@sternberg-foundation.co.uk

STOBIETSKY, Yeshua,

Fdr. Hamodia Newspaper (1999-).

Add Hamodia UK, 113 Fairview Road, London N15 6TS

Tel 020 8442 7777 *Fax* 020 8442 7778

STONE, Andrew Zelig, Baron of Blackheath, H. LLD (Oxford Brookes), H. D. Design (Kingston).
b. Sept. 9, 1942; m. Vivienne née Lee; Ch. Dipex; Patron Gauchers Association; Gov. Weizmann Institute; Gov. British University of Egypt; Mem. Labour Friends of Israel; Dep. Ch. Moon Valley; Dir. Falcon Power Holdings (2012-); form. Jt. Man. Dir. Marks and Spencer plc (1994-2000).
Add House of Lords, London SW1A 0PW

STONE, Richard,
Fdr. and Co-Ch. Alif Aleph (2003-); Pres. Jewish Council for Racial Equality; V. Ch. Runnymede.
Add The Jewish Council for Racial Equality, P.O. Box 47863, London NW11 1AB
Tel 020 8455 0896

STOPPARD, Sir Tom, OM, Kt, FRSL, CBE.
b. July. 3, 1937; Playwright, Journalist and Novelist. Journalist: Bristol Evening World (1958–60). Plays: Rock 'n' Roll (2006); Arcadia (1993); The Real Thing (1982); Rosencrantz and Guildenstern Are Dead (1966). Publ.: Rock 'n' Roll (2006); Heroes (2005); Henry IV (2004).
Add c/o United Agents, 12–26 Lexington Street, London W1F 0LE

STROM, Alex,
Columnist; Jewish Tribune.
Add Jewish Tribune, 215 Golders Green Road, London NW11 9BY
Tel 020 8458 9988

SUDAK, Rabbi Nachman, OBE.
b. Feb. 3, 1936; Principal, Lubavitch Foundation (1959-); Lubavitcher Rebbe's Emissary in Britain.
Add 107-115 Stamford Hill, London N16 5RP
Tel 020 8800 0022 (office) *Fax* 020 8809 7324
Email rabbisudak@chabad.org.uk *Website* www.chabad.org.uk

SUGAR, Lord Alan (Michael), Kt.
b. Mar. 24, 1947; m. Ann neé Simons; Presenter, The Apprentice (BBC TV) (2005-); Exec. Ch. Viglen (1997-), Amstrad Plc (1997-2008); Chief Exec. Tottenham Hotspur (1998–2000); Fdr. Amsair (1993); Owner, Amsprop Estates; Ch. Amscreen. Publ.: The Apprentice: How to Get Hired Not Fired (2005).
Add Brentwood House, 169 King's Road, Brentwood, Essex CM14 4EF
Tel 01277 228 888

SUMBERG, David Anthony Gerald,
b. Stoke-on-Trent, June 2, 1941, m. Carolyn née Franks; Solicitor; form. MEP, North West England (1999-2009); Dir. Anglo-Israel Association (1997-2001); Mem. Foreign Affairs Select Cttee. House of Commons (1992-97); form. MP (Cons) for Bury South (1983-97); Mem. Lord Chancellor's Adv. Cttee. on Public Records (1992); Mem. Home Affairs Select Cttee. House of Commons, (1991-92); Parl. Pte. Sec. Attorney Gen. (1986-90); Jt. Hon. S. Parl. Group, Conservative Friends of Israel, V. Ch. All-Party Committee, Release of Soviet Jewry; V. Ch. All-Party War Crimes Group.
Add 42 Camden Square, London NW1 9XA
Tel 020 7267 9590
Email david@sumberg.fsnet.co.uk

TABICK, Rabbi Jacqueline Hazel (née Acker), BA (Hons.), Dip. Ed.
b. Dublin, Oct. 8, 1948; Convenor, Beit Din for Movement of Reform Judaism; Patron, JCORE; Past Ch. Assembly of Rabbis, RSGB; Past Ch. Council of Reform and Liberal Rabbis; Co. Pres. World Congress of Faiths.
Add Sternberg Centre, 80 East End Road, Finchley N3 2SY
Tel 020 8349 5645
Email jackie.tabick@gmail.com

TABICK, Rabbi Larry Alan, BA, MA, FLBC.

b. Brooklyn, NY, Nov. 24, 1947; Rabbi, Hampstead Reform Jewish Com. (1990-, 1976-81); Rabbi, Leicester Progressive Jewish Community (1994-98); Associate Rabbi, Edgware and District Reform Synagogue (1986-90); Assistant Rabbi, Middlesex New Synagogue (1981-86). Publ.: The Aura of Torah (2014); Growing into your Soul (2005).

Add 1 Ashbourne Grove, Mill Hill NW7 3RS

Tel 020 8959 3129

Email rabtab@tabick.abel.co.uk *Website* www.tabick.abel.co.uk

TAHAN, Ilana Antoinette (née Mattes), OBE, BA (HU), MPhil (Aston) Dip. Lib., CILIP.

b. Bucharest, Dec. 6, 1946; m. Dr Menashe Tahan; Librarian; Lead Curator, Hebrew and Christian Orient Studies (2010-), Hd. of Hebrew Section (1997-) and Hebraica Curator (1989-), British Library; Convenor, Hebraica Libraries Group (2007-12). Publ.: The Golden Haggadah (The British Library Treasures in Focus Series, 2011); Hebrew Manuscripts: the power of script and image (2007); Memorial volumes to Jewish communities destroyed in the Holocaust: a bibliography of BL holdings (2004).

Add APAC, The British Library, 96 Euston Road, London NW1 2DB

Tel 020 7412 7646 *Fax* 020 7412 7641

Email ilana.tahan@bl.uk *Website* www.bl.uk

TAUB, Daniel,

b. London, 1962; m. Zehava; Israeli Diplomat; Ambassador of Israel to the Court of St. James's (2011-); over two decades of experience, Israel's Ministry of Foreign Affairs; expert in International law, with specializations in counter-terrorism and the laws of war; form. legal adviser, Israel's missions to the United Nations in New York and Geneva; form. Deputy Legal Counsel, Israeli Foreign Ministry; form. Education Officer, UJS; form. Pres. Oxford University Israel Soc. and Jewish Soc.; regular speaker, Limmud; lecturer on Middle Eastern issues, international law and negotiation theory; combat medic and reserve officer in the IDF's international law division.

Add Embassy of Israel, 2 Palace Green, London W8 4QB

TAUBE, Prof. (Hirsch) David, BA, BM, BCh.

b. Oct. 4, 1948; m. Dr. Clare Allen; Dir. Imperial College AHSC (2012-); Consultant Nephrologist, Hammersmith and St Mary's Hospital's (1990-); H. Consultant Nephrologist, Royal Brompton Hospital; Prof. of Transplant Medicine, Imperial College.

Add 66 Harley Street, London W1G 7HD

Email davidtaube@msn.com

TAYLOR, Derek Albert Joseph, OBE., MA (Cantab).

b. London, 1932; m. Diane Louise née Milman; Hotel Consultant; Ed. Bd. International Journal of Hospitality Management (1990-2007); Visiting Prof. University of Bournemouth (1997-9), University of Wales (1992-7), University of Surrey (1980-92); Hon. Fel. Oxford Poly. (1983-8); Past Pres. UK Hotel Catering and International Management Association (1983-4); Dir. Grand Metropolitan plc. (1967-81). Author of many books on the Hotel Industry and recently, Jewish Year Book (with Elkan D. Levy) (Ed. 2010-); Thank You For Your Business (2012); Sunderland Beth Hamedrash 1889 - 1999 (with Harold Davis) (2010); Solomon Schonfeld (2009); Don Pacifico (2008); Jewish Parliamentarians (with Lord Janner) (2008); British Chief Rabbis 1664-2006 (2006).

Email derekanddiane@aol.com

TAYLOR, Irving, MD ChM, FRCS, FMed Sci, FHEA.

b. Leeds, Jan. 7, 1945; m. Dr Berenice Penelope née Brunner; Prof. Surgery, V. Dean, UCL Medical School, London; V. Dean (Professional Affairs) and Dir. Medical Studies, University College London (2006-); Elected Council member, Royal College of Surgeons (2004-); Medical Case Examiner, General Medical Council (2003-); Prof. Surgery Hd. Dept. University College London (1993-2006); Prof. Surgery Hd. Dept. University of Southampton (1981-93); Snr. Lecturer, Surgery, University of Liverpool (1977-81); Past Pres. British Association, Surgical Oncology; Past Pres. Society of Academic and Research Surgeons;

Past Pres. European Society of Surgical Oncology. Publ.: Over 600 publications in peer review journal and Ed./Author of 27 books.

Add 43 Francklyn Gardens, Edgware, Middlesex HA8 8RU

Tel 020 895 8364

Email irving.taylor@ucl.ac.uk

TEACHER, Michael,

CEO. Ontex NV (2006-); Norwood Advisory Council (2008-); Ch. Norwood (2004-08), Deputy Ch. (2001-04), T. (1981-2001); Chief Exec. Hillsdown Holdings Plc (1987-1999); Mem. Jewish Leadership Council (2004-08); Ch. Ruralbridge Ltd.

Add Hillsdown House, 32 Hampstead High Street, London NW3 1QD

Email michael.teacher@ruralbridge.com

TEMERLIES, Marc Stephen, ACA, BSc, ALCM.

b. Hove; m. Idit née Herstik; Chartered Accountant and Investment Banker; Conductor, Choirmaster, Arranger and Pianist; Choirmaster, St John's Wood Synagogue (1996-); Fdr. and Conductor, Ne'imah Singers (1993-); Chazan, Hove Hebrew Congregation (1991-2).

Add 6 Sirkin Street, Raanana 43374, Israel

Tel +972 (9) 772 4857

Email marc.temerlies@citigroup.com

TERRET, Norman Harold, JP; Compagnon d'Europe, MBA.

b. Ayr, Scotland, Jan. 10, 1951; Ch. Telecom Associates Group; Ch. Leap2market Ltd.; Ch. Jewish Lads' and Girls' Brigade (JLGB); Snr. Adv. to Somaliland Govt (2008-); Pres. Equant (1984-97).

Tel 020 8866 8587

Email normanterret@btinternet.com

TOWNSLEY, Barry Stephen, CBE.

b. London, Oct. 14, 1946; m. Laura Helen née Wolfson; Stockbroker; Company Dir. Caprice Holdings Ltd. (2005-); United Trust Bank Ltd. (2004-); V. Pres. Weizmann Institute (2004-); Wentworth Group Holdings Ltd. (2004-); Principal Sponsor, Stockley Academic, Hillingdon (2000-); Ch. Oxford Children's Hospital Campaign (2004-09); Bd. Mem. National Gallery East Wing Dev. Project (2002-07); V. Ch. Serpentine Gallery.

Add c/o The United Trust Bank, 80 Haymarket, London SW1Y 4TE

TRAVIS, Anthony Selwyn,

b. June 9, 1932; m. Philippa née Brostoff; Emer. Prof. of Planning, Prof. Urban Regional Studies, University of Birmingham; late Visiting Prof. in Tourism, Glasgow Caledonian University; Dir. East-West Tourism Consultancy; form. Programme Co-ordinator EEC PHARE. Tourism Programme for Poland; Prof and Dir. Centre for Urban and Regional Studies, University of Birmingham; Past Mem. Birmingham and West Midland Jewish Representative Council; Past Ch. 'Grads' ORT, FHU etc. Lecturer on synagogue design, history and Israel. Publ.: 300, including My Life in Travel (2013); Planning for Tourism, Leisure and Sustainability (CABI, 2011); Realising Tourism Potential of the S. Wales Valleys (1985); Recreation Planning for the Clyde (1970); Report on 'Synagogue Design and Siting' (for Board of Deputies).

Add 20 Mead Rise, Birmingham B15 3SD

Tel 0121 454 1215 *Fax* 0121 454 1215

Email tony.travis@btinternet.com

TURNBERG, Lord Leslie Arnold, MB, ChB, MD, Kt Hon D. Sc. Manchester; Salford; Imperial College; Keele.

b. Mar. 22, 1934; m. Edna Barme; British medical professional; T. The Joseph Interfaith Foundation (2006-08); Pres. Medical Protection Society (1997-2007); Pres. Medical Council on Alcoholism (2000-05); Ch. Bd. of the Public Health Laboratory Service (1997-2005); Ch. UK Forum for Genetics and Insurance (1998-2002); Pres. Royal College of

Physicians (1992-97); Prof. of Medicine, University of Manchester (1973-97); Dean, Medical School (1983-86); Scientific Advisor, Association of Medical Research Charities; T. Wolfson Foundation; form. V. Pres. Academy of Medical Sciences; T. Foulkes Foundation; T. Weizmann UK; T. Ovarian Cancer Action; T. Daniel Turnberg Trust Fund. Publ.: 150 articles and books on Medical Science.

Add House of Lords, London SW1A 0PW

TURNER, Rev. Reuben,
b. Karlsruhe; Mem. Chief Rabbis Cabinet (1986-91); Dir. JNF Education Dept. (1973-91); Gen. Sec. Mizrachi-Hapoel Hamizrachi Federation of Great Britain (1970-73); Dir. Zionist Federation Synagogue Council (1967-70); Reader, Brixton Synagogue (1950-68); Min. Finsbury Park Synagogue (1948-50). Publ.: Jewish Living, The Popular Jewish Bible Atlas; Producer, The Four Brothers Kusevitsky (CD), Selections from the Seder service (CD), The Master Chazanim Collection.

Add 13 St Peter's Court NW4 2HG
Tel 020 8202 7023

TYLER, Alan Joseph Lawrence,
b. London, Apr. 2, 1924; m. Jill Naomi née Woolf; Ret. Lieutenant Commander, Royal Navy; Pres. Jewish Committee, HM Forces (2009-), (Ch. 2000-09); Wimbledon Deputy, Board of Deputies (1973-94); Ch. Wimbledon Synagogue (1976-79). Publ: Cheerful and Contented (Autobiography, 2000).

Add 9 Ashcombe Avenue, Surbiton, Surrey KT6 6PX
Tel 020 8399 1542 *Fax* 020 8399 1542
Email jalans@hotmail.co.uk

UNTERMAN, Rev. Alan, BA, B.Phil, PhD.
b. Bushey, Herts., May 31, 1942; form. M. Yeshurun Synagogue, Gatley, Cheshire; form. Lecturer, Comparative Rel. and Chaplain to Jewish Students, Manchester University; Lecturer, Jerusalem Academy of Jewish Studies; Hillel Dir. Victoria, Australia. Publ.: Encyclopaedia Judaica (Contributions); Wisdom of the Jewish Mystics; The Jews: their religious beliefs and practices; Judaism; Penguin Dictionary of Religion (Contributions on Judaism and Hinduism); Penguin Handbook of Living Religions (Contr. Judaism); Dictionary of Jewish Lore and Legend; The Kabbalistic Tradition; Historical Dictionary of the Jews.

Add 5 Rechov Fichman, Jerusalem 92584, Israel
Email unterman_alan@hotmail.com

VAN DEN BERGH, Rabbi Martin, B.ED, M.A.
b. Hilversum, Holland, Dec. 2, 1952; m. Anna Leon; Dir. Yiftach; Rabbi, Bevis Marks Synagogue (2010-12); Welfare Portfolio, Chief Rabbi's Cabinet (1998-); Snr. Rabbi, Ohel Leah Synagogue, Hong Kong (2006-10); Ch. Multi-Faith Group for Healthcare Chaplaincy (2005-06); Snr. Hospital Chaplain, United Synagogue Visitation Cttee. (1995-2006); Communal Rabbi, Wembley United Synagogue (1994-2006); Rabbi, Withington Congregation of Spanish & Portuguese Jews, Manchester (1983-94); Founding Ch. Spanish & Portuguese Congregation in Israel (1981-83).

Add Dolphin House, 12 Beaumont Gate, Radlett WD7 7AR
Tel 07948 916 009
Email rabbimartin@mvdbergh.com

VAN DER ZYL, Nikki, BA (Hons).
b. 1935, Berlin; m. George Rooker; Barrister; Poet; Artist; Singer/Composer; Board of Deputies of British Jews (1997-2009); T. Chipping Barnet Heritage Trust (2000); Presenter on SHALOM FM (1996); Fdr. Sternberg Theatre Actors Repertory Society (STARS); appeared in West End Theatre; Re-voicing Artiste on James Bond films.

Add 5 Greenview Court, 1431-1433 High Road, Whetstone, London N20 9RN
Tel 020 8446 5866 *Fax* 020 8446 5866
Email nikkivanderzyl@waitrose.com *Website* www.nikkivanderzyl.co.uk

VINER, Nicholas Philip, MA (Cantab), MBA (Harvard).

b. July 23 1961; m. Victoria Boyarsky; Dir. Profile Books Ltd. (2013-); Chief Exec. JCC Ventures Ltd (2011-13); Chief Exec. Jewish Community Centre for London (2006-13); Ch. Pop-Up Theatre (2001-08); Snr. Partner, The Boston Consulting Group (1987-2006).

Add 341-351 Finchley Road, London NW3 6ET

Tel 020 7433 8989

Email nick.viner@jw3.org.uk *Website* www.jw3.org.uk

VOGEL, Michele,

Mem. Jewish Leadership Council; Pres. WIZO UK.

Add WIZO House, 107 Gloucester Place, London W1U 6BY

Tel 020 7486 2691

Website www.wizouk.org

VOGEL, Rabbi Shraga Faivish,

b. Salford, Lancs, Apr. 22, 1936; Ch. Centre for Jewish Life; form. Dir. Lubavitch Foundation (1960-2007).

Add 11 Hallswelle Road, London NW11 0DH

Tel 020 8458 9039

Email faivish@thecjl.org

WAGERMAN, Josephine Miriam (née Barbanel), OBE, BA (Hons.), PGCE, Ac. Dip., MA (Ed).

b. London, Sept. 17, 1933, m. Peter; Ch. Legacy Division UJIA (2011-13); Cttee. Women's Interfaith Network (2004-); Independent Assessor NHS Non-Exec. Appointments Panel (1998-2000); Mem. Adv. Bd. UJIA (1997-); Gov. Naima Jewish Prep. School (1996-2012); Inner Cities Religious Council (Dept. of the Environment) (1994-2009); Mem. Academic Panel, Stuart Young Awards (1990-); Hadassah International Volunteer of Distinction (2003); form. Pres. Board of Deputies (2000-3), Snr. V. Pres. (1997-2000), V. Pres. (1994-7); Adv. to the Trustees, Pierre and Maniusia Gildesgame Trust (1996-9); Mem. Council Centre for Study of Jewish Christian Relations, Selly Oak Colleges (1995-8); Jewish Care Woman of Distinction (1996); Gov. Central Foundation Schools London (1996); Chief Exec. Lennox Lewis College (1994-6); form. Hd. JFS (1985-93); Pres. London AMMA (1982-3); form. Mem. ILEA Standing Jt. Adv. Cttee. Working Party on Teachers Service Conditions, History and Social Studies Adv. Cttee.

Add 38 Crespigny Road, London NW4 3DX

Tel 020 8203 7471

Email wagerman@btinternet.com

WAGERMAN, Dr Peter Henry, LDS.RCS (Eng).

b. London, June 10, 1932; m. Josephine Miriam née Barbanel; retired Dental Surgeon; Mem. Blind Veterans UK (2012-); Ch. Friends of Jewish Servicemen and Women (2010-); V. Pres. Association of Jewish Ex-Servicemen & Women (2010-); Nat. Ch. AJEX (2008-10), Nat. Dep. Ch. (2006-8); Mem. Jewish Cttee. HM Forces (2005-); Board of Deputies of British Jews (2003-), Community Issues Division (2003-12); Freeman, City of London (2000); Ch. Hendon Branch, AJEX (1998-2006); Ch. London Dental Cttee. JIA (1984-6); Mem. London Jewish Male Choir (1961-81); General Dental Practitioner (1960-2007); Flt. Lt. Royal Air Force (1956-9); House Surgeon, King's College Hospital (1956).

Add 38 Crespigny Road, London NW4 3DX

Tel 020 8203 7471

Email wagerman@btinternet.com

WAGNER, Leslie, CBE, MA (Econ.) D. University Middx, D. University Leeds Metropolitan, D. Civil Laws, Huddersfield, D. University, Open, D. University Derby.

b. Manchester, Feb. 21, 1943, m. Jennifer; Ch. Commission on Jewish Schools (2008); Chancellor, University of Derby (2003-8); Ch. Education Leeds (2004-7); Ch. Higher Education Academy (2004-7); Ch. University Vocational Awards Council (2001-3); V. Chancellor, Leeds Metropolitan University (1994-2003); Dir. Leeds TEC Ltd (1997-2001);

Ch. Yorkshire and Humberside Universities Association (1996-9); Ch. Higher Education for Capability (1994-8); Ch. Jewish Community Allocation Bd. (1994-6); Ch. Society for Research into Higher Education (1994-96); V. Pres. US (1992-3); V. Chancellor and Chief Exec. University of North London (1987-93); Mem. Council, US; T. Chief Rabbinate Trust; T. Jewish Chronicle. Publ.: Choosing to Learn: Mature Students in Education (with others); The Economics of Education Media; Agenda for Institutional Change in Higher Education (Ed.); Readings in Applied Microeconomics (Ed.).

Add 12 Aminadav, Jerusalem 93549 Israel

Tel +972 (2) 563 9638

Email vcwagner@hotmail.com

WALDMANN, Prof. Herman, BA, MB BChir, PhD, MRCPath, MRCP, FRS.

b. Feb. 27, 1945; m. Judith Ruth Young; Emer. Prof. Pathology, Oxford University (2013-); JDRF Excellence in Clinical Res. Award (2005); José Carreras Award, European Haematology Association (2005); Thomas Starzl Prize in Surgery (2007); Fel. Lincoln College, Oxford (1994); Fel. Royal Society (1990).

Add Sir William Dunn School of Pathology, South Parks Road, Oxford OX1 3RE

Email herman.waldmann@path.ox.ac.uk

WALSH, David, LLB (Hons).

b. Leeds, May 21, 1937; m. Jenny, née Cronin; Solicitor; Dir. Peek Plc, Carlisle Group Plc; Mem. Bd. of UJIA; form. Ch. RSGB, now V. Pres.; Pres. West London Synagogue (1988-91), Ch. (1981-85).

Add 82 North Gate, Prince Albert Road, London NW8 7EJ

Tel 020 7586 1118 *Fax* 020 7483 2598

WARREN, Loraine,

b. London, Dec. 15, 1947; m. Paul Warren; Pres. WIZOuk, (form. Ch. of Trustees (2006-12).

Add WIZOuk, Charles House, 108/110 Finchley Road, London NW3 5JJ

Tel 020 7319 9169 *Fax* 020 7486 7521

Email lorainewarren@yahoo.co.uk

WARRENS, Anthony Nigel, BSc (Glasgow), BM, BCh, DM (Oxon), PhD (London), FRCP, FRCPath, FEBS, FHEA.

b. Glasgow, Oct. 24, 1959; m. Ruth née Burns; Dean for Education; Dir. Institute of Health Sciences Education; Prof. Renal and Transplantation Medicine, Barts and The London School of Medicine and Dentistry, Queen Mary, University of London; Consultant Physician, Royal London Hospital, Wellington Hospital, The Physicians' Clinic, BMI Garden Hospital and BMI London Independent Hospital; Ch. London School of Jewish Studies (2009-); Co-Ch. Immanuel College, Bushey (2001-); Tru. United Jewish Israel Appeal (2004-12), Ch. Educational Leadership Policy Group, Ch. UK programme; Tru. Jewish Continuity (1993-6); previously Bd. Mem. Hampstead United Synagogue and Finchley United Synagogue.

Add Office of the Dean of Education, Barts and The London School of Medicine and Dentistry, Garrod Building, Turner Street, London E1 2AD

Tel 020 7882 2261

Email awarrens@qmul.ac.uk

WASSERSTEIN, Bernard Mano Julius, MA, DPhil, DLitt, FRHistS, FBA.

b. London, Jan. 22, 1948; Meyer Prof. Modern Jewish History, University Chicago (2003-); Guggenheim Fel. (2007-08); Prof. History, University Glasgow (2000-3); Pres. JHSE (2000-02); Pres. Oxford Centre for Hebrew and Jewish Studies (1996-2000); form. Prof. of History, Brandeis University (1982-96), Dean of Graduate School of Arts and Sciences (1990-92); form. Res. Fel. Nuffield College, Oxford. Publ.: The British in Palestine; Britain and the Jews of Europe 1939-1945; The Secret Lives of Trebitsch Lincoln; Herbert Samuel; Vanishing Diaspora; Secret War in Shanghai; Divided Jerusalem; Israel and Palestine; Barbarism and Civilization; On the Eve.

Add History Department, University of Chicago, 1126 East 59th Street, Chicago, IL 60637, USA

Tel +1 (773) 702 3637

Email bmjw@uchicago.edu

WASSERSTEIN, David John, MA, DPhil, FRHistS, FRAS.

b. London, Sept. 21, 1951; Academic; Prof. History and Jewish Studies, Eugene Greener Jnr. Prof. Jewish Studies, Vanderbilt University (2004-), Dir. Program in Jewish Studies (2005-08); Fel. Davis Center, History Department, Princeton University (2008-09); Prof. (1994-2004), Associate Prof. (1990-94), Islamic History, Tel Aviv University; Fel. Institute for Advanced Studies, Jerusalem (2002-03); Fel. Wissenschaftskolleg zu Berlin (1999-2000); Assistant Lecturer (later College Lecturer), Semitic Languages Dept. University College, Dublin (1978-90). Among recent publications: From Hellenism to Islam, Cultural and Linguistic Change in the Roman Near East (Co-Ed. 2009); Language of Religion, Language of People: Medieval Judaism, Christianity and Islam (Co-Ed. 2006); Madrasa: Mamluks and Ottomans (Ed. with A. Ayalon, 2006); The Legend of the Septuagint, from Classical Antiquity to Today (with A. Wasserstein, 2006); Education, Religion and State in the Middle East (Ed. with A. Ayalon, 2004).

Add Dept. of History, Vanderbilt Univ., VU Station B# 351802, 2301 Vanderbilt Place, Nashville TN37235-1802 USA

Tel +1 (615) 322 7801 *Fax* +1 (615) 343 6002

Email david.wasserstein@vanderbilt.edu

WEBBER, Alan, MSc, PhD, FRICS.

b. London, Sept. 5, 1933; m. Roseruth Freedman; Ch. Israel, Britain and Commonwealth Association; V. Ch. New Synagogue Netanya; Deputy Ch. B'nai B'rith Hillel Foundation Executive (2001-05); Ch. B'nai B'rith Hillel Foundation (1998-2001), Hon. S. (1990-98); Ch. of Governors, St. Margaret's School, Hampstead (1990-2001); Pres. First Lodge, B'nai B'rith (1995-97); Ch. Jewish Community Information (1994-97); H. Officer, St. John's Wood Synagogue (1990-91); H. Officer, Hampstead Synagogue (1970-76). Publ.: The B'nai B'rith Hillel Foundation – 1953-1993; B'nai B'rith – 150 years of service to the community; First Century: B'nai B'rith First Lodge of England 1910-2010.

Add 14/1 Ha M'Apilim, Netanya 42264, Israel

Email alanwebber@012.net.il

WEBBER, Anne, BSc (Hons), FRSA.

b. Manchester; Governor, Oxford Centre for Hebrew and Jewish Studies (2012-); Pres. Jewish Book Council (2005-), Ch. (2002-5); Dir. Central Registry of Information on Looted Cultural Property, 1933-1945 (2001-); Fdr. and Co-Ch. Commission for Looted Art in Europe (1999-); Producer and Dir. Legend Films (1994-98); Producer and Dir. BBC TV Documentaries and Features Depts (1980-94).

Add 76 Gloucester Place, London W1U 6HJ

Tel 020 7487 3401 *Fax* 020 7487 4211

Email annewebber@lootedartcommission.com *Website* www.lootedartcommission.com

WEGIER, Michael, MA, BA.

Chief Exec. UJIA (2012-); Exec. Dir. Melitz educational institute in Jerusalem (2009-2012); Dir. Programme and Planning, UJIA (2002-7); Dir. Jewish Education, Jewish Community Centre (JCC), Baltimore, USA (1996-9).

Add UJIA, 37 Kentish Town, London NW1 8NX

Tel 020 7424 6400

Email central@ujia.org *Website* www.ujia.org

WEIDENFELD, George, Baron of Chelsea, GBE, H. MA (Oxon), H. PhD, Ben Gurion University, D.Litt, Exeter; Holder of the Knight Commander's Cross (Badge & Star) of the German Order of Merit; Holder of the Golden Knight's Cross with Star of the Austrian Order of Merit, Austrian Cross of Honour for Arts and Science; Order of Merit of Italian Republic;

Chevalier de l'Ordre National de la Légion d'Honneur, France, Charlemagne Medal for European Media, Italian Order of Merit, Teddy Kollek Life Achievement Award (2009), Italian Grand Officer of the Order of Merit (2005) Fel. King's College London, Honorary Degree, Oxford University (2010), Degree of Doctor of Letters, Honoris Causa, Oxford University 2010.

b. Vienna, Sept. 13, 1919; Publisher; Ch. Weidenfeld and Nicolson, London; Founding Pres. Institute for Strategic Dialogue, Weidenfeld Scholarships and Leadership Programme, Oxford; H. Ch. Bd. of Govs. Ben Gurion University of Negev (2005), Ch. (1995-2004); H. Senator, University Bonn (1996); Hon. Fel. St. Anne's College, Oxford (1993), St. Peter's College, Oxford (1992); Political adv. to Pres. Weizmann of Israel (1949-50); Mem. Bd. Govs. Institute of Human Science, Vienna; Gov. Weizmann Institute of Science; Gov. Tel Aviv University; T. Jerusalem Foundation; Freeman City of London, etc. Awards: Tolerance Ring of the European Academy of Science and the Arts, Frankfurt 2012); Polish Bene Merito Distinction (2011); Order of Merit, Land Baden-Württemberg, Germany (2008); London Book Fair/Trilogy Lifetime Achievement Award for International Publishing (2007). Publ.: The Goebbels Experiment; Remembering My Good Friends (auto).

Add 9 Chelsea Embankment SW3 4LE

Tel 020 7351 0042 *Fax* 020 7379 1604

Email georgeweidenfeld@orionbooks.co.uk

WEIL (BREUER-WEIL), Georges,

b. Vienna, July 7, 1938; Sculptor, painter, jeweller; exhibited UK, US, Israel, Tokyo, Switzerland, South Africa etc.; portrait busts of Ben-Gurion, Churchill, General de Gaulle, etc.; Specialist in Judaica, including Bar-Ilan collection shown in Mann Auditorium, Tel Aviv; collections in British Museum, Antwerp Museum, Royal Museum of Scotland, etc.; H. Mem. Japanese Art Carvers Society.

Add 93 Ha Eshel Street, Herzlia Pituach, Israel

Email gweil@netvision.net.il

WEINBERG, Joanna, BA, PhD (London).

b. London, Nov. 11, 1949; Catherine Lewis Fel. in Rabbinics, Oxford Centre for Hebrew and Jewish Studies (2001-); James Mew Lecturer in Rabbinic Texts, University of Oxford (1999-); Reader in Rabbinics, Leo Baeck College, London (1982-2001). Publ.: Azariah de' Rossi's Observations on the Syriac New Testament (2005); The Light of the Eyes of Azariah de' Rossi: An English translation with introduction and notes (2001).

Add The Oriental Institute, Pusey Lane, Oxford OX1 2LE

Tel 01865 288 213

Email joannaweinberg@orinst.ox.ac.uk

WEINBERG, Sir Mark (Aubrey), BCom, Kt.

b. South Africa, Aug. 9, 1931; m. Anouska Hempel; Ch. Pension Insurance Corporation Holdings (2006-); Ch. Synergy Insurance Holdings (2005-); Pres. St James's Place Group (2004-), Ch. (1991–2004); T. Tate Gallery (1985–92); Hon. T. NSPCC (1983–91); Gov. LSE. Publ.: Weinberg and Blank on Take-overs and Mergers (1962).

Add SJP Head Office, St James's Place House, 1 Tetbury Road, Gloucester GL7 1FP

Tel 0800 0138 137

WEINER, Rabbi Chaim, BA (Hebrew University of Jerusalem), M.A. (Hebrew University of Jerusalem), Rabbinical Ordination Seminary of Judaic Studies Jerusalem (Masorti), European Masorti Bet Din. Av Bet Din.

b. Sydney, Nova Scotia, Nov. 11, 1958; m. Judy; Dir. European Masorti Bet Din (2005-); form. M. New London Synagogue (2000-05); Jerusalem Fel. (1998-2000); form. M. Edgware Masorti Synagogue (1991-98); Dir. Gesher, Masorti Teenage Centre, London (1991-96); National Dir. of Noam, Masorti Youth Movement, Israel (1987-91).

Add c/o Masorti Bet Din, 3 Shakespeare Road, London N3 1XE

Email weiner@masorti.org.uk *Website* www.masorti.org.uk

WEISMAN, Malcolm, OBE, MA (Oxon), OCM.

Barrister-at-Law; Gladstone Pupillage Awardee, Middle Temple; Hd. of Chambers Emer. 1 Grays Inn Square; Recorder, S.E. Circuit; V. Pres. Commonwealth Jewish Trust; T. International Chaplaincy, University Derby; Rel. Adv. to Small Communities; Mem. Chief Rabbi's Cabinet; Chaplain, Oxford University and new Universities; National H. Chaplain, AJEX (2000-); Special Adjudicator, Immigration Appeals (1998-); Pres. Snr. Allied Air Force Chaplains (1993-), Ch. and Sec. Gen. (1980-); Special Interfaith Award, Peterborough Interfaith Council (2011, 2013); Chaplain, London District (2009), 14 Prisons, US Bases (2010); Officiating Chaplain, Military (2009); Co-Chaplain, Basket Makers Company (2008-09); Chaplain to Mayor of Montgomery (2006-7), to Mayor of Redbridge (2005-6), to Mayor of Barnet (1994-5); US Rabbi of the Year Award (2006); Award for Outstanding Leadership, Rabbinical Council, US (2005); ICCJ Gold Medallion (2001); Chief Rabbi's Award for Excellence (1993); Patron, JNF; Patron, Davar; Snr. Jewish Chaplain to H.M. Forces; T. Jewish Music Institute; T. International Multi-Faith Centre, University Derby; Ed. Menorah; Sec. Allied Air Forces Chaplain Cttee.; Tru. Council of Christians and Jews; Ct. Lancaster, East Anglia, Kent, Warwick, Sussex and Essex Universities; Exec. United States Military Chaplains Association; form. JWB, AJEX Exec.; Jewish Youth Fund; Pres. University College Jewish Society; form. Hon. S. IUJF; form. V. Pres. Torah V'avodah Organisation; Provincial Exec. JIA; V. Pres. and Religious Adv. Commonwealth Jewish Council; Small Jewish Community Council; V. Pres. and Religious Adv. Commonwealth Jewish Council.

Add Board of Deputies, 6 Bloomsbury Square, London WC1A 2LP

Tel 020 8459 4372

Email rosalie_weisman@hotmail.com

WEISSBORT, Daniel, MA (Cantab).

b. London, Apr. 30, 1935; m. Valentina Polukhina; Prof.; Research Fel. Dept. of English, King's College, London (2001-); Fdr. Ed. (with Ted Hughes), Modern Poetry in Translation (1965-2004); H. Prof. Centre for Translation and Comparative Cultural Studies, University Warwick (2002); Emer. Prof. of English and Comparative Literature, University of Iowa (2001). Publ.: Contemporary Russian Women's Poetry (with Valentina Polukhina, 2004); From Russian with Love: A Translation Memoir of Joseph Brodsky (2003); Letters to Ted (2003); What was all the Fuss About (2002); Selected Poems of Yehuda Amichai (2000); Selected Poems of Nikolai Zabolotsky (1999), etc.

Add 3 Powis Gardens, London NW11 8HH

Email danielweissbort@ntlworld.com

WEISSER, Jacques,

b. Antwerp, Feb. 7, 1942; m. Judy née Blitz; Exec. Dir. AJEX (2007-), Gen. Sec. (1994-2007); Tru. Yad Vashem - UK Foundation (2004-); Dep. T. Zionist Federation (2004-), Ch. (2007-09), V. Ch. (2006-07); Bd. Man. Radlett US (2002-); Gen. Sec. International Council of Jewish War Veterans (1998-); Bd. Man. Wembley US (1983-2001); T. and Ch. North West London Teenage Centre (1985-94); M. and T. Jewish Lads' and Girls' Brigade.

Email Jacques@ajex.org.uk

WEITZMAN, Peter David Jacob, MA, MSc, D.Phil (Oxon), DSc (Bath), FSB, FRSC.

b. London, Sept. 22, 1935; m. Avis née Galinski; Higher Education consultant; Emer. Prof. University Wales; V. Pres. Bournemouth Hebrew Congregation (2010-12); Ch. South Wales Jewish Representative Council (1997-2003); Pres. Penylan House Jewish Retirement Home, Cardiff (1991-99); Dir. of Academic Affairs, University Wales Institute, Cardiff (1988-93); Prof. of Biochemistry, University Bath (1979-88); Ch. Bournemouth Branch, Friends Israel Sport Centre. Publ.: Scientific writings.

Add 28 Albany, Manor Road, Bournemouth BH1 3EN

Email pdjw@btinternet.com

WESKER, Sir Arnold, Kt., FRSL, D.Litt (H. UEA), DHL (Denison University), H. Fel. Queen Mary & Westfield College London, Fel. award, Royal Central School of Speech and Drama FCSSD.

b. London, May 24, 1932, m. Dusty Bicker; CoP, International Playwrights Cttee. (1980-83); Ch. British Section, International Theatre Institute (1978-83); Dir. Centre 42 (1960-70).

Among recent work - Plays: Amazed and Surprised (2006); Longitude (2002); The Kitchen Musical (2000); Break, My Heart (1997); Denial (1997); Circles of Perception (1996); Circles of Perception (1996); Bluey (1993); The Confession (1993); Wild Spring (1992); Blood Libel (1991); Men Die Women Survive (1990); Letter to a Daughter (1990). Books: Fiction - Honey (2005); The King's Daughters (1998); Non-Fiction - The Birth of Shylock and the Death of Zero Mostel (1997); As Much As I Dare (autobiography) (1994). Film scripts: Letter to Myself (2003); Maudie (1995); Homage to Catalonia (1990). Television: Barabbas (2000); Menace (1961). Radio: Groupie (2001) (later adapted for stage). Libretto: Grief (2008). Collections: Wesker's Comedies (2012); Wesker's Historical Plays (2012); Wesker's Domestic Plays (2012); Joy and Tyrany (2011); Wesker's Political Plays (2010); Wesker's Social Plays (2009) (including Rocking Horse (BBC World Service 75th Anniversary Commission, 2007)); All Things Tire of Themselves (poems) (2008); Wesker's Love Plays (2008); Wesker's Monologues (2008).

Add 14 Champions Row, Wilbury Avenue, Hove BN3 6AZ

Tel 01273 734 013

Email wesker@compuserve.com *Website* www.arnoldwesker.com

WHINE, Michael David, MBE, BA (Hons), FCIM.

b. London, Apr. 4, 1947; m. Ester née Kamenetzky; Dir. Government and Intl. Affairs, Community Security Trust; Consultant, Defence and Security, European Jewish Congress; Dir. Defence and Group Relations Division, Board of Deputies (1986-2012); Hate Crime Independent Advisor Group, Ministry of Justice (2007-); London CPS Hate Crime Security Panel (2012-); Adv. Counter Terrorism Div. CPS (2008-); Metropolitan Police Authority, Hate Crime Forum (2003-12). Publ.: Trans-European Trends in Right-Wing Extremism (2012); Terrorism Against Jewish Communities and Israeli Institution Abroad (2011); The Radicalization of Diasporas and Terrorism (2009); The Homegrown Terrorist Threat in Europe (2008); An Unholy Alliance: Nazi Links with Arab Totalitarianism (2006); Holocaust Denial in the UK (2006); Islamism and Totalitarianism: Similarities and Differences (2001).

Add P.O. Box 35501, London NW4 2FZ

Tel 020 8457 9960

Email mikew@thecst.org.uk *Website* www.thecst.org.uk

WHITESON, Adrian Leon, OBE, MBBS (Hons.), MRCS, LRCP.

b. London, Dec. 12, 1934; m. Myrna; Med. Practitioner; V. Pres. of the British Paralympic Association; form. Ch. World Boxing Council and European Boxing Union Med. Commission; form. Chief Med. Off. British Boxing Bd. of Control; Pres. (form. Ch.), The Teenage Cancer Trust; Mem. Govt. Review Body for Sport for People with Disabilities.

Add 2 Welbeck Mansions, 35a Wellbeck Street, London W1G 8EZ

Tel 020 7842 5789

WIESEL, Elie, D.Lett (hc), D.Hum.Lett (hc), D.Hebrew.Lett. (hc), PhD (hc), DL (hc), etc.

b. Sighet, Romania, Sept. 30, 1928; m. Marion; Survivor of Auschwitz and Buchenwald; Fdr. Elie Wiesel Foundation for Humanity; Andrew W. Mellon Prof. in the Humanities, Boston University; Bd. Dirs. International Rescue Cttee. Grand-Croix, Legion of Honour; International Peace Prize Royal Belgian Acad.; Presidential Medal of Freedom (1992); Nobel Peace Prize (1986); US Congress Gold Medal (1986); Ch. US Holocaust Memorial Council (1980-86); Ch. US Pres. Com. on Holocaust (1979-80); District Prof. Judaic Studies, City University, N.Y. (1972-76). Among recent publications: The Sonderberg Case (2010); A Mad Desire to Dance (2009); Confronting Antisemitism: essays (with Kofi Annan 2006); Night (new translation 2006); Time of the Uprooted (2005); Wise Men and Their Tales (2003); Memoirs: All Rivers Run to the Sea; Vol. II: And the Sea is Never Full (1999); From the Kingdom of Memory; Reminiscences; The Forgotten, etc.

Add Boston University, 147 Bay State Road, Boston, MA 02215 USA

WINEMAN, Vivian, MA (Cantab).

b. London, Feb. 14, 1950; m. Naomi Helen née Greenberg; Solicitor; Consultant, DWFM Beckham (2010-); Ch. JLC (2009-); Pres. Board of Deputies (2009-), Snr. V. Pres. (2006-09);

V. Pres. European Jewish Congress (2009-); Advisory Bd. Three Faiths Forum (2007-); V. Ch. UK Inter Faith Network (2007-); H. Legal Counsel High Premium LLoyd's of London Group (2004-); Ch. Defence and Group Relations Div. (2006-09); Partner, David Wineman (1981-2008); Ch. New Israel Fund (1992-94). Publ.: Contracts (Rights of Third Parties) Act, 1999 (2001).

Add 76 Meadway, London NW11 6QH

WINER, Rabbi Dr Mark L, PhD, DD.

b. Logan, Utah, Dec. 12, 1942; m. Suellen née Mark; V. Ch. WUPJ (2005-); Ch. International Interfaith Task Force (1998-); Snr. Rabbi, West London Synagogue (1998-2010); Chaplain to Lord Mayor of Westminster (2008-09, 2000-01); Pres. National Council of Synagogues (USA) (1995-98); Mem. International Jewish Cttee. for Interreligious Consultations (1987-98); V. Pres. Synagogue Council of America (1993-94). Publ.: articles in Manna, European Judaism, etc.

Add West London Synagogue, 33 Seymour Place, London W1H 5AU

Tel 020 7723 4404 *Fax* 020 7224 8258

Email rabbi@wls.org.uk

WINNICK, David, MP.

b. Brighton, June 26, 1933; Mem. Home Affairs Cttee. (2005-); MP (Lab.), for Walsall North (1979-), Croydon South (1966-70).

Add House of Commons, London SW1A 0AA

Tel 020 7219 5003 *Fax* 020 7219 0257

Email winnickd@parliament.uk

WINSTON, Clive Noel, BA (Cantab).

b. London, Apr. 20, 1925; m. Beatrice Jeannette née Lawton; V. Pres. (form. Ch.) LJ; form. T. European Bd. of WUPJ; form. Dep. Solicitor, Metropolitan Police.

Add 2 Bournwell Close, Cockfosters, Hertfordshire EN4 0JX

Tel 020 8449 5963

WINSTON, Robert Maurice Lipson, Baron of Hammersmith, FMed Sci, Hon. FREng, FRCSE, DSc., FRCP, FRCOG.

b. London, July 15, 1940; Prof. Science and Society and Emer. Prof. Fertility Studies, Imperial College London; Ch. Royal College of Music (2007-); Consultant Obstetrician and Gynaecologist, Hammersmith Hospital, London (-2003); Chancellor, Sheffield Hallam University (2001-); Ch. Science and Technology Select Cttee. House of Lords (1999-); Dean, Institute of Obstetrics and Gynaecology (1995-); Chief Rabbi's Open Award for Contribution to Society (1993); Prof. of Gynaecology, Texas University (1980-81); Vis. Prof. Leuven University, Belgium (1976-77). Publ.: Reversibility of Female Sterilization; Tubal Infertility; Infertility: a Sympathetic Approach; Scientific writings on aspects of reproduction; The Story of God (2005).

Add House of Lords, London SW1A 0PW

Email r.winston@imperial.ac.uk *Website* robertwinston.org

WISEMAN, Debbie, MBE, H. Fel. Trinity College of Music and Guildhall School of Music and Drama.

b. London, May 10, 1963. Currently one of the busiest composers and conductors in the UK; Commissioned to compose a movement of new 'Water Music' for The Queen's Diamond Jubilee Pageant (June 2012). Scores: Father Brown; Lost Christmas; The Passion; Jekyll; Flood; Stephen Fry in America; Judge John Deed; Joanna Lumley's Nile; Tom and Viv; Freeze Frame; The Guilty; Land Girls; Before You Go; Othello; Arsene Lupin; He Knew He Was Right; Michael Palin's New Europe; Sherlock Holmes and the Baker Street Irregulars; My Uncle Silas; Tom's Midnight Garden; Wilde, WPC 56; and many more.

Tel Roz Colls Music Matters Intl. 020 8979 4580

Email wisemaninfo@aol.com *Website* www.debbiewiseman.co.uk

WISTRICH, Robert Solomon, BA, MA (Cantab, 1970), PhD (London, 1974).

b. Lenger (USSR), Apr. 7, 1945; University Professor; First Holder of the Jewish Chronicle Ch. in Jewish Studies, University College, London; Dir. Vidal Sassoon International Centre for the Study of Antisemitism (2002-); Neuberger Ch. of Modern Jewish History, Hebrew University of Jerusalem (1985-). Awards: Journal for Antisemitism Lifetime Achievement (2011); Austrian State Prize for Danubian History (1992); H.H. Wingate/Jewish Quarterly Prize for Non-Fiction (1992); James Parkes Prize (1984). Among recent publications: From Ambivalence to Betrayal: The Left, The Jews and Israel (2012); A Lethal Obsession: Antisemitism from Antiquity to the Global Jihad (2010); Laboratory of World Destruction: Germans and Jews in Central Europe (2007); Obsession: Radical Islamic War Against the West (film, 2006); Blaming the Jews (film, 2003); Nietzsche: Godfather of Fascism (2002); Hitler and the Holocaust (2001); Demonizing the Other: Antisemitism, Racism and Xenophobia (1999).

Add Aliyat Hanoar Street 6/3, Ramot Alon Jerusalem, Israel

Email sicsa@mail.huji.ac.il *Website* http://sicsa.huji.ac.il

WITTENBERG, Rabbi Jonathan, MA, PGCE.

b. Glasgow, Sept. 17, 1957; m. Nicola Solomon; Snr. Rabbi, Assembly of Masorti Synagogue (2008-); Rabbi, New North London Masorti Synagogue (1987-). Publ.: Walking with the Light: From Frankfurt to Finchley (2013); The Silence of Dark Water: An Inner Journey (2008); The Eternal Journey: Meditations on the Jewish Year (2001); A Pesach Companion (Ed. and co-author, 1997); The Laws of Life: A Guide to Traditional Jewish Practice in Times of Bereavement (1997); A High Holyday Companion (Ed. and co-author, 1996); The Three Pillars of Judaism: A Search for Faith and Values (1996).

Add 10 Amberden Avenue, London N3 3BJ

Tel 020 8343 3927 *Fax* 020 8346 1914

Email rabbi@nnls-masorti.org.uk

WOLFF, David,

Ch. JC Maccabi (Southern) Football League (1970-); V. Pres. London FA (1970-); V. Pres. MaccabiGB.

Add 36 Poplar Way, Barkingside, Essex IG6 1EN

Tel 020 8551 2384

Email dawolff@gotadsl.co.uk

WOLFSON, Dianna (née Sherry), BA, DCE.

b. Birmingham, June 29, 1938; Hd. (retd.); Mem. Scottish Inter Faith Council (2004-); H. Pres. Glasgow Jewish Representative Council (2001-), Pres. (1998-2001); Hd. Calderwood Lodge Jewish Primary School (1976-98); Ch. West of Scotland Council of Christians and Jews (1992-95).

Add 22 Park Court, Giffnock, Glasgow G46 7PB

Tel 0141 620 0650

Email dwolfson@tinyworld.co.uk

WOOLF, Lord Harry, PC, LLB, H. FBA, DLL (H.).

b. Newcastle upon Tyne, May 2, 1933; m. Marguerite née Sassoon; UCL Laws 1954; Fellow 1981; Ch. UCL Council (2005–08); called to the Bar (1955); Judge 1979; Law Lord (1992); Master of the Rolls (1996–2000); Lord Chief Justice of England and Wales (2000–05); President of the Courts of England and Wales; Chancellor, Open University of Israel (2004-13); Ch. Bank of England Financial Markets Law Cttee. (2006-09); Ch. Judging Panel, annual FIRST Magazine Responsible Capitalism Awards; Patron, The Woolf Institute; Mem. Blackstone Chambers, accredited mediator and Chartered Arbitrator (Cairn); Ch. Prison Reform Trust (2011-); non-permanent judge, Court of Final Appeal of Hong Kong (2003-12); First Pres. Qatar Financial Centre Civil and Commercial Court (2006-12); Mem. Select Cttee. on Inquiries Act (2005); Mem. Crossbench Peers (1992); served on House of Lords Constitution Cttee; Ch. Sub-Cttee. Members' Interests; Patron, Rehabilitation for Addicted Prisoners Trust; form. Ch. Institute of Advanced Legal Studies; Ch. network of the

Presidents of the Supreme Judicial Courts of the EU Working Group on mediation and the Financial Markets Law Cttee; produced The Woolf Reforms (1999), Strangeways Report into the British Prison System (1990), Access to Justice report (1996); The Woolf Committee, produced report, Ethical Business Conduct in BAE Systems plc: the way forward (2008). Ch. independent inquiry into the LSE's relationship with Libya and with Saif Gaddafi (published 2011); Lifetime Achievement Award by the IAM (International Academy of Mediators) (2009); Hon. Degrees from twelve universities; Hon Fel. British Academy, the Academy of Medical Sciences, The Royal Society of Medicine, (2012), of UCL and the US College of Trial Lawyers and is an Hon Member of the American Law Institute. Among recent publications: various editions (jointly) of De Smith's Judicial Review of Administration (7th ed); An Independent Governance Review of the International Cricket Council (2012); The Pursuit of Justice (2008).

Add House of Lords, London SW1A 0PW

WOOLFSON, Michael Mark, MA, PhD, DSc, FRS, FRAS, FInstP.

b. London, Jan. 9, 1927; Emer. Prof. Theoretical Physics, York University; form. Reader in Physics, Manchester Institute of Science and Technology. Publ.: Direct Methods in Crystallography; An Introduction to X-ray Crystallography; The Origin of the Solar System; Physical and Non-physical Methods of Solving Crystal Structures; An Introduction to Computer Simulation; The Origin and Evolution of the Solar System; Planetary Science; Mathematics for Physics; The Formation of the Solar System; Everyday Probability and Statistics; Time, Space, Stars and Man; Materials, Matter and Particles; On the Origin of Planets; The Fundamentals of Imaging.

Add Physics Dept., University of York, York YO10 5DD

Tel 01904 432 230

Email mmw1@york.ac.uk

WOUK, Herman, BA, Columbia University, 1934; LHD (H.), Yeshiva University; LLD (H.), Clark University; DLitt (H.), American International College; PhD (H.), Bar-Ilan University, Hebrew University; DLitt (H.) Trinity College; DLitt George Washington University.

b. New York, May 27, 1915; Writer. Publ.: Non-fiction: This is My God; The Will to Live On; The Language God Talks. Novels: Aurora Dawn; Marjorie Morningstar; The Winds of War; War and Remembrance; Youngblood Hawke; Don't Stop the Carnival; The Caine Mutiny; Inside, Outside; City Boy; The Hope, The Glory; A Hole in Texas; The Lawgiver. Plays: The Caine Mutiny Court-Martial, etc. TV Screenplays: The Winds of War, War and Remembrance.

Add c/o B.S.W. Literary Agency, 303 Crestview Drive, Palm Springs CA 92264 USA

Website www.hermanwouk.com

WRIGHT, Rabbi Alexandra (née Levitt), MA, PGCE.

b. London, Dec. 10, 1956; Snr. Rabbi, The Liberal Jewish Synagogue (Associate M. 1986-89); Jewish Chaplain, North London Hospice (1997-2005); M, Radlett and Bushey Reform Synagogue (1990-2003); Lecturer in Classical Hebrew, Leo Baeck College (1987-97). Publ.: 'An approach to feminist theology' in Hear Our Voice (1994); 'Judaism' in Women in Religion (1994).

Add Liberal Jewish Synagogue, 28 St John's Wood Road, London NW8 7HA

Email awright@ljs.org *Website* www.ljs.org

WRIGHT, Rosalind (née Kerstein), CB, QC (Hon Causa), LLB (Hons) (London).

b. London, Nov. 2, 1942; m. Dr David J. M. Wright; Barrister; Mem. Regulatory Bd. ACCA (2012-); Mem. Cttee. UKAJLJ (2012-); Complaints Com. London Metal Exchange (2010-); form. Non-Exec. Dir. Insolvency Service Steering Bd. (2006-11); Mem. Supervisory Cttee. of OLAF (European anti-Fraud Office) (2005-12); Ch, Fraud Adv. Panel (2003-); Tru. Jewish Association for Business Ethics (2002); Non-Exec. Dir. DTI Legal Services Group (2001-09); Non-Exec. Dir. Office of Fair Trading (2003-07); Dir. Serious Fraud Office (1997-2003); Hd. Prosecutions, Exec. Dir. Securities and Futures Authority (1987-97); Assistant Dir. Hd. of Fraud Investigation Group, DPP (1985-87).

Add Fraud Advisory Panel, P.O. Box 433, Chartered accountants Hall, Moorgate Place, London EC2R 6EA

Tel 020 7920 8721

Email info@fraudadvisorypanel.org *Website* www.fraudadvisorypanel.org

YENTOB, Robert,
Delegate Ch. Spanish and Portuguese Jews' Congregation; Mem. Jewish Leadership Council; T. Maimonides Foundation.

Add 6 Bloomsbury Square, London WC1A 2LP

YOUNG, Rt. Hon. David Ivor, Baron of Graffham, PC, LLB (Hons.).
b. London, Feb. 27, 1932; Solicitor; Dir. Salomon Inc. (1990-); Exec. Ch. Cable and Wireless plc (1990-); Pres. Jewish Care (1990-); Ch. Oxford Centre for Hebrew and Jewish Studies (1989-92); Dep. Ch. Conservative Party (1989-90); Sec. of State for Trade and Industry (1987-9); Ch. National Economic Development Organisation (1982-9); Sec. of State for Employment (1985-7); Min. without Portfolio, Min. in Cabinet (1984-5); Ch. Manpower Services Com. (1982-4); Ch. Admin. Cttee. World ORT Union (1980-4); Ch. International Council, Jewish Social and Welfare Services (1982-83); Dir. Centre for Policy Studies (1979-82); Gov. Oxford Centre for Post-Graduate Heb. Studies; Pres. Chai Cancer Care; T. Coexistence Trust; Ch. Jewish Museum, London; form. Pres. British ORT. Publ.: The Enterprise Years: A Businessman in the Cabinet (1990).

Add Young Associates, Harcourt House, 19 Cavendish Square, London W1G 0PL

ZALUD, Rabbi Norman, APhS, FRSA.
b. Liverpool, Oct. 5, 1932; Rabbi Emer. Liverpool Reform Synagogue; M. Sha'arei Shalom Synagogue, Manchester; M. Blackpool Reform Jewish Congregation; Jewish Chaplain to H.M. Prisons.

Add Blackpool Reform Jewish Congregation, Raikes Parade, Blackpool FY1 4EX

Tel 01253 623 687

ZARUM, Rabbi Dr Raphael E.S., BSc, MA, PhD.
b. London, Nov. 22, 1968; m. Jacqueline Nicholls; Educator; Dean, London School of Jewish Studies. Publ.: Torah L'Am; The Jampacked Bible.

Add c/o LSJS, Wohl Campus for Jewish Education, Schaller House, 44a Albert Road, London NW4 2SJ

Tel 020 8203 6427 *Fax* 020 8203 6420

Email info@lsjs.ac.uk *Website* www.lsjs.ac.uk

Twitter @SuperSedra

ZEIDMAN, His Honour Judge Martyn, QC, LLB.
b. Cardiff May 30, 1952; m. Verity née Owen; Circuit Judge (2001-); Pres. Mental Health Tribunal (1999-); Ch. Jewish Marriage Council (2004); Recorder (1995). Publ.: Making Sense of the Leasehold Reform Housing and Urban Development Act 1993 (1994); A Short Guide to the Road Traffic Act 1991 (1991); A Short Guide to the Courts and Legal Services Act 1990 (1990); Steps to Possession (1989); A Short Guide to the Housing Act 1988 (1988); A Short guide to the Landlord and Tenant Act 1987 (1987).

Add The Crown Court at Snaresbrook, The Court House, Hollybush Hill, London E11 1QW

Tel 020 8530 0000 *Fax* 020 8530 0073

ZELLICK, Graham John, CBE, QC (Hon), MA, PhD (Cantab), H. LHD (NYU), AcSS, H. LLD (Richmond, Birm), H. FSALS, Hon.FRAM H. FBS, H. DLit (London, QM).
b. London, Aug. 12, 1948; Barrister; Mem. Investigatory Powers Tribunal (2013-); Pres. Valuation Tribunal for England (2009-); Ch. Senate, West London Synagogue (2006-); H. Prof. of Law, University Birmingham (2004-11); Hon. Fel. Gonville and Caius College, Cambridge (2001-); Emer. Prof. of Law, University of London (1998-), Prof. (1982-98); Master, Drapers' Company (2009-10); Gov. Tel Aviv University (2000-09); Ch. Criminal Cases Review Commission (2003-08); H. Fel. Leo Baeck College (2007), Ch. Bd. Gov. (2005-06); Pres. West London Synagogue (2000-06); Electoral Commissioner (2001-04); V.

Chancellor and Pres. University London (1997-2003), Dep. V. Chancellor (1994-97); V. Ch. National Adv. Council, Academic Study Group for Israel and The Middle East. (1995-2003); Master of the Bench, Middle Temple (2001, Reader 2013); Principal, Queen Mary and Westfield College, University of London (1991-8); Freeman, City of London.

Add 63 Hampstead Way, London NW11 7DN

Tel 020 7426 3916 (office) *Fax* 020 7247 6598

Email graham.zellick@gmail.com

ZERMANSKY, Victor David, LLB (H.).

b. Leeds, Dec. 28, 1931, m. Anita née Levison; Solicitor; Past Pres. Leeds Law Society (1988-9); form. Immigration Appeals Adjudicator (1970-8); H. Life. V. Pres. (Pres. 1974-7), Leeds Jewish Rep. Council; form. Assistant Recorder; Life Pres. Leeds Z.C.; form. Ch. Leeds Kashrut Authority, Beth Din Admin. Cttee.

Add 52 Alwoodley Lane, Leeds LS17 7PT

Tel 0113 267 3523 *Fax* 0113 267 3523

Email victor.zermansky@virgin.net

ZIFF, MICHAEL,

Ch. Maccabi GB.

Add Shield House, Harmony Way, London NW4 2BZ

ZIMMELS, Erla (née Broekema), Dip.Lib.

b. Amsterdam, Aug. 16, 1947; m. Judge Martin Zimmels; Librarian, London School of Jewish Studies (1999-); Librarian, Jews' College, London (1974-76); Librarian, Ets Haim Library, Sephardi Community, Amsterdam (1969-73); Librarian, Bibliotheca Rosenthaliana, Amsterdam (1968-73).

Add London School of Jewish Studies, Schaller House, Wohl Campus for Jewish Education, 44a Albert Road, London NW4 2ST

Tel 020 8203 6427 *Fax* 020 8203 6420

Email erla.zimmels@lsjs.ac.uk

ZIMMERMAN, Stephen, BA.

Ch. Jewish Care (2006-11); Ch. NewSmith Asset Management (2003-); Ch. Royal Marsden Hospital Cancer Campaign (2001-03); V. Pres. Merrill Lynch and Co. Inc. and Mem. Executive Management Cttee. (1997-2001); Dep. Ch. Mercury Asset Management Group (1995-97); Fund Manager, SG Warburg (1971-95); Mem. Jewish Leadership Council; Chief Operating Officer, Merrill Lynch Investment Managers.

Add 6 Bloomsbury Square, London WC1A 2LP

ZISSMAN, Sir Bernard Philip, H. LLD (B'ham), H. D. (BCU).

b. Birmingham, Dec. 11, 1934; Ch. Millennium Point Trust (2006-13); Pres. Representative Council of Birmingham and Midland Jewry (2005-); T. City of Birmingham Symphony Orchestra (1992-); Pres. Council Birmingham Hebrew Congregation (1999-2004); Ch. Good Hope Hospital NHS Trust (1998-2003); Dir. BRMB radio station (1995-2000); Leader, Conservative Group, Birmingham City Council (1992-5); Mem. Birmingham City Council (1965-95); Ch. Alexandra Theatre (Birmingham) Ltd (1986-93); Freeman of the City of London (1991); Lord Mayor, City of Birmingham (1990-1); Ch. Cttee. to establish Birmingham International Convention Centre/Symphony Hall (1982-6); Council Mem. Birmingham, Chamber of Commerce and Industry; Mem. Appeal Council National Memorial Arboretum; Tru. Birmingham Jewish Community Care; Marie Curie Hospice Development Appeal. Publ.: Herzl's Journey (2008); Knight out with Chamberlain (2002).

Add 4 Petersham Place, Richmond Hill Road, Birmingham B15 3RY

Tel 0121 454 1751 *Fax* 0121 454 1751

Email sirbernardz@aol.com *Website* www.bernardzissman.com

ZNEIMER, Rabbi Saul, MA (Oxon), DipPFS.

b. Wokingham, Berkshire, Oct. 12, 1960; m. Elizabeth née Colman; Consultant, HBFS Wealth Management (2011-); Hd. of Business Dev. at Bank Hapoalim UK (2008-11); Chief

Operating Officer, Lyons Presentations Group (2007-08); Chief Executive of the US (2001-07); Dir. Jewish Outreach Network (1999-2001); Rabbi, Kenton US (1994-2000); Rabbinic Liaison Officer, Office of the Chief Rabbi (1993-94); Dir. Informal Education, US Bd. of Religious Education (1992); Dir. of Youth Programme, Yakar (1984-86); form. Mem. Chief Rabbi's Cabinet.

Add HBFS Financial Services Ltd, 3 Theobald Court, Theobald Street, Borehamwood, Herts WD6 4RN

Email saul@hbfs.co.uk *Website* www.hbfs.co.uk

ZUCKER, Kenneth Harry, MA, QC.

b. London, Mar. 1935; m. Ruth Erica née Brudno; Retired; Circuit Judge (1989-2005); Recorder (1981-89).

Add 60 Gurney Drive, London N2 0DE

Email kenneth.zucker@btinternet.com

Leon Abrams, Cardiac surgeon with a love of gadgetry who developed and fitted the first variable-rate heart pacemaker. At 89.

John Burgh, Austrian Jewish refugee who arrived in this country, unable to speak a word of English. He went on to become Director of the British Council, having risen through the ranks of the Civil Service to work for some of this country's leading cabinet ministers. He also became President of Trinity College, Oxford. At 87.

Alan Cohen, Lecturing technique expert. At 78.

Eta Cohen, Violin teacher and author of a bestselling series of books, The Eta Cohen Violin Method. In 2012, she was presented with a European String Teachers Association lifetime achievement award. At 96.

Isaac Cohen, Cardiff stalwart. At 88.

Norman Cohen, Cardiff Senior Warden 1956-1995. At 89.

Dana Coleman, Yavneh College founder and much loved headteacher. At 60.

Michael Copeland, Co-founder of World Union of Jewish Students. Director of the Hillel Foundation of Great Britain and Ireland 1975-1978. Later worked in publishing and translation. At 74.

Morton Creeger, Chairman of the Royal National Orthopaedic Hospital Charity, Stanmore. His vocal and heartfelt support of the charity enabled it to increase significantly in both size and profile. He was former chairman of Edgware Ward Panel, and dedicated his life to making Edgware safer for the local community, and a better place for young people to live. At 71.

Sally Davis, Television journalist. She became a correspondent for BBC television, and spent her career as an entertainment writer for magazines and newspapers around the world. She interviewed a number of well-known figures, including The Beatles, Ronald Reagan, Gene Kelly and many others. At 71.

Barry Dobson, English eminent medieval Jewish historian who was expert on the church and its clergy. At 82.

Esther Farber, Distinguished travel agent, travelled the world with her husband Jack and together they pioneered holidays to new destinations, such as Riccione in Italy. At 91.

Naomi Felder, Immanuel College schoolgirl. At 18.

Peter Fisher, Jewish Chronicle Photographer for 40 years, one of the best known photgraphers of the Jewish Community. At 83.

Agnes Freeman, Psychic and healer, author of 3 books on spiritualism. At 72.

Joseph Friedman, Dunstan Road stalwart. At 71.

Maurice Garretts, Consultant dermatologist. At 85.

Evelyn Gee, Much loved president of the Jewish Deaf Association. At 91.

Leon Gerlis, Pathologist and Paediatric cardiologist who added enormously to the scientific understanding of congenital heart defects. At 93.

David Glass, Paediatrician. At 70.

Peter Goldstone, Circuit judge who, as a Manchester solicitor, fought for the underprivileged. At 86.

Geoffrey Goodman, British journalist, broadcaster and writer. He was the founding editor of the quarterly British Journalism Review in 1989, and remained its editor until 2002. At 92.

Cyril Gordon, Oil refinery designer. At 84.

Percy Grosberg, Leading authority in the field of textile engineering. He was noted for his groundbreaking research on the formation, structure and mechanical behaviour of textile yarns and fabrics. His work helped modernise production methods in the industry. At 87.

Peter Gross, St. Johns Wood Synagogue stalwart. At 97.

Norman Heller, Esteemed Freemason, member of the Lodge of Israel since 1952. Served as honorary treasurer and vice president of the North West Furniture

Manufacturers' Association. Norman was an honorary life president of the Merseyside Jewish Representative Council, At 87.

Eric Hobsbawm, British Marxist historian of the rise of industrial capitalism, socialism, and nationalism. At 95.

Stanley Horesh, Sephardi stalwart. At 89.

John Jackson, Former High Sheriff of West Yorkshire who was awarded the CBE in 2002, was a popular entrepreneur, philanthropist and civic figure in his home city for more than half a century. At 79.

David Jacobs, Broadcaster and presenter, whose career spanned several decades. At 87.

Sidney Jacque, Western Synagogue President for 25 years. At 100.

Rene Jordan, Birmingham community stalwart. At 81.

Betty Joseph, Widely considered to be one of the great psychoanalysts of her day. Winner of the Sigourney Award for Psychoanalysis. At 96.

Shirley Kleiman, Hampstead Garden Suburb Synagogue stalwart. At 86.

Ed Koch, An American lawyer, politician, political commentator, movie critic and reality television arbitrator. He served in the United States House of Representatives from 1969-1977 and three terms as mayor of New York. At 88.

Norman Kreitman, Psychiatric researcher and academic, primarily known for coining the term parasuicide. He was also a published poet, and wrote perceptively on the philosophy of art - in particular, on the psychology of metaphor. At 85.

Gertrude Landy, Bnai Brith Emunah Founder President. Established and promoted children's homes and rehabilitation centres in Israel and in the UK. At 100.

Adrian Leftwich, Politics lecturer, writer and activist. Leftwich had been at the forefront of contemporary political research and had written and edited numerous publications, including his 2004 book 'What is Politics?'. At 73.

Trudi Levi, Holocaust educationalist and writer. At 88.

Rita Levi-Montalcini, Italian neurologist who, together with colleague Stanley Cohen, received the 1986 Nobel Prize in Medicine for their discovery of nerve growth factor. From 2001 until her death she also served in the Italian Senate as a Senator for Life. At 103.

Montague Levine, Invariably known as Monty, he started his career as a general practitioner, was appointed assistant deputy coroner for Southwark in 1974 and took over the senior position at the court in 1987. He presided over some 500 inquests a year. At 90.

Herbert Loebl, Co-founder of Joyce, Loebl & Co, the company making high-specification scientific instruments. Of particular importance was the Joyce-Loebl optical microdensitometer, which is used to visualise and quantify the properties of DNA and other biological molecules such as haemoglobin and viruses. At 89.

David Lomon, Last known survivor in Britain of the International Brigades that fought in the Spanish civil war, against General Francisco Franco and his German and Italian backers. At 94.

Olga Lowe, Actress. At 93.

Harry Lubasz, Radical historian. In 1972 he helped found the University of Essex's history department, which he later chaired. At 84.

Susan Lustig, Combined Services Detailed Interrogation veteran. At 91.

Stella Mann, Established one of Britain's best-known professional dance schools after escaping Nazi persecution in her native Austria. At 100.

Bernard Marks, Developed the employment agency founded by his father Alfred into a high-street name that became synonymous with office job opportunities for women in the post-war decades. At 89.

Sam Maritz, Bournemouth stalwart. At 95.

Elizabeth Maxwell, Holocaust Educationalist. In 1987, she started the journal Holocaust and Genocide Studies. At 92.

Stanley Medicks, Founder of World Machal Memorial for the 123 UK volunteers who died in the 1948 War of Independence. At 87.

Norman de Mesquita, Broadcaster and a writer whose career revolved around an unlikely pairing of sports – ice hockey and cricket. At 81.

Sybil Michelow, Contralto. She sang a wide range of works, at the core of which was the oratorio repertoire from Handel to Elgar. At 88.

Yehuda Mindel, Regarded as Israel's leading Vetinary surgeon, and recognised expert on English catchphrases. At 91.

Hilda Mitchell, Leeds stalwart, heavily involved in volunteer and community work. At 89.

Alan Naftalin, Consultant in Obstetrics and Gynaecology at Newham Hospital from 1985, and Hon. Senior Lecturer at the Royal London and St Bartholomew's School of Medicine. He became a FRCOG in 1991. His special areas of clinical interest were in Colposcopy and Fertility Control At 63.

Sarah Overlander, Student Rebbetzin. At 53.

Irvine Patnick, British businessman and former Conservative Party politician. At 83.

Peter Plesch, Chemist and Polymer scientist who helped to found Keele University. At 95.

Charlotte Robson, Represented the Great Britain hockey team in the first Maccabiah Games – known as the "Jewish Olympics", in Palestine in 1932. At 98.

Warren Rose, Research scientist. At 63.

Manusia Rosmarin, Lodz Ghetto survivor. At 87.

Charlotte Saunders, Domestic violence author. At 58.

David Salik, Parachuter and wartime hero. Trained as a medic during national service in the Polish Army. Having survived deportation to a labour camp in the Soviet Union, he volunteered for the Independent Polish Parachute Brigade and took charge of a medical unit during Operation Market Garden at the Battle of Arnhem. He was awarded the Polish Military Cross of Merit with Swords for his initiative in action. At 98.

Bernard Schreier, Left his native Austria for Palestine to avoid the Nazi threat before coming to England to become an industrial entrepreneur and hotelier. Knighted for services to trade. At 95.

Gertrud Seidmann, Linguist who enjoyed a second career in retirement as a historian of jewellery and particularly of English 18th-century gem engraving. At 93.

Cornelia Shane, League of Jewish Women award winner, active in community work. At 94.

Peter Shaw, Federation of Boys Clubs stalwart. At 77.

Michael Sherrard, Barrister. In 1962, he defended James Hanratty in a highly controversial capital case. At 84.

Leslie Sohn, Became a world expert on the psychotic mind during his 62 years as an NHS psychiatrist and, later, psychoanalyst. At 93.

Geza Vermes, Dead Sea Scrolls scholar. Director, Forum for Qumran Research, Oxford Centre for Hebrew and Jewish Studies. At 88.

Joyce Waley-Cohen, Chair, Girls School Association. For 16 years she was on the board of governors at Westminster Hospital and a Chair of Westminster Children's Hospital. At 93.

Michael Webber, Cheltenham stalwart, involved in multi-faith education. Former chairman of Cheltenham Hebrew Congregation and Head of Art at the Jewish Free School. At 86.

George Whyte, Writer, composer and art collector. Author of Dreyfus trilogy. Founder of Dreyfus Society for Human Rights. Active campaigner against anti-Semitism. At 84.

Michael Winner, English film director and producer, and a restaurant critic for The Sunday Times. Police Memorial charity founder. At 77.

Mike Winters, Entertainer who became a household name in a comedy double-act with his brother Bernie. At 82.
Murray Wrobel, Wartime intelligence interrogator. At 92.
Ovadia Yosef, Israel's Sephardi Chief Rabbi. At 93.
Leon Yudkin, University Lecturer and author of many books. At 73.

As Jews we commemorate our defeats - Yom Kippur and Tisha b'Av - as we celebrate our victories - Chanukkah and Purim. The list below marks major anniversaries and some which have been overlooked in years gone by. To all those who still carry on the traditions of their founders, we offer our congratulations and hope you will enjoy many more years of success.

Anniversaries

1345th   First mention of the Jews in English Chronicles.

870th   Norwich Jews accused of ritual murder.

825th   Jews attacked at coronation of Richard I.

820th   Hanakdan Hebrew Grammar.

815th   Jacob of London appointed Presbyter.

780th   Jews prohibited from living in Newcastle.

770th   Jews of London accused of ritual murder.

350th   Sephardi Gates of Hope School founded.

350th   Jacob Sasportas appointed first Haham.

340th   Charles II's Jewish charter confirmed by Order in Council.

265th   Portsmouth cemetery opened.

260th   Nationalisation bill repealed.

195th   Institution for the Relief of the Indigent Blind founded.

185th   Society for Relieving the Aged Needy founded.

175th   Sir David Salomon appointed High Sheriff of Kent.

170th   Nathan Marcus Adler appointed Chief Rabbi.

165th   Baron Lionel de Rothschild elected member for City of London.

165th   Board of Guardians for the Relief of the Jewish Poor founded.

160th   Sandys Row synagogue founded.

150th   Dundee Hebrew Congregation founded.

150th   Sir John Simon created Serjeant at Law.

140th   Death of Haham Benjamin Artom.

135th   Opening of St. Petersburg Place New West End synagogue.

130th   Montefiore centenary.

130th   Great Synagogue, Glasgow founded.

125th   Foundation of Home & Hospital for Jewish Incurables.

125th   Birmingham Jewish Literary & Arts Society founded.

125th   Brynmawr synagogue founded.

125th   Edmonton cemetery opened.

120th   Bristol Talmud Torah opened.

120th   Home for Aged Jews founded.

115th   English Zionist Federation founded.

115th   North Manchester synagogue founded.

115th   Derby synagogue founded.

110th   Belfast synagogue founded.

110th   Bolton Hebrew Congregation founded.

105th   Foundation of Jewish Ministers Conference.

100th	Rufus Isaacs elected to Peerage.
100th	Jewish Peace Society founded.
100th	Stoker William Stern first Jewish world war fatality.
100th	Liberal cemetery opened.
95th	East Ham cemetery opened.
85th	South London Liberal synagogue founded.
80th	Golders Green Beth Hamedresh founded.
80th	Edgware & District Reform synagogue founded.
65th	Hendon Reform synagogue founded.
65th	Wimbledon & District Reform synagogue founded.
50th	St. Johns Wood synagogue founded.
50th	New London synagogue founded.
50th	The Jacobs affair.
50th	Southampton University acquires the Parkes collection.
50th	Carmel College Synagogue founded.
50th	Bromley Reform synagogue founded.
40th	New North London synagogue founded.
30th	Edgware Masorti synagogue founded.

JEWISH STUDIES COURSES IN 2014

The following courses are available on Jewish Studies:

Centre for German-Jewish Studies, University of Sussex, Brighton
Website www.sussex.ac.uk
History (Modules include: 1938 Kristallnacht, 1942 Holocaust; Philosopher of Israel's Mission: An Intellectual Biography of David Einhorn, 1809-1879; Jewish Studies in Europe: Comparative Perspectives; The Zionists among the "Prague Circle" of German-Jewish Intellectuals and their Role in the Debates about Jewish Nationalism: The Case of Robert Weltsch, Hans Kohn and Shmuel H. Bergman)

Heythrop College, University of London, London
Website www.heythrop.ac.uk
BA Abrahamic Religions
BA Philosophy, Religion and Ethics
MA Biblical Studies
MRes Biblical Studies

King's College London, London
Website www.kcl.ac.uk
MA Jewish Studies

Leo Baeck College - Centre for Jewish Education, London
Website www.lbc.ac.uk
BA Jewish Education
Graduate Diploma Hebrew and Jewish Studies 1 and 2
MA Jewish Education
MA Applied Rabbinic Theology
MA European Jewish History (taught jointly with Queen Mary University of London)
MPhil/PhD Hebrew and Jewish Studies
Postgraduate Diploma Hebrew and Jewish Studies
Advanced Diploma Professional Development: Jewish Education

Liverpool Hope University, Liverpool
Website www.hope.ac.uk
MA Jewish Studies

London School of Jewish Studies (LSJS), London
Website www.lsjs.ac.uk
MA Jewish Studies
MA Jewish Education

Nottingham University, Nottingham
Website www.nottingham.ac.uk
BA Biblical Studies and Theology
MA Jewish History and Thought

Oxford Centre for Hebrew and Jewish Studies, Oxford
Website www.ochjs.ac.uk
MSt Jewish Studies (for course options, see website)

The Parkes Institute, University of Southampton, Southampton
Website www.southampton.ac.uk/parkes
BA History Pathways in Jewish History and Culture

MA Jewish History and Culture
MRes Jewish History and Culture
MPhil/ PhD Jewish Studies

Queen Mary University, London
Website www.qmul.ac.uk
MA European Jewish History (taught jointly with Leo Baeck College)

Royal Holloway, London
Website www.rhul.ac.uk
MA Holocaust Studies

School of Oriental and African Studies (SOAS), London
Website www.soas.ac.uk
BA Hebrew and Israeli Studies
BA Hebrew (along with another subject)
BA Middle Eastern Studies
MA Israeli Studies

Stanley Burton Centre for Holocaust Studies, University of Leicester, Leicester
Website www2.le.ac.uk/centres/stanley-burton-centre
MA Holocaust Studies

Trinity College Dublin, Dublin
Website www.tcd.ie
BA Jewish and Islamic civilisations

University of Aberdeen, Aberdeen
Website www.abdn.ac.uk
Jewish Studies MLitt

University of Birmingham, Birmingham
Website www.birmingham.ac.uk
MA/PhD Jewish and Holocaust Studies

University College London, London
Website www.ucl.ac.uk
BA Hebrew & Jewish Studies

University of Edinburgh
Website www.ed.ac.uk
Mth/MSc Biblical Studies

University of Manchester, Manchester
Website www.manchester.ac.uk
BA Hebrew and Israel Studies
MA Biblical Studies
MA Jewish Studies

The Woolf Institute, Cambridge, Center for the study of Christian-Jewish relations
Website www.woolf.cam.ac.uk
MA Master of Arts in Jewish–Christian Relations
MSt Master of Studies in the Study of Jewish–Christian Relations

PUBLICATIONS & PUBLISHERS

The following is a list of notable books of Jewish interest published between November 2012 and October 2013.

THE ARTS
Hadley Freeman: Be Awesome: Modern Life for Modern Ladies, Fourth Estate.
Michael Hall: The Harold Samuel Collection: A Guide to the Dutch and Flemish Pictures at the Mansion House, Paul Haberta Publishing.

BIOGRAPHY
Kate Bassett: In Two Minds: a Biography of Jonathan Miller, Oberon Books.
Renata Calverley: Let Me Tell You a Story: A Memoir of a Wartime Childhood, Bloomsbury.
Anthony J. Dunn: The Worlds of Wolf Mankowitz: Between Elite and Popular Cultures in Post-War Britain, Vallentine Mitchell.
Michael Freedland: Man on the Rock: Mayor Solomon Levy and the Jews of Gibraltar, Vallentine Mitchell.
Donna-Lee Frieze (Ed):Totally Unofficial: The Autobiography of Raphael Lemkin, Yale University Press.
Hilary Heilbron: Rose Heilbron: The Story of England's First Woman Queen's Counsel and Judge, Hart Publishing.
Yudit Kiss: The Summer My Father Died, Telegram Books.
Ariel Saber: My Father's Paradise: A Son's Search for His Family's Past, Algonquin Books.
Oliver Sacks: Hallucinations, Picador.
Avi Shilon: Menachem Begin: A Life, Yale University Press.
Sylvie Simmons: I'm Your Man: The Life of Leonard Cohen, Vintage.

EDUCATION
Stephen Frosh: Hauntings: Psychoanalysis and Ghostly Transmissions, Palgrave Macmillan.
Stephen Grosz: The Examined Life: How We Lose and Find Ourselves, Chatto & Windus.
Otto Dov Kulka: Landscapes of the Metropolis of Death: Reflections on Memory and Imagination, Allen Lane.
Nate Silver: The Signal and the Noise: The Art and Science of Prediction, Penguin Books.

FILM STUDIES
E. Eforgen: Leslie Howard: The Lost Actor, New in PB, Vallentine Mitchell.

HISTORY
Glenda Abramson: Soldiers' Tales: Two Palestinian Jewish Soldiers in the Ottoman Army during the First World War, Vallentine Mitchell.
Peter C. Appelbaum: Loyalty Betrayed: Jewish Chaplains in the German Army During the First World War, Vallentine Mitchell.
Daniel Jonah Goldhagen: Worse Than War: Genocide, eliminationism and the ongoing assault on humanity, Abacus.
Lawrence Joffe: An Illustrated History of the Jewish People, Lorenz Books.
Tony Kushner: The Battle of Britishness: Migrant Journeys, 1685 to the Present, Manchester Universtiy Press.
Laura Arnold Leibman: Messianism, Secrecy and Mysticism: A New Intrepretation of Early American Jewish Life, Vallentine Mitchell.
Anthony Lentin: Banker, Traitor, Scapegoat, Spy?: The Troublesome Case of Sir Edgar Speyer, Haus Publishing.

Clare Mulley: The Spy Who Loved: The secrets and lives of Christine Granville, Britain's first special agent of World War II, Macmillan.

Selina O Grady: And Man Created God: Kings, Cults and Conquests at the Time of Jesus, Atlantic Books.

Mark Roseman: The Wannsee Conference and the Final Solution: A Reconsideration, Picador.

Edward Stourton: Cruel Crossing: Escaping Hitler Across the Pyrenees, Doubleday.

Martin Sugarman: Under the Heel of Bushido: Last Voices of the Jewish POWs of the Japanese in the Second World War Jewish, Vallentine Mitchell.

Daniel Trilling: Bloody Nasty People: The Rise of Britain's Far Right, Verso Books.

HOLOCAUST

Jenni Adams, Sue Vice (Eds): Representing Perpetrators in Holocaust Literature and Film, Vallentine Mitchell.

Jan Láníček, James Jordan: Governments in Exile and the Jews during the Second World War, Vallentine Mitchell.

Margaret Taft: From Victim to Survivor, The Emergence and Development of the Holocaust Witness, 1941-1949, Vallentine Mitchell.

ISRAEL

Shani Bolanjiu: The People of Forever are not Afraid, Hogarth.

Sayed Kashua: Exposure, Chatto & Windus.

Antony Lerman: The Making and Unmaking of a Zionist: A Personal and Political Journey, Pluto Press.

Joseph Millis: Jerusalem: The Illustrated History of the Holy City, Andre Deutsch Ltd.

Patrick Tyler: Fortress Israel: The Inside Story of the Military Elite Who Run the Country - and Why They Can't Make Peace, Portobello.

LITERATURE

Hava Bromberg Ben-Zvi: Portraits in Literature: The Jews of Poland, An Anthology, New in PB, Vallentine Mitchell.

Henry Hardy, Mark Pottle (Eds): Isaiah Berlin: Building, letters 1960-1975, Chatto & Windus.

Giulia Miller: Reconfiguring Surrealism in Modern Hebrew Literature: Menashe Levin, Yitzhak Oren and Yitzhak Orpaz, Vallentine Mitchell.

Frederic Raphael, Joseph Epstein: Distant Intimacy: A Friendship in the Age of the Internet, Yale University Press.

Joseph Sherman (Ed): From Revolution to Repression: Soviet Yiddish Writing 1917-1952, Five Leaves.

Amos Oz, Fania Oz-Salzburger: Jews and Words, Yale University Press.

POLITICS

Adam Gopnik: Winte: Five Windows on the Season, Quercus.

Robert S. Wistrich: From Ambivalence to Betrayal: The Left, the Jews, and Israel, University of Nebraska Press.

SPORT

Anthony Clavane: Does Your Rabbi Know You're Here?, Quercus.

The following list are Publishers of books of Jewish interest.

CUP (Cambridge University Press)
University Printing House, Shaftesbury Road, Cambridge, CB2 8BS
Tel 01223 358 331
Email information@cambridge.org *Website* www.cambridge.org
(Est. 1584)

FIVE LEAVES PUBLICATIONS
PO Box 8786, Nottingham NG1 9AW
Tel 0115 969 3597
Email info@fiveleaves.co.uk *Website* www.fiveleaves.co.uk
Publishes 15 or so books a year. Our main areas of interest are fiction and poetry, social history, Jewish secular culture, with side orders of Romani, young adult, Catalan and crime fiction titles.

LITTMAN LIBRARY OF JEWISH CIVILIZATION
PO Box 645, Oxford OX2 0UJ
Tel 01865 790 740
Email info@littman.co.uk *Website* www.littman.co.uk
(Est. 1965. Reg. Charity No. 1000784) Established for the purpose of publishing scholarly works aimed at disseminating an understanding of the Jewish heritage and Jewish hist., and making Jewish religious thought and literary creativity accessible to the English-speaking world. *Dirs.* Mrs C. C. Littman, R. J. Littman; *Contact* Connie Webber (Editorial); *Chief Exec. Off.* Ludo Craddock

OUP (Oxford University Press)
Great Clarendon Street, Oxford, OX2 6DP
Tel 01865 556 767 *Fax* 01865 556 646
Email WebEnquiry.UK@oup.com *Website* www.oup.com
(Est 1478) Oxford University Press is a department of the University of Oxford. It furthers the University's objective of excellence in research, scholarship, and education by publishing worldwide.

SCHOCKEN BOOKS
1745 Broadway, New York, NY 10019, USA
Tel +1 (212) 782 9000
Email pantheonpublicity@randomhouse.com
Website www.randomhouse.com/schocken
(Est. 1931) Schocken Books joined Random House Publishing in 1987. Books are on Jewish literature, non-fiction, cookbooks, and more.

SUSSEX ACADEMIC PRESS
PO Box 139, Eastbourne, East Sussex, BN24 9BP
Tel 01323 479 220
Email edit@sussex-academic.com   *Website* www.sussex-academic.com
Contact Editorial Dir. Anthony V. P. Grahame

URIM PUBLICATIONS
9 HaUman Street, 2nd floor, P.O.Box 52287, Jerusalem 91521 Israel
Tel +972 (2) 679 7633 *Fax* +972 (2) 679 7634
Website www.urimpublications.com
(Est. 1997) Independent publishing house based in Jerusalem and New York. Publishes books of wide Jewish interest. Main areas of interest include: Jewish Thought, Spiritual or Meditative Works, Women and Judaism, Jewish Law and Modernity, Bible Commentary, Israel Studies, Modern Biographies, and Children's Illustrated Books. Publisher, Tzvi Mauer *Email* Publisher@UrimPublications.com; Ed., *Email* Editor@UrimPublications.com; Children's Book *Ed.* Shari Dash Greenspan *Email* Children@UrimPublications.com

VALLENTINE MITCHELL PUBLISHERS
Middlesex House, 29/45 High Street, Edgware, Middlesex HA8 7UU
Tel 020 8952 9526 *Fax* 020 8952 9242
Email info@vmbooks.com   *Website* www.vmbooks.com
(Reg. Charity No. 472549) International publisher of books of Jewish interest, both for the scholar and general reader. Subjects published include Jewish history, culture and heritage, modern Jewish thought, biography and reference. *Dir.* His Hon. Sir C.V. Callman, A.E. Cass, S.L. Cass, H.J. Osen

The booksellers listed below specialise in Jewish books. Many also supply religious requisites.

GREATER LONDON

Carmel Gifts
Tel 020 8958 7632 *Fax* 020 8958 6226
Email carmelgifts@aol.com

Brauns Judaica and Gifts
82 Dunsmure Road, London N16 5JY *Tel* 020 8809 9393 *Fax* 020 8809 9494
Email info@braunsjudaica.com *Website* www.braunsjudaica.com

Daunt Books
193 Haverstock Hill, NW3 4QL *Tel* 020 7224 2295
Email contact@dauntbooks.co.uk *Website* www.dauntbooks.co.uk

Divrei Kodesh
13 Edgwarebury Lane, Edgware HA8 8LH *Tel* 020 8958 1133
Email enquiries@divreikodesh.co.uk *Website* www.divreikodesh.co.uk

J. Aisenthal
11 Ashbourne Parade, Finchley Road, NW11 0AD *Tel* 020 8455 0501
Email info@aisenthal.co.uk

Jerusalem the Golden Ltd.
146-148 Golders Green Road, NW11 8HE *Tel* 020 8455 4960 *Fax* 020 8458 3593
Email yechiel@jerusalemthegolden.com *Website* www.jerusalemthegolden.com

Joseph's Bookstore and Café Also
1255-7 Finchley Road, Temple Fortune, NW11 0AD *Tel* 020 8731 7575
Fax 020 8731 6699
Email info@josephsbookstore.com *Website* www.josephsbookstore.com
   Cafe Also *Tel* 020 8455 6890

Kuperard
59 Hutton Grove, N12 8DS *Tel* 020 8446 2440 *Fax* 020 8446 2441
Email office@kuperard.co.uk *Website* www.kuperard.co.uk
publishers and distributors, mail order, educational suppliers, book fairs, book launches

Manor House Books, John Trotter Books
Sternberg Centre, 80 East End Road, London N3 2SY *Tel* 020 8349 9484
Email johntrotterbooks@gmail.com *Website* www.ukbookworld.com/members/trotter
New, used and rare Jewish and Hebrew books

Mesoirah Seforim & Books
61 Old Hill Street, N16 6LU *Tel* 020 8809 4310

M. Rogosnitzky
20 The Drive, NW11 9SR *Tel* 020 8455 7645/4112
Antique Jewish books

Muswell Hill Bookshop
72 Fortis Green Road, N10 3HN *Tel* 020 8444 7588
Website www.muswellhillbookshop.com

On Your Doorstep Jewish Books & Gifts (Sandra E. Breger)
1 Rosecroft Walk, Pinner, Middlesex HA5 1LJ *Tel* 020 8866 6236

Steimatzky Hasifria
46 Golders Green Road, NW11 8LL *Tel* 020 8458 9774 *Fax* 020 8458 3449
Email info@steimatzky.co.uk *Website* www.steimatzky.co.uk

Torah Treasures
16 Russell Parade, Golders Green Road, NW11 9NN
Tel 020 8458 8289
Email sale@torahtreasures.co.uk *Website* www.torahtreasures.co.uk
Waterstones
68 Hampstead High Street, NW3 1QP *Tel* 020 7794 1098
Email enquiries@hampstead.waterstones.com *Website* www.waterstones.com

REGIONS

GATESHEAD
Lehmann's Retail
28-30 Grasmere Street. West, NE8 1TS *Tel* 0191 477 3523
Mail order and wholesale: Unit E, Viking Industrial Park, Rolling Mill Road, Tyne & Wear
NE32 3DP *Tel* 0191 430 0333 *Fax* 0191 430 0555 *Email* info@lehmanns.co.uk

GLASGOW
J & E Levingstone
47 & 55 Sinclair Drive, G42 9PT *Tel* 0141 649 2962 *Fax* 0141 649 2962

LIVERPOOL
Jewish Book & Gift Centre
Harold House, Dunbabin Road, L15 6XL (Orders) *Tel* 0151 722 3303
Sunday only, 11am-1pm

MANCHESTER & SALFORD
B. Horwitz (wholesale & retail Judaica)
2 Kings Road, Prestwich, M25 0LE *Tel/Fax* 0161 773 4956
Hasefer
18 Merrybower Road, Salford M7 4HE *Tel* 0161 740 3013 *Fax* 0161 721 4649
J. Goldberg
11 Parkside Avenue, Salford, M7 0HB *Tel* 0161 740 0732
Jewish Book Centre (Mr. Klein)
25 Ashbourne Grove, Salford, M7 4DB *Tel* 0161 792 1253 *Fax* 0161 661 5505

OXFORD
B. H. Blackwell Ltd.
48-51 Broad Street, OX1 3BQ *Tel* 01865 792 792 *Fax* 01865 794 143
Email oxford@blackwell.co.uk *Website* www.blackwell.co.uk
Has a Jewish book section

SOUTHEND
Dorothy Young
21 Colchester Road, SS2 6HW *Tel* 01702 331 218 for appointment
Email dorothy@dorothyyoung.co.uk *Website* www.dorothyyoung.co.uk

The Jewish Calendar is a lunar one, adapted to the solar year by various expedients. The hour is divided into 1,080 portions or *minims*, and the month between one new moon and the next is reckoned as 29 days, 12 hours, 793 minims. The years are grouped in cycles of 19. The present calendar was fixed by the post-Biblical Jewish Patriarch, Hillel II, in 358 C.E. In early Talmudic times the new moons were fixed by actual observation, and were announced from Jerusalem to the surrounding districts and countries by messenger or beacon.

If the time elapsing between one new moon and another were *exactly* 29½ days, the length of the months could be fixed at alternately 29 and 30 days. But there are three corrections to make which disturb this regularity: (1) The excess of 793 minims over the half day, (2) the adjustment to the solar year (civil), (3) the requirement that the incidence of certain Jewish festivals shall not conflict with the Sabbath. To overcome these difficulties the Jewish Calendar recognises six different classes of years; three of them common and three leap. Both the common and the leap years may be either regular, "minimal", or full. The regular year has an alternation of 30 and 29 days. The "minimal" year gives Kislev only 29 days instead of 30, while in a full year Marcheshvan has 30 instead of 29 days. The leap years, which are the 3rd, 6th, 8th, 11th, 14th, 17th, and 19th of the Metonic cycle of 19 years, are composed of thirteen months, an additional month being added. It is usually stated that this leap month is inserted after the month of Adar which in the ordinary year is of 29 days, but in a leap year has 30 days. In reality though the inserted month precedes the ordinary Adar and always has 30 days.

Besides the lunar cycle of 19 years there is a solar cycle of 28 years. At the beginning of this the *Tekufah* of Nisan (the vernal equinox) returns to the same day and the same hour. There are 4 periods to the year - the Vernal Equinox, the Summer Solstice, the Autumnal Equinox and the Winter Solstice.

The chief disturbing influence in the arrangement of the Jewish Calendar is to prevent the Day of Atonement (Tishri 10th) from either immediately preceding or immediately succeeding the Sabbath, and Hoshana Rabba (Tishri 21st) from falling on the Sabbath. Consequently the New Year (Tishri 1st) cannot fall upon Sunday, Wednesday or Friday. A further complication of a purely astronomical character is introduced by the consideration that the Jewish day formally commences six hours before midnight. If the Molad (or lunar conjunction) for the month of Tishri, i.e. the exact moment of the moon's renewal, occurs at noon or later, the new moon will be seen only after 6pm and the Festival is postponed to the next day. When, after paying regard to these and certain other considerations, the days upon which two successive New Year Festivals fall are determined, the number of days in the intervening year is known and the length of Marcheshvan and Kislev is fixed accordingly.

It is customary to describe the type of Jewish year by a "Determinative" consisting of three Hebrew letters. The first of these indicates the day of the week upon which the New Year Festival falls, the second whether the year is regular, "minimal", or full, and the third the day of the week upon which Passover occurs. To this "Determinative" is added the Hebrew word for "ordinary" or "leap".

Authorities differ regarding the manner in which the figure employed for the Jewish Era (this year 5774) is arrived at. It is sufficient to describe it as the "Mundane Era" (dating from the Creation of the World) or the "Adamic Era" (dating from the Creation of Man). The chronology is based on Biblical data.

For the beginning of Sabbaths and Festivals, rules were laid down for the latitude of London by David Nieto, Haham of the Sephardi Community (1702-1728). The hours for nightfall given here are based on those fixed by Nathan Marcus Adler, Chief Rabbi, 1844-1890 in accordance with the formula of Michael Friedlander, Principal of Jews' College, but adjusted to take account of the movement of the Jewish population within the Metropolis since their day.

THE JEWISH YEAR

The times in this calendar for the beginning and ending of Sabbaths, Festivals and Fasts in London are given in Greenwich Mean Time (from January 1 to March 29 and October 26 to the end of the calendar), and in British Summer Time (from March 30 to October 25, 2014). The times will differ according to how far you are from London (*See* p. 448 for an approximate time for the ending of the Sabbath)

5774

is known as **774** on the short system, and is a full leap year of 13 months, 55 Sabbaths and 385 days. Its 1st of Tishri is on a Thursday, and the first day of Passover is on a Tuesday.

It is the seventeenth year of the 304th minor or lunar cycle (of 19 years each) since the Era of Creation, and the sixth of the 207th major or solar cycle (of 28 years each) since the same epoch.

The year began on Wednesday evening, September 4, 2013, and concludes on Wednesday, September 24, 2014.

5775

is known as **775** on the short system, and is a regular common year of 12 months, 51 Sabbaths and 354 days. Its 1st of Tishri is on a Thursday, and the first day of Passover is on a Sabbath.

It is the eighteenth year of the 304th minor or lunar cycle (of 19 years each) since the Era of Creation, and the seventh of the 207th major or solar cycle (of 28 years each) since the same epoch.

The year begins on Wednesday evening, September 24, 2014, and concludes on Sunday, September 13, 2015.

CALENDAR NOTES

Pent. denotes Pentateuchal readings; **Proph.** denotes Prophetical readings.

Parentheses in either of the above denote Sephardi ritual.

Times for the commencement of the Sabbath during the summer months are, as is the tradition in Britain, given as 20.00. The actual times for London are given in parentheses.

PRINCIPAL FESTIVALS AND FASTS 2013–2021 (5774–5781)

Festival or Fast	Hebrew Date	5774 2013-14	5775 2014-15	5776 2015-16	5777 2016-17	5778 2017-18	5779 2018-19	5780 2019-20	5781 2020-21
New Year	Tishri 1	Sept. 5	Sept. 25	Sept. 14	Oct. 3	Sept. 21	Sept. 10	Sept. 30	Sept. 19
Day of Atonement	Tishri 10	Sept. 14	Oct. 4	Sept. 23	Oct. 12	Sept. 30	Sept. 19	Oct. 9	Sept. 28
Tabernacles, 1st Day	Tishri 15	Sept. 19	Oct. 9	Sept. 28	Oct. 17	Oct. 5	Sept. 24	Oct. 14	Oct. 3
Tabernacles, 8th Day	Tishri 22	Sept. 26	Oct. 16	Oct. 5	Oct. 24	Oct. 12	Oct. 1	Oct. 21	Oct. 10
Simchat Torah	Tishri 23	Sept. 27	Oct. 17	Oct. 6	Oct. 25	Oct. 13	Oct. 2	Oct. 22	Oct. 11
Chanucah	Kislev 25	Nov. 28	Dec. 17	Dec. 7	Dec. 25	Dec. 13	Dec. 3	Dec. 23	Dec. 11
Purim	Adar[1] 14	Mar. 16	Mar. 5	Mar. 24	Mar. 12	Mar. 1	Mar. 21	Mar. 10	Feb. 26
Passover, 1st Day	Nisan 15	Apr. 15	Apr. 4	Apr. 23	Apr. 11	Mar. 31	Apr. 20	Apr. 9	Mar. 28
Passover, 7th Day	Nisan 21	Apr. 21	Apr. 10	Apr. 29	Apr. 17	Apr. 6	Apr. 26	Apr. 15	Apr. 3
Israel Indep. Day	Iyar 5[2]	May 6	Apr. 23	May 12	May 2	Apr. 19	May 9	Apr. 29	Apr. 15
Shavuot	Sivan 6	June 4	May 24	June 12	May 31	May 20	June 9	May 29	May 17
Fast of Ab	Ab 9	Aug. 5	July 26[3]	Aug. 14[3]	Aug. 1	July 22[3]	Aug. 11[3]	July 30	July 18

1. Adar Sheni 14 in Leap Years.
2. When this date occurs on Friday or Sabbath, Israel Independence Day is observed on the previous Thursday, and when it occurs on Monday, Independence Day is postponed to Tuesday (to avoid Remembrance Day beginning when Sabbath ends).
3. Ab 10 (Ab 9 being Sabbath).

ABRIDGED JEWISH/BRITISH CALENDAR 2014 (5774-5775)

New Years Day/ Bank Holiday, UK	Wednesday	2014 January 1
Rosh Chodesh Shevat 5774	Thursday	2
Tu B'Shevat - New Year for Trees	Thursday	16
National Holocaust Memorial Day	Monday	27
Rosh Chodesh Adar I, 1st day	Friday	31
Purim Katan -Minor Purim	Friday	February 14
Shushan Purim Katan - Minor Shushan Purim	Saturday	15
Rosh Chodesh Adar II, 1st Day	Sunday	March 2
Fast of Esther	Thursday	13
Purim	Sunday	16
Shushan Purim	Monday	17
British Summer Time begins	Sunday	30
Rosh Chodesh Nisan	Tuesday	April 1
Fast of Firstborn	Monday	14
First Day Pesach (Passover)	Tuesday	15
Second Day Pesach	Wednesday	16
Good Friday/ Bank Holiday, UK	Friday	18
Easter Day	Sunday	20
Seventh Day Pesach/ Bank Holiday, UK	Monday	21
Eighth Day Pesach	Tuesday	22
Yom Hashoah - Holocaust Memorial Day	Sunday	27
Rosh Chodesh Iyar, 1st day	Wednesday	30
Bank Holiday, UK	Monday	May 5
Yom Ha'Atzmaut - Israel Independence Day	Tuesday	6
Pesach Sheni - Minor Passover	Wednesday	14
Lag Ba'Omer - Thirty-third day of the Omer	Sunday	18
Bank Holiday, UK	Monday	26
Yom Yerushalayim - Jerusalem Day	Wednesday	28
Rosh Chodesh Sivan	Friday	30
First Day Shavuot (Pentecost/ Feast of Weeks)	Wednesday	June 4
Second Day Shavuot	Thursday	5
Rosh Chodesh Tammuz, 1st day	Saturday	28
17th Tammuz (Fast)	Tuesday	July 15
Rosh Chodesh Av	Monday	28
Tisha B'Av (Fast of 9th Av)	Tuesday	August 5
15th Av (Festival)	Monday	11
Bank Holiday, UK	Monday	25
Rosh Chodesh Elul, 1st day	Tuesday	26
First Day Rosh Hashanah (New Year), 5775	Thursday	September 25
Second Day Rosh Hashanah	Friday	26
Fast of Gedaliah	Sunday	28
Yom Kippur (Day of Atonement)	Saturday	October 4
First Day Succot (Tabernacles)	Thursday	9
Second Day Succot	Friday	10
Hoshana Rabba	Wednesday	15
Shemini Atzeret (Eighth Day of Assembly)	Thursday	16
Simchat Torah (Rejoicing of the Law)	Friday	17
Rosh Chodesh Marcheshvan, 1st day	Friday	24
British Summer Time ends	Sunday	26
Remembrance Sunday, UK	Sunday	November 9
Rosh Chodesh Kislev	Sunday	23
First Day Chanucah	Wednesday	December 17
Rosh Chodesh Tevet, 1st day	Monday	22
Christmas Day	Thursday	25
Boxing Day	Friday	26

ABRIDGED JEWISH/BRITISH CALENDAR 2015 (5775-5776)

Fast of Tevet, 5775/New Years Day/Bank Holiday, UK . Thursday	2015 January	1
Rosh Chodesh Shevat .... Wednesday		21
Tu B'Shevat - New Year for Trees .... Wednesday	February	4
Rosh Chodesh Adar, 1st day .... Thursday		19
Fast of Esther .... Wednesday	March	4
Purim .... Thursday		5
Shushan Purim .... Friday		6
Rosh Chodesh Nisan .... Saturday		21
British Summer Time begins .... Sunday		29
Fast of Firstborn/ Good Friday/ Bank Holiday, UK . Friday	April	3
First Day Pesach (Passover) .... Saturday		4
Second Day Pesach/ Easter Day .... Sunday		5
Bank Holiday, UK .... Monday		6
Seventh Day Pesach .... Friday		10
Eighth Day Pesach .... Saturday		11
Holocaust Memorial Day .... Thursday		16
Rosh Chodesh Iyar, 1st day .... Sunday		19
Yom Ha'Atzmaut - Israel Independence Day ...... Thursday		23
Pesach Sheni - Minor Passover .... Sunday	May	3
Bank Holiday, UK .... Monday		4
Lag Ba'Omer - Thirty-third day of the Omer ...... Thursday		7
Yom Yerushalayim - Jerusalem Day .... Sunday		17
Rosh Chodesh Sivan .... Tuesday		19
First Day Shavuot (Pentecost/ Feast of Weeks) ..... Sunday		24
Second Day Shavuot/Bank Holiday, UK .... Monday		25
Rosh Chodesh Tammuz, 1st day .... Wednesday	June	17
Fast of Tammuz .... Sunday	July	5
Rosh Chodesh Av .... Friday		17
Tisha B'Av (Fast of 9th Av) .... Sunday		26
15th Av (Festival) .... Friday		31
Rosh Chodesh Elul, 1st day .... Saturday	August	15
Bank Holiday, UK .... Monday		31
First Day Rosh Hashanah (New Year), 5776 .... Monday	September	14
Second Day Rosh Hashanah .... Tuesday		15
Fast of Gedaliah .... Wednesday		16
Yom Kippur (Day of Atonement) .... Wednesday		23
First Day Succot (Tabernacles) .... Monday		28
Second Day Succot .... Tuesday		29
Hoshana Rabba .... Sunday	October	4
Shemini Atzeret (Eighth Day of Assembly) .... Monday		5
Simchat Torah (Rejoicing of the Law) .... Tuesday		6
Rosh Chodesh Marcheshvan, 1st day .... Tuesday		13
British Summer Time ends .... Sunday		25
Remembrance Sunday, UK .... Sunday	November	8
Rosh Chodesh Kislev, 1st day .... Thursday		12
First Day Chanucah .... Monday	December	7
Rosh Chodesh Tevet, 1st day .... Saturday		12
Fast of Tevet .... Tuesday		22
Christmas Day .... Friday		25
Boxing Day .... Saturday		26
Bank Holiday, UK .... Monday		28

JANUARY, 2014

Tekufah Mon Jan 6 16.30

TEBET 29–SHEBAT 30, 5774

Molad Shevat Wed Jan 1 13h 42m 20s
Molad I Adar Fri Jan 31 2h 26m 23s

			Tebet
1	W	Yom Kippur Katan	29
			Shebat
2	Th	Rosh Chodesh. **Pent** Num **28**, 1-15	1
3	F	Sabbath commences 15.49	2
4	**S**	Sabbath ends 16.59. **Pent** Bo, Ex **10-13**, 16. **Proph** Jer **46**, 13-28.	**3**
5	S		4
6	M		5
7	T		6
8	W		7
9	Th		8
10	F	Sabbath commences 15.58	9
11	**S**	Sabbath ends 17.07. **Pent** Beshallach, Shabbat Shirah, Ex **13**, 17-17. **Proph** Judges **4**, 4-**5** (**5**, 1-31)	**10**
12	S		11
13	M		12
14	T		13
15	W		14
16	**Th**	**New Year for Trees.**	**15**
17	F	Sabbath commences 16.09	16
18	**S**	Sabbath ends 17.17. **Pent** Yitro, Ex **18-20**. **Proph** Is 6-**7**,6; **9**, 5-6 (**6**, 1-13)	**17**
19	S		18
20	M		19
21	T	.	20
22	W		21
23	Th		22
24	F	Sabbath commences 16.20.	23
25	**S**	Sabbath ends 17.28. **Pent** Mishpatim, Ex **21-24**. **Proph** Jer **34**, 8-22 and **33**, 25-26. Benediction of Adar Rishon	**24**
26	S		25
27	M	National Holocaust Day	26
28	T		27
29	W		28
30	Th	Yom Kippur Katan	29
31	F	Sabbath commences 16.33. Rosh Chodesh first day. **Pent** Num **28**, 1-15	30

Liturgical notes – Jan 1, omit Tachanun in Minchah. – Jan 2, Half Hallel. – Jan 15, omit Tachanun in Minchah. – Jan 16, omit Tachanun. - Jan 30, omit Tachanun in Minchah. - Jan 31, Half-Hallel.

FEBRUARY, 2014   ADAR RISHON 1-28, 5774

			Adar Rishon
1	S	Sabbath ends 17.39. Rosh Chodesh second day. **Pent** Terumah, Ex **25-27**, 19; Num **28**, 9-15. **Proph** Is **66**	1
2	S		2
3	M		3
4	T		4
5	W		5
6	Th		6
7	F	Sabbath commences 16.45	7
8	S	Sabbath ends 17.51. **Pent** Tetsaveh, Ex **27**, 20-**30**, 10. **Proph** Ezek **43**, 10-27	8
9	S		9
10	M		10
11	T		11
12	W		12
13	Th		13
14	F	Sabbath commences 16.58. Minor Purim	14
15	S	Sabbath ends 18.03. **Pent** Ki Tissa, Ex **30**, 11-**34**. **Proph** I Kings **18**, 1-39 (20-39). Minor Shushan Purim	15
16	S		16
17	M		17
18	T		18
19	W		19
20	Th		20
21	F	Sabbath commences 17.11	21
22	S	Sabbath ends 18.15. **Pent** Vayakhel, Ex **35-38**, 20. **Proph** I Kings **7**, 40-50 (**7**, 13-26)	22
23	S	.	23
24	M		24
25	T		25
26	W		26
27	Th	Yom Kippur Katan	27
28	F	Sabbath commences 17.24	28

Liturgical notes – Feb 1, Half-Hallel; omit Tsidkatcha Tsedek in Minchah. – Feb 13, omit Tachanun in Minchah. – Feb 14, omit Tachanun and Lamenatse'ach. – Feb 15, omit Tsidkatcha Tsedek in Minchah.

MARCH, 2014   ADAR RISHON 29–ADAR SHENI 29, 5774

Molad II Adar Sat Mar 1 15h 10m 27s
Molad Nisan Mon Mar 31 3h 54m 30s

			Adar Rishon
1	S	Sabbath ends 18.28. **Pent** Pekudei, Parshat Shekalim, Ex **38**, 21 to end of Book; and Ex **30**. 11-16. **Proph** II Kings **12**, 1-17 (**11**, 17-**12**, 17 and I Sam **20**, 18 and 42). Benediction of Adar Sheni.	29
2	S	Rosh Chodesh first day. **Pent** Num **28**, 1-15	30

			Adar Sheni
3	M	Rosh Chodesh second day. **Pent** Num **28**, 1-15	1
4	T		2
5	W		3
6	Th		4
7	F	Sabbath commences 17.36	5
8	S	Sabbath ends 18.40. **Pent** Vayikra, Lev **1-5**. **Proph** Is **43**, 21-**44**, 23	6

9	S		7
10	M		8
11	T		9
12	W		10
13	Th	**Fast of Esther** ends 18.42. **Pent** morning and afternoon Ex **32**, 11-14 and **34**,1-10. **Proph** afternoon only Is **55**, 6-**56**, 8 (none)	11
14	F	Sabbath commences 17.49	12
15	S	Sabbath ends 18.52. **Pent** Tsav, Parshat Zachor, Lev **6-8** and Deut **25**, 17-19. **Proph** I Sam **15**, 2-34 (**15**, 1-34)	13

16	S	**Purim. Pent** Ex **17**, 8-16	14
17	M	**Shushan Purim**	15
18	T		16
19	W		17
20	Th		18
21	F	Sabbath commences 18.01.	19
22	S	Sabbath ends 19.04. **Pent** Shemini, Parshat Parah, Lev **9-11** and Num **19**. **Proph** Ezek **36**, 16-38 (16-36)	20

23	S		21
24	M		22
25	T		23
26	W		24
27	Th		25
28	F	Sabbath commences 18.12.	26
29	S	Sabbath ends 19.16. **Pent** Tazria, Parshat Hachodesh, Lev **12-13** and Ex **12**, 1-20. **Proph** Ezek **45**, 16-46, 18 (**45**,18-**46**,15). Benediction of Nisan.	27

30	S		28
31	M	Yom Kippur Katan	29

Liturgical notes – March 1, omit Tsidkatcha Tsedek in Minchah. - March 2 and 3, Half-Hallel. - March 13, Selichot, Aneinu. - March 15, omit Tsidkatcha Tsedek in Minchah; Al Hannissim is said in Maariv; Book of Esther is read. - March 16, Half-Shekel is given; say Al Hannissim; Book of Esther is read in morning; omit Tachanun and Lamenatse'ach. - March 17, omit Tachanun, El Erech Appayim and Lamenatse'ach. - March 31 omit Tachanun in Minchah.

APRIL, 2014
NISAN 1-30, 5774

Tekufah Mon Apr 7 24.00   Molad Iyar Tue Apr 29 16h 38m 33s

			Nisan
1	T	Rosh Chodesh. **Pent** Num **28**, 1-15	1
2	W		2
3	Th		3
4	F	Sabbath commences 19.24.	4
5	**S**	Sabbath ends 20.29. **Pent** Metsora, Lev **14-15**. **Proph** II Kings **7**, 3-20	**5**
6	S		6
7	M		7
8	T		8
9	W		9
10	Th		10
11	F	Sabbath commences 19.36	11
12	**S**	Sabbath ends 20.41. **Pent** Acharei Mot, Shabbat Haggadol, Lev **16-18**. **Proph** Mal **3**, 4-24	**12**
13	S		13
14	M	**Fast of Firstborn.** Festival commences 19.41. **First Seder** in evening	14
15	**T**	**Passover first day** ends 20.47. **Second Seder** in evening. **Pent** Ex **12**, 21-51; Num **28**, 16-25. **Proph** Josh **5**, 2-6, 1 (and **6**, 27)	**15**

			Omer days	
16	W	**Passover second day** ends 20.49. **Pent** Lev **22**, 26-23, 44; Num **28**, 16-25. **Proph** II Kings **23**, 1-9 and 21-25	1	**16**
17	Th	**Pent** Ex **13**, 1-16; Num **28**, 19-25	2	17
18	F	Sabbath commences 19.48. **Pent** Ex **22**, 24-23, 19; Num **28**, 19-25	3	18
19	S	Sabbath ends 20.55. **Pent** Ex **33**, 12-34, 26; Num **28**, 19-25. **Proph** Ezek **37**, 1-14	4	**19**
20	S	Festival commences 19.51. **Pent** Num **9**, 1-14 and **28**, 19-25	5	20
21	**M**	**Passover seventh day** ends 20.58. **Pent** Ex **13**, 17-15, 26; Num **28**, 19-25. **Proph** II Sam **22**	6	**21**
22	**T**	**Passover eighth day** ends 21.00. **Pent** Deut **15**, 19-16, 17; Num **28**, 19-25. **Proph** Is **10**, 32-12, 6	7	**22**
23	W	Issru Chag	8	23
24	Th		9	24
25	F	Sabbath commences 19.59	10	25
26	**S**	Sabbath ends 21.08. **Pent** Kedoshim, Lev **19-20**. **Proph** Amos **9**, 7-15. (Ezek **20**, 2-20). Benediction of Iyar. Ethics 1	11	**26**
27	S	**Holocaust Memorial Day**	12	27
28	M		13	28
29	T		14	29
30	W	Rosh Chodesh first day. **Pent** Num **28**, 1-15	15	30

Liturgical notes - April 1, Half-Hallel. During whole month of Nisan omit Tachanun (weekdays) and Tsidkatcha Tsedek (Sabbaths). - April 12, read from Haggadah and discontinue Barachi Nafshi in Minchah; omit Vihi Noam in Maariv. - April 13, Bedikat Chamets in evening. - April 14, omit Mizmor Letodah, El Erech Appayim and Lamenatse'ach; abstain from Chamets by 10.43; Biur Chamets; discontinue Tal Umatar after Minchah. - April 15, discontinue Mashiv Haruach in Mussaf; in the evening commence counting the Omer. - April 15 and 16, Whole-Hallel. - April 17 to 22, Half-Hallel. - April 17 to 20, omit Mizmor Letodah. - April 19, read Song of Songs; omit Vihi Noam in Maariv. - April 30, Half-Hallel.

MAY, 2014

IYAR 1 - SIVAN 2, 5774

Molad Sivan Thur May 29 5h 22m 37s

			Omer days	Iyar
1	Th	Rosh Chodesh second day. **Pent** Num **28**, 1-15	16	1
2	F	Sabbath commences 20.00 (20.11)	17	2
3	**S**	Sabbath ends 21.21. **Pent** Emor, Lev **21-24**. **Proph** Ezek **44**, 15-31. Ethics 2.	18	**3**
4	S		19	4
5	M	First fast day ends 21.19	20	5
6	**T**	Yom Ha'atsma'ut – Israel Independence Day.	21	**6**
7	W		22	7
8	Th	Second fast day ends 21.24	23	8
9	F	Sabbath commences 20.00 (20.22).	24	9
10	**S**	Sabbath ends 21.34. **Pent** Behar, Lev **25-26**, 2. **Proph** Jer **32**, 6-27, Ethics 3.	25	**10**
11	S		26	11
12	M	Third fast day ends 21.32	27	12
13	T		28	13
14	W	**Minor Passover**	29	14
15	**Th**		30	15
16	**F**	Sabbath commences 20.00 (20.33).	31	16
17	**S**	Sabbath ends 21.47. **Pent** Bechukkotai, Lev **26**, 3 to end of Book. **Proph** Jer 16,19-17, 14. Ethics 4	32	**17**
18	**S**	Lag b'Omer - Scholars' festival	33	**18**
19	M		34	19
20	T		35	20
21	W		36	21
22	Th		37	22
23	F	Sabbath commences 20.00 (20.43)	38	23
24	**S**	Sabbath ends 21.59. **Pent** Bemidbar, Num **1-4**,20. **Proph** Hosea **2**, 1-22 Benediction of Sivan. Ethics 5.	39	**24**
25	S		40	25
26	M		41	26
27	T		42	27
28	W	**Yom Yerushalayim - Jerusalem Day**	43	28
29	Th	Yom Kippur Katan	44	29
				Sivan
30	F	Sabbath commences 20.00 (20.52). Rosh Chodesh. **Pent** Num **28**, 1-15	45	1
31	**S**	Sabbath ends 22.10 **Pent** Naso, Num **4**, 21-7. **Proph** Judges **13**, 2-25, Ethics 6	46	**2**

Liturgical notes – May 1, Half-Hallel.- May 6, see Order of Service and Customs for Israel Independence Day (pubd. Routledge & Kegan Paul, 1964). - May 5, 8 and 12, Selichot; if there be present a Minyan who fast, Vayechal is read. - May 17, omit Tsidkatcha Tsedek in Minchah. - May 18, omit Tachanun. - May 29, omit Tachanun in Minchah. - May 30, Half-Hallel. - May 31, say Av Harachamim in morning service; omit Tsidkatcha Tsedek in Minchah and Vihi Noam in Maariv.

JUNE, 2014

SIVAN 3 - TAMMUZ 2, 5774

Molad Tammuz Fri June 27 18h 6m 40s

			Omer days	Sivan
1	S		47	3
2	M		48	4
3	T	Festival commences 20.00 (20.56).	49	5
4	**W**	**Feast of Weeks** first day ends 22.16. Pent Ex **19-20**; Num **28**, 26-31. **Proph** Ezek **1** and **3**, 12		6
5	**Th**	**Feast of Weeks** second day ends 22.17. Pent Deut **15**, 19-16, 17; Num **28**, 26-31. **Proph** Habak **2**, 20-3, 19		7
6	F	Sabbath commences 20.00 (20.59). Issru Chag		8
7	S	Sabbath ends 22.19. Pent Beha'alot'cha, Num **8-12**. **Proph** Zech **2**, 14-4, 7. Ethics 1		9
8	S			10
9	M			11
10	T			12
11	W			13
12	Th			14
13	F	Sabbath commences 20.00 (21.04).		15
14	S	Sabbath ends 22.25. Pent Shelach Lecha, Num **13-15**. **Proph** Joshua **2**. Ethics **2**.		**16**
15	S			17
16	M			18
17	T			19
18	W	.		20
19	Th			21
20	F	Sabbath commences 20.00 (21.07).		22
21	S	Sabbath ends 22.28. Pent Korach, Num **16-18**. **Proph** I Sam **11**, 14-12, 22. Benediction of Tammuz. Ethics 3		**23**
22	S			24
23	M			25
24	T			26
25	W			27
26	Th	Yom Kippur Katan		28
27	F	Sabbath commences 20.00 (21.08).		29
28	S	Sabbath ends 22.27. Rosh Chodesh first day. Pent Chukkat, Num **19-22**, 1 and **28**, 9-15, **Proph** Is **66** (add I Sam **20**, 18 and 42). Ethics 4.		**30**
				Tammuz
29	S	Rosh Chodesh second day. Pent Num **28**, 1-15		1
30	M			2

Liturgical notes – June 1 to 6, omit Tachanun. – June 4 and 5, Whole Hallel. - June 5, Book of Ruth is read. - June 28 and 29, Half-Hallel. - June 28, omit Tsidkatcha Tsedek in Minchah.

JULY, 2014

TAMMUZ 3 - AB 4, 5774

Tekufah Tue July 8 07.30

Molad Sun July 27 6h 50m 43s

			Tammuz
1	T		3
2	W		4
3	Th		5
4	F	Sabbath commences 20.00 (21.06).	6
5	S	Sabbath ends 22.24. **Pent** Balak, Num **22**, 2-**25**, 9. **Proph** Micah **5**, 6-**6**, 8. Ethics 5	**7**
6	S		**8**
7	M		9
8	T		10
9	W		11
10	Th		12
11	F	Sabbath commences 20.00 (21.01).	13
12	S	Sabbath ends 22.17. **Pent** Pinchas, Num **25**, 10-**30**, 1. **Proph** I Kings **18**, 46-**19**, 21. Ethics 6	**14**
13	S		15
14	M		16
15	T	**Fast of Tammuz** ends 22.07. **Pent** Morning and afternoon Ex **32**, 11-14 and **34**, 1-10. **Proph** afternoon only Is **55**, 6 -**56**, 8 (none)	**17**
16	W		18
17	Th		19
18	F	Sabbath commences 20.00 (20.54).	20
19	S	Sabbath ends 22.08. **Pent** Mattot, Num **30**, 2-**32**, **Proph** Jer **1-2**, 3. Ethics 1	**21**
20	S		22
21	M		23
22	T		24
23	W		25
24	Th		26
25	F	Sabbath commences 20.00 (20.45).	27
26	S	Sabbath ends 21.56. **Pent** Massei, Num **33** to end of Book. **Proph** Jer **2**, 4-28 and **3**, 4 (Jer **2**, 4-28 and **4**, 1-2). Benediction of Ab. Ethics 2	**28**
27	S	Yom Kippur Katan.	29
			Ab
28	M	Rosh Chodesh. **Pent** Num **28**, 1-15	1
29	T		2
30	W		3
31	Th		4

Liturgical notes – July 15, Selichot, Aneinu. - July 27, omit Tachanun in Minchah. - July 28, Half-Hallel.

AUGUST, 2014

AB 5–ELUL 5, 5774

Molad Mon Aug 25 19h 34m 47s

			Ab
1	F	Sabbath commences 20.00 (20.35).	5
2	S	Sabbath ends 21.43. **Pent** Devarim, Shabbat Chazon, Deut **1**, 1-**3**, 22. **Proph** Is **1**, 1-27. Ethics 3.	6
3	S		7
4	M	Fast commences 20.43	8
5	T	**Fast of Ab** ends 21.31. **Pent** morning Deut **4**, 25-40, afternoon Ex **32**, 11-14 and **34**, 1-10; **Proph** morning Jer **8**, 13-**9**, 23; afternoon Is **55**, 6-**56**, 8 (Hosea **14**, 2-10 and Micah **7**, 18-20)	9
6	W		10
7	Th		11
8	F	Sabbath commences 20.00 (20.22).	12
9	S	Sabbath ends 21.29. **Pent** Va'etchanan, Shabbat Nachamu, Deut **3**, 23-**7**, 11. **Proph** Is **40**, 1-26. Ethics 4.	13
10	S		14
11	M	**Festival of Ab**	15
12	T		16
13	W		17
14	Th		18
15	F	Sabbath commences 20.00 (20.09).	19
16	S	Sabbath ends 21.13. **Pent** Ekev, Deut **7**, 12-11, 25. **Proph** Is **49**, 14-**51**, 3. Ethics 5.	20
17	S		21
18	M		22
19	T		23
20	W		24
21	Th		25
22	F	Sabbath commences 19.55.	26
23	S	Sabbath ends 20.57. **Pent** Re'eh, Deut **11**, 26-**16**, 17. **Proph** Is **54**, 11-**55**, 5. Benediction of Elul. Ethics 6.	27
24	S		28
25	M	Yom Kippur Katan	29
26	T	Rosh Chodesh first day. **Pent** Num **28**, 1-15	30
			Elul
27	W	Rosh Chodesh second day. **Pent** Num **28**, 1-15	1
28	Th		2
29	F	Sabbath commences 19.39.	3
30	S	Sabbath ends 20.41. **Pent** Shof'tim, Deut **16**, 18-**21**, 9. **Proph** Is **51**, 12-**52**, 12. Ethics 1	4
31	S		5

Liturgical notes – Aug 2, say Av Harachamim in morning service. - Aug 4, omit Tachanun in Minchah; Book of Lamentations is read in Maariv. - Aug 5, read Kinot; omit Tachanun and Lamenatse'ach; say Aneinu and insert Nachem in Minchah. – Aug 10, omit Tachanun in Minchah. - Aug 11, omit Tachanun. - Aug 25, omit Tachanun in Minchah. - Aug 26 and 27, Half-Hallel. - Aug 27 to 31, the Shofar is blown on weekdays.

SEPTEMBER, 2014

ELUL 6, 5774–TISHRI 6, 5775

Molad Wed Sept 24 8h 18m 50s

			Elul
1	M		6
2	T		7
3	W		8
4	Th		9
5	F	Sabbath commences 19.24.	10
6	S	Sabbath ends 20.24. **Pent** Ki-Tetsei, Deut **21**, 10-**25**. **Proph** Is **54**, 1-10. Ethics 2.	**11**

7	S		12
8	M		13
9	T		14
10	W		15
11	Th		16
12	F	Sabbath commences 19.08.	17
13	S	Sabbath ends 20.07. **Pent** Ki-Tavo, Deut **26**-**29**, 8. **Proph** Is **60**. Ethics 3 and 4.	**18**

14	S		19
15	M		20
16	T		21
17	W		22
18	Th		23
19	F	Sabbath commences 18.52	24
20	S	Sabbath ends 19.51. **Pent** Nitsavim-Vayelech, Deut **29**, 9-**31**. **Proph** Is **61**, 10-**63**, 9. Ethics 5 and 6.	**25**

21	S		26
22	M		27
23	T		28
24	W	Festival commences 18.40. Eruv Tavshilin	29
			Tishri
25	Th	**New Year 5775 first day** ends 19.39. **Pent** Gen **21**; Num **29**, 1-6. **Proph** I Sam 1-**2**, 10.	1
26	F	**New Year second day.** Sabbath commences 18.35. **Pent** Gen **22**; Num **29**, 1-6. **Proph** Jer **31**, 2-20.	2
27	S	Sabbath ends 19.34. **Pent** Ha'azinu, Shabbat Shuvah, Deut **32**. **Proph** Hosea **14**, 2-10; Joel **2**, 15-27 (Hosea **14**, 2-10; Micah **7**, 18-20).	3

28	S	**Fast of Gedaliah** ends 19.26. **Pent** morning and afternoon, Ex **32**, 11-14 and **34**, 1-10. **Proph** afternoon only Is **55**, 6-**56**, 8 (none).	4
29	M		5
30	T		6

Liturgical notes – Sept 1 to 23, the Shofar is blown on weekdays. – Sept 20, omit Vihi Noam in Ma'ariv. – Sept 21 to 24, Selichot. – Sept 24, omit Tachanun. – Sept 25, Tashlich. - Sept. 28 to 30, Selichot. - Sept. 28, Aneinu.

OCTOBER, 2014   TISHRI 7–MARCHESHVAN 7, 5775
Tekufah Tue Oct 7 15.00   Molad Thur Oct 23 21h 2m 53s

			Tishri
1	W		7
2	Th		8
3	F	Sabbath and **Fast** commence 18.19; service 18.30.	9
4	**S**	Sabbath and **Day of Atonement** end 19.18	**10**
		Pent morning Lev 16; Num 29, 7-11, Afternoon Lev 18. Proph morning Is 57, 14-58, 14. Afternoon Book of Jonah and Micah 7, 18-20.	
5	S		11
6	M		12
7	T		13
8	W	Festival commences 18.08. Eruv Tavshilin.	14
9	**Th**	**Tabernacles first day** ends 19.07. Pent Lev 22, 26-23, 44; Num 29, 12-16. Proph Zech 14.	**15**
10	**F**	Sabbath commences 18.04. **Tabernacles second day.**	**16**
		Pent Lev 22, 26-23, 44; Num 29, 12-16. Proph I Kings 8, 2-21.	
11	**S**	Sabbath ends 19.03. Pent Ex 33, 12-34, 26; Num 29, 17-22. Proph Ezek 38, 18-39, 16.	**17**
12	S	Pent Num 29, 20-28	18
13	M	Pent Num 29, 23-31	19
14	T	Pent Num 29, 26-34	20
15	W	**Hoshana Rabba.** Festival commences 17.53. Eruv Tavshilin.	21
		Pent Num 29, 26-34	
16	**Th**	**Eighth Day of Solemn Assembly** ends 18.52.	**22**
		Pent Deut 14, 22-16, 17; Num 29, 35-30. 1. Proph I Kings 8, 54-66.	
17	**F**	Sabbath commences 17.49. **Rejoicing of the Law.**	**23**
		Pent Deut 33-34; Gen 1, 1-2, 3; Num 29, 35-30. 1. Proph Joshua 1, (1 1-9).	
18	**S**	Sabbath ends 18.48. Pent Bereshit, Gen 1, 1-6, 8. Proph Is 42, 5-43, 10 (42, 5-21)	**24**
		Benediction of Marcheshvan. Issru Chag.	
19	S		25
20	M		26
21	T		27
22	W		28
23	Th		29
24	F	Sabbath commences 17.34. Rosh Chodesh first day. Pent Num 28, 1-15	30
			Marcheshvan
25	**S**	Sabbath ends 18.35. Rosh Chodesh second day	1
		Pent Noach, Gen 6, 9-11 and Numbers 28, 9-15. Proph Is 66.	
26	S		2
27	M		3
28	T		4
29	W		5
30	Th		6
31	F	Sabbath commences 16.21.	7

Liturgical notes – Oct 1 to 3, Selichot. – Oct 3, omit Mizmor Letodah, Tachanun and Lamenatse'ach; Vidduy said in Minchah. - Oct 5 to 18, omit Tachanun. - Oct 9 to 17, Whole Hallel. - Hoshanot: Oct 9, Lema'an Amitach; Oct 10, Even Shetiyah; Oct 11, Om Netsurah; Oct 12, E'eroch Shu'i; Oct 13, El Lemoshaot; Oct 14, Adon Hammoshia. - Oct 11, Ecclesiastes is read; omit Tsidkatcha Tsedek in Minchah and Vihi Noam in Maariv. – Oct 16, Mashiv Haruach commenced in Mussaf. - Oct 18, Barachi Nafshi commenced in Minchah and Tsidkatcha Tsedek omitted therein. – Oct 23, omit Tachanun in Minchah.- Oct 24 and 25, Half-Hallel. - Oct 25, omit Tsidkatcha Tsedek in Minchah.

NOVEMBER, 2014 MARCHESHVAN 8–KISLEV 8, 5775

Molad Sat Nov 22 9h 46m 57s

			Marcheshvan
1	S	Sabbath ends 17.22. Pent Lech Lecha, Gen 12-17. Proph Is 40, 27-41, 16.	8
2	S		9
3	M		10
4	T		11
5	W		12
6	Th		13
7	F	Sabbath commences 16.08.	14
8	S	Sabbath ends 17.11. Pent Vayera, Gen 18-22. Proph II Kings 4, 1-37 (4, 1-23)	15
9	S		16
10	M	**First fast day** ends 17.03	17
11	T		18
12	W		19
13	Th	**Second fast day** ends 16.58	20
14	F	Sabbath commences 15.58.	21
15	S	Sabbath ends 17.02. Pent Chayei Sarah, Gen 23-25, 18. Proph I Kings 1, 1-31	22
16	S		23
17	M	**Third fast day** ends 16.54	24
18	T		25
19	W		26
20	Th	Yom Kippur Katan	27
21	F	Sabbath commences 15.49	28
22	S	Sabbath ends 16.54. Pent Tol'dot, Gen 25,19-28, 9. Proph Machar Chodesh I Sam 20, 18-42. Benediction of Kislev.	29

			Kislev
23	S	Rosh Chodesh. Pent Num 28, 1-15.	1
24	M		2
25	T		3
26	W		4
27	Th		5
28	F	Sabbath commences 15.42.	6
29	S	Sabbath ends 16.49. Pent Vayetsei, Gen 28, 10-32, 3. Proph Hosea 12, 13-14, 10 (11, 7-12, 12).	7
30	S		8

Liturgical notes – Nov 10, 13 and 17, Selichot are said in some communities and, if there be a Minyan who fast, Vay'chal is read. – Nov 22, omit Tsidkatcha Tsedek in Minchah. – Nov 23, Half-Hallel.

DECEMBER, 2014

KISLEV 9—TEBET 9, 5775

Molad Sun Dec 21 22h 31m 0s

			Kislev
1	M		9
2	T		10
3	W		11
4	Th		12
5	F	Sabbath commences 15.38.	13
6	**S**	Sabbath ends 16.46. **Pent** Vayishlach, Gen **32**, 4-**36**. **Proph** Hosea **11**, 7-**12**, 12. (Others, Book of Obadiah)	**14**
7	S		15
8	M		16
9	T		17
10	W		18
11	Th		19
12	F	Sabbath commences 15.36.	20
13	**S**	Sabbath ends 16.46. **Pent** Vayeshev, Gen **37-40**. **Proph** Amos **2**, 6-**3**, 8.	**21**
14	S		22
15	M		23
16	T	First Chanucah Light in the evening	24
17	**W**	**Chanucah first day. Pent** Num **7**, 1-17	**25**
18	**Th**	**Chanucah second day. Pent** Num **7**, 18-29.	**26**
19	**F**	**Chanucah third day.** Sabbath commences 15.38. **Pent** Num **7**, 24-35.	**27**
20	**S**	**Chanucah fourth day.** Sabbath ends 16.47. **Pent** Mikkets, Gen **41-44**, 17 and Num **7**, 30-35. **Proph** Zech **2**, 14-**4**, 7. Benediction of Tebet.	**28**
21	**S**	**Chanucah fifth day. Pent** Num **7**, 36-47	**29**
22	**M**	**Chanucah sixth day.** Rosh Chodesh first day. **Pent** Num **28**, 1-15 and **7**, 42-47.	**30**
			Tebet
23	**T**	**Chanucah seventh day.** Rosh Chodesh second day. **Pent** Num **28**, 1-15 and **7**, 48-53.	**1**
24	**W**	**Chanucah eighth day. Pent** Num **7**, 54-**8**, 4.	**2**
25	Th		**3**
26	F	Sabbath commences 15.41	**4**
27	**S**	Sabbath ends 16.52. **Pent** Vayiggash, Gen **44**, 18-**47**, 27. **Proph** Ezek **37**, 15-28.	**5**
28	S		**6**
29	M		**7**
30	T		**8**
31	W		**9**

Liturgical notes – Dec 4, Tal Umatar commenced in Maariv. – Dec 16, omit Tachanun in Minchah. – During Chanucah say Al Hannissim and Whole-Hallel; omit Tachanun, El Erech Appayim and Lamenatse'ach, and on Sabbath Tsidkatcha Tsedek in Minchah.

JANUARY, 2015

Tekufah Tue Jan 6 22.30

TEBET 10–SHEBAT 11, 5775

Molad Tue Jan 20 11h 15m 3s

			Tebet
1	Th	**Fast of Tebet** ends 16.50. **Pent** morning and afternoon, Ex **32**, 11-14 and **34**, 1-10. **Proph** afternoon only Is **55**, 6-**56**, 8 (none).	**10**
2	F	Sabbath commences 15.48.	11
3	S	Sabbath ends 16.58. **Pent** Vay'chi, Gen **47**, 28 to end of Book. **Proph** I Kings **2**, 1-12.	**12**
4	S		13
5	M		14
6	T		15
7	W		16
8	Th		17
9	F	Sabbath commences 15.57.	18
10	S	Sabbath ends 17.06. **Pent** Shemot, Ex **1**, 1-**6**, 1. **Proph** Is **27**, 6-**28**, 13; **29**, 22-23 (Jer **1**, 1-**2**, 3)	**19**
11	S		20
12	M		21
13	T		22
14	W		23
15	Th		24
16	F	Sabbath commences 16.07.	25
17	S	Sabbath ends 17.16. **Pent** Va'era, Ex **6**, 2-**9**. **Proph** Ezek **28**, 25-**29**, 21. Benediction of Shebat.	**26**
18	S		27
19	M		28
20	T	Yom Kippur Katan	29
			Shebat
21	W	Rosh Chodesh. **Pent** Num **28**, 1-15	1
22	Th		2
23	F	Sabbath commences 16.19.	3
24	S	Sabbath ends 17.27. **Pent** Bo, Ex **10**, 1-**13**, 16. **Proph** Jer **46**, 13-28	**4**
25	S		5
26	M		6
27	T	National Holocaust Day	7
28	W		8
29	Th		9
30	F	Sabbath commences 16.31.	10
31	S	Sabbath ends 17.38. **Pent** Beshallach, Shabbat Shirah, Ex **13**, 17-17. **Proph** Judges **4**, 4-**5**, 31 (**5**, 1-31)	**11**

Liturgical notes – Jan 1, Selichot Aneinu. - Jan 20, omit Tachanun in Minchah. - Jan 21, Half-Hallel.

FEBRUARY, 2015

SHEBAT 12-ADAR 9, 5775

Molad Wed Feb 18 23h 59m 7s

			Shebat
1	S		12
2	M		13
3	T		14
4	**W**	**New Year for Trees**	**15**
5	Th		16
6	F	Sabbath commences 16.44.	17
7	**S**	Sabbath ends 17.50. Pent Yitro, Ex **18-20**. Proph Is **6**, 1-7, 6 and **9**, 5-6 (**6**, 1-13)	**18**

			Shebat
8	S		19
9	M		20
10	T		21
11	W		22
12	Th		23
13	F	Sabbath commences 16.57.	24
14	**S**	Sabbath ends 18.02. Pent Mishpatim, Parshat Shekalim, Ex **21-24** and **30**, 11-16. Proph II Kings **12**, 1-17 (**11**, 17-**12**, 17). Benediction of Adar.	**25**

			Shebat
15	S		26
16	M		27
17	T		28
18	W	Yom Kippur Katan	29
19	Th	Rosh Chodesh first day. Pent Num **28**, 1-15	30

			Adar
20	F	Sabbath commences 17.09. Rosh Chodesh second day. Pent Num **28**, 1-15	1
21	**S**	Sabbath ends 18.14. Pent Terumah, Ex **25-27**, 19. Proph I Kings **5**, 26-**6**, 13	**2**

			Adar
22	S		3
23	M		4
24	T		5
25	W		6
26	Th		7
27	F	Sabbath commences 17.22.	8
28	**S**	Sabbath ends 18.26. Pent Tetsaveh, Parshat Zachor, Ex **27**, 20-**30**, 10 and Deut **25**, 17-19. Proph I Sam **15**, 2-34 (**15**, 1-34).	**9**

Liturgical notes – Feb 3, omit Tachanun in Minchah. – Feb 4, omit Tachanun. - Feb 18, omit Tachanun in Minchah. - Feb 19 and 20, Half-Hallel.

EVENING TWILIGHT VARIATION FOR REGIONS

This table shows the number of minutes required to be added to, or substracted from, the times for London, in order to determine the time of the termination of Sabbath, Festival, or Fast. For dates between those indicated here, an approximate calculation must be made.

Acknowledgement is made to the Royal Greenwich Observatory for valued co-operation in the compilation of this table.

		BIRMINGHAM	BOURNEMOUTH	GLASGOW	LEEDS	LIVERPOOL	MANCHESTER	NEWCASTLE
Jan.	1	+ 9	+15	0	+ 4	+11	+ 8	0
	11	+ 9	+14	+ 1	+ 4	+11	+ 8	0
	21	+ 9	+14	+ 3	+ 5	+12	+ 9	+ 2
	31	+ 9	+13	+ 6	+ 6	+12	+ 9	+ 3
Feb.	10	+ 9	+12	+ 9	+ 7	+13	+10	+ 5
	20	+ 9	+11	+12	+ 8	+14	+11	+ 7
Mar.	2	+10	+10	+16	+10	+16	+13	+10
	12	+10	+ 9	+20	+12	+18	+15	+13
	22	+10	+ 7	+22	+12	+18	+15	+14
Apr.	1	+11	+ 7	+27	+15	+20	+17	+18
	11	+12	+ 7	+31	+17	+22	+19	+22
	21	+13	+ 7	+35	+20	+24	+21	+26
May	1	+16	+ 7	+40	+23	+27	+24	+30
	11	+18	+ 7	+46	+26	+30	+27	+35
	21	+20	+ 7	+52	+30	+34	+31	+42
	31	+23	+ 7	+57	+34	+37	+34	+48
June	10	+25	+ 7	+63	+38	+40	+38	+55
	20	+26	+ 7	+64	+40	+41	+39	+58
	30	+26	+ 7	+62	+38	+40	+38	+55
July	10	+23	+ 7	+57	+35	+38	+35	+50
	20	+21	+ 7	+51	+31	+34	+31	+43
	30	+19	+ 8	+46	+27	+30	+27	+38
Aug.	9	+17	+ 8	+40	+24	+27	+24	+32
	19	+16	+ 8	+35	+20	+25	+22	+27
	29	+16	+ 8	+30	+18	+23	+20	+23
Sept.	8	+14	+ 8	+26	+15	+20	+17	+18
	18	+13	+ 8	+23	+12	+18	+15	+15
	28	+13	+10	+20	+12	+18	+15	+14
Oct.	8	+12	+10	+16	+10	+16	+13	+10
	18	+11	+12	+13	+ 9	+15	+12	+9
	28	+11	+12	+10	+ 8	+14	+11	+6
Nov.	7	+10	+13	+ 7	+ 6	+13	+10	+4
	17	+10	+14	+ 4	+ 5	+12	+ 9	+3
	27	+10	+14	+ 2	+ 4	+11	+ 8	+1
Dec.	7	+10	+15	0	+ 4	+11	+ 8	0
	17	+ 9	+15	0	+ 3	+11	+ 7	- 1
	27	+ 9	+15	0	+ 3	+11	+ 8	- 1
	31	+ 9	+15	0	+ 4	+11	+ 8	0

SIDROT AND HAFTAROT FOR 2015

(5775-5776)

Haftara parentheses indicate Sephardi ritual.

2015		5775	HAFTARA	SIDRA
Jan.	3	Tebet 12	I Kings **2**, 1-12	.*Vay'chi*
	10	19	Isaiah **27**, 6-**28**, 13; and **29**, 22-23	
			(Jeremiah **1**, 1-**2**, 3)	.*Shemot*
	17	26	Ezekiel **28**, 25-**29**, 21	.*Va'era*
	24	Shebat 4	Jeremiah **46**, 13-28	.*Bo*
	31	11	Judges **4**, 4-**5**, 31(**5**, 1-31)	.*Beshallach (Shirah)*
Feb.	7	18	Isaiah **6**, 1-**7**, 6; **9**, 5-6 (**6**, 1-13) . . . . .*Yitro*	
	14	25	II Kings **12**, 1-17 (**11**, 17-**12**, 17) . . .*Mishpatim (Shekalim)*	
	21	Adar 2	I Kings **5**, 26-**6**, 13	.*Terumah*
	28	9	I Samuel **15**, 2-34 (1-34)	.*Tetsaveh (Zachor)*
Mar.	7	16	I Kings **18**, 1-39, (20-39)	.*Ki Tissa*
	14	23	Ezekiel **36**, 16-38 (16-36)	.*Vayakhel-Pekudei*
			. . . .	.*(Parah)*
	21	Nisan 1	Ezekiel **45**, 16-**46**, 18 (**45**, 18-**46**, 15;	
			Is **66**, 1 and 23)	.*Vayikra (Hachodesh)*
	28	8	Malachi **3**, 4-24	.*Tsav (Haggadol)*
Apr.	4	15	Joshua **5**, 2-**6**, 1 (and **6**, 27)	.*Pesach (1st Day)*
	11	22	Isaiah **10**, 32-**12**, 6	.*Pesach (8th Day)*
	18	29	I Samuel **20**, 18-42	.*Shemini (Machar Chodesh)*
	25	Iyar 6	II Kings **7**, 3-20	.*Tazria-Metsora*
May	2	13	Amos **9**, 7-15 (Ezek **20**, 2-20) . . . . . .*Acharei Mot-Kedoshim*	
	9	20	Ezekiel **44**, 15-31	.*Emor*
	16	27	Jeremiah **16**, 19-**17**, 14	.*Behar- Bechukkotai*
	23	Sivan 5	Hosea **2**, 1-22	.*Bemidbar*
	30	12	Judges **13**, 2-25	.*Naso*
June	6	19	Zechariah **2**, 14-**4**, 7	.*Beha'alotecha*
	13	26	Joshua **2**, 1-24	.*Shelach Lecha*
	20	Tammuz 3	I Samuel **11**, 14-**12**, 22	.*Korach*
	27	10	Judges **11**, 1-33	.*Chukkat*
July	4	17	Micah **5**, 6-**6**, 8	.*Balak*
	11	24	Jeremiah **1**, 1-**2**, 3	.*Pinchas*
	18	Ab 2	Jeremiah **2**, 4-28 and **3**, 4	
			(**2**, 4-28 and **4**, 1-2)	.*Mattot-Massei*
	25	9	Isaiah **1**, 1-27	.*Devarim (Chazon)*

Sidrot and Haftarot

2015	5775		HAFTARA	SIDRA

Aug. 1 Ab 16 Isaiah **40**, 1-26 . . . . *Va'etchanan (Nachamu)*
    8   23 Isaiah **49**, 14-**51**, 3 . . . . *Ekev*
   15   30 Isaiah **66**, 1-24 (Is **54**, 11-**55**, 5; **66**, 1
                      and 23; I Sam **20**, 18 and 42) . . . . *Re'eh (Rosh Chodesh)*
   22 Elul   7 Isaiah **51**, 12-**52**, 12 . . . . *Shof'tim*
   29   14 Isaiah **54**, 1-**55**, 5 (**54**, 1-10) . . . . *Ki-Tetsei*

Sept. 5   21 Isaiah **60**, 1-22 . . . . *Ki-Tavo*
   12   28 Isaiah **61**, 10-**63**, 9 . . . . *Nitsavim*

       5776
   19 Tishri   6 Hosea **14**, 2-10 and Joel **2**, 15-27
                    (Hosea **14**, 2-10 and Micah **7**, 18-20) *Vayelech (Shuvah)*
   26   13 II Samuel **22**, 1-51 . . . . *Ha'azinu*

Oct. 3   20 Ezekiel **38**, 18-**39**, 16 . . . . *Chol Hamo'ed Succot*
   10   27 Isaiah **42**, 5-**43**, 10 (**42**, 5-21) . . . . . . *Bereshit*
   17 Cheshvan 4 Isaiah **54**, 1-**55**, 5 (**54**, 1-10) . . . . *Noach*
   24   11 Isaiah **40**, 27-**41**, 16 . . . . *Lech Lecha*
   31   18 II Kings **4**, 1-37 (1-23) . . . . *Vayera*

Nov. 7   25 I Kings **1**, 1-31 . . . . *Chayei Sarah*
   14 Kislev   2 Malachi **1**, 1-**2**, 7 . . . . *Tol'dot*
   21   9 Hosea **12**, 13-**14**, 10 (**11**, 7-**12**, 12) . . *Vayetsei*
   28   16 Hosea **11**, 7-**12**, 12 (Obadiah) . . . . . . *Vayishlach*

Dec. 5   23 Amos **2**, 6-**3**, 8 . . . . *Vayeshev*
   12   30 Zechariah **2**, 14-**4**, 7 (and Is **66**,
                    1 and 23; I Sam **20**, 18 and 42) . . . *Mikkets (Chanucah)*
   19 Tebet   7 Ezekiel **37**, 15-28 . . . . *Vayiggash*
   26   14 I Kings **2**, 1-12 . . . . *Vay'chi*

According to the regulations valid among Orthodox Jews, marriages may not be solemnised on the following dates:

2014		2015
———	Fast of Tebet	1 January
13 March	Fast of Esther	4 March
16 March	Purim	5 March
14 April	Day before Pesach	3 April
15-22 April	Pesach	4-11 April
2-16 May	Sephirah	21 April-6 May
19-29 May	Sephirah	8-18 May
3 June	Day before Shavuot	23 May
4-5 June	Shavuot	24-25 May
15 July-5 August	Three Weeks	5-26 July
24 September	Day before Rosh Hashana	13 September
25-26 September	Rosh Hashana	14-15 September
28 September	Fast of Gedaliah	16 September
3 October	Day before Yom Kippur	22 September
4 October	Yom Kippur	23 September
8 October	Day before Succot	27 September
9-17 October	Succot	28 September- 6 October
———	Fast of Tebet	22 December

Nor on any Sabbath

Among Reform Jews, marriages are solemnised during the Sephirah, from the Fast of Tammuz until the Fast of Ab (but not on the Fast of Ab itself), on the days that precede Festivals, on the Second days of Festivals, and on Purim, but not on the other prohibited days mentioned above.

JEWISH CALENDAR FOR THIRTY YEARS

5759–5788 (1998–2028)

INSTRUCTIONS FOR USE

The following Table shows on one line the civil date and the day of the week on which every date of the Jewish year falls during the thirty years which it covers; those dates which occur on Sabbath are printed in *heavier* type. Thus, Tishri 10, 5773, coincides with September 26, 2012, and this is a Wednesday, since September 22 is marked as being Sabbath. The civil dates on which the festivals and fasts (or any other occasion of the Jewish Calendar) occur in any particular year may be ascertained in the same manner. The Table is arranged according to the months of the Hebrew Year, the day of the month being shown in the left-hand column.

YAHRZEIT. – This is always observed on the Jewish date on which the parent died. It has never been customary under the jurisdiction of the Chief Rabbi of the United Hebrew Congregations of the British Commonwealth to observe the Yahrzeit after the death on the anniversary of the burial as is enjoined, in certain circumstances, by some authorities. If the death took place after dark, it must be dated from the next civil day, as the day is reckoned among Jews from sunset to sunset. This date must be located in the Table, according to the month and day, and the civil date of the Yahrzeit in any particular year will be found on the same line in the column beneath the year in question. It should be noted, however, that if a parent died during Adar in an ordinary year, the Yahrzeit is observed in a leap year in the first Adar. (Some people observe it in both Adars.) If the death took place in a leap year the Yahrzeit is observed in a leap year in the same Adar (whether First or Second) during which the death happened. The Yahrzeit begins and the memorial light is kindled on the evening before the civil date thus ascertained.

BARMITZVAH. – A boy attains his Barmitzvah (religious majority) when he reaches his thirteenth birthday, i.e., on the first day of his fourteenth year, this being computed according to the Jewish date on which he was born. The date and year of birth being located in the Table, the corresponding civil date of the first day of his fourteenth year will be found on the same line in the 13th column. If this be a Sabbath, he reads his *Parsha* on that day; if a week-day, he reads it on the following Sabbath. By consulting the Calendar the scriptural portion of the week may be ascertained. It should be noted, however, that if a boy be born in Adar of an ordinary year and become Barmitzvah in a leap year, the celebration falls in the second Adar. If he were born in a leap year and becomes Barmitzvah in a leap year it is celebrated in that Adar (whether First or Second) during which his birth occurred. If he were born in a leap year and the Barmitzvah is in an ordinary year, it is observed in Adar.

The 30 year calendar is updated every 5 years. It starts from at least 13 years ago to enable barmitvah dates to be accurately pinpointed.

TISHRI (30 days)

Tish	88	87	86	85	84	83	82	81	80	79	78	77	76	75	74	73	72	71	70	69	68	67	66	65	64	63	62	61	60	5759
	27	26	25	24	23	22	21	20	19	18	17	16	15	14	13	12	11	10	09	08	07	06	05	04	03	02	01	2000	99	1998
	October	Sept-Oct	Sept-Oct	Oct-Nov	Sept-Oct	Sept-Oct	Sept-Oct	Sept-Oct	Sept-Oct	Sept-Oct	Sept-Oct	Oct-Nov	Sept-Oct	Sept-Oct	Sept-Oct	Sept-Oct	Sept-Oct	Sept-Oct	Sept-Oct	Sept-Oct	Sept-Oct	Sept-Oct	Oct-Nov	Sept-Oct	Sept-Oct	Sept-Oct	Sept-Oct	Sept-Oct	Sept-Oct	Sept-Oct
1	**2**	**12**	23	3	**16**	26	7	**19**	30	10	21	3	14	25	5	17	29	9	**19**	30	13	**23**	4	16	**27**	**7**	18	**30**	**11**	21
2	3	13	24	4	17	27	8	20	1	11	22	4	15	26	6	18	30	10	20	1	14	24	5	17	28	8	19	1	12	22
3	4	14	25	**5**	18	28	9	21	2	12	**23**	5	16	**27**	**7**	19	**1**	**11**	21	2	**15**	25	6	**18**	29	9	20	2	13	23
4	5	15	26	6	19	29	10	22	3	13	24	6	17	28	8	20	2	12	22	3	16	26	7	19	30	10	21	3	14	24
5	6	16	**27**	7	20	30	**11**	23	4	14	25	7	18	29	9	21	3	13	23	**4**	17	27	**8**	20	1	11	**22**	4	15	25
6	7	17	28	8	21	**1**	12	24	**5**	**15**	26	**8**	**19**	30	10	**22**	4	14	24	5	18	28	9	21	2	12	23	5	16	**26**
7	8	18	29	9	22	2	13	25	6	16	27	9	20	1	11	23	5	15	25	6	19	29	10	22	3	13	24	6	17	27
8	**9**	**19**	30	10	**23**	3	14	**26**	7	17	28	10	21	2	12	24	6	16	**26**	7	20	**30**	11	23	**4**	**14**	25	**7**	**18**	28
9	10	20	1	11	24	4	15	27	8	18	29	11	22	3	13	25	7	17	27	8	21	1	12	24	5	15	26	8	19	29
10	11	21	2	**12**	25	5	16	28	9	19	**30**	12	23	**4**	**14**	26	**8**	**18**	28	9	**22**	2	13	**25**	6	16	27	9	20	30
11	12	22	3	13	26	6	17	29	10	20	1	13	24	5	15	27	9	19	29	10	23	3	14	26	7	17	28	10	21	1
12	13	23	**4**	14	27	7	**18**	30	11	21	2	14	25	6	16	28	10	20	30	**11**	24	4	**15**	27	8	18	**29**	11	22	2
13	14	24	5	15	28	**8**	19	1	**12**	**22**	3	**15**	**26**	7	17	**29**	11	21	1	12	25	5	16	28	9	19	30	12	23	**3**
14	15	25	6	16	29	9	20	2	13	23	4	16	27	8	18	30	12	22	2	13	26	6	17	29	10	20	1	13	24	4
15	**16**	**26**	7	17	**30**	10	21	**3**	14	24	5	17	28	9	19	1	13	23	**3**	14	27	**7**	18	30	**11**	**21**	2	**14**	**25**	5
16	17	27	8	18	1	11	22	4	15	25	6	18	29	10	20	2	14	24	4	15	28	8	19	1	12	22	3	15	26	6
17	18	28	9	**19**	2	12	23	5	16	26	**7**	19	30	**11**	**21**	3	**15**	**25**	5	16	**29**	9	20	**2**	13	23	4	16	27	7
18	19	29	10	20	3	13	24	6	17	27	8	20	1	12	22	4	16	26	6	17	30	10	21	3	14	24	5	17	28	8
19	20	30	**11**	21	4	14	**25**	7	18	28	9	21	2	13	23	5	17	27	7	**18**	1	11	**22**	4	15	25	**6**	18	29	9
20	21	1	12	22	5	**15**	26	8	**19**	**29**	10	**22**	**3**	14	24	**6**	18	28	8	19	2	12	23	5	16	26	7	19	30	**10**
21	22	2	13	23	6	16	27	9	20	30	11	23	4	15	25	7	19	29	9	20	3	13	24	6	17	27	8	20	1	11
22	**23**	**3**	14	24	**7**	17	28	**10**	21	1	12	24	5	16	26	8	20	30	**10**	21	4	**14**	25	7	**18**	**28**	9	**21**	**2**	12
23	24	4	15	25	8	18	29	11	22	2	13	25	6	17	27	9	21	1	11	22	5	15	26	8	19	29	10	22	3	13
24	25	5	16	**26**	9	19	30	12	23	3	**14**	26	7	**18**	**28**	10	**22**	**2**	12	23	**6**	16	27	**9**	20	30	11	23	4	14
25	26	6	17	27	10	20	1	13	24	4	15	27	8	19	29	11	23	3	13	24	7	17	28	10	21	1	12	24	5	15
26	27	7	**18**	28	11	21	**2**	14	25	5	16	28	9	20	30	12	24	4	14	**25**	8	18	**29**	11	22	2	**13**	25	6	16
27	28	8	19	29	12	**22**	3	15	**26**	**6**	17	**29**	**10**	21	1	**13**	25	5	15	26	9	19	30	12	23	3	14	26	7	**17**
28	29	9	20	30	13	23	4	16	27	7	18	30	11	22	2	14	26	6	16	27	10	20	31	13	24	4	15	27	8	18
29	**30**	**10**	21	31	**14**	24	5	**17**	28	8	19	31	12	23	3	15	27	7	**17**	28	11	**21**	1	14	**25**	**5**	16	**28**	**9**	19
30	31	11	22	1	15	25	6	18	29	9	20	1	13	24	4	16	28	8	18	29	12	22	2	15	26	6	17	29	10	20

In the left-hand margin figures in **black type** denote major Holy-days; elsewhere they denote Sabbaths.
1st and 2nd, New Year; 3rd, Fast of Gedaliah (if on Sabbath, postponed to Sunday); 10th, Day of Atonement;
15th to 23rd, Tabernacles, etc.; 30th, First day of New Moon of Marcheshvan.

CHESHVAN or MARCHESHVAN (29 or 30 days)

Chesh	5759	60	61	62	63	64	65	66	67	68	69	70	71	72	73	74	75	76	77	78	79	80	81	82	83	84	85	86	87	88
	1998	99	2000	01	02	03	04	05	06	07	08	09	10	11	12	13	14	15	16	17	18	19	20	21	22	23	24	25	26	27
	Oct-Nov	Oct-Nov	Oct-Nov	Oct-Nov	Oct-Nov	Oct-Nov	Oct-Nov	Nov-Dec	Oct-Nov	Oct-Nov	Oct-Nov	Oct-Nov	Oct-Nov	Oct-Nov	Oct-Nov	Oct-Nov	Oct-Nov	Oct-Nov	Nov	Oct-Nov	Oct-Nov	Oct-Nov	Oct-Nov	Oct-Nov	Oct-Nov	Oct-Nov	Nov-Dec	Oct-Nov	Oct-Nov	Nov
1	21	11	30	18	7	27	16	3	23	13	30	19	9	29	17	5	25	14	2	21	10	30	19	7	26	16	2	23	12	1
2	22	12	31	19	8	28	17	4	24	14	31	20	10	30	18	6	26	15	3	22	11	31	20	8	27	17	3	24	13	2
3	23	13	1	20	9	29	18	5	25	15	1	21	11	31	19	7	27	16	4	23	12	1	21	9	28	18	4	25	14	3
4	24	14	2	21	10	30	19	6	26	16	2	22	12	1	20	8	28	17	5	24	13	2	22	10	29	19	5	26	15	4
5	25	15	3	22	11	31	20	7	27	17	3	23	13	2	21	9	29	18	6	25	14	3	23	11	30	20	6	27	16	5
6	26	16	4	23	12	1	21	8	28	18	4	24	14	3	22	10	30	19	7	26	15	4	24	12	31	21	7	28	17	6
7	27	17	5	24	13	2	22	9	29	19	5	25	15	4	23	11	31	20	8	27	16	5	25	13	1	22	8	29	18	7
8	28	18	6	25	14	3	23	10	30	20	6	26	16	5	24	12	1	21	9	28	17	6	26	14	2	23	9	30	19	8
9	29	19	7	26	15	4	24	11	31	21	7	27	17	6	25	13	2	22	10	29	18	7	27	15	3	24	10	31	20	9
10	30	20	8	27	16	5	25	12	1	22	8	28	18	7	26	14	3	23	11	30	19	8	28	16	4	25	11	1	21	10
11	31	21	9	28	17	6	26	13	2	23	9	29	19	8	27	15	4	24	12	31	20	9	29	17	5	26	12	2	22	11
12	1	22	10	29	18	7	27	14	3	24	10	30	20	9	28	16	5	25	13	1	21	10	30	18	6	27	13	3	23	12
13	2	23	11	30	19	8	28	15	4	25	11	31	21	10	29	17	6	26	14	2	22	11	31	19	7	28	14	4	24	13
14	3	24	12	31	20	9	29	16	5	26	12	1	22	11	30	18	7	27	15	3	23	12	1	20	8	29	15	5	25	14
15	4	25	13	1	21	10	30	17	6	27	13	2	23	12	31	19	8	28	16	4	24	13	2	21	9	30	16	6	26	15
16	5	26	14	2	22	11	31	18	7	28	14	3	24	13	1	20	9	29	17	5	25	14	3	22	10	31	17	7	27	16
17	6	27	15	3	23	12	1	19	8	29	15	4	25	14	2	21	10	30	18	6	26	15	4	23	11	1	18	8	28	17
18	7	28	16	4	24	13	2	20	9	30	16	5	26	15	3	22	11	31	19	7	27	16	5	24	12	2	19	9	29	18
19	8	29	17	5	25	14	3	21	10	31	17	6	27	16	4	23	12	1	20	8	28	17	6	25	13	3	20	10	30	19
20	9	30	18	6	26	15	4	22	11	1	18	7	28	17	5	24	13	2	21	9	29	18	7	26	14	4	21	11	31	20
21	10	21	19	7	27	16	5	23	12	2	19	8	29	18	6	25	14	3	22	10	30	19	8	27	15	5	22	12	1	21
22	11	22	20	8	28	17	6	24	13	3	20	9	30	19	7	26	15	4	23	11	31	20	9	28	16	6	23	13	2	22
23	12	23	21	9	29	18	7	25	14	4	21	10	31	20	8	27	16	5	24	12	1	21	10	29	17	7	24	14	3	23
24	13	24	22	10	30	19	8	26	15	5	22	11	1	21	9	28	17	6	25	13	2	22	11	30	18	8	25	15	4	24
25	14	25	23	11	31	20	9	27	16	6	23	12	2	22	10	29	18	7	26	14	3	23	12	31	19	9	26	16	5	25
26	15	26	24	12	1	21	10	28	17	7	24	13	3	23	11	30	19	8	27	15	4	24	13	1	20	10	27	17	6	26
27	16	27	25	13	2	22	11	29	18	8	25	14	4	24	12	31	20	9	28	16	5	25	14	2	21	11	28	18	7	27
28	17	28	26	14	3	23	12	30	19	9	26	15	5	25	13	1	21	10	29	17	6	26	15	3	22	12	29	19	8	28
29	18	29	27	15	4	24	13	1	20	10	27	16	6	26	14	2	22	11	30	18	7	27	16	4	23	13	30	20	9	29
30	19	30	—	—	5	25	—	—	21	—	—	17	7	—	—	3	—	12	—	—	8	28	—	—	24	—	1	—	10	30

Figures in **black type** denote Sabbaths.
30th, First day of New Moon of Kislev.

KISLEV (29 or 30 days)

Kis	5759	60	61	62	63	64	65	66	67	68	69	70	71	72	73	74	75	76	77	78	79	80	81	82	83	84	85	86	87	88
	1998	99	2000	01	02	03	04	05	06	07	08	09	10	11	12	13	14	15	16	17	18	19	20	21	22	23	24	25	26	27
	Nov-Dec	Nov-Dec	Nov-Dec	Nov-Dec	Nov-Dec	Nov-Dec	Nov-Dec	Dec	Nov-Dec	Nov-Dec	Nov-Dec	Nov-Dec	Nov-Dec	Nov-Dec	Nov-Dec	Nov-Dec	Nov-Dec	Nov-Dec	Dec	Nov-Dec	Nov-Dec	Nov-Dec	Nov-Dec	Nov-Dec	Nov-Dec	Nov-Dec	Dec	Nov-Dec	Nov-Dec	Dec
1	20	10	28	16	6	26	14	2	22	11	28	18	8	27	15	4	23	13	1	19	9	29	17	5	25	14	2	21	11	1
2	21	11	29	17	7	27	15	3	23	12	29	19	9	28	16	5	24	14	2	20	10	30	18	6	26	15	3	22	12	2
3	22	12	30	18	8	28	16	4	24	13	30	20	10	29	17	6	25	15	3	21	11	1	19	7	27	16	4	23	13	3
4	23	13	1	19	9	29	17	5	25	14	1	21	11	30	18	7	26	16	4	22	12	2	20	8	28	17	5	24	14	4
5	24	14	2	20	10	30	18	6	26	15	2	22	12	1	19	8	27	17	5	23	13	3	21	9	29	18	6	25	15	5
6	25	15	3	21	11	1	19	7	27	16	3	23	13	2	20	9	28	18	6	24	14	4	22	10	30	19	7	26	16	6
7	26	16	4	22	12	2	20	8	28	17	4	24	14	3	21	10	29	19	7	25	15	5	23	11	1	20	8	27	17	7
8	27	17	5	23	13	3	21	9	29	18	5	25	15	4	22	11	30	20	8	26	16	6	24	12	2	21	9	28	18	8
9	28	18	6	24	14	4	22	10	30	19	6	26	16	5	23	12	1	21	9	27	17	7	25	13	3	22	10	29	19	9
10	29	19	7	25	15	5	23	11	1	20	7	27	17	6	24	13	2	22	10	28	18	8	26	14	4	23	11	30	20	10
11	30	20	8	26	16	6	24	12	2	21	8	28	18	7	25	14	3	23	11	29	19	9	27	15	5	24	12	1	21	11
12	1	21	9	27	17	7	25	13	3	22	9	29	19	8	26	15	4	24	12	30	20	10	28	16	6	25	13	2	22	12
13	2	22	10	28	18	8	26	14	4	23	10	30	20	9	27	16	5	25	13	1	21	11	29	17	7	26	14	3	23	13
14	3	23	11	29	19	9	27	15	5	24	11	1	21	10	28	17	6	26	14	2	22	12	30	18	8	27	15	4	24	14
15	4	24	12	30	20	10	28	16	6	25	12	2	22	11	29	18	7	27	15	3	23	13	1	19	9	28	16	5	25	15
16	5	25	13	1	21	11	29	17	7	26	13	3	23	12	30	19	8	28	16	4	24	14	2	20	10	29	17	6	26	16
17	6	26	14	2	22	12	30	18	8	27	14	4	24	13	1	20	9	29	17	5	25	15	3	21	11	30	18	7	27	17
18	7	27	15	3	23	13	1	19	9	28	15	5	25	14	2	21	10	30	18	6	26	16	4	22	12	1	19	8	28	18
19	8	28	16	4	24	14	2	20	10	29	16	6	26	15	3	22	11	1	19	7	27	17	5	23	13	2	20	9	29	19
20	9	29	17	5	25	15	3	21	11	30	17	7	27	16	4	23	12	2	20	8	28	18	6	24	14	3	21	10	30	20
21	10	30	18	6	26	16	4	22	12	1	18	8	28	17	5	24	13	3	21	9	29	19	7	25	15	4	22	11	1	21
22	11	1	19	7	27	17	5	23	13	2	19	9	29	18	6	25	14	4	22	10	30	20	8	26	16	5	23	12	2	22
23	12	2	20	8	28	18	6	24	14	3	20	10	30	19	7	26	15	5	23	11	1	21	9	27	17	6	24	13	3	23
24	13	3	21	9	29	19	7	25	15	4	21	11	1	20	8	27	16	6	24	12	2	22	10	28	18	7	25	14	4	24
25	14	4	22	10	30	20	8	26	16	5	22	12	2	21	9	28	17	7	25	13	3	23	11	29	19	8	26	15	5	25
26	15	5	23	11	1	21	9	27	17	6	23	13	3	22	10	29	18	8	26	14	4	24	12	30	20	9	27	16	6	26
27	16	6	24	12	2	22	10	28	18	7	24	14	4	23	11	30	19	9	27	15	5	25	13	1	21	10	28	17	7	27
28	17	7	25	13	3	23	11	29	19	8	25	15	5	24	12	1	20	10	28	16	6	26	14	2	22	11	29	18	8	28
29	18	8	26	14	4	24	12	30	20	9	26	16	6	25	13	2	21	11	29	17	7	27	15	3	23	12	30	19	9	29
30	19	9	—	15	5	25	—	31	21	—	27	17	7	26	—	3	22	12	—	18	8	28	—	4	24	—	31	20	10	30

Figures in **black type** denote Sabbaths.

25th to 29th or 30th, Chanucah (opening days); 30th, First day of New Moon of Tebet.

TEBET (29 days)

Teb	5759	60	61	62	63	64	65	66	67	68	69	70	71	72	73	74	75	76	77	78	79	80	81	82	83	84	85	86	87	88
	1998/1999	99/2000	2000/01	01/02	02/03	03/04	04/05	06	06/07	07/08	08/09	09/10	10/11	11/12	12/13	13/14	14/15	15/16	16/17	17/18	18/19	19/20	20/21	21/22	22/23	23/24	25	25/26	26/27	27/28
	Dec-Jan	Dec-Jan	Dec-Jan	Dec-Jan	Dec-Jan	Dec-Jan	Dec-Jan	Jan	Dec-Jan	Dec-Jan	Dec-Jan	Dec-Jan	Dec-Jan	Dec-Jan	Dec-Jan	Dec-Jan	Dec-Jan	Dec-Jan	Dec-Jan	Dec-Jan	Dec-Jan	Dec-Jan	Dec-Jan	Dec-Jan	Dec-Jan	Dec-Jan	Jan	Dec-Jan	Dec-Jan	Dec-Jan
1	20	10	27	16	6	26	13	1	22	10	28	18	8	27	14	4	23	13	30	19	9	29	16	5	25	13	1	21	11	31
2	21	11	28	17	7	27	14	2	23	11	29	19	9	28	15	5	24	14	31	20	10	30	17	6	26	14	2	22	12	1
3	22	12	29	18	8	28	15	3	24	12	30	20	10	29	16	6	25	15	1	21	11	31	18	7	27	15	3	23	13	2
4	23	13	30	19	9	29	16	4	25	13	31	21	11	30	17	7	26	16	2	22	12	1	19	8	28	16	4	24	14	3
5	24	14	31	20	10	30	17	5	26	14	1	22	12	31	18	8	27	17	3	23	13	2	20	9	29	17	5	25	15	4
6	25	15	1	21	11	31	18	6	27	15	2	23	13	1	19	9	28	18	4	24	14	3	21	10	30	18	6	26	16	5
7	26	16	2	22	12	1	19	7	28	16	3	24	14	2	20	10	29	19	5	25	15	4	22	11	31	19	7	27	17	6
8	27	17	3	23	13	2	20	8	29	17	4	25	15	3	21	11	30	20	6	26	16	5	23	12	1	20	8	28	18	7
9	28	18	4	24	14	3	21	9	30	18	5	26	16	4	22	12	31	21	7	27	17	6	24	13	2	21	9	29	19	8
10	29	19	5	25	15	4	22	10	31	19	6	27	17	5	23	13	1	22	8	28	18	7	25	14	3	22	10	30	20	9
11	30	20	6	26	16	5	23	11	1	20	7	28	18	6	24	14	2	23	9	29	19	8	26	15	4	23	11	31	21	10
12	31	21	7	27	17	6	24	12	2	21	8	29	19	7	25	15	3	24	10	30	20	9	27	16	5	24	12	1	22	11
13	1	22	8	28	18	7	25	13	3	22	9	30	20	8	26	16	4	25	11	31	21	10	28	17	6	25	13	2	23	12
14	2	23	9	29	19	8	26	14	4	23	10	31	21	9	27	17	5	26	12	1	22	11	29	18	7	26	14	3	24	13
15	3	24	10	30	20	9	27	15	5	24	11	1	22	10	28	18	6	27	13	2	23	12	30	19	8	27	15	4	25	14
16	4	25	11	31	21	10	28	16	6	25	12	2	23	11	29	19	7	28	14	3	24	13	31	20	9	28	16	5	26	15
17	5	26	12	1	22	11	29	17	7	26	13	3	24	12	30	20	8	29	15	4	25	14	1	21	10	29	17	6	27	16
18	6	27	13	2	23	12	30	18	8	27	14	4	25	13	31	21	9	30	16	5	26	15	2	22	11	30	18	7	28	17
19	7	28	14	3	24	13	31	19	9	28	15	5	26	14	1	22	10	31	17	6	27	16	3	23	12	31	19	8	29	18
20	8	29	15	4	25	14	1	20	10	29	16	6	27	15	2	23	11	1	18	7	28	17	4	24	13	1	20	9	30	19
21	9	30	16	5	26	15	2	21	11	30	17	7	28	16	3	24	12	2	19	8	29	18	5	25	14	2	21	10	31	20
22	10	31	17	6	27	16	3	22	12	31	18	8	29	17	4	25	13	3	20	9	30	19	6	26	15	3	22	11	1	21
23	11	1	18	7	28	17	4	23	13	1	19	9	30	18	5	26	14	4	21	10	31	20	7	27	16	4	23	12	2	22
24	12	2	19	8	29	18	5	24	14	2	20	10	31	19	6	27	15	5	22	11	1	21	8	28	17	5	24	13	3	23
25	13	3	20	9	30	19	6	25	15	3	21	11	1	20	7	28	16	6	23	12	2	22	9	29	18	6	25	14	4	24
26	14	4	21	10	31	20	7	26	16	4	22	12	2	21	8	29	17	7	24	13	3	23	10	30	19	7	26	15	5	25
27	15	5	22	11	1	21	8	27	17	5	23	13	3	22	9	30	18	8	25	14	4	24	11	31	20	8	27	16	6	26
28	16	6	23	12	2	22	9	28	18	6	24	14	4	23	10	31	19	9	26	15	5	25	12	1	21	9	28	17	7	27
29	17	7	24	13	3	23	10	29	19	7	25	15	5	24	11	1	20	10	27	16	6	26	13	2	22	10	29	18	8	28

Figures in **black type** denote Sabbaths.
1st to 2nd or 3rd, Chanucah (final days); 10th, Fast of Tebet.

SHEBAT (30 days)

Sheb	5759 (1999)	60 (2000)	61 (01)	62 (02)	63 (03)	64 (04)	65 (05)	66 (06)	67 (07)	68 (08)	69 (09)	70 (10)	71 (11)	72 (12)	73 (13)	74 (14)	75 (15)	76 (16)	77 (17)	78 (18)	79 (19)	80 (20)	81 (21)	82 (22)	83 (23)	84 (24)	85 (25)	86 (26)	87 (27)	88 (28)
	Jan-Feb	Jan-Feb	Jan-Feb	Jan-Feb	Jan-Feb	Jan-Feb	Jan-Feb	Jan-Feb	Jan-Feb	Jan-Feb	Jan-Feb	Jan-Feb	Jan-Feb	Jan-Feb	Jan-Feb	January	Jan-Feb	Jan-Feb	Jan-Feb	Jan-Feb	Jan-Feb	Jan-Feb	Jan-Feb	Jan-Feb	Jan-Feb	Jan-Feb	Jan-Feb	Jan-Feb	Jan-Feb	Jan-Feb
1	18	8	25	14	4	24	11	30	20	8	26	16	6	25	12	2	21	11	28	17	7	27	14	3	23	11	30	19	9	29
2	19	9	26	15	5	25	12	31	21	9	27	17	7	26	13	3	22	12	29	18	8	28	15	4	24	12	31	20	10	30
3	20	10	27	16	6	26	13	1	22	10	28	18	8	27	14	4	23	13	30	19	9	29	16	5	25	13	1	21	11	31
4	21	11	28	17	7	27	14	2	23	11	29	19	9	28	15	5	24	14	31	20	10	30	17	6	26	14	2	22	12	1
5	22	12	29	18	8	28	15	3	24	12	30	20	10	29	16	6	25	15	1	21	11	31	18	7	27	15	3	23	13	2
6	23	13	30	19	9	29	16	4	25	13	31	21	11	30	17	7	26	16	2	22	12	1	19	8	28	16	4	24	14	3
7	24	14	31	20	10	30	17	5	26	14	1	22	12	31	18	8	27	17	3	23	13	2	20	9	29	17	5	25	15	4
8	25	15	1	21	11	31	18	6	27	15	2	23	13	1	19	9	28	18	4	24	14	3	21	10	30	18	6	26	16	5
9	26	16	2	22	12	1	19	7	28	16	3	24	14	2	20	10	29	19	5	25	15	4	22	11	31	19	7	27	17	6
10	27	17	3	23	13	2	20	8	29	17	4	25	15	3	21	11	30	20	6	26	16	5	23	12	1	20	8	28	18	7
11	28	18	4	24	14	3	21	9	30	18	5	26	16	4	22	12	31	21	7	27	17	6	24	13	2	21	9	29	19	8
12	29	19	5	25	15	4	22	10	31	19	6	27	17	5	23	13	1	22	8	28	18	7	25	14	3	22	10	30	20	9
13	30	20	6	26	16	5	23	11	1	20	7	28	18	6	24	14	2	23	9	29	19	8	26	15	4	23	11	31	21	10
14	31	21	7	27	17	6	24	12	2	21	8	29	19	7	25	15	3	24	10	30	20	9	27	16	5	24	12	1	22	11
15	1	22	8	28	18	7	25	13	3	22	9	30	20	8	26	16	4	25	11	31	21	10	28	17	6	25	13	2	23	12
16	2	23	9	29	19	8	26	14	4	23	10	31	21	9	27	17	5	26	12	1	22	11	29	18	7	26	14	3	24	13
17	3	24	10	30	20	9	27	15	5	24	11	1	22	10	28	18	6	27	13	2	23	12	30	19	8	27	15	4	25	14
18	4	25	11	31	21	10	28	16	6	25	12	2	23	11	29	19	7	28	14	3	24	13	31	20	9	28	16	5	26	15
19	5	26	12	1	22	11	29	17	7	26	13	3	24	12	30	20	8	29	15	4	25	14	1	21	10	29	17	6	27	16
20	6	27	13	2	23	12	30	18	8	27	14	4	25	13	31	21	9	30	16	5	26	15	2	22	11	30	18	7	28	17
21	7	28	14	3	24	13	31	19	9	28	15	5	26	14	1	22	10	31	17	6	27	16	3	23	12	31	19	8	29	18
22	8	29	15	4	25	14	1	20	10	29	16	6	27	15	2	23	11	1	18	7	28	17	4	24	13	1	20	9	30	19
23	9	30	16	5	26	15	2	21	11	30	17	7	28	16	3	24	12	2	19	8	29	18	5	25	14	2	21	10	31	20
24	10	31	17	6	27	16	3	22	12	31	18	8	29	17	4	25	13	3	20	9	30	19	6	26	15	3	22	11	1	21
25	11	1	18	7	28	17	4	23	13	1	19	9	30	18	5	26	14	4	21	10	31	20	7	27	16	4	23	12	2	22
26	12	2	19	8	29	18	5	24	14	2	20	10	31	19	6	27	15	5	22	11	1	21	8	28	17	5	24	13	3	23
27	13	3	20	9	30	19	6	25	15	3	21	11	1	20	7	28	16	6	23	12	2	22	9	29	18	6	25	14	4	24
28	14	4	21	10	31	20	7	26	16	4	22	12	2	21	8	29	17	7	24	13	3	23	10	30	19	7	26	15	5	25
29	15	5	22	11	1	21	8	27	17	5	23	13	3	22	9	30	18	8	25	14	4	24	11	31	20	8	27	16	6	26
30	16	6	23	12	2	22	9	28	18	6	24	14	4	23	10	31	19	9	26	15	5	25	12	1	21	9	28	17	7	27

Figures in **black type** denote Sabbaths.
15th, New Year for Trees; 30th, First day of New Moon of Adar.

ADAR (29 days); in Leap Year, known as ADAR RISHON — 1st ADAR (30 days)

Adar	88	87	86	85	84	83	82	81	80	79	78	77	76	75	74	73	72	71	70	69	68	67	66	65	64	63	62	61	60	5759
	28	27	26	25	24	23	22	21	20	19	18	17	16	15	14	13	12	11	10	09	08	07	06	05	04	03	02	01	2000	1999
	Feb-Mar	Feb-Mar	Feb-Mar	March	Feb-Mar	Feb-Mar	Feb-Mar	Feb-Mar	Feb-Mar	Feb-Mar	Feb-Mar	Feb-Mar	Feb-Mar	Feb-Mar	Feb-Mar	Feb-Mar	Feb-Mar	Feb-Mar	Feb-Mar	Feb-Mar	Feb-Mar	Feb-Mar	March	Feb-Mar	Feb-Mar	Feb-Mar	Feb-Mar	Feb-Mar	Feb-Mar	Feb-Mar
1	28	8	18	1	10	22	2	13	26	6	16	27	10	20	1	11	24	5	15	25	7	19	1	10	23	3	13	24	7	17
2	29	9	19	2	11	23	3	14	27	7	17	28	11	21	2	12	25	6	16	26	8	20	2	11	24	4	14	25	8	18
3	1	10	20	3	12	24	4	15	28	8	18	1	12	22	3	13	26	7	17	27	9	21	3	12	25	5	15	26	9	19
4	2	11	21	4	13	25	5	16	29	9	19	2	13	23	4	14	27	8	18	28	10	22	4	13	26	6	16	27	10	20
5	3	12	22	5	14	26	6	17	1	10	20	3	14	24	5	15	28	9	19	1	11	23	5	14	27	7	17	28	11	21
6	4	13	23	6	15	27	7	18	2	11	21	4	15	25	6	16	29	10	20	2	12	24	6	15	28	8	18	1	12	22
7	5	14	24	7	16	28	8	19	3	12	22	5	16	26	7	17	1	11	21	3	13	25	7	16	29	9	19	2	13	23
8	6	15	25	8	17	1	9	20	4	13	23	6	17	27	8	18	2	12	22	4	14	26	8	17	1	10	20	3	14	24
9	7	16	26	9	18	2	10	21	5	14	24	7	18	28	9	19	3	13	23	5	15	27	9	18	2	11	21	4	15	25
10	8	17	27	10	19	3	11	22	6	15	25	8	19	1	10	20	4	14	24	6	16	28	10	19	3	12	22	5	16	26
11	9	18	28	11	20	4	12	23	7	16	26	9	20	2	11	21	5	15	25	7	17	1	11	20	4	13	23	6	17	27
12	10	19	1	12	21	5	13	24	8	17	27	10	21	3	12	22	6	16	26	8	18	2	12	21	5	14	24	7	18	28
13	11	20	2	13	22	6	14	25	9	18	28	11	22	4	13	23	7	17	27	9	19	3	13	22	6	15	25	8	19	1
14	12	21	3	14	23	7	15	26	10	19	1	12	23	5	14	24	8	18	28	10	20	4	14	23	7	16	26	9	20	2
15	13	22	4	15	24	8	16	27	11	20	2	13	24	6	15	25	9	19	1	11	21	5	15	24	8	17	27	10	21	3
16	14	23	5	16	25	9	17	28	12	21	3	14	25	7	16	26	10	20	2	12	22	6	16	25	9	18	28	11	22	4
17	15	24	6	17	26	10	18	1	13	22	4	15	26	8	17	27	11	21	3	13	23	7	17	26	10	19	1	12	23	5
18	16	25	7	18	27	11	19	2	14	23	5	16	27	9	18	28	12	22	4	14	24	8	18	27	11	20	2	13	24	6
19	17	26	8	19	28	12	20	3	15	24	6	17	28	10	19	1	13	23	5	15	25	9	19	28	12	21	3	14	25	7
20	18	27	9	20	29	13	21	4	16	25	7	18	29	11	20	2	14	24	6	16	26	10	20	1	13	22	4	15	26	8
21	19	28	10	21	1	14	22	5	17	26	8	19	1	12	21	3	15	25	7	17	27	11	21	2	14	23	5	16	27	9
22	20	1	11	22	2	15	23	6	18	27	9	20	2	13	22	4	16	26	8	18	28	12	22	3	15	24	6	17	28	10
23	21	2	12	23	3	16	24	7	19	28	10	21	3	14	23	5	17	27	9	19	29	13	23	4	16	25	7	18	29	11
24	22	3	13	24	4	17	25	8	20	1	11	22	4	15	24	6	18	28	10	20	1	14	24	5	17	26	8	19	1	12
25	23	4	14	25	5	18	26	9	21	2	12	23	5	16	25	7	19	1	11	21	2	15	25	6	18	27	9	20	2	13
26	24	5	15	26	6	19	27	10	22	3	13	24	6	17	26	8	20	2	12	22	3	16	26	7	19	28	10	21	3	14
27	25	6	16	27	7	20	28	11	23	4	14	25	7	18	27	9	21	3	13	23	4	17	27	8	20	1	11	22	4	15
28	26	7	17	28	8	21	1	12	24	5	15	26	8	19	28	10	22	4	14	24	5	18	28	9	21	2	12	23	5	16
29	27	8	18	29	9	22	2	13	25	6	16	27	9	20	1	11	23	5	15	25	6	19	29	10	22	3	13	24	6	17
30	—	9	—	—	10	—	—	—	—	7	—	—	10	—	2	—	—	6	—	—	7	—	—	11	—	4	—	—	7	—
		R			R					R			R		R			R			R			R		R			R	

Figures in **black type** denote Sabbaths.

13th, Fast of Esther (if on Sabbath, observed the preceding Thursday); 14th, Purim; 15th, Shushan Purim.

NOTE. — In a Jewish leap year, indicated by the letter R (for Adar Rishon) at the foot of a column, the above days are observed in 2nd Adar.

In a leap year, 30th day is First day of New Moon of the 2nd Adar.

2nd ADAR — ADAR SHENI, also known as VE-ADAR (29 days)

2nd Adar	5759 / 1999	60 / 2000	61 / 01	62 / 02	63 / 03	64 / 04	65 / 05	66 / 06	67 / 07	68 / 08	69 / 09	70 / 10	71 / 11	72 / 12	73 / 13	74 / 14	75 / 15	76 / 16	77 / 17	78 / 18	79 / 19	80 / 20	81 / 21	82 / 22	83 / 23	84 / 24	85 / 25	86 / 26	87 / 27	88 / 28
	Mar-Apr	Mar-Apr			Mar-Apr		Mar-Apr			Mar-Apr			Mar-Apr			March		Mar-Apr			Mar-Apr			Mar-Apr		Mar-Apr			Mar-Apr	
1	8	8			5		12			8			7			3		11			8			4		11			10	
2	9	9			6		13			9			8			4		12			9			5		12			11	
3	10	10			7		14			10			9			5		13			10			6		13			12	
4	11	11			8		15			11			10			6		14			11			7		14			13	
5	12	12			9		16			12			11			7		15			12			8		15			14	
6	13	13			10		17			13			12			8		16			13			9		16			15	
7	14	14			11		18			14			13			9		17			14			10		17			16	
8	15	15			12		19			15			14			10		18			15			11		18			17	
9	16	16			13		20			16			15			11		19			16			12		19			18	
10	17	17			14		21			17			16			12		20			17			13		20			19	
11	18	18			15		22			18			17			13		21			18			14		21			20	
12	19	19			16		23			19			18			14		22			19			15		22			21	
13	20	20			17		24			20			19			15		23			20			16		23			22	
14	21	21			18		25			21			20			16		24			21			17		24			23	
15	22	22			19		26			22			21			17		25			22			18		25			24	
16	23	23			20		27			23			22			18		26			23			19		26			25	
17	24	24			21		28			24			23			19		27			24			20		27			26	
18	25	25			22		29			25			24			20		28			25			21		28			27	
19	26	26			23		30			26			25			21		29			26			22		29			28	
20	27	27			24		31			27			26			22		30			27			23		30			29	
21	28	28			25		1			28			27			23		31			28			24		31			30	
22	29	29			26		2			29			28			24		1			29			25		1			31	
23	30	30			27		3			30			29			25		2			30			26		2			1	
24	31	31			28		4			31			30			26		3			31			27		3			2	
25	1	1			29		5			1			31			27		4			1			28		4			3	
26	2	2			30		6			2			1			28		5			2			29		5			4	
27	3	3			31		7			3			2			29		6			3			30		6			5	
28	4	4			1		8			4			3			30		7			4			31		7			6	
29	5	5			2		9			5			4			31		8			5			1		8			7	

Figures in **black type** denote Sabbaths.

13th, Fast of Esther (if on Sabbath, observed on the preceding Thurday); 14th, Purim; 15th Shushan Purim.

NISAN (30 days)

88	87	86	85	84	83	82	81	80	79	78	77	76	75	74	73	72	71	70	69	68	67	66	65	64	63	62	61	60	5759	
28	27	26	25	24	23	22	21	20	19	18	17	16	15	14	13	12	11	10	09	08	07	06	05	04	03	02	01	2000	1999	
Mar-Apr	Apr-May	Mar-Apr	Mar-Apr	Apr-May	Mar-Apr	Apr-May	Mar-Apr	Mar-Apr	Apr-May	Mar-Apr	Mar-Apr	Apr-May	Mar-Apr	April	Mar-Apr	Mar-Apr	Apr-May	Mar-Apr	Mar-Apr	Apr-May	Mar-Apr	Mar-Apr	Apr-May	Mar-Apr	Apr-May	Mar-Apr	Mar-Apr	Apr-May	Mar-Apr	Nis
28	8	19	30	9	23	2	14	26	6	17	28	9	21	1	12	24	5	16	26	6	20	30	10	23	3	14	25	6	18	1
29	9	20	31	10	24	3	15	27	7	18	29	10	22	2	13	25	6	17	27	7	21	31	11	24	4	15	26	7	19	2
30	10	21	1	11	25	4	16	28	8	19	30	11	23	3	14	26	7	18	28	8	22	1	12	25	5	16	27	8	20	3
31	11	22	2	12	26	5	17	29	9	20	31	12	24	4	15	27	8	19	29	9	23	2	13	26	6	17	28	9	21	4
1	12	23	3	13	27	6	18	30	10	21	1	13	25	5	16	28	9	20	30	10	24	3	14	27	7	18	29	10	22	5
2	13	24	4	14	28	7	19	31	11	22	2	14	26	6	17	29	10	21	31	11	25	4	15	28	8	19	30	11	23	6
3	14	25	5	15	29	8	20	1	12	23	3	15	27	7	18	30	11	22	1	12	26	5	16	29	9	20	31	12	24	7
4	15	26	6	16	30	9	21	2	13	24	4	16	28	8	19	31	12	23	2	13	27	6	17	30	10	21	1	13	25	8
5	16	27	7	17	31	10	22	3	14	25	5	17	29	9	20	1	13	24	3	14	28	7	18	31	11	22	2	14	26	9
6	17	28	8	18	1	11	23	4	15	26	6	18	30	10	21	2	14	25	4	15	29	8	19	1	12	23	3	15	27	10
7	18	29	9	19	2	12	24	5	16	27	7	19	31	11	22	3	15	26	5	16	30	9	20	2	13	24	4	16	28	11
8	19	30	10	20	3	13	25	6	17	28	8	20	1	12	23	4	16	27	6	17	31	10	21	3	14	25	5	17	29	12
9	20	31	11	21	4	14	26	7	18	29	9	21	2	13	24	5	17	28	7	18	1	11	22	4	15	26	6	18	30	13
10	21	1	12	22	5	15	27	8	19	30	10	22	3	14	25	6	18	29	8	19	2	12	23	5	16	27	7	19	31	14
11	22	2	13	23	6	16	28	9	20	31	11	23	4	15	26	7	19	30	9	20	3	13	24	6	17	28	8	20	1	**15**
12	23	3	14	24	7	17	29	10	21	1	12	24	5	16	27	8	20	31	10	21	4	14	25	7	18	29	9	21	2	**16**
13	24	4	15	25	8	18	30	11	22	2	13	25	6	17	28	9	21	1	11	22	5	15	26	8	19	30	10	22	3	17
14	25	5	16	26	9	19	31	12	23	3	14	26	7	18	29	10	22	2	12	23	6	16	27	9	20	31	11	23	4	18
15	26	6	17	27	10	20	1	13	24	4	15	27	8	19	30	11	23	3	13	24	7	17	28	10	21	1	12	24	5	19
16	27	7	18	28	11	21	2	14	25	5	16	28	9	20	31	12	24	4	14	25	8	18	29	11	22	2	13	25	6	20
17	28	8	19	29	12	22	3	15	26	6	17	29	10	21	1	13	25	5	15	26	9	19	30	12	23	3	14	26	7	**21**
18	29	9	20	30	13	23	4	16	27	7	18	30	11	22	2	14	26	6	16	27	10	20	1	13	24	4	15	27	8	**22**
19	30	10	21	1	14	24	5	17	28	8	19	1	12	23	3	15	27	7	17	28	11	21	2	14	25	5	16	28	9	23
20	1	11	22	2	15	25	6	18	29	9	20	2	13	24	4	16	28	8	18	29	12	22	3	15	26	6	17	29	10	24
21	2	12	23	3	16	26	7	19	30	10	21	3	14	25	5	17	29	9	19	30	13	23	4	16	27	7	18	30	11	25
22	3	13	24	4	17	27	8	20	1	11	22	4	15	26	6	18	30	10	20	1	14	24	5	17	28	8	19	1	12	26
23	4	14	25	5	18	28	9	21	2	12	23	5	16	27	7	19	31	11	21	2	15	25	6	18	29	9	20	2	13	27
24	5	15	26	6	19	29	10	22	3	13	24	6	17	28	8	20	1	12	22	3	16	26	7	19	30	10	21	3	14	28
25	6	16	27	7	20	30	11	23	4	14	25	7	18	29	9	21	2	13	23	4	17	27	8	20	1	11	22	4	15	29
26	7	17	28	8	21	1	12	24	5	15	26	8	19	30	10	22	3	14	24	5	18	28	9	21	2	12	23	5	16	30

In the left-hand margin figures in **black type** denote major Holy-days; elsewhere they denote Sabbaths. 14th, Fast of the Firstborn (if on Sabbath, observed on the preceding Thursday); 15th to 22nd, Passover; 30th, First day of New Moon of Iyar.

IYAR (29 days)

Iyar	5759 1999 Apr-May	60 2000 May-Jn	61 01 Apr-May	62 02 Apr-May	63 03 May	64 04 Apr-May	65 05 May-Jn	66 06 Apr-May	67 07 Apr-May	68 08 May-Jn	69 09 Apr-May	70 10 Apr-May	71 11 May-Jn	72 12 Apr-May	73 13 Apr-May	74 14 May	75 15 Apr-May	76 16 May-Jn	77 17 Apr-May	78 18 Apr-May	79 19 May-Jn	80 20 Apr-May	81 21 Apr-May	82 22 May	83 23 Apr-May	84 24 May-Jn	85 25 Apr-May	86 26 Apr-May	87 27 May-Jn	88 28 Apr-May
1	**17**	**6**	24	**13**	**3**	22	10	**29**	19	6	**25**	15	5	23	11	1	20	9	27	16	6	**25**	13	2	**22**	9	29	**18**	**8**	27
2	18	7	25	14	4	23	11	30	20	7	26	16	6	24	12	2	21	10	28	17	7	26	14	3	23	10	30	19	9	28
3	19	8	26	15	5	**24**	12	1	**21**	8	27	**17**	**7**	25	**13**	**3**	22	11	**29**	18	8	27	15	4	24	**11**	1	20	10	**29**
4	20	9	27	16	6	25	13	2	22	9	28	18	8	26	14	4	23	12	30	19	9	28	16	5	25	12	2	21	11	30
5	21	10	**28**	17	7	26	**14**	3	23	10	29	19	9	27	15	5	24	13	1	20	10	29	**17**	6	26	13	**3**	22	12	1
6	22	11	29	18	8	27	15	4	24	11	30	20	10	**28**	16	6	**25**	**14**	2	**21**	**11**	30	18	**7**	27	14	4	23	13	2
7	23	12	30	19	9	28	16	5	25	12	1	21	11	29	17	7	26	15	3	22	12	1	19	8	28	15	5	24	14	3
8	**24**	**13**	1	**20**	**10**	29	17	**6**	26	13	**2**	22	12	30	18	8	27	16	4	23	13	**2**	20	9	**29**	16	6	**25**	**15**	4
9	25	14	2	21	11	30	18	7	27	14	3	23	13	1	19	9	28	17	5	24	14	3	21	10	30	17	7	26	16	5
10	26	15	3	22	12	**1**	19	8	**28**	15	4	**24**	**14**	2	**20**	**10**	29	18	**6**	25	15	4	22	11	1	**18**	8	27	17	**6**
11	27	16	4	23	13	2	20	9	29	16	5	25	15	3	21	11	30	19	7	26	16	5	23	12	2	19	9	28	18	7
12	28	17	**5**	24	14	3	**21**	10	30	17	6	26	16	4	22	12	1	20	8	27	17	6	**24**	13	3	20	**10**	29	19	8
13	29	18	6	25	15	4	22	11	1	18	7	27	17	**5**	23	13	**2**	**21**	9	**28**	**18**	7	25	**14**	4	21	11	30	20	9
14	30	19	7	26	16	5	23	12	2	19	8	28	18	6	24	14	3	22	10	29	19	8	26	15	5	22	12	31	21	10
15	**1**	**20**	8	**27**	**17**	6	24	**13**	3	20	**9**	29	19	7	25	15	4	23	11	30	20	**9**	27	16	**6**	23	13	**1**	**22**	11
16	2	21	9	28	18	7	25	14	4	21	10	30	20	8	26	16	5	24	12	1	21	10	28	17	7	24	14	2	23	12
17	3	22	10	29	19	**8**	26	15	**5**	22	11	**1**	**21**	9	**27**	**17**	6	25	**13**	2	22	11	29	18	8	**25**	15	3	24	**13**
18	**4**	**23**	**11**	**30**	**20**	**9**	**27**	**16**	**6**	**23**	**12**	**2**	**22**	**10**	**28**	**18**	**7**	**26**	**14**	**3**	**23**	**12**	**30**	**19**	**9**	**26**	**16**	**4**	**25**	**14**
19	5	24	**12**	1	21	10	**28**	17	7	24	13	3	23	11	29	19	8	27	15	4	24	13	**1**	20	10	27	**17**	5	26	15
20	6	25	13	2	22	11	29	18	8	25	14	4	24	**12**	30	20	**9**	**28**	16	**5**	**25**	14	2	**21**	11	28	18	6	27	16
21	7	26	14	3	23	12	30	19	9	26	15	5	25	13	1	21	10	29	17	6	26	15	3	22	12	29	19	7	28	17
22	**8**	**27**	15	**4**	**24**	13	1	**20**	10	27	**16**	6	26	14	2	22	11	30	18	7	27	**16**	4	23	**13**	30	20	**8**	**29**	18
23	9	28	16	5	25	14	2	21	11	28	17	7	27	15	3	23	12	31	19	8	28	17	5	24	14	31	21	9	30	19
24	10	29	17	6	26	**15**	3	22	**12**	29	18	**8**	**28**	16	**4**	**24**	13	1	**20**	9	29	18	6	25	15	**1**	22	10	31	**20**
25	11	30	18	7	27	16	4	23	13	30	19	9	29	17	5	25	14	2	21	10	30	19	7	26	16	2	23	11	1	21
26	12	31	**19**	8	28	17	**5**	24	14	31	20	10	30	18	6	26	15	3	22	11	31	20	**8**	27	17	3	**24**	12	2	22
27	13	1	20	9	29	18	6	25	15	1	21	11	31	**19**	7	27	**16**	**4**	23	**12**	**1**	21	9	**28**	18	4	25	14	3	23
28	14	2	21	10	30	19	7	26	16	2	22	12	1	20	8	28	17	5	24	13	2	22	10	29	19	5	26	14	4	24
29	**15**	**3**	22	**11**	**31**	20	8	**27**	17	3	**23**	13	2	21	9	29	18	6	25	14	3	**23**	11	30	**20**	6	27	**15**	**5**	25

Figures in **black type** denote Sabbaths.
18th, 33rd Day Omer, Scholars' Festival.

SIVAN (30 days)

88	87	86	85	84	83	82	81	80	79	78	77	76	75	74	73	72	71	70	69	68	67	66	65	64	63	62	61	60	5759	Sivan
28	27	26	25	24	23	22	21	20	19	18	17	16	15	14	13	12	11	10	09	08	07	06	05	04	03	02	01	2000	1999	
May-Jn	Jn-July	May-Jn	May-Jn	Jn-July	May-Jn	May-Jn	May-Jn	May-Jn	Jn-July	May-Jn	May-Jn	Jn-July	May-Jn	May-Jn	May-Jn	May-Jn	Jn-July	May-Jn	May-Jn	Jn-July	May-Jn	May-Jn	Jn-July	May-Jn	June	May-Jn	May-Jn	Jn-July	May-Jn	Sivan
26	6	17	28	7	21	31	12	24	4	15	26	7	19	30	10	22	3	14	24	4	18	28	8	21	1	12	23	4	16	1
27	7	18	29	**8**	22	1	13	25	5	16	**27**	8	20	**31**	**11**	23	**4**	**15**	25	5	**19**	29	9	**22**	2	13	24	5	17	2
28	8	19	30	9	23	2	14	26	6	17	28	9	21	1	12	24	5	16	26	6	20	30	10	23	3	14	25	6	18	3
29	9	20	**31**	10	24	3	**15**	27	7	18	29	10	22	2	13	25	6	17	27	**7**	21	31	**11**	24	4	15	**26**	7	19	4
30	10	21	1	11	25	**4**	16	28	**8**	**19**	30	**11**	**23**	3	14	**26**	7	18	28	8	22	1	12	25	5	16	27	8	20	5
31	11	22	2	12	26	5	17	29	9	20	31	12	24	4	15	27	8	19	29	9	23	2	13	26	6	17	28	9	21	**6**
1	**12**	**23**	3	13	**27**	6	18	**30**	10	21	1	13	25	5	16	28	9	20	**30**	10	24	**3**	14	27	**7**	**18**	29	**10**	**22**	**7**
2	13	24	4	14	28	7	19	31	11	22	2	14	26	6	17	29	10	21	31	11	25	4	15	28	8	19	30	11	23	8
3	14	25	5	**15**	29	8	20	1	12	23	**3**	15	27	7	**18**	30	**11**	**22**	1	12	**26**	5	16	**29**	9	20	31	12	24	9
4	15	26	6	16	30	9	21	2	13	24	4	16	28	8	19	31	12	23	2	13	27	6	17	30	10	21	1	13	25	10
5	16	27	**7**	17	31	10	**22**	3	14	25	5	17	29	9	20	1	13	24	3	**14**	28	7	**18**	31	11	22	**2**	14	26	11
6	17	28	8	18	1	**11**	23	4	**15**	**26**	6	**18**	**30**	10	21	**2**	14	25	4	15	29	8	19	1	12	23	3	15	27	12
7	18	29	9	19	2	12	24	5	16	27	7	19	31	11	22	3	15	26	5	16	30	9	20	2	13	24	4	16	28	13
8	**19**	**30**	10	20	**3**	13	25	**6**	17	28	8	20	1	12	23	4	16	27	**6**	17	31	**10**	21	3	**14**	**25**	5	**17**	**29**	14
9	20	31	11	21	4	14	26	7	18	29	9	21	2	13	24	5	17	28	7	18	1	11	22	4	15	26	6	18	30	15
10	21	1	12	**22**	5	15	27	8	19	30	**10**	22	3	**14**	**25**	6	**18**	**29**	8	19	**2**	12	23	**5**	16	27	7	19	31	16
11	22	2	13	23	6	16	28	9	20	31	11	23	4	15	26	7	19	30	9	20	3	13	24	6	17	28	8	20	1	17
12	23	3	**14**	24	7	17	**29**	10	21	1	12	24	5	16	27	8	20	31	10	**21**	4	14	**25**	7	18	29	**9**	21	2	18
13	24	4	15	25	8	**18**	30	11	**22**	**2**	13	**25**	**6**	17	28	**9**	21	1	11	22	5	15	26	8	19	1	10	22	3	19
14	25	5	16	26	9	19	31	12	23	3	14	26	7	18	29	10	22	2	12	23	6	16	27	9	20	2	11	23	4	20
15	**26**	**6**	17	27	**10**	20	1	**13**	24	4	15	27	8	19	30	11	23	3	**13**	24	7	**17**	28	10	**21**	**1**	12	**24**	**5**	21
16	27	7	18	28	11	21	2	14	25	5	16	28	9	20	31	12	24	4	14	25	8	18	29	11	22	2	13	25	6	22
17	28	8	19	**29**	12	22	3	15	26	6	**17**	29	10	**21**	**1**	13	**25**	**5**	15	26	**9**	19	30	**12**	23	3	14	26	7	23
18	29	9	20	30	13	23	4	16	27	7	18	30	11	22	2	14	26	6	16	27	10	20	1	13	24	4	15	27	8	24
19	30	10	**21**	1	14	24	**5**	17	28	8	19	31	12	23	3	15	27	7	17	**28**	11	21	**2**	14	25	5	**16**	28	9	25
20	1	11	22	2	15	**25**	6	18	**29**	**9**	20	**2**	**13**	24	4	**16**	28	8	18	29	12	22	3	15	26	6	17	29	10	26
21	2	12	23	3	16	26	7	19	30	10	21	3	14	25	5	17	29	9	19	30	13	23	4	16	27	7	18	30	11	27
22	**3**	**13**	24	4	**17**	27	8	**20**	1	11	22	4	15	26	6	18	30	10	**20**	1	14	**24**	5	17	**28**	**8**	19	**1**	**12**	28
23	4	14	25	5	18	28	9	21	2	12	23	5	16	27	7	19	1	11	21	2	15	25	6	18	29	9	20	2	13	29
24	5	15	26	**6**	19	29	10	22	3	13	**24**	6	17	**28**	**8**	20	**2**	**12**	22	3	**16**	26	7	**19**	30	10	21	3	14	**30**

In the left-hand margin figures in **black type** denote major Holy-days; elsewhere they denote Sabbaths.
6th and 7th, Pentecost; 30th, First day of New Moon of Tammuz.

TAMMUZ (29 days)

Tam	88	87	86	85	84	83	82	81	80	79	78	77	76	75	74	73	72	71	70	69	68	67	66	65	64	63	62	61	60	5759
	28	27	26	25	24	23	22	21	20	19	18	17	16	15	14	13	12	11	10	09	08	07	06	05	04	03	02	01	2000	1999
	Jn-July	July-Au	Jn-July	Jn-July	July-Au	Jn-July	Jn-July	Jn-July	Jn-July	July-Au	Jn-July	Jn-July	July-Au	Jn-July	Jn-July	Jn-July	Jn-July	July	Jn-July	Jn-July	July-Au	Jn-July	Jn-July	July-Au	Jn-July	July	Jn-July	Jn-July	July-Au	Jn-July
1	25	6	16	27	7	20	30	11	23	4	14	25	7	18	29	9	21	3	13	23	4	17	27	8	20	1	11	22	4	15
2	26	7	17	**28**	8	21	**1**	**12**	24	5	15	26	8	19	30	10	22	4	14	24	**5**	18	28	**9**	21	2	12	**23**	5	16
3	27	8	18	29	9	22	2	13	25	**6**	**16**	27	**9**	**20**	1	11	**23**	5	15	25	6	19	29	10	22	3	13	24	6	17
4	28	9	19	30	10	23	3	14	26	7	17	28	10	21	2	12	24	6	16	26	7	20	30	11	23	4	14	25	7	18
5	29	**10**	**20**	1	11	**24**	4	15	**27**	8	18	29	11	22	3	13	25	7	17	**27**	8	21	**1**	12	24	**5**	**15**	26	**8**	**19**
6	30	11	21	2	12	25	5	16	28	9	19	30	12	23	4	14	26	8	18	28	9	22	2	13	25	6	16	27	9	20
7	**1**	12	22	3	**13**	26	6	17	29	10	20	**1**	13	24	**5**	**15**	27	**9**	**19**	29	10	**23**	3	14	**26**	7	17	28	10	21
8	2	13	23	4	14	27	7	18	30	11	21	2	14	25	6	16	28	10	20	30	11	24	4	15	27	8	18	29	11	22
9	3	14	24	**5**	15	28	**8**	**19**	1	12	22	3	15	26	7	17	29	11	21	1	**12**	25	5	**16**	28	9	19	**30**	12	23
10	4	15	25	6	16	29	9	20	2	**13**	**23**	4	**16**	**27**	8	18	**30**	12	22	2	13	26	6	17	29	10	20	1	13	24
11	5	16	26	7	17	30	10	21	3	14	24	5	17	28	9	19	1	13	23	3	14	27	7	18	30	11	21	2	14	25
12	6	**17**	**27**	8	18	**1**	11	22	**4**	15	25	6	18	29	10	20	2	14	24	**4**	15	28	**8**	19	1	**12**	**22**	3	**15**	**26**
13	7	18	28	9	19	2	12	23	5	16	26	7	19	30	11	21	3	15	25	5	16	29	9	20	2	13	23	4	16	27
14	**8**	19	29	10	**20**	3	13	24	6	17	27	**8**	20	1	**12**	**22**	4	**16**	**26**	6	17	**30**	10	21	**3**	14	24	5	17	28
15	9	20	30	11	21	4	14	25	7	18	28	9	21	2	13	23	5	17	27	7	18	1	11	22	4	15	25	6	18	29
16	10	21	1	**12**	22	5	**15**	**26**	8	19	29	10	22	3	14	24	6	18	28	8	**19**	2	12	**23**	5	16	26	**7**	19	30
17	11	22	2	13	23	6	16	27	9	**20**	**30**	11	**23**	**4**	15	25	**7**	19	29	9	20	3	13	24	6	17	27	8	20	1
18	12	23	3	14	24	7	17	28	10	21	1	12	24	5	16	26	8	20	30	10	21	4	14	25	7	18	28	9	21	2
19	13	**24**	**4**	15	25	**8**	18	29	**11**	22	2	13	25	6	17	27	9	21	1	**11**	22	5	**15**	26	8	**19**	**29**	10	**22**	**3**
20	14	25	5	16	26	9	19	30	12	23	3	14	26	7	18	28	10	22	2	12	23	6	16	27	9	20	30	11	23	4
21	**15**	26	6	17	**27**	10	20	1	13	24	4	**15**	27	8	**19**	**29**	11	**23**	**3**	13	24	**7**	17	28	**10**	21	1	12	24	5
22	16	27	7	18	28	11	21	2	14	25	5	16	28	9	20	30	12	24	4	14	25	8	18	29	11	22	2	13	25	6
23	17	28	8	**19**	29	12	**22**	**3**	15	26	6	17	29	10	21	1	13	25	5	15	**26**	9	19	**30**	12	23	3	**14**	26	7
24	18	29	9	20	30	13	23	4	16	**27**	**7**	18	**30**	**11**	22	2	**14**	26	6	16	27	10	20	31	13	24	4	15	27	8
25	19	30	10	21	31	14	24	5	17	28	8	19	31	12	23	3	15	27	7	17	28	11	21	1	14	25	5	16	28	9
26	20	**31**	**11**	22	1	**15**	25	6	**18**	29	9	20	1	13	24	4	16	28	8	**18**	29	12	**22**	2	15	**26**	**6**	17	**29**	**10**
27	21	1	12	23	2	16	26	7	19	30	10	21	2	14	25	5	17	29	9	19	30	13	23	3	16	27	7	18	30	11
28	**22**	2	13	24	**3**	17	27	8	20	31	11	**22**	3	15	**26**	**6**	18	**30**	**10**	20	31	**14**	24	4	**17**	28	8	19	31	12
29	23	3	14	25	4	18	28	9	21	1	12	23	4	16	27	7	19	31	11	21	1	15	25	5	18	29	9	20	1	13

Figures in **black type** denote Sabbaths.

17th, Fast of Tammuz (if on Sabbath, postponed to Sunday).

AB (30 days)

Ab	5759	60	61	62	63	64	65	66	67	68	69	70	71	72	73	74	75	76	77	78	79	80	81	82	83	84	85	86	87	88
	1999	2000	01	02	03	04	05	06	07	08	09	10	11	12	13	14	15	16	17	18	19	20	21	22	23	24	25	26	27	28
	July-Au	August	July-Au	July-Au	July-Au	July-Au	Au-Sep	July-Au	July-Au	August	July-Au	July-Au	August	July-Au	July-Au	July-Au	July-Au	Au-Sep	July-Au	July-Au	August	July-Au	July-Au	July-Au	July-Au	Au-Sep	July-Au	July-Au	Au-Sep	July-Au
1	14	2	21	10	30	19	6	26	16	2	22	12	1	20	8	28	17	5	24	13	2	22	10	29	19	5	26	15	4	24
2	15	3	22	11	31	20	7	27	17	3	23	13	2	21	9	29	18	6	25	14	3	23	11	30	20	6	27	16	5	25
3	16	4	23	12	1	21	8	28	18	4	24	14	3	22	10	30	19	7	26	15	4	24	12	31	21	7	28	17	6	26
4	17	5	24	13	2	22	9	29	19	5	25	15	4	23	11	31	20	8	27	16	5	25	13	1	22	8	29	18	7	27
5	18	6	25	14	3	23	10	30	20	6	26	16	5	24	12	1	21	9	28	17	6	26	14	2	23	9	30	19	8	28
6	19	7	26	15	4	24	11	31	21	7	27	17	6	25	13	2	22	10	29	18	7	27	15	3	24	10	31	20	9	29
7	20	8	27	16	5	25	12	1	22	8	28	18	7	26	14	3	23	11	30	19	8	28	16	4	25	11	1	21	10	30
8	21	9	28	17	6	26	13	2	23	9	29	19	8	27	15	4	24	12	31	20	9	29	17	5	26	12	2	22	11	31
9	22	10	29	18	7	27	14	3	24	10	30	20	9	28	16	5	25	13	1	21	10	30	18	6	27	13	3	23	12	1
10	23	11	30	19	8	28	15	4	25	11	31	21	10	29	17	6	26	14	2	22	11	31	19	7	28	14	4	24	13	2
11	24	12	31	20	9	29	16	5	26	12	1	22	11	30	18	7	27	15	3	23	12	1	20	8	29	15	5	25	14	3
12	25	13	1	21	10	30	17	6	27	13	2	23	12	31	19	8	28	16	4	24	13	2	21	9	30	16	6	26	15	4
13	26	14	2	22	11	31	18	7	28	14	3	24	13	1	20	9	29	17	5	25	14	3	22	10	31	17	7	27	16	5
14	27	15	3	23	12	1	19	8	29	15	4	25	14	2	21	10	30	18	6	26	15	4	23	11	1	18	8	28	17	6
15	28	16	4	24	13	2	20	9	30	16	5	26	15	3	22	11	31	19	7	27	16	5	24	12	2	19	9	29	18	7
16	29	17	5	25	14	3	21	10	31	17	6	27	16	4	23	12	1	20	8	28	17	6	25	13	3	20	10	30	19	8
17	30	18	6	26	15	4	22	11	1	18	7	28	17	5	24	13	2	21	9	29	18	7	26	14	4	21	11	31	20	9
18	31	19	7	27	16	5	23	12	2	19	8	29	18	6	25	14	3	22	10	30	19	8	27	15	5	22	12	1	21	10
19	1	20	8	28	17	6	24	13	3	20	9	30	19	7	26	15	4	23	11	31	20	9	28	16	6	23	13	2	22	11
20	2	21	9	29	18	7	25	14	4	21	10	31	20	8	27	16	5	24	12	1	21	10	29	17	7	24	14	3	23	12
21	3	22	10	30	19	8	26	15	5	22	11	1	21	9	28	17	6	25	13	2	22	11	30	18	8	25	15	4	24	13
22	4	23	11	31	20	9	27	16	6	23	12	2	22	10	29	18	7	26	14	3	23	12	31	19	9	26	16	5	25	14
23	5	24	12	1	21	10	28	17	7	24	13	3	23	11	30	19	8	27	15	4	24	13	1	20	10	27	17	6	26	15
24	6	25	13	2	22	11	29	18	8	25	14	4	24	12	31	20	9	28	16	5	25	14	2	21	11	28	18	7	27	16
25	7	26	14	3	23	12	30	19	9	26	15	5	25	13	1	21	10	29	17	6	26	15	3	22	12	29	19	8	28	17
26	8	27	15	4	24	13	31	20	10	27	16	6	26	14	2	22	11	30	18	7	27	16	4	23	13	30	20	9	29	18
27	9	28	16	5	25	14	1	21	11	28	17	7	27	15	3	23	12	31	19	8	28	17	5	24	14	31	21	10	30	19
28	10	29	17	6	26	15	2	22	12	29	18	8	28	16	4	24	13	1	20	9	29	18	6	25	15	1	22	11	31	20
29	11	30	18	7	27	16	3	23	13	30	19	9	29	17	5	25	14	2	21	10	30	19	7	26	16	2	23	12	1	21
30	12	31	19	8	28	17	4	24	14	31	20	10	30	18	6	26	15	3	22	11	31	20	8	27	17	3	24	13	2	22

Figures in **black type** denote Sabbaths.
9th, Fast of Ab (if on Sabbath, postponed to Sunday); 30th, First Day of New Moon of Elul.

ELUL (29 days)

Elul	88	87	86	85	84	83	82	81	80	79	78	77	76	75	74	73	72	71	70	69	68	67	66	65	64	63	62	61	60	5759
	28	27	26	25	24	23	22	21	20	19	18	17	16	15	14	13	12	11	10	09	08	07	06	05	04	03	02	01	2000	1999
	Au-Sep	Sep-Oct	Au-Sep	Au-Sep	Sep-Oct	Au-Sep	Au-Sep	Au-Sep	Au-Sep	Sept	Au-Sep	Au-Sep	Sep-Oct	Au-Sep	Au-Sep	Au-Sep	Au-Sep	Au-Sep	Au-Sep	Au-Sep	Sept	Au-Sep	Au-Sep	Sep-Oct	Au-Sep	Au-Sep	Au-Sep	Au-Sep	Sept	Au-Sep
1	23	3	14	25	4	18	28	9	21	1	12	23	4	16	27	7	19	31	11	21	1	15	25	5	18	29	9	20	1	13
2	24	**4**	**15**	26	5	**19**	29	10	**22**	2	13	24	5	17	28	8	20	1	12	**22**	2	16	**26**	6	19	**30**	**10**	21	**2**	**14**
3	25	5	16	27	6	20	30	11	23	3	14	25	6	18	29	9	21	2	13	23	3	17	27	7	20	31	11	22	3	15
4	**26**	6	17	28	**7**	21	31	12	24	4	15	**26**	7	19	**30**	**10**	22	**3**	**14**	24	4	**18**	28	8	**21**	1	12	23	4	16
5	27	7	18	29	8	22	1	13	25	5	16	27	8	20	31	11	23	4	15	25	5	19	29	9	22	2	13	24	5	17
6	28	8	19	**30**	9	23	2	**14**	26	6	17	28	9	21	1	12	24	5	16	26	**6**	20	30	**10**	23	3	14	25	6	18
7	29	9	20	31	10	24	**3**	15	27	**7**	**18**	29	**10**	**22**	2	13	**25**	6	17	27	7	21	31	11	24	4	15	26	7	19
8	30	10	21	1	11	25	4	16	28	8	19	30	11	23	3	14	26	7	18	28	8	22	1	12	25	5	16	27	8	20
9	31	**11**	**22**	2	12	**26**	5	17	**29**	9	20	31	12	24	4	15	27	8	19	**29**	9	23	**2**	13	26	**6**	**17**	28	**9**	**21**
10	1	12	23	3	13	27	6	18	30	10	21	1	13	25	5	16	28	9	20	30	10	24	3	14	27	7	18	29	10	22
11	**2**	13	24	4	**14**	28	7	19	31	11	22	**2**	14	26	**6**	**17**	29	**10**	**21**	31	11	**25**	4	15	**28**	8	19	30	11	23
12	3	14	25	5	15	29	8	20	1	12	23	3	15	27	7	18	30	11	22	1	12	26	5	16	29	9	20	31	12	24
13	4	15	26	**6**	16	30	9	**21**	2	13	24	4	16	28	8	19	31	12	23	2	**13**	27	6	**17**	30	10	21	**1**	13	25
14	5	16	27	7	17	31	**10**	22	3	**14**	**25**	5	**17**	**29**	9	20	**1**	13	24	3	14	28	7	18	31	11	22	2	14	26
15	6	17	28	8	18	1	11	23	4	15	26	6	18	30	10	21	2	14	25	4	15	29	8	19	1	12	23	3	15	27
16	7	**18**	**29**	9	19	**2**	12	24	**5**	16	27	7	19	31	11	22	3	15	26	**5**	16	30	**9**	20	2	**13**	**24**	4	**16**	**28**
17	8	19	30	10	20	3	13	25	6	17	28	8	20	1	12	23	4	16	27	6	17	31	10	21	3	14	25	5	17	29
18	**9**	20	31	11	**21**	4	14	26	7	18	29	**9**	21	2	**13**	**24**	5	**17**	**28**	7	18	**1**	11	22	**4**	15	26	6	18	30
19	10	21	1	12	22	5	15	27	8	19	30	10	22	3	14	25	6	18	29	8	19	2	12	23	5	16	27	7	19	31
20	11	22	2	13	23	6	16	28	9	20	31	11	23	4	15	26	7	19	30	9	**20**	3	13	24	6	17	28	8	20	1
21	12	23	3	14	24	7	**17**	29	10	**21**	**1**	12	**24**	**5**	16	27	**8**	20	31	10	21	4	14	25	7	18	29	9	21	2
22	13	24	4	15	25	8	18	30	11	22	2	13	25	6	17	28	9	21	1	11	22	5	15	26	8	19	30	10	22	3
23	14	**25**	**5**	16	26	**9**	19	31	**12**	23	3	14	26	7	18	29	10	22	2	**12**	23	6	**16**	27	9	**20**	**31**	11	**23**	**4**
24	15	26	6	17	27	10	20	1	13	24	4	15	27	8	19	30	11	23	3	13	24	7	17	28	10	21	1	12	24	5
25	**16**	27	7	18	**28**	11	21	2	14	25	5	**16**	28	9	**20**	**31**	12	**24**	**4**	14	25	**8**	18	29	**11**	22	2	13	25	6
26	17	28	8	19	29	12	22	3	15	26	6	17	29	10	21	1	13	25	5	15	26	9	19	30	12	23	3	14	26	7
27	18	29	9	**20**	30	13	23	**4**	16	27	7	18	30	11	22	2	14	26	6	16	**27**	10	20	**1**	13	24	4	15	27	8
28	19	30	10	21	1	14	**24**	5	17	**28**	**8**	19	**1**	**12**	23	3	**15**	27	7	17	28	11	21	2	14	25	5	16	28	9
29	20	1	11	22	2	15	25	6	18	29	9	20	2	13	24	4	16	28	8	18	29	12	22	3	15	26	6	17	29	10

Figures in **black type** denote Sabbaths.

ARTICLES IN FORMER ISSUES OF THE YEAR BOOK

Below is a list of the essays that have appeared in the Jewish Year Book

1999
BERMANT, Judy - *Chaim Bermant 1929-1998*
FRIEDLANDER, Evelyn & JACOBS, David - *Anglo-Jewish Landmarks*
MASSIL, Stephen - *The books of Anglo-Jewry*
VERMES, Geza - *The Dead Sea Scrolls Fifty Years On*

2000
COSGROVE, John A. - *Scottish Jewry*
FRANKEL, William - *Anglo-Jewish Attitudes and Minhag Anglia*
GOEHR, Alexander - *Yehudi Menuhim, 1916-1999: An Appreciation*
GORSKY, Jonathan - *Christian-Jewish Relations*
JACOBS, Louis - *Four Positions in Anglo-Jewry*
KRAMER, Lotte - *Reflections*
ROTHSCHILD, Miriam - *Sir John Foster And The Jews*
SPIRO, Robin & SPIRO, Nitza - *Education And The Future of Anglo-Jewry*
VEIL, Simone - *The Shoah*
WEITZMAN, Hal & WEITZMAN, David - *The Jews In Wales*

2001
BAYFIELD, Tony - *The Rabbi's View: The Sternberg Centre*
BLACK, Gerry – *The Jews of Hackney Downs School*
GREENBURY, Jonathan - *Polack's House*
LAWTON, Clive - *Limmud And Adult Education*
LEVY, Abraham - *The Rabbi's View: The English Sephardim*
PATTERSON, David - *The Oxfrod Centre For Hebrew and Jewish Studies*
ROSEN, Jeremy - *The View From Yakar*
WAGERMAN, Jo - *What Is Jewish Education For?*
WEBBER, Alan - *A Perspective On Jewish Education*

2002
FELDBERG, Michael - *Can Five Jewish Organisations Actually Live Together? The   Centre For Jewish History in New York*
GREEN, Marc - *JNF 'Supporting Israel For Life', 1901-2001: A Centenary Of Success*
JOFFE, Lawrence - *Chaim Weizman And Lessons For Today?*
MIDDLEBURGH, Charles H. - *One Hundred Years Of Liberal Judaism In Great Britain*

2003
BERKOVIC, Sally - *Daughters Of The Revolution: What Has Changed For Orthodox   Women In Britain?*
BLOOM, Cecil - *Leonard Bernstein: A Jewish Composer*
GELLER, Mark - *The Institute Of Jewish Studies, University College London: A Brief History*
RAU, Diana - *The 1901 Census: A Source For Demographic Research*
SONNTAG, Ruth - *Jacob Sonntag: A Personal Memoir*

2004
SCHMOOL, Marlena - *British Jewry In 2001: First Impressions From The Censuses*
SCHONFIELD, Jeremy - *The Jewish Year: Vignette Of A Marriage*

2005
FRIEDMAN, Edie - *Black-Jewish Relations In The UK*
GOLDMAN, Lawrence - *Jewish Lives In The Oxford Dictionary Of National Biography*
GREEN, Geoffrey L. - *The Two-Hundredth Anniversary Of The Battle Of Trafalgar*
KLUG, Brian - *The Other Balfour: Recalling The 1905 Alien Act*

2006
JOLLES, Michael - *British Jews: Their Biographical Record*

2007
LANGHAM, Raphael - *Suez 1956*
SCHMOOL, Marlena - *Pointes To The Future Of The Community: Ethnicity, Mariage And Migration*
WITTENBERG, Jonathan - *Rabbi Dr Louis Jacobs*

2008
BECKMAN, Jonathan - *Sigmund Freud In London, 1938*
BLACK, Gerry - *Frank Cass Publisher, 1930-2007*
DAVIS, Bernard - *'Judaism Without Enforcement' - Reflections On The Clapton Jewish Youth Centre Sixty Years On*
DUNN, A. J. - *Wolf Mankowitz, 1924-1998 An Appreciation*
MOONMAN, Eric - *Reflections On Liverpool Jewry*

2009
APELOIG, Yitzchak - *Israel And Science*
CONWAY, David - *Short Dark And Jewish Looking': Felix Mendelssohn In Britain*
MASSIL, Stephen & **Winston**, Willow - *Ruth Winston Fox And The Jewish Way Of Life*
SHINDLER, Colin - *The Centenary Of Tel Aviv Founded In 1909*

2010
BUDD, Sidney – *Edgware & District Reform Synagogue*
GRUNWALD, Henry - *The Board Of Deputies at 250*
LEVY, Elkan D. - *The Communities That Nobody Knows About*
NEWMAN, Col. Martin & **MORRIS**, Henry - *The Jews In The British Armed Forces*
PINNICK, Jeffrey - *Yom Hashoah - The Annual Jewish Rememberence Day For Victims Of The Holocaust*
TAYLOR, Derek - *The Chareidim*
ZIMMELS, Erla – *The Jews' College Library: 1860-2010*

2011
CHINN, CVO, Sir Trevor – *Well done the British community*
GARDNER, Mark - *CST and the history of Jewish self-defence*
LEVY, Rabbi Abraham - *The way things are now*
SCHMOOL, Marlena - *Reflections on the 2011 Census of England and Wales*
WINEMAN, Vivian - *Getting on with the neighbours*

2012
SACKS, CHIEF RABBI LORD – *Community Transformation*
TAYLOR, Derek - *Schechita*
LAWTON, Clive - *Limmud*
BRAYBROOKE, Revd Dr Marcus - *CCJ: Seventy Years On*
LEVY, Elkan D. - *The Next Chief Rabbi*
LEE, PETER – *Plymouth: The Oldest Synagogue in the English-speaking World*
TAYLOR, Derek - *Cambridge Synagogue: 75th Anniversary*
BLOOM, Cecil - *The Jewish Libraries of Leeds*

2013
GOULD, MATTHEW – *The View from the Foreign Office*
NEWMARK, Jeremy - *The Jewish Leadership Council*
JACOBS-SARIG, Katrina - *Jewish Genetic Disorders UK*
TAYLOR, Derek – *The Hertz Centenary*
JULIUS, Lyn - *The Sephardi Revolution*
LANGHAM, Raphael - *South Hampstead Synagogue at 75*

INDEX

Entries beginning 'Friends of' and 'British Friends of' will be filed under the first significant word.

Z

Please complete and return the form to us by 29th August 2014

Please reserve the following advertising space in

The Jewish Year Book 2015:

FULL COLOUR AVAILABLE

☐ Full Page   £675   182 x 115 mm

☐ Half Page   £395   90 x 115 mm

☐ Quarter Page   £225   90 x 55 mm

(UK advertisers please note that the above rates are subject to VAT)

Special positions by arrangement

☐ Please insert the attached copy (If setting is required a 10% setting charge will be made.)

☐ Copy will be forwarded from our Advertising Agents (*see below*)

Contact Name: _____

Advertisers Name: _____

Address for invoicing: _____

_____

Tel: _____ Fax:_____

Signed: _____ Title: _____

VAT No:_____

Date: _____

Agency Name (if applicable): _____

Address: _____

_____

Tel: _____ Fax: _____

All advertisements set by the publisher will only be included if they
have been signed and approved by the advertiser.

To the Advertising Department
The Jewish Year Book
Vallentine Mitchell

Middlesex House, 29/45 High Street, Edgware, Middlesex HA8 7UU
Tel: +44 (0)20 8952 9526 Fax: + 44(0)20 8952 9242
www.vmbooks.com

Update for Jewish Year Book 2015

Readers are asked kindly to draw attention to any omissions or errors. If errors are discovered, it would be appreciated if you could give up-to-date information, referring to the appropriate page, and send this form to the Editor at the address given below. Alternatively, you can email us: info@vmbooks.com

With reference to the following entry:

Page:

Entry should read:

Kindly list on separate sheet if preferred.

Signed: _____ Date: _____ .

Name (BLOCK CAPITALS) _____

Address: _____

_____ .

Telephone: _____ .

The Editor
Jewish Year Book
Vallentine Mitchell & Co. Ltd.
Middlesex House, 29/45 High Street,
Edgware, Middlesex HA8 7UU
Tel: + 44(0)20 8952 9526   Fax: + 44(0)20 8952 9242
www.vmbooks.com

WIZO UK

Caring for the people of Israel

50,000 children in day care centres and after school facilities **6** youth villages attached to secondary day schools **1** golden age home **5,000** women receive free legal aid annually **16** warm home facilities for teenage girls at risk **70** support groups nationwide for single parent families **180** day care centres **900,000** meals delivered a month to families in need **2** shelters for victims of domestic violence & their children **53** community centres **5,500** students in schools & youth clubs

www.wizouk.org   020 7319 9169   central@wizouk.org

...changing lives

WIZO uk Registered Office, 108-110 Finchley Road London NW3 5JJ Registered Charity No. 1125012 Registered Company No. 6634748

How does Chai care?

Advisory Services
Counselling
Children, Teenage and Family Service
Therapies
Medical Outpatient Rehabilitation and Palliative Care Service
Complementary Therapies
Home Support Service
Group Activities
Support Groups
Volunteer Services

Thanks to the generosity of the community, Chai Cancer Care provides specialised support to thousands of people across the UK who have been affected by a cancer diagnosis.

To find out more please call our Freephone Helpline on **0808 808 4567** or **020 8202 2211** or visit **www.chaicancercare.org**

Services are available at:

North West London
Redbridge
Hackney
South London
Southend

Leeds
North Manchester
South Manchester
Glasgow
Clients' Homes

chai cancer care
together we can cope

Chai Lifeline Cancer Care Registered Charity No. 1078956